LUST FOR INCA GOLD

The Llanganati Treasure Story & Maps

Steven J Charbonneau

ISBN - 10:1478146060
ISBN - 13:978-1478146063
First Paperback Edition (6" x 9")

Cover design by Steven J. Charbonneau. Cover image taken from the map of Don Pedro Maldonado, *Carta de la Provincia de Quito y de sus adjacentes*, published posthumously in 1750. Digital map image provided by the US Library of Congress.

Grateful acknowledgments to: the Instituto Geográfico Militar of Ecuador, the U.S. National Imagery and Mapping Agency, the CIA and the University of Texas Perry Castañeda Library for the production, maintenance and digitization of the Series J721 1:50,000 scale topographic maps of Ecuador; the Royal Geographical Society and Blackwell Publishing (JSTOR) for the production, digitization, maintenance and preservation of the Don Atanasio *Guzmán Map*, Spruce & Stabler papers, and the Brooks correspondence; the University Libraries and the benevolent staffs of the University of South Florida (USF), University of Nevada Las Vegas (UNLV), University of Vermont (UVM) and University of Michigan (U-M) for the preservation of *Notes of a Botanist on the Andes and Amazon* and/or The Royal Geographic Journal's; Jane Dolinger for *inca gold find it if you can touch it if you dare*; Eric Erskine Loch for *Fever, Famine and Gold*; Rolf Blomberg for *Buried Gold and Anacondas*; Peter Lourie for *Sweat of the Sun, Tears of the Moon*; Mark Honigsbaum for *Valverde's Gold*; Anita Isaacs for *Military Rule and Transition in Ecuador 1972-1992*; Dr. Bruce Farcau for *The Coup: Tactics in the Seizure of Power*; Latin America Bureau for *Ecuador:Fragile Democracy*; and british-history.ac.uk for *A History of the County of Stafford: Vol 14: Lichfield*. With special thanks to Michael Dyott, Pamela Collier PhD, and the Miño family.

Please direct corrections, comments, questions or requests to:
lustforincagold@yahoo.com

Disclaimer: The information contained within this book is for scholastic and informational purposes only. The events and characters are real. This book is not intended to publically disclose private and embarrassing facts, to defame or invade personal privacy. Many character's names have been altered or omitted for the protection of their privacy. Factual representations and statements contained herein are true and correct to the best of the author's knowledge, except for opinions and any matters stated upon information and belief, and as to those matters, he believes them to be true. There are no guarantees, express or implied, as to the existence or location of the Llanganati treasure deposit.

Disclaimer: The author is not a lawyer. Legal issues are highly factual and time sensitive matters. Any legal issues or process referenced herein (laws, regulations, contracts, partnerships, investments, divorce, treasure salvage, permits, travel requirements etc...) are for informational purposes only. A countries laws and relevant legal advice are highly dependent on timing and the facts of a particular case or situation. It is therefore highly recommended that should the need arise, contact the appropriate government or agency, and retain counsel with experience in any particular legal situation that you may encounter. The reader is responsible for the inherent risks of travel, treasure hunting, investing and the results and consequences of their own actions, the author therefore disclaims any and all responsibility.

Brunner's Helicopter Cartoon Sketch
(1970s)

"Hey ... I cannot lift off!
Eugene ... why did you have to find the cursed treasure of Llanganati?"

Table of Contents & Illustrations

INTRODUCTION

Prepare yourself to embark on a journey back in time, as *Lust for Inca Gold* relates a historical story of an indigenous people and their conquest. A subjugation leading to the creation of, search for, and localization of the world's greatest treasure deposit, the Llanganati Treasure. Travel into the realm of the unknown with the conquistadores and on expeditions with latter day explorers the likes of Richard Spruce Esq., Major Edwards C. Brooks, Captain Eric Erskine Loch, Commander George M. Dyott and Eugene K. Brunner, whose stories are related and illustrated through their own words and maps.

This narrative spans a time-line of nearly five centuries, going well beyond historical background and what has been written previously. New evidence is disclosed, while misinformation, misdirection and erroneous factual representations are corrected or dispelled. For the novice, the entire Llanganati story is set out in chronological order with the history, terminology, places and events utilized in the narrative clearly explained. The more advanced reader or explorer will find this definitive work an indispensable reference or guide book.

What you are about to read is a true story based upon historical events, documents, records and maps, combined with the forty-six years of exhaustive research, explorations and writings of Eugene Konrad Brunner, all coalesced by the research, experiences and memories of the author. The maps included in this book have not been altered to hide any details. The story itself is as I know it to be and no details have been omitted, changed or altered to conceal the location of this treasure. Certain characters names have been altered, while some events have been generalized in order to protect the identities and privacy of the innocent ... or guilty.

Two years of my life from mid-1986 through mid-1988 were spent negotiating a contract and archeological permit with the Government of Ecuador for the recovery of this enormous treasure deposit. At the time gold was hovering around $350 an ounce and the treasure was estimated to be worth seventy billion dollars. In today's market of $1500 gold, the treasure's value has increased more than four hundred percent and the treasure could well be worth in excess of two hundred-eighty billion dollars!

Lust for Inca Gold, search if you must, find it if you can! Personally, the realization came to me in 1988 that the world's greatest treasure was already in my possession ... my children. It is to my children, Katie-Jean, John-Anthony, Steven Jr., Tiffany-Michelle, and Christopher Robin, that I dedicate this book with love.

Steven James Charbonneau

PROLOGUE

I found myself on a high and cold mountain, standing to one side of a gloomy and obscure lake. On the far side of the lake rose a great pinnacle from the back of which fell a large waterfall. At the foot and to one side of the waterfall I saw the black mouth of a cave. I went around the lake and entered the cave that from some site not visible, received the light of day. Cautiously I descended stairs that were carved into the solid rock that led to an enormous underground cavern illuminated by the brilliant radiance of gold!

My heart was racing from the lack of oxygen consistent with high altitudes that combined with the excitement and paranoia of what I had discovered. Before me, lay a vast store of treasure greater than could be imagined. I could not remove it alone or with thousands of men. There were life-sized statues of what I assumed to be Incas themselves, figures of shepherds, sheep and their lambs, birds, llamas, fruits, vegetables and plants, all crafted from solid gold! Large vases and receptacles full of multicolored stones were piled on top of stacks of gold plates, twelve inches wide and three inches thick, these must have been used to decorate Inca temples and palaces, with lumps of gold nuggets direct from the mines scattered everywhere.

Upon recovering from the initial shock of this great discovery, my first thought was to empty my knapsack and fill it with a small portion of my fortune before I was discovered. What should I take? ... What should I take my mind raced ... crafted gold objects would be more valuable than slabs of gold, and much lighter! Weight would be a problem. I decided to take as many precious stones as could be stuffed into my pockets, and to fill my knapsack with small golden objects.

From an enormous golden vessel I grabbed headbands and bracelets of solid gold set with precious stones and emeralds while tossing the silver objects to the floor. Next to this was another vessel, both were large enough to hold an entire cow cut in pieces, which was overfilled with idols of gold, llamas of gold, and figures of women, all small, and many jewels. I thrust a few objects into my now half full knapsack as another smaller cave behind a mountainous link of solid gold chain caught my attention. Perhaps I was missing even greater riches hidden within ...

I returned to where I had emptied my knapsack and picked up my flashlight, the second cave did not seem to receive the light of day that illuminated the great wealth that lay before me. After struggling over the pile of solid gold chain, I cautiously entered the cave with my flashlight flickering to life. Instantly the first rays of illumination revealed hundreds of human skeletons. The gruesome corpses frightened me! I lurched back almost falling, startling me from my sleep ... another childhood dream soon to be forgotten.

Eugene Konrad Brunner

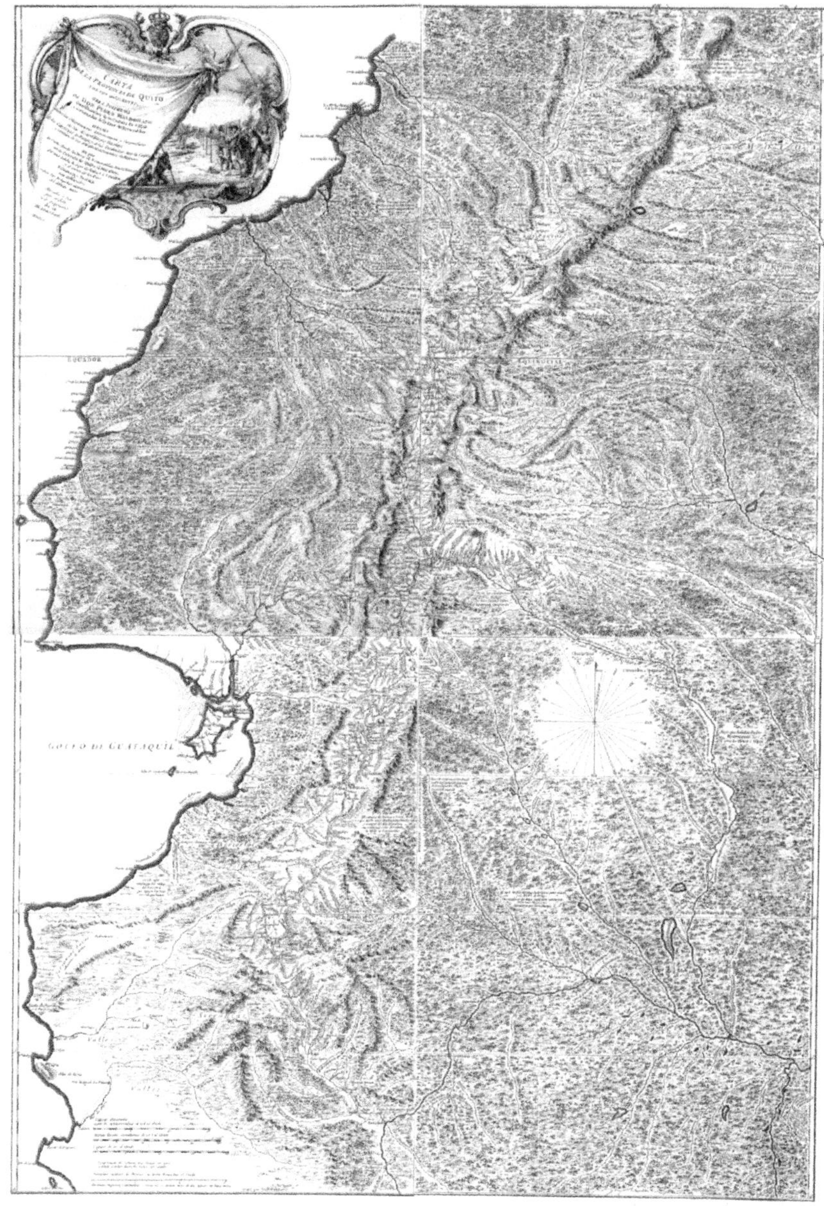

Carta de la Provincia de Quito y de sus adjacentes

By: Don Pedro Maldonado

Published posthumously in 1750

A small section of this map was utilized for the cover of this book.

THE INCAS: A HISTORY

Gold lore and the use of gold predate written history. Gold has been considered a precious metal since ancient times, and the search for gold has stimulated world exploration and trade for more than six thousand years. Mankind's lust for gold did not originate or terminate with the conquests of the new world. Nevertheless, the epoch of conquest, pillaging, looting, kidnapping, torture, murder, rape and destruction of cultural heritage, fueled by the Kingdom of Spain's insatiable lust for Inca gold, has never been paralleled.

Imagine reading a story straight out of a book of fairy tales about a King and his lands awash in the radiance and abundance of precious metals. A land where certain buildings are gilded in gold! While still others are adorned with plates of gold! Golden temples and palaces are abundant and have decorative gardens hung with golden fruit and vegetables. Some gardens are planted with stalks of corn that are of golden-stalk, the leaves and ears of precious metals. Life-size golden statues of domestic animals, llamas and shepherds are dispersed throughout these imaginary gardens. Throughout this fantasy land one encounters many tubs of gold, silver and emeralds, and goblets, pots and every kind of vessel, all made of fine gold or silver.

As with most fairy tales this narrative has a villain that lusts after the King's gold and riches. The dastardly villain captures the King, who offers a ransom of gold and silver for his own release. During the ensuing months the King's loyal subjects deliver more than thirteen thousand pounds of gold and twice as much silver for the release of their sovereign. Just prior to the completion of the monarch's ransom, the villain accuses the King of a crime, finds him guilty and executes him. Upon hearing of the death of their King, his loyal subjects divert and conceal the gold and silver destined to complete his ransom. The villain and his cohorts then melt the King's twenty-ton ransom of gold and silver into bars and ingots, dividing it amongst themselves. After the murder or their monarch, and having seen the villain's lust for these precious metals, the King's loyal subjects secrete untold quantities of gold and silver throughout the realm.

Closing the book, you might well be thinking that never before have you read a fairy tale where the villain prevails. Looking at the cover you realize that you had mistakenly picked up the wrong book. Even though the story had all the hallmarks of a fairy tale, novel or even a movie script, you had been reading a historical record of events, first hand accounts of the Spanish discovery and conquest of "Peru" by Francisco Pizarro in the early sixteenth century, from *The Incas of Pedro Cieza de León*.

■ ■ ■

The Llanganati treasure story and the journey on which the reader is about to embark, is based on actual places, events and people from the past and present. Characters' within our story, from Francisco Pizarro and William "The Buccaneer" Dampier, through Ecuador's modern day military leaders and presidents, will all be introduced as they relate to the story's time-line. Other integral characters, the last of the true explorers of the Llanganati region, great adventurers such as Richard Spruce Esquire, Jordan Stabler, Colonel Edwards Cranston Brooks, Captain Eric Erskine Loch, Commander George Miller Dyott and Eugene Konrad Brunner are introduced through short biographies that explore the true qualities distinctive to each individual.

Through the first hand accounts of these intrepid explorers you shall attain a visual image of the conditions, hardships, deprivations, successes and failures these explorers faced on their expeditions into the mysterious Llanganati mountains. Numerous original maps and illustrations will provide a means to trace the explorers' expedition routes as you travel with them into the unknown. Witness the explorers' insatiable quest for knowledge concerning the solution to the riddle of Atahualpa's gold hidden in the Llanganatis, the thrill of discovering the unknown that drove these personal quests, or in some cases ... their lust for Inca gold.

Lust for Inca Gold will be your personal expedition into the mysterious mountains of Llanganati. Relive the history, follow the expeditions and share in the discoveries of those who have gone before you. In the end ... from the comfort of your home ... you will comprehend why Atahualpa's treasure still lays hidden on Cerro Hermoso, a mountain deep within the Llanganatis of Ecuador. The more adventurous spirit within may also compel you to analyze the knowledge attained over the past century and commence your own personal quest for this enormous unrecovered treasure. Yet before you set out on the journey to Cerro Hermoso, our story must begin with a short history and explanation of the Incan people, their social structure, culture, religion, architecture, military, their empire and its administration.

■ ■ ■

Throughout history the radiance, reverence and lust for gold, has created enormous excitement, wealth and power. Gold has also caused great hardships and tragedies, for nations, its peoples and for individuals. This story is no exception. The Incas [1] had an enormous reverence for gold which in their religion represented the "sweat of the sun," while silver represented the "tears of the moon," both purely revered for holy not monetary value. Spanish Conquistadores and the Crown on the other hand had an even greater lust for gold and silver's monetary value, to create personal wealth, or finance wars and conquests. It is here that our story begins, brought to us in detail through the chronicles of the conquistadores, who were seeking not only individual wealth ... but ... the Royal Fifth.[2]

---

[1] Inca - This term referred solely to the King or Emperor, the Inca, who was also identified as the "Son of the Sun." It was not until modern times that the term has been broadened to describe the people as a whole.

[2] Royal Fifth - The Spanish Crowns one-fifth royal tax paid upon all treasure; gold, silver, emeralds, pearls, fine cloths and the like, obtained by the conquistadors.

The chronicles of the conquest indicate that no kingdom in the world was so rich in precious ores, for every day great deposits were discovered both of gold and silver. Gold was washed from the rivers in many of the provinces and silver was found in the mountains and it all was for the benefit of a single Inca, his ruling class and their religion. The Incas esteemed silver and gold so highly, they ordered it mined in many parts of the provinces in great quantity where they got silver out of the mountains with little trouble. Just one of the thousands of Indian laborers could mine five or six marcs [3] in a single day. The same Indians were not continuously in the mines, every so often they were sent away and others came in their place. So well had the Incas organized this, that the amount of gold and silver mined throughout the kingdom was so great that there must have been years when they took out more than fifty thousand arrobas [4] of silver, and over fifteen thousand of gold, and all this metal was for their [the Incas] use. The Incas treasury in Cuzco alone, was said to contain one hundred thousand clumps of gold taken from the mines, each lump weighing fifty castellanos.[5] All the precious metals that were mined served no other purpose than that of decorating and furnishing the temples, convents and royal palaces.

■ ■ ■

The Incas believed that there was a Creator of all things. The sun was their sovereign god, represented as a man, Viracocha, to whom they erected great temples and effigies of solid gold, while the reigning Inca was the divine incarnation of the deity and revered as the "Son of the Sun" for whom great palaces and effigies were constructed as well. Once the "Son of the Sun" died, his palace and effigies were left intact and new ones were created for the next Inca. Temples of the Sun were found in every province of the realm, which to list one by one the temples, would be a long and prolific task. Temples and palaces of the Incas were adorned with gold and silver to the extent that even the household service was constructed of these revered metals.

In *The Incas of Pedro Cieza de León* [6] edited by Victor Wolfgang von Hagen,[7] the temple of the sun in Cuzco was described as "among-the richest

---

[3] Marc (Marco de Oro or Marco de Plata) - A weight for commodities, especially gold (Oro) and silver (Plata), commonly used in European Countries equaled 8 ounces.

[4] Arroba - A traditional unit of weight in Spain and similar in Latin America, equal to 25.36 pounds.

[5] Castellanos - A Spanish weight of measurement. One Marco de Oro equaled 50 castellanos.

[6] Pedro Cieza de León published eight books on the Incas and Peru printed between the years of 1553 and 1554.These books were written during his seventeen years in Peru (modern Columbia, Ecuador, Peru and Chile) from May1535 until 1552.

[7] Victor Wolfgang von Hagen [1908-1985] - Acclaimed explorer, archaeological historian, anthropologist and travel writer had this to say about *The Incas of Pedro Cieza de León* ... "This chronicle, which had been often

in gold and silver to be found anywhere in the world." Pedro Cieza de León went on to describe this temple in detail as "...having a circumference of over four hundred feet, halfway up the wall ran a stripe of gold two hand spans wide and four fingers thick. The gateway and doors were covered with sheets of this metal. Inside there were four buildings, not very large, fashioned in the same way, and the walls inside and out were covered with gold, and the beams too, and the openings set with precious stones and emeralds. In one of these houses, which was the richest, there was an image of the sun, of great size, made of gold, beautifully wrought and set with many precious stones. This house also held some of the statues of the Incas who had reigned in Cuzco, with a vast store of treasure. There was a garden in which the earth was lumps of fine gold, and it was planted with stalks of corn that were of gold-stalk, leaves and ears. Within the temple there were more than thirty bins made of silver in which they stored the corn. There were more than twenty sheep of gold with their lambs, and the shepherds who guarded them, with their slings and staffs, all of this metal. There were many tubs of gold and silver and emeralds, and goblets, pots and every kind of vessel, all of fine gold. On the other walls there were carved and painted other still greater things. I make no mention of the silver work, beads, golden feathers and other things which would not be believed."

Virgins of the Sun in Cuzco were housed in a convent close by, but not within the Temple of the Sun. The convent, similar to the temple, had a garden hung with golden fruit and vegetables of precious metals, was literally tapestried with plates of gold and silver, with all the table service of the same material. Virgins were the elite women, typically chosen at birth for beauty and lineage. It was the occupation of the virgins to care for the temple, service the mamacunas (which a virgin became at maturity), and to spin and weave the garments of the Inca and his Coya.[8] If a woman was particularly beautiful or showed exceptional ability in weaving or feminine craft, she was chosen to attend school at Cuzco or one of the provincial capitals. They then had the opportunity to marry into nobility or become one of the "daughters of the sun," a royal concubine, living a life of segregation and at the disposal of the Inca alone.

The Inca Garcilaso de la Vega[9] wrote that ... "When the Inca wished to possess one or other of these women, he had her summoned and she was

---

republished throughout the sixteenth century, is not alone one of the most widely printed books on Peru's conquest; it also-in this all scholars agree-possesses the greatest objectivity of any history ever written about the Incas."

[8] Coya - Means queen. The Inca's wife after about 1450 was his full sister, who was called "coya." The nobles of Inca society were polyandrous; a harem of wives provided the ruler with an enormous number of progeny.

[9] Garcilaso de la Vega - Historian of partial Inca heritage whose Mother was Incan from the Cuzco area and his father was Spanish. Garcilaso's writings provide an Incan point of view that counterbalances the chroniclers and historians versions of events. However, one must consider that Garcilaso's knowledge of history was tainted with a bias toward the Cuzco area and

brought to wherever he happened to be ... Those who once had relations with him could not go back to the convent. They were brought to the royal palace, served as attendants or ladies in waiting to the Coya."

Should a virgin ignore her vow of chastity and was caught, she was buried alive and her lover hung. Her accomplice would bear an even greater burden, if married his wife and children would also be put to death, along with his servants, all his close relations, and even his llamas. In order to complete the punishment and set an example, his house was razed to the ground while his fields were destroyed and strewn with stones so that nothing could grow again.

■ ■ ■

Pedro Cieza de León also chronicled the grandeur of Cuzco's buildings, palaces and lodgings in great detail ... "These palaces were a grand thing; when one of the Lord-Incas died, his successor did not abandon or destroy them, but, on the contrary, improved and added to them; for each built his own palace, leaving that of his predecessor adorned and standing as he had left it. Accumulating such a fortune, and with the heir being obliged to leave the possessions of his predecessor untouched, that is to say, his house, his household, and his statue, the treasure piled up over many years, so that all the service of the king's house, even water jars and kitchen utensils, was of gold and silver; and not only in a single place, but in many, especially the capitals of the provinces.[10] These famous lodgings were among the finest and richest to be found in all Peru.

As these Incas were so rich and powerful, some buildings were gilded and others were adorned with plates of gold. The fronts of many of the buildings are beautiful and highly decorative, some of them set with precious stones and emeralds, and, inside, the walls of the temple of the sun and the palaces of the Lord-Incas were covered with sheets of the finest gold and incrusted with many statues, all of this metal. Inside the dwellings there were sheaf's of golden straw, and on the walls carved figures of the same rich metal, and birds, and many other things.

In addition to this, it was said that there was a great sum of treasure in jugs and pots and other receptacles, and many rich blankets covered with silver and beadwork. In their palaces and lodgings there were bars of these metals,

---

factions that **Error! Main Document Only.**supported Huáscar. Garcilaso had no first hand knowledge of events that had transpired in the Northern portion of the empire.

[10] Provincial Capitals - Partially listed by Pedro Cieza de León as Tomebamba, Tacunga, Quito and Caranqui ... "They served as the head of the provinces or regions, and from every so many leagues around the tributes were brought to one of these capitals, for in all these places there were larger and finer lodgings than in most of the other cities of this great kingdom, and many storehouses. In all these capitals the Incas had temples of the sun, mints and many silversmiths who did nothing but work rich pieces of gold or fair vessels of silver."

and their garments were covered with ornaments of silver, and emeralds and turquoise, and other precious stones ... and their litters were all encrusted with silver and gold and jewels. Aside from this, they had a vast quantity of ingots of gold, and unwrought silver, and tiny beads, and large vessels for their drinking feasts and for their sacrifices still more of these treasures. Whatever I say, I cannot give an idea of the wealth the Incas possessed in these royal palaces ... we can well believe that what the Incas were said to possess is true."

■ ■ ■

The Incas forged a mighty empire, subdued kingdoms and sculpted mountains creating a realm known as Tahuantinsuyu,[11] which meant the four quarters or four corners. The quarters or regions of the realm were represented by the four provinces whose four corners met in their capital, Cuzco. This expansive empire that ran along the mountainous spine of South America was denoted by the conquistadors solely as "Peru," actually encompassed some 300,000 square miles, the majority of modern day Columbia, Ecuador, Peru, Bolivia, Argentina and Chile. An empire so vast, roughly 2500 miles from North to South, that was created over a period of three hundred years through a combination of diplomacy, intermarriage and military coercion, had developed a population of six to twelve million at its peak.

The Incas actually preferred to assimilate different tribes and regions avoiding bloodshed whenever possible, absorbing these tribes into the Empire. This system appeared incapable of going wrong or being misused and worked to perfection, with the Inca's conquering first mountain peoples, valley by valley, each valley or grassy upland almost completely isolated by the nature of the terrain which the Incas would then have connected by royal roads. Later the more thickly populated coastal strip was conquered, where each river oasis had developed a city or small state, at the least, some organization that was controlling irrigation and water supplies. Some came voluntarily in this manner and still others by brute force ... there was no failed conquest, if you opposed, you died.

Once part of the empire every assimilated province, every city, every town and every village was reorganized on the Inca system. Essential and functional Inca building [12] was on an enormous scale with temples and fortresses buttressing each newly acquired province, side by side with municipal buildings. Incan officials were superimposed over the existing

---

[11] Tahuantinsuyu - Name of the Incan Empire which means "The Four Quarters." Anti-suyu was the Eastern quarter. Chinchay-suyu was the Northern quarter. Cunti-suyu was the Western quarter, loosely defined lay between the Andes and the Pacific and consisted of many tribes. Colla-suyu was the Southern quarter.

[12] The Incas themselves learned a great deal from assimilated tribes and cultures and put that knowledge to great use, with building techniques being a good example. The stones were of uneven courses and interlocking, keyed stone, in order to survive prevalent earthquakes in the Andean region.

local administrators, whose future loyalty was secured by removing their sons as hostages to Cuzco, who would then also become indoctrinated in the Inca pattern. If a population proved difficult to influence or remained stubbornly defiant of Inca authority or restraint after being conquered, the entire city, town or village was removed and resettled in another docile area of the realm previously pacified and indoctrinated. The population was then supplanted with settlers absolutely loyal to the Incan regime.

Every portion of the empire once assimilated paid tribute to the Inca. Upon conquest taxation included the conscription of one-tenth of the population for service in the army. Tribute amounted to any commodities your community had available, be it one of the twenty varieties of corn or two hundred-forty varieties of potato cultivated in the realm from farming communities, salt produced by the evaporation method, fish or pearls from a seaside village, gold or silver from a mining community, weapons, cloth, tools, in short any commodity required to sustain life in the empire, that was then stockpiled in storehouses throughout the realm. People were also considered tribute, virgins for the temples of the sun, labor conscripts for the mines, fields or construction projects if you had no other resource.

Everyone had to work but they lacked for nothing, even if they became ill, they received all that was needed from the storehouses. Even game throughout the empire was protected and property of the Inca with royal hunts being organized, utilizing up to 30,000 warriors. The vicuña and guanaco (a wild llama) were shorn for their fine wool while the llama was used for transport. Predatory animals were slaughtered while poor stock was culled to provide meat for the villages.

The realm had an extensive system of thousands of miles of supreme interlinking roads with shelters or rest houses (tambos) and storehouses located about every twelve miles or a days walk apart. Larger accommodations and storehouses were found five to six days apart. Thus when the Inca and his retinue would travel the empire there was always at hand food and lodging. Some were in fact fortresses with magazines containing arms and everything else required for the supply of an army traveling fast and light in order to deal with an insurrection. The Incas excelled at inventory control, tracking storehouse contents throughout the realm. As supplies were used from one storehouse or region, they would be replaced from others keeping a constant and equal diversification of supplies throughout the realm.

Communications were made easily and rapidly throughout the empire on the Inca road system which connected isolated communities with cities, by Indian messengers or couriers called Chasqui. These messengers were agile runners that delivered messages and goods throughout the empire using a relay system. Runners were stationed every few miles apart on the road, once another runner arrived and relayed his message, the next runner would depart at top speed to the next station, on and on until the message was delivered. A message from Cuzco the southern capital, to Quito the northern capital, would have taken merely five to seven days utilizing the Incas relay system. It is also said that due to the speed of the Chasqui the Inca and nobility could dine on fruit from the Amazon in the morning and have fresh fish at night from the Pacific Ocean.

■ ■ ■

Complete subservience to the Inca, and absolute loyalty of the military and elite ruling class was assured through royal blood. Even the officers of the army were all chosen from the elite of the Incas own households or lineage. These officers were dependent on the Inca for their position, and this guaranteed absolute loyalty within the tight-knit society.

Centralized form of government and the pyramidal governing bureaucracy, whose apex was the Inca, was the perfection of the society's organization both politically and militarily. This social system required a severe authoritarian government backed by ritual and divine compulsion. It is estimated that the Inca bureaucratic system required roughly 1300 officials per 10,000 in population. Therefore, increased productivity was essential and required through the ruthless exploitation of the labor force or commoners. This gulf between commoners and nobles was absolute and widened as the empire grew.

Orejónes, the big-eared ones, were the administrators in this two cast system, who were also born of royal blood. Given a good education in mathematics, language, religion and indoctrinated with the Inca version of history, they lived and died within the ayllu [13] of the Inca. To mark them out from the rest of the population their ears were pierced and the hole enlarged to accept gold or jeweled earplugs that indicated their station, thus "big-eared ones." A second class of administrators, called curacas, was necessitated by the rapid growth and expansion of the empire. A commoner could climb to the level of curaca based on his abilities, but this was his limit. Orejónes and curacas had a monopoly on high administrative and religious appointments. They paid no taxes and ate off gold and silver, lived in fine houses, were dressed in fine cloth and had several wives, for this as well, their loyalty to the Inca was without question.

The basis of the two cast system in the Inca state was the worker, without which there would have been no society or realm. Upon its conquest or assimilation, the village or ayllu's land would be appropriated by the Inca state and reallocated; part for the ayllu to be self sufficient, part to the state and a portion to the sun god. Thereafter the ayllu would pay a form of labor tax by tilling, planting and harvesting on the state and religious lands. Additionally, the ayllu was responsible for washing gold from the areas placer deposits [14] and getting silver from the local mountain mines.

---

[13] Ayllu - A self sufficient unit. The Incas ayllu consisted of his lineage, the upper class or nobility. Throughout the realm for commoners their ayllu was a village grouping of families.

[14] Placer deposit - A deposit of sand or gravel of a river or lake, containing particles of valuable minerals.

Labor forces were well organized in each ayllu for working on state and religious lands. A group of ten workers made up a field unit under a leader, every ten units had a foreman, every ten foremen had a headman and so on, from a village unit to the tribal unit, tribal unit to provincial, then to regional which was one of the four quarters, and ultimately to the Inca himself.

■ ■ ■

The reign of the Incas' began with the First Inca Manco Capac I around 1200 AD, running through the Twelfth Inca Huayna Capac who succeeded his father Topa Inca (Tupac Yupanqui) on his death in 1493. As was custom, each new sovereign would have built a city palace and country estate for himself and his lineage shortly after assuming power. Pedro Cieza de León writes ... "Most of the treasures of the dead Incas, and their lands, which are called chacaras (huacas) were kept intact from the very first one and none ventured to touch or spend any part of them, for they had no wars or needs which required money [in utter contrast to the Spaniards lust for gold]."

Cieza de León continues to indicate that ... "Topa Inca was buried with so much treasure and precious stones that it must have amounted to more than a million gold pesos." This was consistent with the Incas' religious belief of an afterlife and second coming. Therefore, the estate was revered and left untouched to sustain the deceased Inca, his family and servants, who typically joined him in death.The Inca, similar to a biblical figure as the "Son of the Sun" and the patriarch of the family or tribe, chose their successors based on the rule of inheritance of the firstborn male child, but this was not absolute. Their main concern was that the Inca was of royal blood and fit to rule. If the firstborn son proved weak or incompetent, he would soon be deposed by a more aggressive brother through a civil war or palace rebellion. In fact, most of the previous eleven Incas had succeeded only after such a conflict.

Huayna Capac inherited an empire so firmly established, successful, orderly and obedient that the only opposition he faced to his rule was from the recently conquered Quito, Columbia, Pasto and Popayán tribes in the North, where he would spend a great part of his thirty-four-year reign[15], long absent from Cuzco. Huayna Capac was in Quito with his favorite son Atahualpa [16] at his side throughout, at the head of the empires most experienced warriors, with his two greatest Generals Quizquiz and Calicuchima also at his side, would lose his life to an epidemic fever in 1527.[17]

---

[15] Differing accounts state that Huayna Capac spent at least twelve to fourteen years in the North.

[16] Atahualpa - Born in Quito during Huayna Capac's second year of reign, to his fourth wife the Shyri Paccha, Queen of the Kingdom of Quito. They had a second son together, Atahualpa's younger brother Illescas.

[17] Some historians dispute the year of Huayna Capac's death and place it earlier in 1525, most specifically Juan de Velasco.

After the customary pomp and circumstance of Inca funeral ceremonies, as a sign of his deep love for the Kingdom of Quito,[18] in accordance with Huayna Capac's last testament, Atahualpa had his father's heart removed and interned in a golden vase to be retained in the temple of Quito. Huayna Capac's mummified body was transported to Cuzco to be interned in the lands of his ancestors, accompanied by more than a thousand women and servants into the afterlife.

Huayna Capac [19] was the father of half-brothers Huáscar and Atahualpa. Pedro Cieza de León painted a clear picture of the status these step-brothers held ... "Atahualpa was loved by the old captains of his father and the soldiers, because he went to the wars with him as a child, and because Huayna Capac had so loved him during his lifetime, allowing him to eat nothing except what he left on his plate. Huáscar was clement and pious; Atahualpa, ruthless and vengeful; both were generous, but Atahualpa was a man of greater determination and endeavour."

It has been said that the demise of Huayna Capac's empire commenced prior to his death. Suffering from an epidemic fever under great pain and suffering throughout his entire body, Huayna Capac returned to Quito after hearing of the foreigners encamped on Isla de Gallo and attempted to cure his fever in vane. Living day by day in great pain, considering death and the future of his beloved empire, Huayna Capac summoned his advisors, generals, orejónes and nobles to court. In their presence with all sincerity and formality, as was customary with the Incas, Huayna Capac made his testament, his ultimate declaration and disposition of the realm.

Huayna Capac declared each of these sons to rule a part of the empire as regent during his reign.[20] Huáscar's primogeniture was not in question, the legitimate heir, being Huayna Capac's first born son from his first wife Rava-ocllo, was to rule the south, being all that had pertained to the old empire of Peru and its respective treasures, from Cuzco with his militia army. Atahualpa his favorite son, from his fourth wife Queen Paccha, as

---

[18] Kingdom of Quito - Before the Inca conquest in about 1450, Ecuador was broken up into a series of tribes. The Panzaleo tribe, called Quitos, lived where the modern capital city Quito, Ecuador exists today. The Inca's also purportedly established their northern capital here, historians and archeologists remain divided on this issue. It appears historians of the nineteenth and twentieth century dispute the finds of historians of the sixteenth, seventeenth and eighteenth centuries on the issue.

[19] Huayna Capac's children - Historians vary on the number of children Huayna Capac had, from one to two hundred offspring. Among his prominently known sons were Nanque Yupanqui, Tupac Inca, Huanca Auqui, Tupac Hualpa, Titu, Huaman Hualpa, Manco Inca, Cusi Hualpa, Paullu Tupac Yupanqui, Conono, Huáscar, Atahualpa and Rumiñahui.

[20] There is a dispute among chroniclers and modern historians whether there was a dividing of the empire or not. We may never know for certain the exact nature of Huayna Capac's legacy.

heir to the Kingdom of Quito, was to rule in Quito consistent with all that was possessed by his maternal grandparents with the support and loyalty of his fathers trusted generals and professional armies. The Inca had spoken, his divine declaration, although breaking with custom, was implemented and accepted by all.

Huayna Capac must have realized that any threat to his empire would probably come from the north. Surely the first notice received by the Inca in mid-1525 while he was at Tomebamba,[21] of the pale skinned bearded strangers appearing from the north on the sea, landing near Atacames, must have given him great concern. Was this not a sign from the prediction of Viracocha that some foreign people from a faraway land would come to wage war on them and become their masters?

Logically, the best way for Huayna Capac to deal with any possible future threat from the north, was to ensure that it would be confronted by an army in the north of his empire. Who best to lead an army in a time of war than his favorite son Atahualpa, on whose ability in a time of war he could rely. Whatever Huayna Capac's reasons or motives for dividing his Empire, it shall remain, unfortunately, unclear.

■ ■ ■

After a few years the step-brothers went to war. Not over animosities concerning who would succeed their father, as Huayna Capac's testament was the unquestionable law of the land, but to dispute the boundaries of their respective empires at the instigation of third parties. Padre Juan de Velasco [22] in *Historia Del Reino de Quito (1789)* makes the point very clearly that Huáscar and Atahualpa ruled their respective monarchies in peaceful coexistence nearly four years before hostilities broke out between them.

Death again would play a critical role in the fate of the empire. Chamba, principal chief of the Province of Cañar, one of the nobles at court to witness Huayna Capac's testament, died. Chamba had administered his province faithfully to the testament and was also partial to Atahualpa who was viewed as his legitimate sovereign. Chamba's son, who would follow in his reign, instigated the subordinate and inferior chiefs of the province, those that were more inclined toward the old Peruvian Empire from the time when the province had been conquered by Topa Inca, to political insurrection. Simply put, the position was taken that the province was outside that which belonged to the Kingdom of Quito and Atahualpa's reign. That according to Huayna Capac's testament, the province was the rightful inheritance of Huáscar. However, to take this position was to ignore

---

[21] Tomebamba - Today known as Cuenca located some miles south of Quito. The Inca's had grand palaces here that were among the finest and richest to be found in all Tahuantinsuyu.

[22] Juan de Velasco [1727-1792] - Jesuit priest, historian and author of *Historia Del Reino de Quito en la América Meridional* published in 1789. Native of what once was the Kingdom of Quito, born in Riobamba.

the fact that long before the Province of Cañar was conquered by Topa Inca, it had been conquered by the Shyri Cacha Duchicela [23] and therefore had been a part of the Kingdom of Quito for many years.

Huáscar had apparently been disinterested or oblivious to events in the Province of Cañar, until it was brought to his attention by his mother Rava-ocllo, a very ambitious woman who was to say the least, extremely upset over the division of her first born son's rightful empire. Under his mother's direction and prodding Huáscar ultimately ordered a new governor to administrate this province as part and portion of his Empire.

Atahualpa in the meantime had convened his court, which included all of the generals, orejónes and nobles that had been present for Huayna Capac's testament. A court from which Atahualpa sought and obtained an ultimate declaration of the boundaries of his reign in the Kingdom of Quito. The declaration of the court went well beyond the Province of Cañar, even encompassing Tomebamba, consistent with his father's testament. It was also decided to be necessary that troops be mobilized to put down the insolence and insurrection of the new Chief of Cañar, in order to warn other provinces and set an example against further similar insurrections. Atahualpa and his troops marched toward the Province of Cañar under the command of Generals Quizquiz and Calicuchima.

Upon learning of Atahualpa's troops march, the son of Chamba found himself placed in a position to save hisself from war, retired. Subordinate chiefs and others who had been part of the insurrection, out of fear and to escape confrontation, protested their innocence and unwitting involvement in any insurrection. Quizquiz and Calicuchima diligently made inquires' to discover where the son of Chamba had retired to. The torment that was meted out fell on the shoulders of his sons and daughters who were all empaled, their houses were demolished and the stones scattered. The Province of Cañar had been recuperated with minimum opposition.

Atahualpa arrived at Tomebamba, which at the time was the most beautiful and celebrated city in all the Kingdom due to the royal buildings that had been built here by Huayna Capac and his paternal grandfather Topa Inca. Six months had passed since Atahualpa had made an example of the Province of Cañar, with only minor protests and contestations on the part of Huáscar, apparently the matter was settled.

---

[23] Shyri Cacha Duchicela - Was the sixteenth Shyri of the Kingdom of the Shyris of Caranqui. The Caranqui Indians occupied what is now the province of Imbabura Ecuador, extending southward into the territory of Quito. They were led by their Chieftain or Shyri. Shyri Cacha Duchicela reigned from 1463 to 1487. Her reign was followed by that of Paccha and Huayna Capac from 1487 to 1525, then by Atahualpa the seventeenth Shyri from 1525 to 1533, Hualpa Capac for two months of 1533 and finally by Rumiñahui for one year and five months until his death. (From *Historical Dictionary of Ecuador*, 1973)

Inca Atahualpa

General Rumiñahui

It was here in Tomebamba that Atahualpa set out to build a new palace and residence to enjoy the devotion and fruits of the land from the surrounding provinces that were part of his heredity. Notice of Atahualpa's action irritated and infuriated the ambitious Rava-ocllo, who forced and prodded Huáscar to action once again.

Huáscar attempted to invade Tomebamba and Quito. After initial success Huáscar and his militia army were driven back south during the Battle of Chimborazo, in which Huáscar's entire army on the field was killed or disbanded. Huáscar was left with a smaller army in the south, which was finally defeated during the Battle of Quipaipan in April 1532 at the hands of Atahualpa's Generals Calicuchima and Quizquiz in command of just a small army of 50,000 to 100,000 warriors, as General Rumiñahui had already returned to Quito with Atahualpa's larger army after the Battle of Chimborazo the year before.

With the defeat and capture of Huáscar, General Quizquiz and some 30,000 professional troops held Cuzco. Atahualpa's supreme commander Calicuchima held the central Andes with another 35,000 troops at Jauja, while his General and step brother Rumiñahui [24] held the Quito homeland. At this time Atahualpa was marching triumphantly southward in the wake of his Generals with still another 40,000 troops. Whether by mere coincidence or not, Atahualpa encamped at the thermal baths in Cajamarca, some say to recover from a wound received in battle. Apparently, what neither Atahualpa nor Huáscar knew was that a far greater threat to the Empire was approaching.

The Spanish Conquistador's were indeed very fortunate to find the Inca Empire involved in this civil war at the precise moment when by chance they commenced their conquest of Peru. Had Francisco Pizarro attempted to conquer Peru on either of his previous expeditions or had not been delayed in Spain for a year, he would have encountered a completely different undivided empire and clearly would have failed.

Huayna Capac also had other sons that played a major role in history, one of whom was later crowned Inca by the Governor Francisco Pizarro in 1534, Manco Capac II. Another son was the intrepid Rumiñahui, a celebrated captain of the empire. Well known for his bravery and military success's during his fathers reign, who had also served his younger step-brother Atahualpa with honor throughout the civil war, would end up resisting Pizarro's conquest of the empire and inhibit his lust for Inca gold.

■ ■ ■

In Peru at about the same time that Francisco Pizarro was planning his third voyage, Atahualpa was consolidating his control over the Inca Empire. Our story begins prior to this point in history on 25 Sep 1513 when a force of

---

[24] Rumiñahui - Born to Huayna Capac and his wife Princess Nary, daughter of Ati Pillahuazo, King of the Choazanquil Kingdom.

Spanish explorers, led by Vasco Núñez de Balboa, crossed the Isthmus.[25] For twenty-five days their line of march [26] took them over hills covered with dense forests, through swamps and the lush tropical green jungles of Panama (an area that would later be well known for malaria and yellow fever), across the crocodile infested Chagres River and ultimately to be confronted by the Pacific Ocean or Mar del Sur, the South Sea. A senior officer on this expedition was the thirty-five-year-old captain, Francisco Pizarro.

Six years later the Spanish established the town of Panama on the Pacific shore of this isthmus, which became their base to build ships to explore, exploit and if need be, conquer this unknown sea. Ships were dismantled on the Atlantic shore and transported in sections across the isthmus on the backs of Indian labor to be reassembled on the shores of the South Sea. This proved to be the threshold of yet another vast expansion for Spain and the rest of the world. Once again, as in Mexico with Cortez, this expansion would be at the expense of another unknown people, the Incas.

With the support of Diego de Almagro, Spanish cleric Fernando de Luque and a financial partner, Pizarro made his first voyage of expedition following the coast southward in 1524 with a small contingent of eighty men and four horses. The expedition was not a success as no riches of any sort were found.

Pizarro's second expedition in November of 1526, still with partners Diego de Almagro and Fernando de Luque, was better financed and equipped with a new financial partner Gaspar de Espinosa. The expedition of one hundred-sixty men and a few horses, set sail in two small ships, Pizarro commanding one with Ruiz as his pilot, Almagro in the other. It was on this voyage that the first Inca contact was made, the conquistadors' lust for Inca gold commenced in earnest and the demise of the Inca Empire was set in motion.

Pizarro's expedition split, with Almagro sailing south to the equator. Pizarro captured an ocean going balsa raft outfitted with fine cotton sails and twenty Inca men on board that were on a trading mission. Of the men on board, perhaps for fear of the pale and bearded strangers, or for fear of the unknown, eleven jumped overboard into the sea presumably to their deaths. Nine of them were captured, of which six were let go and three were kept to be taught Spanish as interpreters, for the Indians could not understand Spanish nor could their Incan Quichua language or numerous other Indian dialects be understood.

A report to King Charles I described in detail the Inca artifacts that were discovered on board ... "They were carrying many pieces of silver and gold

---

[25] Isthmus - A narrow strip of land with sea on either side, linking two larger areas of land, specifically modern day Panama.

[26] Line of march was well east of the present day canal and the "Camino Real," which was the pack mule route that the conquistadors would later use to transport their gold and treasure from the Pacific Ocean to the Atlantic on its way to Spain.

as personal ornaments ... including crowns and diadems,[27] belts and bracelets, armour for the legs and breastplates, tweezers and rattles and strings and clusters of beads and rubies; mirrors decorated with silver, and cups and other drinking vessels. They were carrying many wool and cotton mantles and Moorish tunics ... and other pieces of clothing coloured with cochineal,[28] crimson, blue, yellow and all other colours, and worked with different types of ornate embroidery, in figures of birds, animals, fish and trees. They had some tiny weights to weigh gold. There were small stones in hand bags, emeralds and chalcedonies and other jewels and pieces of crystal and resin."

Almagro and Pizarro continued southward exploring along the coast of modern day Ecuador for a period of time until they returned north as far as the Tumaco estuary and the uninhabited Isla del Gallo (Island of the Rooster), a movement that had been observed and reported to Huayna Capac. Here the Spaniards would suffer a dreadful, intense, almost indescribable period of about four weeks, many dying of hunger and disease. It was here that Pizarro purportedly drew a line in the sand as the morale, contentment and condition of his men deteriorated, thirteen brave souls crossed the line and stayed with Pizarro while the others returned to Panama with Ruiz.

It would be the next year, by mere coincidence the year of Huayna Capac's death, that Pizarro and his faithful crew sailed south again as far as the Gulf of Guayaquil where they sighted their first Inca city, Tumbez. Many were the riches observed by the conquistadores in this city. With such a small expedition, Pizarro made no attempt to conquer this city, instead he traded with and befriended its occupants, obtaining evidence of Inca civilization and culture such as pottery, metal vessels, fine clothing and llamas for display in Spain. They sailed further down the coast as far as the modern Santa River ultimately turning north again toward Panama. Pizarro crossed the isthmus and embarked for Spain where he would attempt to gain royal approval, men and money, for the conquest of this vast new world, the Inca Empire.

■ ■ ■

It would be mid-1528 when Pizarro was received by King Charles I in Toledo Spain. Nevertheless, Spanish bureaucracy moved at a snails pace. It would not be until 26 Jul 1529 when in the name of the King, the Queen signed a *Capitulación* which granted Pizarro an authorization for his third voyage to discover and conquer "Peru," the titles of Governor and Captain-General of Peru, a generous salary and extensive territorial concessions in this New World. Another six months would pass though, until Pizarro was able to depart Spain for Panama in January of 1530.

---

[27] Diadems - A jeweled crown or headband worn as a symbol of sovereignty.

[28] Cochineal - A scarlet dye used for coloring food, made from the crushed dried bodies of a female scale insect.

Driven by greed and lust for Inca gold and power, Pizarro's third expedition embarked from Panama onboard three vessels, two large and one small, in January of 1531,[29] the discovery and conquest of an empire two thousand sea miles long commenced. With some one hundred-eighty men[30] and twenty-seven horses Pizarro landed on the coast of modern day Ecuador thirteen days later, where they procured their first treasure from a small undefended town. Gold and silver in the form of clumsily wrought ornaments were looted in the amount of 20,000 pesos. Emeralds were taken as well, however only Pizarro and a few others appreciated their value. Many were the towns and villages, with great riches being found in them, that were pillaged, and they brought away more specimens of gold and silver. In one large village called Coaque, as chronicled in *Reports on the Discovery of Peru*, the conquistadors took fifteen thousand pesos [31] of gold, fifteen hundred marcs of silver and many emeralds. These initial riches were sent back to Panama to encourage others to join the expedition.

Pizarro arrived at Tumbes to find none of the riches that had been observed on his previous visit. Huáscar and Atahualpa's struggle for power had been resolved shortly before his arrival and Tumbes had been completely destroyed as a result of the Inca civil war. Huáscar had withdrawn the city's garrison to fight Atahualpa and the city had paid a stiff price for this action. Cautious, Pizarro left Tumbes in May of 1532 after having killed the local Chief Amotape and set out to establish the first Spanish settlement, San Miguel de Piura near Tangarara, roughly 1300 miles from Cuzco and only 350 miles from the town of Cajamarca.

After the settlement of San Miguel, all the gold and silver objects the Spaniards had obtained up to that point were converted to ingots. Pizarro somehow persuaded his men to forego their own shares. After deducting the Royal Fifth, Pizarro was able to send the treasure back to Panama in two vessels and thereby settle the expedition's accounts. Atahualpa, informed of the appearance of strangers surely must have been aware of and concerned about the looting and pillaging along the coast, the killing of the Chief Amotape and the construction of a town within his empire. Whether concerned or just curious, Atahualpa sent a noble to investigate and discover the Spaniards' strength and intentions. It was at this time and place however, where the Spaniards were most disorganized and this must have been the impression the noble passed on to Atahualpa, as for some unknown reason he did not confront them or inhibit their movement.

■ ■ ■

---

[29] Pizarro's third voyage - Some sources indicate instead that he sailed 27 Dec 1530.

[30] Seventy men short of the two-hundred-fifty authorized in the Queen's *Capitulación.*

[31] Peso de Oro - The Peso or Castellano was not a coin but a weight of measure of gold, equal to 0.162 of an avoirdupois ounce (British) or 4.59 grams (Metric) per Peso de Oro. Therefore approximately 6 Pesos de Oro equaled an avoirdupois ounce.

"Peru" would ultimately prove to be the richest of the New World prizes taken in the name of the Spanish Crown. A beautiful land so geophysically fantastic where geography is vertical and the climate is governed by height rather than latitude, when it is summer on the coast it is winter in the Andes. It contained coastal plain, the world's greatest mountain chains, the Andes, and extended inland to the rain forests of the Amazon. Its ocean is fed by the Humbolt current from the cold southern latitudes and abounds with fish. The currents effect on the warm air of the coastal tropics, reduces the temperature and produces clouds, high humidity, even fog in the winter months of June through November, but no rain except when the El Niño current is running southward. This arid coastal plain in the south of the empire, modern day Peru, is crossed by river beds sourced in the melting snows of the Andes, which reach like fingers into the sea.

Although the Incas had conquered many coastal civilizations of these hot and humid coastal valleys, they were a mountain people. "El Dorado" sought by the Spaniards, the true Inca Empire, ran along the spiny ridges of the Andes and it would be here in the sierra, through the foothills, mountains, passes and gorges, in the breathlessness of altitude, that the conquistadors must travel to confront them. The Spaniards' unabated lust for Inca gold, with a portion of all treasure from this vast empire, the gold, silver, emeralds, pearls and fine cloths, being set apart as a tax belonging to his Majesty, the "Royal Fifth," would not be quenched on the coastal plains.

Pizarro received intelligence of an inhabited valley called Caxamalca [32] where Atahualpa supposedly resided, who was known to be the greatest lord among the natives. The Governor marched out of San Miguel for this town on 24 Sep 1532 with a force of sixty-two horsemen, one hundred-six foot soldiers [33] and four cannons.

Pizarro's line of march was not direct or hurried, but more at a leisurely pace, spending ten days at Piura and pausing at Zarán [34] and Motux (Motupe) until he reached Sáña on the 6th of November. Finally Pizarro left the coastal plain on November 8th and commenced the arduous march into the sierra, not on the Inca Road, but by following the River Zaña into a gap in the foothills, mountains and gorges to a 12,000 foot pass. Throughout long days march up the precipitous slopes of the Nancho gorge, so steep that in places they had to ascend in steps, the Spaniards had been at the mercy of Atahualpa's warriors, however the pass was not defended. Pizarro had penetrated the mountains in a region rarely penetrated and found the gateway to the empire unbarred. Atahualpa had allowed them to advance without opposition and thus sealed his fate and that of the mighty Inca Empire.

---

[32] Caxamalca - Current day Cajamarca located in Peru, spelling changed throughout for ease of reading.

[33] Force size is listed as one hundred-ten foot and sixty-seven horse by another source.

[34] Zarán - Modern day Serrán.

Suffering as everyone does from the suddenness of an altitude, caught breathless on the slopes below the pass, the Spaniards would have had little chance of survival against seasoned warriors attacking from above, such as occurred in battles later in the conquest. The fortress at the top, had it been defended, would have stopped them in their tracks. Even after passing by the fortress, for the five days march across the high sierra, the conquistadors' were still vulnerable. At any moment during that exhausting week Atahualpa could have destroyed them. This threat to his empire could have easily been destroyed or at the minimum, its advance impeded. Even Hernando Pizarro would write ... "The road was so bad that they could very easily have taken us there or at another pass which we found between here and Cajamarca. For we could not use the horses on the roads, not even with skill, and off the roads we could take neither horses nor foot soldiers."

Pizarro and the conquistador's emerged from the hills that looked down on the valley of Cajamarca, a few miles wide and flat with rivers rushing through precipitous canyons. Pizarro halted on the edge of the valley to await his rear guard and camped on the high ground, a grassy plain looking down from the rounded hills that appear to hang above and surround Cajamarca. Across the valley and beyond the town, spread out across the opposite hillside, were the tents of Atahualpa's 40,000 strong army. One can easily imagine the fear and confusion that must have filled the minds of one hundred- sixty-eight exhausted Spaniards' upon being confronted with the majestic vision of their enemies enormous encampment. It must have appeared to all that it would be here where their insatiable lust for Inca gold would finally be confronted.

The Spaniards', a throng of soldiers with their clanking armor and horses across the valley must have also presented a visual sensation that startled the Indians' senses. Perhaps over prepared for this country and enemy, the Spaniards' were armored head to foot, in what would prove to be an invulnerable steel shell that weighed sixty pounds. The horsemen were armed with lances, long wooden spears with iron or steel points, and swords of steel about three feet long, relatively narrow and sharp on both sides. The foot soldiers were armed with the same Spanish steel, some also carried a crossbow, others a harquebus, which were a sort of an early musket, not very effective but feared by the natives, as it was a source of thunder.

The Inca weaponry that the conquistadores would soon confront consisted of bronze or bone tipped spears, two handed wooden swords with serrated edges, clubs with stone and spiked metal heads, stone or copper headed battle axes, woolen slings for stones, and bolas (stones fastened to lengths of cord). Though these weapons proved to be formidable against human flesh, tens of thousands having died in single Incan battles, they could inflict very little damage to a conquistador covered in armor. The Spaniards, ultimately outnumbered roughly two hundred-forty to one at Cajamarca, were still destined to obtain the greatest spoils and ransom of treasure ever known, and subsequently, to create the greatest treasure cache ever known.

■ ■ ■

Governor Pizarro arrived in Cajamarca, where the town with its central triangular square had been vacated for the Spaniards to use, on Friday, 15 Nov 1532. The next day, on Pizarro's second attempt, Atahualpa was summoned from the nearby thermal baths. Atahualpa, accompanied by several thousands of his best troops, went to Cajamarca's central plaza. The sheer magnitude and majesty of Atahualpa's entourage and the treachery that followed, was recorded for posterity by Pizarro's secretary, Francisco de Xeres[35] [1530-1534], in *Narrative of the Conquest of Peru* republished in *Reports on the Discovery of Peru* by Sir Clements R. Markham. Thus an eyewitness account ... "First came a squadron [300] of Indians dressed in a livery of different colors, like a chessboard. They advanced, removing the straws from the ground and sweeping the road. Next came three squadrons in different dresses, dancing and singing. Then came a number of men with armour, large metal plates, and crowns of gold and silver. Among them was Atahualpa [who wore a collar of large emeralds] in a litter lined with plumes of macaws' feathers of many colors and adorned with plates of gold and silver. Many Indians [80] carried it on their shoulders on high. [It was borne by eighty chiefs, all dressed in a very rich blue livery] . On reaching the center of the open space, Atahualpa remained in his litter on high, and the others with him, while his troops did not cease to enter.

"A captain [Indian captain] then came to the front and, ascending the fortress near the open space, where the artillery was posted, raised his lance twice, as for a signal. Seeing this, the Governor asked the Father Friar Vicente if he wished to go and speak to Atahualpa, with an interpreter. He replied that he did wish it, and he advanced, with a cross in one hand and the Bible in the other, and going amongst the troops up to the place where Atahualpa was, thus addressed him: 'I am a priest of God, and I teach Christians the things of God, and in like manner I come to teach you. What I teach is that which God says to us in this Book. Therefore, on the part of God and of the Christians, I beseech you to be their friend, for such is God's will, and it will be for your good. Go and speak to the Governor, who waits for you.'

"Atahualpa asked for the Book, that he might look at it, and the priest gave it to him closed. Atahualpa did not know how to open it, and the priest was extending his arm to do so, when Atahualpa, in great anger, gave him a blow on the arm, not wishing that it should be opened. Then he opened it himself, and, without any astonishment at the letters and paper, as had been shown by other Indians, he threw it away from him five or six paces, and, to the words which the monk had spoken to him through the interpreter, he answered with much scorn, saying: 'I know well how you have behaved on the road, how you have treated my chiefs, and taken the cloth from my storehouses.' The monk replied: 'The Christians have not done this, but some Indians took the cloth without the knowledge of the Governor, and he ordered it to be restored.' Atahualpa said: 'I will not leave this place until they bring it all to me.' The monk returned with this reply to the Governor.

---

[35] Francisco de Xeres - Listed as Francisco de Jeres in the chronicles.

"Atahualpa stood up on the top of the litter, addressing his troops and ordering them to be prepared. The monk told the Governor what had passed between him and Atahualpa, and that he had thrown the Scriptures to the ground. Then the Governor put on a jacket of cotton, took his sword and dagger, and, with the Spaniards who were with him, entered amongst the Indians most valiantly; and, with only four men who were able to follow him, he came to the litter where Atahualpa was, and fearlessly seized him by the arm, crying out, 'santiago!' Then the guns were fired off, the trumpets were sounded, and the troops, both horse and foot, sallied forth. On seeing the horses charge, many of the Indians who were in the open space fled, and such was the force with which they ran that they broke down part of the wall surrounding it, and many fell over each other. The horsemen rode them down, killing and wounding, and following in pursuit. The infantry made so good an assault upon those that remained that in a short time most of them were put to the sword. The Governor still held Atahualpa by the arm, not being able to pull him out of the litter because he was raised so high. Then the Spaniards made such a slaughter amongst those who carried the litter that they fell to the ground, and, if the Governor had not protected Atahualpa, that proud man would there have paid for all the cruelties he had committed. The Governor, in protecting Atahualpa, received a slight wound in the hand. During the whole time no Indian raised his arms against a Spaniard.

"So great was the terror of the Indians at seeing the Governor force his way through them, at hearing the fire of the artillery, and beholding the charging of horses, a thing never before heard of, that they thought more of flying to save their lives than of fighting. All those who bore the litter of Atahualpa appeared to be principal chiefs. They were all killed, as well as those who were carried in the other litters and hammocks.

"The Governor went to his lodging, with his prisoner Atahualpa despoiled of his robes, which the Spaniards had torn off in pulling him out of the litter. It was a very wonderful thing to see so great a lord taken prisoner in so short a time, who came in such power. The Governor presently ordered native clothes to be brought, and when Atahualpa was dressed, he made him sit near him, and soothed his rage and agitation at finding himself so quickly fallen from his high estate. Among many other things, the Governor said to him: 'Do not take it as an insult that you have been defeated and taken prisoner, for with the Christians who come with me, though so few in number, I have conquered greater kingdoms than yours, and have defeated other more powerful lords than you, imposing upon them the dominion of the Emperor, whose vassal I am, and who is King of Spain and of the universal world. We come to conquer this land by his command, that all may come to a knowledge of God, and of His Holy Catholic Faith ...'

"In the square and on the plain there were over two thousand killed [other references indicate up to ten thousand were killed], besides wounded Indians. The Governor asked whether the Spaniards were all well. His Captain-General, who went with them, answered that only one horse had a slight wound. The Captain, with his horsemen, collected all that was on the plain and in the tents of Atahualpa, and returned to the camp before noon with a troop of men, women, sheep, gold, silver, and cloth. Among these spoils there were eighty thousand pesos of gold, seven thousand marcs of silver and fourteen emeralds. The gold and silver were in immense pieces, great and small plates and jars, pots, cups, and various other shapes. Atahualpa [seeing the Spaniards lust for gold] said that all this was the furniture of his service, and that the Indians who fled had taken a great deal more away with them."

"Atahualpa feared that the Spaniards would kill him, so he told the Governor, that he would give his captors a great quantity of gold and silver. The Governor asked him: 'How much can you give, and in what time?' Atahualpa said: 'I will give gold enough to fill a room twenty-two feet long and seventeen wide, up to a white line which is half way up the wall.' The height would be that of a man's stature and a half. He said that, up to that mark, he would fill the room with different kinds of golden vessels, such as jars, pots, vases, besides lumps and other pieces.[36] As for silver; he said he would fill the whole chamber with it twice over. He undertook to do this in two months. The Governor told him to send off messengers with this object, and that, when it was accomplished, he need have no fear."

Pizarro and Atahualpa also came to the agreement that the treasure would be accounted for in its original form, not being melted into bars, as the Inca could benefit from its magnitude when filling the room. Even so, it is important to note that a great portion of the ransoms treasures were flat wall, roof and decorative tiles, although of a lower overall karat, they would quickly amass great weight.

Atahualpa sent messages to his captains, who were in the city of Cuzco, ordering them to send thousands of Indians laden with gold and silver, without counting that which was coming with his captains and brother. It has also been said that in accordance with Inca custom Atahualpa had ordered his captains not to touch his fathers or predecessors gold and for that reason it appeared as Huáscar would later state, that Atahualpa was ... "reduced to stripping our temples of their ornaments." Atahualpa had also said that he would deliver his brother Huáscar, whom his captains were bringing from Cuzco as prisoner to Cajamarca, into the hands of the Governor, to do with him as he pleased. Atahualpa, hearing rumors that Huáscar attempted to send a message to Pizarro offering three times the treasure than that offered by Atahualpa, perhaps fearing that Pizarro might depose him, ordered Huáscar killed en route along with hundreds of his nearest kin. Quoting Huáscar, Garcilaso states ... "I know where the

---

[36] To place the massiveness of Atahualpa's offer in context, consider the following statement made by J.M.Lucas, physical scientist for the US Department of the Interior's Bureau of Mines Division of Nonferrous Metals in *Bulletin 675 Mineral Facts and Problems* [1985] ... "Total world production to date (of gold up to 1985) is estimated at about 3.1 billion ounces ... equivalent to a cube roughly 55 feet on a side."

incalculable riches amassed by my father and all his predecessors are hidden, whereas my brother [Atahualpa] does not know this, and he is therefore reduced to stripping our temples of their ornaments in order to fulfill his promise."

After some days the ransom began to arrive from Cuzco. The first installment that entered Cajamarca consisted of two hundred loads of gold and twenty-five of silver, another sixty loads arrived, then more than three hundred loads of gold and silver in jars and great vases and in divers other shapes arrived, one hundred loads of gold and seven loads of silver arrived, the accounts go on and on. *Reports on the Discovery of Peru* gives us an eyewitness account ... "The brother brought many vases, jars and pots of gold, and much silver, and he said that more was on the road; but that, as the journey is so long, the Indians who bring the treasure become tired, and cannot all come so quickly, so that every day more gold and silver will arrive of that which now remains behind. Thus on some days twenty thousand, on others thirty thousand, on others fifty thousand or sixty thousand pesos of gold arrived, in vases, great pots weighing two or three arrobas, and other vessels. The Governor ordered it all to be put in the house where Atahualpa had his guards, until he had accomplished what he had promised."

Again *Reports on the Discovery of Peru* gives us another account ... "With the gold that was brought from Cuzco, there were some straws made of solid gold, with their spikes, just as they grow in the fields. If I was to recount all the different varieties in the shape of the pieces of gold, my story would never end. There was a stool of gold that weighed eight arrobas. There were fountains with their pipes, through which water flowed into a reservoir on the same fountains, where there were birds of different kinds, and men drawing water from the fountain, all made of gold."

■ ■ ■

It was decided that all the gold should be melted down that had been brought to Cajamarca by order of Atahualpa, as well as all that might arrive before the smelting was finished. The commencement of the smelt took place on 3 May 1533 [37] and proceeded until almost every Incan artifact of silver and gold had fed the furnaces at a rate of up to six hundred pounds a day, the destruction of which was sadly an irreparable artistic loss. The smelting process had two purposes, as the artifacts were of different fineness and karats, melting separated and refined the metals to 26,000 pounds of "good" or pure silver [38] and 13,420 pounds of 22 ½ karat "good" gold,[39] thereby making the treasure easier to record, value, distribute and

---

[37] Smelt took place May 13th according to Juan de Velasco.

[38] The purity of silver is expressed by its fineness or parts per thousand. Pure or fine silver is 1,000 parts fine, or 100% silver. Sterling silver for example is 925 fine, or 925 parts silver and 75 parts copper, or 92.5% silver.

[39] The purity of gold is expressed by its fineness or parts per thousand just as silver. The term "karat" or "carat" refers to purity but is expressed in 24ths,

verify payment of the Royal Fifth. Once the "good" gold and silver emerged from the furnaces it was cast into bars and officially marked with the royal mark or seal of the Crown and meticulously recorded indicating that the Royal Fifth had been paid.

A division and distribution of the gold, silver, pearls and emeralds from the ransom of Atahualpa, of which the majority had come from the Temples of the Sun, Royal Treasury and Lodgings of Cuzco was made, setting aside the Royal Fifth. After the fees of the founder were deducted, the Royal Fifth amounted to some 262,259 pesos of gold and 10,121 marcs of silver! A portion of the Royal Fifth was left in its original form, so that the King of Spain might bear witness to the artistic value of treasures from New Castille. It was decided that Hernando Pizarro should return to Spain with a portion of the Royal Fifth and the samples set aside for his Majesty. He departed on 13 Jun 1533 with roughly half of the Royal Fifth, more than 100,000 castellanos and the Kings artistic samples. Pizarro arrived safely in Seville, Spain with his treasure cargo of Inca gold in February of 1534.

This ship and others that later arrived in Seville carried the Royal Fifth in bars and planks, and in pieces of gold and silver enclosed in large boxes. It was here that the young Pedro Cieza de León witnessed the arrival of gold and artifacts from the New World and like many others, was drawn to the El Dorado of Peru. One account in *Reports on the Discovery of Peru* states ... "A ship brought, for his Majesty, thirty-eight vases of gold and forty-eight of silver, among which there was an eagle of silver. In its body were fitted two vases and two large pots, one of gold and the other of silver, each of which was capable of containing a cow cut into pieces. There were also two sacks of gold, the size of a child four years old; and two small drums. The other vases were of gold and silver, each one capable of holding two arrobas and more. In the same ship passengers brought home forty-four vases of silver and four of gold."

Ultimately nothing would survive the furnaces of Spain and the demand for gold to finance the Kings wars with France and England. An official in Seville would write a report to the King in 1535 that they had completed the melting down of the objects brought by Hernando Pizarro. The objects were listed as "...thirty-four large urns, two kettledrums, one figure of a bust of an Indian, another similar of an Indian woman, a small retable, two platters, an idol in the form of a man, gold in powder and golds of 21 to 9 karats.[40]"

This report continues to list the value of these priceless artifacts after melting, as roughly three thousand marks or 150,070 pesos, yet another irreparable artistic loss unequaled in modern times. Very few gold or silver artifacts from the time of the Inca exist even today and can only be replaced

---

thus 24 karat gold is 1000 fine or pure gold, while 14 karat gold is 14/24 or 58.3% gold.

[40] The most complete report of objects brought to the King in *Nouvelles certaines des Isles de Peru [Lyon 1534].*

through the possible discovery of great treasures lost within the depths of the earth.

■ ■ ■

After receiving the huge ransom from Atahualpa, Pizarro charged the Inca with conspiring against him. Xeres reports further ... "Now I must mention a thing which should not be forgotten. A chief, who was Lord of Cajamarca, appeared before the Governor and said to him through the interpreters: 'I would have you to know that, after Atahualpa was taken prisoner, he sent to Quito, his native land, and to all the other provinces, with orders to collect troops to march against you and your followers, and to kill you all; and all these troops are coming under the command of a great captain called Rumiñahui. This army is now very near to this place. It will come at night and attack the camp ...' At the time Rumiñahui was indeed very near Cajamarca, however whether he had planned an attack or been ordered to do so remains unclear. Perhaps through inadequate interpretation or even deceit there was also no mention that Rumiñahui and his army were transporting a purported 4000 cargas of treasure for the ransom of Atahualpa.

"The Governor then spoke to Atahualpa, saying: 'What treason is this that you have prepared for me? For me who have treated you with honor, like a brother, and have trusted in your words!' Then he told him all the information he had received. Atahualpa answered, saying: 'Are you laughing at me? You are always making jokes when you speak to me. What am I and all my people that we should trouble such valiant men as you are? Do not talk such nonsense to me.' He said all this without betraying a sign of anxiety; but he laughed the better to conceal his evil design, and practiced many other arts such as would suggest themselves to a quick-witted man. After he was a prisoner, the Spaniards who heard him were astounded to find so much wisdom in a barbarian ...

"Then the Governor, with the concurrence of the officers of his Majesty, and of the captains and persons of experience, sentenced Atahualpa to death. His sentence was that, for the treason he had committed, he should die by burning, unless he became a Christian.

"They brought out Atahualpa to execution [August 29, 1533]; and, when he came into the square, he said he would become a Christian. The Governor was informed, and ordered him to be baptized. The ceremony was performed by the very reverend Father Friar Vicente de Valverde. The Governor then ordered that he should not be burned, but that he should be fastened to a pole in the open space and strangled. This was done, and the body was left until the morning of the next day, when the monks, and the Governor with the other Spaniards, conveyed it into the church, where it was interred with much solemnity, and with all the honors that could be shown it. Such was the end of this man, who had been so cruel. He died with great fortitude, and without showing any feeling ..."

■ ■ ■

History of the Conquest of Peru (1847) by the historian William Prescott provides us with a vivid picture after the Incas death ... "Atahualpa expressed a desire that his remains might be transported to Quito the place of his birth, to be preserved with those of his maternal ancestors ... The body of the Inca remained on the place of execution through the night. The following morning it was removed to the church of San Francisco, where his funeral obsequies were performed with great solemnity ... The ceremony was interrupted by the sound of loud cries and wailing, as of many voices at the doors of the church. These were suddenly thrown open, and a number of Indian women, the wives and sisters of the deceased, rushing up the great aisle, surrounded the corpse. This was not the way, they cried, to celebrate the funeral rites of an Inca; and they declared their intention to sacrifice themselves on his tomb, and bear him company to the land of spirits ... They then caused the women to be excluded from the church, and several, retiring to their own quarters, laid violent hands on themselves, in the vain hope of accompanying their beloved lord to the bright mansions of the Sun." ... "Atahualpa's remains, notwithstanding his request, were laid in the cemetery of San Francisco. But from thence, as is reported, after the Spaniards left Cajamarca, they were secretly removed, and carried, as he had desired, to Quito. The colonists of a later time supposed that some treasures might have been buried with the body. But, on excavating the ground [in Cajamarca], neither treasure nor remains were to be discovered ... "*Oviedo* [41]*, Historia. de las Indias, Ms., Parte 3, lib. 8, cap. 22.*

■ ■ ■

We owe to the meticulous record keeping and accounting of the Spanish Conquistadores, the knowledge that has survived the centuries concerning this unfathomable ransom paid by Atahualpa in 1533. Not inclusive of previous or subsequent plunder, this immense ransom amounted to an unimaginable 1,326,539 pesos of good gold and 51,610 marcs of good silver! [42] Which is to say 13,431 pounds of gold and 25,805 pounds of silver, roughly twenty tons of precious metals, worth well over $250,000,000 US dollars in today's precious metals market!

Governor Francisco Pizarro did quite well for himself as he received "a present" of Atahualpa's 15 karat gold litter that weighed 183 pounds or 83 kilos, valued at some 25,000 pesos of gold. Additionally the Governor received 57,220 pesos of gold and 2,350 marcs of silver which was roughly seven times that of a horseman's share. Hernando Pizarro received roughly three and a half times that of a horseman's quota, while Hernando Soto received double.

The base share or quota for each horseman was 8880 pesos of gold and 362 marcs of silver, whereas the base share of a foot soldier was only half as

---

[41] Gonzalo Fernández de Oviedo - Spanish chronicler born 1478, died 1557. Well known for his work *La historia general y natural de los Indias.*

[42] Rolf Blomberg, Swedish travel/adventure writer and explorer, in his book *Buried Gold and Anacondas (1955)*, placed a lower value on the distribution and states that ... "Francisco Pizarro got the lion's share." Both of these representations are confuted by historical documents and evidence.

much, 4440 pesos of gold and 181 marcs of silver. Pizarro however, adjusted these shares based on the performance, accomplishments or lack thereof for each conquistador. Xeres for example, would receive a full horseman's share for himself, and he shared in 94 marcs of silver and 2220 pesos of gold which was divided between Xeres and Pedro Sancho the notary, for secretary's work.

Consider for a moment that the conquistadors, unlike modern explorers and soldiers, were paid only in gold and silver, not paper money, script, check or electronic deposit as is custom today. Each horseman received ninety pounds of gold and one hundred eighty pounds of silver while the foot soldier received half as much. Gold was so prevalent that horsemen and foot soldiers went around settling debts without regard to its size or value, often overpaying. Up to the point of distribution the treasure had been under the constant guard and authority of the Governor. After the treasure distribution, each conquistador was responsible for the transport, storage and security of his own share. One can only imagine the animosities, paranoias and unexpected new set of problems that arose for the individual conquistadores upon the ransom's distribution.

■ ■ ■

The Spaniards lust for Inca gold was not quenched by this massive treasure division and they set out to complete their conquest of Peru. The lust for Inca gold continued under the cloak of religion. The raping, pillaging, looting and murder continued, more ruthless than before, torture was commonly practiced in an attempt to discover hidden treasures. Armed with the knowledge that the vast wealth already acquired predominately originated from Huáscar's capital Cuzco the conquistadors sought even greater treasures from the rest of Peru. However, Cuzco would still be their first destination after the death of Atahualpa. In just one location on the march to Cuzco, Pedro Pizarro reported encountering ten planks or bars of solid silver twenty feet long by one foot wide and two to three inches thick that had been used to decorate the dwelling of an Indian noble.

Upon arriving in Cuzco the Spaniards did not find as much plunder as they had expected and received many accounts of riches having been secreted prior to their arrival. Even so, reports from Pedro Pizarro and others indicate that the Cuzco treasure distribution amongst the four hundred-eighty soldiers exceeded that from the ransom of Atahualpa, with each horseman receiving six thousand Pesos de Oro and each infantryman half as much. The official account to the Crown of The Royal Fifth however, as reported in Prescott's *History of the Conquest of Peru*, indicates the treasure in Cuzco to have been only 580,200 Pesos de Oro and 215,000 marks of silver. Either way, the Cuzco treasure was larger than that of the ransom paid at Cajamarca!

The historian Rafael Loredo published a detailed comparison of the Cajamarca and Cuzco treasure distributions where the values of both meltings were converted into Maravedis.[43] On one hand the Cajamarca ransom amounted to a grand total of 697,994,930 Maravedis and consisted mainly of gold. Converted at a rate of 450 Maravedis per Peso de Oro, the gold equaled the sum of 596,942,550 Maravedis, while the silver that was converted at a rate of 1958 Maravedis per marc, only amounted to 101,052,380 Maravedis.

Cuzco's treasure of 700,113,880 Maravedis on the other hand, consisted mainly of silver of varied purity. Even so, the Cuzco treasure contained almost five times as much silver than was collected at Cajamarca. Cuzco's silver consisted of two grades ... poor, valued at the rate of 1125 Maravedis per marc for the sum of 71,721,000 Maravedis ... and good silver, valued at a rate of 2210 Maravedis per marc for the sum of 363,673,180 Maravedis. Gold of course was also found in Cuzco. Still being valued at 450 Maravedis per peso de oro, the gold added 264,719,700 Maravedis to the treasures valuation.[44] Regardless of value or mass, the Cuzco treasure clearly exceeded the astronomical ransom paid by Atahualpa and yet, the conquistadors' lust for Inca gold was not quenched ... but fueled!

The effect of such an overabundance of precious metals in Peru was instantly felt on prices. Precious gold and silver became common and common articles became precious. Ordinary articles were only to be had for outrageous sums ... a bottle of wine for sixty pesos de oro; a sword for fifty; a cloak for a hundred and a good horse could not be had for less than twenty-five hundred, some brought a still higher price! Iron used to make horseshoes was in such short supply that horses were shod in silver. Every article rose in value as gold and silver declined. In short, gold and silver seemed to be the only things in Peru that were not wealth. Those wise enough to return contented with their present gains to Spain, found these riches brought them sufficient consideration and competence for a life of leisure outside of Peru.

■ ■ ■

The conquistadores were also aware of numerous ransom shipments en route that never made it to Cajamarca after the death of Atahualpa. Many were the treasures that they were aware of in other towns, villages, cities, provincial capitals and Quito, Atahualpa's capital. Numerous were the consistent accounts on the riches of Quito and her seven shipments of Atahualpa's ransom, none of which arrived in Cajamarca. The gold and

---

[43] Maravedi - The basic Spanish monetary unit of the period which dependent upon the year, was worth between 450 - 490 per Peso de Oro. Other Spanish coins of the period were the real or tomin, a silver coin of 0.6 grams worth 34 maravedis, the real de a ocho or patacon (commonly known as the piece of eight) worth 8 reals or 272 maravedis, the ducado or ducat was a gold coin of 23.75 carats worth 375 maravedis and the escudo, a 22 carat gold coin worth 350 maravedis from 1537 through 1566, thereafter it was valued at 400 maravedis.

[44] Rafael Loredo's calculations from Los Repartos; bocetos para la nueva historia de Peru (Lima 1958)

silver concealed by the natives was affirmed to greatly exceed in quantity that which fell into the hands of the Spaniards. Oviedo writes in *Historia de las Indias* ... "That which the Inca gave the Spaniards, said some of the Indian nobles to Benalcazar, the conqueror of Quito, was but a kernel of corn, compared with the heap before him."

It was known that as a matter of custom, the Inca dispersed his treasures and wealth throughout his entire realm. *The Incas of Pedro Cieza de León* demonstrates ... "Thus, when Huayna Capac was in Quito and possessed of such wealth that he had ordered brought to Quito more than five hundred loads of gold and some thousand of silver, and many jewels and fine raiment."

Not only was wealth transferred to Quito by Huayna Capac, more tribute was paid and accumulated throughout the years before his death. One must not forget that after Huayna Capac's death, Atahualpa had many more years to accumulate and consolidate his own wealth in Quito, as the Inca, prior to the Spaniards arrival.

The Incas of Pedro Cieza de León also gives note to lost treasures ... "Huayna Capac's full life-sized image of gold, has never been found ... Other known objects have not been found, nor is there an Indian or Spaniard who knows or can guess where they are; but much as this is, it is little compared with what is buried in Cuzco and the shrines and other places of this great kingdom ... To be sure, the Spaniards had already taken a great part of the treasure and the rest was hidden and concealed in places which few or perhaps none know of ... "

In further conquests the Spaniards arrived after treasure was removed or in the process of being removed. One such case from the same chronicle was reported ... [Governor Pizarro] "sent Captain Hernando Pizarro, his brother, with a force of Spaniards, to this valley to remove all the gold from that cursed temple , and return to Cajamarca. And although Captain Hernando Pizarro made his way to Pachacamac with all possible speed, it is common knowledge among the Indians that the headmen and priests of the temple carried away more than four hundred loads of gold which was never seen again. Not withstanding, Hernando Pizarro found considerable gold and silver."

Something that perplexed the conquistadores, was a custom generally observed by all the Indians to bury with the bodies of the dead, all those possessions they most prized, and certain of their most beautiful and best-loved women. This occurred especially with the wealthy or Incas, who were mummified like the Egyptians ... "The Incas tombs had been described as magnificent and sumptuous, in them they placed great treasures and a greater number of women and servants with victuals and fine attire. None of the tombs of these Incas has been discovered, but the only proof needed as to whether they were rich or not is to know that in ordinary graves as much as sixty thousand gold pesos, more and less, have been found."

■ ■ ■

Upon hearing news of Atahualpa's execution, his faithful step brother, the great General Rumiñahui, en route from Quito with a purported four thousand cargas of gold for the ransom, ordered his men to withdraw with the treasure to the north of the Incan Empire, back to Quito, in the Andean Region of modern day Ecuador. Rumiñahui reportedly remained behind and upon the Spaniards advance to Cuzco he entered Cajamarca and disinterred Atahualpa.

Rumiñahui embalmed Atahualpa as was custom and re-interred Atahualpa and the gold of Quito and Latacunga where the Spaniards would never find it, in the remote Llanganati Mountains. There exists a dispute among historians whether Atahualpa was embalmed in Cajamarca or Quito, either way Atahualpa was embalmed. Clearly through customs, legend and myth, Rumiñahui's intent was to recover the Inca and his gold after the Spanish departed.

Rumiñahui organized resistence against the Spaniards, fighting them every step of the way back to Quito with little success, with the last major battles being on the plains of Riobamba. The eruption and accompanying earthquake of the Cotopaxi Volcano,[45] disrupted one of these battles between the Spanish and Rumiñahui in 1534. A previous eruption was purported to have occurred when Atahualpa was imprisoned in Cajamarca, an ominous event that had been forewarned and verification to the superstitious Incas of Viracocha's prophecy that when the volcano erupted, some foreign people from a faraway land would come to wage war on them and become their masters. Adding to both armies' distress in battle, the ground was completely covered in volcanic ash and sand while the air was filled for several days with thick clouds of earthy particles and cinders, which blinded the men and made respiration exceedingly difficult.

Rumiñahui's troops disbanded and retreated to the heavily populated Province of Caranqui, reportedly one of the richest provinces in the kingdom, with a spectacular royal palace and temple of the sun, which had been Huayna Capac's first priority to construct at the beginning of his reign. Both held an immense treasure of gold and silver that was easily taken from the surrounding mountains.

■ ■ ■

When in 1534 the Spaniard Sebastian Benalcazar finally arrived at Quito, he was once again faced with the scorched earth policy that Rumiñahui had practiced in Riobamba, Mocha, Muli-ambato [46] and in the Province of Latacunga. Some would say barbarous operations against his own people, but in reality an excellent military tactic depriving the Spaniards of food, supplies and lodging.

---

[45] From 1534 until 1877 there have occurred numerous eruptions of Cotopaxi that on three occasions have destroyed the nearby city of Latacunga.

[46] Muli-ambato - Brunner in his manuscript states that Muli-ambato today is known as San Miguel de Salcedo.

Rumiñahui had been in Quito and was gone. Quito's Temples of the Sun and Moon, royal treasury, palaces, lodgings and storehouses with everything that could provide aid and comfort to the enemy, had been emptied, burned, destroyed, and their countless treasures removed. The concubines and virgins of the temples were given the choice to flee the city or remain. Those who chose to remain and take their chances with the conquistadores, in order to preserve their honor, were ordered killed by Rumiñahui. Speaking of Benalcazar in Quito, Prescott relates in *History of the Conquest of Peru* ... "But great was his mortification on finding that either the stories of its riches had been fabricated, or that these riches were secreted by the natives."

We do not have the benefit of a Spanish chronicler traveling with Rumiñahui who kept eyewitness accounts, as was the case with the conquistadores. Reports between the chronicles and histories of Cieza, Herrera, Garcilaso, Fernández, Oviedo and Velasco, on the size of Rumiñahui's treasure convoy vary considerably from 600 to 70,000 cargas,[47] with six hundred cargas being slightly more than the twenty ton ransom of Atahualpa. Accounts of Rumiñahui's activities are far and few between, and most have been reduced to myth and legend. However, I am sure that if or when these lost treasures are discovered, that the Incas will have left records of their own, documented in the quipus [48] that most definitely will be found with any deposit, if they can ever be deciphered.

Shortly after Rumiñahui's death it appears that the Spaniards gave up on their ambitious quest for hidden treasure. The conquistadors were more preoccupied with lands to be acquired, people, land and mines to be exploited, cities, towns and churches to establish or rebuild and an empire that they had just begun to explore. Many were the stories and expectations of further "El Dorados" in this new world, which appeared easier for them to grasp, as lust for Inca gold continued.

■ ■ ■

Eugene Konrad Brunner wrote his early version of the history of the Inca and the Llanganati deposit that was derived from legends, myth, lore, historical research and his lifelong explorations into the treasures of Ecuador. These early writings are presented in their entirety without correction or adjustment except that footnotes have been added for ease of following his story … "In order to relate my adventures and misadventures in the search of the cursed treasure of Llanganati,[49] it is necessary to go

---

[47] Chroniclers and historians various treasure convoy sizes - Pedro de Cieza de León states 600 cargas, Gonzalo Fernández de Oviedo states 60,000 cargas while the Inca Garcilaso de la Vega states 70,000 cargas.

[48] Quipus - An Incan recording device that usually consisted of cords spun from llama or alpaca hair. Quipus mostly contained numeric and other values encoded by knots in a base ten positional system.

[49] Llanganati - Mountain range in the Andes of Ecuador encompassed within the Llanganati National Park. This park is 219,707 hectares in size and is

back in the past and become acquainted with the people and events that intervened in the history of this treasure. The Ati's were the royal family of the Kingdom's of Píllaro and Muli-ambato. Ati I was named Pillahuazo "the lightning conqueror," and he was the grandfather of Ati II, who was named Rumiñahui.

"Ati Pillahuazo made a great defense and war in the first invasion of the Kingdom of Quito by Tupac-Yupanqui, defeating the Inca in many battles. Later the son of Tupac-Yupanqui, Huayna-Capac, attempted yet another invasion. He too was defeated and repelled until on his third intent at conquering the Kingdom of Quito, Huayna-Capac finally defeated the lightning conqueror of Píllaro and Muli-ambato.

"In place of taking up arms in retribution, understanding the great value held for him in the warlike knowledge of Ati Pillahuazo and to consolidate the victory, Huayna-Capac married with the only daughter of Ati I, and of the Choazanguil Kingdom, with the princess Nary. Of this marriage was born Huayna-Curi ATI II, named Rumiñahui, which means "eye of stone," the name that forever enters in the history of Quito and of the Republic of Ecuador. Rumiñahui's lineage was superior to that of the son of Huayna-Capac in Cuzco, Huáscar. Rumiñahui was a son of the same father but as well he was the son of a royal princess. While Huáscar was not the son of a carnal sister of Inca Huayna-Capac but only of a relative. Therefore Huáscar's mother was not Coya but Nusta ... she was only nobility and not a queen.

"Eight years later, when Huayna-Capac defeated the aged Shyri (chieftain) Cacha at Jatuntaqui, by killing him in battle, the generales and Quiteño chiefs named Paccha (daughter of Cacha) Shyri and considered her to be Queen of the Caranqui. Huayna-Capac took her as a concubine and from this union was born the son named Atahualpa,[50] whose lineage was greater than that of Rumiñahui, due to his mother being a Queen.

■ ■ ■

"Before Huayna-Capac died, perhaps to please his two most loved sons, he divided Tahuantinsuyu in half. The southern portion from Macara and below was for Huáscar. The northern part above Macara and into Columbia was for Atahualpa. The Cañaris Indians that since the time of Tupac-Yupanqui had been the elite troops and the Kings Guard in Cuzco, rebelled against this division and declared themselves faithful subjects of Huáscar, and for this fraction originated the war between Huáscar and Atahualpa.

"Atahualpa went to Tomebamba to protest the action of the Cañaris, but with difficulty was able to flee and save his life. Huáscar, knowing what was going on, sent his general Atoco in command of a great army toward Quito to punish Atahualpa. However, Atoco suffered at Muli-ambato a

---

located between the provinces of Tungurahua, Cotopaxi, Napo and Pastaza. The parks highest peak is Cerro Hermoso.

[50] Huayna Capac had another son through this union, Atahualpa's younger brother Illescas also known as Hualpa Capac.

terrible defeat at the hands of the troops from Quito. Atoco was killed and threaded on a pointed stick. Historians talk of up to 25,000 dead in this battle.

"From here started the glorious march of the soldiers and generals Quiteños for the camps of battle at Cajamarca, Chachapoyas, Moyobamba, Huanuco and the final and ultimate battle in Quipaypan. The general's Quiz-Quiz, Razo-Razo, Calicuchima and Rumiñahui, along with the Inca Atahualpa, defeated the armies of Cuzco. Huáscar, along with his family, was imprisoned in the interior of the fortress of Jauja. Atahualpa having gone to punish the Indians of the island of Puna, suffered here a wound in his thigh. He was recuperating in the thermal baths of Cajamarca when the Spaniards arrived.

"The legends affirm that Atahualpa, in his victorious advance to Tomebamba, punishing the treason of the Cañaris, commanded the death of a thousand young men and scattered their hearts in a plain to see what fruits would grow from the hearts of traitors. It is for this reason alone that when Sebastian de Benalcazar advanced in his conquest of the Kingdom of Quito, he was accompanied by more than 35,000 Cañaris Indians, thirsty for vengeance and full of hatred. Solely due to their intervention, the Spaniards reached Quito.

"Many were the battles that the worthy warriors supported to defend the kingdom from the conquistadors. From among them they detached those of Tiocajas and those of the plain of Lasso against the small hill of Callo, it is here where one of the volcanos, I don't know precisely if it was the Tungurahua or the Cotopaxi, the truth is that it formed a grand cross of smoke in the sky that the Indians connected to the prophecy of the Seventh Inca, the Inca Yahuar-Huacac (he of the eyes of blood because he cried blood ... the bloody weeper), that said when it formed a great cross in the sky, the Indians would be conquered by bearded men with white complexions that came from the seas. The Indians disbanded and not even Rumiñahui, he with the determination of stone, could detain them.

■ ■ ■

"When the ultimate Inca and son of the Kingdom of Quito, Atahualpa, having made his offer to pay a ransom of gold and silver in exchange for his liberty, an offer that consisted of filling one room of his prison quarters to the height of his raised arm with gold and another room three times with silver, hundreds of Chasqui departed for all four corners of the great empire Tahuantinsuyu that extended for twelve hundred leagues [51] from Chile well into southern Columbia, with an order to ship the gold and silver from the temples and royal coffers to Cajamarca, where the Son of the Sun (Atahualpa) was imprisoned, or better stated, under house arrest with guards under orders to shoot to kill if the sovereign attempted to flee.

---

[51] A Spanish league was measured by the distance a horse could walk in an hour, about 2 ½ to 3 miles.

"The gold and silver began to arrive, thousands and thousands of Indians arrived day and night loaded down with precious metals, but this property arrived solely from the North of Chile, from certain regions of Peru, but none arrived from Quito, for the distance was excessively long. I am sure and the history confirms that the seven huandos [52] that initially departed from Quito, not one of them arrived in Cajamarca.

"Because the Spaniards killed the Son of the Sun, the Indians, in place of delivering the gold to Cajamarca, they concealed it. I must clarify that they hid it and did not throw it away or abandon it. Portions of the same, for orders received, went to rest on the slopes of the volcano Sangay, the Tunguru Sangay where it is said that the spirits roam. Another shipment that was closest to Cajamarca was hidden by Captain Quinara in the Valley of Piscombamba between Yangana and Vilcabamba in the province of Loja. It is also known that another shipment left Achupallas in the province of Chimborazo but never arrived on the other side of the mountains in Cañar. It is rumored constantly that another shipment had been concealed in the area of the Indian settlement Nisag between Alausi and Cuasuntos also in the province of Chimborazo.

"But the largest of all, the treasures from the Temples of Tacunga,[53] the treasures from the Temples of Quito, the treasures of the royal coffers and household, that all belonged to Atahualpa, the greatest portion was taken to the mysterious mountains of Llanganati, by Ati II, named Rumiñahui, the glorious defender of Quito, of noble lineage.

■ ■ ■

"Rumiñahui, after the death of Atahualpa,[54] took his place, eliminated Quilliscacha or better Illescas, brother of Atahualpa's father and mother, because he was very feminine and cowardly, he wanted to give up the Kingdom of Quito without a fight. He was executed and with his skin was made a drum of war [55] to demonstrate to the other chiefs and regulate them. There were many royal chiefs that accompanied Rumiñahui in his struggle to save Tahuantinsuyu from the false white gods the viracochas. Sota-Scre, Raze-Razo, Cosopango (governor of Quito), Zopo-Zopanqui, Quimbalembo of Sangolqui, Imbaquingo, Tucumango of Tacunga, Jacho of Sigchos and Nazacota-Puento of Cayambe, just to mention a few, all of whom helped in

---

[52] Huandos - Shipments carried by thousands of Indians.

[53] Tacunga - Today known as Latacunga located approximately forty miles south of Quito. During the reign of the Inca it contained a temple of the sun where the virgins dedicated to the service of the temple lived. A high steward was stationed in this village that was in charge of collecting the tribute of the neighboring provinces and storing it here.

[54] Atahualpa was the 17th Shyri of the Kingdom of the Shyris of Caranqui for eight years, Illescas followed as the 18th Shyri for a period of two months and then Rumiñahui for 1 year and 5 months until his death in 1534. From *Historical Dictionary of Ecuador, Appendix 1.*

[55] Rumiñahui killed Illescas and made a drum from his skin, his bones were made into panpipes and his teeth were strung into a necklace.

the struggle as well as with the concealing of the gold and silver treasures, eagerly desired by the Spaniards.

"Here, with his heart shattered and with the rest of his followers, he retired to Quito. There he began to destroy and burn the old capital of the Shyris, while his captain concealed part of the treasures of Quito in the surrounding area, like the Nina-Huilcas. In addition to this, Rumiñahui commenced the long march toward the lands of his grandfather on his mother's side, toward Píllaro, but heading for the plains behind of Cotopaxi and of Quilindana. When the Spaniards and Cañaris advanced for Machachi, Rumiñahui exited for the Vicentina toward Cuangopolo. Like always, when many people march carrying heavy loads, there are strong and the weak, it is for this reason that it was necessary to leave part of the treasures in a cave of the Cerro of Ilalo and the Indians of Cuangopolo until today are the guardians of this gold. The poor man that attempts to reach the site where is the entrance of the cave ...

"Afterwards Rumiñahui advanced with his people for Uyumbicho, Sangolqui, Batichubamba, Llavepungo following the riverbed of the river Pita al Pedregal, and it is consistently reported that in the slopes of the Cerro they left portions of the treasure. From here they went around Cotopaxi and Quilindana to reach the plains of Chalupas, where they were awaited by the two Huandos of gold that was commanded to take from Latacunga and with all this they marched for the Llanganatis." ... here ends Brunner's short history of the Inca.

■ ■ ■

Over the past centuries it has not been the story of the Inca Atahualpa's ransom and murder that has captured the hearts and minds of Ecuadorians. Curiously, it was the story of his half-brother Rumiñahui, the glorious defender of Quito,[56] who was tortured appallingly by the Spaniards in an attempt to make him reveal the secret of Quito's treasures, who is still alive in the hearts of the people of Ecuador even today, nearly five hundred years later.[57]

One of the oldest romantic treasure legends of Quito reads [58] … "The great treasures which the unfortunate Inca, Atahualpa, delivered to Pizarro as his ransom, are said to have come from Cuzco and other Peruvian towns. The treasure at Quito is said to have remained intact, and to have been seized upon by Rumiñahui, one of the Inca's generals, who, after the capture of his master by the Spaniards, had usurped the government of Quito, and with a view to his own elevation to the throne, had put to death all the members of

---

[56] By other accounts usurper of the thrown.

[57] During modern times Rumiñahui's face has been the prominent image on the face of the country's 1000 Sucre bank note. In 1985 the Ecuadorian legislature also voted to create a national Rumiñahui remembrance day on December first of every year.

[58] Velasco's version recorded in *Four Years among Spanish-Americans (1868)* by Friedrich Hassaurek.

his master's family whom he could get into his power. On the approach of the victorious Spaniards under Benalcazar, Rumiñahui set fire to the town, and evacuated it with the rest of the army. Some say he carried the treasure away with him; others, that he buried it at Quito before he left the city. And here our legend begins :.. 'Hualca, a partisan and follower of Rumiñahui, was one of the officers who superintended the burying of the treasure. In this he was assisted by his son Catuña, a boy of tender age. After the town had commenced to burn, a wall, near which Hualca's party had been at work, fell in, apparently crushing the child, so that his father left him, supposing him to be dead. Catuña, however escaped, and was taken care of by one of the Spaniards, who entered Quito immediately after Rumiñahui had left it. The boy's injuries were so severe that his features remained distorted and his limbs dislocated, and he became a hunchback of frightful ugliness. He was at last taken into the service of a Captain Hernan Suarez, who took a fancy to the poor cripple, taught him to read and write, and instructed him in the doctrines of the Christian religion. Suarez, having been unfortunate in his speculations, soon afterwards was reduced to great distress, and about to sell his house in order to meet the claims of some of his most pressing creditors, when Catuña told him to have a secret vault constructed under his residence, and to furnish it with all the implements necessary for smelting gold; adding, that he was able and willing to give him enough of the precious metal in bars, but that he would not let him see it in its original form. He also made his master promise never to reveal to any body from whom he had received it. Suarez complied with these instructions, and soon became a rich man. A great part of the wealth his servant had bestowed on him, he applied to charitable and religious purposes, and when he died, in 1550, leaving neither wife nor children, he made Catuña heir of his real and personal property.

'In the mean time, the change in the circumstances of Suarez had aroused suspicion. It was surmised by many that he owed his sudden unaccountable prosperity to Catuña, the ugly Indian imp who served him. This suspicion was confirmed by the great sums of money which Catuña subsequently bestowed on churches and convents, and distributed among the poor. He was taken into custody, and required to declare from what source he had derived his wealth. The Indian knew well enough that, should he declare the truth, his riches would be seized upon by the first conquerors, who considered any part of the treasure of Atahualpa as their lawful spoils. He, therefore, resorted to a most daring stratagem. He said it was true that he had been the benefactor of Suarez, and a great many others, but that he could have as much gold as he wanted, having made a compact with the Evil One, to whom he had sold his soul. Under other circumstances, this confession would not have improved his case, and he would probably have been dispatched by the tribunals of the Inquisition; but his munificent generosity had gained him the good-will of the priests and rabble, and probably of his own judges, who did not wish to dry up the source from which so much liberality flowed. They affected to pity his misery, and set him free. His statement was the more readily credited, as the Indians were then generally believed to have intercourse with the Prince of Darkness.

'Many of the priests, and especially the Franciscans, exhorted him to renounce his pact with the devil and make his peace with the Lord; but he remained unmoved, and insisted that he wanted to have gold as long as he lived. 'secretly,' says Father Velasco, the chronicler of Quito, he 'laughed at the exhortations of the monks, being at heart a good Christian and extremely devoted to the sufferings of the most holy Virgin." After his death, his premises were searched, and with considerable difficulty the vault was discovered, with a great quantity of gold in ingots, bars, and in vessels, and the tools with which Suarez had provided him. Still the people continued to believe in the story of his pact with the Evil One, 'and the truth,' adds Father Velasco, 'would never have been discovered, if it had not been for a Franciscan monk who had secretly been his confessor, and, on his death, left a written account of what Catuña had confided to him.'"

■ ■ ■

As detailed and accurate as the historical references have been in describing the riches of Cuzco, would it not stand to reason that the reports of treasures in the provincial capitals and Quito, whether lost or hidden, were as accurate? Another legend and myth surrounds the son of Píllaro Rumiñahui, which was passed from generation to generation within his hometown. What follows is the indigenous people's Spanish language version of the legend that provides a guide to the riches of Atahualpa's treasure that is ..."lost behind the ranges."[59] …

"Si quieres tener la ambición del blanco barbudo español, enemigo de nuestra raza pura, nunca des este derrotero que te voy a dejar, pues habiendo ido hasta nuestros cerros del sol los tres Llanganates, meterás las manos en la laguna encantada y sacarás el oro, ambición del barbudo blanco y corregidores de Tacunga y Ambato, que nuestras razas siempre les mandarás oprobios y maldiciones pidiendo a Dios Viracucha haga justicia para que siempre queden en poder de nuestra tierra y que nunca descubran los barbudos. Así te doy y te indico el derrotero que debes seguir sin avisar ni notificar a ninguno de los blancos que quieren vencer nuestros dominios.

"Te pondrás en el pequeño pueblo de Píllaro suelo de nuestro gran Rumiñahui, allí preguntarás por el Moya que era de Rumiñahui, seguirás hacia las alturas frías hasta llegar a nuestro cerro del Guapa a cuya punta, si es que el día fuese de bueno, mirando siempre el lado de donde sale el sol o sea el pueblo de Ambato que tendrás siempre a las espaldas y fijándote tus ojos verás siempre, al lado donde sale el sol, los tres cerritos que se llaman los Llanganatis que están en forma de tres, como el de callo el Tacunga, que dan las tolas en línea recta las del cerro Hermoso. Siguiendo este derrotero bajarás hasta llegar a la laguna verde que es la misma que se hizo a mano, ordenado por Rumiñahui, quien mandó a su hermano el cacique de Panzaleo se arroje allí todo el oro metal que quisieron los ambiciosos guiracochas para liberar a nuestro Padre Atahualpa con motivo de la orden que dio el guiracocha blanco. Seguirás, te digo, el cerro de Guapa, siempre con la montaña hasta que llegues al gran manchón de las grandes sangurimas que

---

[59] Rudyard Kipling from his poem *The Explorer*.

hacen de la confundir a los que anden por allí porque desvían del derrotero flechas.

"Pues te diré que ese manchón es el guía que llevarás siempre hasta la mano izquierda hasta cuando llegues al juncal grande; desde el juncal grande, a media ladera pasarás por medio de él, donde verás dos lagrimitas que llamamos 'laguna de los anteojos', por tener nariz al medio, una punta de arena semejante al Cuilcoche de Otavalos; desde este sitio volverás los ojos donde sale el sol y verás otra vez los Llanganates como lo viste otra vez desde el alto del gran Guapa y te prevengo que no te engañes porque dichas lagunitas has de dejar siempre a tu izquierda y siguiendo siempre con mano izquierda de nariz o punta verás un gran llano de paja donde es dormida del segundo días donde se deja las bestias y seguirás con pie hasta llegar a la laguna negra llamada Yanayacu, la cual dejarás a la izquierda, bajando con mucho cuidado a la ladera, llegando a la quebrada, llegando a la gran Chorrera que es el golpe del agua o Chorrera del Golpe, donde pasarás por puente de tres palos. Y si éstos no halla ya, buscarás sitio poniendo otro puente donde verás la choza donde sirve de dormida, unida a la gran piedra donde están trazados los derroteros.

"Al otro día seguirás el viaje por el mismo derrumbe de la montaña, llegando a la quebrada cerca muy honda donde pondrás palos para poder pasar con mucho tiento, porque es muy honda. Así llegarás a los pajonales donde braman los rayos del cielo, siguiendo los grandes llanos; y viendo que termina el gran llanete entrarás en una grande cañada entre los tres cerritos, donde toparás con camino empedrado del Inca y donde verás las puertas del socavón que está hecha como si fuera de iglesia; caminarás un buen trecho hasta topas con chorrera que sale de un hijo del cerro de Llanganates más grande haciendo tembladeras donde hay bastante oro que metiendo la mano sacarás otro granado.

"Pero para subir el cerro dejarás la tembladera y tomarás mano derecha por encima de chorrera, subiendo para dar vuelta el hijuelo y si acaso esta boca del hijuelo está tapada ha de ser con salvaje o musgo. Quita con las manos y darás con la puerta donde verás la guaira donde está horno para fundir metal. Si quieres regresar procura coger el río que queda a mano derecha, cogiendo playa para el hato siguiendo siempre el cañón del desagüe de la laguna; luego seguirás a mano derecha hasta cuando veas la nariz de las lagrimitas de anteojos y el gran Guapa que siempre deja atrás al pueblo de Ambato; seguirás cerro de mayordomo siguiendo pajonales fríos para bajar a Píllaro."

As with any translation, the human factor can interpret and infer many different meanings to the same words. For this reason I have provided both the Spanish version of the guide and my translation in English which follows ...

"If you yearn to achieve the wealth desired by the bearded white Spaniard, enemy of our pure race, never divulge this route that I am going to provide you. Because having gone to the three Llanganatis, our hills of the Sun, and by putting your hands into the enchanted lagoon you will get gold, the desire of the bearded white men and magistrates of Tacunga and Ambato, those who our lineage have always expressed disapproval and disappointment with, uttering curses urging God Viracocha for justice, so that the gold will always remain in the possession of our land and that it will never be discovered by the bearded ones. So here I bequeath and describe the path you must follow without warning or notifying any of the whites who want to overcome our domains.

"Placed in the small town of Píllaro, soil of our great Rumiñahui, there ask for the "Moya of Rumiñahui," continue toward the cold heights until you reach our peak of "Guapa," from whose top, if the day is good, always watching in the direction where the sun rises, or to say that you will always have the town of Ambato to your backs and your eyes will always focus to the side where the sun rises, toward the three mountains called the Llanganatis that are in the form of a triangle, like that of the "Callo of Tacunga,"putting the mounds in a straight line toward those of "Cerro Hermoso." Follow this course downhill until you reach the green lagoon that is the same that was made by hand, ordered by Rumiñahui, who sent his brother the Chieftain of Panzaleo to throw all the gold metal desired by the ambitious white gods to free our father Atahualpa, owing to the order that the white god gave. I say continue to follow the "Cerro Guapa," always with the mountain until you arrive at the great patch of dense vegetation of large "sangurimas" that will confuse those who walk by there because they are diverted from the route by "flechas."

"I will tell you that this spot where vegetation grows thick is the guide that you will always follow on the left hand until you reach the large "juncal" in the middle of the slope, pass through it, and from the large "juncal" you will see two small lakes that we call "Los Anteojos", from having a nose in the middle, a tip of sand resembling the "Cuilcoche de Otavalos." From this site focus your eyes where the sun rises and you will see again the Llanganatis just as you saw them from the height of the great "Guapa" and I warn you do not be deceived because these lagoons you must leave always on your left and proceeding with the nose or point on your left hand you will see a large plain of straw which is the second days sleeping place. This is where you will leave the beasts and proceed on foot to reach the Black Lake called "Yanayacu," which you leave to the left, descending very carefully along the hillside, arriving at a ravine, reaching the great waterfall that is the drain or "Chorrera del Golpe," where you will pass over a bridge of three poles. And if they do not already exist, search for a site to place another bridge where you will see the hut that serves to sleep in, attached to the large stone where many routes have been drawn out.

"The next day, continue to travel by the same landslide of the mountain, reaching a very deep gorge where you put poles in order to pass with much caution, because it is very deep. This way you can always get to the pasture where the rays of heaven roar, follow the great plain; and seeing that the plain ends you come into a large canyon between the three mountains, where you come across a trail paved by the Inca and from where you will see the entrance of the "socavón" (tunnel) which is made like the outside of a Church. You will walk a good way up coming across a waterfall coming out of a son (offshoot) of the largest Cerro of Llanganati creating a soft boggy area where there is more than enough gold so that by inserting your hand you will extract grains of gold.

"But to climb the mountain leave the soft boggy area and go along to the right hand passing above the waterfall, climbing to go around the offshoot and if by chance the mouth of the offshoot is covered as it should be with "salvaje" or wild moss, remove this with your hands and encounter the entrance, from where you will see the "guayra" (furnace) which is the oven to melt metal. If you want to return, seek the river and follow it on the right bank, taking to the beach toward the confluence, always following the canyon of the drainage of the lagoon; that you will follow on the right side until you see the nose of the "Lagunas de Anteojos" and the great "Guapa" that always resides behind the town of Ambato. Continue along to this mountain, your principal steward, then follow the cold pasture down to Píllaro."

This indigenous legend or guide, directs the benefactor to a lake made by hand where Rumiñahui ordered the gold destined for the ransom of Atahualpa to be thrown. Although many landmarks on the route to the treasure lake are clearly identified, the guide indicates there is also gold within a bog. The guide instructs the follower to remove the moss from the entrance of a tunnel, without mention of entering it. Continuing on, the guide further provides directions on how to ascend the mountain. However, the location of the treasure lake does not follow, instead the guide describes the route to return to Píllaro. Therefore, once the mountain has been ascended, you must decipher the treasure lake's location from the clues provided in the beginning of the guide.

It might be deduced that only upon correctly translating, deciphering and understanding this cryptic message contained in the beginning of the guide, will the treasure lake of Rumiñahui ultimately be discovered: "...los tres cerritos que se llaman los Llanganatis que están en forma de tres, como el de callo [60] el Tacunga, que dan las tolas en línea recta las del cerro Hermoso. Siguiendo este derrotero bajarás hasta llegar a la laguna verde que es la misma que se hizo a mano, ordenado por Rumiñahui ..."

Alternatively, one might also consider that Rumiñahui died in 1535 taking the secrets of Latacunga and Quito's treasures with him, or did he we ponder ... as lust for Inca gold continues.

■ ■ ■

---

[60] "Callo" - Callus in English, the term used in the context of geology refers to a protruding mass of hardened plant tissue.

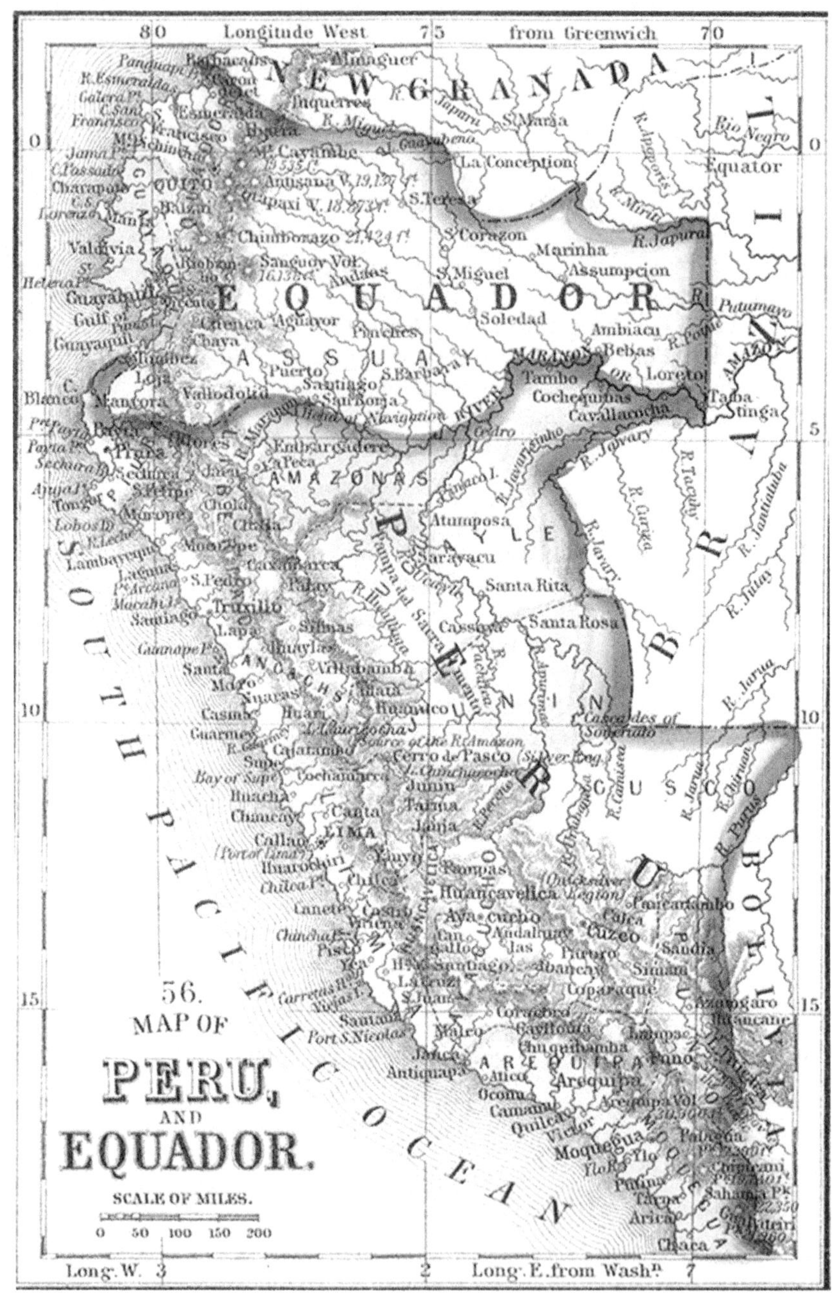

1860 Map of Equador & Peru

Samuel Augustus Mitchell

THE BOTANIST: RICHARD SPRUCE

The Spaniards lust for Inca gold so vividly detailed in *The Incas of Pedro Cieza de León*, unquestionably the most interesting and detailed account of the Incas, sadly has become more and more difficult to obtain with the passage of centuries. Book three is hard to acquire and book four relating to the conquest of Quito, is almost nonexistent. Rumiñahui's transport of treasure and perhaps Atahualpa's mummy into the Llanganatis would have been lost to memory, myth and legend, if not for the involvement of a young Spaniard named Valverde, his Indian wife, the King of Spain and Richard Spruce.

■ ■ ■

Travel and adventure author Jane Dolinger [1932-1995] wrote numerous books, including *Inca Gold find it if you can touch it if you dare (1968* [61]*)*. Chapter five entitled *Secret of the Golden Condor*, is an enthralling romantic account based in fact, yet related with great use of literary license, concerning Rumiñahui's treasure, a young Spaniard named Valverde, his Indian wife and the King of Spain.

Dolinger lays the basis for her story ... "For many centuries, it was believed that a great quantity of Inca treasure had been spirited away by the followers of Atahualpa, and buried in a remote area deep in the desolate, little-explored Llanganati Mountains of Central Ecuador."

Jane continues an account of Valverde where the lines between fact and fiction are extremely blurred, but it makes interesting and easy reading. Dolinger relates that the legend of the Llanganatis has a "solid basis" in fact through the *Derrotero de Valverde*. An account dictated for "His Majesty King Philip II"[62] of Spain by the "semi-illiterate young Spanish Conquistador Juan Valverde" concerning the source of his wealth that was brought back to Spain "in crude gold bars" and which had elevated his status and standing in the community.

The story is set in the small town of Píllaro in the foothills of the Llanganati Mountains, southeast of Quito, Ecuador. It began in 1584 when a young eighteen-year-old Spanish soldier named Juan Valverde arrived in the New World, drawn by the lust for Inca gold just as so many others before him. Lonely and homesick Valverde sought out the companionship of a woman, met and fell in love with a young seventeen-year-old named "Catla," whose

---

[61] Dolinger's source for portions of this book, by her own admission, was Eugene K. Brunner. Dolinger does indicate however that her story has its basis in "various documents and other written material in the Indian Archives and Madrid's National Library." Whether Dolinger actually researched in Spain, or this is what Brunner had told her, is unclear.

[62] King Phillip II reigned from 1554-1598. Historians and researchers have not concretely ascertained for which specific King the *Derrotero* was dictated.

father was a "high chieftain" among the Salasaca Indians.[63] Valverde had chosen to desert his army post in Ambato in order to be with his love, and they were married.

Later, in order for Valverde to correct his situation with the authorities, for which the penalty was death, and to travel to Spain with his young wife and live comfortably thereafter, it was decided by the chieftains of the Salasacas whom he had befriended, that they would break their solemn vow never to disclose the location of Rumiñahui's treasure. A dozen Indians and eight burros transported Valverde into the vastness of the Llanganatis in early May of 1589, returning three weeks later laden with pieces of golden treasure that was later hammered into "twelve large bars, each weighing approximately one hundred pounds, enough gold to make Valverde one of the richest and most respected men in Spain."

Once in Spain Valverde's gold was sold and converted to cash and "almost overnight he became a rich man." News and rumors of Valverde's great and instantaneous wealth spread throughout Spain ultimately reaching the ears of the King. Valverde was summoned to "Granada" where under threat of confiscation and imprisonment he dictated his famous *Derrotero* containing the "exact instructions one must follow to the site of the Inca treasure," the source of his wealth.

Dolinger delves further into specifics than most other authors on this subject providing specific names, dates, locations and the amount of Valverde's wealth, further blurring fact with fiction. Absolutely apparent though, is the fact that Dolinger concludes her story eloquently ... "The golden treasure of Rumiñahui may never be found, but it is certain that man, in his eternal quest for gold and riches, will continue to seek it."

■ ■ ■

As with any narrative that has been passed down throughout the centuries, there can be many versions of the same story. Another interesting account that was passed down throughout the generations of Píllaro occurs nearly two centuries later. This version indicates that José Valverde was married to a daughter of the Chieftain of Píllaro during 1770. At some point Valverde came to the knowledge of the secret of the Llanganatis and discovered the exact site of the treasure. Valverde returned with a small portion of his discovery to Píllaro, taking note of the landmarks in order to return. Valverde later traveled to Spain, sometime after 1788, but would never return to Píllaro and the Llanganatis. Instead, while in Spain Valverde would dictate his infamous deathbed *Derrotero* for his King, Carlos IV.[64]

Yet another contradictory account, which if true would invalidate the previous version, indicates that Valverde's deathbed *Derrotero* was not dictated in Spain, but in Ecuador, as Valverde never returned to Spain with

---

[63] The Salasaca Indians were known as the finest agriculturists of the realm and had been resettled from Bolivia to northern Ecuador by the Incas in the early 1500s.

[64] The reign of Carlos IV was from 1788 through 1808.

his wife. Valverde's *Derrotero*, this version indicates, consisted of two parts, the written guide and a companion map. The guide was delivered to the King of Spain and the map was kept by the church for safe keeping in Guayaquil. The remainder of the story mirrors what has previously been related, except for two points. A Padre Longo had obtained a copy of the map from the church in Guayaquil prior to his famed expedition on behalf of the Church and the King of Spain,[65] for this reason he was murdered while on the expedition. Many years later in 1684, the English Buccaneer William Dampier looted this exact same church in Guayaquil and pillaged the original map of Valverde.

■ ■ ■

Valverde's story based on the discovery of historic documents, hearsay, rumor and legend was brought to modern understanding in a very brief and straightforward scientific account through the botanist Richard Spruce, which will be related in this chapter. It is perhaps best to start our story with a brief sketch of Spruce's life and work. Strangely, there is no full length biography of such a remarkable man, which would easily fill volumes. Richard Spruce the man was by any reckoning one of the greatest botanical explorers of the nineteenth century.

Richard Spruce, named after his father and grandfather, was born in September 1817 at Ganthorpe near Terrington in England, in the West Midland region of England, the only child of Richard [66] and Ann.[67] Richard's mother having died, his father was remarried to Mary Priest shortly thereafter and the couple went on to have a family of eight daughters including Anne, Elizabeth, Sarah, Mary, Louisa and Harriet.[68] Three of Spruce's stepsisters died of scarlet fever in 1845, but at least one stepsister Anne, went on to have a family of her own, presenting Richard Spruce with six nephews and nieces; John Spruce, Harry, Alfred, Annie, Frances Elizabeth and Mary.[69] Remember this point as it will become extremely relevant later in our story.

Spruce took lessons in Latin and Greek from a retired schoolmaster, taught himself to read and write French, and in his latter years acquired Portuguese, Spanish and three Indian languages including Quichua. It appears however that Richard was mainly educated by his father who was a respected schoolmaster as evidenced by his gravestone in Terrington Churchyard which reads ... "Richard Spruce [the father] having been, during upwards of 40 years, schoolmaster upon the Estates of the Earl of Carlisle, who put up this stone as a memorial of the faithful and conscientious

---

[65] The story of which is related later in this chapter.
[66] Born 1782, died circa 1851.
[67] Born 1792, died circa 1832.
[68] Anne was born in 1833, Elizabeth in 1835, Sarah in 1838, Mary in 1840, Louisa in 1848 and Harriet circa 1851.
[69] John Spruce born circa 1859, Harry born circa 1860, Alfred [1862-1946], Annie circa 1866, Frances Elizabeth circa 1868 and Mary circa 1873.

manner in which he discharged the duties of that responsible and honorable office."

With such an epitaph ... what more need be said about Spruce's father?

■ ■ ■

A student of Spruce's father, George Stabler [1839-1910] born in Wellburn, would also become for a short period of time a student of Richard Spruce. Stabler was the son of James [70] and Elizabeth who provided him with two sisters, Hannah [1842-1917] and Mary [1845]. George was married in 1869 and had five children of his own,[71] James, Harold, Edgar, Oswald and Bertha Elizabeth. Stabler's lineage ended with his children, as they all went on in their lives without having any children of their own. George followed in Spruce's footsteps becoming a school teacher, schoolmaster of Levens Boys School and ultimately a botanist. Even given their drastic age difference of some twenty-two years, George was friendly his entire life with his teacher's son, Richard Spruce. Especially in his latter forty years of life, Richard Spruce would come to view Stabler not only as a very close friend, but as his confidant.

■ ■ ■

Spruce had developed a great love of nature at an early age and had taken up botany by the 1830s and by 1834, when merely sixteen years old, had produced a list of 403 species that he had found around Ganthorpe. In 1837 Spruce had drawn up yet another *List of the Flora of the Malton District* containing 485 species of flowering plants.

Following his father's footsteps into teaching, Spruce obtained the position of mathematical master at the Collegiate School of York at the end of 1839, which he retained until the school was closed in mid 1844. Spruce's teaching position had provided him with the benefits of a regular salary and spare time, which allowed him to continue and explore many parts of York where he made numerous botanical discoveries. Once Spruce found himself without a job, he became determined to find employment as a botanist. In the end Spruce decided to go to the French Pyrenees. Spruce left England in May 1845 and returned in April of the following year. Spruce had collected more than three hundred species of plants and mosses, of which seventeen were new to science and many not previously recorded from the Pyrenees.

After some consideration Spruce later became determined to conduct a botanical exploration of the Amazon. Spruce finally left England in June 1849 and arrived at Pará [72] in the northern part of Brazil in July. After arriving at Belém Spruce spent three months working in the forests of the area. Spruce went further afield mapping and collecting in the basin of the previously unexplored Río Trombetas. Spruce also explored and mapped

---

[70] Born circa 1813, died 1893.

[71] George Stabler's children; James born 1870, Harold born 1872 died 1945, Edgar born 1874, Oswald born 1876 and Bertha Elizabeth born 1878 died 1917.

[72] Pará now Belém: A city on the banks of the Amazon estuary.

the Río Negro and some of its tributaries. In 1855 Spruce explored some of the Amazon headwaters, the Huallaga, Pastaza and Bombonasa rivers which were particularly difficult and dangerous to navigate.

In 1857 Spruce left Tarapotó, Peru, bound for Canelos, Ecuador, ultimately arriving by foot at the town of Baños in the Andes of Ecuador, where he stayed for six months before heading to Ambato in January of 1858. Spruce found Ecuador to be in a revolutionary state during this entire period which limited his travels.

■ ■ ■

The Ecuadorian-Peruvian Territorial Dispute of 1857-1860 began when Ecuador attempted to sell Amazonian land claimed by Peru and the Peruvian government headed by President Ramón Castilla ordered a blockade of Ecuador's ports in order to force the cancellation of the sale. By late 1859 Ecuadorian President Francisco Robles had fled the country and control of Ecuador was consolidated between General Guillermo Franco in the city of Guayaquil and a provisional government in Quito headed by Gabriel García Moreno.

Due to the temporary occupation of Ecuadorian territory by Castilla's forces upon his arriving in Guayaquil during October 1859 with a few thousand troops to negotiate and sign a treaty with Ecuadorian General Franco in January 1860, this dispute is sometimes referred to as the Ecuadorian–Peruvian War of 1859. No fighting took place between the troops of the two countries within the duration of the dispute. However, in September 1860, the forces of the provisional government, commanded by García Moreno and General Juan José Flores defeated Franco's government at the Battle of Guayaquil, ending the civil war in Ecuador.

■ ■ ■

In Ecuador throughout 1860, Spruce collected seeds and living plants of the Peruvian Cinchona [73] tree for the Government of India because they were concerned about the supply of quinine, which was essential for safeguarding the health of the Indian army. Spruce collected these plants in the rain forest below the Chimborazo volcano, packed and dispatched the material, which was then established in southern India.

While at Ambato, Spruce was suffering from the effects of rheumatic fever and also suffered a stroke and found himself partly paralyzed in the neck, back and legs. For a while Spruce struggled with his collecting, but the following year he had yet another disaster, the failure of a mercantile house in Guayaquil in which Spruce had invested most of his savings that left him almost bankrupt. After a few more years on the coast of Ecuador and in Peru, Spruce found it impossible to continue his work and returned to England in May of 1864. Spruce arrived back in England almost penniless

---

[73] Cinchona - The medicinally active bark, which is stripped from this tree, dried and powdered, contains a variety of alkaloids, including the anti-malarial compound quinine.

and in very poor health due to the effects of his stroke and an intestinal disease.

Spruce however had survived all kinds of dangers, illnesses and deprivations, working for long periods alone except for his Indian assistants. His nearly fifteen-year expedition resulted in Spruce collecting more than seven thousand species of plants and fungi. Spruce's work added enormously to the scientific knowledge of Amazonian botany. The high quality of the specimens Spruce sent to England and the scrupulous care with which they were collected, labeled and annotated was clearly evident throughout his work. Spruce's contributions involved not only botany, he added much to the scientific description of the Andean Indians and his mapping of little known parts of Amazonia was recognized by his election as a fellow of the Royal Geographical Society in 1866.

Spruce never attended a university but in 1864 he was awarded a PhD. by the Academy of Sciences in Berlin in recognition of his published work and eminence as a botanist and explorer. His most important non-bryological work was his classical account of the palms of the Amazon (1870), but purportedly his greatest work was the *Hepaticae Amazonicae et Andinae (1884-85).*

The importance of any work however, can ultimately be attributed to the relevance and benefit it may provide the reader. For the purposes of our story, Spruce's greatest work was the presentation to the Royal Geographical Society and subsequent publication of his twenty-fifth paper; *On the Mountains of Llanganati in the Eastern Cordillera of the Quitonian Andes.* This work would later be edited and condensed by Alfred Russell Wallace and republished with footnotes and commentary in Spruce's *Notes of a Botanist on the Amazon & Andes; Being Records of Travel on the Amazon and its Tributaries, The Trombetas, Río Negro, Uaupés, Casiquiara, Pacimoni, Huallaga, and Pastasa; as also to the cataracts of the Orinoco, along the eastern side of the Andes of Peru and Ecuador, and the shores of the pacific, during the years 1849-1864,* published posthumously in 1908.

Never married, Spruce died of influenza in December 1893 and is buried beside his parents in the churchyard at Terrington in accordance with his directions to the executor of his estate, Matthew B. Slater. Although a great portion of Spruce's journals and papers have been preserved for posterity, Spruce's Ecuadorian journals (1858-1864), have to my knowledge never been found.

■ ■ ■

While Spruce was still in Ecuador, one of his papers was presented to the Royal Geographical Society (RGS) and communicated by a third party. On 12 Mar 1860 a paper entitled *On the Mountains of Llanganati, in the Eastern Cordillera of the Quitonian Andes, illustrated by a map constructed by the late Don Atanasio Guzmán by RICHARD SPRUCE, Esq* [74] was presented on Spruce's behalf to the RGS by Sir W. J. Hooker. This paper [75] and accompanying map was later published, as is customary, in the *Geographical Journal* of the same society, volume XXXI of 1861. Spruce's paper is reproduced here in its entirety.

XI. *On the Mountains of Llanganati,*
in the Eastern Cordillera of the Quitonian Andes,
illustrated by a map constructed by the late
Don Atanasio Guzmán.
By Richard Spruce, Esq.

"IN the year 1857 I travelled from Tarapoto, in Peru, to Baños, in Ecuador, along the rivers Huallaga, Marañon, Pastasa, and Bombonasa to Canelos, and thence overland through the forest to Baños---a journey which occupied me exactly a hundred days. At the Indian village of Andoas, near the confluence of the Bombonasa with the Pastasa, a distant view is sometimes obtained of the Andes of Quito, but during my stay there the sky was too much obscured to allow of any but near objects being seen. On the 21st of May I reached Paca-yacu, below Canelos, and was detained there three weeks in getting together Indians for conveying my goods through the forest, and procuring the necessary provisions for the way. This village stands on a plateau elevated 240 feet above the river Bombonasa, and about 1800 feet above the sea. In fine weather there is a magnificent view of the Cordillera, looking westward from the plateau, but I saw it only once for about a couple of hours in all its entirety. It takes in an angle of about 60°, bounded left and right by forest on adjacent elevations. At my feet lay the valley of the Bombonasa, taking upwards a northwesterly direction; the stream itself was not visible, and audible only when swollen by rains. Beyond the Bombonasa stretched the same sort of boldly undulated plain I had remarked from Androas upwards, till reaching one long low ridge of remarkably equable height and direction (north to south): this is the watershed between the Bombonasa and Pastasa, and the latter river flows along its western foot. A little northward of west from Paca-yacu the course of the Pastasa bends abruptly, and is indicated by a deep gorge stretching westward from behind the said ridge. This gorge has on each side steep rugged hills---spurs of the Cordillera---of from 5000 to 7000 feet high; one of those on the right is called Abítagua, and the track from Canelos to Baños passes over its summit. All this was frequently visible, but it was only when the mist rolled away from the plain, a little after sunrise, that the lofty Cordillera beyond lay in cloudless majesty. To the extreme left (south)

---

[74] Esquire is a term of British origin used as an unofficial title of respect, having no precise significance, used to denote a high but indeterminate social status.

[75] For reasons to be explained later, I have taken the liberty to highlight portions of Spruce's paper in **bold** print. The footnotes are Spruce's.

rose Sangáy, or the volcano of Macas, remarkable for its exactly conical outline, for the snow lying on it in longitudinal stripes (apparently of no great thickness), and for the cloud of smoke continually hovering over it. A good way to the right was the loftier mountain called "El Altar" its truncated summit jagged with eight peaks of nearly equal elevation, and clad with an unbroken covering of snow, which glittered in the sun's rays like crystal---an altar to whose elevated purity no mortal offering will perhaps ever attain.[76] Not far to the right of El Altar, and of nearly equal altitude, stood Tunguragua, a bluff irregular peak with a rounded apex capped with snow, which also descends in streaks far down its sides.[77] To the right of Tunguragua and over the summit of Abitagua appeared lofty blue ridges, here and there pointed with white, till on the extreme right was dimly visible a snowy cone of exactly the same form as Sangáy, but much more distant and loftier; this was Cotopaxi, one of the most formidable volcanoes on the face of our globe. Far behind Tunguragua, and peeping over its left shoulder, was distinctly visible a paraboloidal mass of unbroken snow; this was Chimborazo, long considered the monarch of the Andes, and though latterly certain peaks in Bolivia are said to have out topped it, it will be for ever immortalized in men's memories by its association with such names as Humboldt and La Condamine. Thus to right and left of the view I had an active volcano---Cotopaxi I never saw clearly but once, but Sangáy was often visible when the rest of the Cordillera was veiled in clouds, and on clear nights we could distinctly see it vomiting forth flame every few minutes. The first night I passed at Paca-yacu I was startled by an explosion like that of distant cannon, and not to be mistaken for thunder; it came from Sangáy, and scarcely a day passed afterwards without my hearing the same sound once or oftener.

In the month of July 1857 I reached Baños, where I learnt that the snowy points I had observed from Paca-yacu, between Tunguragua and Cotopaxi, were the summits of a group of mountains called Llanganati, from which ran down to the Pastasa the densely-wooded ridges I saw to northward. I was further informed that these mountains abounded in all sorts of metals, and that it was universally believed the Incas had deposited an immense quantity of gold in an artificial lake on the flanks of one of the peaks at the time of the Spanish Conquest. They spoke also of one Valverde, a Spaniard, who from being poor had suddenly become very rich, which was attributed to his having married an Indian girl, whose father showed him where the treasure was hidden, and accompanied him on various occasions to bring away portions of it; and that Valverde returned to Spain, and, when on his death-bed, bequeathed the secret of his riches to the king. Many

---

[76] El Altar seen from the western side---from Riobamba, for instance---is very distinctly perceived to be a broken-down volcano, which is by no means the case when seen from the east.

[77] Tunguragua seen from the north and north-west is an almost symmetrical truncated cone, and the most picturesque peak in the Andes.

expeditions, public and private, had been made to follow the track indicated by Valverde, but no one had succeeded in reaching its terminus; and I spoke with two men in Baños who had accompanied such expeditions, and had nearly perished with cold and hunger on the páramos of Llanganati, where they had wandered for thirty days. The whole story seemed so improbable that I paid little attention to it, and I set to work to examine the vegetation of the adjacent volcano Tunguragua, at whose north-eastern foot the village of Baños is situated. In the month of September I visited Cotaló, a small village on a plateau at about two thirds of the ascent of Guayrapáta, the hill in front of Tunguragua and above the confluence of the rivers Patate and Chambo. From Cotaló, on a clear night of full moon, I saw not only Tunguragua, El Altar, Condorasto, and the Cordillera of Cubilliú, stretching southwards toward the volcano Sangáy, but also to the eastward the snowy peak of Llanganati. This is one of the few points from which Llanganati can be seen; it appears again, in a favourable state of the atmosphere, a good way up the slopes of Tunguragua and Chimborazo.

At Baños I was told also of a Spanish botanist who a great many years ago lost his life by an accident near the neighbouring town of Patate, and that several boxes belonging to him, and containing dried plants and manuscripts, had been left at Baños, where their contents were finally destroyed by insects. In the summers of the years 1858 and 1859 I visited Quito and various points in the Western Cordillera, and for many months the country was so insecure, on account of internal dissensions, that I could not leave Ambato and Riobamba, where my goods were deposited, for more than a few days together. I obtained, however, indisputable evidence that the *Derrotero* or Guide to Llanganati of Valverde had been sent by the King of Spain to the Corregidors of Tacunga and Ambato, along with a Cedula Real (Royal Warrant) commanding those functionaries to use every diligence in seeking out the treasure of the Incas. That one expedition had been headed by the Corregidor of Tacunga in person, accompanied by a friar, Padre Longo, of considerable literary reputation. The *Derrotero* was found to correspond so exactly with the actual localities, that only a person intimately acquainted with them could have drawn it up; and that it could have been fabricated by any other person who had never been out of Spain was an impossibility. This expedition had nearly reached the end of the route, when one evening the Padre Longo disappeared mysteriously, and no traces of him could be discovered, so that whether he had fallen into a ravine near which they were encamped, or into one of the morasses which abound all over that region, is to this day unknown. After searching for the Padre in vain for some days, the expedition returned without having accomplished its object.

The Cedula Real and *Derrotero* were deposited in the archives of Tacunga, whence they disappeared about twenty years ago. So many people were admitted to copy them that at last some one, not content with a copy, carried off the originals. I have secured a copy of the *Derrotero*, bearing date August 14, 1827; but I can meet with no one who recollects the date of the original documents.

I ascertained also that the botanist above alluded to was a Don Atanasio Guzmán, who resided some time in the town of Píllaro, whence he headed many expeditions in quest of the gold of Llanganati. He made also a map of the Llanganatis, which was supposed to be still in existence. Guzmán and his companions, although they found no deposit of gold, came on the mouths of several silver and copper mines, which had been worked in the time of the Incas, and ascertained the existence of other metals and minerals. They began to work the mines at first with ardour, which soon, however, cooled down, partly in consequence of intestine quarrels, but chiefly because they became disgusted with that slow mode of acquiring wealth when there was molten gold supposed to be hidden close by; so the mines were at length all abandoned. This is said to have taken place early in the present century, but the exact date I can by no means ascertain. Guzmán is reported to have met with Humboldt, and to have shown his drawings of plants and animals to that prince of travellers. He died about 1806 or 1808, in the valley of Leytu, about four leagues eastward of Ambato, at a small farmhouse called now Leytillo, but marked on his map San Antonio. He was a somnambulist, and having one night walked out of the house while asleep, he fell clown a steep place and so perished. This is all I have been able to learn, and I fear no documents now exist which can throw any further light on the story of his life, though a botanical manuscript of his is believed to be still preserved in one of the archives of Quito. I made unceasing inquiries for the map, and at length ascertained that the actual possessor was a gentleman of Ambato, Señor Salvador Ortega, to whom I made application for it, and he had the kindness to have it brought immediately from Quito, where it was deposited, and placed in my hands; I am therefore indebted to that gentleman's kindness for the pleasure of being able to lay the accompanying copy of the map before the Geographical Society.

The original map is formed of eight small sheets of paper of rather unequal size (those of my copy exactly correspond to them), pasted on to a piece of coarse calico, the whole size being 3 feet 10 ½ inches by 2 feet 9 inches. It is very neatly painted with a fine pencil in Indian ink the roads and roofs of houses red but it has been so roughly used that it is now much dilapidated, and the names, though originally very distinctly written, are in many cases scarcely decipherable: in making them out I have availed myself of the aid of persons familiar with the localities and with the Quichua language. The attempt to combine a vertical with a horizontal projection of the natural features of the country has produced some distortion and dislocation, and though the actual outline of the mountains is intended to be represented, the heights are much exaggerated, and consequently the declivities too steep. Thus the apical angle of the cone of Cotopaxi (as I have determined it by actual measurement) is 121°, and the slope (inclination of its surface to the horizon) 29 ½°; while on Guzmán's map the slope is 69 ¼°, so that the inclination is only three-sevenths of what he has represented it, and we may assume a corresponding correction needed in all the other mountains delineated [78].

The whole map is exceedingly minute, and the localities mostly correctly named, but there are some errors of position, both absolute and relative, such that I suppose the map to have been constructed mainly from a simple view of the country, and that no angles and very few compass-bearings have been taken. The margins of the map correspond so nearly with the actual parallels and meridians, that they may be assumed to represent the cardinal points of the compass, as on an ordinary map, without sensible error.

The country represented extends from Cotopaxi on the north to the base of Tunguragua on the south, and from the plain of Callo (at the western foot of Cotopaxi) on the west to the river Puyu, in the forest of Canelos, on the east. It includes an area of something less than an equatorial degree, namely, that comprised between 0° 40' and 1° 33' S. lat., and between 0° 10' W., and near 0° 50' E. of the meridian of Quito. In this space are represented six active volcanoes (besides Cotopaxi), viz.--

1. El Volcan de los Mulatos, east a little south from Cotopaxi, and nearly on the meridian of the Río de Ulva, which runs from Tunguragua into the Pastasa. The position of this volcano corresponds to the Quilindaña of most maps a name which does not occur on Guzmán's, nor is it known to any of the actual residents of the country. A group of mountains running to north-east, and terminating in the volcano, is specified as the Cordillera de los Mulatos: it is separated from Cotopaxi by the Valle Vicioso.

2. El Volcan de las Margasitas, south-east by east from Los Mulatos, and a little east of north from the mouth of the Río Verde Grande. "Margasitas" (more properly Marquesitas) corresponds nearly to the term "pyrites," and is a general name for the sulphates of iron, copper, &c.

3. Zunchu-urcu, a smaller volcano than Margasitas, and at a short distance south-south-east of it. "Zunchu" is the Quichua term for mica or talc.

4. Siete-bocas, a large mountain, with seven mouths vomiting flame, south-west by south from Margasitas, west by south from Zunchu. Its southern slope is the Nevado del Atilis.

5. Gran Volcan del Topo, or Yurag-Llanganati, nearly east from Siete-bocas and south-west from Zunchu. A tall snowy peak at the head of the river Topo, and the same as I saw from Cotaló. It is the only one of the group which rises to perpetual snow, though there are many others rarely clear of snow; hence its second name Yurag (White) Llanganati.[79]

---

[78] The apical angle of Tunguragua—the steepest mountain I ever climbed—is 92 ½° and the slope 43 ¼°

[79] Villavicensio gives its height as 6520 varas (17,878 English feet) in his *Geografia del Ecuador*, from a measurement (as he says) of Guzmán, but does not inform us where he obtained his information.

[This mountain is partly shown on the extreme right margin of the map here given.]

The last four volcanoes are all near each other, and form part of what Guzmán calls the Cordillera de Yurag-urcu, or Llanganatis of the Topo.

North-east from the Volcan del Topo, and running from south-east to north-west, is the Cordillera de Yana-urcu, or the Llanganatis of the Curaray, consisting chiefly of a wooded mountain with many summits, called Rundu-uma-urcu or Sacha-Llanganati.

6. Jorobado or the Hunchback, south-southwest half west from Yurac-Llanganati, and between the river Topo and the head of the greater Río Verde.

I have conversed with people who have visited the Llanganati district as far as forty years back, and all assure me they have never seen any active volcano there; yet this by no means proves that Guzmán invented the mouths vomiting flame which appear on his map. The Abbé Velasco, writing in I77O,[80] says of Tunguragua, "It is doubtful whether this mountain be a volcano or not," and yet three years afterwards it burst forth in one of the most violent eruptions ever known. I gather from the perusal of old documents that it continued to emit smoke and flame occasionally until the year 1780. Many people have assured me that smoke is still seen sometimes to issue from the crater. I was doubtful about the fact, until, having passed the night of November 10, 1857, at the height of about 8000 feet on the northern slope of the mountain, I distinctly saw at daybreak (from 5 ½ to 6 ½ A.M.) smoke issuing from the eastern edge of the truncated apex.[81] In ascending on the same side, along the course of the great stream of lava that overwhelmed the farm of Juivi and blocked up the Pastasa, below the mouth of the Patate, for eight months, we came successively on six small fumaroli, from which a stream of thin smoke is constantly issuing. People who live on the opposite side of the valley assert that they sometimes see flame hovering over these holes by night. The inhabitants of the existing farm of Juivi complain to me that they have been several times alarmed of late (especially during the months of October and November 1859) by the mountain "bramando" (roaring) at night. The volcano is plainly, therefore, only dormant, not extinct, and both Tunguragua and the Llanganatis may any day resume their activity.

Returning to the map, let us trace briefly its hydrography. The actual source of the Napo is considered to be the Río del Valle, which runs northward through the Valle Vicioso, on the eastern side of Cotopaxi. Its large tributary the Curaray (written Cunaray by Guzmán) rises only a few miles more to the south, in the Cordillera de los Mulatos, in

---

[80] Historia de Quito

[81] The same morning (Nov. 11), at 4 A.M., I observed a great many shooting-stars in succession, all becoming visible at the same point (about 40° from the zenith), proceeding along the arc of a circle drawn through Orions Belt and Sirius, and disappearing behind the cone of Tunguragua.

several small streams which feed the lake Zapalá (a mile or more across) and issuing from its eastern extremity run east-south-east to Yana-cocha (Black Lake), a large body of water a league and a-half long by two miles broad. After passing this lake the river takes the name of Desaguadero de Yana-cocha, and lower down that of Río de las Sangurimas, receiving in its course (besides smaller streams) the Río de los Mulatos from the north, and a good way farther down the Río de los Llanganatis, coming from the south along a deep ravine (Cañada honda) between Rundu-umu and the Volcan del Topo. Beyond this and nearly north by east from the Volcan del Topo it is joined from the north by a considerable stream, the Curaray Segundo or Río de las Flechas, and takes the name of Río Grande de los Curarayes. The general course of the Curaray is eastward, as is also that of the Napo, and although the two rivers diverge so little from each other, they run as it were side by side through four degrees of longitude ere they meet.

The map is traversed from the north-western corner by a large stream, the Patate, rising in the western cordillera near Ilinisa, and running east-south-east through the central *callejon* (the lane between the two cordilleras) to a little south of Cotopaxi, where it reaches the base of the eastern cordillera, which it thenceforth separates from the callejon until it unites with the Chambo, at the foot of Tunguragua, to form the Pastasa. It receives all the streams flowing from the eastern side of the western cordillera, from Ilinisa to Chimborazo, of which the principal is the Ambats. From Cotopaxi the western edge of the eastern cordillera has a general direction of south by east. It consists of elevated páramos sown with lakes and morasses, and rarely covered with snow, which sink down to the river Patate, and from Píllaro southward have many deep-wooded ravines on the slope. From Píllaro northward they sink down into the plain quite bare of wood. The whole range is vulgarly called "Páramos de Píllaro." The principal tributaries of the Patate entering from these mountains are the Aláquis, which comes in a little north of Tacunya, and whose bed is subject to sudden enlargement from the melting of the snows on Cotopaxi, interrupting all communication with the capital; the Guapanti, whose sources are a number of lakes lying south of Lake Zapalá, their united waters flowing westward through the large lake Pisayambu, and entering the Patate near the village of San Miguel; and the Cusatágua, which comes down through a black wooded valley from the Cerro de los Quinua1es; on the left it is joined by a stream which, about midway, forms a high cascade of two leaps, called Chorrera de Chalhuaurca (Fish-hill Fall): this cascade is visible from and nearly east of Ambato.

As the great mineral districts of Llanganati, occupying the northern half of the map, was repeatedly travelled over by Guzmán himself, it is fuller of minute detail than the rest; and I am assured by those who have visited the actual localities that not one of them is misplaced on the map; but the southern portion is much dislocated; and, as I have traversed the whole of it,

I will proceed to make some remarks and corrections on this part of the map.

From Chimborazo (lying a few miles to westward of the village of Mocha) a spur or knot is sent off to the eastward, containing the mesetas or páramos of Sanancajas and Sabañán and the heights of Igualáta. Guambaló, Múlmúl, and Guayrapata, which last slopes abruptly down to the junction of the Chambo and Patate. These are so much transposed in Guzmán's map that I have omitted them in my copy, with the exception of the last. Even the environs of Ambato are much distorted; for the river Pachanlica actually unites with the Ambato a little above the mouth of the latter, instead of running direct into the Patate, some distance below the Ambato, as it is made to appear on the map.

Let us now descend the valley of the Pastasa from Guayrapata.[82] **The easterly wind, due to the earth's rotation, is distinctly felt along the Amazon so long as that river preserves an enormous width, and its course presents no abrupt sinuosities; but in its upper part, and on most of its tributaries, the wind is variable, and owes its modifications partly to local circumstances. In ascending the valley of the Pastasa from the roots of the Andes, one begins to feel the general wind again at a height of about 4000 feet, and, on coming out on the top of Guayrapata (9000 to 10,000 feet), the easterly wind (blowing up the gorge of Baños) strikes with tremendous force against that barrier, which is almost continually veiled in mist. The forest which crowns it is so densely hung with mosses as to be almost impenetrable; and one is forcibly struck by the contrast on emerging from the humidity and vigorous vegetation of Guayrapata to the arid sandy plains extending toward Píllaro and Ambato.**

The Chambo, which flows at the base of Guayrapata, is a larger stream than the Patate (though Guzmán's map represents it much smaller), and takes its origin from the volcano Sangáy. The steep descent from Guayrapata to the river is 3000 feet in perpendicular height, and occupies the traveller two hours to descend whether mounted or on foot; but from the opposite margin of the river rises the majestic cone of Tunguragua in an unbroken slope of full 11,000 feet perpendicular! Proceeding eastwards from the confluence of the two rivers, the first stream which enters to swell their united waters is the Lligua coming from the north. Below this, and on the right bank, near the village of Baños, a small stream of tepid water, the Vascún, comes from Tunguragua. Before the last eruption of Tunguragua (April 23rd, 1773) a larger stream came down from the mountain and watered the farm of Juívi, in the angle between the Chambo and Pastasa; but the lava which descended on that side buried the farm, and since then the rivulet has

---

[82] Guayra-pata = margin (or beginning) of the wind; thus, sacha-pata = edge of the wood; Cocha-pata = margin of the lake.

been dry, though its bed is still traceable wherever not covered up by the lava. The water now finds its way through a subterranean channel, and bursts out in considerable volume on the very margin of the Pastasa, beneath the lava which is there heaped up to the height of more than a hundred feet. Not a single stream waters now the northern side of Tunguragua, all the way from Baños to Puela (half a day's journey), though several gush out of the cliff on the right bank of the Chambo.

A little above Baños, and on the same side of the river, stand a few cottages called Pitíti (the cleft), because the Pastasa at that point foams through a narrow, tortuous chasm from 150 to 200 feet deep.

Below Baños, and on the opposite (the left) bank, enters the Illúchi, whose course is parallel to that of tbe Lligua. The next stream, the Río de Ulva, is of considerable volume, and comes down from the snows on the north-eastern side of Tunguragua.

A very little below the mouth of the Ulva, and on the opposite bank enters a still larger stream, the Río Verde Primero, which descends from the páramos of Llanganati.

Thus far there has been little to correct in this part or the map; but the next tributary of the Pastasa therein indicated is now called the Río de Agoyán, and the farm of Agoyán occupies the site marked on the map "La Yunguílla." There is no river called Yunguílla, and the farm known by that name is actually on the farther side of the next river (the Río Blanco); while the farm of Antombós is at the eastern foot of the hill called El Sapotal, and on a smaller stream than the Río Blanco. Exactly opposite Antombós the river Chinchin falls over a high cliff into the Pastasa.

The last bridge across the Pastasa is above the mouth of the Agoyán: on passing it we have fairly entered the Montaña, or Forest, of Canelos. A little above the mouth of the Río Blanco is the Chorrera de Agoyán, one of the finest waterfalls in South America, where the Pastasa is precipitated over a semicircular cliff, deeply excavated to the left of the fall, a height of about 150 feet.

Continuing along the left bank of the Pastasa, we next reach the Río Verde Segundo---now better known as the Río Verde Grande---which comes from the Cordillera de Pucarumi (Red-stone Ridge), running south of the snowy Llanganati. There is now a fine cane-farm near the mouth of the Río Verde, where the existing track to Canelos passes. The river is unfordable, and has to be crossed at a narrow place by throwing poles across from cliff to cliff.

The prevailing rock in the Gorge of Baños (as this deep, narrow valley may well be called) is mica-schist, though a hard, compact, black, shining, volcanic rock protrudes in many places, especially at the bridges of Baños and Agoyán.

The next river marked on the map is the Río Colorado, now known as the Río Mapóto, but well meriting its ancient name by its red margins and the red stones in its bed, coloured by a ferruginous deposit. At its mouth a broad beach (Playa de Mapóto) extends down the Pastasa for near 2 leagues: this beach is never entirely covered with water even in the highest floods; and it bears great quantities of the wax-tree called "laurél" (*Myrica cerifera*). But the Río Colorado, instead of being at the short distance from the Río Verde represented in the map, is as far apart from it as the Río Verde is from the bridge of Agoyán; and from the Río Verde to Mapóto is a good day's journey, as is also the distance from Mapóto to the river Topo. It is true that the Río Verde and Topo, though so wide apart at the mouth, may converge in the upper part (as is represented in the map); but I much suspect that the eastern portion of the map is much contracted in longitude, although, from the comparative paucity of details, the contrary might seem to be the case.

The Topo is the largest of all the upper tributaries of the Pastasa. In the time of Guzmán it seems to have been passed by a Taravita [83] a good way up, but the modern track to Canelos crosses it at only 200 yards from the mouth. The Topo, as far as anyone has been up it, is one continued rapid; and where it is crossed nothing is to be seen but rocks and foam, while the shock of its waters makes the very ground tremble. To pass over it bridges of bamboo have to be thrown from the margin to rocks in the middle, and thence to the opposite side, so that in all four bridges are needed; but a very slight flood lays one of the rocks under water, and then it is impossible to rest a bridge on it.

Only a league below the mouth of the Topo enters the Shuña, a river of little less volume than the former; but as there is a point on each side, where the rocks advance considerably into the stream, it admits of being passed by a single bridge. A flood, however, renders it equally impassable as the Topo.

When I journeyed from Canelos to Baños, I found the Shuña somewhat swollen, and crossed it with difficulty; but when I reached the Topo, I found one of the rocks, on which it is customary to rest a bridge, covered with water. My party consisted of sixteen persons, for whose sustenance every article of provision had to be carried along with us. We waited two days: the river, instead of lowering, continued to rise; our provisions were nearly exhausted, and we saw ourselves exposed to perish of hunger. In this dilemma we found a place a little higher up the river, where we determined to attempt the passage by means of three bridges. On making the experiment, we found the distance between the two rocks in the middle so great that the bamboos barely rested with their points against the side of the opposite rock instead of on the top of

---

[83] Taravita - an aerial ferry, consisting of a number of stout thongs stretched across a river from cliff to cliff, and a sort of basket slung on them, wherein a person sits to be drawn over.

it; and when a man walked over them they bent with his weight into the water, whose foaming surges threatened to wash him off; and there was obviously no hope of any one passing with the load of one of my boxes. However, a thunderstorm with heavy rain came on, and, seeing no other chance of saving our lives except by risking the passage of the frail bridges, without loss of time I resolved to abandon my goods and get over to the other side. We had barely all crossed in safety when the river rose and carried away our bridges. On the third day afterwards we reached Baños, where I sought out practised cargueros, and sent them off to the Topo; but for fifteen days from the date of my crossing it the waters did not subside sufficiently to allow of bridges being thrown over; and when the cargueros, at the end of that time, succeeded in passing to the opposite side, they found the leather covering of my boxes completely soaked and full of maggots! We had left them under ranchos of *Anthurium*-leaves (for the palms have long ago been exhausted between the Topo and the Shuña); and as the rains had been almost unceasing, the leaves had fallen off the roof upon the boxes and were rotting there. Fortunately the contents of the boxes had sustained very little injury.

Many lives have been lost in the Shuña and Topo; and of those who have fallen into the latter only one has come out alive. But the fate is more horrible of those who, shut up between the Shuña and Topo when both are so much swollen as to be impassable, perish of hunger.

The Shuña, though approaching so near the Topo at its outlet, diverges considerably in its upper part; and, as well as I can make out, its source is not far from those of the Ashpa-yacu and Pindu. When the Topo and Shuña are passed under favourable circumstances, the traveller on his way to Canelos arrives at an early hour the same day at the Cerro Abitagua, a steep mountain ending to the south in perpendicular cliffs, along the very base of which runs the Pastasa; so that the track is made to pass over the summit of Abitagua; and the ascent and descent on the other side occupy a whole day. The great mass of Abitagua seems alluvial; and from this point downwards no more primitive or igneous rock is seen *in situ*, nor indeed all the way down the Amazon until reaching the volcanic districts of Villa Nova and Santarem. Abitagua is also the last hill of any elevation on the eastern side of the Andes (following the valley of the Pastasa): beyond it the ground sinks in gentle undulations down to the great Amazonian plain. From its summit there is a near view of Llanganati, toward the sources of the Topo; but on two occasions that I have ascended Abitagua the summit of Llanganati has been hidden by clouds, and only its wooded flanks and deep, savage valleys have been visible. The valley of the Shuña can be traced to west and north of Abitagua. In descending the eastern slope of the mountain a fine view is obtained of the Great Plain, extending as far as the sight can reach to the south-east like a sea of emerald, in one part of which the Pastasa is seen winding like a silver band, but at so great a distance that it is impossible to discern whether

its course be still obstructed by rocks and whirlpools as at the base of Abitagua.

A good day's journey beyond Abitagua brings us to the Ashpa-yacu, which is also sufficiently large to become unfordable after heavy rains: it does not appear at all on Guzmán's map. On the following day the Pindu and Púyu are reached; these rivers are equal in size to Ashpa-yacu, and the two unite at a short distance before they reach the Pastasa. In the space between them are a few huts and chacras of Jívaro Indians, the only habitations between the Río Verde and Canelos.

Beyond the Río Púyu (River of Mists) the track diverges from the Pastasa, within hearing of whose surges it has run thus far. It also passes the limits of Guzmán's map, and continues with an easterly course along the ridges which seperate the basin of the Púyu from that of the Bombonasa, which latter river is finally crossed to reach the village of Canelos situated near its left bank.

Of the climate of the Forest of Canelos I can only say a few words here. The clouds heaped up against the cordillera by the wind of the earth's rotation descend in daily rains. For three or four months in the year---between November and April---the sun rather predominates over the rain, and this is called "summer ;" while for the rest of the year the heavy rains allow the sun to be seen for a very brief interval each day, so they call it "winter," though the climate is in reality a perpetual spring. From the Topo eastward the mist looks as if it were permanently hung up in the trees; and beyond Abitagua wind is scarcely ever felt, except rarely an occasional hurricane; and yet after heavy rains it is customary to find the forest strewed with large green branches. Immense bunches of moss depend from the trees, hiding the very foliage; and when saturated with moisture (which no wind ever shakes out) their weight breaks off the branches whereon they are hung. I am assured by the cargueros that from this cause alone they pass through the forest with fear and trembling after heavy rains; for their load obliges them to travel in a stooping posture, so that they are unable to see the impending danger. Yet with all this moisture the climate is healthy, and I have nowhere suffered so little from going all day in wet clothes.

The track above described is one of the two routes from Ecuador to the Amazon; the other proceeds from Quito to the Indian villages on the Napo, and presents almost equal dangers and difficulties. It is easy to see that the commerce carried on by such routes must be of very slight importance. In another paper I may perhaps discuss the facilities offered and the difficulties to be overcome in the attempt to establish a safe and speedy communication between the Pacific and the Amazon by the various routes which depressions in the Cordillera seem to offer us.

I am unable to give, from personal observation, any account of the geological structure of the country represented in the central and

northern portion of the map. The form of the mountains and the rugged peaks leave no doubt that trachyte is the prevailing formation; but some of the rocks seem so regularly columnar that I suppose them to be basaltic; for instance, La Mesa de Ushpa Yuras, La Capilla del Sol and El Docel de Ripalda, all near each other, and a little north of the Volcano Margasitas; El Pulpito, on the south side of the lakes at the head of the river Guapanti; El Castillejo, north-west of Sieté Bocas, &c.

"The parts of the map covered with forest are represented by scattered trees, among which the following forms are easily recognizable: ---

No. 1 is the Wax palm (*Palma de Ramos* of the Quitonians; *Ceroxylon andicola*, H. et B.[84]), which I have seen on Tunguragua up to 10,000 feet. Nos. 2 and 3 are Tree-ferns (*Helechos*) the former a *Cyathea*, whose trunk (sometimes 40 feet high) is much used for uprights in houses; the latter an *Alsophila* with a prickly trunk, very frequent in the forest of Canelos about the Río Verde. No. 4 is the *Aliso* (*Betula acuminata*, Kunth), one of the most abundant trees in the Quitonian Andes; it descends on the beaches of the Pastasa to near 4000 feet, and ascends on the páramos of Tunguragua to 12,000. But there is one tree (represented thus), occupying on the map a considerable range of altitude, which I cannot make out, unless it be a *Podocarpus*, of which I saw a single tree on Mount Abitagua, though a species of the same genus is abundant at the upper limit of the forest in some parts of the Western Cordillera. A large spreading tree is figured here and there in the forest of Canelos which may be the *Tocte* a true Walnut (*Juglans*), with an edible fruit rather larger than that of the European species. The remaining trees represented, especially those toward the upper limit of the forest, are mostly too much alike to admit of the supposition that any particular species was intended by them.

The abbreviations made use of in the map are : *C°* for *Cerro* (mountain), *Cord*^{a} for *Cordillera* (ridge), *Mont*^{a} for *Montana* (forest), *A°* for *Arroyo* (rivulet), *L*^{a} for *Laguna*, and *C*^{a} for *Cocha* (lake), *Far*^{n} for *Farallón* (peak or promontory), *H*^{a} for *Hacienda* (farm), and *C*^{l} for *Corral* (cattle or sheep-fold).

Mule-tracks (called by the innocent natives "roads") are represented by double red lines, and footpaths by single lines. I have copied them by dotted lines.

Having now passed in review the principal physical features of the district, let us return to the *Derrotero of Valverde*, of which the following is a translation. The introductory remark, or title (not in very choice Castilian), is that of the copyist: ---

---

[84] I am doubtful if later writers are correct in referring this palm to the genus *Iriarten*.

I have adhered closely to the sense and style of the original. (Guide, or Route, which Valverde left in Spain, where death overtook him, having gone from the mountains of Llanganati, which he entered many times, and carried off a great quantity of gold; and the king commanded the corregidors of Tacunga and Ambato to search for the treasure: which order and guide are preserved in one of the offices of Tacunga.)

■ ■ ■

"Placed in the town of Píllaro, ask for the farm of Moya, and sleep (the first night) a good distance above it ; and ask there for the mountain of Guapa, from whose top, if the day be fine, look to the east, so that thy back be toward the town of Ambato, and from thence thou shalt perceive the three Cerros Llanganati, in the form of a triangle, on whose declivity there is a lake, made by hand, into which the ancients threw the gold they had prepared for the ransom of the Inca when they heard of his death. From the same Cerro Guapa thou mayest see also the forest, and in it a clump of *sangurimas* standing out of the said forest, and another clump which they call *flechas* (arrows), and these clumps are the principal mark for the which thou shalt aim, leaving them a little on the left hand. Go forward from Guapa in the direction and with the signals indicated, and a good way ahead, having passed some cattle-farms, thou shalt come on a wide morass, over which thou must cross, and coming out on the other side thou shalt see on the left hand a short way off a *jucál* on a hill-side, through which thou must pass. Having got through the *jucál*, thou wilt see two small lakes called 'Los Anteojos' (the spectacles), from having between them a point of land like to a nose.

"From this place thou mayest again descry the Cerros Llanganati, the same as thou sawest them from the top of Guapa, and I warn thee to leave the said lakes on the left, and that in front of the point or "nose" there is a plain, which is the sleeping-place. There thou must leave thy horses, for they can go no farther. Following now on foot in the same direction, thou shalt come on a great black lake, the which leave on thy left hand, and beyond it seek to descend along the hill-side in such a way that thou mayest reach a ravine, down which comes a waterfall: and here thou shall find a bridge of three poles, or if it do not still exist thou shalt put another in the most convenient place and pass over it. And having gone on a little way in the forest, seek out the hut which served to sleep in or the remains of it. Having passed the night there, go on thy way the following day through the forest in the same direction, till thou reach another deep dry ravine, across which thou must throw a bridge and pass over it slowly and cautiously, for the ravine is very deep ; that is, if thou succeed not in finding the pass which exists. Go forward and look for the signs of another sleeping-place, which, I assure thee, thou canst not fail to see in the fragments of pottery and other marks, because the Indians are continually passing along there. Go on thy way, and thou shalt see a mountain which is all of *margasitas* (pyrites), the which leave on thy left hand, and I warn thee that thou must go round it in this fashion:

On this side thou wilt find a *pajonál* (pasture) in a small plain, which having crossed thou wilt come on a *cañon* between two hills, which is the Way of the Inca. From thence as thou goest along thou shalt see the entrance of the *socabón* (tunnel), which is in the form of a church porch.

Having come through the cañon and gone a good distance beyond, thou wilt perceive a cascade which descends from an offshoot of the Cerro Llanganati and runs into a quaking-bog on the right hand; and without passing the stream in the said bog there is much gold, so that putting in thy hand what thou shalt gather at the bottom is grains of gold. To ascend the mountain, leave the bog and go along to the right, and pass above the cascade, going round the offshoot of the mountain. And if by chance the mouth of the socabón be closed with certain herbs which they call "Salvaje," remove them, and thou wilt find the entrance. And on the left-hand side of the mountain thou mayest see the 'guayra' (for thus the ancients called the furnace where they founded metals), which is nailed with golden nails.[85] And to reach the third mountain, if thou canst not pass in front of the socabón, it is the same thing to pass behind it, for the water of the lake falls into it.

If thou lose thyself in the forest, seek the river, follow it on the right bank; lower down take to the beach, and thou wilt reach the canon in such sort that, although thou seek to pass it, thou wilt not find where; climb, therefore, the mountain on the right hand, and in this manner thou canst by no means miss thy way."

■ ■ ■

With this document and the map before us, let us trace the attempts that have been made to reach the gold thrown away by the subjects of Atahualpa as useless when it could no longer be applied to the purpose of ransoming him from the Spaniards.

Píllaro is a somewhat smaller town than Ambato, and stands on higher ground, on the opposite side of the river Patate, at only a few miles distance, though the journey thither is much lengthened by having to pass the deep quebrada of the Patate, which occupies a full hour. The farm of Moya still exists; and the Cerro de Guapa is clearly visible to east -north -east from where I am writing. The three Llanganatis seen from the top of Guapa are supposed to be the peaks Margasitas, Zunchu, and el Volcan del Topo. The "*sangurimas*" in the forest are described to me as trees with white foliage; but I cannot make out whether they be a species of Cecropia or of some allied genus. The "*flechas*" are probably the gigantic arrow-cane, *Gynerium saccharoides* (*Arvoré de frecha* of the Brazilians), whose flower-stalk is the usual material for the Indian's arrows.

---

[85] [Query — sprinkled with gold—ED.] (Wallace)

The morass (Cienega de Cubillin), the Jucál,[86] and the lakes called "Anteojos," with the nose of land between them, are all exactly where Valverde places them, as is also the. great black lake (Yanacocha) which we must leave on the left hand. Beyond the lake we reach the waterfall (Cascada y Golpe de Limpis Pongo), of which the noise is described to me as beyond all proportion to the smallness of the volume of water. Near the waterfall a cross is set up with the remark underneath, "Muerte del Padre Longo" - this being the point from which the expedition first spoken of regressed in consequence of the Padre's sudden disappearance. Beyond this point the climate begins to be warm; and there are parrots in the forest. The deep dry quebrada (Quebrada honda), which can be passed only at one point difficult to find, unless by throwing a bridge over it is exactly where it should be ; but beyond the mountain of Margasitas, which is shortly afterwards reached, no one has been able to proceed with certainty. The *Derrotero* directs it to be left on the left hand; but the explanatory hieroglyph puzzles everybody, as it seems to leave the mountain on the right. Accordingly, nearly all who have attempted to follow the *Derrotero* have gone to the left of Margasitas, and have failed to find any of the remaining marks signalized by Valverde. The concluding direction to those who lose their way in the forest has also been followed; and truly, after going along the right bank of the Curaray for some distance, a stream running between perpendicular cliffs (Cañada honda y Rivera de los Llanganatis) is reached, which no one has been able to cross; but though from this point the mountain to the right has been climbed, no better success has attended the adventurers.

"Socabón" is the name given in the Andes to any tunnel, natural or artificial, and also to the mouth of a mine. Perhaps the latter is meant by Valverde, though he does not direct us to enter it. The 'salvaje'which might have grown over and concealed the entrance of the socabón is *Tillandsia usneoides*, which frequently covers trees and rocks with a beard 30 or 40 feet long.

Comparing the map with the *Derrotero*, I should conclude the cañon, '-which is the Way of the Inca,' to be the upper part of the Rivera de los Llanganatis. This cañon can hardly be artificial, like the hollow way I have seen running down through the hills and woods on the western side ot the Cordillera, from the great road of Azuáy, nearly to the river Yaguachi. 'Guayra' said by Valverde to be the ancient name for a smelting - furnace,

[86] *Júco* is the name of a tall, solid-stemmed grass, usually about 20 feet high, of which I have never seen flower, but I take it to be a species of *Gynerium*, differing from *G. saccharoides* in the leaves being uniformly disposed on all sides and throughout the length of the stem, whereas in *G. saccharoides* the stem is leafless below and the leaves are distichous and crowded together (almost equitant) near the apex of the stem. The Júco grows exclusively in the temperate and cool region, from 6000 feet upwards, and is the universal material for laths and rods in the construction of houses in the Quitonian Andes.

is nowadays applied only to the wind. The concluding clause of this sentence, 'que son tachoneados de oro,'is considered by all competent persons to be a mistake for 'que es tachoneado de oro.'

If Margasitas be considered the first mountain of the three to which Valverde refers, then the Tembladá or Bog, out of which Valverde extracted his wealth, the socabón and the guayra are in the second mountain, and the lake wherein the ancients threw their gold in the third.

Difference of opinion among the gold-searchers as to the route to be pursued from Margasitas would appear also to have produced quarrels, for we find a steep hill east of that mountain, and separated from it by Mosquito Narrows (Chushpi Pongo), called by Guzmán "El Peñon de las Discordias."

If we retrace our steps from Margasitas till we reach the western margin of Yana-cocha, we find another track branching off to northward, crossing the river Zapalá at a point marked Salto de Cobos, and then following the northern shore of the lake. Then follow two steep ascents, called respectively 'La Escalera' and 'La Subida de Ripalda,' and the track ends suddenly at the river coming from the Inca's Fountain (La Pila del Inca), with the remark, 'sublevacion de los Indios--- Salto de Guzmán,' giving us to understand that the exploring party had barely crossed the river when the Indians rose against them, and that Guzmán himself repassed the river at a bound. These were probably Indians taken from the towns to carry loads and work the mines; they can hardly have been of the nation of the Curarayes, who inhabited the river somewhat lower down.

A little north and east of the Anteojos there is another route running a little farther northward and passing through the great morass of Illubamba, at the base of Los Mulatos, where we find marked El Atolladero (the Bog) de Guzmán, probably because he had slipped up to the neck in it. Beyond this the track continues north-east, and after passing the same stream as in the former route, but nearer to its source in the Inca's Fountain, there is a tambo called San Nicolas, and a cross erected near it marks the place where one of the miners met his death (Muerte de Romero). Another larger cross (La Cruz de Romero) is erected farther on at the top of a basaltic mountain called El Sotillo. At this point the track enters the Cordillera de las Margasitas, and on reaching a little to the east of the meridian of Zunchu-urcu, there is a tambo with a chapel, to which is appended the remark, "Destacamento de Ripalda y retirada per Orden Superior." Beyond the fact thus indicated, that one Ripalda had been stationed there in command of a detachment of troops, and had afterwards retired at the order of his superiors, I can give no information.

There are many mines about this station, especially those of Romero just to the north, those of Viteri to the east, and several mines of copper and silver which are not assigned to any particular owner. Not far to the east of the Destacamento is another tambo, with a cross, where I find written, 'Discordia y Consonancia con Guzmán,' showing that at this place Guzmán's fellow-miners quarreled with him and were afterwards reconciled. East-north-east from this, and at the same distance from it as the

Destacamento, is the last tambo on this route, called El Sumadal, on the banks of a lake, near the Río de las Flechas. Beyond that river, and north of the Curaray, are the river and forests of Gancaya.

Another track, running more to the north than any of the foregoing, sets out from the village of San Miguel, and passes between Cotopaxi and Los Mulatos. Several tambos or huts for resting in are marked on the route, which ends abruptly near the Minas de Pinel (north-east from Los Mulatos), with the following remark by the author 'Conspiracion contra Conrado y su accelerado regreso,' so that Conrado ran away to escape from a conspiracy formed against him, but who he was, or who were his treacherous companions, it would now perhaps be impossible to ascertain.

Along these tracks travelled those who searched for mines of silver and other metals, and also for the gold thrown away by the subjects of the Inca. That the last was their principal object is rendered obvious by the carefulness with which every lake has been sounded that was at all likely to contain the supposed deposit [87].

The mines of Llanganati, after having been neglected for half a century, are now being sought out again with the intention of working them; but there is no single person at the present day able to employ the labour and capital required for successfully working a silver mine, and mutual confidence is at so low an ebb in this country that companies never hold together long. Besides this, the gold of the Incas never ceases to haunt people's memories; and at this moment I am informed that a party of explorers who started from Tacunga imagine they have found the identical Green Lake of Llanganati, and are preparing to drain it dry. If we admit the truth of the tradition that the ancients smelted gold in Llanganati, it is equally certain that they extracted the precious metal in the immediate neighbourhood; and if the socabón of Valverde cannot at this day be discovered, it is known to every one that gold exists at a short distance, and possibly in considerable quantity, if the Ecuadoreans would only take the trouble to search for it and not leave that task to the wild Indians, who are content if, by scooping up the gravel with their hands, they can get together enough gold to fill the quill which the white man has given them as the measure of the value of the axes and lance-heads he has supplied to them on trust.

The gold region of Canelos begins on the extreme east of the map of Guzmán, in streams rising in the roots of Llanganati and flowing to the Pastasa and Curaray,[88] the principal of which are the Bombonasa and Villano. These rivers and their smaller tributaries have the upper part of their course in deep ravines, furrowed in soft alluvial sandstone rock, wherein blocks and pebbles of quartz are interspersed, or interposed in distinct layers. Toward their source they are obstructed by large masses of quartz and other rocks; but as we descend the stones grow fewer, smaller,

---

[87] The soundings of the lakes are in Spanish varas, each near 33 English inches.

[88] The name Curaray itself may be derived from "curi," gold.

and more rounded, until toward the mouth of the Bombonasa, and thence throughout the Pastasa, not a single stone of the smallest size is to be found. The beaches of the Pastasa consist almost entirely of powdered pumice brought down from the volcano Sangáy by the river Palora. When I ascended the Bombonasa in the company of two Spaniards who had had some experience in mining, we washed for gold in the mouth of most of the rivulets that had a gravelly bottom, as also on some beaches of the river itself, and never failed to extract a few fragments of that metal. All these streams are liable to sudden and violent floods. I once saw the Bombonasa at Pucayacu, where it is not more than 40 yards wide, rise 18 feet in six hours. Every such flood brings down large masses of loose cliff, and when it subsides (which it generally does in a few hours) the Indians find a considerable quantity of gold deposited in the bed of the stream.

The gold of Canelos consists almost solely of small particles (called 'chispas,' sparks), but as the Indians never dig down to the base of the wet gravel, through which the larger fragments of gold necessarily percolate by their weight, it is not to be wondered at that they rarely encounter any such. Two attempts have been made, by parties of Frenchmen, to work the gold-washings of Canelos systematically. One of them failed in consequence of a quarrel which broke out among the miners themselves and resulted in the death of one of them. In the other, the river (the Lliquino) rose suddenly on them by night and carried off their canoes (in which a quantity of roughly-washed gold was heaped up), besides the Long Tom and all their other implements.

I close this memoir by an explanation of the Quichua terms which occur most frequently on the map. Spanish authors use the vowels *u* and *o* almost indiscriminately in writing Quichua names, although the latter sound does not exist in that language ; and in some words which have become grafted on the Spanish, as spoken in Peru and Ecuador, the *o* has supplanted the *u* not only in the orthography but in the actual pronunciation, as, for instance, in Pongo and Cocha, although the Indians still say "Chimbu-rasu," and not "Chimborazo" "Cutupacsi" or "Cutu-pagsi," and not "Cotopaxi." The sound of the English *w* is indicated in Spanish by *gu* or *hu*; that of the French *j* does not exist in Spanish, and is represented by *ll*, whose sound is somewhat similar; thus "Lligua" is pronounced "Jiwa." "Llanganati" is now pronounced with the Spanish sound of the *ll,* but whether this be the original mode is doubtful. An unaccented terminal *e* (as in Spanish "verde") is exceedingly rare in Indian languages, and has mostly been incorrectly used for a short *i* ; thus, if we wish to represent the exact pronunciation, we should write "Casiquiari," "Ucayáli," and "Llanganati" ---*not* Casiquiare, Ucayale, Llanganate.

"Llanganati" may come from "llanga," to touch, because the group of mountains called by that name touches on the sources of the rivers all round; thus, on Guzmán's map, we find "Llanganatis del Río Verde" "Llanganatis del Topo" "Llanganatis del Curaray," for those sections of the group which respectively touch on the Río Verde, the Topo, and the Curaray. The following are examples of the mode of using the verb “llanga.” “Ama llángaichu!”—“Touch it not!” “Imapág llancángui?” -“Why do you touch it”; or “Pitag lláncaynirca?” -“Who told you to touch it?” And the answer might be “Llancanatág chári cárca llancarcáni.”—“[Thinking] it might be touched, I touched it.”

It is to be noted that the frequent use of the letter *g*, in place of *c*, is a provincialism of the Quitonian Andes, where (for instance) they mostly say “Inga” instead of “Inca.” But in Maynas the *c* is used almost to the exclusion of the *g*; thus “yúrag,” white, and “pítag,” who, are pronounced respectively “yurac” and “pitac” in Maynas.

“Tungurágua” seems to come from “tungúri,” the ankle-joint, which is a prominence certainly, though scarcely more like the right-angled cone of Tunguragua than the obtuse-angled cone of Cotopaxi is like a wen (“coto” or “cutu”).

Of the termination “agua” (pron. “awa”) I can give no explanation.

“Cungúri,” in Quichua, is the knee; thus an Indian would say “Tungúri-mánta cungúli-cáma llustirishcáni urmáshpa,” *i.e.* “In falling ('urmáshpa') I have scrubbed off the skin from the ankle to the knee.”

Among rustics of mixed race, whose language partakes almost as much of Quichua as of Spanish, it is common to hear such expressions as “De tunguri á cunguri es una cola llaga.”- “From the ankle to the knee is a continuous sore.”

The following words occur repeatedly on the map:

“Ashpa” (in Maynas “Allpa”), earth. “Urcu,” mountain. “Rumi,” stone. “Cócha (cucha),” lake. “Yácu,” river. “Ucsha,” grass or grassy place (“Pajonál,”Sp.). “Póngo (pungu),” door or narrow entrance. “Cúchu,” corner. “U'ma,”head. “Paccha,” cataract. “Cúri,” gold. “Cúlqui,” silver. “Alquímia,” copper. “Ushpa,” ashes. “Chíri,” cold. “Yúnga,” warm, from which the Spaniards have formed the diminutive “Yungúilla,” warmish, applied to many sites where the sugar-cane begins to flourish. “Yúrag,” white. “Yána,” black. “Púca,” red. “Quílla,” yellow.

"I’shcai," two; ex."I’shcai-guáuqui," the Two Brothers, a cloven peak to the east of Los Mulatos. "Chunga," ten; ex. "Chunga-uma," a peak with ten points, a little to south of “Ishcaiguauqui.”

“Parca,” double; thus a hill which seems made up of two hills united is called “Parca-urcu.”

“Angas,” a hawk. “Ambátu,” a kind of toad. “Sácha,” forest. “Cáspi,” tree. “Yúras,” herb. “Quínua,” the “Chenopodium Quinoa,” cultivated for its edible seed. “Pujín,” hawthorn (various species of Crataegus) ; thus “Montaña de Pujines,” Hawthorn Forest; “Cerro Pujin el chico,” Little Hawthorn-hill. “Cubiliín,” a sort of Lupine, found only on the highest páramos. It gives its name to a long ridge of the Eastern. Cordillera, mostly covered with snow, extending from Condorasto and El Altar toward Sangay. “Totorra,” a large bulrush from which mats are made; hence “Totorrál,” amarsh full of bulrushes. “Sara,” maize.

"Tópo" is the name given in Maynas to the Raft-wood trees, species of Ochroma (of the N.O. Bombaceae). They begin to be found as soon as we reach a hot climate, say from 3000 feet elevation downwards.

"Rundu," sleet; thus "Rundu-uma" Sleety Head. "Rásu" is snow, and occurs in "Chimbu-rasu,""Caraguai-rasu" (Carguairago), and many other names. The vulgar name for snow as it falls is "Papa-cara," *i.e.* potato peelings.

"Pucará" indicates the site of a hill-fort of the Incas, of which a great many are scattered through the Quitonian Andes."

■ ■ ■

Here would be the opportune place to reproduce the hand-traced copy of the *Guzmán Map*, which was "Copiada de Original por Ricardo Spruce in Ambato," dated 1 Aug 1860, as it was presented to the Royal Geographic Society with Spruce's foregoing paper. However, Spruce's penciled copy was purportedly rough and faint, almost indistinct.[89] The Society therefore commissioned a new version from the engraver A. Findlay, to be published with Spruce's paper in volume XXXI of the *Journal of the Royal Geographical Society* in 1861. In reworking the map, Findlay reduced its scale to three-eighths of the original, and sharpened the details of every peak, river, tree and hacienda, with each place-name clearly indicated.

Some interesting details concerning Findlay's map have captured my attention and in my mind have raised certain questions. It has been widely stated by authors over the years that Spruce himself had made the copy of Guzmán's map. However, in Spruce's paper he does not specifically make any such claim, instead Spruce just refers to "my copy." The notation on the maps lower left hand corner, written in Spanish states: "Copiada de Original por Ricardo Spruce," which could be translated with two separate meanings ... either ... "Copied from original for ..." or "Copied from original by ..." If Spruce actually made the copy himself, why would he sign his work with the notation and his name in Spanish? It would appear more reasonable that a third party actually copied the map for Spruce and presented it to him.

Another detail that raises a question is the map's date ... 1 Mar 1860. Was it possible in 1860, prior to the advent of air travel, for a document (Spruce's paper and the *Guzmán Map*) to be transported from the Andes in Ecuador to England in a mere eleven days, in order to be read before the Royal Geographical Society on March 12th of the same month?

■ ■ ■

---

[89] I believe copies of this map at one time were available from the RGS, but as of publication have not been able to confirm this or obtain a copy.

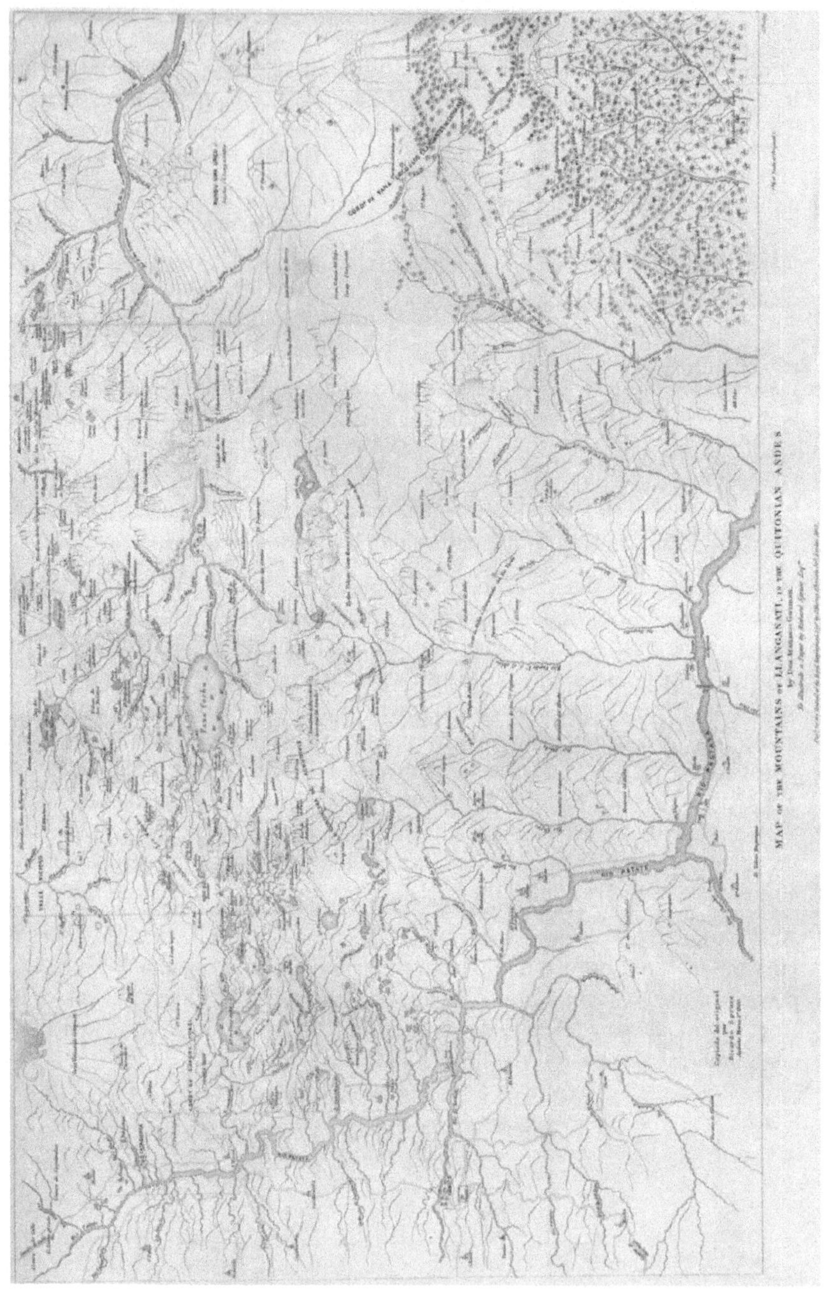

Findlay's Engraving of the Guzmán Map

After Richard Spruce's return to England in 1864 he was in poor health due to intestinal disease caught in South America and spent much of the rest of his life in near poverty, in and around Yorkshire, working on his papers and manuscripts.

Spruce's continuous labors for science and humanity provided him with many friends, some of whom were influential in obtaining for Spruce a civil pension of £50 a year in 1864. Clements R. Markham (later Sir) was relentless on Spruce's behalf in seeking a supplemental pension from the Government of India in recognition of Spruce's work on the Cinchona. Markham pleaded on Spruce's behalf that ... "One hundred pounds a year would enable him to exist in his present sad condition, fifty pounds would not. The grant, therefore, of this trifling pension of 500 rupees a year for a few short years, will make all the difference between absolute want and comparative comfort." This claim was denied in 1866, ultimately in 1877 Spruce's pension in England was supplemented by an additional £50 from India.

From 1864 on Spruce published some twenty-nine papers which were in addition to the twenty-five papers he had published previously. Spruce's voluminous work *Notes of a Botanist on the Amazon & Andes* covering his fifteen years in Peru and Ecuador, was not completed prior to Spruce's death. This manuscript would ultimately be edited and condensed by Alfred Russel Wallace and published posthumously in two volumes, each containing more than five hundred pages, in 1908.

Spruce's paper, *On the Mountains of Llanganati, in the Eastern Cordillera of the Quitonian Andes* would also be edited and condensed, footnotes and commentary added and republished in part. Wallace himself has been credited with creating an enthralling new title for Spruce's paper ... *A HIDDEN TREASURE OF THE INCAS, IN THE MOUNTAINS OF LLANGANATI, ECUADOR; AN AUTHENTIC GUIDE TO ITS LOCALITY; ILLUSTRATED BY A MAP, THE MAP COPIED AND THE GUIDE TRANSLATED BY RICHARD SPRUCE.*

Ultimately, Wallace had omitted the first two pages of Spruce's paper and as noted by Wallace, the "description of the various rivers and tributaries as shown on the map" along with Spruce's remarks and corrections on the map. In all, more than nine pages of text from Spruce's paper were deleted! Spruce's entire paper reproduced herein displays the **deleted portions highlighted in bold print**. The paper was then included as Chapter XXVIII in *Notes of a Botanist on the Amazon & Andes.* Wallace commenced Chapter XXVIII with the following headline and comment ...

A HIDDEN TREASURE OF THE INCAS

"THE following narrative forms one of the most curious pieces of genuine history in connection with the never-ceasing search for buried treasure in the territory of the Incas. We owe to the persevering exertions of Richard Spruce the discovery and the translation of one of the few remaining copies of the official order of the Spanish king to search for this treasure, with the accompanying detailed 'Guide' to its locality. Still more are we indebted to his generally esteemed character and ingratiating manners for obtaining permission to copy the unique map of the district containing the treasure, and for undertaking the considerable labour of copying in the minutest detail so large and elaborate a map, without which both the "Guide" and the story of the search for the treasure would be unintelligible.

"The essential portions of this map, containing the whole of the route described in the 'Guide,' as well as the routes of the various explorers (marked in red), have been reproduced here (see the end of the chapter). The portions farther east and south, which have no immediate relation to the quest for the treasure, having been omitted in order to make it more convenient for reference here. The scale of the map is, approximately, six miles to an inch.

"In Dr. Theodore Wolff's *Geografia et Geologia de Ecuador (1892)*, the region of Llanganati is still referred to as the most unknown part of the whole of Ecuador."

Wallace concludes the chapter by adding the following "critical note of the editor" ... "The preceding account of the various routes of the gold-seekers among the Llanganati Mountains leads to the conclusion that only the earliest, that led by the Corregidor of Tacunga and the friar Padre Longo, made any serious attempt to follow the explicit directions of the 'Guide', since the others departed from it so early in the journey as the great black lake 'Yana Cocha', going to the left instead of to the right of it. No doubt they were either deceived by Indian guides who assured them that they knew an easier way, or went in search of rich mines rather than of buried treasure. The first party, however, and those who afterwards followed it, kept to the route, as clearly described, to the sleeping-place beyond the deep ravine where Padre Longo was lost; but beyond this point they went wrong by crossing the river, and thus leaving the district of the three volcanoes, which twice at the beginning of the 'Guide' are indicated as the locality of the treasure.

"Although no route to these mountains is marked on the map, Spruce tells us that other parties did take the proper course, and found the 'deep dry ravine' (marked on the map as Quebrada honda), and after it the mountain of Margasitas ; but here they were all puzzled by the 'Guide' directing them to leave the mountain on their left while the hieroglyph seems to leave it on the right, and following this latter instruction they have failed afterwards to find any of the other marks given by Valverde in his 'Guide'. Spruce himself suggests that the upper part of the Rivera de los Llanganatis (which is outside the portion of the map here given) is the 'Way of the Inca' referred to in the 'Guide'. But this is going quite beyond the area of the three mountains, so clearly stated as the objective of the 'Guide.'

"It seems to me, however, that there is really no contradiction between the 'Guide' and the map, and that the route so clearly pointed out in the former has not yet been thoroughly ('Quebrada honda' of the map), we are directed to 'go forward and look for the signs of another sleeping-place.' Then, the next day 'Go on thy way, and thou shalt see a mountain which is all of margasitas, the which leave on thy left hand.' But looking at the map we shall see that the mountain will now be on the right hand, supposing we have gone on in the same direction as before, crossing the deep ravine. The next words, however, explain this apparent contradiction: they are 'and I warn thee that thou must go round it in this fashion,' with the explanatory hieroglyph, which, if we take the circle to be the mountain and the right-hand termination of the curve the point already reached, merely implies that you are to turn back and ascend the mountain in a winding course till you reach the middle of the south side of it. So far you have been going through forest, but now you are told 'On this side thou wilt find a pajonál (pasture) in a small plain' (showing that you have reached a considerable height), 'which having crossed thou wilt come on a cañon between two hills, which is the way of the Inca.' This cañon is clearly the upper part of the 'Chushpi pongo,' while the 'Encañado de Sacha pamba' is almost certainly the beginning of the 'Way of the Inca.' The explorers will now have reached the area bounded by the three volcanoes of the 'Guide' -the Margasitas will be behind them, Zunchu urcu on his right, and the great volcano Topo in front, and it is from this point only that they will be in a position to look out for the remaining marks of the 'Route' -the socabón or tunnel 'in the form of a church porch,' and evidently still far above them, the cascade and the quaking-bog, passing to the right of which is the way to 'ascend the mountain,' going 'above the cascade' and 'round the offshoot of the mountain' to reach the socabón. Then you will be able to find the Guayra (or furnace), and to reach the 'third mountain,' which must be the Topo, you are to pass the socabón 'either in front or behind it, for the water of the lake falls into it.' This evidently means the lake mentioned in the first sentence of the 'Guide' as being the place where the gold prepared for the ransom of the Inca was hidden. The last sentence of the 'Guide' refers to what must be done if you miss the turning shown by the hieroglyph, in which case you have to follow the river-bank till you come to the cañon (on the map marked 'Chushpi pongo'), up the right hand side of which you must climb the mountain, 'and in this manner thou canst by no means miss thy way'; which the map clearly shows, since it leads up to the 'Encañado,' which is shown by the other and more easy route to be the 'Way of the Inca .'

"I submit, therefore, that the 'Guide' is equally minute and definite in its descriptions throughout, that it agrees everywhere with Guzmán's map, and that, as it is admitted to be accurate in every detail for more than three-fourths of the whole distance, there is every probability that the last portion is equally accurate. It will, of course, be objected that, if so, why did not Guzmán himself, who made the map, also complete the exploration of the route and make the discovery? That, of course, we cannot tell; but many reasons may be suggested as highly probable. Any such exploration of a completely uninhabited region must be very costly, and is always liable to fail near the end from lack of food, or from the desertion of the Indian porters when there was doubt about the route. Guzmán had evidently been diverted from the search by what seemed the superior promise of silver and gold mines, from which he may have hoped to obtain wealth enough to carry out the other expedition with success. This failing, he apparently returned home, and may have been endeavouring to obtain recruits and funds for anew effort when his accidental death occurred.

"It is to be noted that beyond the point where the hieroglyph puzzled all the early explorers there is a complete absence of detail in Guzmán's map, which contains nothing that might not have been derived from observations made from the heights north of the river, and from information given by wandering Indians.

"It is also to be noted that only four sleeping-places are mentioned in the 'Guide,' so that the whole journey occupied five days. The last of the four sleeping-places is before reaching the spot where the path turns back round the Margasitas Mountain, so that the whole distance from this place to the 'lake made by hand' must be less than twenty miles, a distance which would take us to the nearer slopes of the great Topo Mountain. In this part of the route the marks given in the 'Guide' are so many and so well-defined that it cannot be difficult to follow them, especially as the path indicated seems to be mostly above the forest-region.

"For the various reasons now adduced, I am convinced that the 'Route' of Valverde is a genuine and thoroughly trustworthy document, and that by closely following the directions therein given, it may still be possible for an explorer of means and energy, with the assistance of the local authorities, to solve the interesting problem of the Treasure of the Incas. The total distance of the route, following all its sinuosities, cannot exceed ninety or a hundred miles at most, fully three-fourths of which must be quite easy to follow, while the remainder is very clearly described. Two weeks would therefore suffice for the whole expedition.

"I have written this in the hope that someone who speaks Spanish fluently, has had some experience of the country, and is possessed of the necessary means, may be induced to undertake this very interesting and even romantic piece of adventurous travel. To such a person it need be but a few months' holiday."

So here we have in Spruce's own words, edited and commented on by Alfred Russel Wallace, everything that they wished to make public. Spruce's work has been the basis and background for the ensuing one hundred-fifty years of treasure exploration in the Llanganati Mountains of Ecuador which resulted from Spruce's 1857 discovery, copying, translation and publication of the infamous *Derrotero de Valverde* and the *Guzmán Map*. We also have Wallace's observations, interpretations, theories and opinions on the *Derrotero* and map. Every subsequent explorer and treasure hunter has interpreted these documents and developed their own theories, opinions and conclusions about this lost Inca Treasure.

Today no one doubts that there exists a famous *Derrotero* or guide to reach the treasure. Richard Spruce's discovery and translation of more than a century past, provided clear evidence that his copy was written by a Spaniard. One of the older Spanish versions translated and reproduced in the previous chapter, is quite similar to Spruce's version. On the other hand, there exist many inconsistencies or irregularities. The most obvious contradiction is having been dictated by an indigenous person, for an indigenous person, not by a Spaniard. This observation is clearly supported by several paragraphs contemptuously making reference to the ... "white bearded Spanish enemy of our pure race."

In reality, it is the interpretation of the data and theories that defines the Llanganati treasure hunt ... until of course ... the day it is recovered. Only then will the interpretations and theories be confirmed or dispelled once and for all.

■ ■ ■

Guzmán's map that had been copied from the original by (or for) Richard Spruce in Ambato, Ecuador, was completed March 1860, then reworked by the engraver A. Findlay and published by J. Murray in 1862 for the *Journal of the Royal Geographical Society,* once again the map was reworked and edited by Wallace for publication in *Notes of a Botanist.*

Just as Wallace had taken great liberties editing Spruce's original paper, the *Guzmán Map* would meet the same fate, with a large portion of the map ending up on the proverbial cutting room floor. The southern portions and entire right side (eastern portions) of the map, up to fifteen miles of territory, including half of the Volcan del Topo, the Sacha Llanganatis, Cordillera de Yana-Urcu (Cerro Negro), Rivera de los Llanganatis and even the southern flowing rivers including the all important Río Topo, Río Verde Chico and Río Verde Grande, were deleted from Wallace's version.

It is also widely believed, that Wallace was responsible for the addition to Guzmán's map of the meandering red lines, which indicate three expedition routes in search of the treasure. Perhaps it is a bit ironic, but this edited version of Guzmán's map, entitled *Map of the mountains of Llanganati, in the Quitonian Andes,* being more easily accessible than other versions over the past century, has been the map of the region most utilized by many explorers of the Llanganatis.This map appeared in the very back of Volume Two of Spruce's oversized book, *Notes of a Botanist on the Amazon & Andes* published in 1908.

■ ■ ■

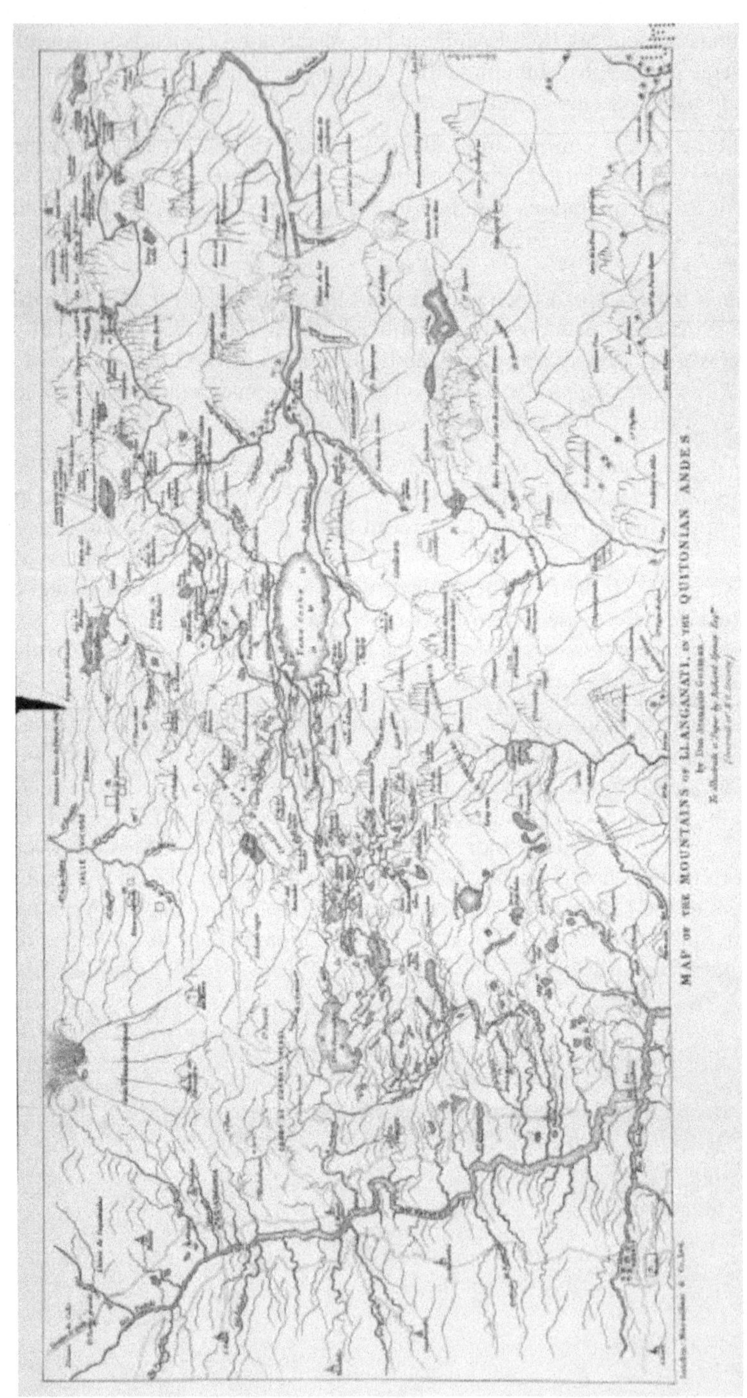

Guzmán Map from Notes of a Botanist

Eugene Konrad Brunner wrote the following history of the *Derrotero de Valverde, Guzmán Map* and Richard Spruce that he again derived from legends, myth, lore, historical research and his lifelong explorations into the treasures of Ecuador. These early writings are presented in their entirety without correction, interpretation or adjustment ... "To explain the significance of the name Llanganati given some mountains East-South-East of the high plains of Píllaro in the province of Tungarahua, and whose highest elevation is Cerro Hermoso or Yurac-Llanganati (4639 meters above sea level), almost always entangled in dense fog and covered by ice and snow; ... it's worthwhile to speak of the Spaniard that mentioned this name for the first time in a document in the Spanish language, for this document we can understand something of the treasure of the Inca hidden in the Mountains of Llanganati ... coming from Valverde, that would have arrived in Quito at the end of the fourteenth century or the beginning of the fifteenth. Little is known of his origin, perhaps he was a descendant of Don Francisco Valverde, brother of the famous priest Valverde that accompanied Francisco Pizarro during the conquest of Peru, and that was one of the principal actors in the successes of Cajamarca. Don Francisco was the conqueror of the newly founded Guayaquil and was the first advisor of the Cazicazgo of Daule. What is known is that Valverde was a clerk in the military barracks in the city of Quito and that he was a well instructed man.

"One fine day, perhaps bored of receiving orders from the officers, he deserted and went to hide in the mountains of Píllaro, where he was helped by the Indians with his work and needs. He married a young native girl, direct descendant of the family of Ati and of Rumiñahui. From that moment on the fortune of Valverde changed, he that was totally poor, suddenly paid his debts and corrected his situation with the authorities in Quito.

"The legends and myths that are passed mouth to mouth say that the wife and father-in-law took Valverde to a site in nearby Llanganati and showed him the treasure of Atahualpa, hidden by the relentless defender of Quito, Rumiñahui-Ati II. Later Valverde and his wife embarked for the voyage to Spain, and that the young girl and noble Indian woman of Píllaro got sick and died on the high seas where the daughter of the Ecuadorian Andes received a Christian burial in the damp depths of the ocean. Once upon returning to Spain, Valverde changed into one of the wealthiest men of his time, and personal friend to His Majesty the King.

"When Valverde felt that his health, which had weakened during his years in the colonies of the Indies, grew worse and being nearly at the brink of death, Valverde wrote his very famous *Derrotero* or guide to reach the site where the treasure was hidden in the mountains of Llanganati. This document was delivered by the hand of a friend of confidence to the King.

"The *Derrotero* begins ... 'Placed in the town of Píllaro, ask for the farm of Moya, and sleep (the first night) a good distance above it; and ask there for the mountain of Guapa, from whose top, if the day be fine, look to the east, so that thy back be toward the town of Ambato, and from thence thou shalt perceive the three Cerros Llanganati, in the form of a triangle, on whose declivity there is a lake, made by hand, into which the ancients threw the gold they had prepared for the ransom of the Inca when they heard of his death.' ... It is here that the name Llanganati is mentioned for the first time in a Spanish document.

"The King of Spain immediately dispatched his proxy to America, who was a catholic priest, the Padre Longo. Supplied with a copy of the *Derrotero* and a Cedula Real (Royal Certificate) to the Corregidores (Spanish magistrates) of Tacunga and of Ambato, ordering that with the greatest of secrecy they organize an expedition to the mountains mentioned in the *Derrotero*, in order to verify the truthfulness of the Valverde document and of the treasure mentioned therein.

"Quickly they left Píllaro, well supplied with food, necessary equipment, hundreds of Indian carriers, and soldiers. The surprise of the magistrates and Padre Longo must have been great when they saw the lakes of the spectacles (Lagunas de Anteojos), swamps, the black lake (Yana-cocha), the chasm, in total everything mentioned in the *Derrotero*!

"Camped the third night at the drain of Yana-cocha, during the night Padre Longo disappeared. Until today it is not known with scientific certainty why. But it is possible that upon the padres giving notice that on the following day they would reach the site of the treasure, the magistrates may have been thinking of taking the gold for themselves, in which case Padre Longo would have been a troublesome witness, so that the magistrates ordered the padre killed. Or perhaps the father left the encampment for a necessity of the body and suffered an accident, something very possible in these wild zones.

"In the end the expedition was unable to advance further, because the *Derrotero* no longer agreed with landmarks. It could have been that Padre Longo learned certain parts to memory and this part died with him, no one knows. Within three days they found the body of the Father and buried it in the same place. With him as well died a portion of the *Derrotero* and this misfortune cost dearly through the centuries. Due to this, hundreds of lives were lost, great sums of money were expended and hundreds of expeditions ended in failure. I as well wasted nearly thirty years searching to reach the mountain mistakenly.

"The original documents worn out by Padre Longo, were deposited in the archives of the Corregidor, from where later they passed to the municipal archives of the government, where everyone was able to make a copy, but it always lacked one piece and no one reached the treasure. Later only a few people knew of the existence of this document and of the history of Valverde, and almost everything about the Treasure of Atahualpa in the mountains of Llanganati. Everything became legend and myth.

"We know that many people went in search of the treasure and that some of them found rich mineral deposits, like for example the Parish priest of Píllaro Enriquez de Guzmán that worked a silver mine in 1793. We know this for the discovery of a document in Quito. Here like the scientific explorer and great Spanish botanist Atanasio or Antanasio Guzmán, that lived for many years in the area containing Píllaro, Sucre, and Patate. He that made many expeditions to the northern part of the Llanganatis, better stated the mountain ranges of Mulatos and the Roncadores. He was accompanied by many Indians and mestizos. They discovered many mineral deposits of gold, silver, copper, and rock crystal in the area in the form of abandoned mines from the ancient pre-Inca Indians.

"Atanasio Guzmán made the first map of the mountains of Llanganati and of others that surround them. Starting with Cotopaxi in the north, it extends toward the south and ends in the valley of Río Pastaza. For the west it goes to the plain of Callo for Latacunga, San Miguel (Salcedo), Ambato, Quero until Mocha. For the east it extends through the mineral hills of Mulatos, Loma Pelada, Cordillera de las Torres (Runda-Uma-Urco), the Cerro Negro (Yana-Llanganati), until the forests and jungles at the headwaters of Río Puyo and of Abitagua (mountains of Tapasi).

"The map, in as much as it refers to hills and mountains, is a miracle of exactness. It must be taken into consideration that it was drawn more than two hundred years ago in a time when there were no roads, and when the mountains of Llanganati were only white blemishes on the maps. Some rivers are not in their proper location (in many modern maps as well), but the hills and up to certain coordinates in the land, concur with the modern aerial photographs of today.

"Now then, Guzmán and his companions found valuable deposits of precious minerals and abandoned mines of the ancient natives. While in the *Derrotero de Valverde* it is mentioned of the third Cerro of Llanganati as follows ... 'And on the left hand side of the mountain thou mayest see the guayra [90] (for thus the ancients called the furnace where they founded metals), which is nailed with golden nails'. . . mineral deposits, abandoned mines, and furnaces for founding metals. All of this indicates an enormous mineral zone, or say that the Llanganatis must be found to contain mines, and for as much, the name Llanganati refers to or signifies something relative to mines.

■ ■ ■

"The premature disappearance of scientist, historian, writer and linguist Don Luciano Andrade Marin [1893-1972] was said to be the greatest authority in the native languages, for example the Ketchua of Peru, the Ketchua or Quichua of Ecuador and the Aymara of Bolivia. He made extensive studies into the meaning of the name Llanganati, breaking down the word in every possible sentiment, and later as he explains in the end, that Llanganati or Llanganan-Ati means or signifies: The stone workshop or

---

[90] Guayra - Wind ovens for smelting gold, silver, and copper ore. The primitive bellows of the Incas could not produce sufficient heat to melt metals, gold's melting point is 1,063 degrees C, silver 1,420 degrees C, and copper is 1,083 degrees C. The Inca's located these ovens on the south - east slope of high mountains in order that the strong winds would produce sufficient draft to obtain the needed temperatures.

Mineral Works of Ati, or of the Ati's. I should clarify that the Ati's were the Kings of Píllaro and Muli-Ambato, for the least the only ones that could have mineral works.

"Luciano Andrade in his book *Llanganati*, second edition of 1970 page 198, speaking about Valverde's *Derrotero* and Richard Spruce the English Botanist, states the following: '. . . Spruce finally states that he had secured a copy of the *Derrotero* bearing the date August 14, 1827.' Spruce continued on to state that the Cedula Real and the copy of the *Derrotero* had disappeared from the archives of Latacunga about twenty years before he arrived in the Andes of Ecuador, in July of 1857. Therefore, according to Spruce, the disappearance of the original documents would have occurred in 1837.

"Marin continue's ... 'However, the most important point is the emphatic declaration from a man as serious and sensible as Spruce, before the very respectable Royal Geographical Society in London, stated ... 'I obtained, however, indisputable evidence that the *Derrotero* or Guide to Llanganati of Valverde had been sent by the King of Spain to the Corregidores of Tacunga and Ambato.' This would mean to say, that in 1857 it was still possible to obtain in Ecuador indisputable evidence about the sending of the *Derrotero* from Spain together with the royal warrant.'

"In Richard Spruces book *Notes of a Botanist on the Amazon & Andes*, edited and condensed after Spruce's death by Alfred Russel Wallace, Volume II, Chapter XXVIII entitled *A Hidden Treasure of the Incas*, Wallace states in an editor's footnote ... 'We owe to the persevering exertions of Richard Spruce the discovery and the translation of one of the few remaining copies of the official order of the Spanish king to search for this treasure, with the accompanying detailed Guide to its locality. Still more are we indebted to his generally esteemed character and ingratiating manners for obtaining permission to copy the unique map of the district containing the treasure, and for undertaking the considerable labour of copying in the minutest detail so large and elaborate a map, without which both the Guide and the story of the search for the treasure would be unintelligible.'

"The author Eugene K. Brunner asks ... Why did Wallace not publish the famous Cedula Real (Royal Warrant) and its content, as he had published the information about the official search for the treasure as ordered by the King of Spain? I also question ... Why did Marin in his book make no mention about Spruce's notes? Marin additionally made no mention that Spruce had copies of the Cedula Real and an account of the official search ordered by the King of Spain. The content of which no one knows even today! What we do have is the *Derrotero de Valverde* as published in *Notes of a Botanist on the Amazon & Andes*." [At this point Brunner recites the *Derrotero*, which has previously been presented, so it is not reproduced again here.]

Brunner continues ... "And here ends the famous *Derrotero* of the Spaniard Valverde that certainly is only a portion of the truth that disappeared from the archives of Latacunga. All of the explorers of Llanganati have been guided by the indications of this *Derrotero* that was translated from Spanish to English, then published in Spruce's *Notes of a Botanist on the Amazon & Andes*. Nevertheless, though Spruce did not relate the complete truth, it is for his notes, that the history of the Inca treasure in the Llanganati Mountains has survived until our time, and has reached my understanding."...here ends Brunner's short story of the *Derrotero de Valverde*, the *Guzmán Map* and Richard Spruce.

■ ■ ■

Brunner would write later much more specifically concerning Spruce. Contained within his 1979 manuscript *El Tesoro en las Misteriosas Montañas de Llanganati* Brunner relates the following story of Richard Spruce ... "One Englishman [91] came to understand that in the mountains of Llanganati a treasure was hidden. It was through this same son of Albion [92] that the Royal Geographical Society in London also came to understand, and through the publication of a pamphlet in the *Geographical Journal* of this society that all of Great Britain came to understand, that in the Mountains of Llanganati a treasure was hidden.

"In the year 1849 the young botanist Richard Spruce arrived at the city of Belém [Bethlehem] a few miles above the delta of the majestic Amazon River in Brazil. He was twenty-seven years old, and proposed to study the vegetation of the lush and ancient hardwood forests along the Amazon River and portions of its tributaries. Taking the city of Belém as a starting point, Spruce traveled for more than 3,000 miles of the rivers Amazonas, Negro, Uapés, Casiquiare, the headwaters of the Orinoco River and its connection with the Amazon Basin. From there back to the Amazonas and Marañon, going up the Huallagua in Peru, to the river port of Moyobamba, from where he traveled the spine of the beast to the town of Tarapotó. Here he spent two years collecting plants, flowers and mosses of wet evergreen forests of the ridges in the subtropics, and it is here in Tarapotó where he receives mail from his beloved England.

"Among these letters there was one that changed Spruce's plans, situation and stay in Latin America completely. The letter read ... 'In the name of Her Majesty Queen Victoria of Great Britain, the Secretary of State of her Majesty and of India, reports that she has entrusted the Honorable Richard Spruce Esq. the commission to immediately procure the seeds and seedlings of the Red Bark Tree [*Cinchona succirubra*], which contains the chemical ingredient known as quinine, and hereby informs him, to proceed to Ecuador, that once there, with the help of a Mr. Cross, and the money deposited in the form of letter of credit in her Majesty's Consulate in Guayaquil, to carry out in the best way possible and under the conditions allowed with this commission.'

---

[91] Brunner is referring to Richard Spruce.
[92] Albion - The oldest known name of the island of Great Britain.

"Spruce was pleasantly surprised and grateful, realizing that back in his country it was finally recognized how valuable his studies of botany were. But at the same time his situation became more difficult and his problems were quite serious, the principal was his transfer to Ecuador. How could he travel from this small site in the subtropical forests, on the edge of the Peruvian Amazon to the Republic of Ecuador? High snowy peaks and enormous frigid wastelands stood between Tarapotó and the city of Lima on the Pacific coast. Although Spruce could have reached the city of the viceroys, today he was separated by only a few hundred miles from the Ecuadorian forests where the Cinchona trees grow. The outbreak of a revolution in Peru and a yellow fever epidemic in Tarapotó decided for him, forcing Spruce to travel by water. He returned to Moyobamba by mule and pack animals, from there descended the river Huallaga to the Marañon, then ascended the Pastaza and the Bobonaza and entered Ecuador through the back door.

"His journey through the Pastaza was an adventure in itself, but Spruce finally arrived at the port of Andoas, where he recalled the exploits and adventures lived by Madame Isabel Godin des Odonais of Riobamba. Almost a century before Spruce in 1769, after twenty years of separation from her husband, French surveyor Jean Godin, whom she believed dead, Isabel and thirty-one Indians traveled the same waterway to reunite with the man for whom she had cried so long. In her journey from Riobamba in the Republic of Ecuador, to the city of Cayenne in French Guiana, she suffered a host of mishaps, death, betrayal and outrages that marked her path.

"All this reminded Spruce while at the same time made him realize that he was about to make the same trip but in reverse. Even with Indians more civilized, he also had to pass through the territories of the terrible Jibaro headhunters of the Pastaza and Bobonaza. If the ascent up the rivers mentioned to Canelos was difficult and dangerous, the journey by land through the forest of Canelos and onto Baños would be worse still. Finally, accompanied by his faithful porters Spruce arrived on foot at the resort of Baños safe and sane, remaining there for a short break of six months. After which Spruce traveled on to Ambato and from there to Guayaquil.

"Unfortunately for Spruce the revolution in Peru had succeeded and the new President of that nation, Ramón Castillo, was at war with Ecuador, occupying the port of Guayaquil with a contingent of Peruvian troops under the command of General Franco an Ecuadorian traitor, therefore Ecuador was also at war. The preparations for which, degenerated into a revolution in Ecuador. Spruce's expedition became all but impossible, since it was not possible to obtain workers or laborers for his business. All were mobilized to fight in the war against the enemy outside, or for the revolution against the enemy within. The others which no one could catch for either service, were of no use to Spruce as well, for they hid in the mountains to protect their families and loved ones.

"As circumstances didn'allow Spruce to pursue the *Cinchona succirubra*, Spruce collected samples of plants, flowers and rare mosses in the surroundings of Baños and other places in the valleys of the rivers Pastaza, Patate, Chambo and Ambato. While involved in these matters and collecting samples of very rare mosses in the surroundings of Cotaló, ascending toward Guayrapata in the month of August 1857, the Indians' who were with Spruce, indicating a snowy hill in the east across the valley Pastaza and almost in front of the Tungurahua volcano, stated ... 'Llanganati, Llanganati, there is the treasure of Atahualpa.' Days later on another occasion, the Indians of Penipe and Baños, while working on the slopes of Tungurahua, told Spruce exactly the same in nearly the same words.

"We must not forget that Richard Spruce Esquire belonged to a group of great Englishmen that during the nineteenth century transformed the Kingdom of England into an enormous Empire, comparable only with that of the Spanish Empire of Charles V, on which the sun never set. Therefore, no matter where in the world they were, when men like Spruce investigated, nothing was left to chance, everything was checked thoroughly and our friend Spruce was no exception. For this reason Spruce opened a serious investigation into the legend of the treasure of Atahualpa, hidden in the mountains of Llanganati.

"In one of Spruce's notes written to some friends that he had in the city of Quito, he aimed to find out if they knew anything concerning the supposed treasure of the Incas in the Llanganatis. One of his friends told him that he should go to the city of Tacunga (Latacunga today) because he knew that in the municipal archives there were important papers on the subject. That these documents consisted of a *Cédula Real*, in which the King of Spain ordered the magistrates of Tacunga and Ambato to verify the veracity of a guide to the Llanganati Mountains, and thence to a site where there was a hidden treasure, and the guide of the Spanish Valverde which was the purpose of the *Cédula Real*.

"In another of his notes Spruce tells us that when reaching Tacunga he did not find any authentic documents in the archives. That the same had been stolen some twenty years before his arrival, but luckily he obtained a copy dated 14 Aug 1827 which he translated into English. Unfortunately, in the most important parts of this copy it was ruined (look) and what was written could almost not be read, that is why sometimes the text does not fit from one line to another.

Brunner's copy of Guzmán Map

"Still another note reports that Spruce also came to know that a gentleman in Ambato, a Señor Salvador Ortega, kept a map of the mountains of Llanganati, drawn by a Spanish colleague, and this distinguished gentleman of Ambato had the politeness to place the map in Spruce's hands allowing him the opportunity of copying it. It is for this reason that Spruce had the possibility of accompanying the translation of the *Derrotero de Valverde* with this formidable map. Spruce indicated that the original map was formed by eight small pieces of paper of unequal proportions and that his copy is the size of 3 feet and 10 ½ inches by 2 feet 9 inches and is three-eighths of scale of the original map of Atanasio Guzmán.[93]

"Guzmán was a botanist, explorer and an adventurer in his own way and why not also say a little fanatic. According to what you can see on your map, Anastasio Guzmán, in the company of many men from San Andrés, San José de Poaló of Tungipamba and elsewhere, made an endless number of expeditions into the Llanganatis, especially to the mountains of Mulatos and the Roncadores. Finally ruling out this area and transferring their explorations to the hills of Limpio-Pungo and Ainchilibi, the rocky outcrops of Jaramillo, the snowy Atilis, and Yurac Llanganati or Cerro Hermoso, which incidentally was the snowy hill that the Indians of Cotaló, Penipe and Baños had earlier indicated to Richard Spruce.

"While they were exploring this area, Guzmán who was a sleepwalker, fell or better stated walked into a deep ravine on the ranch of Leytillo near Leyte. They found him the next morning badly injured, and he was transported to the settlement of Patate, where he succumbed to injuries and loss of blood in the same year of 1807. His death was deeply felt because Guzmán was a good man, wise and above all very humane. With all the above, we know clearly that the seasoned Guzmán also came to the conclusion that the lagoon and treasure should be in the vicinity of Cerro Hermoso and not in the mountains that he and his men had explored for many years. In reality, Guzmán and his associates had found in the Mulatos and Roncadores countless deposits of minerals and mines worked by pre-Inca Indians. There were minerals of copper, gold, silver, as well as old abandoned mines and so on. But why were they going to work the mines, if somewhere in these mountains was a huge treasure trove?

"Spruce came to know that in Baños was still kept some personal items of Atanasio Guzmán. Above all was a large collection of dried and pressed plants, but when Spruce arrived, insects had destroyed almost everything. As the war with Peru continued on and the port of Guayaquil was still in the hands of the Peruvians, Spruce had plenty of spare time in which to make

---

[93] "Ebru" was Brunner's synonym for his signature. Brunner would sign some of his artwork, documents and manuscripts in this manner. What I assumed to have been Brunner's hand copied *Guzmán Map,* appears exactly as explorer/author Rolf Blomberg's copy that was published in *Buried Gold and Anacondas* [1955]. Both of these mens map source, was clearly Wallace's version as published in *Notes of a Botanist.*

inquiries about the treasure of Atahualpa and perhaps even make expeditions. I am convinced that Spruce was in some of the sites mentioned in the *Derrotero de Valverde*, because one of his notes said ... 'Through the window of my room, I can distinguish clearly the Cerro de Guapa.' From which room I ask? From the room in Ambato, or from the room in Píllaro? I believe or rather I am sure that this small note is proof that, Richard Spruce was not only dedicated to translating the route and copying the map, but although he does not say so, also had made explorations in the surrounding lands, almost certainly within these same Llanganati Mountains.

"For me it is a fact that Spruce knew much more about the treasure and the site at which this is hidden, which I have noted in Spruce's notes of yore. We will never know how many interesting things more that he knew, but definitely it was a lot. Why this almost fanatical obsession toward the treasure of the Llanganatis? To this question there is no answer, but for an unusual event in the year 1861, while Spruce was still in Ecuador, he published in the *Geographical Journal* of the Royal Geographical Society in London, a paper with the title; *A hidden treasure of the Incas in the Mountains of Llanganati, Ecuador, an authentic guide to its locality, illustrated by a map. The map copied and the Guide translated by Richard Spruce.*[94]

"I wonder how is it possible that a man with such prolixity, responsibility and above all a personality like Richard Spruce, had published his paper concerning a treasure of the Incas, in remote unknown mountains, before he published something relative to his real work that was undertaken for the Queen? To find out how things really were, let history do the talking and discover that what at first appears improbable, becomes plausible and then becomes logical and true.[95]

"In 1860 General Juan José Flores, accompanied by the legitimate President of the country, Doctor Don Gabriel García Moreno, managed to free the city of Guayaquil. The flight of the Peruvian forces with the traitor Franco at its head, finished the war. The port of Guayaquil reopened to maritime traffic and international trade. Finally Spruce obtained workers and all the people he needed for the collection of seeds and seedlings of the *Cinchona succirubra*.

---

[94] Here Brunner is erroneously stating the title of Spruce's paper which was; *On the Mountains of Llanganati, in the Eastern Cordillera of the Quitonian Andes, illustrated by a map constructed by the late Don Atanasio Guzmán*. The title Brunner quotes was given to this same paper by Alfred Russel Wallace, editor of *Notes of a Botanist on the Amazon & Andes*, which was not published until 1908.

[95] Here again Brunner is clearly in error. Spruce had actually published papers prior, including; *Notes on a Visit to the Chinchona Forests on the Western Slopes of the Andes (1860)* and shortly thereafter *Report on the Expedition to procure Seeds and Plants of the Chinchona succirubra or Red Bark Tree (1862).*

"In the beginning of October Spruce arrived in Guayaquil, where he awaited Mr. Cross who was coming with the first shipment of plants and seeds. This project required them to travel constantly between Guayaquil, Bodegas de Babahoyo, Ventanas and Cataram, which during these times could be deadly. Spruce was sick with Malaria, infested with vermin, in total, he was a very sick man. Finally in early 1861 the steamship departed and carried the cargo of seeds and plants of the *Cinchona succirubra,* under the care of Mr. Cross to Panama. From there they undertook the long journey to India and the Island of Ceylon where the English commenced cultivation. *Cinchona succirubra* is a plant blessed by God. It was the only plant that could cure the millions of patients with malaria and for this reason Spruce's work was so important.

"Spruce traveled to Duale and from there back to Guayaquil, where he tried to salvage some of his fortune that was lost in the collapse of the mercantile house "Gutierrez" in which he had invested. Spruce passed the month of January 1862 at the Hacienda "Chonana" of the late General John Hunt Illingworth, or in other words, in the care of Doctor Matins Destruge Alcides, son-in-law of the General and Spruce's personal physician.

"On the advice of Dr. Destruge Spruce traveled to the Chanduy resort on the seacoast, in the Santa Elena Peninsula. Here Spruce spent several months very sick, but even this ill Spruce collected a great amount of plants and flowers. In August Spruce returned to Guayaquil where he continued trying to salvage something of the property he had lost. The first of January 1863 Spruce embarked on a steamship traveling to Paita in Peru, where he spent the whole year of 1863 and the first four months of 1864. On the first of May Spruce embarked again, this time for his return to England. Spruce landed at Southampton almost fifteen years after his departure. In the end, Richard Spruce's trip had lasted ten days less than fifteen years, of which almost six years were in the mountains and subtropical forests of Ecuador. Spruce retired to his native Yorkshire, where he spent the remaining nineteen years of his life, poor among the poor, with a state pension that was too much to let him die and too little to live on.

"During these last years working on his notes, Spruce wrote his book and spent as much time as possible in the botanical gardens, sorting and taking care of more than 30,000 species and varieties of plants obtained throughout the Amazon, that he had sent to England. His journey of 3000 miles through the rivers of Brazil, Venezuela, Peru and Ecuador, facing the dangers and diseases of the virgin forests of the tropics alone, is a feat unmatched (the Baron von Humboldt had at least his companion Aimé Jacques Alexandre Bonpland). One of those great feats that only men of decision make with tenacity and honesty toward oneself." ... here ends Brunner's short story.

■ ■ ■

The story of the *Derrotero de Valverde* and the *Guzmán Map*, first came to my attention in May of 1986 through Eugene Konrad Brunner's documentation. I wanted to verify through my own research the history of the Inca's and the source and accuracy of the information presented by Brunner. At the time I lived in Temple Terrace Florida, with my wife and our then three children, not far from the University of South Florida. I assumed that the library would be a great starting point in my quest.

Within the stacks and shelves of the university's library, I found numerous books on the Incas that were quite informative and exciting as I knew nothing of their history. Having grown up in the Northeastern United States, Vermont to be exact, my school's curriculum didn't encompass Inca History or for that matter Spanish, as French and Latin were the only languages' offered at the time. The French and Indian Wars along with the Lewis and Clark Expedition were some of the subjects I enjoyed learning about, my family roots being French Canadian. However, I never was able to ascertain whether Toussaint Charbonneau born in Montreal, having been the husband of Sacagawea, being hired as an interpreter and guide on the expedition, was a distant relative or not. Perhaps the need to discover the unknown through travel and exploration was in my blood ... perhaps not.

I decided to search the library's catalog for *Notes of a Botanist on the Amazon & Andes* by Richard Spruce and to my great surprise the University had a reference copy. After some difficulty deciphering the call numbers and location, I finally discovered both volumes on the shelf. Turning to the back of Volume II, CHAPTER XXVIII, page 489 the words "A HIDDEN TREASURE OF THE INCAS" grabbed my attention. I thumbed through the chapter and to my astonishment, bound in the back was a large tri-fold map, the *Guzmán Map*, with red lines marking out the three expedition routes that had been added by Wallace! My first adrenalin induced instinct was to tear out the map and run ... morality and reason prevailing, I settled for photocopies, as the map's size required that it be copied in sections.

■ ■ ■

When I first read the last chapter in *Notes of a Botanist* it appeared that Richard Spruce had become an avid treasure hunter even to the point of being obsessed with it, but upon reading his paper in its entirety without Wallace's commentary, it appears more accurately that Wallace was the one enthralled. Spruce in my opinion had remained scientific, studious and sincere.

Question's still lingered ... Why did Spruce not publish the *Cédula Real* [Royal Decree] or the account of the official search ordered by the King of Spain? What information was contained in Spruce's missing Ecuadorian journals and could there have been a map by Valverde along with his famous *Derrotero* as most believe? It stands to reason that making a detailed search of the Archivo General de Indias in Seville Spain could verify the *Derrotero de Valverde*, *Cédula Real*, report to the King on the expedition, and the *Valverde Map* if one exists [96]. . . unless of course ... these documents have met the same fate as those in Ecuador.

---

[96] The theory goes that the purported *Valverde Map* is actually depicted in part by an 1887 map of Barth Blacke, referred to later in this text as Blacke's first map.

One wonders, did Spruce confide information or tell stories to his friend George Stabler, which were passed down throughout the family over the years? What information may have been lost or embellished over the centuries, perhaps even innocently through translation, copying or editing? It would have appeared extremely relevant for Wallace to publish Spruce's paper in its entirety, which he did not do. The knowledge contained within those omitted nine and a half pages clarified a great deal of the *Guzmán Map* and similar data that has been collected by numerous explorers over the ensuing decades. These omitted pages, although previously published, were not available to all of those who chose to follow in Valverde's footsteps, including Eugene Brunner, creating unnecessary expenditures of time, effort and money.

The *Guzmán Map* [97] as well, although a detailed map of the area, was produced hundreds of years after the *Derrotero* and had been copied by Spruce, an engraver and Wallace. In the chapter introduction Wallace acknowledges portions of the map have been "omitted in order to make it more convenient for reference here." Spruce himself acknowledges that not only was the original "much dilapidated" and "scarcely decipherable" in locations, but that he made them out with the aid of other persons. Most importantly Spruce indicates that in some locations Guzmán's map was so transposed that ... "I omitted them in my copy."

■ ■ ■

Explorers and treasure hunters get caught up in the excitement and paranoia inherent in this field of endeavor. Without a doubt, every single person believes they are destined to decipher the location of the treasure or that they have exclusive data, which may have been acquired by any means. If someone else makes a discovery, they do all that is possible to add reasonable doubt to others successes. If information is shared, something is always held back, or there is misdirection ... I am familiar with these situations as they have all occurred to me as well.

Like Wallace before me, I have never set foot in the Llanganatis, and similarly, based on the exhaustive and extensive work of another, Eugene K. Brunner, I have made observations, interpreted data, developed theories and made conclusions about this treasure. Of certain things I am positive, without setting a foot in any archive ... the *Derrotero* is absolutely accurate. Guzmán's map as well ... is absolutely accurate in the areas he actually visited, both having been verified up to a certain point by countless explorers and expeditions over the centuries.

---

[97] Richard Spruce's copy from the "original" map of Don Atanasio Guzmán was completed in Ambato Ecuador in early 1860. This map was utilized to illustrate Spruce's paper *On the Mountains of Llanganati, in the Eastern Cordillera of the Quitonian Andes* and later reworked and published in the *Geographic Journal*. Ultimately, only a portion of this reworked map was republished in *Notes of a Botanist.*

Without question the landmarks mentioned within the first half of the *Derrotero,* up to the hieroglyph ... Píllaro, the farm of Moya, the mountain of Guapa, the three Cerros Llanganati in the form of a triangle, the two small lake's Los Anteojos, the great black lake Yana Cocha and the mountain of Margasitas ... all exist and are accurately depicted in the *Derrotero* and *Guzmán Map.* Another explorer in the footsteps of Valverde, to be introduced in our next chapter, E. C. Brooks, was quite clear and concise when he wrote ... "I had no trouble in finding all of the landmarks of the guide up to and beyond the "Way of the Inca," and I had no trouble about the correct side on which to pass the "mountain which is all margasitas."

It has always stuck in the back of my mind however, that hundreds of years after the *Derrotero* was written Spruce translated and interpreted the document to the best of his scientific ability. What if even a portion Spruce's interpretation and subsequent theory was erroneous? Spruce writes ... "If" and I must reiterate ... "If" Margasitas be considered the first mountain of the three to which Valverde refers, then the Tembladá or Bog, out of which Valverde extracted his wealth, the socabón and the guayra are in the second mountain, and the lake wherein the ancients threw their gold in the third."

Spruce further states ... "The three Llanganatis seen from the top of Guapa are supposed to be the peaks Margasitas, Zunchu, and el Volcan del Topo." ... these mountains, just as many others in the Llanganatis, could form a triangle. But what if ... three Cerros Llanganati did not mean three mountains ... instead the *Derrotero* was referring to a main peak and two secondary peaks of one mountain, as the ancient guide appears to indicate?

Valverde's *Derrotero* plainly and simply appears to be a direct and concise guide to the source of his wealth. However, it is this "inhospitable" region that presents a problem for the explorer following Valverde's guide. The Llanganati is a region in which the human imagination can discern numerous locations of three peaks in the form of a triangle and is peppered with hundreds' if not thousands' of lakes and caves. It is a region that has been transformed throughout hundreds of years by massive earthquakes, rock falls, mud slides, erosion and rapid botanical growth.[98]

What becomes clearly self-evident is that where the ancient indigenous guide and the *Derrotero de Valverde* concur, those landmarks, Guapa, sanguirimas, flechas, Lagunas de Anteojos, and the great black lake are all easily discovered. The description of the landmarks, the waterfall, quaking bog, socavón or tunnel, and how to ascend the mountain are also quite similar. It is only within the portions of the *Derrotero de Valverde* that are

---

[98] Explorers of this region are required to constantly cut new trails, yard by yard, through this massive growth. An expedition trail cut one year, will be required to be re-cut the next year. Consider then, the effect that hundreds' of years of growth alone would have, not just on travel in the region, but on the vistas one would encounter ... or not.

not mentioned in the ancient guide, or vice versa, that confusion and misdirection abound. The *Derrotero de Valverde* for instance makes no mention of Cerro Hermoso as does the ancient guide. While on the other hand the guide makes no mention of "a mountain which is all of margasitas" or of a hieroglyph, the two clues that have confused explorers' for decades.

In the end, you must follow the *Derrotero de Valverde* , keeping in mind that Guzmán's map is just an important tool, not a companion map ... it will be the interpretation of the hieroglyph found within Spruce's version of the *Derrotero de Valverde,* or the translation of the cryptic clue within the Spanish version, that remains the key. Remember, certain areas of Guzmán's map, such as Cerro Hermoso, were drawn from a distance and not visited, it is for this reason the map contains inaccuracies. Spruce's reproduction of the *Guzmán Map* was not published due to size limitations, yet Wallace included most of the relevant portions. Through Brunner's relentless explorations and discoveries verifying both the *Derrotero de Valverde* and the *Guzmán Map* on location, I know that the "socavón" exists, as does the "lake made by hand" ... all of which I shall share with you later ... as lust for Inca gold continues.

■ ■ ■

Richard Spruce, Esq.

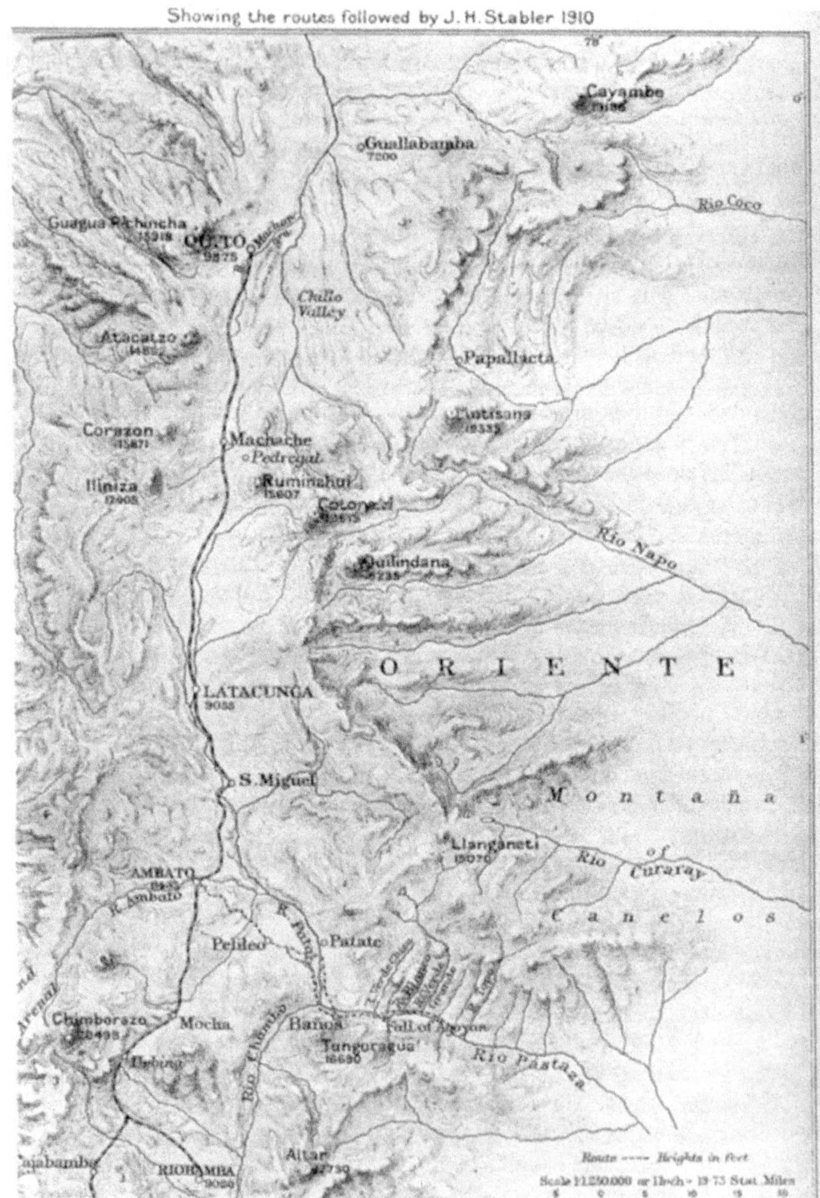

Stabler's Expedition Map

THE ROYAL GEOGRAPHICAL SOCIETY: STABLER & BROOKS

The Royal Geographical Society of England is the learned society and professional body for geography and geographers. The society was founded in 1830 under the name Geographical Society of London, as an institution to promote the "advancement of geographical science." Like many learned societies, it had started as a dining club in London, where select members held informal dinner debates on current scientific issues and ideas. Under the patronage of King William IV the society later became known as The Royal Geographical Society and was granted its Royal Charter under Queen Victoria in 1859.

The society has been a key associate and supporter of many famous explorers and expeditions, including those of Charles Darwin, James Kingston Tuckey, David Livingstone, William Ogilvie, Robert Falcon Scott, Richard Francis Burton, John Hanning Speke, George W. Hayward, Percy Fawcett, George M. Dyott, Henry Morton Stanley, Ernest Shackleton, and Sir Edmund Hillary to name but a few. From the middle of the 19th century until the end of World War I, expeditions sponsored by the Royal Geographical Society were frequently front page news, and the opinions of its President and Council would be avidly sought by journalists and editors.

The early history of the Society was interlinked with the history of British Geography,[99] exploration and discovery. Information, maps, charts and knowledge gathered on expeditions were either deposited with, or presented to, the Royal Geographical Society through lectures given at the societies meetings, making up its now unique geographical collections. The Society published its first journal in 1831 and from 1855 accounts of meetings and other matters were published in the *Proceedings of the Royal Society of London*. In 1893, this was replaced by the *Geographical Journal* which is still published today.

The Society supports and promotes many aspects of geography including geographical research, education and teaching, field training and small expeditions, the public understanding and popularization of Geography, and the provision of geographical information. The Society also works together with other existing bodies serving the geographical community, in particular the Geographical Association and the Royal Scottish Geographical Society.

Fellowship of the Society is currently conferred to anyone over twenty-one who has a deep involvement with geography through research, publication, profession, or who has been an ordinary member of the society for the five previous years. The applicant must be proposed and seconded by existing Fellows and elected by the Council. Fellows are granted the right to use the initials 'F.R.G.S.' after their names.

■ ■ ■

---

[99] Especially "colonial" exploration in Africa, the Indian subcontinent, the polar regions and central Asia.

Our story continues years later in the early 1900s with some of the first expeditions in the footsteps of Richard Spruce, perhaps even with a connection through the family of Spruce's life-long friend George Stabler. The surname may possibly be just a coincidence, but in May of 1916 a paper entitled *Travels in Ecuador* was read before the Royal Geographical Society by fellow Jordan Stabler and was subsequently published in the societies *Geographical Journal*, Volume 50, October of 1917.

Very little has been written about Jordan Herbert Stabler [1885-1938], an American Citizen, the son of Jordan [born 1840] and Carrie Stabler. Stabler's paternal grandparents were Edward [born 1794] and Ann Stabler. Jordan's great grandparents were Dr. William and Deborah Stabler, the Doctor's father was also named Edward Stabler [born 1732], and had emigrated to the United States from England in 1753. Edward's father's name was Edward as well, and his father was Ishmael Stabler, the son of a George and Ann Stabler. As previously indicated it might be just coincidental, but it would also seem logical that in this family tree, somewhere, there might just be a connection to Spruce's young friend, George Stabler.

Jordan was educated at Country School at Homewood in Maryland and graduated Johns Hopkins University in 1907 with a Bachelors Degree. He became the private secretary to the Honorable Henry Lane Wilson, at the time US Minister to Belgium, where he remained until the spring of 1909. In June of 1909 Stabler was appointed Secretary of the American Legation [100] at Quito, Ecuador, where he remained through at least June of 1911.

In March of 1911 Stabler had been appointed Second Secretary of the US Embassy at Berlin, however an emergency situation arose and he was transferred to the US Legation at Guatemala as acting Chargé d'Affairs during the absence of the US Minister. From there Stabler was appointed as Secretary of Legation at Stockholm Sweden in 1912, served as Assistant to Chief of Division for Latin-American Affairs during 1913-1914 and in 1915 under President Woodrow Wilsons administration was appointed as Chief of Division for Latin-American Affairs. Mr. Stabler apparently spent the first two years of World War I in London, retired and became affiliated with the Gulf Oil Corporation in Venezuela and Europe. Jordan died at the young age of fifty-three, in Paris.

■ ■ ■

Similar to Spruce's writings describing his travels in Ecuador, Stabler, himself a fellow of the Royal Geographical Society, reported on his own Ecuadorian travels during the period of 1909 through 1911, making specific references to Spruce's observations as well. Stabler read his paper entitled *Travels in Ecuador* at the Society meeting of 8 May 1916 and it was published with a frontispiece map entitled ... *Part of Ecuador Showing the routes followed by J. H. Stabler 1910* (which is reproduced on page 101),

[100] Legation was a diplomatic representative office lower than embassy, the use of this term was dropped after World War II.

two sections, and six Plates in the *Geographical Jour* October 1917.

The first pages of Stabler's paper are not directly relate story, although they do make for interesting read country's territorial dispute with Peru, and place the lifestyles and difficulty of travel in Ecuador during the ... clear perspective. Stabler's entire paper as published in the *Geographical Journal* follows ... "AT the time of the discussion in the Spanish Council of State concerning the decision of the Ecuadorian-Peruvian Boundary dispute, upon which His Majesty the King of Spain had been asked to arbitrate, the President of the Council is said to have remarked, 'Beyond the natural boundaries, raised by the hand of God, it will be difficult for Ecuador to hold territory, for she is the Switzerland of the Americas.' This remark is indeed true, for a striking similarity exists between the Alpine Republic and this country in the Andes — both having as common features lofty snow-clad peaks, deep ravines, and broad valleys enclosed by great mountain ranges — and the comparison enables one to form a topographical idea of Ecuador.

"The Republic of Ecuador, which with the exception of Uruguay is the smallest of all the South American Republics, lies between 2° N. and 6° S. lat. The longitudinal extension of the Republic is as yet undecided, for, although many years of discussion have passed and many decisions have been made, the Eastern and Southern frontier limits are still in dispute with the neighbouring Republic of Peru, and some territory is in litigation with Colombia.

"One is almost safe in claiming that Ecuador has more boundaries than any other country, for there are maps of the Republic showing six different frontiers according to six different opinions. There are the limits claimed by the Government of the Republic, which take in the greatest extent of territory and stretch far to the east, including a vast portion of the 'Oriente,' that territory lying to the east in the great Amazonian plain. This delineation of the frontier was made by Restrepo and Humboldt in the eighteenth century. Another frontier line is that known as the Pedemonte Mosquera line, and was drawn in 1830. The third is the provisional boundary made according to Menendez-Pidal, the Spanish High Commissioner, in 1887. The fourth is the line drawn according to the ideas set forth in the Garcia Herrera agreement. The fifth is the boundary as outlined in 1909 by the Spanish Council of State. The sixth is that claimed by the Government of Peru. These limits of Ecuador are embodied in a chart issued by order of the President of the Republic. When rumours were circulated as to what the decision of the King of Spain would be, both countries made objections; the King resigned his position as arbitrator, and the boundaries still remain in *statu quo*.

"The Republic is divided into three distinct divisions from west to east, clearly defined by the great Cordilleras of the Andes. They are the Pacific littoral sloping up to the Western Range some 60 to 80 miles; the great

-Andine plateau, at an altitude of from 7250 to 9200 feet, in some aces over 100 miles broad, fertile, cultivated, good grazing country; and, thirdly, the country known as the 'Oriente' stretching from the Eastern Cordillera to the farthest border of Ecuador, tropical jungle country, unexplored to a great extent and known only to the semi-savage Indian tribes, to a few travellers, to the Ecuadorian officials at government posts, and to the "Caucheros," rubber hunters, who make a yearly trip to the interior.

"From Guayaquil; the principal port of Ecuador, on the Guayas River, 2° South, the journey to Quito, the capital, is now made in two days by the trans-Andine railroad, a much easier trip than in Whymper's time in 1880, when it necessitated from six to fifteen days by mule according to season, over almost impassable trails, with no accommodation, and with but little or no food to be found on the way. Nevertheless the trip is still full of interest and of the unexpected. One must be provided with an abundant supply of food and warm blankets, for landslides and derailments are frequent, and a night spent on an Andine Pass without warm covering and nourishment is none too pleasant.

"From the banks of the Guayas River the railway runs inland some 60 miles through coco, banana, and tagua plantations, and through thick tropical jungles, abounding in palms of all descriptions; and then begins, to ascend the Andine slopes through the valley of the Chan-chan River, which has its source in the lower hills of Chimborazo. Reaching the outer walls of the Cordillera it quickly mounts to the high plains by means of a 'switchback' track cut into the side of an almost perpendicular cliff by a skillful feat of engineering.

"The western wall of the Andes once surmounted, the track runs north, crossing at an altitude of 11,362 feet the sandy wind-swept plain known as the 'Grand Arenal,' which is, at almost all seasons of the year, a prey to the snow and wind storms that come with deadly blasts from the high slopes of Chimborazo. Here, in the days before the railway, many travellers were frozen to death in the severity of these storms, and it present the trail is dotted with the bones of pack-animals.

"Leaving the sandy plateau and winding through the valleys of the outlying slopes of the mighty Chimborazo, the railway at length comes out upon a broad plain, at the end of which is the capital of the Province of Chimborazo, Riobamba by name, a quaint old colonial Spanish town with streets exceptionally wide as a precaution against earthquake, built on sandy soil, at an altitude of some 9030 feet. Here the night is passed, for travelling by rail at night in Ecuador is not considered safe. The volcano of Altar, rising to 17,730 feet according to the observations of Reiss and Stübel, lies almost due east of the town and surmounts this part of the eastern Cordillera.

"From Riobamba the railway passes due north along the Inter-Andine plain, leaving the great mass of the ranges of Chimborazo to the west until it reaches the town of Ambato. From this point the road-bed descends a little until the town of Latacunga is reached, and passing over the Páramos of Cotopaxi, winds up through the ridges of the eastern slopes of the Andes, where an excellent view is obtained of the great peaks of Iliniza, Corazon, Antisana, Rumiñahui, and Atacatzo. The run into Quito from there on is down grade, and one arrives at the small wooden station on the outskirts of the town, barring landslides and derailments, in the late afternoon of the second day of the journey.

"Quito, the capital of Ecuador, is at an altitude of 9342 feet, according to the observations of Whymper, while the survey of the railway engineer makes it some 250 feet higher. It lies close south of the equator at a distance of about 15 English miles. It is beyond doubt one of the most interesting and picturesque cities in the western hemisphere, for it still retains the charm of colonial days, and the modernizing influence of the outside world has as yet touched it but lightly. The northern capital of the Inca Empire, captured by the Conquistadores after their almost unbelievable marches over the Andes, the seat of the Vice-Regal Governor of the Presidency of Quito, the scene of some of the earlier of the attempts for independence, and, after the formation of the Republic, the theater of much revolutionary activity, Quito has a history of great importance, in the development of Spanish America.

"The many plazas; the monasteries of the Dominicans, the Mercedarios, the Franciscans, and other of the great Orders; the great patios of the houses of the descendants of noble Spanish families; the religious processions frequently passing through the streets; the variegated colour scheme formed by the bright ponchos of the Indians of the city and the orange-coloured Macanas of the tribes of the hills and north country, imprint an indelible picture upon the mind. Looking down upon the city from the slopes of the volcano of Pichincha---the mountain which dominates the town---one sees below a wide extent of closely joined roofs, with here and there the tower of some great church or monastery; for Quito is for its size one of the strongest Catholic cities in South America, having some two hundred churches, chapels and monasteries. The city covers a wide area; but it is very difficult to form an idea of its population, as is so often the case in Spanish-American cities where no regular census can be taken. Although a population of some eighty thousand is claimed, I should consider a conservative estimate was from forty to fifty-five thousand.

"The population may be divided into three distinct classes: the pure Indian, the descendant of the Quichua tribes speaking that language and a little Spanish, who are in the majority; the 'Cholos,' or mixed class---Indian and Spanish; and lastly, the pure Spanish families, who have come down in direct line from the Conquistadores. The principal streets show very well the general character of the city: the two-storied houses and the flag-paved streets, under almost all of which run streams of water from the sides of Pichincha, draining the city through the deep volcanic ravines or 'quebradas.'

“The hill known as the ‘panecillo’ or ‘little loaf’ at the south-west end of the town, rises some 300 feet in height. It is reputed locally to have been built by order of the Inca as a tomb of one of the kings. The peaks of Cayambe, Imbabura, Cotocachi, all to the north, and Atacatzo, Corazon, Antisana, and Cotopaxi to the south, are visible from this point on a clear morning of the dry season.

“Quito has one of the most regular climates of any capital in the world, and this has been proved by the observations made at the observatory erected by the French mission in the park of the city. The mean annual temperature is 58.8° Fahr., the maximum annual is 70°, and the minimum annual is 45°. The average range in the twenty-four hours is some 10°.

“During the two years I spent there I found that I never had to worry about what the weather was going to be. One rarely made a mistake, as the weather conditions seemed to change as if by clockwork. In the summer months, from October to April - the rainy season - the rain commences to fall in a torrential downpour regularly at a little after two p.m., and by five or six it has usually cleared off and the nights are almost always cloudless. From May until the latter part of September it is clear and very dry, and quite cold in the early morning and late evening. I have known an occasional shower and once or twice a hailstorm in the winter months. There were very few rainy mornings, even in the wet season, during all the time I was in the highlands of Ecuador, and I noted very few days when it rained all day even in the middle of the wet season. Hailstorms are fairly frequent, but only last for a quarter to half an hour.

“My travels from Quito into the little-known parts of the Republic were almost always made with Dr. Pierre Reimbourg, a Frenchman who has spent some years in Ecuador and has made travels from Quito into the little-known parts of the Republic were almost always made with Dr. Pierre Reimbourg, a Frenchman who has spent some years in Ecuador and has made observations for the Ministère de l'Instruction Publique, and with M. Paul Suzor, the Secretary of the French Legation. These companions of many excellent and interesting expeditions are both serving their country at the Front, and I have no doubt that they are as hardy and unflinching in the supreme test as they were in former moments of minor difficulties on the Andine trails.

“One of the most interesting trips which may be made from Quito, in a very short time and with but little hardship, is the ascent of the now extinct volcano of Pichincha, the summit of which is at an altitude of 15,918 feet. The ascent may be made to one of the lower peaks almost all the way on horseback, and if one goes the night before to a hacienda some three hours from the city one may sleep there and go up to the summit and back in a day.

“On the ascent four distinct belts of vegetation may be observed: (1) The lower slopes---with some few myrtles and Eucalyptus trees, and fields under cultivation with wheat, barley, and potatoes. (2) Shrubs of many varieties. (3) The Páramo---between 12,000 and 14,000 feet---pasture country. (4) Grass; this is intermingled with some hardy shrubs distributed in scattered patches. The plant known as *Lupinus alopecuriodes* is characteristic of this region.

"As one climbs over the outlying slopes a superb view of the Andine plain is obtained. A large waterfall is passed far up the side of the mountain, and, one reaches quite soon a height overlooking a sea of clouds.

"The expedition necessitates much more time if one desires to make a descent into the crater of the now extinct volcano. Indian guides must be procured, and a camp made just below the summit of the Guagua Pichincha, one of the two peaks of the mountain. According to the observation of Dr. Reimbourg the diameter of the crater is about 1500 feet, but it was impossible to obtain an exact measurement, as the clouds prevented observations to a great extent. The greatest depth of the crater, according to Professor W. Jameson, who visited Pichincha, is 2460 feet. One may descend by means of ropes to a floor some 500 feet in depth where there are traces of sulphur and some small shrubs.

"A two days' journey to the north-east brings one to the great mountain of Cayambe on the equator. For several miles the route follows the Camino del Norte, which runs from Quito to the Colombian frontier then on to Santa Fé de Bogata, a journey of some thirty-five days on horseback. It is always full of interest and typical of the life in the high Andes. Indians in bright costumes run along at their regular trot; women with babies on their backs, and men bending under their loads, which are held by a broad strap over their forehead, are continually passing or are to be seen drinking 'chicha' as the national beer is called, at the little posadas on the side of the road. Leaving the Camino del Norte the road to Cayambe runs to the east and crosses the great 'quebrado' of Guallabamba, 7200 feet, which Whymper considered to be the biggest earthquake fissure in Equatorial America. This ravine is infamous for its fevers, and many prayers are said before any native crosses it in the rainy season. In this valley are grown sugar-cane, chiromoya, lemons, and other fruit of the temperate zone.

"Cayambe is a wonderful mass, rising to an altitude of 19,186 feet in eastern Cordillera. It is so immense that one easily imagines that it covers the greater part of the northern half of the Republic. Its lower slopes are considered among the best pastures in the highlands, and great herds of cattle and wiry Ecuadorian horses graze here. Some Ecuadorians say that there are over 40,000 head of cattle on the haciendas on the slopes of the mountain.

"The smaller variety of the Ecuadorian deer are to be found in the páramos of Cayambe (9000 to 11,000 feet), and are tracked with the aid of the big hounds bred on this mountain. The Indians of this region are good hunters, and one is surprised at their hardiness and strength. The typical costume is a pair of cotton trousers and a cotton shirt, and one or two ponchos of varying thicknesses. They all wear the native sandal 'alpargata' and a wide felt hat. But in spite of the thinness of their covering they never seem to feel the extreme cold of the páramos.

"The expedition to the mountain of Iliniza, a large mountain in the western chain to the south-west of Quito, is one of the most interesting from the point of view of sport. The route out of Quito leads along the Camino Real, the Vice-Regal 'royal road' running to Riobamba. This road was built in the early days of the Conquest, and crosses in several places parts of the Inca road from Cuzco to Quito. It was remade in 1872 by Garcia Moreno, then President of Ecuador.

"Arriving at Machache, a small town close to the railroad, one takes a trail leading to the right and ascends from the valley to the western slopes. The peak known to Whymper as the 'Little Iliniza' rises to an altitude of 16,936 feet, and is one of the most prominent of the western Cordillera. On its lower slopes deer and wood-pigeons and sometimes partridges are to be found.

"To the south-east of the capital, between the hamlet and hacienda of Pedregal (11,629 feet) and the mountain of Antisana, one of the greatest peaks of the eastern range (19,335 feet), lies some of the best shooting country in the Andes. Besides the Andine deer are found tapir, known in Ecuador as danta, and a lake affords wild duck. The páramos in this region are very exposed, there is much rain and snow, and the journey is a difficult one. The deer which are found on the páramos of the Ecuadorian Andes are the *Odocoileus peruvianus*. This is an ally of the Virginian deer. The Andine tapir is the *Tapirus pinchaque*, allied to the Amazonian tapir, but with a thicker coat. The turkey is probably the *Meleagris gallopavo*.

"In the month of September, 1910, M. Suzor, Dr. Reimbourg and I set out from Quito to make a trip to the town of Baños, the southern gateway to the Oriente on the Pastaza River, and lying under the slopes of the volcano of Tunguragua. Dr. Reimbourg wished to make certain observations on the volcano for the Ministère de l'Instruction Publique, and I had the intention of continuing further on down the Pastaza river [101] into the Montaña of Canelos, as this part of the Oriente is called.

"We left Quito in the early morning by train and arrived at the town of Ambato, where we were to procure horses and pack-animals for our trip. At about 10 o'clock, passing close by the active volcano of Cotopaxi, we were afforded a somewhat rare view of the cone, the summit of the mountain being free from clouds. Great volumes of black smoke were pouring out, and a portion of the side of the mountain was jet black where the ashes and lava had melted the snow---a striking contrast to the other sides, which were dazzling white in the sunlight. Cotopaxi is a most satisfactory volcano in that one is rarely disappointed in seeing it in eruption; and from the higher parts of Quito one can see almost every day in the sky a long line of black made from its smoke and by night a red glare on the horizon.

"Ambato is a pleasant town some 45 miles south of Quito. It lies in the Inter-Andine plain at an altitude of about 8435 feet on a sandy plateau. In

[101] In his paper and on the *Guzmán Map*, Spruce utilized the English spelling for this river ... the Pastasa.

the dry season the town is wind-swept and dusty. There are few trees in the town itself, but the outskirts have been irrigated, and there are orchards and gardens and trees along the banks of the Río Ambato, a small stream which runs through a narrow valley close to the town. Ambato is considered by the Ecuadorian's to be by far the prettiest city in the Republic, and is famous for its fruits, which are excellent and abundant. Oranges, chirimoyas, aguacates, granadillas, are grown here, as well as pears and peaches and other fruits of a more temperate zone.

"The people of Ambato lay claim to a population of ten thousand, but the most careful estimates I have seen do not concede it over six thousand inhabitants. The climate is healthy, and numbers of people come to Ambato from Quito and from the coast for a change of air.

"Notwithstanding the claims which the people of Ambato make as to the longevity of its citizens and the healthfulness of the place, when rumours spread about that a foreign physician was in the town, Dr. Reimbourg had many calls made upon him for medical advice, and his kindness was rewarded by gifts of 'dulce de guyava,' a sweet made from the guyava, for which Ambato is famous. These sweets formed a valuable addition to our stock of provisions later on in our journey, as we found that tough beef and a watery potato-soup called 'locro' constituted the principal diet of the people of Baños.

"We left Ambato at 6 a.m. by the road leading to the east. Winding up out of the valley of the Río Ambato one obtained an excellent view of the mountains of Chimborazo and Tunguragua, and looking down upon the town all that was seen was a green spot in the waste.

"The trail to Pelileo runs south-west from Ambato through almost desert country. Both sides of the sandy road are lined with cactus plants and a species of American aloe. The air is exceedingly dry and the glare of the sunlight so strong that I found a pair of smoked spectacles and a sun-helmet indispensable. Ecuadorians cover their faces with veils or with large handkerchiefs when travelling through this country, as they consider sunburn dangerous.

"Pelileo, which we reached at midday, is a small town with some 1500 to 2000 inhabitants as far as we could ascertain; and almost every person we saw was either pure Indian or had Indian blood. Its principal houses and churches are built of a volcanic rock and grey pumice stone. It is an old Spanish town and some of the churches are good examples of colonial architecture.

"On the banks of a small stream, which, flowing from a spring in the ridges above Pelileo runs into the Río Patate, we stopped for lunch and lifted our cups and drank to the Amazonas, for were we not practically at its very headwaters? The Patate flows into the Pastaza, the Pastaza into the Marañon, and the Marañon further along its course becomes one with the Amazon itself. Following the course of this stream we came to the Río Patate, which we crossed and continued along its valley which is beautiful and enjoys a delightful climate, being some 3500 feet below Quito and sheltered from the cold winds by the ridges of Tunguagua, which with its snow-capped peak towers far above this region. In this valley coffee and sugar-cane are grown in abundance and one of the wealthy families of Quito owns several haciendas along the banks of the river. Not far from the junction of the Río Patate and the Río Chambo, which unite to form the great Río Pastaza, the trail ascends from the valley and follows the contour of the slopes above the 'Puente del Union,' as the bridge at the meeting-place of the two rivers is called. It then leads along the hills above the Pastaza, being in some places almost impassable, and further on winds down to the bank of the river. The Pastaza is crossed a mile and a half from Baños by means of a small bridge across the gorge 300 feet deep, which it has cut through the solid rock, and where it rushes through the narrow channel churning up white foam.

"Baños, which derives its name from the hot baths which are located close to the town under the foothills of Tunguragua, is a small village of some nine hundred to one thousand souls, lying close under the volcano, and according to our aneroid at an altitude of 8750 feet. The inhabitants are mostly of the Cholo type, but on market days the town is crowded with Indians from the hill villages. Jivaro Indians from the Oriente, usually in parties of three or four, often come into the town to trade. Their settlements are along the Pastaza River and its tributaries. They are semi-savage but quite friendly to white men, and those who come as far west as Baños have picked up a few words of Spanish. They are stocky well-built men, with rather round faces and blunt features of a dark bronze colour. Their faces are usually painted with a few marks of some sort of black paint, and they wear their straight black hair cut just below the base of their neck. They wear little or no clothing in the Montaña, but on reaching a town dress themselves in what looks like a football jersey and cotton trousers. They carry long poles of bamboo, and some bring with them their blowpipes---six or seven feet in length---through which they blow clay pellets or darts. They always carry on their backs a finely woven basket which contains their food for the journey.

"The houses of Baños are made of bamboo and mud, with palm-leaf roofs, and everything is of most primitive nature. There is a small church and a little four-roomed monastery in charge of two Belgian priests of the Dominican order, one of whom, Padre Van Schoote, formerly an officer in the Belgian army, had spent nineteen years as a preaching Father among the Indians of the Oriente. He had passed eight years at Maccas, which lies far to the east of Ríobamba in the heart of the slopes of the Eastern Andes, among the head-hunting tribes, and eleven years among the Jivaros at Cañelos in the Oriente.

"A small hospicio or rest-house, a well-built stone building with several small bare rooms, is attached to the monastery, and here we made ourselves comfortable during our stay at Baños. We were very content to install ourselves in such a shelter; as this region is exceedingly damp and there is a great deal of rain. It is never very warm, and in the early morning the temperature is between 40° and 50° Fahr., and the thermometer does not even rise above 70° at midday.

"The waters which come out at a high temperature from the springs in the hills under the volcano are said to be a cure for rheumatism and gout. The baths are prepared in a primitive manner. An Indian is sent to dig a deep hole close to the streams of hot water, and by making a little canal for the hot water and a similar one for the water from a cold stream close by, the bath is filled and regulated.

"The patron saint of Baños, known as 'La Virgen de las Aguas Santas,' has a great reputation all over Ecuador as a worker of miracles, and on her festival the town is crowded with Indians who come many days' journey from the northern and southern parts of the Republic.

"The eastern Cordillera of the Andes, which runs approximately north and south throughout the length of Ecuador, forms an almost impenetrable barrier between the Inter-Andine Plain and the Oriente. Through this barrier there are but few passes and the three most accessible are those by way of the town of Papallacta and the Río Napo, east of Quito, by way of Cuenca and the Río Paute to the far south of the Republic, and via Baños and the Río Pastaza. This last is probably the most practicable gateway to the Oriente. Through these passes the Ecuadorian Government must send its officials and soldiers and provisions, and the task is a very difficult one. To get to the centre of the Oriente takes from three to six weeks, and ten to fifteen days at least must be made on foot over trails so deep in mud that it takes many hours to go a few miles. The question of transportation is also a large factor in any expedition into this country. An Indian bearer can only carry from twenty-five to forty pounds over these trails, and all provisions must be carried into the Oriente; but bearers are not plentiful and are most unsatisfactory. On the other hand, the Peruvians have a relatively easy access to the Amazon Plain, for their launches run from Iquitos up and down the rivers flowing into the Marañon, and men and supplies may be moved with facility. It is said that there are now many Peruvians in the part of the Oriente claimed by Ecuador who have settled on the smaller rivers, and who are armed to resist ejection by the Ecuadorian officials. What the final boundary of the Republic will be it is hard to say, but Peru has lost no time in endeavouring to send as many of her citizens as she is able into the disputed territory.

"A railway from Ambato along the valley of the Pastaza to the Curaray River has been projected and a survey made of certain parts. The road construction was commenced at Ambato under the direction of two engineers, Messrs. Moore and Fox, in 1912, and I understand it has been graded for a few miles to the east. It will probably be a great many years before such railway is completed, for this route presents almost unsurmountable difficulties.

"From Baños I set out to the east over the Oriente trail which leads to the village of Canelos on the Río Bombonasa. The road, which is passable for mules as far as the waterfall of Agoyan, keeps close to the banks of the

Pastaza after leaving the town. There are three bridges over the river just below Baños. These are some 250 feet above the river, and are built by means of great logs pushed out from each side, and another log or two logs spliced together between. It is rather ticklish work crossing them, especially if there is a strong wind in the gorge, as often happens. The road leads close by the river, through sugar-cane plantations, with here and there a 'trapiche' or cane mill, by the side of groves of plantains and palm trees and by patches of *camote*, as a vegetable of the potato family is locally known.

"Some miles further on the Pastaza is crossed by a well-built bridge constructed by Padre van Schoote, and the waterfall of Agoyan is reached. This point in the trail is at an altitude of about 5500 feet. This waterfall is the largest in the Oriente, and as the river has cut a deep channel into the solid rock and comes down with great force, it is a beautiful sight from the trail. This waterfall marks the beginning of the Montaña of Canelos, the entrance into the real Oriente.

"The Montaña of Canelos, the forest on the edge of the Amazon plain which Richard Spruce, according to Mr. Wallace's *Notes of a Botanist*, claimed was 'the most cryptogamic locality on the surface of the globe,' is bounded on the west by the volcanoes of Cotopaxi, Llanganati, and Tunguragua, and on the east by the slopes of the Amazonian lowlands. Through this forest Gonzalo Pizarro wandered nearly two years in search of cities 'as rich in gold as those of all Peru,' and returned with only 80 members out of a company of Spaniards and Indians numbering 4500. Ferns, mosses, and lichen grow in the forest in great profusion. Of the ferns the Genera *Marattia* and of the mosses the Genera *Hookeria* were most abundant.

"After leaving Agoyán the trail becomes a track 3 feet wide, very rough and with deep mud holes, and the progress is slow. The undergrowth is very thick, all or the jungle is moist, and it rains at frequent intervals. There is a light mist continually overhead. The palm trees are numerous all through the region. Spruce found that the *Iriartea ventricosa* was the most abundant species. There are also some wax palms, the *Iriartea andicola*. There are many plantains, and the undergrowth is very thick. In the season I was there I noticed very few orchids. Several small rivers are crossed on the way from Baños to the Río Verde, notably the Río Blanco and the Río Verde Chico; but all may be forded.

"At 15 English miles from Baños the Río Verde Grande joins the Pastaza and near its bank there is a 'trapiche' for grinding sugar-cane and making aguardiente. This is the last building to the east in the Montaña of Canelos with any pretensions to civilized architecture. These 15 miles from Baños to the Río Verde are the longest I have ever travelled, for the mud of the narrow trail is so deep and sticky that to go a mile sometimes takes over an hour. In the bad rains the trip can hardly be made under two days, and this trail is typical of all trails in the Oriente [102]. One must travel as lightly equipped as possible.

"The Río Verde, as its name implies, is of a deep green colour, and flows due south from the Llanganati Mountains along a steep valley, the course of which has yet to be explored. The junction of this river with the Río Pastaza is remarkable, for it comes with great force down a hanging valley whose sill is some 60 feet above the bed of the Pastaza. The momentum of the water carries it across, forming an arc, which cuts the far bank of the Pastaza where it has eroded a bay, whence the water of the Verde is turned into the Pastaza.

"Spruce states in his notes [103], made in 1857, that the cascade formed by the Río Verde at this point is some 200 feet in height. I think that this is an overestimate, and that the erosion of the river valley cannot have progressed as rapidly as would be implied.

"The Río Verde is locally reputed to have its source in the lake in the Llanganati Mountains, at the bottom of which the golden vessels which formed the ransom of King Atahualpa were thrown by the Incas when news reached Quito that their ruler had been murdered.

"In the paper by Richard Spruce read before this Society in 1860, and published in the *Proceedings R. G. S.*, 1861, p. 163, the story of the Inca treasure in the Llanganati is told at length. A short résumé of the story is as follows: The contents of 'the Chamber filled with Gold' stored in Quito for the ransom of the king from the Spaniards was carried swiftly into the Eastern Andes by Inca runners when the messengers announced the murder of the ruler. A river which flows through a valley among these mountains was dammed and the gold thrown into the artificial lake so formed. A Spaniard Valverde by name who many years afterward married an Indian woman, or as some say an Indian princess, was given the secret of this treasure by his wife. He made many trips to the lake and must have been successful in his search, for he returned to Spain a very wealthy man and bequeathed the secret of the lake to his king upon his death. The key to the treasure, or the *Derrotero of Valverde* as the guide is called, was sent by the King of Spain to officials at the town of Latacunga with instructions to make a search. Many attempts were made in colonial days as well as later; but as yet it appears that no one has found the hidden lake. During my stay in Ecuador, and some months prior to my trip to the Montaña of Canelos, a compatriot of mine ... Major Brooks by name ... was able to procure a copy of the *Derrotero* at Latacunga, and from it constructed a map with the purpose of searching for the lake.

"He made two attempts, starting from the town of Ambato; but on the first attempt his Indian carriers deserted him in the heart of the mountains, and

[102] Oriente - The name given to the vast eastern most regions of Ecuador, also known as the Amazon.

[103] Interestingly Stabler refers to Spruce's notes ... not Spruce's paper submitted to the Royal Geographical Society ... or *Notes of a Botanist.*

he was only able after great difficulty and with the aid of his personal servant to return to his starting-point. His second attempt was not more successful, for while he was able to find his way to certain points in the Llanganati range marked in the guide, and reached a lake, his camp was flooded and most of his provisions ruined or lost by a sudden rising of the lake, and he had to give up the search. On his return he told me that he was not sure whether he had reached the lake containing the treasure, for he himself, as well as all the other treasure-seekers who had followed Valverde's guide, had been mystified by certain directions.

"These are, to quote from Spruce's translation, 'Go forward and look for the signs of another sleeping-place, which I assure thee thou canst not fail to see in the fragments of pottery and other marks, because the Indians are continually passing along there. Go on thy way, and thou shalt see a mountain which is all of margasitas (pyrites), the which leave on thy left hand, and I warn thee that thou must go round it in this fashion: (*Diagram showing clockwise direction of motion, inconsistent with what precedes.)* On this side thou wilt find a pajonal (pasture) in a small plain, which having crossed thou wilt come on a cañon between two hills, which is the Way of the Inca.' The question of turning to the left or right of the mountain appears as yet to be unanswered.

"I hoped to be able to push up along the bank of the Río Verde in the direction of the Llanganati Range, but this project had to be given up as I was called back to Baños by a messenger sent by the good padres, to find that I must return at once to Quito.

"To the geographer, the traveller, and explorer Ecuador presents a great range of interest. Most of the country has not been mapped, a great deal is still unexplored, and a vast amount of valuable work remains to be done. In concluding this paper I wish to add that I most heartily recommend the 'switzerland of the Americas' as a field for geographical investigations the result of which I feel sure will be of lasting service to the science."

"As is customary, at the end of Stabler's reading, the President of the Royal Geographical Society expressed his sentiment's concerning the lecture and lecturer thus ... "the admirable use he made of his opportunities during the two years he was in country. Very few people sent on a diplomatic mission would have wandered about so much."

■ ■ ■

Stabler's map, *Part of Ecuador Showing the routes followed by J. H. Stabler 1910*, provides a general view of the area discussed in the foregoing paper. Stabler's route can also be viewed and traced on the 1750 map of Don Pedro Maldonado reproduced on the cover. The modern J721 Series Topographic Maps of Ecuador; *Baños (3989-IV)*, *Mera (3989-I), Río Negro (3990-II)* and *Sucre (3990-III),* would not become available to explorers of the region for another five decades!

Stabler's route followed along the Río Pastaza past the town of Baños and the tributaries that flow from the north, the Río Verde Chico, Río Blanco and Río Verde on the western and eastern sections of the *Baños* map, toward the mighty Río Topo and its junction with the Pastaza, which is located on the left hand corner of the adjacent *Mera* map. The Topo can then be traced north onto the south western and north western sections of the *Río Negro* 1:50,000 scale map, until the river veers northwest around Cerro Hermoso onto the *Sucre* map. These maps provide a detailed perspective of the area transversed first by Spruce westbound and later by Stabler eastbound.

Another topographic map entitled 1:250,000 Scale CIA Joint Operations Graphic AIR, Series 150, AIR Sheet SA17-8 Edition 1, was compiled in 1993 with data available from 1990. The maps source was graciously the University of Texas Libraries and can be viewed online. Almost every map explained in this book lies within the boundaries of this modern day map. The map clearly depicts the Llanganati region previously explored in our story and described by Spruce, Wallace, Stabler and Brooks. Looking closely one can ascertain the location of the previously cited landmarks of Ambato, Píllaro, Baños, El Triunfo, Cerro Hermoso, Río Pastaza, Río Topo, Río Verde Chico and Río Verde Grande

■ ■ ■

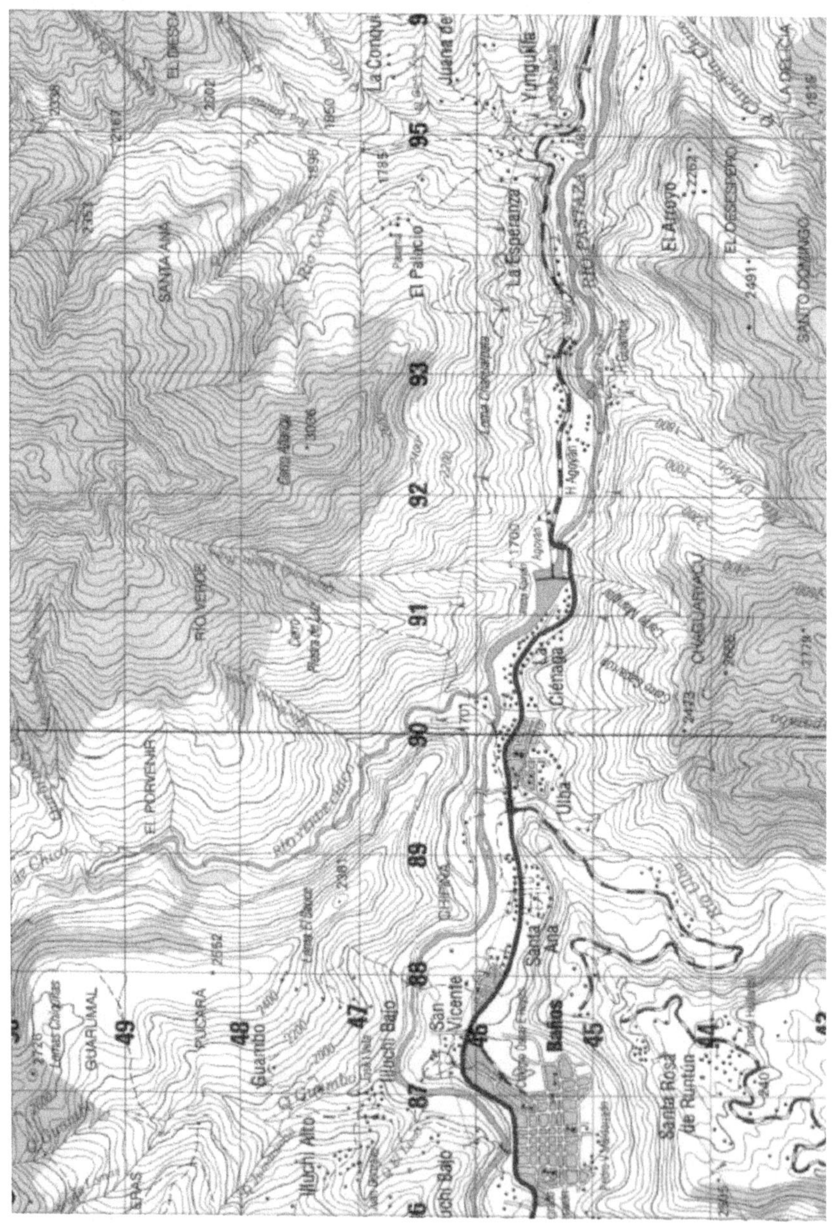

Baños Topographic Map
(Western Section)

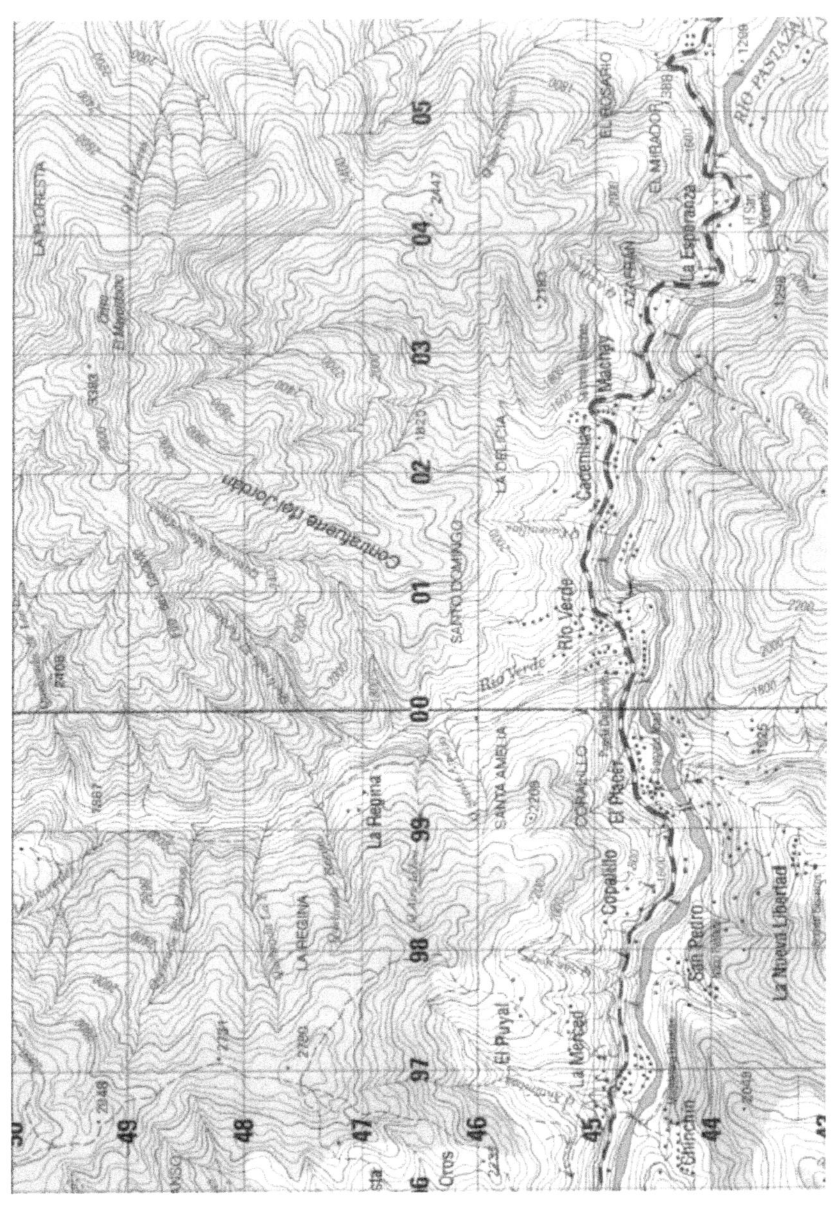

Baños Topographic Map
(Eastern Section)

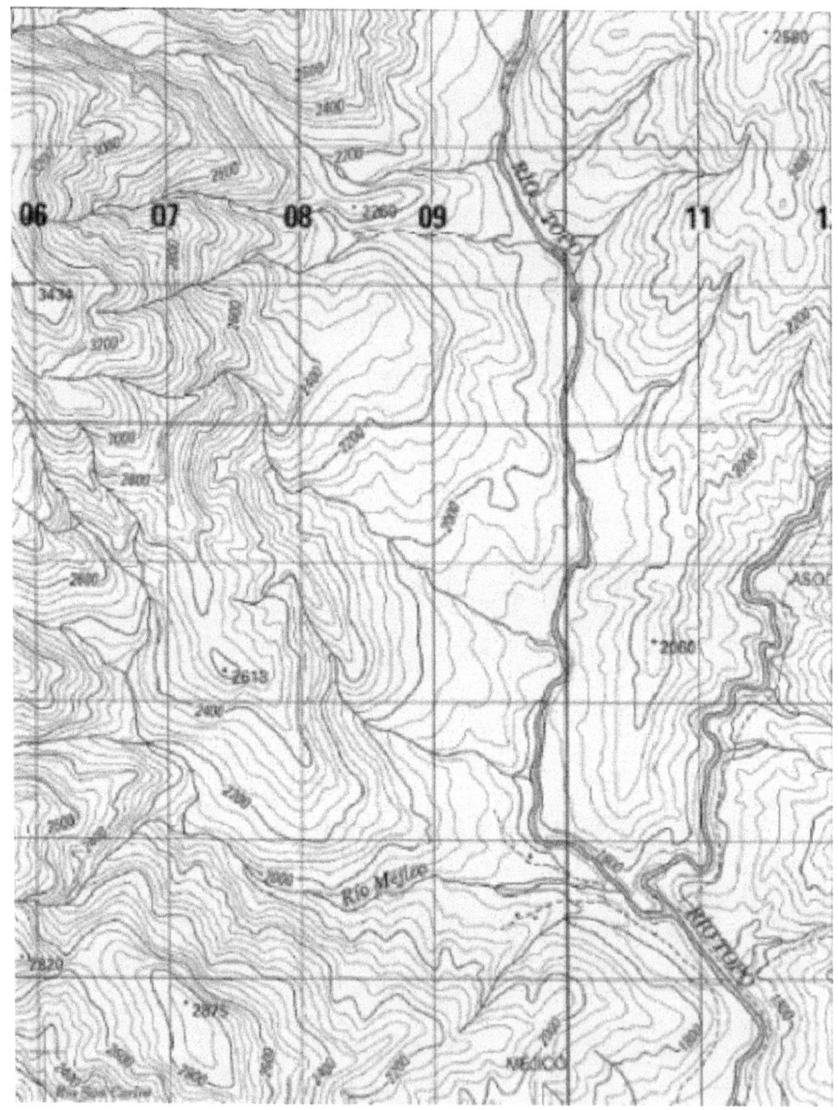

Río Negro Topographic Map

(Enlarged Southern Section)

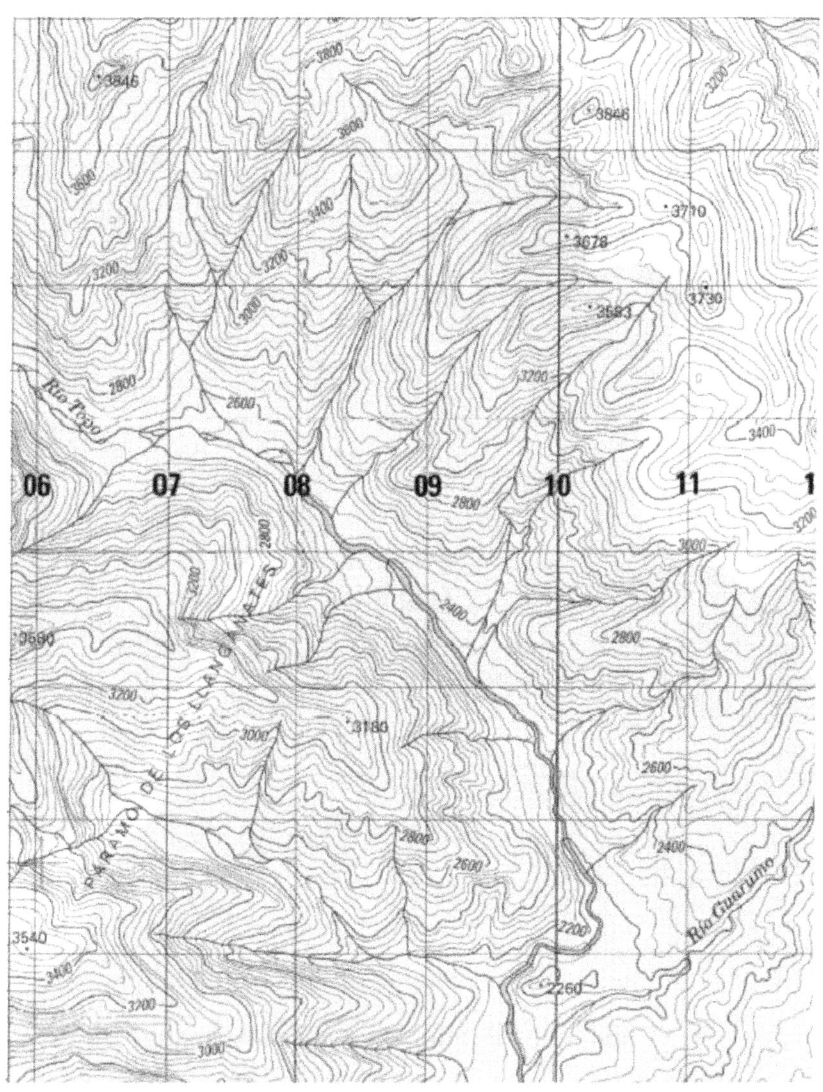

Río Negro Topographic Map
(Enlarged Northern Section)

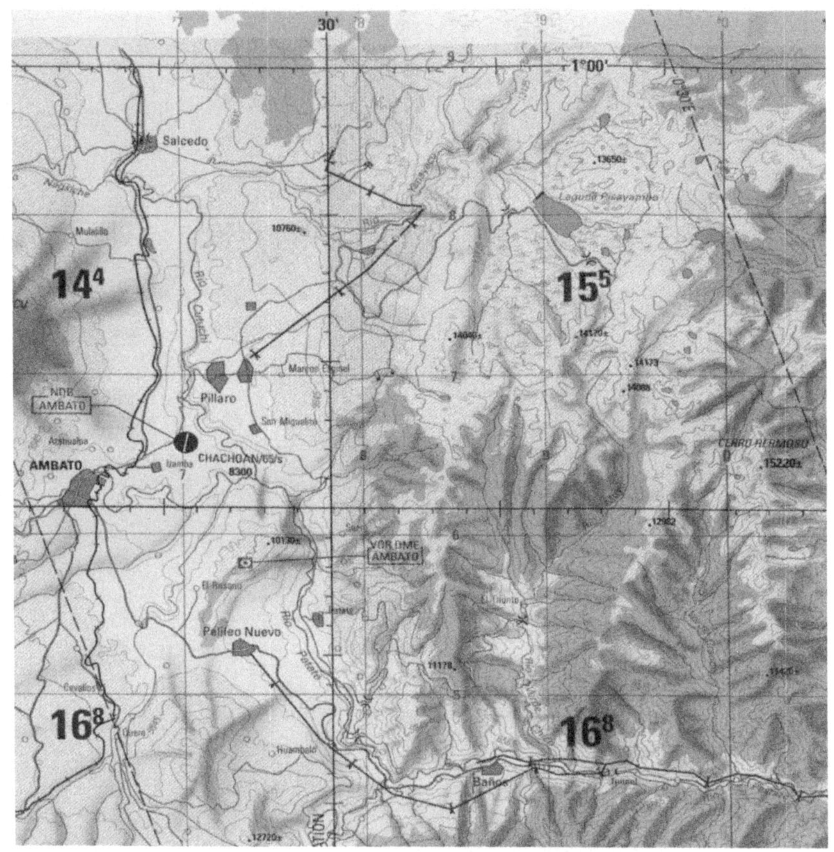

Llanganati Region Topographic Image

(Section of 1:250,000 Scale CIA Joint Operations Graphic AIR)

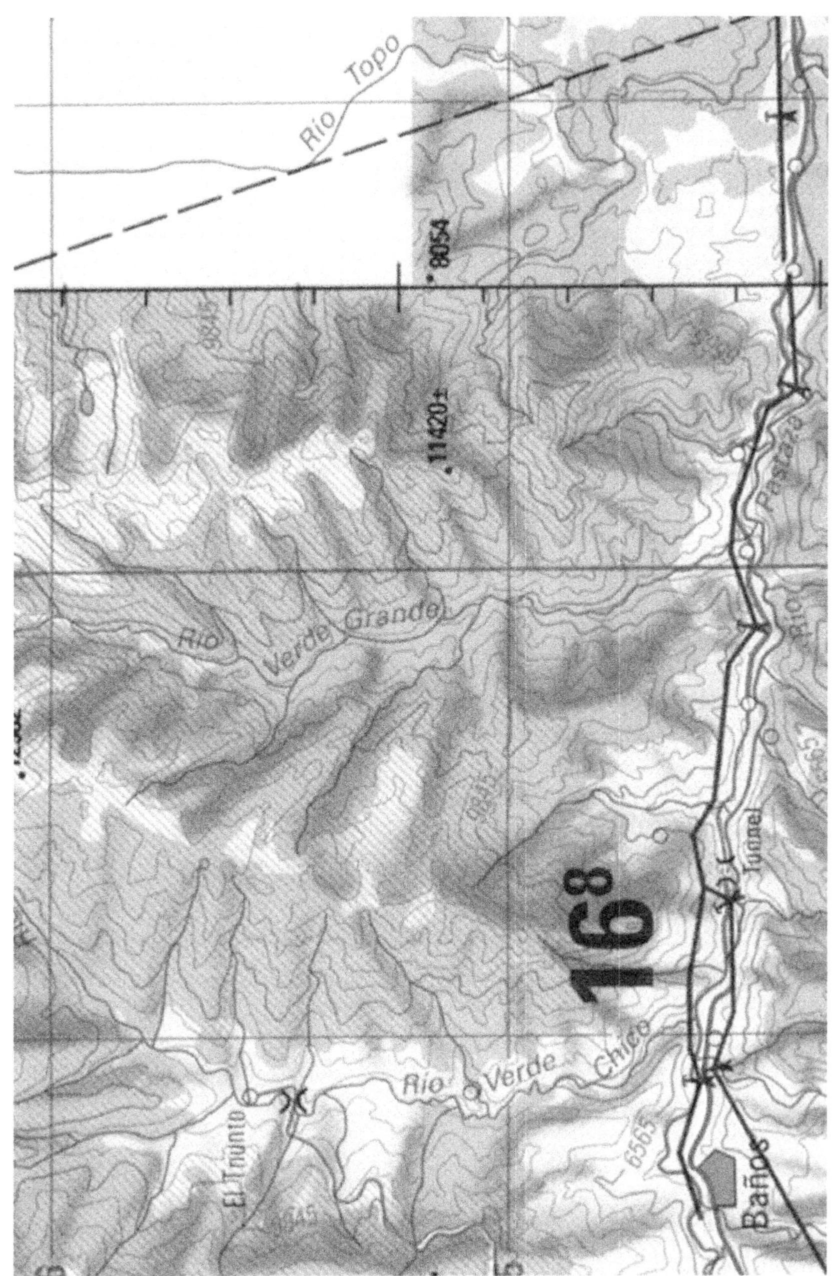

Image of Ríos Pastaza, Topo, Verde Chico & Grande
(Enlarged Section of 1:250,000 Scale CIA Joint Operations Graphic AIR)

Stabler's paper drew an almost immediate response from an American ... E. C. Brooks, apparently a friend from the period of Stabler's assignment in Quito Ecuador. The Royal Geographical Society quickly published Mr. Brooks correspondence in its January 1918 *Geographical Journal*, volume 51, No.1, page 59, entitled *The Inca Treasure of Llanganati*, reproduced below in its entirety ... "I beg to bring to the attention of your society the enclosed copy of an editorial in the *New York Sun* for November 4 and my reply thereto in the issue of the 14th, which I also enclose.

"Since it was in your journal that Mr. Spruce's article and Señor Guzmán's map were first published, I have always intended to send you a report of my discoveries; but I hoped to make a third journey; and, indeed, for the last three years plans have been made each autumn for my going. The financial man has, however, each time been prevented from going, although last year he bought the outfit recommended by me, and now has it ready for next year. Mr. Stabler's article has taken me by surprise and has rather forced my hand before I was ready to go into print. However, I think well, in case anything happened to me, to have it go on record that the Valverde *Derrotero* as published first in your *Journal* (about March 1860) is substantially correct and surprisingly so considering that it was written on a deathbed in Spain and after some years of absence of the writer from Ecuador."

[The article in the *New York Sun* of November 4 is based on the passages in Mr. Stabler's paper (*G. J.*, October 1917, 50, 251) which summarize the story of the Inca treasure, and mention the unsuccessful search made by Major Brooks, whose letter to the *Sun* of November 12 we have the pleasure to print below. Major Brooks has kindly undertaken to give us further news of his quest at a later date. --- Ed. *G. J.*][104]
[*New York Sun*, 12 Nov. 1917.]

THE WAY TO THE GOLD OF THE INCA LIES OPEN TO ALL
A Hunter of the treasure which was to ransom Atahualpa tells of his adventures in Ecuadorean Mountains.

"More than anyone else, perhaps, I was interested. in the editorial article in *The Sun* of Sunday, 4 November 1917, entitled *The Way to the Gold of the Inca*, because I am the Major Brooks spoken of, who made two expeditions into that part of the Ecuadorean Andes called the Llanganati Mountains, in which there is much reason to believe the hidden treasure of the Incas is located.

"I wish to correct some errors which seem to be in the original article which you discuss. I make these corrections with the most kindly feelings toward Mr. Stabler, the author, whose friendship. I esteem most highly. His memory is a little at fault as to some parts of what I related to him, but he cannot be blamed for this, considering the time that has elapsed since 1910, when I made my trips into that wilderness.

---

[104] I have searched the *Geographic Journals* through 1922 and have found no further correspondence from Major Brooks.

"It must be conceded that the one who underwent the peculiar hardships of climbing in those rough and uninhabitable regions must have had the incidents more indelibly impressed upon his memory than they could have been impressed upon the memory of anyone by mere narration. During my first and second expeditions Mr. Stabler was the secretary of our legation in Quito, Ecuador, where I was well acquainted. In fact for my protection in case I should find the treasure, I fully consulted the American Minister before starting on my second expedition, because from the results of my first expedition I felt sure of locating the treasure in my second trial.

"My first journey was a failure because I went not sufficiently provided to stay long, and because, while climbing the 'margasitas' mountain to get a look-out to see where the three Llanganati peaks were I had a fall that caused a stick to be thrust in my eye. The eye became quite irritated and swollen, although I bathed it frequently in cold water of which in those high regions there was more than an abundance. On my return to Quito the doctor prescribed hot water and an eye wash which cured it. It was the second journey when my Indian bearers deserted me---and this was when I had just pitched my camp on the edge of a lake-that proved my undoing.

"This small lake lay at the base of one of the three Llanganati peaks, and since it had no visible outlet must have had a subterranean one. It was bordered on one side by a somewhat dangerous morass or swamp. I broke through the sod of this swamp and went down the full length of one leg without touching terra firma. This lake was very much like the one described in the *Derrotero* or itinerary, and since, on account of continual fogs, I had not yet seen the third and most beautiful peak (Llanganati is the Quichua or Inca word for 'beautiful') I wanted carefully to examine this mysterious lake and marsh.

"I had no more than constructed a rude shelter for my party when the Indians, on account of the rains and hardships, deserted me, and from these rains the lake rose gradually, finally coming up about 25 feet---way above what would have been the roof of my shelter had it remained standing instead of floating off on the surface of this little lake.

"I had employed a young Ecuadorean and I had brought my servant or valet with me. These did not desert. We remained three days without fire, and after five days a relief party came out to bring me back, but on condition of not remaining in those regions.

"Before this I had seen the third or most beautiful peak and found that I was within about 6 or 8 miles of it. The day that I started back was clear, and I got such a beautiful view of the third mountain that I could have cried at having to return, but I resolved to go again in a better season of the year. I had unwittingly gone in the rainy season. The seasons there in the interior were reversed, strange to say.

"Regarding the *Derrotero* or itinerary of Valverde, I wish to correct the statement that I had been mystified by part of the directions in the itinerary, I had gone in there fully aware of this possible mystification, because I had read of so many people going astray by being unable to understand the diagram or hieroglyphic and make it fit the other directions. But, on account of my military education and training in map making and topography I was conceited enough to believe that I could do better than any one before me and follow the itinerary correctly.

"I did not construct a map from the *Derrotero* or guide, but I made a tracing of the map that appeared in the *Geographical Journal* of the Royal Geographical Society of London about March 1860.[105] By the way, this map is by no means according to scale—in one day I walked what was represented by about 4 inches on the map. The next day, going just as far, I covered only 1 inch on the map.

"I had no trouble in finding all of the landmarks of the guide up to and beyond the 'Way of the Inca,' and I had no trouble about the correct side on which to pass the 'mountain which is all margasitas.' By the way, this proved to be one of the 'three peaks' mentioned in the *Derrotero.*

"The *Derrotero* or guide was for the purpose of guiding a party over the most practicable way of reaching the three peaks. I reached two of these peaks and plainly saw the third from its church spire-like top to its very base. This third---the beautiful mountain---is somewhat like Trinity Church with a saddle in the roof and this part snow covered, but the peak or tower mica schist, and, black, is so steep that snow cannot lie on it.

"Let me make this clear and emphatic that the *Valverde Derrotero* or guide is correct and that the 'three Llanganati peaks in the form of a triangle' do exist [106]; and that a person in good health and of ordinary strength can reach them if properly provisioned and properly guided.

"It took me two journeys to find the right way, but now I do not need the *Derrotero.* Those who wish to see part of the map from which I made my tracing will find this and also the full *Derrotero* in the appendix to the second volume of' *Notes of a Botanist of the Ecuadorean Andes*, by Richard Spruce, a copy of which is in the New York Public Library."

E. C. Brooks

Mr. Brooks will be further analyzed and discussed in depth later in this chapter. One fact however is abundantly clear ... all three men ... Richard Spruce, Jordan Stabler and E. C. Brooks ... had at least one common connection ... the Royal Geographical Society. Before we delve into the explorations of other explorers' following Spruce's translated *Derrotero* and *Guzmán Map*, perhaps it is best to review the story of these two explorers', clearly the first explorers' of the Llanganatis in the twentieth century ... Jordan Stabler [107] and E. C. Brooks.[108]

---

[105] Clearly mistaken, March 1860 is when the map was copied and presented to the society, the *Journal* was not published until 1861.

[106] Brooks clearly establishes his opinion that the "three Llanganati peaks in the form of a triangle" are ... Margasitas, Cerro Negro and Cerro Hermoso.

[107]**Error! Main Document Only.**It must be clarified that Stabler's expedition did not extend into the Llanganatis. Stabler followed the Río Pastaza from

■ ■ ■

Jordan Stabler appeared to have committed numerous errors in his paper as it related to his "compatriot" Major E. C. Brooks, which were subsequently corrected by Brooks himself. I find myself asking whether Stabler was also committing errors throughout other sections of his article ... utilizing literary license ... or ... did Stabler have access to some information or knowledge that others did not?

Four points in Stabler's article instantly seized my attention. Let us for a moment explore Spruce's paper in the plainest and simplest of terms without over thinking. Most important, Spruce speaks in singular form of ..."the snowy peak of Llanganati" ... "one of the few points from which Llanganati can be seen" ... "a near view of Llanganati, toward the sources of the Topo" ... "running south of the snowy Llanganati" ... and ... "the *Derrotero* or Guide to Llanganati." Then Spruce continues to describe Gran Volcan del Topo, or Yurag-Llanganati as ... "A tall snowy peak at the head of the river Topo"..."It is the only one of the group which rises to perpetual snow"..."a near view of Llanganati, toward the sources of the Topo" ... and ... "the summit of Llanganati has been hidden by clouds, and only its wooded flanks and deep, savage valleys have been visible."

Not only is it a proven scientific fact that there is only one mountain with perpetual snow in the Llanganatis ... Cerro Hermoso ... but Jordan Stabler's map of the period, showing the route of his 1910 expedition, clearly depicts Cerro Hermoso entitled Llanganati, with an estimated elevation of 15070 feet. Stabler ... just as Spruce had a half century prior ... not only referred to Llanganati in singular form when mentioning the Volcano Llanganati, but Stabler also published his period map.

Secondly was Stabler's statement that ... "The Río Verde is locally reputed to have its source in the lake in the Llanganati Mountains, at the bottom of which the golden vessels which formed the ransom of King Atahualpa were thrown by the Incas when news reached Quito that their ruler had been murdered." Spruce, it must be noted, never expressed this sentiment in his paper. Therefore the question arises ... Is this statement actually a legend or myth Stabler had heard in Ecuador as he implied, Stabler's use of literary license, or information received from another source?

The third point that captured my interest was contained in Stabler's "résumé" of Spruce's story of the Inca treasure in the Llanganatis that ... "A river which flows through a valley among these mountains was dammed, and the gold thrown into the artificial lake so formed." Spruce unquestionably had been the source that brought the Llanganati story,

---

west to east skirting the zones southern border in the opposite direction of Richard Spruce's route (Spruce's route along the Pastaza one might recall was from east to west).

[108] Brooks' expedition routes entered the Llanganatis from the north west. Commencing from Ambato Brooks traveled to Píllaro and from there followed the exact route into the Llanganatis as described in the *Derrotero*.

Derrotero and *Guzmán Map* to light in the twentieth century, yet Spruce never specified in his paper how the artificial lake of the *Derrotero* had been formed. So once again I am left to question ... Is this statement Stabler's use of literary license, a legend or myth Stabler had heard in Ecuador or information received from another source?

Lastly, but possibly most importantly is Stabler's reference ... "Spruce states in his notes, made in 1857." Had Stabler mis-spoken, intending to refer to Spruce's paper instead? Or, did Stabler actually have access to Spruce's missing journals?

The questions also arise ... Why would Stabler, an educated young man half Brooks' age, write an account of Brooks' expeditions that deviates so drastically from that of Brooks himself? ... Was this some form of misinformation and misdirection to discredit or divert future explorers from the region of Brooks' discoveries? ... Why would two "friends" and "compatriots" that held a common interest in solving the riddle of the Inca treasure of the Llanganatis, men that obviously shared an adventurous spirit and the tenacity and grit of explorers to discover the unknown ... why would some partnership between the two not have been developed? Why was Brooks advancing from the north and Stabler from the south?

■ ■ ■

The immediate response to Mr. Stabler's paper published in the *Geographical Journal* and the subsequent editorial article in the *New York Sun*, not only shed light on some of the first major expeditions into the Llanganatis as lust for Inca gold continued into the twentieth century, but it raised as many questions as were answered.

One main point to take away from Stabler's paper, Brooks' correspondence and all future accounts of Brooks' expeditions ... on one very important detail all sources agree ... Brooks entered the Llanganatis following along the route of Valverde utilizing Spruce's translated *Derrotero* and copy of the *Guzmán Map* ... quite uncommonly, Brooks did not seek out a guide to the region for his expeditions ... porters only, just to carry his supplies.

Although published in 1917 and 1918, there was very limited public access (especially in Ecuador) to the *Geographical Journals'* and the information contained therein, concerning Mr. Brooks and his involvement with the Llanganati treasure story. Even in today's technological society, these little known documents have been difficult to acquire or view. When I first learned of their existence and they came under my understanding, not only did I find the discrepancy over Brooks' military rank odd, but many more irregularities became apparent.

The first public appearance of any information concerning Mr. Brooks, after the initial publication by the Royal Geographical Society, apparently was within Luciano Andrade Marín's *Viaje a las misteriosas montañas de Llanganati (1937),* which has been the source, or holy grail if you will, for most explorers and authors on this subject since its publication and reprint.

According to Andrade's listing of explorers of the Llanganatis, "in 1912 the North American Colonel Brooks penetrated the Llanganati twice." By

Andrade's account the source for this information was Don Alfonso Troya. This information however, as I have discovered, conflicts with Brooks' own account of events in the *Geographical Journal* and the verifiable facts, raising questions regarding the balance of the Brooks story as related over the past decades. Misinformation and possible misdirection regarding Brooks' real name, rank, and the years, events and results of his expeditions, has confounded and expanded the story of the Llanganati treasure.

The discrepancy over Brooks' military rank, where Andrade and all authors' post-Andrade refer to Colonel Brooks, while Stabler indicates "Major Brooks," and Brooks himself states ... "because I am the Major Brooks spoken of"...raises questions which to date have not been answered. It has been my opinion that if Brooks had retired as a Colonel, I believe he would have been proud of that rank and clearly would have assumed and utilized that title instead of Major. Brooks also clearly established that his two expeditions into the Llanganatis had occurred in 1910, further conflicting with what has been written.

Captain Eric Erskine Loch D.S.O., explorer and author, would write shortly after Andrade in his book *Fever, Famine and Gold (1938)* mentioning Brooks' title and the year of an expedition into the Llanganatis thus ... "As late as 1912 an American, Colonel E. C. Brooks went in looking for the treasure."

Another author, a partner of Andrade's and friend of Brunner's, Rolf Blomberg, would also give a brief account of ... "an American Colonel named E. C. Brookes"[109] in *Buried Gold and Anacondas (1955)*. Blomberg also erroneously relates that in 1912 Brooks ... "undertook <u>an</u> expedition."

The author Peter Lourie, in *Sweat of the Sun, Tears of the Moon (1991)* purportedly quoting Brunner, relates in his story that "Colonel Brooks" had come to Ecuador and made two expeditions into the Llanganatis, implying that his source, Brunner, was adamant that it was "a lie" that Brooks had died in 1922 as ... "Brooks had been in the Llanganatis in 1924."

Mark Honigsbaum, author of *Valverde's Gold (2004)* states ... "A graduate of West Point, Brooks had served as a colonel in the United States Army during the Spanish-American War and had later been appointed Auditor of Cuba." Although it is a verifiable fact that Brooks went to West Point and served during the Spanish-American War,[110] Honigsbaum's statement on rank is erroneous and will be explained later. Honigsbaum's story continues

---

[109] Notice the misspelling of Brooks' surname and reference to "an" expedition.

[110] Spanish-American War from April 1898 to August 1898, treaty would later be signed in December 1898.

to erroneously relate that "Colonel Edward C. Brooks" had made two expeditions into the Llanganatis and infers that they occurred in 1912.[111]

Only bits and pieces have been written by these numerous authors regarding Jordan Stabler's "compatriot" E. C. Brooks, his background, biography and involvement with the Llanganati treasure story. Much of what has been written tells an incomplete or inaccurate story and misinformation abounds, until now. The complete story of Mr. E. C. Brooks begs to be told ...

■ ■ ■

What can be pieced together and verified after extensive research, is that E. C. Brooks was born Edwards Cranston Brooks [112] on 8 Nov 1860 in Portland, Oregon, to pioneer settlers Major Quincy Adams Brooks and Elizabeth Cranston, an invalid. Young Brooks lived a life of hardships and privations, frugal, he wasted neither words nor money.[113] A bit of a loner with few associates, Brooks made friends with the animals on his family's farm rather than the youth of the neighborhood. Brooks obituary would later describe him "with determination and an indomitable will and perseverance," being "destitute of the feeling of fear," and of an "adventurous spirit."

As a young man of eighteen Edwards C. Brooks entered the State University of Oregon at Eugene, yet within two years a new opportunity opened up before him. Oregon's sole Representative in Congress announced that a competitive examination for cadetship to West Point would be held roughly three hundred miles away in Portland and on a given date. Brooks' journey was later described by his younger sister, whose sentiments speak volumes of the young man that would later explore the Llanganatis ... "Young Brooks' arduous route lay over the Cascade Mountains through a wild unsettled region and had to be made on horseback over a road little better than a trail, there were thick woods to pass, a hundred miles of desert

---

[111] In addition to the apparent errors when compared with Jordan Stabler and Brooks own accounts' as published in the *Geographical Journal* and *The New York Sun*, Honigsbaum writes concerning Brooks in his book "...sometime in 1912 he obtained a copy of *Notes of a Botanist on the Amazon and Andes* and became an avid student of the *Derrotero* ...", while on this same subject Stabler indicates that Brooks obtained "a copy of the *Derrotero* at Latacunga and from it constructed a map." Brooks however disputed Stabler's assertion and clarified the matter by stating ..."I made a tracing of the map that appeared in the *Geographical Journal*." Honigsbaum's version therefore, would erroneously place Brooks' interest in the *Derrotero*, two years after his expeditions. Again, Honigsbaum's incorrect time line is noted on page 155; "...in 1913, one year after Colonel Brooks fateful expedition to the Llanganatis ...", placing the expedition which Brooks clearly stated occurred in 1910, as having occurred during 1912 .

[112] He was given the surnames of his two maternal grandparents, Roxanna Edwards and Ephruim Cranston.

[113] Frugality carried through to Brooks' adult life, partaking of neither alcohol or any form of tobacco.

to cross, he must camp out in the open where not a single human habitation was to be found. Leading a pack horse with blankets and provisions, the young man set his face toward this unknown country he must traverse, without guide or companion, and started on his two-hundred mile ride to the railroad spur to Portland.

"Picture the boy traveler alone on the desert at the approach on night, picketing out his horse, making camp and preparing his evening meal, studying for the examination by the light of his camp fire, spreading his blankets on the ground for a bed, his saddle for a pillow, his tent the dark bowl of the night sky, its converted brim resting on the darker circle of wilderness, at the center of all this desolate waste spread above and beneath him, the one solitary bit of human life for miles around. Picture the boyish outlines as he lay curled up in his blankets in the careless relaxation of sleep, off guard and defenseless, at the dead of night to be startled out of heavy slumber, hardly realizing his whereabouts, to find himself surrounded by a pack of howling wolves drawing nearer and nearer, aroused to his peril, hastily raking together the smoldering embers of his camp fire. Picture again the boyish form silhouetted against the leaping crackling flames, through the long black night while he piled on brushwood to hold the wolves at bay.

"Perhaps no more severe test of endurance could have been deliberately planned, no harsher method devised to develop sinew of mind and mussel than were his experiences hardening him even before his time for the life he seemed destined to follow."[114]

As destiny would have it, out of a class of thirteen competitors for the cadetship, E. C. Brooks won the appointment from Oregon, to the United States Military Academy at West Point, New York. Young Brooks prepared for and took the examination to West Point, which he passed in June of 1882, being admitted on 1 Jul 1882 to the class of 1886.[115]

For some unknown reason, perhaps being merely a typographical error upon admittance, Brooks West Point and military records have him listed as Edward Cranston or E. C. Brooks throughout his career. This error remains on Brooks' military records even today. I wonder though, how much of Brooks' life was spent correcting his name from Edward to Edwards!

An average student, Brooks ranked fortieth in his class of seventy-seven at West Point where his most notable classmate was the elected class president, John J. Pershing,[116] who ranked thirtieth. Upon graduation on 1

---

[114] Eloquent sentiments of Hattie Evelyn Brooks from Edwards Cranston Brooks' obituary of June 1923.

[115] Source: From limited edition of one hundred copies of *1886-1911 In Commemoration of the 25th Anniversary Graduation of the Class of 1886 United States Military Academy (West Point June 1911)* and the *Official Register of the Officers and Cadets of the U.S.M.A.*

[116] Well known for his pursuit of the Mexican Revolutionary General Pancho Villa after Villa's famous raid on Columbus in 1916. US Army General John

Jul 1886, Second Lieutenant E. C. Brooks had his choice of postings, the cavalry or artillery. It has been said he chose the former arm of the service because of his great fondness for horses. Brooks was assigned to the United States 8th Cavalry and served on frontier duty at San Antonio, Texas from late September 1886 to 21 Oct 1887.

During this period Brooks was married to Margaret Anna Gray,[117] daughter of Theodore Gray and Sarah Ann Sourbeck in Chicago, Illinois on 17 Feb 1887. The couple later had two children born on army posts on the frontier ... Margaret Brooks Johnson [1889-1962] and Dorothy Brooks Holcombe [1892-1976]. A third child, Edwards Cranston Brooks Jr. was born in January of 1894, but died in infancy in June of the same year.

Back in Texas, Lieutenant Brooks and his new wife remained at Fort Davis, Texas until 17 May 1888. Brooks was then on the march with his regiment [118] to and served at Fort Yates, North Dakota, until 21 Nov 1891. In actuality, some of Brooks' posting here was spent in the field in South Dakota, where Brooks participated in both of the battles which took place near Pine Ridge in the cavalries winter campaign against hostile Sioux Indians from 14 Dec 1890 to 30 Jan 1891, and his was the cavalry battalion which brought in the body of Sitting Bull.

From there Brooks' military career took him back east, across country to Delaware on college detail, having been assigned to the Delaware College in Newark from 3 Dec 1891 to 27 Jan 1893 as "Professor of Military Science and Tactics." Brooks was then detailed to serve at Girard College, Philadelphia, Pennsylvania as "Instructor of Cadets" from 28 Jan 1893 to 6 Dec 1895, during which period he was promoted to First Lieutenant of Cavalry, 6th Cavalry, on 8 Mar 1893. Oddly enough, Brooks' worst classes at West Point had been military tactics, engineering, ordinance and gunnery, he excelled in the Law and Languages (English, French and Spanish).

Returning from leave in January 1896, Brooks was on garrison duty at Fort Myer, Virginia, until 19 Apr 1898, then with the regiment at Camp Thomas, Georgia, and at Tampa, Florida, until 14 Jun 1898, where he had served as

---

J. Pershing tried unsuccessfully to capture Villa in a nine-month pursuit that ended when Pershing was called back upon the United States entry into World War I. Pershing was a general officer in the United States Army who led the American Expeditionary Forces in World War I and is the only person to be promoted in his own lifetime to the highest rank ever held in the United States Army, that of General of the Armies.

[117] "Margaret had a strong interest in the family history and wrote hundreds of letters to collect information from relatives, pastors, county clerks, etc., and published a genealogy with Hattie Evelyn Brooks." (Pamela Collier, PhD.)

[118] In May of 1888 the regiment prepared for the longest march ever taken by a cavalry regiment. It was ordered to march more than 2600 miles to its new regimental headquarters at Fort Meade, South Dakota. Some of its march was along the famous Santa Fe Trail in New Mexico.

Regimental Adjutant [119] from the first of June. The regiment shipped out to Cuba during the Spanish-American War with Brooks continuing to serve as Regimental Adjutant until 6 Aug 1898 while also being engaged in the campaign against Santiago Cuba up to 17 July 1898 and the Battle of San Juan Hill from 1 Jul to 3 Jul 1898.

On 1 Jul 1898, a combined force of about 15,000 American troops in regular infantry and cavalry regiments that included Brooks' 6th Cavalry, included all four of the army's "colored" regiments, and volunteer regiments, among them Theodore Roosevelt and his "Rough Riders," the 71st New York, the 2nd Massachusetts Infantry, and 1st North Carolina, and rebel Cuban forces attacked 1,270 entrenched Spaniards in dangerous Civil War-style frontal assaults at the Battle of El Caney and Battle of San Juan Hill outside of Santiago. More than two hundred U.S. soldiers were killed, one having been a West Point classmate of Brooks, and nearly 1,200 were wounded in the fighting.

The result of these and other American victories was that Spain was reduced to suing for peace and the 1898 Treaty of Paris, negotiated on terms favorable to the U.S., which allowed temporary American control of Cuba and, following their purchase for twenty-million dollars from Spain, indefinite colonial authority over Puerto Rico, Guam and the Philippines.

Brooks was promoted Captain and Assistant Adjutant General of the United States Volunteers [120] on 17 Sep 1898 but was already on duty as Assistant Adjutant General, US Troops Santiago, Cuba, from 7 August until 2 October 1898. Brooks was also on duty as Assistant Engineer and various other local duties, at Santiago Cuba through March 1899, then on sick leave until May of the same year.

Brooks served as aide-de-camp to Brigadier General Wood U.S. Volunteers, commencing 1 May 1899 and was honorably discharged from volunteer service 12 May 1899.[121] Brooks was promoted and assigned as Major of the

---

[119] A Regimental Adjutant is a staff officer who assists the commanding officer of a regiment, battalion or garrison in the details of regimental, garrison or similar duty.

[120] U. S. V. - United States Volunteers were a special category, being raised exclusively under Federal sponsorship as a temporary wartime augmentation to the Regular Army. Every volunteer regiment, by law, contained at least one Regular Army officer who normally held a volunteer commission one or more grades above his lineal rank in the Regular Army. Such officers normally were selected either because they were native sons of the specific state or because they were serving as Regular Army advisors with the state or teaching in a state's college or university system when war broke out.

[121] Listed on the rolls of the 29th Regiment U. S. V. formed March of 1899 and organized at Fort McPhersen in Atlanta Georgia, through US Army General Order #46 dated 13 Mar 1899; ... "Captain Edward C. Brooks and 159 other officers were ... "By the direction of the President ... are honorably discharged

46th US Volunteer Infantry on 17 Aug 1899 to 20 Apr 1900, an assignment which Brooks declined being also Assistant Adjutant General, Department of Santiago, Cuba, 28 Sep to 30 Dec 1899 and Auditor of the Island of Cuba [122] from 20 Apr 1900 to 6 May 1901.[123]

Major E. C. Brooks returned to the United States and had hardly established himself in his old quarters at Fort Myer, commanding troop from May 1901 to January 1902, when he was ordered to the Philippines [124] with the regiment. Brooks sailed from New York on the transport "Buford" via the Suez Canal for Manila on 21 Jan 1902 and was accompanied by his wife and two small children that had been born at army posts on the western frontier. The route taken, one of two the regiment would take, occupied two months of travel before arriving in their port of destination.

Brooks remained in the Islands [125] "commanding troop" at Vigan, Salamogue, Camp Morrison and San Mateo until 15 Mar 1904 at which time he was en route to the United States where he would be stationed at Fort Sheridan, Illinois in "command of troop" from 15 Apr until 30 Dec 1904. Brooks had been more than once seriously ill and confined to the hospital while in the Philippines and suffered from the trouble he contracted there, which continued to affect him more or less in the years that followed. Brooks however must have considered himself very lucky. Of his seventy-

---

from the Volunteer Army ... their services being no longer required ... as of May 12, 1899."

[122] The United States Military Governor of Cuba established through a Civil Order of the Island of Cuba on 14 Mar 1899, the position of Auditor of the Island of Cuba, with the first auditor being appointed on March 18 of the same year, a Major E. F. Ladd. The position as defined by Major E. C. Brooks in his official report for the fiscal year ending 30 Jun 1900 on 12 Mar 1901 was ... " to have charge of the examination and scrutiny of all accounts arising from the disbursement of funds obtained from the customs receipts of the Island of Cuba." Brooks' official title was "Major and Quartermaster U. S. V., Auditor for the Island of Cuba."

[123] Brooks once again was officially honorably discharged from the volunteers on 1 May 1901 and was returned to the cavalry. The position of Auditor of the Island of Cuba was later abolished on 20 May 1902, as the United States ended its three year military presence in Cuba and the Republic of Cuba was established under its first elected president.

[124] Philippine-American War commenced 4 Feb 1899 when the Philippines declared independence from the United States. The war officially ended in June 1902, but hostilities broke out again in 1906. Sometimes confused with the earlier Spanish-American War, the Philippine-American War was a much more brutal and bloody conflict.

[125] Here the story becomes murky, Brooks is hereafter referred to in the singular sense and no further mention is made of his wife and children. Whether Mrs. Brooks and the children returned to the United States with or prior to the Major's return is unknown. What is clear is that the Brooks' never shared the same legal residence from this point forward.

seven West Point classmates only sixty-one survived, one died in the Battle of San Juan Hill, while fifteen died in the Philippines.[126] Brooks being not in very good health officially went on leave of absence on 31 Dec 1904. Brooks' furlough found him visiting his parents at Port Townsend, Washington. His resignation from the army soon followed and Major Brooks' official resignation was accepted 2 May1905.

Major Brooks' civilian life began with traveling from his parents in Washington State to San Francisco. On 15 May 1905, he took passage by sea, bound for Panama en route to Ecuador, "to look into a business venture he had under consideration."[127] Brooks made a "flying trip"[128] to London, Paris, and back in connection with this new undertaking,[129] and he settled down in Ecuador where he engaged in various business enterprises and lived for some years. From May 1905 to May 1908 [130] Brooks resided in Guayaquil,[131] Ecuador and from thence in Quito until September 1913. [132]It was during his time in Quito, 1910 to be exact, that Major Brooks made two expeditions "on foot with Indians as pack-bearers into the Llanganati spur of the Ecuadorean Andes." It was also during his time in Ecuador that Brooks became connected with the American Bank Note Company[133] of

---

[126] By 1911, of Brooks' seventy-seven West Point classmates, sixteen had been KIA, five had retired from active service and nine, including Brooks, had resigned.

[127] What "business venture" Brooks had under consideration is unknown.

[128] This claim in Brooks' obituary raises questions, being that transatlantic passenger flight, whether by plane or zeppelin, commenced after Brooks' death. Perhaps the explanation could be that this trip was a combination of an ocean voyage and air travel once in England and Europe.

[129] I have found no concrete evidence what Brooks' "new undertaking" was. It could have been his employment with the American Bank Note Company, the Llanganati treasure project, or some other unknown venture.

[130] During this period however and for some unknown reason, on 7 Dec 1907 to be exact, five foot seven Edward C. Brooks, of fair complexion with brown-grayish hair and gray eyes, claiming to be a "railroad man", appeared at the American Legation in Panama seeking an "emergency passport" which was issued. The signature on the application was that of Edwards C. Brooks and signed as such.

[131] Guayaquil was not only Ecuador's main port, but the country's banking system was centered there.

[132] Brooks traveled through Panama arriving at the Port of New York on 6 Oct 1913 and the very next month 12 Nov 1913 was issued a new passport.

[133] The American Bank Note Company was the world's foremost engraver and printer of bank notes and securities (money, stocks and railroad-related certificates).The huge American Bank Note Company was formed from an association of seven competing companies in 1858. The company employed the country's finest engravers, and its images were of the highest and most durable quality. Banknotes were printed for the US government, foreign governments and private banks.

New York City, where he resided upon his return from Ecuador, until his death on 14 Jan 1922.

It is now evident why both Stabler in 1916 and Brooks in 1917 made reference to a "Major" Brooks. Having established the indisputable facts that "Major" Brooks resigned from the army and made two expeditions into the Llanganatis in 1910, one could reasonably assume that we had reached the end of the story, but that is not the case with our Major Brooks. For some unknown reason, whether financial motivation, patriotism, at the bequest of classmate John J. Pershing, or any other grounds, The World War or Great War of 1914-1918 would intervene in our story.

On 30 Aug 1918, *The New York Times* published the following letter to the editor from E. C. Brooks dated 20 Aug 1918 ... "Noticing in several newspapers that there is a general scarcity of labor in the United States and, especially, in the article in your issue of today, that the situation is so serious that there is an 'appeal for volunteers to do unskilled work as a patriotic service,' I wonder why the Department of Labor and the Director General of the Employment Service do not avail themselves of the unskilled and the somewhat skilled labor that, to my personal knowledge, in certain South American countries, are willing and anxious to come here to work. These laborers lack assurances of positions and most frequently lack funds for making the trip to this country, although they would, of course, come as third class passengers. Why has not this labor been arranged for when our war needs should probably have found a means of removing obstacles?

"I also know that quite a number of South American's would enlist in our army and navy, both as officers and enlisted men in various branches. Since they can legally be so employed if they will only declare their intention of becoming United States citizens, why are their services not sought?"

It would be near the end of the war and shortly after E. C. Brooks letter to the editor, in October of 1918 to be exact, more than thirteen years since his resignation, that Major Brooks received an appointment as Colonel of Infantry at Camp Pike, Arkansas, commanding the 2nd Brigade, consisting of infantry replacement troops.[134] Shortly thereafter, once again and for the last time in his life, Brooks, now "Colonel" Brooks, was honorably discharged from the United States Army on 3 Dec 1918.

As a 1921 arriving passenger list clearly shows, just as I had correctly assumed earlier, Brooks, a "single" man certainly proud of his military title, was listed as ... Colonel Edward C. Brooks. However, the Brooks family military legacy would not end with Edwards. The *2002 Genealogical Succession Table* for West Point shows two grandsons, William Henry Holcombe Jr. and Thomas Wesley Holcombe, and one great grandson, Robert Kemp Holcombe, following in Colonel Brooks' footsteps as cadets at West Point.

■ ■ ■

---

[134] Whether Brooks' letter to the editor had any relation to his appointment at Camp Pike remains unclear.

It is in the footsteps of Colonel Brooks that the Llanganati story has traveled this past century, but through the words of others the story has become twisted, with misinformation being related as fact. Once again, to separate fact from fiction, our story must be interpreted through the relations of authors as compared to Brooks own account and verifiable evidence.

On certain issues however, there can now be no dispute ... Brooks' given name, that "Major" Brooks "resigned" from the military, Brooks traveled to Ecuador and returned to New York,[135] worked for the American Bank Note Company, made two expeditions into the Llanganatis in search of hidden Inca treasure, died in New York City in 1922 and was buried at Arlington National Cemetery [136] in Virginia with his wife Margaret Anna Gray, who died five years later in 1927.

Andrade erroneously had assumed that Brooks arrived in Ecuador in 1904 and related that according to his source Don Alfonso Troya ... "The North American Colonel Brooks penetrated the Llanganati, some say, accompanied by a woman, who died on the shores of a lake. The Colonel, demoralized, having lost his head, wandered about, until a rescue expedition from Ambato sent by Alfonso Troya ... having advanced to the previously mentioned small lake, where he remained, later moribund and lost for a long time in the labyrinths, he managed to exit through the region of Mulatos, in the arms of a rescue expedition sent from Ambato by Don Alfonso Troya."

Captain Eric Erskine Loch, D.S.O. in *Fever, Famine and Gold* does not mention a second Brooks expedition but writes with specificity about a Brooks expedition, being the same route which Loch himself traveled, which shall be detailed in the next chapter, ..."he followed the *Derrotero* closely but was flooded out by a cloudburst, deserted by his Indians, and when eventually rescued by a searching party was wandering in the mountains practically out of his mind, and died not long afterwards in New York."

Loch continued to state ... "we came to the lake that popular belief says was the one reached by Colonel E. C. Brooks.[137] Lovely as the spot was, it would become a potential death trap in the event of a cloudburst such as Colonel Brooks met, upon the surrounding mountains ... If I ever had any doubts about the story of Colonel Brooks being flooded out of his Treasure Lake by a cloud-burst, they were quickly dispelled," because Loch himself was similarly flooded out of his own camp. Loch's expedition also dragged

---

[135] Brooks was enumerated during the 1920 U.S. census as a married boarder who was employed "traveling" for a bank note company. (Frederick Ritchie household, 1920 U.S. census, New York County, New York)

[136] It has also been said that General Pershing himself was a pallbearer at Brooks' funeral.

[137] Located just north of the mighty Río Topo slightly north-northeast of Cerro Hermoso, in a valley slightly east of the "Páramo de Soguillas," in the "Valley of Brooks" at the foot of Cerro Negro.

Brooks' "treasure lake"[138] and discovered nothing more than mud and mica ... "fools gold."

Blomberg, continued his account of Brooks stating that he "...undertook an expedition which had a romantic beginning but a tragic end. Colonel Brookes fell in love with a pretty Ecuadorian woman named Isabela. She accompanied him on his expedition but died in Llanganati. The colonel was deserted by his guides and porters and wandered about in the wilds alone till a relief expedition found him half mad and utterly exhausted. He returned to the United States and died there soon afterwards."

Peter Lourie in *Sweat of the Sun, Tears of the Moon,* once again purportedly quoting Brunner, related the story that Colonel Brooks "...had come to Ecuador from New York to establish the Central Bank of Ecuador"[139]. . . and ... "He and his New York firm finally established one currency here where before there had been many. Each bank had printed its own ... it was chaos."[140]

Lourie's story continues to quote Brunner stating that Brooks made two expeditions into the mountains ... "The first time, he was miserably lost and the Indian porters deserted him, but he got out with his Peruvian friend. The second time, he went into the Llanganatis with his wife, an Ecuadorian he met here. They made camp in a beautiful meadow. At the end of the Valverde Guide, just after the Margasitas Mountain. There was a small river, meandering through the lovely valley.[141] But it began suddenly to rain high up in Las Torres Mountain and the camp was flooded. They crawled up the hillside, hanging there all night long, but his wife caught pneumonia and she died right there."

A few interesting last details related in Lourie's version is that one of Brunner's guides, an Amado López, had actually been one of the porters who had carried Isabela Brooks body out of the Llanganatis so that she could be buried in the cemetery of Píllaro.[142] Finally, that due to this tragedy ... "Brooks went crazy" and "He didn't ever go back to the Llanganatis, but

---

[138] Known as "Laguna de Isabela Brooks." Over the years authors have created the popular belief and denoted this lake as Brooks' "treasure lake". Brooks himself never makes any such claim and Stabler states ... "he was not sure whether he had reached the lake containing the treasure."

[139] The Central Bank of Ecuador was not established until the mid-twenties, its first banknotes were printed in 1928.

[140] Up to this point Ecuador's banking system was utter chaos as each bank would print and issue its own currency.

[141] Known as the Valley of Brooks and Laguna de Isabela Brooks located just south east of Margasitas Mountain.

[142] I must interject that throughout Brunner's years of research and explorations, his porters and guides (he would call them his spies), kept him well informed concerning previous and current expeditions of Brunner's competitors.

instead returned to the United States, where he died shortly after in a madhouse."

Mark Honigsbaum in *Valverde's Gold* related a similar version to that of Lourie without indicating his source and was a great deal more specific ... "On his retirement from service Colonel Brooks became the South American representative of the American Bank Note Company of New York and traveled to Ecuador, where he fell in love with and married a local woman, Isabela de Troya."

In Honigsbaum's version as well, Brooks first expedition "was a failure" due to Brooks lack of knowledge of the topography and climate of the region, combined with his setting off ill-equipped during the worst season of the year, returning to Píllaro hungry, wet and exhausted after only a few days. According to Honigsbaum's account, Brooks' second expedition was purportedly with "eight Indian porters and a Peruvian mestizo ... when he set off from Píllaro, Isabela was with him at the front of the line." Honigsbaum continues ... "At first all went well. Brooks had no trouble finding the farm of Moya and Guapa Mountain ... Having descended Guapa, he marched east past the cattle farms mentioned in the guide and the 'wild morass' until he reached Los Anteojos, and in front of them, the 'plain' where the *derrotero* instructed he should sleep the first night. The next morning Brooks continued in the same direction, arriving at the 'great black lake'—which he identified as Yana Cocha on Guzmán's map. Leaving it 'on the left hand,' he then rounded its southern shore to the Desaguadero de Yana Cocha and continued east, eventually reaching what he thought was Valverde's ravine and waterfall—the 'Cascada y Golpe de Limpio Pungu' of Guzmán's map ...but from the third day Brooks found that Valverde's directions became increasingly confusing ... The weather was changing for the worse, and heavy storm clouds were gathering. The porters pleaded with him to return to Píllaro with his wife, but Brooks would not do so ... they arrived at the rim of a water-filled crater near what is known today as the Páramo de Soguillas. Brooks was convinced he'd found the 'lake, made by hand,' into which the ancients had thrown Atahualpa's ransom, and he ordered his men to set up camp near the water's edge.

"It was a tragic misjudgment. In the night the rains came, washing down the rim of the crater in torrents and elevating the level of the lake. Alerted by the cries of their porters, Edward and Isabel dashed to the safety of a ledge high on the rim of the crater, where they spent the night exposed to the freezing wind and rain. The dawn revealed the full extent of their plight: what had been a small and inviting pool was now a vast expanse of water, somewhere below the surface of which lay their food and equipment. Worse, Isabela had caught a severe chill from the soaking she'd received in the night.

"Their only hope was to abandon the search for the treasure and retrace their steps to Píllaro as quickly as possible. Brooks's Indian porters immediately set off at a fast clip. Unfortunately, by now Isabela had become weak and feverish and could not keep pace. The porters ... deserted in the night, leaving Edward and Isabela to fend for themselves.

"Abandoned and hungry, Brooks remained camped on the páramo, praying for his wife's recovery. But Isabela grew steadily sicker until, weakened by cold and hunger, she died the following night.

"Setting off into a snowstorm, with only his compass to guide him, he wandered in a daze. Fortunately, he'd had the foresight to arrange for Isabela's father, Alonso [143] de Troya, to send a relief party in the event of his not returning within a specified time, and it was this that saved his life. Tired and grief-stricken, Brooks returned to the United States. From time to time he talked of mounting another expedition to the Llanganatis, but in 1922 he died—according to his family, of a broken heart."

■ ■ ■

The greatest source available on Brooks, of course is Brooks himself, and luckily the man described his expeditions in great detail to the Royal Geographical Society. In 1917 Brooks put it best and in his own words when he wrote ... "It must be conceded that the one who underwent the peculiar hardships of climbing in those rough and uninhabitable regions must have had the incidents more indelibly impressed upon his memory than they could have been impressed upon the memory of anyone by mere narration."

Clearly in Brooks' correspondence it was established that he had ... "hoped to make a third journey; and indeed, for the last three years plans have been made each autumn for my going." Brooks clearly was intent on returning to the Llanganatis with the "financial man," from the moment he returned to New York in 1913, and states they were "ready for next year" (1918) ... did he ever make the trip or not? We now have verifiable evidence that in the fall of 1918 Colonel Brooks was in Arkansas, not the Llanganatis.

Without question Brooks not only had the intent to make a third expedition, he had also acquired a financial partner for the endeavor. Certainly Brooks not only had the ability to travel under passports issued to him in 1913, 1916, 1920 and 1921, but travel he did. Arriving passenger lists from the Port of New York during this period have Brooks arriving from Panama, Uruguay and Venezuela [144] on at least six occasions right up to the month before he died. Even though an unrecorded third expedition by Brooks could explain some of the discrepancies we have encountered, no evidence can be discovered that one occurred.[145]

---

[143] Spelling error ... should be Alfonso.

[144] Whether mere coincidence or not, Stabler and Brooks appear to have been in Venezuela at the same time during 1915 and 1917.

[145] In his *Geographical Journal* correspondence, according to the journals editor, Brooks had ... "kindly undertaken to give us further news of his quest at a later date." I have searched the *Geographical Journals* from 1918 up until Brooks' death in 1922 and have found no further published correspondence.

One can only wonder what knowledge Brunner thought he had, in order to be so adamant that Brooks had not died in 1922 and had been in the Llanganatis again in 1924? We know now that these statements have been proven completely inaccurate, but what could Brunner's source of information have been? One of his guides or porters from Píllaro perhaps, or ... from the headstone of Isabela de Troya Brooks? Could it be that perhaps Isabela's headstone shows a date of death that does not correspond to the erroneous date of Brooks' expedition? One must recall that common belief placed Isabela's death in 1912, but the expeditions actually took place in 1910. What if the headstone indicates a date after 1922? With all certainty the question would then be answered. It would also be extremely relevant to our story if concrete evidence, a marriage or death certificate for Isabela de Troya could ever be produced and lay these questions to rest once and for all.

Not only did I find the discrepancies over Brooks' military rank odd, but the fact that Stabler and Brooks failed to make any mention of Isabela and her purported death in the Llanganatis seems almost unbelievable.[146] Raising even more concerns is the fact that Andrade's source, Don Alfonso Troya, indicates ... "Brooks penetrated the Llanganati, some say, accompanied by a woman." Why would Alfonso not have said instead ... accompanied by my daughter, Isabela de Troya, Brooks' wife? Lastly, these romanticized versions, quite similar to the literary license taken with Valverde's story, read much more like fiction than not.

Imagine my surprise while researching this book, upon viewing Brooks' headstone for the first time, learning that Brooks was buried with his wife Margaret Anna Gray, not Isabela de Troya! The dilemma presented itself, not realizing that Brooks was married in the United States, if the stories of Isabela de Troya were true, how could one politely approach such a subject with the family and discreetly relate the facts to the world. As luck would have it, Brooks' American wife, a great-great grandchild of Joseph Collier, had an interest in genealogy. The information I discovered on Brooks' grave site had been submitted by a Pamela Collier, PhD., who I would learn shared such an interest and had been writing a book on the family history and even knew one of Brooks' grandsons.

I considered the politist way to breech the matter was with the statement and question ... "I was previously not aware Mr. Brooks had been married to Margaret Anna Gray. Did his wife accompany him to Ecuador, or were they at some point in time divorced?" The response was clear and concise ... "Edwards and Margaret were happily married until Edwards death, Margaret did not remarry. Margaret did not accompany Edwards on his travels abroad."

Before I could structure my next question, Dr. Collier indicated she had discovered an article on the internet that stated in part ... "Later Brooks

[146] Unless of course there existed some moral or legal reason for withholding such information, if true.

decided to take his wife to the Llanganati for a 'romantic getaway', but they were promptly greeted by torrential rains. She died of pneumonia, and he ended up in a madhouse in New York – muttering wildly, one imagines, about gold and silver and emeralds."

Dr. Collier forwarded the article to me with her response ... "This is hilarious! She (meaning of course Margaret) outlived Edwards by about five years so the story of her death from pneumonia is inaccurate, she never went to Ecuador with Edwards."

Reluctantly I had arrived at the point of breeching the uncomfortable subjects of Isabela de Troya , whether Brooks and Margaret had ever been divorced and the possibility of bigamy. Dr. Collier indicated that there was no evidence they were divorced, to the contrary she replied ... "I know that Edwards and Margaret remained married.[147] It looks like he and Margaret lived apart after 1905."[148]

Dr. Collier's final sentiment on the subject ... "It wouldn't surprise me if Edwards had a second wife or family of which the first was unaware."

Once again we are left with questions unanswered. It has been misdirection, misinformation and liberal use of literary license that has consistently, throughout history, added to the story of the Llanganatis.

The facts clearly show though that Brooks remained in Ecuador for three years after his expeditions and as having died twelve years afterward. There is no evidence that Brooks "went crazy," was in "a madhouse" or died "of broken heart." To the contrary, the evidence clearly shows not only a man that remained gainfully employed and continued to travel extensively in conjunction with that employment, but also managed to become an Army Colonel in command of troops. As the family genealogist would later state ... "If Edwards ever ended up in a mad house, it was a well-kept secret from the family."

Throughout history the story of the Llanganatis has raised as many questions as have been answered. Brooks in some aspects is no exception to the rule, but on the other hand, Brooks indicated even more clearly than Spruce and Wallace that ... "I had no trouble in finding all of the landmarks of the guide up to and beyond the 'Way of the Inca,' and I had no trouble about the correct side on which to pass the 'mountain which is all margasitas.' By the way, this proved to be one of the 'three peaks'

---

[147] One must remember that during this time period, women's rights were extremely limited. In a divorce for instance, more often than not, the man would attain custody over any children. Being of "high-society," it would not have been uncommon for Margaret and Brooks to remain married and live apart, while she raised the children. She would then have been buried with her "husband."

[148] This statement is clearly substantiated by the evidence. Brooks lived in New York after his return from Ecuador while Margaret "summered" in Cape Cod and "wintered" in Washington, D.C.

mentioned in the *Derrotero*. The *Derrotero* or guide was for the purpose of guiding a party over the most practicable way of reaching the three peaks. I reached two of these peaks and plainly saw the third from its church spire-like top to it's very base. This third---the beautiful mountain---is somewhat like Trinity Church with a saddle in the roof and this part snow covered, but the peak or tower mica schist, and, black, is so steep that snow cannot lie on it."

As for Brooks ... his correspondence does not appear to be the ramblings of a mad man, but rather an intelligent, articulate and concise account of his experiences that answers many of our questions.[149] I personally found Brooks' correspondence to be refreshing, one of the few explorers of the region that does not appear to have embellished or obscured his discoveries and failures with misinformation and misdirection. Brooks, in the spirit of a true adventurer and explorer, rather than hide his conclusions as to where he thought the treasure lay ... he pointed the way.

■ ■ ■

The story of yet another explorer, or better stated an adventurer, of the period begs to be mentioned at this point. Very little has been written concerning the involvement of Austrian born treasure hunter [150] Paul Thur de Koos [1864 - ? post 1915]. Thur de Koos, an engineer (and a diver) by trade, came to Guayaquil, Ecuador, in 1898. In 1901 he entered into a partnership with another engineer and obtained some very large and important commercial construction contracts. In 1903, nearing the peak of his career, Thur de Koos married Rosa Helena León Velasco and started a family. From 1911, Thur de Koos served as Guayaquil-Playas railway management until 1913, the year in which his life drastically changed course. Thur de Koos quit his job, and traveled to Ambato in order to start preparations for an expedition into the Llanganatis, with the sole purpose to recover the lost treasure of Atahualpa carried into this inhospitable region by Rumiñahui.

During 1914 and 1915 Thur de Koos prepared and conducted two or three expeditions into the Llanganati region. Departing from Ambato, where Thur de Koos would leave his family at his friend's house, he traveled with numerous guides and porters through Píllaro and journeyed up to the valleys of Soquillas and Vanadio. The story goes ... that he continued to explore these valleys until he discovered a quaint little lake which is now called the Laguna Thur Koos or Poza Rendón.[151] Thur de Koos conducted several dives in the lagoon and on his last expedition located a certain amount of

---

[149] Perhaps other writers have our Mr. Brooks confused with another E. C. Brooks that also lived in New York and committed suicide on February 9, 1908. A mere coincidence in similar names, as Edwards Cranston Brooks lived until 1922.

[150] Others have written labeling Thur de Koos an "explorer". In my opinion Thur de Koos does not meet the definition of an explorer, his sole interest in the Llanganatis appears to have been a lust for Inca gold.

[151] After a Colombian named Rendón, who would explore the same area later.

gold, with which he returned to Ambato "extremely thin, with bugs and whiskers" to the point that he was difficult to recognize.

After 1915 Thur de Koos was absent from Ecuador. Traveling to Europe, Thur de Koos conducted research in the Archive of the Indies, where, equipped with personal funds, he hired various researchers, who assisted him in discovering the original of the *Derrotero de Valverde*.[152] This alleged original of the mysterious *Derrotero*, which leads to the location of the treasure, provided Thur de Koos with no benefit what-so-ever. Paul Thur de Koos, on his attempted return to Ecuador, was overcome by severe pneumonia and died in Lisbon, Portugal, far from his family.

One observation becomes apparent … Thur de Koos may have discovered gold in natural form ... but not treasure. Otherwise, if he had found the treasure, there would have been no reason to travel to Europe in search of the original *Derrotero*. Everything else up to this point appears simple enough, but ... when one starts comparing the stories of Thur de Koos and Brooks ... very interesting important facts and circumstances are brought to the light of day.

Brooks arrived in Guayaquil, Ecuador in 1905, where Thur de Koos, at the apex of his lucrative career, lived and worked. In 1907 Brooks applied for a passport calling himself a "railroad man" and at some point became employed by the American Bank Note Company that printed not only banknotes, but stock and "railroad certificates." From 1911 until sometime in 1913, Thur de Koos worked for the Guayaquil-Playas railroad. Given the small tight-knit international community in Ecuador at the time (even today you find the same camaraderie), it appears highly improbable that the paths of these two men did not cross ... they must have been acquainted with each other, socially or on a business level.

Given the plausibility that these men were acquainted, let us examine for a moment their stories further ... Brooks made two expeditions into the Llanganatis in 1910, leaving from Ambato and traveling through Píllaro, ending at a lake ... Laguna de Isabela Brooks. Coincidently, around the same time period that Brooks left Ecuador in 1913, Thur de Koos quit his job to search for treasure in the Llanganatis. Brooks by his own account had been planning a third expedition into the Llanganatis in 1914, with a financial partner. During 1914 and 1915, Thur de Koos made two or three expeditions into the Llanganatis, leaving from Ambato and traveling through Píllaro, ending at a lake ... Laguna de Thur de Koos.

The questions arise ... was Thur de Koos actually Brooks' "financial man"?, ... Did the inexperienced explorer Thur de Koos simply follow in Brooks' footsteps to arrive at a lake where he would ultimately toil and extract a quantity of gold?, ... Are the Laguna de Isabela Brooks [153] and the Laguna de Thur de Koos, also known as Poza de Rendón after yet another explorer

---

[152] According to Luciano Andrade Marin in *Llanganati*

[153] Another explorer in the mid to late 1930s would note that there "was a long narrow cut, an obvious attempt to drain it at some previous time."

... one and the same?, ... If Brooks and Thur de Koos were partners, did Brooks have any knowledge that his partner had advanced into the Llanganatis without him?, ... Is it a mere coincidence that at the time Stabler presented his Royal Geographical Society papers, which surprised Brooks and "forced my (Brooks') hand before I was ready to go to print," Thur de Koos was in the Archives of the Indies?, ... and ... Is it also a coincidence that after the death of Thur de Koos, Brooks appears to go silent, with no further expedition or communication occurring in 1918, 1919, 1920 or 1921?

All the previous questions, coincidences, theories and conjecture could be just that ... but for one small fact. A seemingly small detail from each of these men's stories that if true, unquestionably binds them together with a common thread ... in Ambato. According to popular belief, a relief expedition was sent for Brooks from Ambato, by his wife's father, Alfonso de Troya. Again according to popular belief, during his expeditions, Thur de Koos left his family at the house of his friend ... in Ambato ... that friend was none other than Alfonso de Troya![154]

Of one thing we can now be absolutely certain ... with Valverde, Spruce, Wallace, Brooks and now Thur de Koos pointing the way toward Cerro Hermoso ... lust for Inca gold would continue in earnest throughout the twentieth century ...

■ ■ ■

Edwards Cranston Brooks

[154] It is also important to note that Andrade's source, and therefore all author's that would follow him, for the Thur de Koos and Brooks information, was none other than ... Alfonso de Troya.

THE EXPLORERS CLUB: CAPTAIN ERIC ERSKINE LOCH

The Explorers Club, a sister organization of the National Geographic Society, and quite similar to the Royal Geographical Society, is an international multi-disciplinary professional society dedicated to the advancement of field research and the ideal that it is vital to preserve the instinct to explore. The club, founded in 1904 was ... "Formed to further general exploration, to spread knowledge of the same; to acquire and maintain a library of exploration; and to encourage explorers in their work by evincing interest and sympathy, and especially by bringing them in personal contact and binding them in the bonds of good fellowship."[155]

The Club has served as a meeting point and unifying force for explorers and scientists, whose headquarters are still located in New York City with branches worldwide. The Club promotes the scientific exploration of the Earth, its land, sea, air, and space, by supporting research and education in the physical, natural and biological sciences. Its members have been responsible for an illustrious series of famous firsts; first to the North Pole and South Poles, to the summit of Mount Everest, to the deepest point in the ocean and to the surface of the moon ... all feats accomplished by its members.

Currently, the Club provides expedition resources including funding, online information, and member-to-member consultation. In addition to sponsoring expeditions and lectures, the Explorers Club annual dinners honor accomplishments in exploration and are known for their adventurous, exotic cuisine served at these banquets. But probably the most powerful resource available to those who joined the Club was fellowship with other members ... a global network of expertise, experience, technology, industry, and support. The Explorers Club actively encourages public interest in exploration and the sciences through its public lectures' program, publications, travel program, and other events. The Club also maintains research collections, including a library and map room, to preserve the history of the Club and to assist those interested and engaged in exploration and scientific research.

Many of the founders of the Explorers Club had experience in the Arctic including Adolphus Greely and David Brainard, survivors of the Lady Franklin Bay Expedition, and Frederick Cook. Others, such as Carl Sofus Lumholtz and Marshall Howard Saville, explored the tropics. Famous members of the club have included Robert Peary, Matthew Henson, Roald Amundsen, Edmund Hillary, Neil Armstrong, Rolf Blomberg, Commander George M. Dyott and Captain Eric Erskine Loch.

■ ■ ■

Some Explorers Club members would become an indispensable part of our story, Captain Eric Erskine Loch [1891-1944] for one. Loch attended the Royal Military College Sandhurst and was appointed Second Lieutenant of

---

[155] From The Explorers Club Certificate of Incorporation, 25 Oct 1905.

The Seventy-first Highland Light Infantry on 5 Oct 1910 being promoted to Lieutenant on the 11 May 1913. On 29 Apr 1914 Loch was attached to the Nigerian Regiment and was stationed at Lokoja. When World War I broke out, Loch "served with distinction until his fourth wound forced him to leave the front and enter the intelligence department at the War Office."[156] Loch took part in the Cameroons campaign and was in the attack on Garua, at which time he was wounded. For his conduct there he was awarded England's Distinguished Service Order (D.S.O.).

The following appeared in Brigade Orders, Nigerian Regiment, Kaduna, dated 24 Sep 1919 ... "It is notified for information that the Distinguished Service Order has been awarded to Captain E.E. Loch, The Highland Light Infantry (late 2nd Battalion Nigerian Regiment), for gallantry under the following circumstances: Most conspicuous gallantry in action, during the night operations against Garua on the night 29th-30th August, 1914. On the morning of the 30th August, during the withdrawal Lieutenant and Adjutant Browne was wounded and unable to move. Lieutenant (now Captain) Loch, though himself wounded, went immediately to his assistance and carried him out of action on his back under an extremely heavy fire."

Captain Loch was later removed from active service and appointed to be Adjutant to the Highland Brigade at Norwich.

After the war was over Loch left the Army to take up an adventurous life as an explorer. Loch personally claims to have participated in a dozen expeditions in India, Africa and South America including Commander George M. Dyott's ... "1932 expedition to the Jivaro Indians in eastern Ecuador ... 'I was second-in-command.'"[157] Whether or not Loch was actually, second-in-command has not been independently confirmed. However, there is clear evidence that ... "In 1932-33 Captain Loch accompanied Commander George Dyott to the Upper Amazon and dwelt with the Jivaro Indians, head-shrinkers."[158] Loch (listed as an army officer) departed from La Libertad, Ecuador on 7 Jan 1933 and arrived in New York aboard the ship *Santa Clara* on 24 Jan 1933. Listed on the ships manifest was also the "explorer" ... George Miller Dyott.

Loch became a member of The Explorers Club in 1935. Shortly thereafter, on 8 Jul 1935 Loch announced an upcoming expedition departing New York within a month to study the Ssabela Indians of the Upper Amazon Valley for the Museum of the American Indian (Heye Foundation). *The New York Times* of 9 Jul 1935 carried an article concerning Loch's announcement and indicated ... "The leader of the venture, to be known as the Andes-Amazon Expedition, 1935-36, is Captain E. Erskine Loch, a retired British Army officer, who accompanied Commander George M. Dyott on several expeditions."

---

[156] *The New York Times* 5 Jan 1944

[157] This quote was attributed to Loch on his application to The Explorers Club by Mark Honigsbaum in *Valverde's Gold.*

[158] *The New York Times* 5 Jan 1944

Loch's announcement laid out the expeditions planned itinerary. They would set sail from New York to Guayaquil, Ecuador. From Guayaquil the group would travel by mountain railway to Riobamba, then by truck to Hacienda Leita, Patate, in the Andes. Loch then planned to make the rest of the expedition by mule, on foot and by canoe or raft across the region of the Llanganati Mountains, and down the Napo and Curaray Rivers to the Amazon.

Loch stated that the expedition would collect specimens and attempt to capture various species of animals for the New York Zoo, the Museum of Natural History and other museums. Beyond that point Loch made it perfectly clear, that his expedition's primary purpose "...is to study the Ssabela Indians who dwell in the Upper Amazon Valley and to bring back to the Museum of the American Indian specimens of their ethnological cultures. These specimens are particularly important, as the Museum of the American Indian has none; in fact, we do not know of their existence in any museum today, nor of anyone who has ever visited this tribe. Probably less is known of these Indians than of any tribe living in the Upper Amazon Valley. Early explorers of South America have called the Ssabelas 'the phantom people.' So little is known of them that they may well be called that at the present time. We know that the Ssabelas are an unfriendly people and fight among themselves, but little more than that is known."[159]

Everything did not go just as planned and Loch's expedition was actually split into two separate expeditions. Loch's first expedition would travel through and explore the Amazon, while the second would explore the Llanganatis. Loch spent a total of sixteen months in Ecuador, traversed the Llanganati range from east to west, and mapped vast regions of the interior. Loch departed from Guayaquil on 3 Apr 1937 on the Grace Lines ship *Santa Lucia* [160] and arrived in New York on 14 Apr 1937. The very next day *The New York Times* ran the headline ... *CAPTAIN LOCH HERE AFTER JUNGLE TRIP*, which stated in part ... "Captain Eric Erskine Loch, leader of the Andes-Amazon Expedition under the auspices of the Museum of the American Indian (Heye Foundation), returned yesterday on the Grace liner Santa Rita after sixteen months in Ecuador. He was accompanied by John Ohman of Glen Head, L.I., radio engineer, and Georges Brun, French aviator. Others of the party have either returned or are remaining in South America."

The New York Times article went on to indicate that Loch had returned without making contact with the "dreaded Ssabela Indians," but Captain Loch had discovered what he believed to be ... "...a 400-year-old Indian settlement in the little-known Llanganatis Mountains. There were evidences of a canal system, working implements, some gold trinkets and several gold

---

[159] *The New York Times* 9 Jul 1935

[160] Loch's book states that he traveled aboard the *Santa Lucia,* the ship's manifest and *The New York Times* of 15 Apr 1937 state Loch arrived on the *Santa Rita.*

nuggets, he said. Captain Loch believes this discovery may be connected with ancient legends of Incan treasures."

This statement appears to have been one of the first references to treasure in the reporting on Loch's expedition. The reports on Loch's plans and expedition up to this point, appear to have been more attuned to the scientific aspects and goals of Loch's party. Reports indicated that Loch traversed the Llanganatis from "east to west,"[161] studied a possible air route, and mapped vast regions of the interior. Although Loch's "phantom Indians" were not located, Loch had discovered "many evidences of the famous tribe, and collected ethnological data."

After his return Loch settled in at The Explorers Club in New York, where he wrote a book that told the complete story of the expedition entitled *Fever, Famine, and Gold (1938)*. Previously the public reporting had been more concerned with the scientific aspects of Loch's expedition, perhaps because it was conducted under the auspices of the Heye Fountain. In my opinion, in order to attain funding and support from the scientific community for his expedition, Loch must have had to downplay his true interest in the Llanganatis ... Inca gold. It would be in Loch's forthcoming book where the public would learn of his quest for Incan treasure.

Shortly after completing his manuscript, Loch returned to Ecuador for a short two month visit ... "where he surveyed the extent of the old gold mine workings discovered by the expedition. He said the mines might be developed by an American corporation."[162] Loch then arrived back in New York from this short trip on 10 Jan 1938 aboard the *Santa Lucia* of the Grace Line.

The remaining years of Loch's life were spent in Ecuador, although there is evidence that he returned to the United States for an unknown period on 17 Nov 1940. Arriving by airplane in Miami, Loch's immigration form indicates that the six-foot-one and seven-eights-of-an-inch tall, blond haired, green eyed Scottish man of a fair complexion, was a "mining company president." The remaining years of Loch's life were spent in Ecuador, until he came to a violent end. Suffering from a tropical disease which was masked by the heavy consumption of alcohol, Loch ended his life on 4 Jan 1944 by committing suicide [163] and is buried at the town of Huigra in Ecuador.

■ ■ ■

Eugene Brunner would write of Loch thus ... "During the twentieth century there were countless Englishmen and others who came to explore in these mountains. Some came simply as treasure or gold seekers, while others came as botanists, geologists, surveyors, always camouflaged in some way.

---

[161] Inaccurate statement as Loch traveled from west to east through the Llanganatis.

[162] *The New York Times* 11 Jan 1938

[163] An obituary from London states Loch died ... "following tropical ill-health."

Some made only one expedition others several and some even settled for decades in Ecuador, while still others traveled as a pendulum between Europe and the Republic of Ecuador in South America.

"Some of these explorers I knew personally, such as retired Captain Eric Erskine Loch, Scottish and tall, strong and very smart, brave and with a very commendable tenacity. Loch had belonged to one of the finest regiments of the Army of England, the Uganda Highlanders, who fought in the First World War against the German colony of Cameroon in Africa. Loch for his distinguished service received the highest decorations of the British Empire.

"Here in Ecuador Loch traveled by many rivers in the Oriente on rivers whose real courses until then, almost no one knew. Loch navigated the Curaray, the Nushiño, the Sotano, the Cononaco and on the Napo from Rocafuerte to Puerto Napo. From here Loch penetrated the virgin forests that had never been trodden by the white man to the headwaters of the Rivers' Oglán, Arajuno and Puni Yacu until he reached the hill of Raya Urcu. Loch had been carefully searching for the city of the 'ssabela' Indians, or as he called them, the Aucas. Better stated a tribe, which according to legends spread from mouth to mouth, that govern or at least control the different Auca tribes. But our illustrious English Captain, as he explored navigating by the rivers of the Ecuadorian Amazon, already had a group of compatriots working in the mountains of Llanganati. After completing his explorations in the Oriente, Loch also traveled to Píllaro and thence into the Llanganatis.

"Loch explored the Llanganati for a long time and until today is the only man known to have crossed these mountains from the village of Píllaro until reaching Puerto Napo in the Oriente. Loch's adventures and disappointments on this expedition and his explorations in general, are described in his book *Fever, Famine, and Gold.* A friend of Loch's, the owner of a farm in the Oriente, showed him some gold nuggets that were found after a downpour in a ravine on his property. Loch discovered an old river bed that had changed course in its descent through the Eastern foothills of the Llanganatis. In this same old river bed Loch discovered former placer mining operations of pre-Inca Indians.

"On this site, which Loch called 'The Rainbow's End', he recovered a little more than fifty pounds of gold that according to his own story the largest nugget weighed little more than an ounce (37 grams). Here also were found many objects of wrought gold; hooks, pendants, earrings, nose rings and plaques worked in high relief. Unmistakable proof that this river on its previous course went through some indigenous cemetery or maybe even a city in ruins.

"Based on subsequent results and his work after the first discovery, Loch formed the company Scarloch Mines Incorporated. The company functioned for many years exploring the channels of the rivers that descend from the mountains of Llanganati, including the Topo, the Shuña, the Ila, the Amaron Cachi, the Mulatos, and the Desaguadero; as well as the rivers

Chalupas, Verde Yacu, Cedros, and others that descend from the adjacent ridges of Llanganati.

"In the Llanganatis Loch tried unsuccessfully to drain the Laguna of Thur de Koos or the Rendón, generally known as the lake of mica and mica is all that Loch ever recovered. This is very logical because this small lake was not made by the Indians, it is natural. Valverde clearly stated ' ... there is a lake, made by hand, into which the ancients threw the gold ...' Other explorers also went mistakenly wrong here, including myself.

"While Loch was fulfilling his military service in Africa, he acquired a very rare infirmity which affects the throat and prevented him from swallowing with ease. Probably due to the hot, humid and suffocating weather of the Oriente the disease worsened. Throughout almost two years the poor man's food consisted of whiskey, porridge of oats and wheat semolina. Loch's health worsened and finally he could no longer work. Loch retired to the town of Huigra on the Guayaquil Quito Railway line, which has a mild and dry climate, leaving the functions of his mining company in the Oriente in the hands of his nephew Alasdair Loch.

"Loch's disease progressed and unfortunately no doctor could help him. When Loch could no longer eat anything solid, when to even take a drink was almost impossible, tired of so much suffering and seeing how he was becoming, Loch made a type of an altar. Loch placed Whiskey bottles and candles around him, put a rug in front of himself and knelt on it, he smashed the bottles and blew out the candles. Using the Colt 45 that Captain Bancroft Butler had given him, Loch finally shot himself in the head, dying instantly.

"Whether Loch was creating a Viking ceremony or a type of Japanese Harakiri, I do not know and nobody ever knew, however people started to talk. They spoke of the curse of Llanganati, others stated that his suicide was due to the economic failure of his explorations and expeditions in the Oriente and the Llanganatis, that Loch had no money and that he was in bankruptcy. Nothing is more erroneous. Eric Erskine Loch received a very good military pension and left in the bank on the day of his death, more than 25,000 English pounds, a substantial sum, which reveals that Loch's economic situation was somewhat enviable.

"On the other hand Loch always dreamed of a cure and that someday he could return to the Llanganatis. Loch was sure he could discover the treasure lagoon of the *Derrotero de Valverde*. In one of my last visits with Loch, he said he would soon be well enough to make a new expedition into the Llanganatis together. He also gave me a copy of a report from Scarloch Mines Incorporated that was delivered in 1942 to the Director General of Mines and Petroleum in Quito, which I still have. Thus ended the life of the first Englishmen [Scottish] related to the Llanganatis that I knew."

■ ■ ■

It is in *Fever, Famine, and Gold* where Loch writes the following eloquent sentiments which in some manner, would shape and define Eugene Brunner's methods and goals in his own search for the Llanganati treasure

... "Many people, even today, think there are Indians throughout the whole Inca Empire who know the exact location of these lost treasures and pass the information from father to son on oath that it shall never be divulged. To do so, they claim, is to invoke the curses of their forefathers upon them. In some books containing information given by the old priests shortly after the conquest, one finds the belief mentioned that the Incas or their descendants will never disclose the whereabouts of these treasures except to a man 'of good heart'. This worthy is further warned not to use what he finds to the detriment of the natives, but rather to employ it to their betterment.

It is quite possible that in the secrecy of their hearts some Indians know where hidden treasures lie but will never admit it, for behind their secrecy lie unspeakable atrocities committed against their forbears by the Spanish conquerors."

■ ■ ■

I could write a lengthy overview of Loch's book *Fever, Famine and Gold* but by paraphrasing this man one might lose insight into the man and his intentions. Loch's story as it relates to the treasure of the Llanganatis, in my opinion is best told through excerpts from his book, in his own words. Loch's body of work, like that of Spruce, Stabler and Brooks before him, paints a detailed picture of not only the man, but of the Llanganatis themselves, as he follows in the footsteps of Valverde and his famous *Derrotero*. Only a small portion of Loch's work is reproduced here. Loch's entire book not only is recommended, but it is a must read.[164]

Loch writes an introduction explaining his reasoning and writing style ... "A few years ago the public's ever-increasing demand for thrills forced explorers, often against their will, to give accounts of their explorations that far exceeded their rightful field of truth. Breath-taking escapes and adventures were demanded. Then came a new fashion, that of burlesquing exploration and its risks. It became the mode to return from a trip with stories of having fondled a rhinoceros much as one would a Pekinese and of having fed a lion out of the back of one's car with a ham sandwich or two.

"I trust there still remains the simple middle course. In the narrative of this Expedition I have deliberately shortened a few wearisome lapses of time, and have attempted to minimize the necessarily repetitious accounts of daily routine scientific work and mechanical details in favor of those features of more general interest which we pursued. And in the last chapter I have intentionally withheld the names of two men and of a place for obvious reasons.

"Before leaving New York it had appeared to me, from rumors and conjectures, that the Curaray River had a winding course and that there was

---

[164] *Fever, Famine, and Gold* is available in many libraries and used copies can still be obtained for a few hundred dollars. However, many years have passed since Loch's death and his work is no longer protected by copyright. Being public domain material, one can also view the entire book online at the Hathi Trust Digital Library.

only a small difference in altitude between its headwaters and the frontier. These were indications that it might be free from rapids or falls. If so, I saw no reason why it should not prove to be a safe, navigable waterway right through the Oriente to the frontier. A direct passage then, through the Llanganatis Mountains, from the railroad to the source of the Curaray, with a link to Napo Town, was a logical counterpart; and it was searching for these two things that linked together the whole year and four months of the Expedition's work.

"So little was known about either region that each offered an extremely interesting field for research. Also the itinerary as finally laid out was to take us through an area cloaked with one of the most colorful and romantic stories in the history of South America.

"But I trust that no story of a famous treasure is to alluring to overshadow the other work we did. I wish to say that we brought back many thousands of observations, thermometric and hygrometric readings, ethnological and natural history specimens, which are now in leading institutions in New York, Chicago, Philadelphia, and Great Britain.[165] Such things require constant daily work, arduous and uninspiring, and, under conditions in the field, are most difficult to acquire.

"The scientist, most understandably, does not as a rule care to associate himself with romance, lost treasures, and so forth. Personally, I have no such qualms. But then, I am not a scientist and make no pretensions whatsoever to being one. I'm a British Army Officer, retired, who does things for the love of them, that's all. But a life of travel takes me to far-off places from which I bring back such information as I can.

"Not one single man of us took any part at all in South American politics, nor have we any bias whatever on that score. Any service that our records may contribute toward the Ecuador of the future is given purely out of affection for that country.

"Although months have now passed since those turbulent days spent in the Llanganati Mountains and the Oriente, to me they seem but as yesterday. For at the very moment this book goes to press, the New York newspapers are carrying dispatches of another clash on the Ecuador-Peru frontier, involving people and places directly connected with this Expedition. It was through Rocafuerte, the main garrison on the frontier, and Tarqui, the military post on the Curaray, that the Expedition journeyed.

---

[165] Researching this manuscript I discovered that after Loch's visit to the United States at the end of 1940, and prior to his death in January of 1944, the US Library of Congress, sometime in 1943, acquired a large collection (1000 items in two containers) of Loch's "Correspondence and other papers relating to the organization and personnel of an expedition to the Andes-Amazon to gather information on the Ssabela Indians and the Llanganati Mountains." These items are "open to research" and stored under the title ... "Eric Erskine Loch Papers."

"I regret that it was impossible to record photographically the more exciting happenings of the Expedition. In the Llanganati Mountains the constant clouds, rain, and fog rendered picture-making an all but impossible task."[166]

■ ■ ■

Loch explains the purpose and intention of his expedition thus ... "It was the spring of 1935. As I emerged from the New York Public Library, my mind was aflame with the few startling pages of history I had just been reading. The Valverde Treasure! The Lost Mines of the Incas! The Legend of the Llanganati Mountains of Ecuador! The story stood before me like a beacon. What hidden mysteries, what vast hoards of gold might be secreted in those distant, snowy peaks! Just four hundred years earlier Spain had conquered that mighty Empire of the Incas.

"A vision of that Empire's tragic end sprang up before my mind, and on that instant came a desire ... a sudden determination to reach those far-off Llanganatis, and find a short route to the Amazon. Uncharted territory, rare animals, a tribe of Indians of which little or nothing was known, and a region which offered abundant fields for exploration and research! And with it all, that slender fabric of an ancient legend ... hidden lakes, lost treasure, Llanganatis Gold!

"I knew the 'Valverde Treasure Guide,' copied from the ancient archives of Madrid, almost by heart; and at my own first reading of the detailed instructions for finding the treasure I had been as enthralled as those around me now. But, as time went on, I had come to know the hidden contradictions contained in that Guide ... pitfalls that were not at once apparent at first reading and that were no less disheartening when met with on the scene.

"There are about a hundred lakes on the best maps available and many more that aren't even known about ... at least that's my experience with South American maps. But whether it's a treasure in a lake, a mine, or both, four hundred years of searching leaves it anybody's guess.

"The whole matter was indeed one of great interest, which in the back of my mind subtly exerted its centuries-old magic upon me as much as upon the others. It had been taken very seriously by such recognized authorities as Richard Spruce and Hassaurek,[167] who had given much thought and study to the matter. The original Guide sent to Ecuador by the King of Spain contained old Spanish phraseology, obsolete words, and terms capable of being interpreted in various ways; but, because of the wealth to which it refers, it is one of the best-known treasure stories in the world

---

[166] Regardless of Loch's apologies over the lack of a photographic record, the book includes some very interesting photographs, including shots of the Lagunas de Anteojos, Brooks' Lake and Cerro Hermoso, in all some 605 still photographs were taken.

[167] Friedrich Hassaurek [1831-1885] was appointed as US Minister to Ecuador by Abraham Lincoln and served there from 1861 to 1865. Hassaurek engaged in journalism, politics and the practice of law.

today. To prove or disprove the legend of the Lost Mines or Treasure ... and one should lead to the other ... was a matter of legitimate historical interest and one which wanted dealing with later as soon as opportunity offered. "Ethnological, geographical, and other scientific purposes soon took root as my plans developed. In fact they were soon an obligation on my part, for Mr. Heye, Director of the Museum of the American Indian (Heye Foundation), of New York, knowing the scientific value of the region, placed me under that institution's auspices for ethnological research. Hectic weeks of turmoil followed. Boxes, bales, equipment, men ... all crowded through the panorama of those busy days.

"The summer came. By August we were ready. The Andes-Amazon Expedition was organized, and on its way to South America. It was two expeditions in one and, unlike others which have a single objective in view, its aims were many and diverse."

■ ■ ■

The territory Loch and his party were about to explore ranged from the snow peaks around Ambato and Latacunga directly eastward across the Mulatos and Llanganati Mountains and down the Curaray and Napo Rivers to the Peruvian frontier in the Oriente. In all they would map 360 miles of Rivers in the Oriente, the Llanganati and Mulatos Mountains. They traveled 840 miles in canoes and rafts on rivers and covered 1440 miles on foot and horseback. Loch successfully completed his scientific research which included recording astronomical observations, survey angles and bearings, altitudes, hygrometric, and thermometric readings, as well as collecting 180 ethnological, 470 ornithological and mammalogical specimens.

Loch's collections and reports from the expedition were distributed to The Museum of the American Indian (Heye Foundation), American Museum of Natural History, Academy of Natural Sciences of Philadelphia, Field Museum of Natural History, New York Zoological Society, Central Park Zoo, American Geographical Society, Royal Scottish Geographical Society and of course ... the Royal Geographical Society.

■ ■ ■

Loch's expedition commenced in the Oriente and once completed, moved into the Andes and his second phase of exploration ... the Llanganatis. Loch paints a clear picture after leaving Ambato ... "By late afternoon we had begun descending out of the higher altitudes; suddenly the ground spread open before us like a gigantic bowl, in the center of which stood a small cluster of miniature houses against a background so fantastic as to make one catch his breath. Mighty Chimborazo and Altar stretched their white-capped peaks into the infinite blue; and, in contrast to their majestic splendor, between them lay the little town of Riobamba, like a tiny jewel in a setting beyond the ability of man to conceive. The sun had almost sunk behind the lofty Cordilleras. Beyond us towered the Peaks of Llanganati, grim and forbidding, guarding in their fastnesses an age-old secret that had kindled an enthusiasm which was to carry us, without regret, through two years of toil and hardship to a climax so strange I can scarcely believe I did not dream it all.

"We soon reached Píllaro, where we arranged a base from which to launch our attack on the Llanganatis. Once we were established, the others joined me with that part of our heavy equipment we had left in Ambato months before; and we set about the task of renewing clothing and food supplies, and generally reequipping for the mountains.

"This meant a complete change in attire, camp paraphernalia, etc., from what we had carried into the hot Oriente. Now we should need heavy sheepskins for the high altitudes, different types of condensed foods, waterproofs in abundance, and heavy sleeping bags, to name but a few of our main items of equipment.

"Next morning I set out in high fettle to purchase supplies. John followed me. He seemed to have something on his mind. 'What's the trouble, John?' said I. He produced a book on ... of all things ... old languages. 'Do you know the origin of the name Píllaro?' he asked. 'No, and I don't care a damn,' I retorted without slackening my pace. That was like John. Having a flair for languages, he was forever delving into the origin of things that had far better be left alone. But John was persistent. 'It means,' he said, 'The Place of Thieves.' Then he ran for his life. Approaching me later, he asked, 'How did it go?' John liked to be right. 'You did them an injustice. The inhabitants didn't ask much more for their stuff than it was worth ... at least, not very much more ... 'John, dismayed, turned to his book.' ... only about two hundred per cent more!'

"Everyone was of course convinced that it was only the famous treasure that we sought. The spirit of old Valverde must haunt the place. In truth he should be Píllaro's Patron Saint, for I well believe he has been its principal source of revenue for the last four hundred years. Expedition after expedition has set out from the little place pouring funds, in the form of wages and the purchasing of supplies, into the pockets of its inhabitants. That many have failed before they have gone far does not matter, for a new one comes along. Píllaro should erect a monument to Valverde in its plaza.

"Supplies and equipment now being nearly ready, carriers became the next question. What a problem the question of transportation was! As a rule a carrier could be expected to bear a load of from sixty to eighty pounds. But in the difficult country ahead of us that amount was not to be expected, especially as the carriers' own bedding, which they also carry, would have to be heavier because of the rigors of the climate. Moreover, in the high altitudes the peon is accustomed to foods very heavy in weight. It is difficult, if not impossible, to change him to lighter or more concentrated foodstuffs. To insist on it would cause great discontent, and you would in all probability fail to get men at all.

"They eat three pounds per day and even on reduced rations, two and a half pounds. A carrier therefore eats up all the food he can carry in from fifteen to twenty days, and then becomes of no use to an expedition. But the carrier must eat on his return journey also; consequently he can only go forward for from seven to ten days. Add to this the men incapacitated for carrying by adverse travel conditions but who must be fed while in the field and further losses of food by bad weather, accidents, and unavoidable petty pilfering, and it can readily be seen how difficult the problem is.

"Forbidding as the Llanganatis are themselves, I am sure it is this matter of commissary that, more than anything else, has caused so many failures and disasters. This is nearly always the hazard with an expedition that has to travel on foot in a land that is barren of food resources. But it is doubly true in the case of the Llanganatis because of the immense difficulty of the type of travel one faces.

"At the time we entered the mountains, scarcely anyone knew anything of the region, and such a thing as a guide was not to be had.[168] Every wrong turn, mistake in the way, or accident of weather would mean delay; and delay meant further dwindling of the precious food supplies, an early return, and failure.

■ ■ ■

"Píllaro lies eastwards of Ambato on the western fringe of the Llanganatis Mountains ... a pleasant little country town, its origin lost in a distant past long before the coming of the Spaniards.

"Here, some 9,000 feet up, all of us went off our feed, for we were getting into the more rarefied air of the mountains, a great change from what we had recently been through.

"It was from here that we hoped to locate the pass through the terrific obstacle of the Llanganati Mountains to the Oriente. In the whole of Ecuador there are but two trails that lead from its economic centers to that eastern region. Both of these are widely separated by the Llanganatis and adjacent groups forming two arms of a great semicircle which meet, on the other side of the mountains, at Napo. This causes detours involving the loss of many days of travel. It was our purpose to cut through the center of this semicircle and locate a direct route to Napo and the Curaray which could, when opened up, make it possible to accomplish the journey in little more than a day.

"Unbelievable as it may seem, the distance is less than eighty miles, the first forty-five miles of which lead over the high barren páramo [169] lands at an average altitude of from 10,000 to 12,000 feet. These extend to the eastern rim of the cordillera which marks the commencement of the timberline once more and drops away rapidly to the low jungle country of the Oriente.

"Once Píllaro is left behind, the whole region is completely uninhabited. Even game is very scarce, until the small settlement of Napo, on the first edge of the Oriente, is reached. The high, bleak páramo-lands, broken up amidst the gigantic peaks of the Andes, are great expanses of prairies covered by long wiry grass and weeds interspersed with numerous wild

---

[168] Unlike Brooks who entered the Llanganatis without a guide, Loch did obtain a guide in the form of José Ignacio Quinteros (old Q), who is the basis of yet another story.

[169] Páramo is an alpine plain open to the winds.

morasses and bottomless swamps. On the eastern slopes below these páramos, at about 10,000 feet, the forest country begins and stretches downward to meet the jungle vegetation of the Amazon basin, at about 5,000 feet.

"This intermediate area of forest country (called montaña) is a region of terrific wooded declivities cut through by torrential cascades and mountain streams which fall precipitously to swell the head-waters of the Amazon. The borderlines of the páramos and these dismal forests, continually enshrouded in mist, are the habitat of the rare and seldom-seen hairy tapir and spectacled bear, which are unique to this region.

■ ■ ■

"Much of the area to be explored and mapped would include the territory covered by Valverde's historic Guide to the lost mines,[170] and the little town of Píllaro is the last point of civilization before entering the mountains. It is the place whence Valverde started on his journey so long ago, and interest in the old Guide now revived in all of us, especially in Bill Klamroth. He went through it word for word, carefully enumerating the landmarks in the order Valverde indicated them.

"First he listed the 'Farm of Moya,' then the 'Guapa,'then 'flechas,' then 'sangurimas,' and next the 'forest.' All seemed fairly clear as far as the 'Mountain of Margasitas' [pyrites]. 'After passing the Margasitas the directions in the Guide seem involved,' said Bill. 'Yes,' I replied, 'the end of the Guide is extremely vague and of little help; and it does not even state definitely where the vast treasure is to be found. For, while it implies that it is within a socabón, or tunnel, yet the searcher is directed to the 'third mountain' and is informed that, providing the Guide is correctly interpreted, 'the waters of the lake fall into the tunnel.'[171] 'Neither does Valverde mention whether the treasure is to be found in the form of golden vessels, utensils, ingots, or a mine or deposit of virgin gold,'[172] he broke in.

---

[170] Curiously Loch refers to the *Derrotero* as a guide to "the lost mines" not Atahualpa's ransom treasure. Loch always was of the opinion that the lost mines were the key to discovering the treasure, but still, this statement seems odd.

[171] Loch loses me with his interpretation of these points within the *Derrotero*. Without question Valverde indicates where the treasure is to be found ... "there is a lake, made by hand, into which the ancients threw the gold." I totally disagree with Loch's statement that the *Derrotero* "implies that it (the treasure) is within a socabón." The only "implication" is that one might have to remove the "salvaje" to find the entrance of this landmark, which you must pass, and ascend the mountain to reach the lake, which is at a higher altitude ... because "the waters of the lake fall into it."

[172] Here I would strongly disagree with Loch's conclusion. The *Derrotero* specifically states that ... "the ancients threw the gold they had prepared for the ransom of the Inca." Not only had the majority of Atahualpa's ransom been paid in worked gold, but Valverde clearly does not indicate a "mine deposit or deposit of virgin gold".

'Indications are, however,' I continued, 'that they are ancient gold workings; for he refers to a 'furnace' that is'nailed with golden nails.[173]

"I had always thought that the fact that the Llanganati treasure was thrown into a lake has been given undue prominence, possibly through the romantic features attached to the story. It would appear to be of far greater importance to discover the ancient mines from which the gold had been extracted. An invaluable clue to their location would be the discovery of some ancient roadway."[174]

■ ■ ■

Loch's expedition ultimately sets out from Píllaro. Within *Fever, Famine, and Gold* a "fragment" of Loch's expedition sketch of the Llanganatis is reproduced as a visual aid to track their route and progress. One must remember that the "fragment" Loch published, only represents a small portion of the area the expedition covered. Loch's "key" and "fragment" follow:

KEY TO FRAGMENT OF EXPEDITION SKETCH OF LLANGANATIS
Portion of Expedition's Itinerary

- 1. Old site of Moya Farm.
- 2. Cerro Guapa.
- 3. Pongo (pass) de Guapa.
- 4. Old site of Mamarita cattle corral.
- 5. Wild Morass.
- 6. Twin lakes of Los Anteojos.
- 7. The great black lake.
- 8. The forest.
- 9. The first ravine.
- 10-a-b-c. Ravines.
- 11. Valley deathtrap and fateful pass.
- 12. Old Q's valley of the mountain crowned with gold.
- 13-a. Colonel Brooks Three Peaks and Treasure Lake.
- 13-b. A perfect three peaks in the form of a triangle, with lake. But other stipulations are wanting.
- 14. Signs of what appears to be an ancient roadway.

[]

---

[173] Here I also disagree with Loch's conclusion. I am of the opinion that the "guayra" mentioned in the *Derrotero* is clearly a mere landmark, quite similar to the other landmarks Valverde used within his guide.

[174] Clearly Loch was of the opinion that the riddle of the treasure of Llanganati would be resolved through the "discovery of some ancient roadway." In my opinion this is exactly what the *Derrotero* suggests. Valverde refers to another landmark within his guide as "the Way of the Inca." For what other purpose would one utilize a road in this desolate, inhospitable, uninhabited, mining region ... except to transport ore from the mine to the "guayra" and then out of the region?

Loch's Llanganati Expedition Sketch

In my opinion, at the time Loch published his sketch, it was the best map available of the region. This map clearly depicts not only the route of the *Derrotero* into the heart of the Llanganatis, but adds detail and clarity to the region where Guzmán's map is vague and incomplete. Remember that Loch's map details only a "fragment" of the expedition sketch and a "portion of the expedition's itinerary" within the Llanganatis.

With the passage of time, portions of the *Derrotero* and regional maps have become irrelevant and outdated. It is beyond question that at a minimum, the first third of the riddle of the *Derrotero* has been solved. The landmarks within this portion of the famous guide ... Píllaro, the Farm of Moya, Cerro Guapa, the pass (Pongo de Guapa), cattle farms (Mamarita), Los Anteojos and the Great Black Lake (Yana Cocha), have all been discovered and verified by countless explorers. Today, especially considering the encroachment of civilization upon the Llanganatis, even the novice adventurer or explorer can visit these sites with ease.

It is with the remaining route of the *Derrotero* that Loch's sketch becomes useful. Leaving Yana Cocha (number 7 on Loch's sketch) the expedition follows the route of the *Derrotero* descending to the southeast on the Desaguadero de Yana Cocha, passing its junction with the Golpe de Auca Cocha, continuing east-north-east along the Río Desaguadero toward the Río Niagara. Loch appears to have missed "Margasitas Mountain," or found a "false Margasitas," in any event none is marked on his sketch.

■ ■ ■

Loch continues ... "On March 31, 1936, we set off up the mountain, accompanied for a short distance by the peons' women. On saying good-by they waved, shouted, and wished us 'freedom from disaster.'The veil of superstition in which the whole region of the Llanganatis is cloaked had not affected us while we were in Píllaro, but it was to become apparent later on, as we entered the eerie land ahead of us.

"In the afternoon rain came on, and what a different rain it was from the warm downpours of the Oriente! Biting, cold, and in continuous blasts, it penetrated to the bone. Believe me, as it fell without let-up, I had a longing for the once-bemoaned heat of the Curaray basin. But our spirits were high; for before us lay the final, and in many respects the most important, territory to be explored and in it hopes of Inca gold!

"Here in the Llanganatis the trade winds, sweeping countless miles from the east across the lowlands of the Amazon Valley, strike the great barrier of the Andes only to be forced abruptly upwards to great heights, where they condense into immense banks of gargantuan, weeping clouds. If there is any choice of a good season it would be October to December. Yet here we were in our world of perpetual mists and biting, never-ceasing rains with the worst, the snow months, just ahead.

"By the afternoon we had reached the spot where the 'Farm of Moya' once stood, an open flattish slope covered by knee-high grass and a few stunted trees. Continuing on up the mountain-side, now amid the high open páramo country, we went into camp. The 'Farm of Moya and a short distance above it' ... the first landmark mentioned in Valverde's famous Guide! Suddenly the whole story of Valverde's hoard seemed transformed from a mere legend to a vivid actuality. He and his Inca wife must have stood on this selfsame spot centuries before. Laden with gold, they must have passed along this very trail we were following.

"There above us stood the second landmark, the 'Mountain of Guapa,' looming up through the mist against the sky, and by noon on the next day we had reached the 'Pongo,' or pass, of the Guapa, over which, at an altitude of more than 12,000 feet, a bitter cold wind drove a light rain into our faces.

"It was a faint indication of what lay ahead of us, for the rainy season had now set in. The labyrinth of ridges and snow-covered peaks, considered impassable at all times, was now said to be impossible even to enter, let alone to pass through. As we crossed the pass, it was a desolate, forsaken world that spread before us. Amid mist and rain, sleet, and penetrating cold, the peaks reared their ice-sheathed summits fifteen thousand feet into the air.

"Even after descending from that inhospitable pass, we were afforded slight protection in the valley, nor did the rain show any sign of abating. By late afternoon it let up somewhat; and arriving at a tiny copse,[175] the only timber thereabouts, we took advantage of its shelter and went into camp for the night.

"A short while before sundown the skies cleared, and across the lovely valley lay what was once the tambo (shelter) of Mamarita with the lakes of Pisayambu behind it, all shown on Guzmán's old map. Off to the northeast the peaks of Roncador [176] stood out like a fortress.

"In such localities as the Llanganati Mountains, timbered areas such as the small copse where we were camped are few and far between, but rivers numerous. Here it is timber, rather than water, as in the Oriente, which rules the day's march. This often results in very slow progress. Not infrequently there may be two timbered areas only a few miles apart, with no others for many miles, and thus a day's march may not cover more than two or three miles.

"After a freezing night we left Mamarita behind and had considerable trouble passing the 'wild morass over which thou must cross.' A light rain came on once more, but we were still afforded some protection by the great valley in which we traveled. It all seemed strangely familiar; for here again, after struggling through several morasses and as the ground dropped away on crossing a rise, we finally came upon the small twin lakes of Anteojos.

---

[175] Copse - A small group of trees.

[176] This region is located in the upper north east quadrant of the *Guzmán Map* and is north of the area depicted on Loch's expedition sketch. It is apparent by the extensive details on Guzmán's map that he traveled extensively in this highly mineralized zone of the Llanganatis.

There could be no mistake about them. Between them is a point of land like a nose that gives the lakes an appearance for all the world like a pair of spectacles. So small they were that we could easily have missed them. We stood motionless on a small rise, four strange-looking figures heavily muffled in our sheepskins of brown and white, gazing down over the two sheets of water, each one of us lost in thought.

"Here Valverde had left his horses, unable to take them farther. Here also, a few years later, had passed the ill-fated expedition of the King of Spain. What a motley throng! Spanish soldiers with their clanking armor, priests with flowing robes, pushing onwards through swamp, morass, and river, looking eastwards eagerly, ever hopeful of finding Valverde's cache.

"We continued on in the same direction; and, though hindered by swamps, we were afforded more protection from the weather by the narrowing of this great valley. Ascending an abrupt rise, we looked down to see Yana Cocha, the 'Great Black Lake, the which leave on thy left hand.' Its distance from the Anteojos was a pleasant surprise, for it turned out to be a far shorter distance than the impression given by the curious old *Guzmán Map*. Guzmán certainly must have covered a tremendous amount of ground in this region, a very wonderful achievement under the conditions of his day, but the map that today is attributed to him is drawn on pictorial lines that give no accurate sense of distance or even, in many parts, of direction.

"The immense difficulties under which our own sketching and mapping were now being carried out made us realize how much easier it would be just to remember the country and draw a nice little picture of it afterwards amid the comforts of civilization, as was done in the case of some old maps. The constant bad weather made the chances for 'long shots' to get our bearings few and far between; and the making and preservation of records in that chill, watery climate, without shelter for pencil or paper, was no little effort.

"While fighting one's way on foot, charting the interminable maze of mountains, I thought that here even the high efficiency of modern aerial photographic mapping would be baffled. Dependent upon the caprices of those massive banks of clouds, a flyer might suffer delay after delay, perhaps for months, until a break in the dense atmosphere would happen to lay bare, for a few moments, the labyrinth below.

"From here Bill and I, taking with us old Q and some peons, explored and mapped the region to the southeast. This was rather south of the line which I personally believed Valverde's Guide indicated, but nevertheless previous seekers after the treasure have always followed this southerly course. In any case, at that time, our best chances of finding a west to east pass through the mountains appeared to be in that direction.

"We arrived at a sharp, precipitous drop where we 'descended along the hillside' to reach a 'deep ravine.' Crossing this successfully, we continued our steep descent. By now we had dropped down out of the barren, icy regions above the timber line and, circling a bluff on our right, we saw before us the edge of Valverde's next landmark ... 'the forest.' We plunged in. Dark, dank, and drear, every leaf and hanging strand of moss dripped ceaselessly with moisture from the incessant rains. Not even the hearts of large fallen trees were dry enough to afford fuel for our campfires. We spent days cutting our way through this ghostly world of chill, depressing misery.

"Finally we commenced to ascend, and as we emerged from the edge of the forest once more, we came in sight of a possible 'Margasitas' mountain, the stumbling block of so many searchers for the treasure. We had hoped to pass this and reach a 'grass valley' beyond, but the rain had been unceasing the whole day, and the men became utterly exhausted with climbing the wet and slippery mountain. To add to this, Bill cut his leg badly with his machete while clearing the trail, and so we went into camp perched on the mountain-side.

"It was a miserably cold, rainy night; there was no space to pitch our tents. We were thankful for dawn and a chance to be doing something other than shiver and curse. We tried to find consolation in the thought that a few hours more would find us in a 'grass valley' beyond. But we were over-optimistic. We spent the whole of the next day, amid downpours of rain, striving to find a passable route across the mountain's spur. The country commenced to get more difficult. This way certainly gave no indications of a good route through to the Oriente.

"On the following day we took a somewhat lower line, and after many hours of laborious climbing reached the lip of a small sheltered valley set high up in the mountain. We were now some 10,000 feet up, and the two days' delay on that false 'Margasitas' had been a severe drain on our provisions.

■ ■ ■

"The valley wherein we now pitched camp was almost fantastic.[177] In appearance a small grassy oval, perhaps six hundred yards in length by four hundred in width, it was entirely surrounded by towering mountain peaks except for a narrow cleft on one side where a stream which passed through the center of the valley flowed between the rocky walls to a lip and formed a cascade to plunge several hundred feet to the river below.

"As we entered, the sun chose to make one of its rare appearances. Bees, butterflies, and birds flitted about; and the sudden change from the dismal rain swept mountains and bitter cold revived everyone's spirits. Lovely as the spot was, it would become a potential death trap in the event of a cloudburst such as Colonel Brooks met, upon the surrounding mountains.

"Near the lip was the highest ground in the valley, with a solitary tree growing on it. Bill and I picked one slight rise; old Q and the peons another; all were soon in camp and in our sleeping bags.

"I slept peacefully until midnight, when I was awakened with a start. Someone was calling. Rain drummed heavily on the tent top as I strained

---

[177] Denoted as "11- Valley death trap and fateful pass" on Loch's expedition sketch and key.

my ears to listen. It was Bill. 'Is there any water in your tent?' That seemed an odd question; we had been living in water for the past few weeks. But almost before I could answer, the whole canvas bottom of my tent gave an upward lurch, and rose some four or five inches off the ground.

"I leaped up to find a foot or more of water pouring in, short-circuiting my flashlight, which was on the floor beside my bed. Grabbing up instruments and precious records, I hastily threw them into a haversack and floundered out into the coal-black night, only to be met by a freezing deluge which had already buried the valley floor waist-deep in water.

"I remembered the solitary tree, the only one in the vicinity; and, struggling and wading, I reached it and lashed the haversack high up in the branches. Here I was joined by Bill, and as the flood was gaining every moment and the rain still coming down in torrents, we scrambled up into a fork to spend what was probably one of the coldest nights of our lives.

"The men and old Q were on a knoll further away from the main rush, but in the pitch dark, with arms full of records and instruments, it was impossible for us, in the dark, to cross the now raging torrent and reach it. Within fifteen minutes the water had reached the top of the tent doors. We thanked our stars for that lone tree, whose solitary grandeur had impressed itself on our memories so strongly that even in the darkness we could find it.

"The pitch-black night in the treetop seemed never to end for Bill and myself. The branches in which we were perched were coated with six inches of sopping wet moss. The rain was descending in torrents; and, soaked to the skin and chilled to the bone, we were unable to move sufficiently even to keep warm. The real risk was falling asleep, tumbling out and being carried over the now appalling cascade. We used every artifice to keep each other awake. We were assisted in this by a last-minute thought I had of bringing along our emergency bottle of whisky. This, I assured Bill, was to be used for medicinal purposes only. He acquiesced, and soon an empty bottle plopped into the torrent below to go on the long, long journey to the Amazon and thence to the distant Atlantic Ocean. If I had ever had any doubts about the story of Colonel Brooks being flooded out of his Treasure Lake by a cloudburst, they were quickly dispelled.

"As a dismal dawn finally broke upon us through the mist, we descended to a flooded camp. Rain fell for two days and two nights thereafter; and, when the sun finally shone through and the waters had receded, we found that most of our precious food supplies, which had not been in sealed cans, had perished. The loss of our food supplies made a great difference in our plans for the future, and we waited impatiently for a break in the weather; but the rain continued for several days, and our already sodden bedding had no chance to dry out ... rather, we found signs that it was beginning to rot, a great hardship and cause of suffering even at this altitude; and ahead of us were the lofty peaks of the Llanganatis with their sleet and snow, which would render sleep well-nigh impossible. The peons with us began to show a certain passive resistance and muttered among themselves about going back. The way to circumvent this was to send their food supplies and equipment on ahead of ours, which we proceeded to do. We camped at the end of the day's climb in a freezing fog accompanied by half a gale. We were held in camp by this for two more days.

"However, on the third day we got away, and after a morning of slithering in ankle-deep mud and scaling precipitous walls of rock, we made camp at the foot of a gigantic rock mass towering thousands of feet into the air, over which we had to cross.

■ ■ ■

"The next day, April 17th, we headed for a higher pass at the back of the peaks. En route we encountered a tunnel, or socabón, beside a small lake, which drew forth a few mutterings from old Q. Nothing developed from our examination of the place, however. It was a natural tunnel ... rather a cave with a small outlet at the back ... but we found no signs what-so-ever of man's handiwork anywhere about, nor any site nearby particularly favorable to catch the prevailing winds. This latter is a significant point, for it was the custom of the Incas to smelt their ores in furnaces placed in natural rock crevices, or chimneys, where, at that altitude, the wind created strong drafts which made a natural bellows for the smelting furnaces. These vertical currents of rushing wind carry with them banks of mist which ascend to great heights. This gives these perilous crags the appearance of being volcanoes pouring forth great clouds of smoke. It was this which caused the belief that the whole region was one of active volcanoes, and hence the continued use of the word *Volcán* in Guzmán's map.[178]

"The ascent to the pass was laborious in the extreme, for the surface of the mountain was covered with jucál, a long, stiff, cane-like grass growing to a height of some eight feet, which resisted every attempt to get through. In patches it had dried and fallen to the ground in great masses. This presented an even worse obstacle, for the hard shell casing was as slippery as ice and offered no foothold. The only way we finally reached the pass was by finding a tapir trail which, through constant use, had worn a slight passageway to the top. 'Passageway' is only a relative term, for the precipitous and perilous places up which it led would have been difficult to accept as possible had I not seen them for myself.

"On many occasions these tapir trails were our salvation. In fact, whenever Bill and I were in doubt as to the easiest way to reach a point or scale a hill, we began looking for a tapir trail, for it had been our experience that we could often better trust to the animals' judgment than to our own. They would fool us sometimes, however, and lead us serenely right to a precipice edge down which they had apparently flitted airily. Then there was nothing for us to do except retrace our steps in search of a safer route.

---

[178] Whether fact or fiction, this is the most rational, reasonable and highly plausible explanation that I have seen concerning the discrepancy over Guzmán's erroneous representation of Cerro Hermoso ever having been an active volcano, which we now know to be an impossibility.

"Bill and I, on ahead of the others, finally reached the top of the pass, a narrow ridge but a few feet across, at an altitude of 12,320 feet. Overshadowed by terrific crags, with a drop of many hundred feet on each side, the perilous knife edge, where the wind whistled with tremendous force, seemed like the world's end, from which we gazed beyond into another realm. At our feet was a precipice down which we peered into the swirling mists below, searching for old Q's next landmark.

"The thought of spending a night on this inhospitable knife-edge was an unpleasant one, and we were carefully feeling for a way down when the mist thinned for a few moments to show us below a long pear-shaped lake with an outline impossible to mistake ... old Q's landmark, as described by him and marked on his map. We pushed on toward the cave, hoping it would afford a warm and sheltered camp.

"Progress became easier ... until we committed that ever-tempting folly of taking a short-cut. This time it was a pleasant-looking patch of grass down below which lured us. Forsaking the rugged edge of the cuchillo, a long, narrow, knife-edged ridge, down which we were slowly working our way, we dropped sharply down to the 'green patch.'

"Before we knew it we were imprisoned, not in grass, but in jucál which ran to a height of some two feet over our heads. To retreat back up the steep ascent was impossible, and it took us two hours and a half to force our way through but a few hundred yards of the obstruction to our cave, where, exhausted, we went into camp just as daylight departed.

"But our hopes for a warm shelter here were short-lived, for the shallow cave exuded a dampness that bit into one's bones. The drip, drip, drip of the moisture falling from the roof continued without ceasing.

"By the next morning it was raining hard again. Setting out, we worked our way to a chain of three lakes threaded together like huge beads upon a slender string of river. Here we climbed up 1200 feet to a narrow pass through which we entered a magnificent valley. Open and pasture-like, and covered with a growth of stiff grass, it was of enormous size. On the east it was bounded by very lofty mountains, barring easy progress in that direction, and on the west and southwest by the spurs of the great range over which we had come. Toward the south it fell away gently, stretching far into the distance until it was lost in an abrupt end where it met the great forested area of the Oriente.

"Before leaving that day, old Q had sworn that his 'mountain of gold' lay over this pass, at the foot of this enormous valley. This was borne out by his sketch map. But he now became hopelessly vague. The rugged outline of the mountains surrounding the valley was so outstanding that once seen they could never have been forgotten. We returned to camp wet, disappointed, and disconsolate.

"Our nights spent in the congested space of the damp clammy cave were dismal beyond words, and our food was now reduced to a perpetual diet of lentils ... all that remained with us. This finally drove us back over the pass to our reserve dump to replenish. We soon returned, however, to this forgotten land, but, upon crossing the pass this time, took a higher line toward what appeared to be drier country.

"Dawn came, and we awakened to see right before us, breaking through the mist, the pride and majesty of the Llanganatis, the Cerro Hermoso. This giant peak named 'Beautiful Mountain' has been vested with sacredness in the old legends. We had long since circled this peak, and were now well to the east of it; but, owing to the constant bad weather, this was the first time we had seen it.

"Everyone was soon astir, and we made an early start, old Q ahead and now apparently brisk and eager to show us his great secret. Making a detour somewhat to the south of the line of our entry, however, with the idea of covering that region also, we came to the lake that popular belief says was the one reached by Colonel E. C. Brooks.[179]

"Our reward was an old weather-beaten camp site, presumably his. Near at hand, leading to the edge of the lake, was a long narrow cut, an obvious attempt to drain it at some previous time.[180] Across the water was a strange rock formation which looked for all the world like a replica of a church porch. This expression was used by Valverde in his Guide.

"We decided to drag Brooks' lake with a makeshift raft made of jucál grass wrapped in a waterproof sheet. Bill stretched out face downwards on the contraption and paddled his way into the center of the lake, which, fortunately, was not deep. He used a kerosene can on a rope as a dredge. When the samples had been brought ashore, they were dried off and examined. Bill's work continued apace. But an examination of the samples disclosed that they contained nothing but mica, or fool's gold. So much for that lake."

■ ■ ■

Loch explains further ... "During the earlier stages of the expedition into the mountains the peons did fairly well. To be sure they had taken their time, always anxious to camp long before the end of the day, and delaying the start in the mornings by their leisurely manner of cooking and eating their breakfasts. But they had not grumbled and had given no trouble. However, as time went by, their enthusiasm for the enterprise waned in the face of the difficulties and terrific weather. As I recall it, we had thirty-nine days and nights of almost incessant rain. At times the weather became even worse ... the rain turned to snow. A small taste of this was enough for Luis, the cook, who, while back on the convoy, decamped. This was bad news, for although his loss was of minor importance in itself, his idea of running away would soon spread in spite of all precautions. And so it did. The men could be

---

[179] Represented as "13a - Colonel Brooks Three Peaks and Treasure Lake" on the expedition sketch and key.

[180] It is widely believed that the Austrian explorer Paul Thur de Koos attempted to drain Brooks' treasure lake. However, not once in Loch's book is Thur de Koos ever mentioned.

controlled while actually with the main party, but they had to be sent back on supply convoys, and during these periods it was touch and go, although we exerted all possible vigilance.

"On one occasion, at dawn, on going to the place where the men had spent the night, not a sound was to be heard. The whole party had vanished, taking with them the load ropes and specially made packs. I pulled out then and on a rapid trip to Quito obtained an interview with President Paez. The Government of Ecuador was to gain very materially by our mapping and study of this hitherto uncharted area. Being keenly aware of all this, "President Paez lent a ready ear and offered to call for volunteers from the army. I shall be eternally grateful to him for the speed with which he carried this out. Within thirty-six hours I had an officer and seventeen men from the engineering corps; with these, and a new batch of Indians and half-breeds,[181] we made a fresh start.

"To obviate the extreme loss of efficiency with human transport, I determined to try animals[182] this time for the first stages and form a main supply camp at the farthest forward point we could take them. We hoped that with a certain amount of temporary road making we could get them past the swamps and morasses as far as the more difficult mountain terrain. The value of these animals was due to the fact that they could be fed on the páramo grass and would not, therefore, consume the loads they carried.

"By June 12th we were again on the familiar trail to the Farm of Moya, Guapa, and the Anteojos, pushing on into that land of false lures and dashed hopes. Getting them over the numerous swamps was a problem which occupied everybody's efforts, and here Bill Klamroth did fine work. These swamps are really a series of tufts thrusting out of pools of deep mud. A man could cope with them by stepping carefully from one tuft to another. But, with the horses, they became a real difficulty. Across the more extensive swamps we had actually to make roadways. Timber not being available at that high altitude, it was necessary to construct improvised corduroy roads out of the stiff cane grass (jucál).

"This took a lot of time, and wherever possible in the narrower crossings we would use a very simple device which we called quite affectionately our 'wedding carpet.' It was a long roll of stiff sacking some four feet broad. We would unroll and spread it across a narrow stretch of swamp, and the problem was solved. As the transport animals have a habit of following each other in single file, we would attempt to rush them across at a smart speed in order to get all of them over before the 'carpet' sank down.

---

[181] During the field period of the Andes-Amazon Expedition, Loch would ultimately have employed a total of four hundred-seventy-seven men and fifty-eight animals.

[182] To clarify, some authors erroneously indicate one of Loch's failures being his use of animals on the expedition ... it was only on this latter portion of the expedition that he utilized animal transport in an attempt to resolve his supply issues.

"The ever-increasing rains soon converted even the higher country into an almost impregnable barrier. Do what we might, it was impossible to prevent the transport animals from getting bogged. The unfortunate beasts would wallow up to their middles, when panic would take possession of them; and, plunging frantically, they would sink deeper and deeper into the mire. Meanwhile the loads would have been scattered to the four winds. Then the problem was to save not only them but also the equipment. It required quick work to extricate the animals, and by the time we reached terra firma they were too exhausted to do anything but lie down. The same was true of the men themselves after their desperate efforts. I doubt if ever before any swamps on the entire continent heard such fervent cursing as we gave off during those days.

"By keeping at it, however, we made some progress and reached the stream that, according to Richard Spruce, the botanist, is the one which played a prominent part in the King of Spain's first expedition to solve the riddle. For here it was that the priest accompanying the expedition, Padre Longo, whose presence was relied upon to give moral and religious courage to the party, completely disappeared. Apparently no trace of him was ever found, nor has any explanation of his vanishing been advanced. The superstitions of the day were enough, and almost immediately the expedition broke up without going further. As late as the middle of the last century, when Spruce spent considerable time studying the whole matter of the Valverde Guide and treasure, a cross of wood was said by him to be standing by this river. It seems incredible after so long a time, although in the high altitude the cross would be less likely to rot away than in a low-lying area.

"Meanwhile, we were proceeding higher and higher, our tent floors almost constantly immersed in water. Both the men and the animals had to be kept moving or they would soon crack. The rain now turned to snow, and the swollen rivers made such fords as had existed earlier impassable. The effort of bringing timber for the bridges from the distant valleys became more and more difficult until we reached the point where even this was impossible.

"This was as far as we could use the animals, and when we pushed on we had to change to man power to carry our loads. Not only were the horses suffering, but also such a high proportion of the men that it became evident many would soon have to be sent back.

"At this point Valverde's Guide commenced to grow vague. It gave landmarks of a nature that could be found in different places a dozen times a day. A 'dry quebrada!' Why, the region was nothing else but ... except that they are not dry, at least at the season we were there, and Valverde did not say what time of the year he traveled in.[183]

---

[183] Loch may very well have made an important point here. The time of year that Valverde traveled in the Llanganatis is extremely relevant. For this reason, the route Valverde marked in his *Derrotero*, may not appear the same. What may have been a 'dry quebrada,' or a passable river in certain months of the year, most probably would not be encountered in the rainy season.

"Similarly, his earlier references to 'flechas,' 'sangurimas,' and 'forest,' are little help, for after four hundred years nature's work can make great changes. Lakes with 'cascades' abounded, and very logically so. A breakaway, forming a bowl high up in the sides of these mountains, is a common occurrence. The flow of water into the bowl very naturally forms a lake, the only outlet to which is the narrow lip from which height the outflow pours in a cascade many hundreds of feet to the valley floor below.

"There are several groups of peaks fulfilling some but not all of Valverde's conditions; and they can be looked upon, therefore, as false peaks which have lured many searchers astray. One magnificent group of 'Three Peaks in the form of a triangle' we did come upon; and on its declivities, true enough, was a lake, a narrow outlet, and cascade. But other stipulations of Valverde's did not coincide.

"One morning, however, our hopes ran high. While following a cuchillo, one of those long, narrow, knife-edged ridges, we came upon an extensive, clearly-cut depression. Broad, deep, and plainly marked, it followed a relatively straight course and gave every appearance of being the remains of an ancient roadway.[184]

"Enormously encouraged, we traced this out in both directions, but at both ends it appeared to peter out, and the lay of the land offered no hope for a continuance nor reason for its existence. It may have been a natural freak geological formation or, if once a road, the surrounding country must have undergone some great cataclysm, and attempts on our part to follow the depression came to naught.

"Shortly after this we came upon what is, I think without question, the source of the River Topo, which dashes in a violent winding course through the mountains to join the River Pastaza well to the south.

"Our eyes were ever on the alert for geological specimens that might show signs of gold or other precious metal, but none did we see. In fact the whole region gave little evidence of being a gold-bearing country. Even if the ancients had thrown their treasure in a lake in the Llanganatis, they were en route from the mines at the time; and now more than ever I was convinced that if they existed, they must lie farther over on the eastern slopes.

"The 'Mountain of Margasitas' proved another delusion. No sign of any pyrites whatsoever did we find, until much later on, when I had passed beyond the eastern rim of the mountains.

"Our daylight hours were filled with mapping, sketching, and forever seeking our main objective ... a feasible pass through the mountains to the east to the head of the Curaray River and the Oriente. By now we had mapped an enormous area and learned a great deal of the region. One thing now was certain. No feasible passageway to the Oriente lay on this line. A route further north must be sought.

---

[184] Denoted as "14 - Signs of what appears to be an ancient roadway" on expedition sketch and key.

"In the course of this search we ranged through a vast new territory. For forty days we searched in vain. But at last good fortune favored us. For the first time we awoke to a beautiful clear day. After marching for about three hours Bill and I reached the top of a pass from which we could see the whole surrounding country. Before our incredulous eyes opened out a great indentation which seemed to cut through the barrier made by the mountain ranges, presumably to a river valley below. This gave every indication of a natural passageway to the east. If this proved to be so, our problem was solved.

"We were congratulating ourselves, eagerly intent upon this discovery, when abruptly we saw something that had hitherto escaped us. To the left of where we were standing suddenly loomed a new 'Three Peaks' ... and right on the line given by Valverde! This confirmed in my mind my original belief that previous searchers had misread Valverde's directions, and had gone too far to the south.

"One can imagine the surprise and encouragement which followed the glimpse of this pass through the mountains, heightened as it was by the sight of the new 'Three Peaks.' With all haste we prepared to get under way. True, these peaks lay quite far north, in fact on the border of what is deemed by some to be the Llanganatis proper.[185] The supposed confines of this region are most variable, and the origin of the name by no means certain. So far as I can tell, the first known use of the word 'Llanganatis' is in the Valverde Guide, where he applies it to his particular Three Peaks of the treasure. There is an old Quechua word, Llanga, 'to touch.' It is quite plausible, therefore, that Valverde used it merely to indicate his Three Peaks, which were (Uanganati) 'touching' or joined together by their geological formation, and not as a name for the entire region.[186]

"As we were leaving to follow our new clue, the rain broke afresh, but the pendulum of luck was evidently swinging in our favor; for, scarcely had we started, when we managed to shoot four ducks. The dinner that followed was the best we had known in months in this region where game was so scarce.

"The next day we went up a great valley, only to meet with a downpour that exceeded any we had so far encountered. The Fourth of July, that blistering hot holiday Bill and John had so familiarly known in the States, found us

---

[185] These "new Three Peaks" Loch is making reference to, are not on the "fragment" of expedition sketch published in *Fever, Famine, and Gold*. These peaks lie much further north in the Roncador region of the Llanganatis, the heavily mineralized zone depicted in the north-east quadrant of the *Guzmán Map*.

[186] In my opinion, one of Loch's most astute observations and once again, just as we have discussed previously, yet another "singular" inference to the location of the Incas treasure ... the plausibility that Valverde's "three peaks are joined together by their geological formation."

trapped in a pass on top of a cuchillo, with intermittent rain, snow, or sleet as our constant companions.

"It was then that I felt obliged to give the 'pep' talk of my life, and the outcome was that, after a lengthy palaver among themselves, the Indians decided to stick 'just a little longer.'

"All around us was a dense thicket of chaparral which, though not high, was almost impenetrable. For example, Bill and I had to go down a hill face from our camp in the saddle of a mountain to the valley below. It was only a matter of a few hundred yards, yet it took over an hour and a half to cover.

"Our objective was to find a way through to these new 'Three Peaks,' of which we now seemed to be within striking distance. After two days of effort, our reward was an impasse—a sheer drop impossible to descend or cross. I then turned my attention to trying to find a course over a saddle in the ridge to the southeast, but for several days I failed utterly.

"The rain continued for three days more, and we were held as in a vise. Through most of this period we were unable to see twenty yards away, everything was afloat, and the valley floor had become a lake. But finally the weather relented, and on we shoved in bitter cold and sleet, eventually succeeding in reaching the saddle, which was our destination.

"The weather continued to improve to such an extent that the next day we were able to reach the crest of the main peak, where the altimeter read 12,360 feet. I climbed to the far edge and looked expectantly down below. I was not disappointed. There, cradled in a declivity of the great peak, was a sheet of emerald-green glass ... a lake ... just as Valverde had described it!

"Hastening back, I waved the men to a lower route. Eagerly we made camp on the saddle of the mountain and set out at once to explore the region. From a distance the surrounding country had appeared to be pleasant, easy grassland, but when we reached it we found it to be chaparral so high, tough, and dense that it required an hour to progress but a few hundred feet, its elasticity resisting every blow of our machetes.

"Every yard was a struggle, but despite this we were greatly encouraged. Upon reaching the lip of the lake we found an outlet so narrow we could jump across it and below appeared a flashing cascade, 'green pasture in a small plain' and a 'canon betwixt two hills' ... all agreeing perfectly with the Guide.

"In all our wanderings in the Llanganatis this setting was the only one we encountered that fulfilled so many of Valverde's stipulations. As a climax to it, high up on the mountain-side and dimly discernible to the eye, was a long, narrow depression for all the world like an ancient roadway.

"Our hopes ran high, and excitement coursed through our veins, blinding us to the brutal truth. For, when I summed up the situation, I knew without doubt that the crisis had come. The transport animals had long since been sent back. Right after that all our Indians had abandoned the Expedition, as well as many of the peons. Such had been the ravages of the climate that of the original seventeen soldiers only seven remained in good enough physical condition for me to feel justified in asking them to continue further.

“I had to face the truth. No more work could be expected of these men upon the lake regardless of what treasure might be hidden in its deep recesses. It meant infinite toil with fresh men, more supplies, and much apparatus. To do more than we had done was impossible.

“The bitterness of the blow was great, but it had to be banished from our minds, as all thought had now to be given to the all-important problem of finding the pass through to the east. It was a race against time. Food was appallingly low, and the percentage of men that were now too incapacitated to proceed farther was so high that I realized with foreboding I had but a day or two left in which to find this pass or be forced to give up the whole project after nearly a year in the field. Time after time we scaled the surrounding peaks to try and catch those few moments of clarity which, in this atmosphere, when they do occur, come just after dawn.

“It was a world of infinite solitude, doubly awe-inspiring from the fact that, lost in the constant mist but a few feet away, the mountains dropped into an abyss from the terrifying pinnacle on which we stood. Nothing but mist enveloped us. Bank after bank of heavy, rolling clouds clung to us as if determined to obstruct all our attempts. We could see nothing. We could learn nothing.

“The time for a decisive step rapidly approached. I could not expect to hold the men longer. That night I lay awake in my sleeping bag wondering what the morning would bring. We had traveled miles and miles in face of constant setbacks, and such a short distance remained to complete the last link in the chain to the frontier. Was ours just to be one more name to add to that lengthy list of failures? After so long, defeat seemed impossible to accept.”

By this time most of the expeditions Indian porters had either been sent back or deserted, Brun had been stung by a scorpion and only seven soldiers remained. Loch ultimately chose to push on and complete his mission alone with the aid of a few volunteers, as Loch would state ... “I knew now that our problem was so acute that there was but one solution, one that I had thrust from my mind as long as possible. But it had to be faced. Because of the shortage of carriers and of food it would be impossible to take the whole Expedition through. If the Oriente was to be reached, I would have to continue light. I called for volunteer carriers among our few remaining soldiers and peons to take a chance with me on what lay ahead. Private Pons agreed instantly; and through his example, two others quickly joined, a brother soldier, Pasmino, and Cajas, a peon.”

Just seventy days of living hell and misery,[187] after viewing his long sought after pass through the mountains from the top of his 'Three Peaks', Loch and his two companions made it to civilization.[188]

■ ■ ■

Sadly, Loch's expedition's persistence, the months of hardships they endured and the obstacles they overcame, the discoveries they made and all the work they accomplished, has been overshadowed by great tragedies. The first tragedy occurred near the end of the expedition and Loch describes the harrowing event in vivid detail ... "Our descent to the bottom of the valley took a week, and, on reaching the river bank, we found ourselves in a trap at the junction of two rivers. One was fairly tranquil at this point for a mountain river, but broad ... far too broad for us to bridge ... while the other, narrow enough to permit bridging, was extremely turbulent and in flood. It was exceedingly swift and filled with huge water-worn rocks as slippery as ice. Although my heart sank as I considered the prospect, it appeared the easier of the two, and we fell to work on trying to span it. We commenced our bridge, but before we could make it fast it was lost in the foam. And so with another and another and another.

"According to my diary we made seventeen attempts in all, each crude structure being swept away like its predecessors. Precious days were wasted, and eventually we were forced to turn to the broad river which, though too deep to ford, was calm at one place and gave us a chance to cross by raft with a rope. We soon had knocked together a flimsy raft of sorts and were ready to make the attempt. I feared that our cable was all too short for the broad span, but with the assistance of Cajas and Pons it was eventually stretched to the other bank and secured. This was made possible through Cajas' finding a foothold on a small rock in the middle of the swiftly moving river, while Pons poled and paddled himself across, held from being swept into the rapids by the cable, and was the first to set foot on the far bank. The cable had reached all right, but with little to spare.

"Meanwhile, I had been lying on our side of the river directing them. Inability to shout instructions, owing to my injured lungs, necessitated my speaking them to Pasmino, who, in turn, would yell them across to Cajas. Then they were relayed to Pons, who signaled his arrival by a wave, for a short distance below this calm stretch was a cascade, the roar from which was deafening. Once the ferry line was secure, Pons started back in the raft by means of a short safety rope looped around the cable and secured to the raft.

"On our side we waited eagerly as he started, drawing himself along by his hands. He was perhaps halfway to the rock on which Cajas was waiting for him when suddenly the raft broke free. The safety loop either broke or came

[187] Loch would fall, hurt his leg and brake two ribs.

[188] The author Honigsbaum, having professed to have read *Fever, Famine, and Gold* more than once, erroneously indicates that Loch was accompanied by Brun and three soldiers.

untied. Slowly the raft gathered momentum downstream carrying the helpless Pons toward the boiling rapids. The stream was too broad and the current even here was too strong to paddle the raft to shore before it would be swept into the maelstrom. Like most of the mountain people he could not swim. He called out desperately and our anxiety in that moment was intensified by knowing there was nothing we could do. We watched for what seemed an eternity, as he finally disappeared forever amid the rapids—a frail, bent figure, hands clutching the fatal raft. We never saw him again, although Pasmino and I searched a long distance below the falls on both banks. Some time later we found the raft smashed almost beyond recognition."

Speaking of the personnel chosen for his expedition, Loch had stated earlier in his book that after ... "A dozen expeditions in India, Africa, and South America, eleven years as a British Army Officer in various campaigns have taught me the wisdom of choosing men for themselves and because of certain traits of character often indiscernible by the eye or ear, rather than by a long list of professed abilities."

Loch ultimately dedicates *Fever, Famine, and Gold* thusly ...

"TO THE MEMORY OF
PRIVATE JOSÉ PONS
SOMETIME SOLDIER
OF THE MONTUFAR BATTALION
ECUADOREAN ARMY"

Other tragedies that overshadowed Loch's accomplishments in his military career and explorations would occur later. Sadly it would be these failures and traits for which authors seeking to romanticize and "burlesque" the story have framed our memory of the man. Sure Loch was a heavy drinker and committed suicide ... but it is easy to comprehend his reasons. Was Loch depressed over his financial situation? One cannot say with certainty ... but financial circumstances seem to indicate otherwise. One must remember the man for his successes' not failures. Loch's expedition was not a complete failure. Clearly Loch failed to discover the treasure of the Llanganatis, but this was only a small portion of his mission ... many more goals were met.

Loch would state ... "There's no romance to this, nor to a battle ... while one takes part in it. Great physical effort and discomfort are one's sole companions. Only with the passage of time, when one can relive past scenes amid a life of ease, does the spirit of romance transform those memories into something glamorous and picturesque."

Loch's work and contributions, just as that of those before him, Guzmán, Spruce, Wallace, Stabler, Brooks, Thur de Koos and Andrade, adds to the understanding and clarity of the Llanganati treasure story. Even the minutest bit of data, when viewed alone may appear irrelevant or trivial, but like the pieces of a puzzle fitting together, the riddle of the Llanganatis slowly comes together.

■ ■ ■

Loch makes one odd reference in passing, concerning the Llanganati treasure story ... "It had been taken very seriously by such recognized authorities as Richard Spruce and Hassaurek, who had given much thought and study to the matter." That made me question ... who was Hassaurek and why did Loch mention him? No other author, whom I have read on the subject of the Llanganati treasure, appears to have made any mention of the man.

Friedrich Hassaurek was the US Minister to Ecuador from 15 Jul 1861 through 13 Jan 1866. His book ... *Four Years among the Spanish-Americans (1868),* tells an interesting story of Ecuador's history, legends, peoples, customs, geography and botany, all intertwined with Hassaurek's years of travels in Ecuador. Also, mentioned in detail was Hassaurek's interest in the Llanganati treasure and the story of Richard Spruce's work on the subject.

Hassaurek had arrived in country shortly after the end of Ecuador's civil war and dispute with Peru. Richard Spruce one might recall, was still in Ecuador at this time. Just month's prior to Hassaurek's arrival in Ecuador, Spruce's paper had been published in the *Proceedings of the Royal Society of London.* Three years later, in early1864, Spruce finally leaves Ecuador for England. The questions arise ... Even though he does not make the claim in his book ... Did Hassaurek know Spruce? ... Were copies of Spruce's paper given to friends, circulated or left in Ecuador by Spruce?

Introducing *Four Years among Spanish-Americans*, Hassaurek writes ... "Considering the rapid multiplication of books in every branch of science and literature, it has always been my opinion that no new book should be written unless the author has something new to say, or unless he can present something already known in a new and original light."

A quarter through his book, Hassaurek begins his relation of the Valverde legend and Richard Spruce by writing ... "Latacunga is the starting-point of the most romantic gold legend circulating in Ecuador. As it has a better claim to consideration than any other of the many idle gold-stories in which the interior abounds, and as it has led to many adventurous expeditions into the mountains of Llanganati, where the treasure that enriched Valverde is said to be buried, I will give a full account of it, availing myself of the information contained in a pamphlet written by Mr. Spruce, the celebrated botanist, who made a scientific exploration of the wilderness of Llanganati:"

Hassaurek follows this prologue with an abbreviated version of Spruce's paper including the Valverde story, *Guzmán Map*, *Derrotero* route, hieroglyph and Spruce's observations. Included in the back of the book in the Appendix, Hassaurek reproduces the entire *Derrotero de Valverde* and hieroglyph.

I ask myself ... What was the something new to say that Hassaurek intended to relate, or how did he present something already known in a new and original light? Only one important difference appears between Spruce's material and Hassaurek's account ... differences in the hieroglyph as depicted below ...

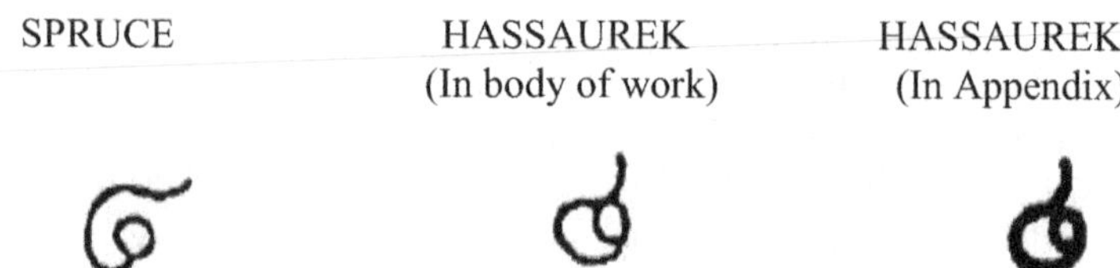

... food for thought as lust for Inca gold continues in the twentieth century.

■ ■ ■

I obtained my copy of Loch's *Fever, Famine, and Gold* from Michael Dyott, a son of another past member of The Explorers Club. The intent of his gift I assumed, was either to establish the reality of the situation one encounters in this inhospitable region, or possibly to dissuade me from going into the mountains by dispelling any thoughts I might have that an expedition into the Llanganatis was going to be a walk in the park. Michael's father, a past member of The Explorers Club, also had connections with the Royal Geographical Society and is an integral part of the Llanganati story ... the famous British Commander George Miller Dyott.

It has been implied by a character in Honigsbaum's *Valverde's Gold*, that Commander "Dyott hated Loch. He thought he was a fool." Also, the book indicates that Dyott by his own account was instrumental in getting Loch to mount his 1936 Andes-Amazon Expedition. Years later Michael Dyott had this to say about the matter ... "My dad liked Loch. I didn't know that my dad went on an ocean voyage with Loch, but he did get Loch interested in the Llanganatis."

Loch did mention Commander Dyott in his book once, and this statement confirms that Loch had been on an expedition with Dyott previously ... "My Indian friends thoroughly enjoyed the whole excursion, but as for me, every bone in my body ached, a torment set in that seemed to continue for an eternity. It was so dark inside that I could neither read nor write, but only reflect bitterly on what the explorer, G. M. Dyott, once said to me during one of his expeditions as he eyed my six feet two acidly: 'Tall men are a great nuisance. They don't fit normal store equipment; their beds have to be longer, therefore heavier; they perpetually knock things down from the tent roof with their heads, and besides' ... with a stony glare at me ... 'they are apt to eat more!'... Commander Dyott is a very short man."

■ ■ ■

Eric Erskine Loch

George Miller Dyott

THE COMMANDER: GEORGE MILLER DYOTT

Wallace's publication of Spruce's *Notes of a Botanist on the Amazon & Andes* would not be the end of English involvement in the Llanganati treasure, merely the beginning. Yet another individual connected with the Royal Geographical Society and The Explorers Club, Commander George Miller (Burnaby) Dyott, would become an intrinsic part of our story. Similar to Spruce, strangely there exists no biography of such a remarkable man, which could easily fill volumes. Without Dyott's involvement, the quest for Inca gold, commonly described as Atahualpa's Treasure hidden by his stepbrother Rumiñahui in the Llanganati Mountains of Ecuador, would have little clarity. If, or better stated when, this Inca treasure is discovered, it will be in no small part to the involvement of Commander G. M. Dyott.

■ ■ ■

An aviator, inventor, adventurer, explorer, writer, film maker and linguist who spoke nine languages, Dyott was born in New York City on 6 Feb 1883, to an American mother and English father. Dyott was raised at his father's home in Freeford, Freeford Hall, a British manor house [189] known as Freeford Manor until the 1930s, located in the West Midland region of England southeast of Lichfield. Most of Freeford, formerly a township in St. Michael's parish, was an estate centered on Freeford Manor.

The Dyott's of Lichfield acquired interests in the manor of Freeford over a period of many years from about 1584. When Richard Dyott, Member of Parliament (M.P.) for Lichfield during 1690-1715 died in 1719, his son, also Richard, decided to move from the city to live at Freeford. His son, another Richard was Recorder of Lichfield and in 1798 High Sheriff of Staffordshire.[190] In 1891 a cousin, Richard Burnaby, who changed his surname to Dyott, inherited the estate. The Dyott family has a chapel dedicated to them in the north end of St Mary's Church in Lichfield. A brief account of the Dyott family lineage, well entrenched in British history and society, appears in the report *A History of the County of Stafford: Volume 14: Lichfield* (©University of London, Victoria County History), a fragment of which follows ... "John Dyott, a barrister and three times bailiff of Lichfield, was probably the original of the 'little John Doit of Staffordshire,' the boon companion of Shakespeare's Justice Shallow in their youth. He was granted a crest in 1560 and a coat of arms in 1563. He was succeeded in 1578 by his son Anthony Dyott, a barrister and M.P. for Lichfield in 1601 and 1603, who died in 1622. He was succeeded by his son Richard, a barrister, who in 1610 had married Dorothy, daughter and heir of

---

[189] Manor - a large country house with lands, chiefly a historical a unit of land consisting of a lord's demesne and lands rented to tenants.

[190] The High Sheriff is the oldest secular office under the Crown. Formerly the High Sheriff was the principal law enforcement officer in the county but over the centuries most of the responsibilities associated with the post have been transferred elsewhere or are now defunct, so that its functions are now largely ceremonial.

Richard Dorrington of Stafford. Knighted in 1635, he was M.P. for Lichfield in the 1620s and in 1640 and a prominent royalist. He was succeeded in 1660 by his son Anthony (d. 1662), another barrister, whose heir was his brother Richard. Richard, who had accompanied Charles II into exile, was elected M.P. for Lichfield in 1667.

"On Richard's death in 1677 his son, another Richard, succeeded. He was M.P. for Lichfield in most parliaments 1690–1715 and died in 1719. His heir was his son Richard, the first of the family to live at Freeford rather than Lichfield. He died in 1769 and was succeeded by his son Richard. In 1776 Richard was living at Ashbourne and in 1784 at Leicester, where he died in 1787. He was succeeded by his son Richard, who lived at Freeford from 1784 and was recorder of Lichfield from 1808. He was succeeded in 1813 by his brother Lt. Gen. William Dyott, a regular soldier who was promoted to full general in 1830. An edition of the diary which William kept from 1781 to 1845 was published in 1907. William was succeeded in 1847 by his son Richard (d. 1891), M.P. for Lichfield 1865–74. Richard was succeeded by Lt. Col. Richard Burnaby, grandson of William Dyott's sister Lucy. Burnaby, who changed his name to Dyott, was succeeded in 1903 by his grandson Richard (d. 1965). He was followed by his grandson Richard Burnaby Dyott, formerly Shaw, who remained the owner in 1985."

George Miller Dyott was educated at Faraday House in London, which was established in 1890 and provided training for electrical engineers. Prior to graduating, Dyott left England and traveled to the United States in August of 1904. He found employment with Westinghouse in Pittsburgh, Pennsylvania, but at some point Dyott was "laid off"[191] and moved to Long Island in New York where he had relatives.

It was in New York where Dyott ultimately became interested in flying. On at least one occasion Dyott had been present and witnessed the Wright brothers' fly. Many years later Dyott would reminisce about his life's exploits with one of his sons, who passed the following account onto me ... "He told me that they (the Wright brothers), essentially, vaulted themselves into the sky and that's why he got into aviation. He said, 'If I couldn't do better than that, I wasn't worth my salt.'"[192] Dyott obtained his pilot's certificate, number 114, in February of 1911 and not only designed but test piloted planes shortly after the Wright brothers.

It had been late 1910 when Dyott teamed up with Dr. Henry Walden, the designer, builder and pilot of the first successful American monoplane flight. Dyott designed two aircraft, one a monoplane built by Hewlett & Blondeau Ltd. with a wing span of twenty-nine feet and twenty-three feet in length, which reached speeds of 45-75 miles per hour. The other plane Dyott designed was a twin-engine biplane, which was never used during the Great War as it was underpowered, although, it reportedly was later used for mapping palm groves in the Congo.

---

[191] Quote from Mark Dyott - February 2006
[192] Quote from Michael Dyott - May 2012

In the autumn of 1911, Dyott and Captain Patrick Hamilton traveled from England to New York with two Deperdussin monoplanes, a two-seater and a single-seater. They made an exhibition tour, stopping for a while in Nassau and in Mexico. A highlight of the Nassau exhibition was a night flight in the two-seater, with Hamilton as passenger, carrying a searchlight powered from the ground via cables.[193] In Mexico the two-seater carried many passengers, including the Mexican Republic's President Madero.[194] Dyott later reported on the different flying conditions in hot climates, particularly the effects of thermals, rotating winds, and the excitement of flying over forest fires.

In November 1913 *Flight Magazine* wrote under the headline *The Dyott Monoplane at Hendon* ... "After an extensive tour of the U.S.A., where he has given numerous exhibition flights, Mr. G. M. Dyott has brought his machine back to this country, and it is now flying at Hendon. When looking at this machine it is difficult to believe that it has just completed a series of exhibition flights, most of them made under anything but ideal conditions, so well has it kept its ship-shape appearance. Not only has it flown over 2,000 miles, but on two occasions the machine was turned upside down when landing without breaking anything of importance, thus testifying to the qualities of the design and the workmanship."

Once in England Dyott joined the Royal Naval Air Service [195] serving during The Great War from 1914 to 1918. Dyott was promoted from Flight Sub-Lieutenant to Flight Lieutenant in September of 1914, then to Flight Commander in January 1916, ultimately achieving the rank of Squadron Commander. I have seen indications that Dyott remained a Squadron Commander until the end of the war in 1918 but this cannot be verified.[196] In 1920 the President of the Royal Geographical Society would state [197] that Dyott ... "has served during the war three years in France, and was invalided and went back to America."

After the war Dyott became a fellow of the Royal Geographical Society and embarked upon a series of expeditions that would establish his name and reputation. In 1922-1923 he joined the Faunthorpe-Vernay expedition to India, Nepal, and Burma, sponsored by the American Museum of Natural History. He then turned to South America with an expedition to Ecuador and Brazil in 1924-1925, another expedition down the Río Roosevelt in 1926-1927, and an expedition to try and find the missing British explorer Percy Fawcett in the Amazon in 1928.

Dyott was also active in the early years of aviation in South America. He set up a company, Dyott & Company Ltd. of Lima, taking aerial photographs,

---

[193] Dyott was certainly one of the first to try night flight.

[194] Dyott traveled to New York from Mexico aboard the ship *Guantanamo* on 23 Feb 1912.

[195] Royal Naval Air Service became the RAF in 1918.

[196] Commander Dyott's official military record was and still is classified.

[197] *Geographic Journal* Volume 56, October 1920.

scenic vistas and native scenes, which were sold as postcards. Dyott pioneered possible air routes across the Andes in Peru, many of which are in use today, detailed in his book *Possibilities of Aerial Transport in Peru (1919)*. On 19 Apr 1920, Dyott gave a lecture on the subject to the Royal Geographical Society reading his paper *An Air-Route Reconnaissance from the Pacific to the Amazon*. Dyott was introduced by the President of the Society thus ... "The lecturer this evening is Mr. Dyott, who was originally a mechanical engineer, but who always took a very keen interest in aviation work, and finding aviation interfered with business, very wisely gave up business and took to aviation."

Colonel Beatty, RFA, in attendence at Dyott's lecture on behalf of England's Civil Aviation Department, had these comments to share; " ...in some ways its (the lectures) outstanding feature has been the modesty of the lecturer. I have known Mr. Dyott for some years, especially in the very early days of aviation. It was something new, and therefore he went into that. When it became a dull and monotonous amusement, as it is nowadays, he proceeded to find more amusement in out-of-the-way parts of South America."

Throughout his life experiences, Dyott, without reservation or exception, appears to have sought the unknown through adventure and discovery, consistently documenting his adventures. In *Silent Highways of the Jungle: Being the Adventures of an Explorer in the Andes and Reaches of the Upper Amazon (1922)*, Dyott begins his narration with an outline of the journey and preliminary arrangements. He describes the climates and altitudes in all of the regions he travels through from Peru to the Amazon. With vivid detail, Dyott talks about his modes of transportation, which include traveling by mule, by foot, and in a canoe. Dyott also relates an account of the natives that he meets and the land all around him.

In Ecuador, Dyott successfully climbed the Tungurahua Volcano in 1924, during which he even witnessed an explosion. The Commander reached the summit of Sumaco Volcano in 1925 and was reportedly the first white man to have attempted to climb the Sangay Volcano also in 1925, having reached 150 meters below the craters rim prior to being turned back on his two attempts.

Two further works were published concerning Dyott's early adventures in Ecuador. The first, entitled *On the Trail of the Unknown: In the wilds of Ecuador and the Amazon. With plates and a map (1926)*,[198] in which Dyott describes his travels in the Ecuadorian Oriente, his stay among the headhunters of the Amazon and travel by jungle and river to Sumacu. The second work, *The Volcanoes of Ecuador Guideposts in Crossing South America,* was published in *National Geographic's* Volume 55, No. 1, January 1929 issue.

---

[198] It was also in 1926 that Dyott was nominated and elected as a member of The Explorers Club.

Dyott was well known for his expedition of 1927, as the second person too transverse the Amazonian "River of Doubt," following in the footsteps of the 1913-14 Roosevelt-Rondon Scientific Expedition.[199] After Roosevelt returned, Dyott was contracted to verify Roosevelt's claim of discovering the river, for which there had been some doubt that he had actually discovered the river and made the expedition. To settle the dispute, Dyott led a second trip down the river, confirming Roosevelt's discoveries.

Dyott was married in 1928 to Persis Stevens Wright, who was from a well-known family in New York Society. *The New York Times* of 11 Feb 1928 announced the couple's plans under the headline *DYOTT TO WED BEFORE SEEKING LOST EXPLORER* which read in part ... "George Miller Dyott, who has done extensive exploring in South America, and Miss Persis Stevens Wright, daughter of Mr. and Mrs. Lawrence W. Wright of Skyfield, Merrick, L.I., whose engagement was announced last July, will be married on Feb. 17 in Old Trinity Church, this city. The couple obtained their marriage license at the Municipal Building yesterday. The day following Mr. Dyott and his bride will sail for Brazil, where the explorer will start on an expedition to find the missing British explorer, Colonel P. H. Fawcett.

"In the interview the bride-to-be, twenty-four year old granddaughter of E. Kellogg Wright and Albert Gallatin Wright, was quoted as saying ... "I shall be with Mr. Dyott in Río de Janeiro for only a short time, for he plans to leave there as soon as possible after our arrival to search for Colonel Fawcett. I feel positive he will find Colonel Fawcett. It may take him six to eight months, and to me that seems like a very long time, but I am sure in the end it will end in success for him in his quest." Miss Wright clarified that her brother, David Hamilton Wright, was to follow them to Brazil on the next steamer and that he would then accompany her back to New York,[200] while her new husband was on expedition. Miss Wright's disappointment was clear ... "I would love to go with Mr. Dyott, but he thinks I should not go."

Commander Dyott at the time of his marriage was forty-five, almost double that of his bride and according to *The New York Times* article ... "Mr. Dyott served in the World War as a squadron commander in the British Naval Air Service. He returned last spring, after an expedition down the River of Doubt."[201]

---

[199] The Roosevelt-Rondon Scientific Expedition was jointly led by Theodore Roosevelt and Cândido Rondon to be the first explorers of the 1000 mile long river which was later renamed Río Roosevelt, located in a remote area of the Brazilian Amazon basin.

[200] Dyott's new bride and her brother would return to the United States sailing from Santos on the *SS Southern Cross* 13 Mar 1928 bound for New York, where they arrived the 28th of the same month.

[201] *The New York Times* 11 Feb 1928

Similar to the Dyott lineage in England, Miss Wright's ancestry was deeply entrenched within early American historical events including the Boston Tea Party, American Revolution, War of 1812, Louisiana Purchase[202] and Lewis & Clark Expedition.[203] Although not related to the Wright brothers as one might assume, Miss Wright was a direct descendant of Albert Gallatin, US Secretary of the Treasury from 1801 until 1814 and Major General Ebenezer Stevens, a Son of the American Revolution.

Always in the public eye, Dyott's expeditions, adventures, exploits and personal life was all well publicized in *The New York Times*. On this occasion, it would appear that his notoriety worked against the Commander, for at the time Dyott was involved in a legal dispute concerning the company Travel Films Incorporated. The following was published in the 24 Mar 1928 issue of *The New York Times* under the headline *DYOTT LOSES HERE IN FILM LAWSUIT* ... "Commander George M. Dyott, explorer, who sailed on Feb. 18 for the Brazilian jungles in an effort to find Colonel Fawcett, English explorer, lost for several years, may find a judgement against him here when he returns if a decision yesterday by Supreme Court Justice Ford in a suit by Gilbert C. Johnston for $3,416 damages for breach of an agreement is upheld."

The article continues to relate how Mr. Johnston of London, was suing Commander Dyott over the liquidation of his holdings in Travel Films Incorporated, a company in which Dyott was a large stockholder and managing director. Johnston alleged that he bought preferred stock and bonds on representations made by Dyott as to the earnings and assets of the company. Johnson further alleged that no payments were made, and nothing was done to make the business a success or to protect the stockholders.

---

[202] The Louisiana Purchase started with a US desire to purchase New Orleans from the French, who in turn chose to sell the entire territory that stretched from New Orleans into Canada. In 1803 the US bought the Louisiana Territory from France, adding over eight hundred thousand square miles to the United States at a cost of approximately fifteen million dollars, about three cents an acre. President Jefferson's Secretary of the Treasury, Albert Gallatin, was able to somehow manage the budget (over eighty-million dollars in debt) so the United States could pay France the fifteen million dollars and still maintain the budget.

[203] Albert Gallatin was not only instrumental in the purchase of the Louisiana Territory, but he also arranged financing for the exploration of these new lands. Gallatin considered the sale of public lands as the best way to rid the nation of its debt and The Louisiana Territory provided the country with the land to sell. Gallatin funded expeditions through the Louisiana Territory so that the territory could be better described increasing its value. Among the explorers of the region were Meriwether Lewis and William Clark, their guide Toussant Charbonneau and his two Indian wives, Hidatsa and Sacagawea. During their travels they found the headwaters of the Missouri River, which was the confluence of three rivers. Lewis and Clark named these rivers after three prominent individuals of their time ... Jefferson, Madison, and Gallatin.

Johnston asserted that the explorer agreed to give Johnston the value of his bonds in return for a release of all claims. A demand for payment was made, but Commander Dyott said he was unable to make payment but he "would try to do so."

It appears that when Johnson's attorneys read in *The New York Times* that Dyott was to be married on Feb. 17 and would sail for Brazil the following day, they wrote to the explorer threatening suit if payment was not tendered. Dyott responded through his attorney that there would be no payment made. On the evening before Commander Dyott's marriage, Johnson's attorney dispatched a law clerk from his office, to serve a summons on Commander Dyott. What happened that night was the subject of a motion by Dyott's attorney attempting to vacate the service. Dyott had claimed he was not served and the process server claimed that Dyott had denied that he was Commander Dyott, purportedly hoping to have service made on the wrong person. According to *The New York Times* article the Judge "...said he believed the process server's version of the incident was the most probable one. Unless an answer is filed within the legal time a judgement can be entered against the explorer by default."

Despite pending legal action and Colonel Fawcett's wishes that no one should come looking for them if they failed to return, Dyott mounted his expedition from Río de Janeiro in search of the missing English explorer Colonel Percy Fawcett, in the Matto Grosso jungle of Brazil. The *Los Angeles Times* of 11 Mar 1928 carried the following short announcement ... "The Royal Geographical Society, famous among British scientific organizations, announces through its official publication, *The Geographical Journal*, that it will follow 'with high expectation' Commander George M. Dyott's expedition to rescue the missing British explorer, Col. P. H. Fawcett."

On expedition Dyott filed dispatches for the North American Newspaper Alliance, which published his accounts. During the expedition Dyott was held captive by Indians and barely escaped with his life. When Dyott and his men finally emerged from the jungle months later they appeared sick, thin, bearded and apparently mosquito ravaged. Dyott believed that he had found evidence that confirmed Fawcett had been killed by the Aloique Indians, but the strength of his evidence appeared to collapse on closer scrutiny by Fawcett's family. The mystery of Fawcett's disappearance remained unresolved. Dyott later published a book about this expedition called *Manhunting in the Jungle, Being the Story of a Search for Three Explorers Lost in the Brazilian Wilds (1930)*. The book was later adapted to film as *Manhunt in the Jungle (1958)*.

In 1929 Dyott trapped wild animals in India, which he later donated to the Bronx Zoo, for a documentary in which he played himself called *Hunting Tigers in India.* Filmed in India on the A. S. Vernay expedition under the auspices of the American Museum of Natural History, the film was billed as "the first all talking nature picture" that was reportedly shown to the First Lady Mrs. Hoover, in the White House theater. A review of the documentary by F.D. Wilson on 23 Dec 1929 stated in part ... "Commander George Dyott who went to India with the Vernay-Faunthorpe expedition talks about his trip and shows you pictures of it. His record is a good travel log, wonderfully vivid ... Some of Dyott's facts are interesting. Indians never kill ordinary elephants, regarding them as almost sacred because of their capacity for work. They kill only rogue elephants, lonely, vindictive bulls who have become killers when driven out of their tribe by the hostility of tribal females. If an Indian kills a rhinoceros without permission, he is fined; if he kills another, he is executed."

Once again *The New York Times* would tout the story of Dyott's exploits and upcoming return to New York under the 14 Jun 1930 headline of *DYOTT IS BRINGING MENAGERIE FOR SON* ... "Commander George M. Dyott, the explorer, is on his way home from India with a baby menagerie which he will present to his 5 months' old son, whom he has never seen. Since the Dyott baby might be at a loss how to take care of a menagerie, it has been arranged to give the animals to the Bronx Zoo, in the boy's name ... The gift has been accepted by the zoo authorities. . . The trip from which Commander Dyott is now returning was an eight month's journey in the jungles of India in which he took sound pictures of the beasts.

"Mrs. Dyott accompanied him on the first part of his journey, but later returned to the home of her mother ... Their son was born on Jan. 22 and was named George Richard Burnaby Dyott. Mrs. Dyott cabled the news to her husband, and he cabled back his joy and his intention to give his son a baby menagerie. The animals which Commander Dyott is bringing include a baby elephant, a baby tiger, two baby bears, a baby monkey, two baby peacocks and two baby leopards. The baby leopards are chaperoned by a full grown leopard, which has an ugly disposition and is known as 'the evil spirit.' None of the crew will go near it, and it has scratched Commander Dyott severely ... 'All the animals have taken to ocean travel except the smallest leopard,' said Mrs. Dyott. 'It became very sick and had to sleep with Commander Dyott in his cabin and be fed every three hours.'"

Dyott's next major expedition occurred in 1932 and took the Commander back to South America and Ecuador, resulting in the film *Savage Gold (1933)*. Based on a true story, *Savage Gold* is a filmed record of Commander Dyott's jungle expedition into the Amazon jungle to find an archaeologist who had vanished three years previously. The expedition runs into a tribe of warlike Jivaro headhunters, who are determined to add the expedition members' heads to their collection.[204] One scene's focus is on the tribe's head shrinking ritual, with the process shown in close gruesome detail. Dyott co-wrote the story and played himself in the film.

Dyott returned to New York on 24 Jan 1933 aboard the *Santa Clara*, which sailed from La Libertad, Ecuador on 7 Jan 1933. Dyott was passenger number eleven on the ships *Manifest of Alien Passengers for the United*

---

[204] In the real story, the archaeologist, a Mr. Schweitzer, was found to have been murdered by a tribe of Brazilian headhunters.

States. Passenger number twelve was none other than Eric Erskine Loch. Dyott's movie finally came out in July of 1933 and for some unknown reason, this was also the year that Dyott resigned his membership in The Explorers Club.

The New York Times ran an article under the headline *DYOTT FINDS WILDS AWAIT COLONISTS* on 25 Jan 1933 which states in part ... "Commander George M. Dyott returned on the liner *Santa Clara* yesterday from an exploration into the forest country of Ecuador to survey the possibilities of colonization. On familiar ground, Commander Dyott spent considerable time with tribes of Shuaros Indians, an ancient race with many strange customs and beliefs. Traveling about 2,000 miles of jungle land during five months, Commander Dyott made moving pictures of everything he saw, including pictures of the hideous Indian custom of head-shrinking, by which heads of slain enemies are prepared for souvenirs. He also brought back with him ornaments and Indian impedimenta, much of which he said he would turn over to the Museum of the American Indian, Heye Foundation. Accompanying Commander Dyott was Captain E. Erskine Loch, retired British Army officer, and Walter Lewisohn, the son of Mrs. H. Bartow Farr, 10 Gracie , New York. They were with him in Ecuador and returned on the same ship yesterday."

While researching Dyott's life story, it quickly became apparent, judging from the passenger lists that I could discover, that travel, adventure and exploration were in Dyott's blood. I counted no less than twenty-six verifiable ocean voyages, but none for more than a year after Dyott's arrival on the *Santa Clara* in January of 1933. It appears that the Commander was actively planning yet another expedition during this time period, to the South Seas ... "In search of giant lizards, wild dogs, hairy-eared rhinoceroses and other strange creatures of the South Seas, the 500-ton steam yacht *Southwind* will sail on a 30,000-mile cruise next week, Commander George M. Dyott, explorer and traveler, announced yesterday."[205]

Dyott's movements continued to elude me, as I have found no evidence that his planned expedition to the South Seas occurred,[206] until Dyott arrived in England on 27 Aug 34 from New York. Dyott then traveled back across the Atlantic aboard the *Pennland*, arriving in New York on 2 Oct 1934.[207] Within months Dyott returned to England arriving from New York on 21 Jan 1935. Somehow ... Dyott had made his way to Ecuador and from there, aboard the *Santa Rita*, Dyott returned to New York and his ever larger family on 15 Oct 1935.

Perhaps as an action to connect with or convey his feelings to his young sons, Dyott's last book appears to have taken on a drastically different tone,

---

[205] *The New York Times* 18 Jan 1934

[206] I would later learn from the Commander's son Michael ... "The *Southwind* never sailed due to an alcoholic skipper."

[207] Ten months prior to the birth of his third son, Michael.

character and genre from his previous works ... a children's book ... *Nip and Tuck: A true story of two little bears (1935)*, is illustrated throughout with black-and-white photos. This book tells the story of Nip and Tuck, two bear cubs Dyott rescued after their mother died. These Himalayan bear cubs were part of the animals from India that Dyott brought back to the United States and donated to New York's Bronx Zoo in the name of his eldest son. It was also quite common for Commander Dyott to donate native items from his expeditions to various museums, including the Smithsonian.

Once again Dyott's method of travel eludes me ... but at some point Dyott had returned to Ecuador, as he departed Guayaquil aboard the *Santa Inez* on 22 Aug 1936 arriving back in New York on 1 Sep 1936. Dyott's occupation on the passenger manifest was noted as an ... "explorer." Besides this manifest, little public record can be found of Dyott's activities after he wrote his last book. What is known is that Dyott retired to Ecuador sometime afterwards, where he lived most of his latter life farming on "Hacienda Delta," Dyott's rain forest plantation and self-built house outside Santo Domingo de los Colorados ... until World War II intervened.

During the World War II years of 1939 through 1945 a substantiated record of Dyott's life, actions and adventures appear almost nonexistent. Three separate unsubstantiated accounts all have Dyott operating throughout the war as a British Intelligence Officer.[208] One account has the Commander operating out of India, another out of South America,[209] while Brunner's account has Dyott moving to London during the war ... ultimately I was able to obtain evidence that substantiates portions of Brunner's account.

After returning to Ecuador in late 1936 or 1937 it appears Dyott remained in Ecuador, until 14 Sep 1942 when the Commander appeared at the US border crossing in Brownsville, Texas. It was then that Dyott entered the United States from Mexico en route to the British Embassy in Washington. From there, Dyott traveled to Trinidad where he caught the Cunard White Star steamship line's *City of Exeter*, which arrived in Liverpool, England, on 23 Nov 1942. From this point forward, on all passenger lists, customs and immigration forms, Dyott is listed as a "British Government Official" with an address in care of the "Ministry of Supply, London."[210]

Shortly thereafter, on 15 Jan 1943, Dyott sailed again, this time from Gourock, Scotland, to Canada, aboard the *SS Andes*. Dyott then entered the

---

[208] The fact that Commander Dyott's military record has been classified, and marked as sealed for 75 years, would seem to indicate Dyott might very well have been in British Intelligence.

[209] Michael Dyott also held this belief, writing ... "My dad did projects in South America for the government, mostly the United States of America, but I don't think he returned to England.

[210] The Ministry of Supply was formed in 1939 to co-ordinate the supply of equipment to all three British armed forces. However, a separate ministry was responsible for aircraft production and with Dyott's background it would have been more plausible for him to have been assigned there instead.

United States by land, crossing the border at St. Albans, Vermont on 23 Jan 1943. As Dyott traveled south on his way to New York on a typically clear, crisp, sunny day in January, he could not help looking to the east and encounter a view of Mount Mansfield with its snow covered wooded slopes and rocky heights, the highest mountain in the State of Vermont.

I cannot ascertain what occurred during the ensuing three years, but the next travel record I encountered shows Dyott departing New York in November of 1945 on the *Queen Elizabeth*, that arrived in Southhampton, England, on 27 Nov 1945. A month later, Dyott again set sail on the *Queen Mary* bound back to New York where he arrived on 3 Jan 1946. Whether Dyott traveled back to Ecuador at this time is unclear. However, at some point he had returned to England as Dyott once again departed aboard the *SS Port Ferry* on 23 Jan 1947, arriving back in New York on 3 Feb 1947.[211]

For reasons to be explained later, Dyott came out of retirement and began a search for Inca gold in Ecuador. Dyott made two expeditions into the Llanganati Mountains of Ecuador during 1947 that continued into 1948.[212] Commencing in early 1947 [213] and departing from Píllaro, the Commander made expeditions into the Llanganatis keeping meticulous records and journals as was his practice. In March of 1947 Dyott suffered a broken leg or ankle in the mountains and was stranded there for five months. Dyott the relentless explorer, returned to the mountains again in November of the same year. Dyott's last expedition into the Llanganatis ended with a stomach malady later to be diagnosed as bowel cancer. Pages of Dyott's meticulous journals covering his Llanganati expeditions, eerily similar to the *Cedula Real*, *Derrotero de Valverde*, *Valverde Map* if one ever existed and Spruces journals, mysteriously vanished.[214]

---

[211] The dates of Dyott's travel play an important role in ascertaining his whereabouts in order to confirm or dispel the plausibility of events that follow.

[212] Discrepancies abound on the exact dates of Dyott's expeditions. Honigsbaum in *Valverdes Gold* indicates Dyott's two expeditions were September 1947 and February 1948. Brunner indicates that he met Commander Dyott in the Llanganatis during 1946. Michael Dyott states that his father's papers and journals of 1948 & 1949, the years of his expeditions, disappeared.

[213] I have changed this date from 1946 ... the date Brunner indicates Dyott made his first expedition, being hurt in March 1946. Judging from the time-line of Dyott's travels, I believe Brunner may be in error on the year, therefore I changed the date to coincide with popular belief.

[214] Michael Dyott had this to say about his fathers missing journals ... "Back in 1968 my dad packed up his Llanganati papers and journals of 1948 & 1949 and put them at the British Embassy for me to pick up. They disappeared." Through other accounts it appears that the Commander's missing journals have resurfaced and appear to be in the possession of Andrés Fernandez Salvador, how or when they were obtained is not clear.

It would be 1963 when the stomach malady that had ended Dyott's last expedition into the Llanganatis would require major medical attention. Dyott's beloved "Hacienda Delta" was signed over to a friend in exchange for payment of the Commander's required prostate cancer operation. In 2012 Michael Dyott would proudly proclaim ... "Hacienda Delta has gone from a rain forest plantation to a muddy slum suburb of Santo Domingo, but my dad's self built house still stands tall and indestructible." Sometime between 1968 and 1970 Dyott left Ecuador returning to New York to live with his wife.[215]

Dyott, totally convinced of the existence of the treasure deposit, whether referred to as the Llanganati, Atahualpa, or Rumiñahui Treasure, having abandoned his own search, passed the mantle to Eugene K. Brunner in 1966. What can be ascertained with certainty is that after World War II and his Llanganati search, Dyott lived most of his latter life farming on his "Hacienda Delta" in Ecuador.

Dyott died at the age of eighty-nine on 2 Aug 1972 in Babylon, Long Island. Commander George Miller Dyott was ultimately laid to rest in Valhalla, New York, leaving three sons that he had rarely seen,[216] George Richard Dyott [1930-1994], Mark Hamilton Dyott [1932-2011], both of New York, and Michael Stevens Dyott [born August 1935] of California. Mark, just like his father, enjoyed an interest in aviation and would later write proudly of the Commander's achievements in the field. Michael on the other hand, as his father before him, has on several occasions entered the Llanganati Mountains of Ecuador. Michael would later relate a childhood memory of his "dad" visiting New York, when Michael was but a twelve-year-old boy ... "I was the one stated by my dad to be the one who would follow in his footsteps."[217]

In all fairness to the memory of the Commander and the Dyott family, it is important to understand that although many might consider Commander Dyott to have been a "no good," someone who had left his wife and children to explore and then retire in Ecuador, they hold a point of view not shared by Mrs. Dyott and her youngest son. Michael would also write ... "It should be understood that being of a British manor house, the life of such a

---

[215] As a family friend and neighbor would state ... "George was an explorer who was absent from home many years at a time. It was only when George became ill and was dying that he returned home and Mrs. Dyott cared for him until his death." *JF 18 Aug 2011*. The Commander's son Michael would later clarify the circumstances ..."Of course it was I who searched out his whereabouts, found him in the monte of Ecuador and, eventually talked him into coming back to his wife and New York."

[216] "I should start by saying I can only remember seeing my father twice in my life, once when I was perhaps three years old at Merrick, Long Island and again when he was eighty-nine years old at Babylon, Long Island." Quote from - Mark Dyott, February 2006.

[217] Letter of Michael Dyott May 2012

person, in 1900, was quite different from what we consider 'responsible' today. That's why I wasn't down on my father like my brothers [218] (but not my mom) were."

I cannot help but find myself reminded of the parallels between the life and times of the adventurers and explorers, Colonel E. C. Brooks and Commander G. M. Dyott. By definition an adventurer thrives on the excitement associated with the danger arising from an unusual, exciting, and daring experience ... while the explorer travels through an unknown area to learn, examine and scrutinize everything about it. It is painfully obvious that the conditions, hardships, deprivations and solitude these explorers, and their families for that matter, faced due to their chosen lifestyle, was not consistent with any desire they might have had to be "family men." Brooks and Dyott to their credit, at least made an attempt to meld family with their chosen occupations. In the end the contradictions between a lifestyle of an adventurer and explorer naturally imposed on their relationships so that any possibility of a "normal family life" ... was destined to fail.

■ ■ ■

Our knowledge concerning Commander Dyott's involvement with the Llanganati treasure, what possessed him to come out of retirement, what he discovered and what he passed on, must be pieced together from the second hand accounts of Andrés Fernandez Salvador and Eugene Konrad Brunner, as related by author's who utilized Salvador, Brunner and others as sources for their own books and stories that record the story of Commander Dyott's involvement. Ultimately, we have available Eugene Brunner's first hand account as written in November 1979 in his manuscript *El Tesoro en las Misteriosas Montañas de Llanganati*. Viewed in their entirety, the reader can develop his or her own theories as to the exact truth, it probably lies somewhere in-between.

■ ■ ■

It is now the opportune moment to provide the reader with a description of another general map of the Cerro Hermoso area. Drafted by Commander Dyott in January 1949, Dyott's map represents the ridge line just across the Río Topo and north-north-east of Cerro Hermoso (Yurac- Llanganati), commencing in the west at Lake Auca Cocha and the Cascada y Golpe de Limpis Pongo on Guzmán's map, and bounded on the east by Cerro Negro (Yana - Llanganati) and Las Torres Mountain. Not represented on Dyott's map is what lies north of the depicted ridge line ... which would be the area detailed on the right upper portion of Loch's expedition sketch mentioned in the previous chapter.

---

[218] "My other two brothers didn't seem to be interested in our dad's life nor that he was somewhere in this world." Michael Dyott letter of May 2012.

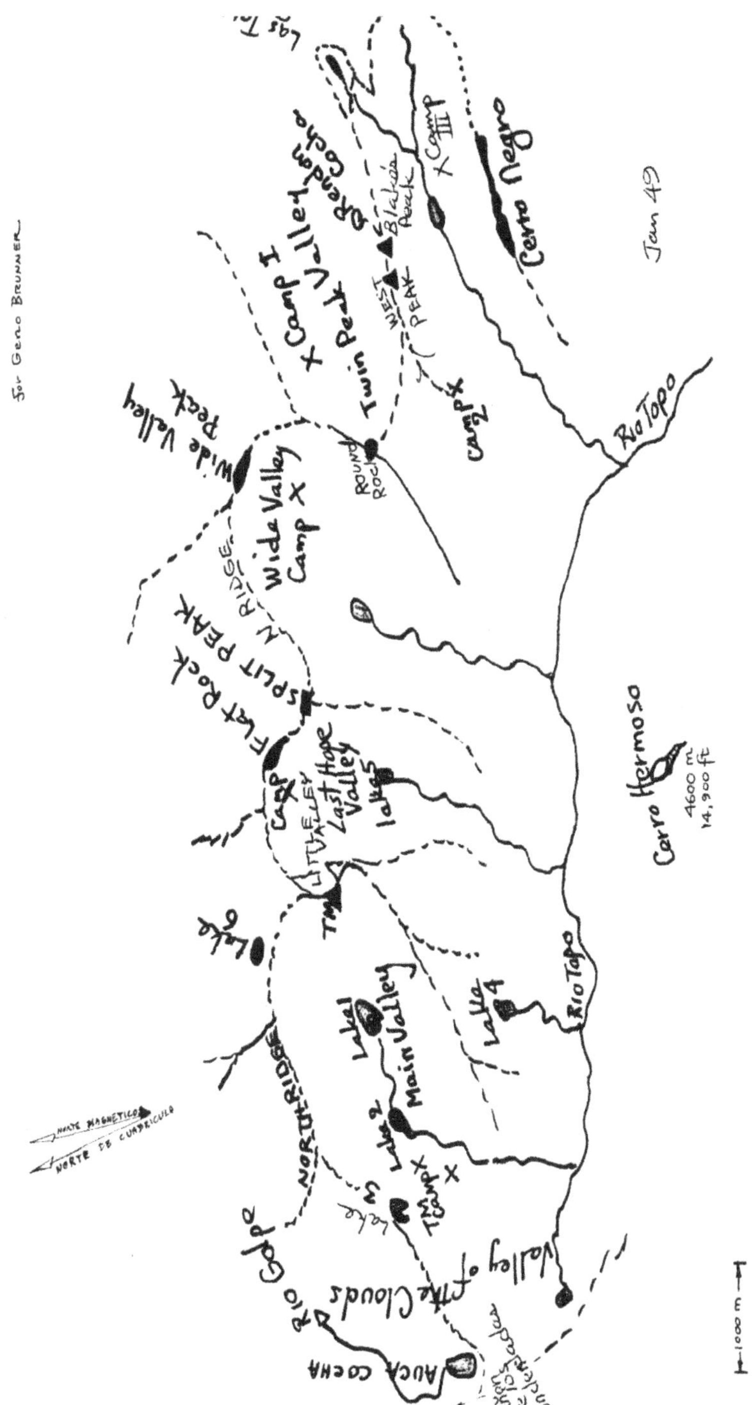

Dyott Map of Area North of Cerro Hermoso

Apparently this map was utilized and annotated, as at least two separate handwriting styles exist on the map, by Dyott's son Michael. Campsites and peaks are clearly detailed on the map, while solid lines represent rivers and dotted lines indicate the routes traveled. This copy was at some point presented to Eugene Brunner, by someone who had attached a note which stated ... "Diego Arias had this map with him on an expedition in the Llanganatis"!

■ ■ ■

Andrés Fernandez Salvador, born in Quito Ecuador on 15 Jun 1924, was a son of Ricardo Fernandez Salvador del Campo. The Fernandez Salvador family, one of the most prominent in Ecuador, was originally from Villoslada in Spain. Andrés parents owned a large ranch with some 44,000 heads of cattle which was sold in 1930. Several transactions over the years were reducing their fortune, so the family acquired the mineral springs in Machachi Ecuador.[219]

Apparently through an article in the *Los Angeles Examiner,* Andrés became aware of the legend of hidden treasure in the mysterious mountains east of Píllaro, the Llanganatis. This interest had reportedly been revived again in 1948 when Andrés Father showed him a copy of Spruce's *Notes of a Botanist.* In Quito Andrés had the opportunity to speak on several occasions with Luciano Andrade Marín Baca [1893-1972], author of *Viaje a las Misteriosas Montanas de Llanganati: Expedicion Italo-Ecuatoriana Boschetti - Andrade Marin 1933-1934*, who appears to have motivated Andrés to take up the search. Since then Andrés has made numerous expeditions into the Llanganatis that commenced from Píllaro. In many of his expeditions the difficulty of the terrain had caused serious events, risks and catastrophes.

In 1952 Andrés went into the Llanganatis for the first time with his cousin Luis del Campo Fernandez Salvador for a month long expedition. They had many difficulties and could not find the "deep dry ravine" and the mountain of Margasitas. Using the map of Atanasio de Guzmán they sometimes lost their way in the dense fog. They saw three peaks, possibly those mentioned in the famous *Derrotero de Valverde,* to the north in the Roncadores region [220] and explored more in that direction, with no success.

Afterwards, Salvador made a few more trips into the Llanganatis, one of which was in 1954 with Guido Boschetti Calle. During this expedition it poured rain for thirteen days in a row, as a result they made little or no

[219] The family marketed the water brand Güitig, slightly salty, carbonated mineral spring water which penetrates, filters and flows through the hard core and subterranean passages of the Cotopaxi Volcano. Güitig is well known in the marketplace and contains an extraordinary combination of the healthy minerals calcium, magnesium, sodium bicarbonate and silica. However, during my travels in Ecuador, I personally could never acquire a taste for Güitig and drank soda or fresh squeezed juices instead.

[220] The same three peaks Loch explored.

progress. The return was tragic, with ice water to the waist in certain sections and one of the porters (cargadores) fell off a deep precipice into a river and died. Again in 1955 Andrés returned to the Llanganatis joining Boschetti and eight porters. For two weeks they tried not to lose their way until finally reaching the Valle Prohibido [221] (Forbidden Valley in English), locating some steps carved in stone, possibly they concluded, leading to an abandoned mine. On the way back they found the frozen corpse of the porter they had lost the previous year.

Later in 1956, with Tulio Boschetti the father of Guido and eight porters, Andrés arrived again at Valle Prohibido using an antique map of the area provided by Andrade Marín. Andrés final expedition with the Boschetti's was in 1958, again with Tulio Boschetti and eleven porters, spending three weeks in the Llanganatis. They explored a lagoon with white stairs and an island in the center which drained through trenches, without finding anything else of significance.

During 1958 Andrés was working for his father at Güitig and traveled frequently between Quito and Guayaquil. One day the story goes, Andrés was asked by his father to deliver some letters or papers to a friend in Santo Domingo de los Colorados, who turned out to be Commander George Dyott. It appears Andrés became enthralled with Dyott's life stories and visited him regularly on his trips to and from the coast. Over time Dyott revealed a portion of the information that had come to his attention and peeked his personal interest in the Llanganati treasure.

Andrés Fernandez Salvador over the years has enjoyed repeating the enchanting stories Dyott related, but to my knowledge has never published that information, although Andrés has professed to have written a manuscript. However, Salvador has given many interviews over the years, most of which appear to be alcohol induced, with authors utilizing him as a source, through which we can ascertain his latest version of Dyott's involvement and material. It appears in my opinion however, that with the passage of time, printed stories as related by Salvador have been embellished, placing himself at the center of the story while taking full credit as the central character and downplaying others involvement, especially that of Eugene Konrad Brunner.

■ ■ ■

Eugene Konrad Brunner, born in Switzerland to a Swiss mother and German father during 1915, moved to Ecuador from Europe in 1938. Almost immediately Brunner heard of the treasure legend and a book published the year before about an expedition into the Llanganatis. In Quito Brunner purchased Luciano Andrade Marín's 1937 Edition of *Viaje a las Misteriosas Montanas de Llanganati.* Over the ensuing years, Andrade's book became Brunner's holy grail, I would not be surprised if he could have recited the entire book word for word.

---

[221] At the base of the "three peaks" previously mentioned.

That same year Brunner made his first expedition into the Llanganatis. Leaving as all treasure hunters before him from the town of Píllaro, with three porters and a guide named José Ignacio Quinteros who had also accompanied Captain Eric Erskine Loch on his first expedition into the Llanganatis in March of 1936. On the second day Brunner's group arrived at the first major landmark of "Lagunas de Anteojos" which appeared exactly as described in the *Derrotero de Valverde*. One can only imagine the exhilaration and adrenaline rush that treasure hunters must experience upon seeing the landmarks of their treasure guide for the first time.

Brunner's expedition advanced to Parca Yacu and Pava Micuna where the weather changed to days of torrential rain. Brunner's first expedition ended an utter failure, the food ran out and he was drenched to the bone having been ill prepared with no rain gear. Brunner would later write that ... "the passion of the Llanganatis had seized me ... and would not let me loose."

Subsequently another expedition was mounted in 1939, under the same conditions, ill prepared and with inappropriate equipment the expedition did not even arrive at Brunner's final camp site of the previous year, once again defeated by the inhospitable rain and fog of the Llanganatis.

Brunner's third expedition into the Llanganatis was in March of 1941 traveling through Auca Cocha and Pan de Azúcar on modern maps, Zunchu Urcu on Guzmáns map, Brunner advanced to Soguillas. In this zone Brunner discovered evidence that the ancient Indians traveled in these mountains. He found portions of the "Camino del Inca" (Inca road) and a large Tola (Inca burial mound) in the form of a round hill, built with pyramids of stones. Once again, Brunner's supplies ran out bringing his expedition to an abrupt end.

Brunner met Dyott deep in the Llanganati Mountains during 1947 [222] and as Brunner would tell, became friends. They met and visited each others camp and as they were competitors didn't share what they knew, although each of them made inquires about the others information. On one such occasion in Dyott's camp slightly north west of Cerro Hermoso on Zunchu Urcu, Brunner recalls Dyott stating that ... "if on your travels in these mountains you find a formation of rocks that resembles a reclining woman, or, if you find a large square hole, do let me know and I will share in the benefits I obtain." It would not be until 1964 that Brunner would make the first of these discoveries, the second discovery coming a year later in 1965.

Bitten by the adventure and explorer bug, Brunner would make more than forty expeditions covering a span of nearly fifty years, investigating the Llanganatis, purportedly becoming the explorer with the best chance of discovering the Llanganati treasure. Brunner's background, involvement, explorations and discoveries relating to the Llanganati treasure are extensively detailed throughout this book, like never before.

■ ■ ■

---

[222] Once again this date has been changed from 1946, when Brunner states the two met.

Brunner and Salvador at some point had met and become extremely close friends as well. Brunner knew nothing specific about Dyott's material until 1962 when Andrés told Brunner a small portion of the story which he had heard from Dyott concerning two mariners ... Barth Blacke [223] and George Edwin Chapman. Brunner writes in his manuscript ... "Andrés Fernandez Salvador met Commander Dyott who over a period of time showed him a portion of Blacke's papers. Andrés then later told me the story more or less and only to a point where it suited him, because at that time we were not partners in the exploration of the Llanganati."

Then in 1963 Andrés told Brunner that he intended to make an expedition to the Llanganatis by helicopter for aerial reconnaissance and to take photographs. Andrés flew into the Llanganatis in a small four person Cessna CH-1C helicopter [224] he had purportedly leased from the Ecuadorian Air Force [FAE] to survey and take photos. Disaster struck Salvador's expedition and the helicopter crashed behind Cerro Hermoso on a small island in the Río Topo, stranding Andrés with his two companions.

Slightly different versions of the crash story appear to exist. Consistent throughout is the year of the crash being 1963,[225] location of the crash site on the northwest face of Cerro Hermoso in the Río Topo, number of people on board was three, that it was a military helicopter of the FAE and that they were stranded for over a month ... beyond that the stories diverge.

Salvador's version of the crash is related through his conversations with the author of *Sweat of the Sun, Tears of the Moon* Peter Lourie and with Mark Honigsbaum author of *Valverde's Gold.* According to Honigsbaum, Andrés was accompanied by a young Indian pilot straight out of flight school and another explorer, while Lourie states an Air Force pilot and an old prospector. Lourie quotes from his conversations with Salvador in early 1980, that Andrés climbed Cerro Hermoso discovering what could be the "socavón" of the *Derrotero de Valverde.* Not having explored inside the tunnel or cave, Salvador sent expeditions later to discover if water ran through it as in the *Derrotero*. Whereas Honigsbaum relates, that in his conversations with Andrés some twenty years later, Salvador himself climbed Cerro Hermoso and discovered the "socavón," explored inside and

---

223 Blacke - Spelled in this manner by Brunner alone, in all other sources the name is spelled Blake. Spelled as Blacke throughout this book unless quoting from other authors. It would seem reasonable to assume that Brunner ... having viewed and copied from the original documents ... is utilizing the correct spelling.

224 Ecuador had recently acquired four to six Cessna CH-1C helicopters through the US Air Forces Military Assistance Program for foreign countries. After a decision to scrap the program, with production ceasing in December of 1962, the helicopters were delivered by Cessna in 1963.

225 Although one author, Peter Lourie, consistently mis-states the year as 1965 in latter portions of his book.

described the interior in detail, including that water ran through it, just as in the *Derrotero*.

It is also related in *Valverdes Gold* where "shortly before Dyott's death"[226] Salvador had chartered a helicopter to fly over Zunchu Urcu. Salvador is quoted as stating ... "I aligned the nose of the helicopter with the mountain to the south, and then instructed the pilot to turn a few degrees to the east. That's when I saw the silhouette of Topo Mountain exactly as it appears on Blake's map."

Neither author offered any indication of Brunner's involvement in the crash, rescue nor subsequent exploration and discoveries in the tunnel. Honigsbaum does relate however in *Valverde's Gold*, in a quote credited to Salvador regarding Brunner ... "I was the one who sent him to Cerro Hermoso, but Eugenio became fixated on the mountain. He wouldn't consider any other possibility." Salvador's mention of Brunner's fixation on Cerro Hermoso was indeed a fact. Similarly Brunner not considering "any other possibility"was also true, as every other possibility had previously been explored by Brunner in depth over a period of twenty-five years. Perhaps this was Salvador's attempt, through misinformation and misdirection, to direct future explorers away from Cerro Hermoso.

Both Lourie and Honigsbaum relate that poor weather conditions combined with the unavailability of parts to repair the helicopter in Ecuador, required that parts be obtained from Miami Florida, delaying Salvador's rescue. This appears to be a major discrepancy that raises two issues. Why wouldn't a helicopter rescue have been attempted considering Ecuador acquired up to five other helicopters at the same time? Even considering that perhaps the FAE's other helicopters were not in service for one reason or another ... why would the required part not be removed from an out of service helicopter to effect a rescue, instead of waiting for a part to arrive from the United States?

■ ■ ■

Brunner's version of events comes from his manuscript *El Tesoro en las Misteriosas Montañas de Llanganati* wherein Brunner relates that he learned weeks after the crash of his friend Andrés' situation in the Llanganatis. Fearing the worst, Brunner immediately left for Píllaro and made contact with Don Ricardo Fernandez Salvador in Quito, an old friend and Andrés father. Plans were made for a rescue or recovery expedition that was financed by Don Ricardo. Brunner set out several days later, after all his supplies were purchased and arrangements were made, to find his friend Andrés. Upon nearly arriving where Andrés had reportedly crashed, Brunner heard the roar of a helicopter heading away from the area toward Shell Mera, he realized that the helicopter had been repaired and able to take off, hopefully his friend was safe, so he returned to Píllaro.

---

226 The helicopter crash in fact took place five years prior to Dyott's leaving Ecuador and nine years prior to his death.

Brunner later traveled to Quito in order to check on his friend Andrés, who was staying with his mother. Andrés indicated that he had been accompanied by the pilot Major Luis Ortega and the brother of the pilot, who had built a camp that was stocked with a large quantity of equipment and supplies that had been parachuted in and they had to leave behind. Brunner also learned that the brother of the pilot had climbed the nearly 3000 foot vertical cliffs of Cerro Hermoso to retrieve one of the parachute drops that had fallen high up on the slopes and in so doing, found a sort of cave or tunnel that he did not explore.

The story goes that Andrés then told Brunner, that if he wanted to explore in the area he would provide funding and that all the supplies they had left behind were Brunner's to use. Brunner chose to utilize this new opportunity to explore a section of Cerro Hermoso that he had not been to before. A gentleman's agreement was entered into with funding being later provided by Andrés.

It would be January 1964 when Brunner returned to Andrés camp in the Llanganatis with five porters. He climbed the northeast slope of Cerro Hermoso,[227] found the tunnel and made an extensive exploration, inside and out. Brunner came to the conclusion that this tunnel was indeed the "socavón" mentioned in the *Derrotero de Valverde.*

■ ■ ■

"From thence as thou goest along thou shalt see the entrance of the socabón (tunnel), which is in the form of a church porch ... And if by chance the mouth of the socabón be closed with certain herbs which they call 'salvaje', remove them, and thou wilt find the entrance" ... so states the *Derrotero de Valverde*. Although I no longer have the photographs in my possession of the "socavón" taken by Eugene Brunner, I do have Brunner's colorful artists rendering. From my observations and recollection, the drawing coincides with Brunner's photographs perfectly, hard for anyone to say that the caves entrance does not look like an archway of a church partially overgrown by "salvaje."

On its own, Brunner's drawing of the "socavón" could represent any of the hundreds, if not thousands of caves to be found in the Llanganatis. What sets Brunner's cave apart, aside from meeting the physical description in the *Derrotero*, is its interior, which comports with the *Derrotero* as well ... "And to reach the third mountain, if thou canst not pass in front of the socabón, it is the same thing to pass behind it, for the water of the lake falls into it."

---

[227] Although the helicopter crash occurred on the northwest quadrant of Cerro Hermoso, the socavón and the route required to ascend the mountain is more to the east in the northeast quadrant. This location concurs with the indigenous guide, *Derrotero de Valverde* and the requirement that a furnace to melt metals was situated on a mountains southeast slope.

Brunner's Drawing of the Socavon

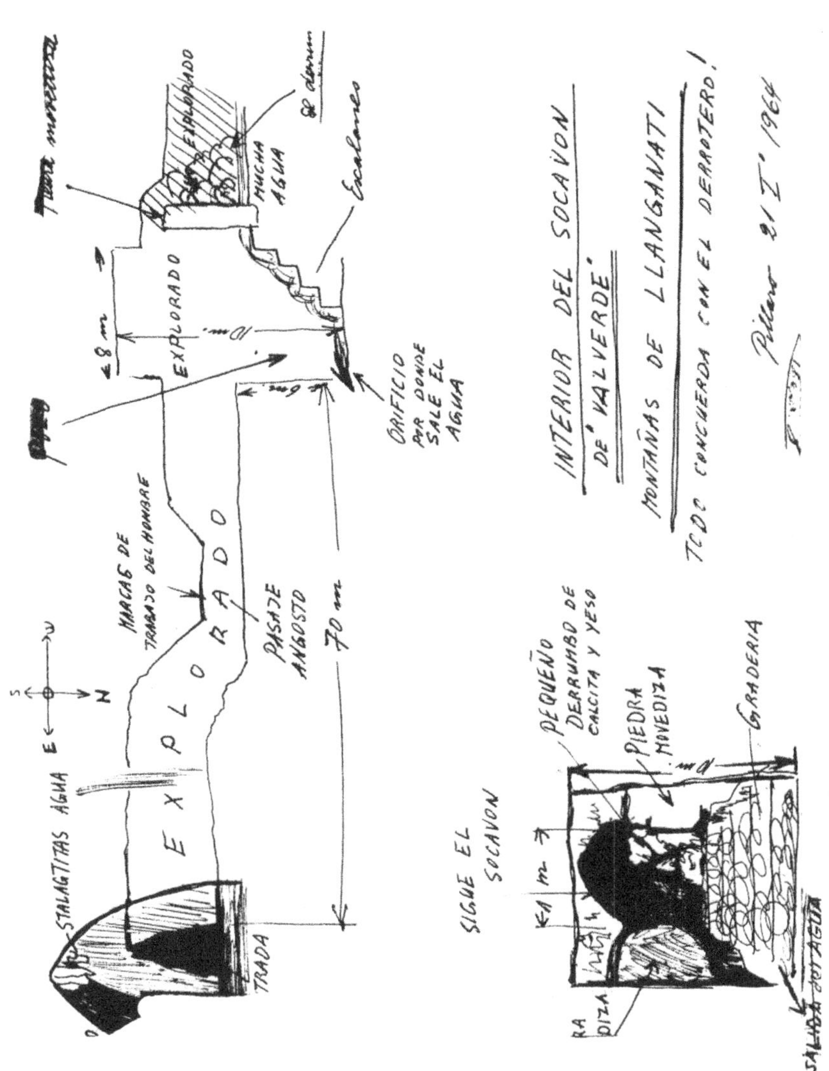

Brunner's Sketch of Socavon Interior

This cave was thoroughly explored, documented and detailed. Brunner explored 78 meters or 256 feet into this cave discovering evidence of the hand or work of man throughout. About 230 feet into the cave there is a large cavern, 33 feet high and 26 feet long with a twenty foot drop-off.

From the bottom of the drop-off, hand carved stairs climb up the other side, with water running down the stairs into an orifice. Brunner could not explore the three-foot wide tunnel any further, due to a small cave-in blocking his way at the top of these stairs. As well, a large perfectly fit moving stone, with water flowing around it, appeared to be some manner of a trap.

■ ■ ■

Higher up on the mountain and almost at the end of the vegetation, Brunner's next great discovery of significance, above the socavón, was the obvious zigzag of an ancient Indian path, cut into solid rock. It was at this point that for the first time, Brunner saw with his keen artist's eye the reclining woman which Dyott had mentioned eighteen years earlier in camp. The reclining woman Brunner had been seeking was not just a formation of rocks as Dyott had stated. Indeed, the reclining woman was the rock formation of the primary and two secondary peaks of the "Tres Cerros Llanganati,"[228] in which the human imagination found an image. Viewed from this specific angle by Brunner, Cerro Hermoso resembled a reclining woman!

Brunner took extensive photographs and made drawings of these discoveries. Again I no longer have the photographs in my possession of the "reclining woman" taken by Eugene Brunner, but I do still have his artists rendering which matches exactly! "Look for the Reclining Woman and all your problems are solved" ... Brunner was closing in on his ultimate destination ... Cerro Hermoso!

Peter Lourie, in his children's book *Lost Treasure of the Inca (1999)*, published Brunner's artist rendering of the reclining woman, in so doing, Lourie made in my opinion three grave errors. First, Brunner's signature and date were omitted, then the sketch was printed in reverse. Thirdly, the photograph Lourie published with the drawing is not the picture Brunner had with the rendering which was from the same angle (NE) and matched exactly. Lourie's photograph appears to be a distant view of Cerro Hermoso from a completely different location and angle, therefore it does not appear similar to Brunner's drawing or photograph.

■ ■ ■

---

[228] "It is quite plausible, therefore, that Valverde used it merely to indicate his Three Peaks, which were (Uanganati) 'touching' or joined together by their geological formation, and not as a name for the entire region."...Eric Erskine Loch in *Fever, Famine, and Gold.*

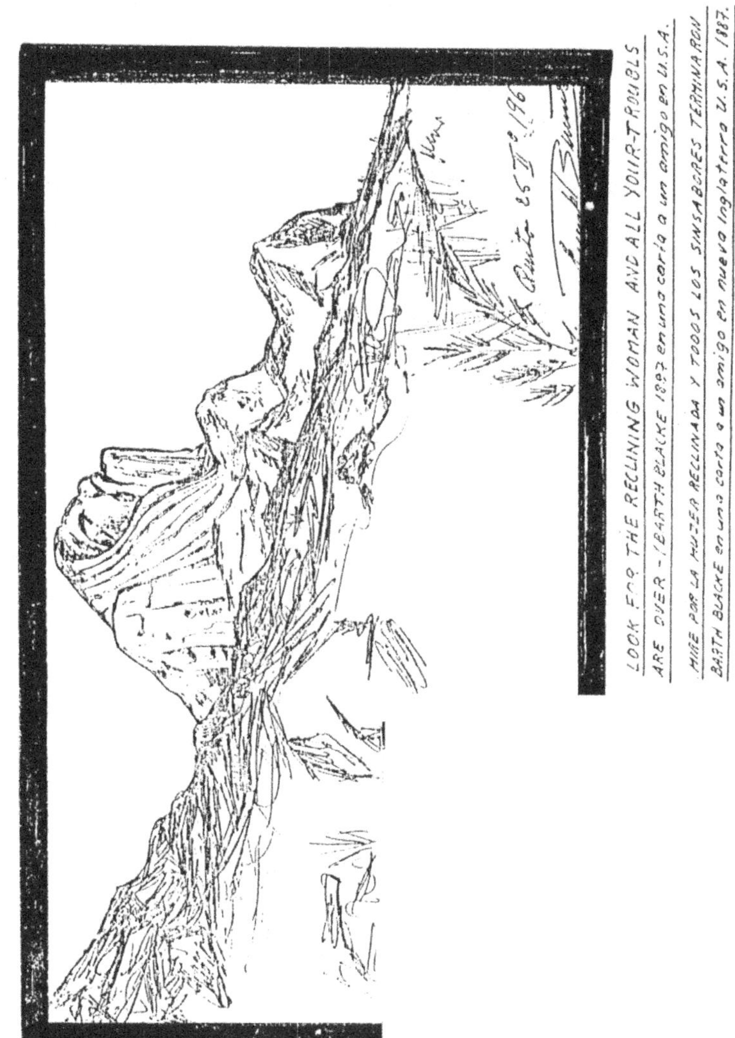

Brunner's Sketch of the Reclining Woman

The following year in 1965 Brunner discovered and documented a pit, or large square hole (guayra), which appeared consistent with the second landmark that Dyott had indicated in his statement at camp in 1946. Another Brunner discovery of 1965 was a small lake, at a higher elevation of roughly 14,500 feet on the southwest quadrant of Cerro Hermoso and southwest of the "socavón," which he named Lake Brunner. This discovery will be discussed in great detail in the next chapter.

■ ■ ■

In order to personally share his discoveries with the Commander, Brunner later traveled to Santo Domingo de los Colorados and Hacienda Delta. Dyott was apparently amazed and so convinced with the validity of Brunner's discoveries of the socavón, Reclining Woman and large square hole, that Dyott, seemingly a man of his word, finally showed Brunner the material that he had acquired and had never disclosed in its entirety to anyone previously. The entire story was laid out before Brunner for the first time, like pieces of a puzzle fitting together.

Brunner was not physically given the Dyott material. Instead, Dyott retained the materials but told Brunner the entire story of his involvement and of the two sailors Blacke & Chapman. Brunner was then allowed to copy the maps and letters [229] in his own artist's hand at "Hacienda Delta," where Brunner remained for a three-week period of time.

It was then, in April of 1966 [230] that the infamous contract between Dyott and Brunner was entered into, when they became partners in the Llanganati treasure hunt. Dyott supplied the Blacke & Chapman materials, Brunner had the time and ability to conduct the expeditions, and Brunner's friend Salvador had disposable funds, it appears to have been a perfect association. A second contract was purportedly entered into between Brunner and Salvador approving the Dyott/Brunner agreement and establishing Salvador's financial support of future Llanganati explorations. The agreement Brunner had in his materials however that I have seen and reproduced below, shows only two signatures with Brunner binding as "his partner" Salvador.

■ ■ ■

AGREEMENT

AGREEMENT made this 12th day of April 1966, at Santa Domingo de los Colorados, Republic of Ecuador, by and between Commander George M.

---

[229] Brunner states that he was holding and copying from the "original" documents, not copies or notes.

[230] Michael Dyott had also expressed to me his belief that Salvador had signed the contract and received a copy of the documents it involved. Salvador would later be quoted by Mark Honigsbaum in *Valverde's Gold* as stating that the three of them, Salvador, Brunner and Dyott, drew up the secret contract and it was in 1965.

Dyott as party of the first part, and Eugene Konrad Brunner as party of the second part, both parts on their behalf.

WHEREAS, both parties have worked for many years trying to reach the so called Atahualpa Treasure or Inca Treasure in the Republic of Ecuador.

WHEREAS, Dyott intends not to continue searching for the Atahualpa Treasure and deems that Brunner has the knowledge and ability to discover it.

THEREFORE, both parties agree on the following provisions:

1. Dyott shall furnish Brunner, actually and permanently with all the advice and information Dyott has in relation with the so called Atahualpa Treasure or Inca Treasure.
2. Brunner agrees to give Dyott, or the person or persons Dyott appoints by his sole decision, ten percent (10%) of everything Brunner could get from Inca Treasure discovery.
3. Brunner agrees to get from his partner, Mr. Andrés Fernandez Salvador, the participation of ten percent (10%) of Salvador's share of the Inca Treasure for Dyott or for the person or persons appointed by Commander George M. Dyott.

Signed: ***G. M. Dyott*** and ***Eugene Brunner***

■ ■ ■

As luck would have it, the complete story that Eugene Brunner learned from Dyott himself, told at Hacienda Delta over that fateful three-week period ... survives today. Brunner's first hand account as written in November 1979, is told in detail within his previously unpublished manuscript *El Tesoro en las Misteriosas Montañas de Llanganati*, unchanged with the passage of time, unaltered by poor memory or narrated in the second or third person. Brunner's story begins ... "One Englishman [231] came to understand that in the Mountains of Llanganati a treasure was hidden. It was through this same son of Albion that the Royal Geographical Society in London also came to understand, and through the publication of a pamphlet in the *Geographical Journal* of this society that all of Great Britain came to understand, that in the mountains of Llanganati a treasure was hidden.

"In the year 1887, two officers of the Royal Navy found the treasure and not having taken the necessary precautions, not having made contact with the Ecuadorian authorities, both lost their lives. The one died, as reported by his companion of a tropical illness, when they wandered lost, and seeking an exit from the Llanganati Mountains. The other died on the high seas when he traveled from England to the United States to meet up with a friend from New England on his way to Ecuador in order to recover the treasure that he had previously found. They are to my knowledge, the last Englishmen who in the late nineteenth century were in the mountains of Llanganati.

---

[231] Richard Spruce

"A nephew [232] of Richard Spruce was a student at the Royal Naval Officer School [233] and had two superior officers who had previously traveled to Guayaquil Ecuador and the Galapagos Islands. I am certain that the nephew of Spruce related his uncle's adventures in Ecuador and the story of the treasure in the mountains of Llanganati to these officers, his professors. The two officers became immediately interested in the matter and ultimately determined to make another trip to Ecuador in South America. Over a period of time they prepared their equipment, obtained the money necessary and naturally prepared their documents required to travel. Here is a small detail and question, why would the British Admiralty grant a license and permission to leave the country immediately, especially naval officers or professors during the school term? Later we will see why.

■ ■ ■

"In January of 1887 ship's Captain Barth Blacke and Frigate [234] Lieutenant [235] George Edwin Chapman, using a special license and on a secret mission, embarked bound for Panama. Once the two sailors crossed the isthmus, they were heading for Guayaquil in the Republic of Ecuador. They arrived in the early days of February and remained in this port a few days.

"Blacke & Chapman then traveled on board a small steamer to Bodegas de Babahoyo, from there by canoe to Catarama, where they traveled by mule along the Río Pita on the old mule track to the Andean town of Guaranda. From which they passed through the very high pass of Gallo Rumi (4150m above sea level) to arrive at Riobamba and Ambato. In Ambato, the two

---

[232] At this point in Brunner's story I must interject, that in order to verify Brunner's account, I attempted to discover if Spruce did indeed have any nephews. Spruce had no brother's, if he did have a nephew, the surname would not be the same. I was able to ascertain as previously stated in chapter two, that indeed Spruce had eight half-sisters from his father's second marriage. At least one sister Anna, provided Spruce with three nephews; John Spruce Crowther born circa 1859, Harry Crowther born circa 1860, and Alfred Crowther [1862-1946]. However, whether Spruce's other sisters had any children or not eluded me, it appears none ever married and at least two were old maids who lived with Anna and her family. However, it is a matter of verifiable fact, that Spruce did indeed have nephews.

[233] Actually The Royal Naval School, which in fact operated from 1833-1910 and was established as a boarding school for sons of officers in the Royal Navy and Marines to receive a primary education. It appears that Brunner may have meant the Royal Naval College which replaced the Royal Naval Academy in 1873 and operated until 1998. Spruce did have nephews' and if one or the other was in the navy, studying to be an officer, this is where he would have been trained.

[234] Frigate - A fast and light warship of the period with three masts and at least twenty eight guns on a single continuos deck.

[235] Frigate Lieutenant - Was a rank used by Spain not Britain, Brunner presumably meant that Chapman was a Lieutenant on a Frigate.

sailors spent several weeks resting and preparing for their expedition into the Llanganatis.

"When everything was ready they set off for Píllaro, where porters, horses and mules were obtained to transport their cargo to the Lagunas de Anteojos (the spectacles). It is to be taken into account and kept in mind, that given the traditional and typical English perseverance in the preparation of an expedition, with tedious attention to minute details, Blacke & Chapman were not concerned with obtaining any information or knowledgeable guides.[236] I believe this clearly indicates that they came with documents and data, maybe even with maps and knowledge, possibly even with precise instructions from Richard Spruce. Very likely they also had letters of recommendation to some person in Ambato or Píllaro.

"The second week of March Blacke & Chapman set off on their expedition, passing directly through the Pongo de Guapa toward the two small lakes 'Los Anteojos' without climbing the hill of the same name and turning their backs to Ambato in order to see the three Cerros Llanganati in the east, in order to obtain the direction of travel, as indicated by Valverde in his guide ... why? Nobody knows for sure, but for me the matter is very clear. Blacke & Chapman did not come to search for anything. They came to get straight to the exact site. They came from England with plans and maps whose directions were perfectly laid out beforehand. Spruce surely must have had information relating to the treasure that he never disclosed and was not published. Blacke & Chapman proceeded directly to the camp site in front of the point or nose between the Lagunas de Anteojos as indicated in the *Derrotero*, spent the night and from there sent the animals back to Píllaro.

"The next morning Blacke & Chapman proceeded on foot, leaving the lagunas on their left heading toward Yana Cocha (Black Lake), which they later passed leaving it well to their left as well. They descended the hillside into a ravine, from which they followed the right bank of the river Desaguadero de Yana Cocha arriving at Parca Yacu (Two Rivers). From there they crossed the Desaguadero following the left shore to a tributary called Cascadas de las Tundas confined there in the dense subtropical forests on the slopes of Roncadores. And there the big surprise ... the sailor Captain Barth Blacke writes in his first map as follows ... 'Location of probably world's biggest gold mine.'

"How is it that two sailors arrived first at a site that does not appear in the *Derrotero de Valverde*, an unknown mine site that legends speak of, but that no one knows where or if it really exists? The answer is simple and clear ... Richard Spruce is the one who directed Blacke & Chapman to this site.

---

[236] Quite similar to the story of Major Brooks, who years later also did not seek out guides.

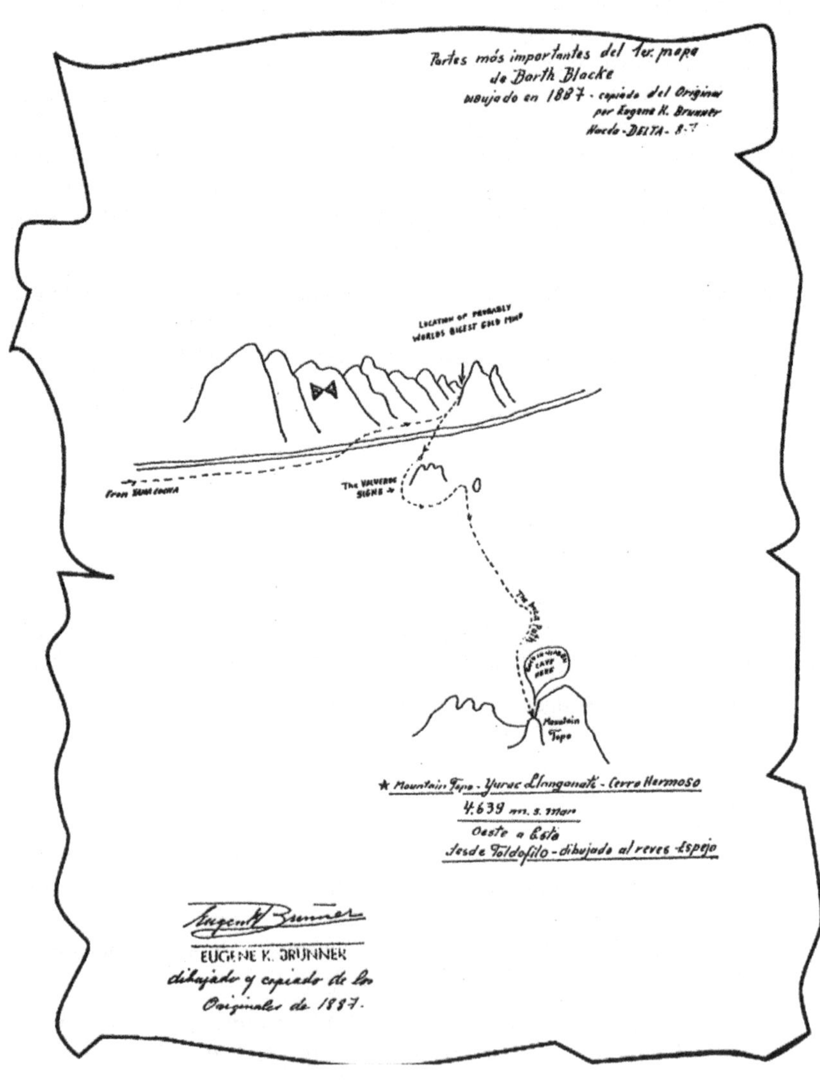

Blacke's First Map

"Spruce knew that from the mine there was a Camino de los Incas [Inca trail] to the third Cerro Llanganati on whose slope there is a Guayra (smelting furnace) in which the ancients melted their metals, just as written in the *Derrotero*. Spruce knew very well that the two Navy officials were not able to work the mine, but he did know that once there, they would find the trail. Nothing is more logical, throughout the world minerals from a mine are carried to where the smelting furnaces exist. The ancient Indians of the Andes had their guayra's or furnaces to melt metals on the highest peaks facing southeast, utilizing the strong trade winds to produce sufficient draft to melt the metals.

"Blacke & Chapman returned to the Parca Yacu, which is the confluence of the rivers Desaguadero and the Rivera de Llanganati on the map of Guzmán. From there the two followed the Rivera de Llanganati until they reached a site called Soguillas, which is a passage in which the water is divided. On one side the water flows south in the Río Topo into Río Pastaza. On the other side the water runs north in the river Desaguadero that flows into Río Mulatos, which in turn disappears into Río Jatun Yacu after it makes its union with the Anzu in the Oriente with the name of Napo. Even today in this passage can be seen traces of the old trail of the Indians. Luciano Andrade Marin said in his book *Llanganati* that it is a trail of the dantas (tapir), but I say that over several centuries' tapir used the ancient Indian trail.

"In Soguillas for many years I had a very good camp and walked hundreds of times by the remnants of the old road, here as well I also walked the señal (sign) of Valverde without realizing it, because it is much larger than I imagined. But to reach the Valley of Brooks and the lagoon Isabela de Brooks, you are obligated to walk in the shape of the sign of Valverde, if not, you will fail to reach the valley between two hills which is the Way of the Inca, mentioned in the *Derrotero*. The two Englishmen walked the path in the same way and Barth Blacke marked the sign of Valverde and also the Inca Path on his first map.

"Definitely Blacke & Chapman must have seen the socavón (tunnel) mentioned in the *Derrotero* as they walked along the Inca Trail before entering into the thick forest that is crossed by the mighty Río Topo. Facing the Valley of Brooks and Inca Trail stands majestically the third Cerro, Yurac Llanganati, the sacred hill of the ancient Indians, the Volcan del Topo on the map of Guzmán, to which Barth Blacke gave the name Mountain Topo, that is known today as Cerro Hermoso.

"Blacke and Chapman climbed this mountain on its east side reaching the summit and the passage that exist between the main peak and secondary peaks, by which you can descend to the west side of the mountain. It is at this site, between the main peak and an adjacent stone pyramid, where Barth Blacke marked on his map one point, with the enigmatic but definitive sentence ... 'Gold in hidden cave here.' In this cave the two sailors found an enormous treasure, which Barth Blacke called Atahualpa's Hoard.[237] This occurred on 4 Apr 1887.

"These two sailors had found what they sought, that which they had traveled to Ecuador for, but at the same time they were in trouble. A problem that resided in their Indian carriers from Píllaro and its environs, that if they came to know of this discovery it could easily have transformed these men into annoying witnesses placing Blacke & Chapman in mortal danger. For this reason I am sure that the Englishmen sent their companions on some pretext back to Píllaro, which would have been by the same route by which they had arrived. When the Indians had departed the two sailors organized their belongings and prepared their backpacks discarding everything that they felt was unnecessary, replacing them instead with figures of gold and emeralds.

"In all probability Blacke & Chapman estimated the maximum time to travel out of the mountains was four days and carried a sufficiently small amount of food. They also carried with them a large canvas sail which served as a tarp or tent. The rest of their possessions and provisions were abandoned in the rugged and uneven terrain of Cerro Hermoso [most probably in the treasure cave itself]. The expedition had not been in vain, Blacke & Chapman headed in the direction of Píllaro, they were sons of the British Empire, full of dreams of grandeur, medals and titles of nobility as counts or barons that this success would bring. They did not depart by the path by which they came, instead they headed west using Blacke's compass, walking the rocky knife blade ridges of the sierra,[238] not descending from the heights, where they could walk relatively easily.

"They passed through the ridge on whose northern slopes are three lakes that are known today by the name of the Tres Marias (Three Mary's) and up until this point everything went well and without incident. But it is there, a little below the hills of Ainjilibi, that a disaster in the form of thick fog, rain and hail, made them lose their way and get lost in the snowy labyrinth of Atilis above the Valle de Auca Cocha. There Blacke & Chapman wandered for days between slopes and deep ravines, dodging bottomless swamps, wet and hungry, the few supplies already exhausted.

---

[237] This has always been an interesting point. Searching for a treasure that was by all accounts in a lake, Blacke & Chapman, by the merest chance discovered Atahualpa's treasure in a cave. The questions arise ... Did Blacke & Chapman discover a second deposit? ... or ... had someone previously removed the treasure from Valverde's lake and placed it within the cave?

[238] Blacke & Chapman presumably headed west-north-west via the rocky ridges known as the Jaramillo Range, marked as "Fallallón y Precipice de Yana Rumi on Guzmán's map.

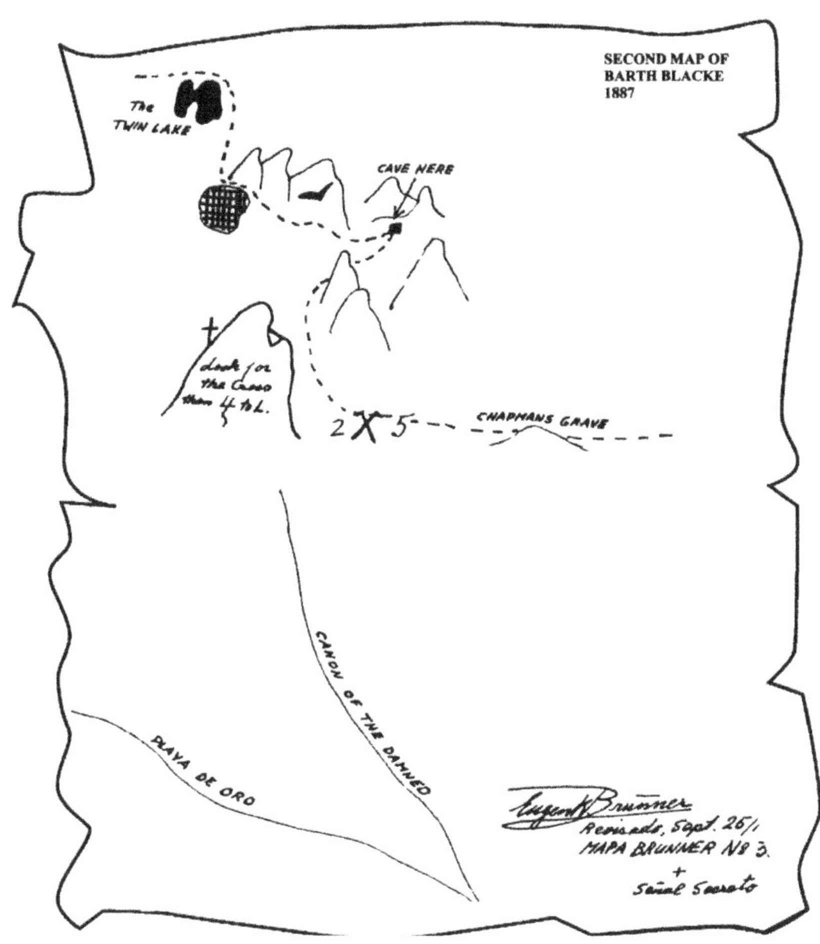

Blacke's Second Map

"For days and days they walked, the few moments when the fog dissipated were not sufficient to orient themselves. On top of all these evils, in a fall Blacke broke his compass, without which the disorientation was worse still. George Edwin Chapman, who presumably suffered from pernicious malaria, became ill and died in the rugged terrain of these inhospitable mountains. Blacke laid Chapman on the ground and covered him with a mound of stones, the location of which Blacke marked on his second map as 'Chapman's Grave'. The grave of Chapman? I have a doubt and certainly a question and wonder thoroughly ... is Chapman really buried at this site? Later we will see why I am asking this question, but if Chapman is in this tomb marked on the map, we do not know if Blacke left Chapman's knapsack there with his dead companion or perhaps Blacke carried his load as well? This I doubt, as I am sure that Blacke was also close to death, that he too was exhausted and at the end of his forces. Blacke certainly must have left the knapsack there and it is for this reason that he marked the site on his second map.[239]

"Nobody knows exactly how many days the two wandered lost, but on his second map Blacke marked 'Cave Here' in the spot where he hunkered down and rested when he was alone. Blacke probably spent some time at this site until he recovered and composed himself, because in his second map he drew to one side of the hill with the cave a row of mountains and hills. On the side of one of them Blacke drew the shape of a bird in flight with outstretched wings, a little further on a swamp in the form of a painter's palette, further still he drew a couple of ponds linked in the middle as though by an umbilical cord, which he labeled 'Twin Lake' or Laguna Melliza. The map indicates that off the chain or line of hills and ridges sits an isolated hill which stands out alone and has written on its right side ... 'Look for the cross then 4 to L.' Arrows outlined on a dotted line show the direction of travel which indicated that this map shows the route from Cerro Hermoso to Píllaro.

"Exhausted and near death Blacke decided to make one last effort to escape these inhospitable mountains, but he could not continue with such a load and would have to leave things behind. Hence to make his load smaller he removed eighteen small pieces of gold and a few emeralds from the backpack and placed them into a small sack, the rest he left somewhere close to the hill with the caption 'Look for the cross then 4 to L.' Blacke leaves behind a navy telescope, a broken navy compass,[240] a piece of sail

---

[239] For what other reason than the recovery of Chapman's body or a knapsack full of treasure, would Blacke have created a second detailed map away from the treasure? If Blacke were to return later for the main treasure, he would have undoubtably intended on following the original easier route in his first map.

[240] The accuracy of this statement raises a question in my mind. It seems to me that in their travels, mariner's of the period would have utilized a small sextant or quintant (which both contain a small telescope), the GPS of the time, instead of or in addition to a compass.

canvas which they had used as a carp or tent, and perhaps either one or two knapsacks loaded with gold and emeralds from the treasure they had found.

"This second Blacke map cost many headaches and an enormous amount of money, to no more than three people. The first was Commander George M. Dyott, the second Señor Andrés Fernandez Salvador and the third is the author [Brunner]. It took me a long time to realize that Barth Blacke created the maps strictly for his personal use, in order that he personally could return to the places he himself marked with the thought of recovering the gold and treasure, of which he believed himself to be the absolute and sole owner.

"I want to clarify that the odyssey of these two sailors occurred at altitudes between 3500 and 4000 meters above the sea, in a deserted wasteland where the fog, humidity, snow and hail reigns, as is typical in the Llanganatis. If there is no proper equipment, hot food and fire, these places become dangerous and deadly. Today I am familiar with this zone, I have enjoyed it in all its beauty on sunny days, and I have suffered in times of fog, storm and snow. But while I was alone, I enjoyed good camps, good tents, gas stoves and everything you need to survive, things that Barth Blacke did not have.

"Blacke took the eighteen pieces of gold and emeralds as proof of his discovery, as well as to finance his return from Europe. Continuing on he was constantly looking for a way out of this maze, until finally, when he arrived at the high peaks above the Laguna Melliza, appearing in the distance, through a gap in the fog, was the two small lakes of Tambuleo and Lake Pisayambo. The certainty of having left the terrible labyrinth of Ainchilibi, which is known today as the Mountains of Limpiopungu, seems to have given wings to the feet of the unfortunate English sailor. A glorious sunset that comes with the last light of day illuminated Blacke's path as he arrived at Tambo de Mama Rita, where he spent the night, which incidentally was the first in a long time spent indoors under a solid roof with something warm in his stomach. We know Blacke arrived safely in Píllaro and Ambato, where he spent a period of time to recover his strength and put some meat on his ribs. Finally he returned to Guayaquil from where he embarked for the journey back to England. Upon arriving back at home in England, Blacke returned to duty in the navy.

■ ■ ■

"I want and need to clarify why I have doubts that Chapman is truly in the grave marked on the second map of Barth Blacke. I doubted and I still have reasonable doubts, because it is the case that in the year 1966 I met the very old grandmother of a waiter at the Hotel Villa Hilda in Ambato. The señora was nearing 118 years of her life, looked well and enjoyed an enviable memory that bordered on the unbelievable.

"Manuel, the waiter and grandson of the old lady took me to meet her, because she had met the two English sailors of this story. The señora told me many things about the 'mysterious gentlemen' as she called them, she knew much about them, because they had come to the house of her parents, when she was bordering on forty years of age. Among other things she told me a story that one had died in the Llanganati having fallen into a precipice because the rope with which he was secured broke (look).

"The other, the Captain, had shown her family eighteen gold pieces and green stones like glass (look), and had told them that they had found the long sought treasure of Atahualpa. The señora also said that no one in her family believed what the Captain told them. They were sure that the Captain bought these things from the looters of Tungipamba or Píllaro, which were the places where Blacke & Chapman got the porters and mules for the trip, and that all people from there were known excavators of the ancient pagans ... so here is the relation of the little old lady in Ambato, who told me her story in confidence.

"Now we have two versions of the death of Chapman, first he died of a tropical illness while lost in the mountains, in the second he died falling headlong into a precipice because the rope on which he was secured broke. There is reason to doubt or not? Moreover, in a letter Barth Blacke sent from Ambato to a friend in the United States he stated ... 'It is impossible for me to describe to you the wealth that now lies in that hidden cave marked on my map, but I could not remove it alone or could thousands of men.' I ask why would Blacke state he could not remove it alone if Chapman was with him? Where was Chapman then? But there is something in common between the accounts of Blacke and the ancient Señora, both indicate that Chapman died in the Llanganatis.

"If indeed Chapman plunged headlong into a precipice on Cerro Hermoso, once back in civilization Blacke understandably could have indicated Chapman died of a tropical disease. After having found such a treasure, to return and say that your companion died because a rope broke, surely no one would have believed him. Everyone would have believed that Blacke killed Chapman for his share of the treasure. I am sure that is why Blacke invented the story of the tropical disease. To be positive of one or the other is only possible when you open the stone mound at the foot of the snowy Atilis. In the meantime I reserve the right to continue doubting. Someday we will see, if not ... who knows?

■ ■ ■

"An employee of the English consulate in Guayaquil, a friend of Barth Blacke, wrote a friend in London, referring to the journey of the two sailors and especially Barth Blacke and what he had told him ... that 'By the merest chance, he (Blacke) found Atahualpa's Hoard in a cave next to an extinct lake.' It could have been that Blacke had told something to this friend in Guayaquil, and what this person revealed in the letter to a stranger in London, may be part of the death sentence issued against this unfortunate ships captain, Barth Blacke. We shall see. Back in England, Blacke delivered a few pieces of worked gold from the treasure to the British Museum, what he did with the rest is not known, but it is very likely that he sold it to finance his return.

"After completing his service in the Royal Navy, Blacke arranged his private affairs and embarked in Liverpool during 1892 on an old sailing boat, one of the last Clippers [241] still offering passenger and freight service. It may be that Blacke, as the old sailor he was, traveled on an old Clipper for the nostalgia of an era that was ending. For that reason it is not beyond comprehension why Blacke was not traveling on a modern steam vessel.

"The Clipper weighed anchor and left the port bound for New York. The ship arrived safely, but Barth Blacke was no longer on board. The Captain of the Clipper reported to the Port Authority of New York that his passenger, retired Navy Captain Barth Blacke, during a storm and due to his advanced state of intoxication fell overboard into the sea. Although they tried, he could not be saved, and on those grounds reported the death of Captain Barth Blacke as drowning at sea.

"Blacke had traveled to the United States to visit a friend in New England who had control of all Blacke's notes, maps and letters regarding the history of the treasure in the mountains of Llanganati, as well as the experiences of his journey with Lieutenant George Edwin Chapman. Blacke had met this friend in New England and knowing he was a good man, incapable of committing treason or felony, Blacke had sent his papers for safekeeping. Blacke also knew too well that he could not send his papers to the aged Richard Spruce in England because in his advanced senility perhaps these documents would have been shown to everyone and especially to unwanted users. Blacke also thought that this friend would be the ideal companion to return to Ecuador and rescue the treasure, which was the goal of this trip, to sneak into the Llanganatis and organize the removal of the treasure of Atahualpa to be taken secretly to his beloved England. When all this happened, Richard Spruce was still alive and perhaps the news of Blacke's death affected Spruce so badly it helped cause his death in 1893.[242]

■ ■ ■

The last three pages of Brunner's manuscript *El Tesoro en las Misteriosas Montañas de Llanganati*, contained extracts of various letters that Barth Blacke wrote between 1886 and 1891 to his friend from New England, in the United States of America. These excerpts are reproduced below ...

1886

"My dear friend, very soon I shall be in South America. I have to make a secret research in the Andes of the Republic of Ecuador. I am not aloud to tell you, but it is something very important. I shall write often, and if I have some very important information, I will send it to you, and you guard it for me."

1887

"It is impossible for me to describe to you the wealth that now lies in that hidden cave marked on my map, but I could not remove it alone, or could

[241] Clipper-a fast sailing vessel powered by the wind used in former times

[242] Whether Brunner's use of literary license or a result of Dyott's research, an interesting analogy.

thousands of men. I have to go back to sea for a while, and I beg of you, to take good care of my maps and papers ..."

1888

"If something should happen to me, and you decide to go and search for that hidden cave marked on my map, LOOK FOR THE RECLINING WOMAN AND ALL YOUR PROBLEMS ARE SOLVED."

1889

"Maybe you cannot believe me when I tell you: There are thousands of gold and silver pieces of Inca and pre-Inca handicraft, the most beautiful goldsmith works you are not able to imagine. Life size human figures made out of beaten gold and silver, birds, animals, corn stalks made out of silver with golden corn ears. Gold and silver flower pots full with the most incredible jewelry. Golden vases full with emeralds and other beautiful stones, golden goblets and a thousand other artifacts."

1891

"Very soon I shall be with you, and then we will go together to Ecuador and the Llanganati Mountains, to get what we know is there."

This appears to be from Blacke's last letter.

■ ■ ■

Brunner continues ... "Years passed and nobody remembered the two officers of the British Royal Navy. But when the children and grandchildren of Barth Blacke's friend in New England [243] decided to restore the old family house, situated on a cliff high above the sea, opposite a small island not far offshore, it was necessary to move furniture from one location to another and this is when they found in an old desk drawer an old yellow paper on which was written ... 'All about the Inca treasure in *Rifles and Knapsack's.*' They read it again and again, but did not understand what the writing meant and threw the paper into the trash.

"Later when the work came to the library they had to pull all the books off the shelves, that's when they found a book whose title seemed familiar, it simply read *Rifles and Knapsack's.* The book was about the last years of the War of Independence in the United States of America. They remembered the old paper they had found previously and carefully browsed the book and found another old paper on which was written ... 'All about the Inca treasure in Ecuador, in the hollow tree on the island.'some of them quickly took the boat and went to the island as they all knew the old oak, rotten inside, on which in their youth they had a swing suspended from one of its still strong branches. One of the youth's climbed the tree and found attached to one of the higher branches a copper wire. This wire had been inserted into the

---

[243] **Error! Main Document Only.**It would not be until the publication of *Valverde's Gold* that the surnames of Albertson and Bermender were applied to "the family." After the publication of *Sweat of the Sun, Tears of the Moon,* Peter Lourie was purportedly contacted by a Donald Bermender who claimed to be a descendent of the family mentioned in his book. Many years later Lourie would pass this information on to Mark Honigsbaum who interviewed Bermender for *Valverde's Gold.*

hollow tree trunk, carefully and curiously he pulled the wire and felt a weight suspended at the other end. He pulled even stronger and finally an old two gallon whiskey bottle emerged. The bottle was well sealed, inside were all the letters, maps and charts that Barth Blacke had sent his friend from Ecuador.

"Logically the restoration of the old house was delayed because they all were devoted to reading and studying the papers and other things found in the bottle. They knew almost as a family tradition that their father and grandfather had a friend who was an officer in the British Royal Navy. One of the sons, now almost sixty years old, remembered that his father once had spoken to him about how he was going to make a trip to South America, with a very good friend of his, who was an Officer of the Navy. Now after so many years it became known that a treasure of the Incas was the object of their father's planned journey. A journey that for reasons we now know was never made. That the documents found were not genuine was out of the question or beyond doubt, but none of them knew anything about Latin America, much less of the Republic of Ecuador.

"The family [244] decided to find out first through the Admiralty of Great Britain, if these two sailors mentioned in the papers and by their father and grandfather, were in fact officers of the Royal Navy in the years between 1880 and 1900. Reading the response they received from the Archives of the Admiralty they were somewhat surprised. The letter stated that both Captain Barth Blacke and Lieutenant George Edwin Chapman appear in the archives of the British Royal Navy. Chapman had died in South America while on a secret mission (look) and after his discharge from the Navy, Captain Barth Blacke lost his life while traveling to the United States in 1892, drowning at sea. The family now knew the reason for the suspension of the journey to South America of their father and grandfather.

"Armed with this data and with the assurance that everything was exactly as the documents indicated, the family wrote to the Royal Geographical Society in London, asking for information on Spruce's pamphlet published in the *Journal* of the Society in 1861.[245] Likewise they wrote the famous Explorers Club asking if the club could recommend a good explorer, that might make an investigation in the Republic of Ecuador in South America for them. The Royal Geographical Society replied that indeed the pamphlet was published but copies were exhausted, but in the British National Library there was a copy. The Explorers Club informed them that they were

---

[244] Utilizing Brunner's time-line and my subsequent research on the Albertson genealogy, part of "the family" at the time would have been Carrie Albertson Bermender, John Adam Bermender, Claude Albertson Bermender and Donald Bermender, Samuel's daughter, son-in-law, grandson and great grandson.

[245] This indicates that Brunner had knowledge of Spruce's paper prior to its inclusion in *Notes of a Botanist*. However, the copy that Brunner had access to was Wallace's edited version in *Notes of a Botanist*, this is the copy I would later find within Brunner's documents, not Spruce's entire paper.

lucky, because one of the best English explorers currently lived in the Republic of Ecuador, he had been a Wing Commander of the Royal Naval Air Service, George Miller Dyott, now retired.

"Continuing with our story, our friends from New England wrote Dyott setting out and explaining the situation as it was. George M. Dyott responded from Ecuador that he was interested in the matter, but for him the take charge of the project, it would be necessary in advance to explore the archives of Great Britain, both at the Royal Geographical Society and in the Archives of the Admiralty in London. Dyott proposed that if the family was ready to cover the expense of this research, he was ready to travel.

"The family in the U.S. accepted Dyott's proposal and after a visit to New England Dyott traveled to London, where he spent two years [246] researching the lives of two sailors from their date of birth, until their death. He also investigated their connection to old Richard Spruce and Spruce's relationship with the Royal Geographical Society in London and on and on. All these investigations ought to have been easy for Dyott as a member of the British Explorer's Club.[247] Incidentally the Explorers Club also has some fabulous files, which may also contain a copy of the pamphlet with Spruce's story on the treasure of the Incas. Already having completed his research, Dyott was prepared to return to Ecuador, when he was surprised by the outbreak of World War II in Europe. Dyott immediately moved to London,[248] where he spent the war years as a senior intelligence service officer.

---

[246] The source for Brunner's story and version of events was of course, the Commander himself. Taking into account the possibility of faulty memories, exaggerated narration or the use of literary license, it is reasonable to assume that at least in general terms, the story is accurate. However, Dyott's travel records listed in the beginning of this chapter do not support the claim that Dyott was in England researching for two years prior to the war breaking out in Europe. It is plausible that the Bermender family originally contacted Dyott by letter in the 1930s and his research on the matter was done during his travels to England during the mid-thirties and prior to World War II. Judging from Dyott's travel records, it is also possible that his research on the matter could have been conducted sometime between November 1942 and January 1947.

[247] Here Brunner is clearly in error as the British Chapter of the Explorers Club was not founded until 1977. However, Dyott was a member of the Explorers Club in New York from 1926 to 1933. It could also be inferred that Commander Dyott may very well have been more successful with research in London than any ordinary researcher. Dyott's military rank, his standing as an explorer and fellow of the Royal Geographical Society, his families position and connections, all could have played a role in opening doors and granting access to confidential documents.

[248] Brunner has been the sole author to make this claim, which has been partially substantiated by Dyott's travel records. The exact year of the initial Bermender family contact with Dyott is unclear. The date Dyott traveled to

■ ■ ■

"Just after the end of the war Dyott returned to Ecuador and his property in Santo Domingo de los Colorados. From there he began his explorations into the Llanganati Mountains and it is there where I met him. Dyott would come to my camp and I to his. Dyott would try to coax information of what I knew and I would do the same. With time explorers became friends, as to say without much effort we drew close with each other.

"In early 1946 [249] visiting Dyott's camp in Zunchu Urcu, talking by a nice warm fire where the heat made us forget that outside roared a torrential hailstorm, Dyott stated ... 'if on your travels in these mountains you find a formation of rocks that resembles a reclining woman, or, if you find a large square hole, do let me know and I will share in the benefits I obtain.' Of course at that time I knew nothing of the Englishman Blacke or his friends in New England.

"In the month of March of that same year,[250] Dyott suffered a nasty accident in the Llanganatis, in the Valley of Brooks to be exact. He rolled down an almost perpendicular hillside and broke an ankle. Dyott had to stay for five months in this location, a period of time equal to all the time Loch remained in the mountains. Later England's Ambassador sent Dyott a doctor and through Luis Villacreses of Píllaro Dyott was supplied food and everything necessary until he could walk out of the mountains on his own power. It is worth clarifying that during this period of time there were no helicopters.

"In November of 1946 [251] a North American friend in the city of Quito asked me to accompany a countryman of his to the Llanganatis. He told me that the person I would be dealing with was a Mr. Gail Mendell [1912-1979] [252] from the small city of Lakeview in the state of Oregon, USA. This good man had been on a flight of Panagra [253] about three or four weeks

---

Philadelphia to meet with the Bermender family can also not be confirmed with absolute certainty. Donald Bermender's story places his families meeting with the Commander in 1946, while Michael Dyott recalls his "dad" traveling to Philadelphia in 1947. Once again reviewing Dyott's travel records, it is clear that the Commander was in New York during January 1946 and February 1947, therefore either date is possible.

[249] As stated earlier, Brunner's recollection of the year may be faulty ... it may very well have occurred in 1947. In *Sweat of the Sun, Tears of the Moon,* Brunner is quoted as placing the event as "...in 1947, I believe it was."

[250] **Error! Main Document Only.**Regardless of the year, the accident occurred after Brunner's initial meeting and contact with Dyott.

[251] Again, as stated earlier, Brunner's recollection of the year may be faulty ... it might well have been 1947. In *Sweat of the Sun, Tears of the Moon,* Brunner is quoted as placing the date as "In November 1947."

[252] Spelled here correctly, Brunner and all other authors mis-spelled the surname using only one letter l.

[253] Panagra - Pan American - Grace Airways.

previously and immediately moved to Ambato and Píllaro,[254] where the lucky gringo discovered the young lady Rosita (Rosa) Elena Alvarez Valdivieso, sister of the then Commissioner of Píllaro.

"Rosita spoke perfect English and helped Gail in preparations for his trip into the Llanganatis. She obtained the laborers and porters seeing that these men did not abuse the gringo charging too much for materials and their salaries. Finally the gringo was ready and walked proudly in front of his long line of porters in the direction of the highland plains of Pongo of Guapa. But something went wrong, Mendell only made it as far as Soguillas, four days' journey from Píllaro. Here they rebuilt a former camp that everyone always used when walking through this area. Perhaps because Gail did not speak Spanish or that the food he provided was not to their liking, and only God knows why, the Indians abandoned him there, returning at night to Píllaro. These same Indians and Mestizos [255] made many trips with me, I never had any trouble with them and they never abandoned me. That is roughly the first adventure in the Llanganatis of Gail Mendell, and when this young man came to Quito, presented to me by my friend, I liked the man and committed to accompanying him on his next trip.

"The first time I entered the mountains' with Mendell we set out first for Soguillas where Gail had hidden a lot of equipment that had to be left behind when the Indians deserted him. But before arriving at Soguillas, in camp at Zunchu Urco we met up with Commander Dyott who was accompanied there by a young Danish friend. We were received very well, but after having been introduced to Gail and having heard the surname, something radically changed in Dyott, as if he had locked himself inside his shell. After dinner Dyott did something very strange, because I knew him very well, he did not come to sit by the heat of fire as was customary to chat like always, this night there was no chatting, no questions, no answers. Dyott got into his sleeping bag and with a dry good night, was speechless.

"Gail and two porters left very early in the morning to hunt for deer. It was then as Dyott, the young Dane and I drank coffee, that the Commander gave me a hard rebuke ... How could you bring this man to the Llanganatis? I was surprised and it bothered me. Dyott must have read in my face that I was upset and explained that this man was a descendant of one of the officers who threw Barth Blacke into the sea under the impression that he had his papers concerning the treasure with him. Excuse me I said ... who is Barth Blacke and what papers did he have relating to the Llanganatis? Dyott replied ... 'Oh I beg your pardon Gene, but I remember that you do not know the history of the English because I met you in these terrible mountains and never told you. Someday I will tell you everything, but to do

---

[254] Sometime after completing his military service in World War II (17 Dec 1943), Mendell lived in Ecuador during the period of 1947 to 1951. A family genealogy site states Gail was "a carpenter in Ecuador."
[255] Mestizo - a person of mixed race.

that I must consult with some friends I have in the United States ... but watch Mendell!'

"Logically from this point on, I watched Gail more closely and realized that occasionally he took a small notebook from his backpack, opened it and checked the surrounding hills with something that was on the pad. Although I never saw it, I am sure that it was a sketch of the Cerros Llanganati, but as I did not know the story, I did not care. As Gail could not achieve or obtain anything on this expedition, I was not going to give myself headaches attempting to deliberate and resolve this issue.

"The second expedition I made with Mendell was in the completely opposite direction following along the Río Desaguadero of Yana Cocha as far as San José. From there we followed the gorge of San José up to reach the cave of Guácharos (in Jíbaro Tallo or Tayo). Gail believed that this cave was the socavón of the *Derrotero de Valverde*, but I explained that a cave is a cave and a socavón was something like a tunnel. From here we followed the small rocky outcrops on the west side of the Cordillera de las Torres. Here Gail suffered a serious misfortune when he went off alone with his secret notebook and was lost in the fog. The porters and I searched over a period of two days and could not find him. On the third day very early in the morning Gail appeared, crawling along the ground all beaten and wet. Gail explained that on several occasions he had fallen for the nearly vertical rocks and it was a miracle that he did not leave his life there.

"On this expedition as well the poor gringo accomplished nothing. His notebook served for nothing. I know this because I was there with him and witnessed it all. The only thing that Gail Mendell took with him when he returned to his ranch in Lake County, Oregon, was the two treasures that he found in Píllaro and San Andrés, the wife he married on 23 Apr 1949, Rosita Alvarez de Mendell and the robust son of two months that she had given him.

"I must explain that at the time I knew nothing of the Englishmen Barth Blacke and George Edwin Chapman. From this point in time it would be another sixteen years before I knew anything concrete about these children of the new empire on which the sun was rising, which was not the Spanish Empire, but the British. Nor was it from the mouth of Commander Dyott, but from my friend Andrés Fernandez Salvador son of the owner of the mineral springs in Machachi, Güitig. Andrés also made his own research concerning the treasure of Atahualpa in the Llanganatis. Andrés had made some expeditions into the Llanganatis but with Americans and with the son of Don Tulio Boschetti, the leader of the Italo-Ecuadorian Llanganati Expedition in 1934. All of them are my friends, but we never traveled together into the Llanganatis."

■ ■ ■

At this point I must interject in Brunner's story. It is true that Gail Mendell's genealogy can be traced back to Plymouth County in Massachusetts. However, the questions arise ... How did Commander Dyott become aware that ... "a descendant of one of the officers who threw Barth

Blacke into the sea under the impression that he had his papers concerning the treasure with him" carried the family name of Mendell? ... Was there some undisclosed form of evidence concerning Blacke's existence and the circumstances of his death that had become available to Dyott? ... Had Dyott perhaps come across an official report, an obituary or a passenger and crew manifest of that fateful last voyage? ... Or, did the family of Blacke's friend in New England receive some form of notification of Blacke's death?

With only a surname to go by, it would appear almost impossible to confirm Dyott's allegation. However, given the fact that the Mendell's could be traced back to New England during the same time period ... on a whim I searched ship passenger lists for the year 1892 containing the surname Mendell. To my surprise I obtained one result. The ship *Yarmouth* departed Nova Scotia bound for Boston where it arrived 1 Sep 1892 with "R. Mendell" on board, passenger 377. Mendell's occupation was listed as "laborer" and his residence was listed as Massachusetts. However, upon examining the balance of the passenger list ... there was no Blake, Blacke or any name even remotely similar listed.

With negative results on the Mendell passenger list, I made one last attempt expanding my search for Blacke in the year 1892, with no result except for an "R. Blake." Having gone this far, I examined this record and to my surprise the coincidences between R. Blake and Barth Blacke were astonishing. Blake, born about 1844, passenger number 205, boarded the same ship that Mendell had previously, the *Yarmouth*. Blake departed Nova Scotia bound for Boston where the *Yarmouth* arrived on 25 Sep 1892. Blake's occupation was listed on the manifest as "sailor," his destination was "Maine," his nationality and last residence was listed as "Nova Scotia."

Sadly, even with all these similarities, there was still no "smoking gun," as no "Mendell" was listed on the Passenger List this voyage. Brunner had also indicated that Blacke was bound for New York not Boston, so there exists yet another discrepancy. However, the question arises ... Is it possible that the "laborer" Mendell was still onboard but not as a passenger ... perhaps as a crew member and therefore not listed on the manifest?

■ ■ ■

Having read Brunner's account we now get a somewhat different version of Brunner's story as related by Peter Lourie in *Sweat of the Sun, Tears of the Moon.* The story begins ... "one day in the 1930s [256] the grandchildren of Blake's friend in New England,[257] while restoring their colonial house

---

[256] Brunner and Lourie adhere to the same time-line and if their date is accurate, Dyott would still have been an active member of The Explorers Club.

[257] Lourie's account differ's from Brunner's original version which indicates the "children and grandchildren" were restoring the family house. Brunner never mentioned Blacke's friend by name in his manuscript and according to Lourie, Brunner would not reveal the name to him as well. The name was purportedly disclosed after the publication of *Sweat of the Sun, Tears of the*

situated above the sea overlooking a small island just offshore [Maine?][258] ... found in their attic, inside a book, a faded piece of paper that said ... "All about the Inca treasure in Ecuador in the hollow tree on the island."

Taking a boat to the island, one of "the boys"[259] climbed the tree and found a copper wire attached to a branch on the end of which was a large two gallon whiskey bottle. Inside the bottle were all the letters, maps, and papers which Barth Blake had sent from Ecuador to his friend concerning Atahualpa's treasure. The boys showed what they had found to their parents and Lourie writes ... "the boys' father remembered that his father [260] had indeed talked from time to time about a treasure and had planned an expedition which, he remembered now, had never come off."

The family [261] decided to write the British Navy to find out if Blake & Chapman were listed in the archives. After receiving word that the two men

---

Moon. The story goes that a great grandson of Samuel "Uncle Sammy" Alberston, "Blake's friend in New England", came forward and contacted Peter Lourie.

258 Here Lourie is apparently guessing that the family's house was in Maine. Research has shown that Samuel Albertson and the "family" appear in numerous Federal Censuses with addresses in New Jersey and Pennsylvania, but not in Maine. Coincidently though, Maine was the destination of the Blake I discovered on the 1892 passenger list.

259 Lourie's version has Samuel Alberston's grandsons, "the boys" (who at the time would have been adults), discovering the Blake documents. Genealogical research indicates that Samuel and Lavina Albertson indeed begat four daughters and in turn grandsons. Extrapolating from Brunner's original version and genealogical research, Brunner indicates that the "children and grandchildren" (which would have included his son-in-law John Adam Bermender, daughter Carrie Albertson Bermender and grandson Claude Albertson Bermender) ... "of Barth Blacke's friend" (Samuel Albertson), restored the family house. Brunner further indicates that "their father and grandfather (Samuel Albertson) had a friend who was an officer in the British Royal Navy (Barth Blacke)." Finally Brunner states that "One of the sons (of Samuel Albertson, in other words Carrie Albertson Bermender's brother), now almost sixty years old, remembered that his father once had spoken to him about how he was going to make a trip to South America ..." Therefore, when Brunner indicates that "one of the youth's climbed the tree", taking into consideration the ages and time-line, Brunner would have been referring to a grandson of Samuel Albertson.

260 Lourie's statement ... "the boys' father remembered that his father" ... would have been consistent with Brunner's original account, referring to Samuel Albertson's grandsons' and their father, Samuel Albertson's son. However, as of publication I have not been able to confirm that Samuel Albertson had any sons.

261 The *1930 United States Federal Census* and other research clearly shows the Bermender "family" at the time, consisted of John Adam Bermender (58) and his wife Carrie Albertson Bermender (59-daughter of Samuel Albertson,

had been in the service, they wrote the Royal Geographical Society in London asking for information about Spruce's translation of the *Derrotero de Valverde* and the history of the treasure. They also wrote The Explorer's Club to see if it might be interested in investigating the Llanganati region based on this new material.

The Club purportedly wrote back that one of England's finest explorers lived in Ecuador, and Commander George Dyott's address was sent along. The family wrote Dyott, sending along the Blake material, hoping the explorer would undertake an exploration for the treasure. Dyott was indeed interested, but World War II intervened. After the war and a few years of research, Dyott became convinced the treasure was real, that it existed somewhere in the Llanganatis, and mounted expeditions into the region.

Lourie continues to describe, purportedly through his conversations with Brunner, how the papers came to New England. That in 1886 a cousin [262] of Richard Spruce, while studying to be an officer in the British Royal Navy, told his superior officers, Captain Barth Blake and Lieutenant George Edwin Chapman, about his uncle's adventures in Ecuador and the lost treasure of Atahualpa. The officers decided to undertake an expedition to Ecuador that commenced in January 1887. In 1886 before Blake left, he purportedly wrote to "a friend in New England" the following ... "Very soon I shall be in South America. I must perform some secret mission in the Republic of Ecuador. I am not allowed to tell you more at this time, but it is a critical operation. I shall write you often, and if I have some information, I will send it to you. You must guard it for me with your life."

Presumably following "special information supplied by Spruce or his family," Blake & Chapman set out on their expedition into the Llanganatis from Píllaro. Lourie continues his story with an almost verbatim account of Blake & Chapman's route as laid out in Brunner's *El Tesoro en las Misteriosas Montañas de Llanganati*, to the point where Blake & Chapman entered a cave on 4 Apr 1887, discovering within "Atahualpa's hoard." Blake later wrote his friend in New England that ... "It is impossible for me to describe to you the wealth that now lies in that hidden cave marked on my map, but I could not remove it alone, nor could thousands of men. I have to go back to sea for a while, and I beg of you to take good care of my maps and papers." Later in 1889 Blake wrote ..."Maybe you don't believe me when I tell you. There are thousands of gold and silver pieces of Inca and pre-Inca handicraft, the most beautiful goldsmith works you can imagine: life-sized human figures beaten out of gold and silver; birds; animals; corn stalks of silver with golden ears of corn; gold and silver

---

born in New Jersey), who lived with their son Claude Albertson Bermender (35), his wife Verna Bermender (34), and their son Donald Bermender (2). In 1930, this Bermender family unit lived together in Philadelphia, Pennsylvania. This was also the year that John Adam Bermender died.

[262] Lourie clearly in error, as he subsequently states "his uncle," should read nephew.

flowers; pots full of the most incredible jewelry; golden vases filled with emeralds in gilded goblets and a thousand other artifacts."

Lourie continues to relate that Blake & Chapman packed their knapsacks with "four days' supplies to lighten their loads for the way out," thereby making room for "eighteen pieces of gold objects and a handful of emeralds. They didn't leave the same way they had come in, instead taking a more direct route to the west using a compass." The story of Blake & Chapman's route out of the Llanganatis, Chapman's death, and Blake's return to England and Blake's death en route to New York in 1892, closely mimics Brunner's account.[263]

Again according to Brunner, Lourie writes ... "Commander Dyott believed that Blake had indeed been drunk and had blabbed the story to some of his shipmates, who then killed him, thinking he had all his papers and maps with him. But they found nothing." Blake had written his friend the New Englander in 1888 ... a clue that Dyott passed on to Brunner while camped in the Llanganatis … "If something should happen to me, and you decide to go and search for that hidden cave on my map, look for the *Reclining Woman* and all your problems are solved."

■ ■ ■

With the benefit of the passage of time, Salvador's version of how Commander Dyott became involved in the Llanganati treasure hunt, is related through Salvador's conversations sometime around the year 2000, with Mark Honigsbaum author of *Valverde's Gold.* Honigsbaum of course, is to be credited with disclosing for the first time in print "the families" surnames' ... Albertson and Bermender.

Andrés version as related by Honigsbaum states that ... "In 1945 [264] when Dyott received a letter from a woman in Philadelphia [265] ... Andy didn't

[263] In this portion one small detail of Brunner and Lourie's account differs ... in Lourie's account there is no mention of Blake depositing a few pieces of treasure in the British Museum.

[264] Dyott receiving the letter in 1945 is also possible. However, if the "family" obtained Dyott's address in Ecuador, from his travel records he does not appear to have been there to receive a letter. According to Dyott's travel records, it cannot be established that he returned to Ecuador until 1947. It is plausible however, that Dyott did somehow receive a letter in 1945 and departed New York in November of that same year for England, perhaps to research the matter. Dyott then departed England after a short month, arriving back in New York at the beginning of January 1946. At some point Dyott returned to England, perhaps to complete his research, arriving back in New York on 3 Feb 1947.

[265] In *Valverde's Gold* it is indicated that Don's (Donald Bermender, born 1928) ... "mother had taken the lead in writing to Dyott, and after an exchange of letters the commander had visited them at their home in Philadelphia." This occurred when Don was eighteen, which would indicate Dyott had visited Philadelphia in 1946. The address for Don's mother ... Verna Bermender

mention her name ... containing a series of letters and two maps. The maps had been disguised so as to make it difficult to identify the region they described ..." The woman had inherited a house on the coast of Maine [266] that overlooked a small island, from her grandfather,[267] an old sea Captain known to the family as "Uncle Sammy."[268] She explained that her husband [269] had discovered inside an old family Bible, a paper stating "find *Rifles and Backpacks*," which they could not find. The following year their sons

---

[born 1896] ... has been confirmed by records from 1950 showing her still residing in Philadelphia.

[266] Yet another unconfirmed reference to Maine, consistent with Lourie's assumption. Honigsbaum states ... "the woman had inherited a house beside the sea from her grandfather, an old sea captain known familiarly as 'Uncle Sammy.' The summer house was located in New England, near the coast of Maine ..." It must be stated that genealogical research on Samuel Albertson does not link the man to Maine. Samuel was born in New Jersey [abt: 1834] and resided in Weymouth, NJ, [1850 & 1860 census] and Millville, NJ, [1870, 1880 & 1900 census]. However, if Carrie Albertson inherited a house from her grandfather, her father is not the "Uncle Sammy" of the story. As of publication I have not been able to establish if her grandfather was indeed another Samuel Albertson and if he was indeed "an old sea captain."

[267] Samuel Albertson [born 1834] - The *1850* and *1860 United States Federal Census*' show young Samuel Albertson as a boarder with the Champoin family in Weymouth, NJ. His occupation was listed as "laborer" on both censuses. The *1880* and *1890 United States Federal Census'* (which is the time frame of Blacke's letters) show a family man living in Millville, NJ working in the Wheaton Glass Factory.

[268] This purported term of affection ... "Uncle Sammy" has always bewildered me ... it just does not seem plausible that any family would call a grandfather or great-grandfather ... uncle. It must be stated that I had no success locating any evidence (not to say I couldn't be wrong) that "this Samuel Albertson" had ever been "an old sea Captain", ever lived in or had any property in Maine to bequeath. However, even though I could not ascertain Samuel's parentage or genealogy ... I did uncover two additional possibilities, with Samuel Albertson being a common name during the period. One of the Samuel Albertson's [born about 1810] was from Egg Harbor, NJ, and was "employed in the navigation of the ocean" (*1840 United States Federal Census*). The second possibility, listed as "a male from 5-20 years", was discovered in the *1885 New Jersey Census* living in a different ward of Millville, NJ, the same town as the Samuel Albertson of our story. Considering the time period, proximity of residences and ages, it could be possible that "Uncle Sammy" ... was just that ... either Carrie Albertson's or her father's brother ... an uncle.

[269] Claude Albertson Bermender [1895-1948] - Single in 1917, served in WWI as a Sergeant in the 45th Balloon Company from Dec 1917 to May 1918. Born in Millville, N.J., appears as the "head of household" in the *1930 United States Federal Census*, which shows the family living in Philadelphia, Pennsylvania with his parents and two year old son Donald.

[270] had found the missing book in the attic. In its interior was another paper stating ... "All about the Inca treasure in Ecuador in the hollow tree on the island." Connected to the branch of the tree on the island the boys discovered a wire with a whiskey bottle attached at the end, inside of which they found the letters addressed to "Uncle Sammy" from a Barth Blake and two maps.[271]

Salvador indicated that Blake was a "sailor from Nova Scotia" and recited excerpts of Blake's letters from memory. These letters were written in English to Blakes's friend in New England, and indicated Blake had discovered the treasure of Atahualpa in April 1887 ... "You will recall that I've been looking for the treasure of Atahualpa all these years without success, but now I am pleased to inform you that, only by the merest chance, I have found it in a cave on a mountain in Ecuador."..."It is impossible for me to describe to you the wealth that now lies in that distant cave marked on my map but I could not remove it alone, nor could a thousand men."...and "Maybe you cannot believe me when I tell you. There are thousands of gold and silver pieces of Inca and pre-Inca handicraft, the most beautiful goldsmith works you are not able to imagine."

The letter's further indicated Blake had used Valverde's map [272] that included the lost Inca gold mine. Blake stated that he had removed eighteen of the best artifacts and a handful of emeralds from the treasure cave and that he had traveled to the Llanganatis with his friend George Edwin Chapman, who died of a tropical disease in the mountains.

Blake later sent another letter with a second map telling his friend that he ... "had to go back to sea for awhile ... take good care of my maps and papers." Blake traveled to Europe but on his voyage back to New York, five years later in 1892 he disappeared, having fallen overboard or been thrown into the sea. One important main detail in his last letter ... "If something should

---

[270] Donald Bermender [born 1928] ... once again I must admit that I had no success locating any evidence that the Bermender's had more than one son (not to say that I couldn't be wrong as the 1940 Census had not yet been released) . However, I did discover a John F. Bermender [born 6 Aug 1933], but could not confirm any connection with Verna, Claude or Donald. It must be noted that this version also appears to skip a generation.

[271] Throughout *Valverde's Gold,* whenever Honigsbaum refers to Blake's "first map" or "second map" his representations are incorrect. Honigsbaum has the two maps confused. What is referred to as the "first map" is actually Blake's second map showing the route out after the discovery of the treasure. What is referred to as the "second map" is actually the map Blake used to reach the treasure. Some have also referred to this map as the *Valverde Map*, which is plausible but has not been confirmed. It is also plausible that this map was provided by or through Richard Spruce or his family.

[272] *Valverde's Map* that Blacke & Chapman purportedly utilized to reach the treasure, is referred to by Brunner and myself as Blacke's first map.

happen to me ... look for the Reclining Woman and all your problems are solved."

Again according to Andrés, Commander Dyott traveled to Philadelphia to interview the woman and examined the letters, maps and Bible. Holding the Bible up to the light, Dyott noticed pinpricks under certain letters, that when combined spelled out "Atahualpa's gold in the lake of Marcasitas" and "treasure in dead volcano by extinct lake." Dyott supposedly came to the conclusion that "Uncle Sammy" had never been to South America and could not have had the knowledge of names and places in the Llanganatis to forge the documents. Dyott, after careful consideration of the letters and maps, came to the conclusion that Blake was a sailor from Nova Scotia [273] who might have been a Captain in the Royal Navy or merchant marine and had perhaps planned an expedition with his friend to remove the treasure. Dyott himself, Andrade stated ... "had gone into those mountains in 1947 and again in 1948." Honigsbaum further related that ... "According to Andy (Salvador) Dyott loved mysteries ... The treasure appealed to Dyott's love of cloak-and-dagger ... It was a puzzle he just couldn't leave alone."

■ ■ ■

Later in *Valverde's Gold*, Honigsbaum relates the story of how he contacted Donald Bermender through Peter Lourie and tells the family's story from Don's viewpoint. Honigsbaum indicates that ... "Don explained that Sam Albertson had been his maternal grandfather"[274] and related that his family contacted the National Geographic Society in Washington with their information and they were advised to contact Commander Dyott in Ecuador and given his address. His mother wrote Dyott. They corresponded and when Don was eighteen, Dyott visited them in Philadelphia.

Apparently an agreement was made for Dyott to make an expedition into the Llanganatis utilizing the Blake material. Don indicated that Dyott had mistrust for the Ecuadorian authorities stating ... "Dyott said the government would make all sorts of promises, but if we found the treasure, we would be out on the sidewalk." Don also provided a letter dated 17 May 1947 from Dyott to his mother that stated in part ... "Your letter of May 10th arrived this morning and afforded me much interest in view of the fact that I was instrumental in getting Captain Loch to come to Ecuador some years ago on a similar mission.[275] Captain Loch however had nothing to base his search on except Valverde's guide which always seemed to me to be very inadequate. I cannot enter into reasons in this letter but to have anything to do with the government is absolutely fatal to almost any plan ... you will never get a cent of your enterprise even if you should find what you seek."

---

[273] Which Nova Scotia I ask ... the port on the Gulf of Maine in Canada, or the village in Cheshire, England?

[274] Samuel Albertson was not Don's "maternal grandfather" as stated, but paternal great-grandfather.

[275] Dyott is making reference to Loch's 1936 Andes-Amazon Expedition. It is plausible that the two explorers may have discussed possible future expeditions while in Ecuador or during their January 1933 ocean voyage.

■ ■ ■

Dyott, Brunner and Salvador all excellent story tellers, through the years have related portions of their stories to all who would listen. All three also put a great deal of this story on paper. Unlike Salvador, Brunner published portions of his story and both men allowed authors to utilize them as a source. One such author utilizing Brunner as a source, Jane Dolinger, published her book *inca gold; find it if you can touch it if you dare (1968)*, a short two years after Brunner discovered the socavón and Reclining Woman on Cerro Hermoso. Discoveries that allowed Brunner access to the Blacke & Chapman material and the ensuing Dyott partnership. Dolinger's book however, makes no mention of Blacke or Chapman and as for Dyott, only one short paragraph ... "Among the better-known explorers of this century who have tried their hand at unearthing the golden loot of Rumiñahui was the famous Britisher, Commander G. N. Dyott,[276] who spent fifteen fruitless months in the Llanganatis. Dyott, it will be remembered, led an official expedition many years ago in search of the missing Colonel Fawcett who had mysteriously disappeared in the wilds of Brazil's Matto Grosso."

■ ■ ■

Another author whom I would describe as Ecuador's version of Richard Spruce, Luciano Andrade Marín Baca, published his Spanish language manuscript *Viaje a las Misteriosas Montanas de Llanganati. Expedicion Italo-Ecuatoriana, Boschetti-Andrade Marin 1933-1934* in 1937, which was updated and re-released in a 1970 version. Unlike the previous edition, this second release included the story of Dyott and Blake & Chapman in a short addendum. I wonder who the source was for this update ... was it Salvador whom Andrade had apparently befriended and mentored, was it Brunner who was enthralled with Andrade's writings, or was it Dyott himself. Of two things we can be sure, Andrade states that his "anonymous" third party source spoke with Dyott in the 1960s, and Andrade was the first to actually publish any account of Blake & Chapman. However, similar to Andrade's account of Brooks, his version is replete with erroneous information.

Andrade's version has Commander Dyott being contacted by Spruce's grandson, who had shown Dyott a note from a Dutchman named Blake to Richard Spruce, posted from Panama, stating that the map Spruce had lent him was completely accurate, that he and Chapman, who had been in the Royal Navy, had found Valverde's treasure cave. Going through his grandfather's papers he had come across more of Blake's papers, letters and maps. Knowing of Dyott's reputation, the grandson hired Dyott to conduct an expedition to the Llanganatis on his behalf.

Through these stories and others, we arrive at numerous different accounts of Dyott's involvement with the Llanganati treasure hunt. Perhaps Dyott, Brunner or Salvador have given slightly different versions or even obscured

---

[276] Note Dolinger's incorrect middle initial for Dyott, should read Commander G. M. Dyott. Author Rolf Blomberg had committed this exact same error in *Buried Gold and Anacondas*.

certain details, we may never know. One thing we do know, Spruce never married or had any children, he had no "grandson."

■ ■ ■

During one of my initial trip's to Quito on this project in 1986, I took a leisurely walk to Libri Mundi on the street Juan León Mera. Well known in Ecuador as a bookstore and publisher, I thought perhaps they might have an interest in publishing Brunner's manuscript. I had a short conversation with the owner, Enrique Grosse-Luemern, who was familiar with Brunner's work. It appears Brunner had previously attempted to get his manuscript published through Libri Mundi, but I was advised, just as Brunner must have been previously, that the draft was not complete and the writing quite rough, so Enrique would not have an interest in publishing it at that time. While in the store browsing the Ecuadorian subject matter, I came across a book on archaeology written in English that on first appearance would give me a historical background on Incan artifacts. I purchased the recently published *Digging up prehistory: The Archaeology of Ecuador* by Karl Dieter Gartelmann.

Upon arriving at my hotel I sat down and browsed through the nearly four hundred page book. To my surprise, similar to Spruce's *Notes of a Botanist*, this serious work on archaeology in Ecuador, the digs, finds and history, included a short two page story on the Llanganati treasure that provided an erroneous version of Blacke & Chapman ... "It is said that two European sailors, one an Englishman by the name of Chapman, and the other a Dutchman, Blake, who had gone into the Llanganatis in 1887 at the behest of the famous English botanist Richard Spruce, were able to discover the hiding place and managed to take a few pieces of the treasure away with them. As they had found so much that 'not even a hundred men would be enough to move it' (according to a letter sent to Spruce), they decided to return and organize a better equipped expedition so as to be able to take much more of the treasure. However, Chapman was struck down with pneumonia while still in the mountains, and died a short time later in Quito. Blake talked too much on his way back to Europe. Having probably had one drink too many he began to talk about his adventures in Ecuador and about the golden treasure hidden in the Llanganatis. It appears that one of his fellow-travellers took advantage of the first available opportunity to heave Blake over the ship's side, in order to acquire the maps and papers that he had in his possession."

And the following story of Commander Dyott's involvement ... "Knowing this [Dyott's] background, a grandson of Richard Spruce offered to finance an expedition to the Llanganatis under Dyott's leadership, and he handed over all his grandfather's documents, including the letter that Blake had sent him. Dyott went into the Llanganatis twice: the first time in 1946, and again the following year. He broke a leg during the first expedition, and a severe nasal hemorrhage and a stomach complaint led him to abandon the second. During his convalescence in a Quito hospital, he had a lot of time to think about the matter of the treasure, and he finally decided to abandon the search. Dyott was utterly convinced that the treasure exists, but, as he told a visitor to Quevedo, he finally decided that 'a man can live more happily and more at peace without it.'"

In this version we are confronted with numerous inconsistencies, Spruce did not have a grandson, a quote has been changed from "a thousand men" to "not even a hundred men would be enough to move it," Chapman did not die in Quito, Blacke did not die on his return trip to England, and Dyott did not live in Quevedo his visitors would have been to Santo Domingo de los Colorados. At least with Gartelmann's version, through reference and content material, we know that his source was Luis Andrade's 1970s edition of *Viaje a las Misteriosas Montañas.*

■ ■ ■

Mark Honigsbaum's prologue to *Valverde's Gold* relates another account of Blake & Chapman, parallel to Brunner's, yet quite dissimilar. Whereas Brunner's account has Blacke & Chapman embarking in England (as passengers "using a special license and on a secret mission") bound for Panama in January of 1887, whose route of travel would take them across the isthmus and onto Guayaquil, Honigsbaum tells a completely different story, related here in part ... "Shortly after Christmas 1886, an American merchant ship weighed anchor at Callao, the port of Lima, and drifted into the cool waters of the Humbolt Current. The current swept the vessel into the Pacific and northwest along the slanting coast of Peru toward Ecuador. Bound for the steamy port of Guayaquil, the four-masted schooner had already called at Buenos Aires and Valparaiso. Guayaquil was to be its last stop before rounding Cape Horn once more and setting sail for Boston and home. That, at least, was the plan. But as the ship inched up the Ecuadorian coast early in 1887, disaster struck. A navigational error had brought the schooner perilously close to shore. Alerted to the danger too late by his pilot, Captain Barth Blake attempted to heave his vessel back into open waters. But near the Gulf of Guayaquil the ship grazed an underwater reef—perhaps the very same reef that had claimed the Spanish treasure ship *La Capitana* 232 years before—and the rudder shattered on a rock. As the schooner listed in the shallows, Blake frantically ordered his men to cut the rigging. But before they could do so, a high wind caught the ship's mainsail, snapping the mast in two. Fortunately, the Guayaquil port authorities heard the schooner's distress signals, and the ship was pulled free from the reef before it suffered further damage. But the crew's hopes of being back in Boston by the summer were gone."

Honigsbaum's account has Blake & Chapman sailing around Cape Horn in search of Atahualpa's hoard. The two mariners' "first heard about the treasure from a young English colleague in the Royal Navy." Apparently the sailor was a nephew of Richard Spruce, who then placed Blake & Chapman in contact with his uncle. Spruce hoped that "with the mariners help" and his secret copy of the *Valverde Map*, he would be made wealthy. The pair then traveled to Ecuador at Spruce's behest, discovered the treasure, Chapman died, Blake returned to England and reported the results back to Richard Spruce.[277]

■ ■ ■

The more versions that are told, the further they seem to diverge and the more confusing it gets. Certain points however remain quite consistent throughout. The names of Barth Blacke and George Edwin Chapman haven't changed or been disputed, except for the spelling of Blacke as Blake. Taking into consideration that Brunner actually viewed and copied the Blacke materials over a three-week period, I have accepted Brunner's spelling of the surname Blacke. It has always bothered me however, the probability of not knowing Blacke's entire name. What if Barth was merely a middle name or nickname, as was customary during the period?

Blacke & Chapman all agree, had some form of connection with Richard Spruce as the source of their material. Everyone also concurs that Atahualpa's gold was discovered in a "hidden" cave in the Llanganatis. One apparently misinformed author has Chapman dying in Quito while every other source states that Chapman died in the mountains while Blacke died at sea. Ultimately, the fact that Commander Dyott was the initial source of the Blacke & Chapman material in Ecuador has never been in dispute.

Treasure stories like any other story, have a beginning, middle and an end. Throughout any story there can be misdirection, misinformation and the liberal use of literary license, authors fictionalize for more continuity and interest, even adding themselves into the story as a central character. If a reader believes or knows a portion of the story to be true, does it not follow that the reader would then believe the entire story to be true?[278] Some people, myself included, would have preferred to verify this story's base in fact, prior to accepting it as fact.

It stands to reason that just as the archives in Seville should hold records of the *Derrotero de Valverde* and related documents, similarly the National Archive of the United Kingdom, formerly the Public Record Office in Kew, holds old Admiralty service registers and the Navy Lists,[279] Lloyd's register holds merchant marine records and the Royal Geographic Society would be a good source to search for Spruce's journals. Examining Dyott's journals if they could be attained would also prove invaluable. On the other hand, does

---

[277] However, if this account were accurate, the question arises ... why then did Spruce living in near poverty not receive his share of treasure, that by all accounts Blacke had returned to England with?

[278] Michael Dyott is partially quoted in these sentiments which derived from conversations we had and he is similarly quoted in *Valverde's Gold.*

[279] In response to a query, The National Archives of the United Kingdom advised that ... "A schoolmaster at the Royal Naval College who was commissioned, in uniform or not in uniform, would normally be included in the Navy List." It is also true that "confidential editions" of the Navy list exist, an example being the World War I and II periods.

it matter whether Blacke & Chapman were Dutch, American,[280] English or from Nova Scotia. Is it really that relevant to our search how Spruce and Dyott became involved, who found the Blacke maps, the pinpricks in the bible or who has the original documents?

Eugene Brunner did not rely on one source of information. His painstaking, although financially limited methods, involved a combination of historical research in Ecuador, the interpretation of stories and legend, and many years of exploration and expeditions into the Llanganati Mountains themselves. Brunner astutely deduced that from narration to narration a story changes and evolves with the use of literary license.[281] The one constant over the centuries has been the landmarks within the *Derrotero de Valverde*, *Guzmán Map* and Blacke's maps. Therefore, Brunner's modus operandi became analyze the guide and maps, discover and confirm the landmarks, thereby confirming or dispelling the story.

The *Derrotero* and *Guzmán Map* have been unequivocally verified as accurate by countless explorers, up to a certain point. Brunner's discoveries on the ground in this desolate area have gone beyond that point confirming the remainder. In addition, Brunner verified the points of reference and signs indicated on Blacke's maps as well. Once all this data is combined and viewed in its entirety, it becomes apparent why Brunner would accept the *Derrotero* and Blacke's maps as fact, not considering any location as holding the deposit of Atahualpa's gold, other than Cerro Hermoso.

■ ■ ■

Brunner's explorations in the Llanganatis for almost thirty years followed the *Derrotero* exactly to the hieroglyph which diverted him to the north, into the region of the Roncadores, as it had almost every explorer previously. Not until Brunner's discovery of the "Reclining Woman" and further access to the Blacke material was it that ... "all his problems were solved." Brunner makes it very clear that he had been exploring the wrong mountains ... Cerro Negro, Zunchu-urcu and the entirety of the Roncadores.

According to Andrés Salvador as quoted in *Valverdes Gold*, Dyott on his first expedition followed the *Derrotero*, *Guzmán Map* and Blacke's maps, on a route that "led him down the gorge marked "Encañada de Sancha

---

[280] Researching this manuscript an interesting theory came to mind. What if Blacke or Blake was indeed an American? As was customary during the period, is it plausible that Samuel had a father and/or brother with the same forename? How or where would Blake have become friends with our Samuel Albertson considering that Millville, NJ, is not a coastal town? Interestingly, the *1850 United States Federal Census* indicates that Blake, like Albertson was a very common name in New Jersey during the period. Millville, with a population of 1771 in 1844, coincidentally was the residence of two William Blake's, one born in 1815 and another in 1840. Could it be our Blake was from Millville?

[281] Brunner himself, when it suited the situation, was known as a flagrant user of literary license as well.

Pamba" on Guzmán's map. But when he reached the spot where Guzmán had marked "Gran Volcán del Topo" ("Topo Mountain" on the Blacke map), "Dyott found himself staring up at the ramparts of Cerro Hermoso." Dyott had incorrectly assumed that the maps were wrong. Indeed as Brunner and Salvador discovered, Gran Volcán del Topo, Topo Mountain, Yurac Llanganati and Cerro Hermoso are one and the same mountain, drawn on Blacke's map in reverse from the direction of Toldofilo which is northeast of Cerro Hermoso.

■ ■ ■

One can only image the emotional rush that Brunner, or any explorer for that matter, must have encountered with each new discovery, especially with the last piece of the puzzle being Dyott's large square hole (I have seen these photos as well but alas, no longer have them). Consider Dyott's astonishment and excitement at the age of eighty-three when Brunner visited him in his Hacienda Delta, opening his folio and pulling out a folder with photographs and drawings not only of the "reclining woman and square hole," ... but of the socavón as well! Brunner records this moment in time as follows ... "The man's mouth fell open in astonishment and he believed what he saw" ... just as Brunner's must have ... when Commander Dyott laid out Blacke's maps!

The reader now has before them the material that Brunner presented Dyott in 1966. Placing yourself in Dyott's shoes, would it not be accurate to say that you too would believe Brunner was very near the discovery of Atahualpa's treasure and entrust him in return with Blacke's two maps, which have previously been described in detail. Brunner's subsequent discoveries alluded to previously, will be described in detail in the next chapter ...

Eugen Konrad Brunner

THE EXPLORER: EUGENE K. BRUNNER

By definition an adventurer thrives on the excitement associated with the danger arising from an unusual, exciting, and daring experience ... while the explorer travels through an unknown area to learn, examine and scrutinize everything about it. Spruce, Brooks, Loch, Dyott and Brunner were men that possessed the unique qualities required of true explorers and adventures. These men endured great deprivations and solitude in their quest for knowledge and Inca gold.

Perhaps due to the factors of the personal experiences of being an only child, his mother's death when he was just a teenager, his father's quick remarriage, eight stepsisters and the death of three of them due to scarlet fever, Spruce remained a bachelor his entire life, married to his chosen life's work. Loch as well lived his life in solitude as an adventurer and explorer, an occupation that seems to require a disposition toward being alone, without family for extended periods of time.

Brooks and Dyott on the other hand both made an attempt to meld family with their chosen occupations. Both men married and had three children. Brooks dragged his family from territorial military outposts to numerous different postings including the Philippines, until the couple separated. Dyott as well tried to become a "family man" whose younger wife wanted to join him on his expeditions and exploits.[282] Dyott sadly spent very little time at "home" and his boys would grow up having very few memories of "dad," never really getting the opportunity of knowing their father. Brunner as well attempted to settle down and have a family, which resulted in one child and divorce. To be fair, one must consider that the contradictions the lifestyle of an adventurer/explorer, that these men had freely chosen, naturally imposed on their relationships so that any form of a "normal family life" ... was destined to fail.

The lust for Inca gold found within the personas of all these men was not their sole motivating factor. The inherent qualities and characteristics of these men embodied the true spirit of an adventurer and explorer. As a matter of nature they all found the thrill of the search, to learn the unknown, to see the unseen, to discover what no man has discovered before, as the true treasure they sought. Eugene Brunner, in my opinion, was the last of these true explorers of the Llanganati.

■ ■ ■

---

[282] Dyott's new wife wanted to join him on his expedition into the wilds of Brazil searching for Colonel Fawcett, which in my opinion Dyott appropriately rejected. However, Dyott's wife did accompany him on a portion of his expedition to India. Mrs. Dyott would later remain at home raising the couple's family.

Eugene Brunner [283] the man was quite an enigma. Little can be ascertained and verified regarding Brunner's life and background prior to his arrival in Ecuador on the first day of January in 1938, where he arrived at twenty-two and a half years of age. Brunner was born in the afternoon on 18 Jun 1915 in Zurich, Switzerland, to a Swiss mother Berta Luise Willen, and a German father Eugen Brunner, a well-to-do family connected in high society. Brunner's father was apparently a wealthy German businessman with strong social and political contacts in the military and government, although his father would later lose the family wealth. Brunner's grandfather had been a Major General in the German army during World War I on the Russian front and his father was in "war service" when Eugene was born.

Brunner at some point studied commercial drawing in Switzerland where he spent most of his early years, his illustrations clearly showing a keen artists eye and aptitude for drawing. The only other fact that can be positively ascertained is that Brunner died in the military hospital on 3 Jun 1984, in Quito, Ecuador. The following biography of Brunner's life prior to his arrival in Ecuador is based on second and third hand accounts that cannot be verified but appear to be consistent.

■ ■ ■

Apparently Brunner was in Berlin during the infamous "Night of the Long Knives" that took place between 30 Jun and 2 Jul 1934. The story goes that seven of Brunner's young friends were killed by the Nazis during the purge. Brunner supposedly had been part of an organization that smuggled people out of Nazi Germany and into Switzerland when he was caught and spent six months in a concentration camp.

The Night of the Long Knives occurred during Hitler's rise to power in the Nazi Party and was a series of rapid executions and purge of the paramilitary SA or Brownshirts. The SA in the beginning of the Nazi Party had been organized into an armed band of several hundred thousand men to protect Nazi meetings, to break up the meetings of others and to terrorize those who opposed Hitler. Later, Chief of the SA Roehm, proposed to make the SA the foundation of a new peoples army supplanting the regular army should Hitler come to power. Hitler however could not afford to offend the army and gave no support to this proposal. In Germany as in latter day Ecuador, the republic and its leadership's continued existence depended on the will of the officers' corps.

Relations between Roehm of the SA and Army High Command continued to deteriorate. The army was pressing for a purge but would not participate, Hitler chose to pay for his elevation to power and the armies support by the sacrifice of Roehm and the SA. Roehm's two most powerful enemies, Göring and Himmler, had in mind not only to purge the SA, but to liquidate other opponents. Long lists were drawn up of present and past enemies to eliminate, including political activists. "Many were killed out of pure

---

[283] Born Eugen, known as Eugene in English and Eugenio in Spanish, Gino to his friends.

vengeance and having opposed Hitler in the past, others murdered apparently because they knew too much and at least one because of mistaken identity."[284]

Hitler made a call to Göring in Berlin with the prearranged code word "Kolibri" (hummingbird) that unleashed a wave of murderous violence in Berlin and more than twenty other cities. Nazi SS execution squads under Himmler along with Göring's private police force roared through the streets hunting down SA leaders and anyone on the prepared list of political enemies, the *Reich List of Unwanted Persons*. Estimates of the dead vary widely from two hundred to a thousand. Thousands more were arrested, with only half of the dead being actual members of the SA.

Hitler himself acknowledged in a speech that sixty-one had been shot including nineteen SA leaders, thirteen more died resisting arrest for a total of seventy-four killed, while three more had committed suicide. *The White Book of the Purge* published in Paris, indicates that four hundred and one were shot, yet it only identifies one hundred-sixteen. However, during the Munich trials the figure of more than a thousand having been killed was more commonly given.

■ ■ ■

At some point Brunner had also been shot and spent time in a hospital in Switzerland. It would be shortly after his release from the hospital that Brunner returned to Germany, where ultimately Brunner chose to flee the Nazism that was overtaking Germany. Brunner had chosen as his destination the Republic of Ecuador, for which he departed by rail from Zurich in mid-December 1937. Brunner traveled through France to La Rochelle [285] on the coast, from where he caught an English freighter or steamship [286] for the trans-Atlantic crossing, then on to Ecuador. [287]

During World War II Brunner did not answer the Fuhrer's call for all German countrymen to return to the Fatherland as many Germans' did, after all Brunner had fled Germany to avoid Nazism. Instead Brunner remained in Ecuador and supplied information to the United States on German activities there. Supposedly, this involvement nearly cost Brunner his life on

---

[284] From *The Rise and fall of the Third Reich (1960)* by William L. Shirer.

[285] La Rochelle - City in western France and a seaport on the Bay of Biscay, a part of the Atlantic Ocean.

[286] Trans-Atlantic crossings took between twelve days and two weeks during the late 1930s. Brunner's exact route to Ecuador upon leaving France is not perfectly clear.

[287] The author Honigsbaum, on page 227 of his book writes about Brunner thus ... "On June 30, 1934, 'the Night of the Long Knives', he'd been in Berlin when the Nazis killed seven of his close friends. He escaped by jumping out a window, but they caught up with him soon afterward and threw him into a concentration camp. It was when he got out, six months later, that he fled to Ecuador." Brunner in fact arrived in Ecuador on the first day of 1938 three years after his release from the concentration camp.

two separate occasions, as the Nazis in Ecuador tried to kill him. If Brunner truly was, or believed he was spying for the United States, this would have added greatly to the paranoia that one develops as a treasure hunter.

Brunner married twice in Ecuador. His first wife bore him a daughter and at some point they became separated and/or divorced. Brunner lived in the "Old Quito" historical district until sometime around 1983 [288] when he moved to the "La Vicentina" sector of Quito. Brunner remarried shortly thereafter and just month's prior to his death, with Brunner's second wife being this author's mother-in-law. Brunner and my mother-in-law spent hours, days, weeks and months pouring over his charts, maps, and notes rewriting from memory Brunner's manuscript chapter *El Tesoro en las Misteriosas Montañas de Llanganati* that had apparently been stolen. Brunner would be working on recreating these exact papers in the hospital prior to his death.

Brunner had assembled a three inch thick, brown, three ringbinder, stuffed with personal memorabilia, on the cover of which Brunner had mounted a large medallion of the Ecuadorian Ejército (army). Inside were newspaper stories and clippings relating Brunner's expeditions into the Llanganatis and other parts of Ecuador. The binder contained clippings about plane crashes where Brunner was sent by the military on rescue missions in rugged mountain passes, or to recover bodies. Also included were newspaper stories concerning Brunner's search for sunken treasure off the coast, his salvage contracts with the Navy, and articles about his training of navy divers. I would learn that Brunner himself had spent more than five thousand hours diving in the coastal and inland waters of Ecuador.

From Brunner's writings and through comments made by people that knew him personally, it is obvious to see how deeply Brunner cared for the indigenous peoples of Ecuador. A poor man in his own right, Brunner always took great care of his indigenous porters. These hardy mountain men would cut trail and transport eighty to ninety pound packs [289] of rubber and canvas on Brunner's expeditions in exchange for food and fair wages. Brunner not only supplied his porters with provisions, he made sure the provisions consisted of their regular diet.[290] When Brunner was financially

---

[288] Peter Lourie writes in his book that he visited Brunner in Old Quito in 1982 so it would have been sometime after this.

[289] When packing for an expedition the intent is to divide your supplies and equipment evenly between all of your carriers. In this manner each porter carries an equal load, and if a pack should be lost in one way or another, the expedition would only lose a portion of its supplies and could continue on. (For example ... with ten porters and twenty pounds of sugar, each pack has two pounds of sugar, etc ...)

[290] By providing his porters with the diet they were accustomed to eating, to some degree Brunner was able to avoid sickness and discontent among his porters while on expedition. For this reason Brunner was not plagued as others before him had been, by the desertion of porters.

capable, he went as far as helping them with clothing and necessities as well. His attitude toward the indigenous porters appeared to be to treat these people with respect and never ask them to do anything he could not or would not do himself.

Not only did Brunner empathize with the poverty of the Indians, but he was disappointed by Ecuador's wealthy many times and taken advantage of by partners, authors and others throughout his quest. Brunner loved his life's work, while working on an idea he disappeared, buried in his papers, lost in thought he forgot everything else. His life's work, the stories and discoveries that he held so dear, over the past thirty years have been minimized and trivialized by others and regrettably his involvement and discoveries are slowly fading from existence.

■ ■ ■

Lust for Inca gold continues with the following stories from Eugene K. Brunner's unpublished manuscript *Ecuador y Sus Tesoros* (*Ecuador and Her Treasures*) and his personal papers which are presented here in their entirety. Brunner's manuscript is a compilation of stories concerning many of Ecuador's lost treasures, of which the Llanganati treasure was only a part. Brunner's manuscript also includes chapters on the Nisag and Tunguru Sangay treasure deposits, two more of the seven treasure shipments of the undelivered ransom of Atahualpa, and chapters on Mar Bravo and Isla de la Plata concerning sunken treasure off the coast of Ecuador to name a few. These and other chapters are not relevant to our story and therefore are not included in this book.

■ ■ ■

Brunner writes ... "In Europe on the other side of the seas, a young child of seven years had a strange dream. He found himself in a high and cold mountain, standing to one side of a gloomy and obscure lake. On the far side of the lake rose a great promontory from the back of which fell a large waterfall. At the foot and to one side of the waterfall the boy saw the black mouth of a cave. The boy went around the lake and entered the cave, that from some site not visible, received the light of day. Here he went down some stairs to an underground cavern full of strange things. There were life-sized figures of men, women, birds, animals and plants, large vases and receptacles' full of multicolored stones, and all of this created a brilliant radiance because everything was gold and silver! But, as well there were a great number of human skeletons, the terrible corpses frightened the child that awoke, nearly jumping from his bed crying. [291]

---

[291] This was Brunner's original version of his dream story, written prior to the second version reproduced in the beginning of this book. Brunner's second version of this story includes an exact description of Lake Brunner and it's landmarks, an expanded description of the treasure, obviously culled straight from his dog eared copy of *The Incas of Pedro Cieza de León*, and includes Blacke's quote ... "I could not remove it alone or with thousand's of men" ... with references to the treasure that was removed in a backpack.

"Later his mother calmed him down with a kiss while saying ... 'Face it you have had a nightmare, tomorrow don't eat so much for dinner,' covered him and retired. The child returned to sleep and the following morning it was almost completely forgotten. Until, when on the first day of the year 1938 he set a foot in the Puerto de la Libertad, for the first time in the land of Ecuador.

"Young at twenty-two and a half years of age, he came to work for the Swiss company of Scottoni that was building the railroad from Ibarra to San Lorenzo in Esmeraldas. But when he arrived the Scottoni Company was not working, there had been a change in government and Scottoni was left without a contract. And I found myself in a country where they spoke a language that I couldn't understand and was unemployed. [292]

"An Austrian naturalized Ecuadorian Francisco Mike Solis and an old North American Charles W. Fredericks, were installing in the country house of the Acosta-Velasco family in Sangolqui, electricity and water, they gave me work. They were good friends and they knew a great deal of legends and stories about hidden treasures, Tolas and Tumbas of the ancient Indians.

"There in the country house once you completed the day's work, in the afternoon and night there was no place to go. Mike told me stories and things of the past about Ecuador. One night he told me the history of the treasure of Llanganati and of a book about an Italian expedition that had been there, written by Luciano Andrade Marin. Naturally on my first trip to Quito I purchased the book and from that moment on Mike had no free time. Night after night he had to read and translate for me the contents of the book. I am sure that he quickly repented telling me about the book. At least he asked me with emphasis, that I hurry up and learn Spanish.

"One afternoon he asked me why I had this uncomprehensible interest in the history of Llanganati, but his question was left unanswered. I didn't want him to consider me crazy, but from the first day that he told me about the lake in a high mountain, mentioned in the *Derrotero de Valverde*, I remembered that strange dream of my childhood.

"The work in the country house of the Acosta family I liked very much and here I learned how to ride a horse. On Sundays I passed for every direction in the Valley de los Chillos and here as well I met the first Ecuadorian friends, and as well started to stutter Spanish. Being that I didn't learn Spanish in a classroom, but across days of contact with people, and more or less of necessity. I learned as well a large amount of bad words, and I believe it is for this that sometimes I am called the bad speaking gringo.

"One nice day, early in the morning the young Jaime Acosta Velasco, who passed the weekends in the country house, opened the closed windows and

---

[292] Brunner had traveled to Ecuador with the prospect of a job with the Scottoni Company through a family friend of his well connected family. When Brunner was confronted with no job prospects, he survived by taking on odd jobs and painting murals.

pointed to a mountain, better stated a hill illuminated for the first rays of sunlight and said 'Llanganati, Cerro Hermoso, much gold.' (I should indicate that the hill was the Sincholahua and not Cerro Hermoso.) It was on this fine day when it was born inside me the idea and the plan for my first expedition to the mysterious mountains of Llanganati, to search for the lake and cave of the dream of my early childhood, in search of the treasure.

"Many years later, when I learned that some Englishmen had discovered a treasure in a cave in Llanganati, I was very sure that the destiny with which one was born, that is the karma of each person, in one form or another wanted that I intervene in the discovery of this treasure. There have been others that dreamt in their childhood about certain historical discoveries. For example the German Heinrich Schliemann, discoverer of the ruins of the city of Troy the base of the *Illiad* of the Greek poet Homer (2500 AC).

"I am positive, that the dream of my infancy, the book *Llanganati* of Luciano Andrade Marin and my insatiable desire to know the unknown, to see what is beyond the horizon, behind the next mountain, are the principal means that pushes and pushes me totally to be for forty-two years the most hardened and constant explorer of Llanganati. Much have I suffered and have made to suffer my family and others during these years owing to my obsession to continue exploring these inhospitable mountains. But something greater than my own determination keeps pushing and calling, that which pertains to the glorious son of the Kingdom of Quito, the ultimate legitimate Inca Atahualpa, hidden by his older brother by the same father, Ati II named Rumiñahui.

"Be it good or bad, but Llanganati is my destination. Of one thing I am positive, if I should be surprised and one day discover the treasure, this could serve to scatter blood and be cause of fights and disagreements. In which case, it would be better if it stayed where it is. The gold of Atahualpa once recovered should serve so that the Ecuadorian Indian could integrate into the national life with dignity and with guarantees, in that case and only in that case, I am ready to deliver the treasure to the government of Ecuador."

■ ■ ■

Two of Brunner's maps are published at this point in our story as an aid to the reader in understanding the general area described in Brunner's writings and to trace some of his, and others, expedition routes into this inhospitable region.[293] Drawn and revised by Brunner in 1973, the maps detail the northern region and other landmarks of the Llanganatis as they relate to our story.

---

[293] Notice that for this different route into the Roncadores, Yana Cocha is on thy right hand, not "thy left hand" as indicted in the *Derrotero*.

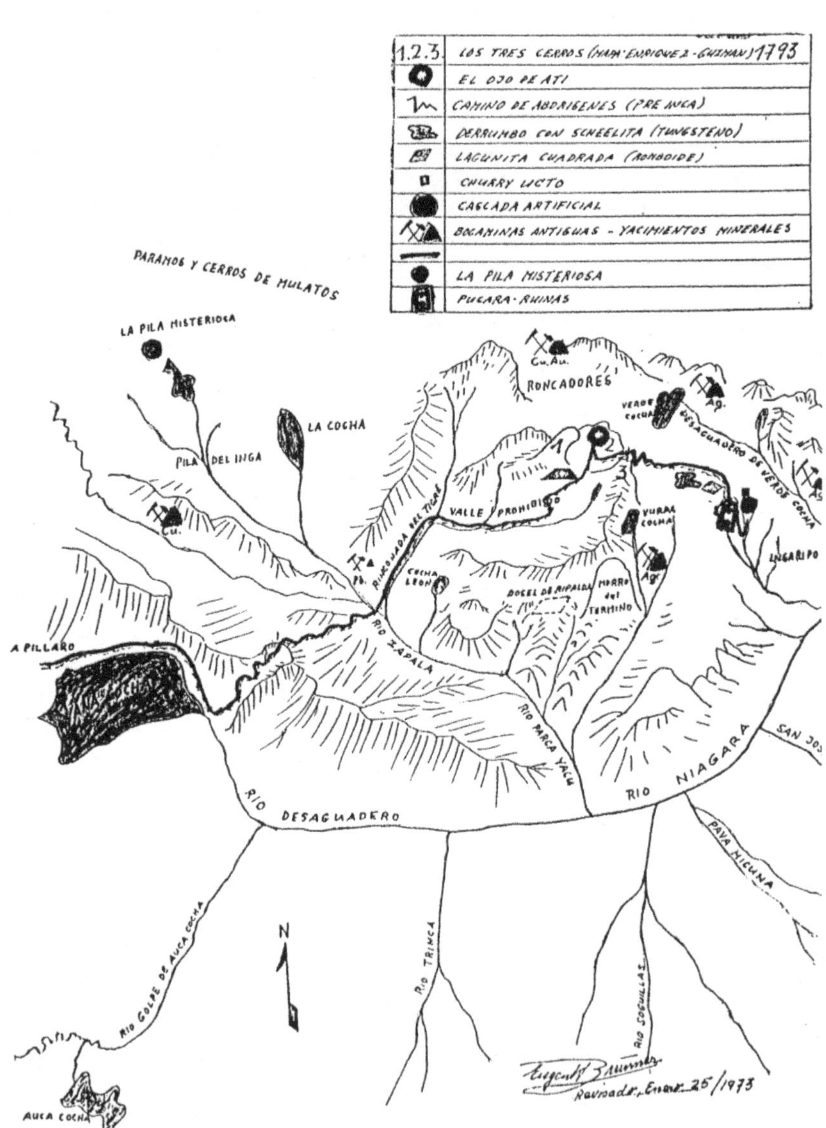

Brunner's Roncadores Map

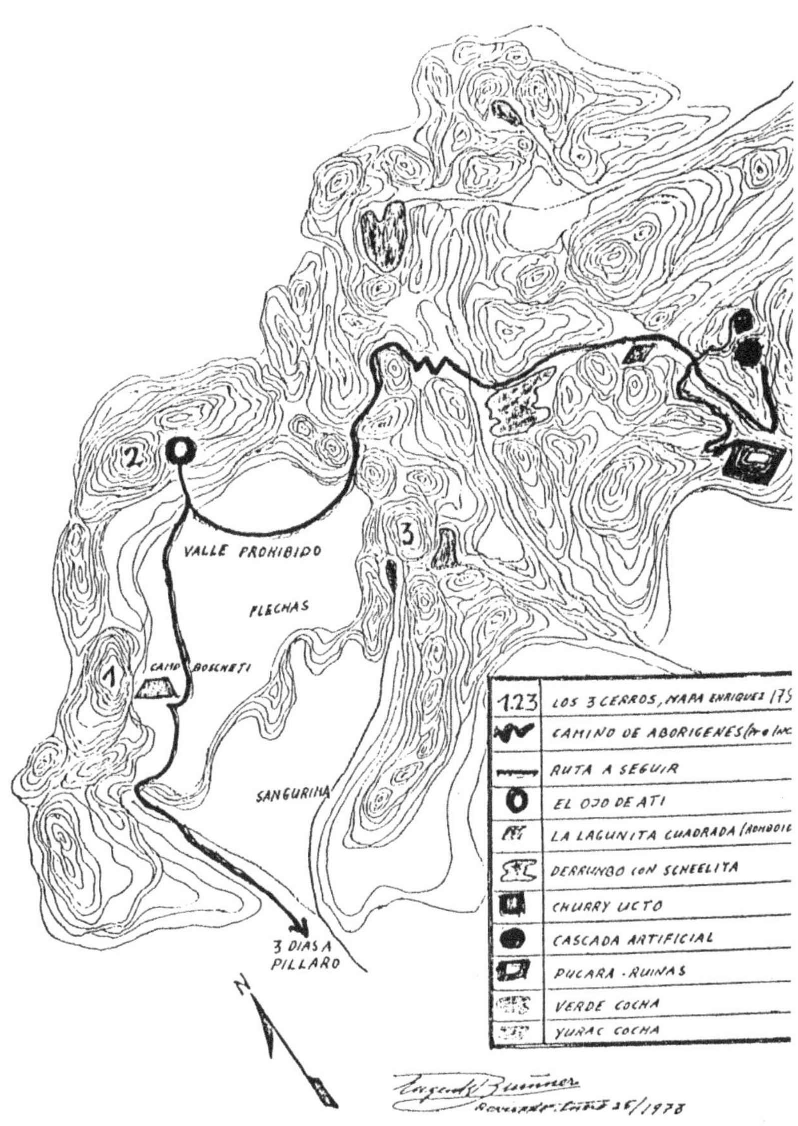

Brunner's Tres Cerros Map

The subject area of these maps contain the northern most trail on Guzmán's map which travels through the highly mineralized mining zone of the Llanganatis known as the Roncadores. The trail ends in the top northeast quadrant of Guzmán's map, which is the area depicted in Brunner's two maps. Cerro Hermoso, Cerro Negro and Zunchu-Urcu are not located in this quadrant, but are found in the southeast quadrant of Guzmán's map, which would be oriented below the area Brunner has represented in these maps.

Most if not all of the rivers depicted at the bottom of Brunner's Map flow north, having as their source and descending from, the ridges' south of Río Desaguadero, which are clearly depicted on Loch's expedition sketch and the Dyott map. When these three maps are viewed in conjunction with each other, a clearer picture of the region can be attained.

The big black lake Yana Cocha [294] sits on the far left of Brunner's map on the *Derrotero's* route from Píllaro, the major rivers and lakes of the region, the purported three Cerros Llanganati and the region known as the Roncadores with its numerous mineral deposits ... all included on Brunner's drawings.

Many interesting discoveries that Brunner made over the years appear on these two map illustrations and their index legends. Enriquez Guzmán's [295] purported "Tres Cerros Llanganati," the three Llanganati Mountains (peaks) in the form of a triangle, are clearly located and numbered by Brunner along with Camp Boschetti in Valle Prohibido (Forbidden Valley).

On the purported second Cerro Llanganati Brunner has placed a black circle and the legend ... "Ojo de Ati [Ati's Eye or the Eye of Ati in English]. On the face of this mountain is a large bare rock circle. Below this circle Brunner discovered evidence of pottery shards and fire. The Incas Brunner theorized, would light a large fire at night under the "Eye" and the light would illuminate off the bare rock giving the Indians a point of direction in the mountains for travel at night, to and from the mines, similar to the function of a light house.

Another important discovery, a very small square lake and trench. This small lake or pit and trench with a wall at one end containing a gate or sluice could very well have been a "guayra" where the Indians smelted their metals. The southeast quadrant of a mountain is exactly where history and

---

[294] "The big black lake Yana Cocha"- This landmark that is mentioned briefly by Valverde, Spruce, Andrade, Loch, Dyott, Blomberg and Brunner, is clearly viewed on Guzmán's map. In order to give the reader a sense of scale to the map and place in perspective the accounts of expeditions into these inhospitable mountains, one must recall that Spruce estimates Yana Cocha to be roughly four miles long by two miles wide!

[295] Not to be confused with Spruce's map copied from the map drawn by the botanist Atanasio Guzmán who died in 1806 or 1808. There is a second map drawn in 1793 by the Píllaro curate Enríquez de Guzmán. This map places the "Tres Cerros Llanganati" north of the Desaguadero de Yana Cocha.

science establish that a guayra [296] was required to be placed in order to produce sufficient heat to melt metals ... exactly the spot where Brunner had located this discovery ... labeled as "la lagunita cuadrada" on his map.

Other points of interest on Brunner's maps include the route to ascend the mountain "ruta a seguir" ... the zig zag path of an Indian trail "camino de aborigenes"...the small lakes "Verde Cocha and Yurac Cocha"...the ruins of a fortress "pucara en ruinas"...an artificial waterfall "cascada artificial"...a spiral staircase carved in rock "churry ucto" ... trees with white foliage "sangurimas" ... gigantic arrow-cane "flechas" ... and the fact that the trail from the base of the mountain was only three days to Píllaro.

Even though certain landmarks that coincide with the *Derrotero* were discovered in the zone, this last fact alone ... that the trail from the base of the mountain is only three days travel from Píllaro ... should have indicated to all the explorers of the area ... Guzmán, Loch, Boschetti, D'Orsay, Andrade, Salvador and Brunner to name just a few ... that they were searching in the wrong area.[297] Not only does the route traveled in the *Derrotero de Valverde* require four nights and five days travel, the hieroglyph and its explanation direct the explorer south ... away from the Roncadores in the direction of three other peaks in the form of a triangle. The author/explorer Rolf Blomberg makes my point most succinctly in *Buried Gold and Anacondas* ... "But I assure you that all who have searched for the Valverde treasure north of the Río Llanganati[298] have searched in vain!"

■ ■ ■

Brunner's maps, along with those of Guzmán, Loch, Dyott and Blacke, provide the reader with points of reference and orientation, but only a one-dimensional view and understanding of these "inhospitable" Llanganatis, a zone in which Mother Nature is continually changing its appearance. Maps alone do not provide the true sense of what explorers to this region must have endured obtaining these maps. These explorers' faced a toilsome march over difficult almost impenetrable ground, whose distances were

---

[296] Rolf Blomberg in *Buried Gold and Anacondas* incorrectly translates and misquotes the *Derrotero* stating ... "on the western side of the mountain you ought to find a guayra" ... guayra's were located on a mountains eastern declivity.

[297] This zone is the same area where the landmark ... "location of probably world's biggest gold mine" of Blacke's first map should be discovered.

[298] Blomberg, having made six expeditions into the Llanganatis (three with his partner Andrade), further describes Río Llanganati as the river that starts in the Black Lake (Yana-cocha). Spruce however is much more specific in the portion of his 1860 paper omitted from *Notes of a Botanist* by Wallace ... "After passing this lake the river takes the name Desaguadero de Yana-cocha, and lower down that of Río de las Sangurimas, receiving in its course the Río de los Mulatos from the north, and a good way further down the Río de los Llanganatis, coming from the south along a deep ravine (Cañada honda) between Rundu-umu and the Volcan del Topo."

covered and explored under the greatest of hardships, exhaustion and even death.

One can also study the topographic maps and satellite images of today and not get a true understanding of this region. Its desolate peaks, snow covered in the winter, are lofty peaks constantly buffeted by biting cold wind, sleet and snow. Its precipitous walls of rock, perilous perpendicular slippery rock faces, crags, hillsides, precipices and ravines are all transversed in perpetual mists, freezing fogs and never ceasing rains that descend in biting cold soaking torrents that penetrate to the bone. The regions labyrinth of passages through bamboo thickets and subtropical valleys, almost primeval forests with dense boughs and roots, its rivers with their fierce and swift currents or rapids, its bogs and omnipresent mud, cannot be appreciated ... until they are endured.

Tramping along, cutting their way foot by foot, yard by yard, sinking into the mud that was everywhere and on everything, sucking them down and holding on with every step they took, these explorers had the fortitude to struggle on year after year, knife or machete in hand, plagued by biting bloodsucking flies, sopping wet ... "soaked to the skin and chilled to the bone."

Rolf Blomberg in *Buried Gold and Anacondas* provides a vivid account of the conditions he encountered in the Llanganatis ... "Trees, stones and rocks were covered with thick moss, and taking hold of them was like taking hold of a sponge full of water. It was impossible to tell whether the branches and trunks were sound or rotten, nor was it possible to see the deep holes with which the ground was pitted: everything was hidden under the moss."

■ ■ ■

Brunner writes ... "My first expedition into the Llanganatis during 1938 was somewhat terrible and an utter failure. In the company of three porters and José Ignacio Quinteros,[299] I left Píllaro poorly equipped and badly protected, above all from everything that clothing against the rain refers! In the beginning the time was very good and full of sun. The first day we arrived at Tambo de Mama Rita [300] [Inn or Lodging of Mama Rita] which is the ultimate dairy farm. Each year in the dry months, as to say in the spring of the narrow Inter-Andean plain between the mountains, the people of Píllaro, San Andrés and San José de Peale bring their cattle here and return for them in Autumn.

"Here there is an Indian woman well over one hundred years of age. This woman still works everyday herding the cows, taking care of the pigs and other farm chores. She had a fantastic memory and great teeth for her age. She said she recalled many explorers and travelers. Her eyes kept holding a strange path when she spoke of what the ancients had touched.

---

[299] The same guide utilized by Captain Eric Erskine Loch two years prior.

[300] Blomberg describes Tambo de Mama Rita in *Buried Gold and Anacondas* as "a few grass huts about 11,500 feet above sea level, on the shore of lake Cocha de Tambo."

Unfortunately at that time my Spanish, if the few words I cackled could be called that, was awful. Of one thing I am sure, the old woman knew a lot and liked me, however every other word I did not understand. For example yurac is one of the words that she repeated and repeated, gesturing and pointing vaguely to the southeast, Yurac, Yurac Llanganati she would say. José Ignacio and Amador Lopez tried to explain me, with signs, but at the time Spanish was like Chinese for me.

"It was here I ate my first beans cooked with fresh cheese, beaten and strained of machica [301] which I liked a lot. The things that I liked the least on my expedition were the bugs and lice. Lice came quick and in great number as they did not yet have DDT.[302] The only defense against lice was the bath and in these altitudes bathes were quite short, considering the tremendous cold that exists in these mountains. Myself, I preferred the lice over pneumonia.

"The second day we continued our trek and in the middle of the day, leaving a gorge and passing through a Jucal [forest of reeds], we saw in front of us the small lakes that appear as eyeglasses [Lagunas de Anteojos] exactly as Valverde described centuries ago. 'The Anteojos'. . . José and Amador shouted at me! My emotion was great and I hurried my pace, within no time we were on the edge! It was very marshy but be that as it may, I climbed to the nose of land in-between the lakes but the fog closed every view and soon it began to rain. We assembled the tent, if that's what you could call the piece of canvas that we had and spent a very bad night.

"Early in the morning we were found to be on our way again. It was no longer raining but the fog was very dense. We passed the great black lake Yana Cocha, which is to say we imagined that we saw it in the fog, we went around a swamp and suddenly we found ourselves on an embankment, undoubtedly a road. José Ignacio pointed to a stretch of rocks, which had been to my surprise cut by hand. The road of the Inca Amador reported to me. From this point we had to descend the slope toward the outlet, this is what you call the stream that descends from Yana Cocha, the outlet or Desaguadero de Yana Cocha. The rain fell incessantly and it made me completely wet to the bone. My teeth began to chatter and I lacked only a flamenco song to keep me company.

"We arrived at the end of the descent and here was another river that came from the other side of the valley that had a waterfall whose thunder could be heard from afar, the outlet of Auca Cocha, the lake of the unfaithful. My guides mentioned in passing that previously some men had made camp there. Soon the laborers cut sticks and grass with long leaves and with them they built a shelter. We placed the tent inside on the ground, my surprise was great that not a drop of water penetrated and the rain sang to us tapping

---

[301] Machica is a type of corn or wheat flour.

[302] Dichloro Diphenyl Trichloroethane is one of the most well-known synthetic pesticides whose insecticidal properties were not discovered until 1939.

on the roof. We reflected listening to the beat of the rain drops at the same time expectant with anxieties for something but to eat. I got into a change of clothes and a strange well being unexpectedly came over me. At last I was in the Llanganatis, the waterfall that roared to one side of the camp had also been heard by Valverde and Padre Longo! That night I reflected ... two outlets, in one of them died Padre Longo, but in which one?

"The situation that bothered me was not being able to converse with my companions. I knew that Amador had accompanied innumerable expeditions with Boschetti, Re, Puch, the English Captain Loch and others, he must have known a great deal! Also José Ignacio knew a lot, but a strange thing, here in these mountains' José turned uncommunicative, reserved and removed, with a strange look in his eyes. Today I know what caused his sadness in the Llanganatis, but later you will hear more about this.

"Very early in the morning, we were again on our way, in the direction of Parca Yacu (Río Saco) here in the valley it did not make much cold and we advanced rapidly. The trail was terrible with swamps on the side and fallen trees obstructing our feet. It did not rain and even a little sun brought us joy. At midday we were at the Parca Yacu and José Ignacio said there was enough time for us to advance to Pava Micuna. At five in the afternoon we arrived there and we found the remainder of an old camp ... Boschetti and Puch said Amador, quickly repairing the old shelter. The rain fell again torrentially and the river rose and rose. The same thing occurred with the water that descended from Pava Micuna! We waited three days and it did not stop raining, the food supplies diminished and we had no choice but to return.

"We walked and walked in the Rancho del Golpe until I was no longer able. Now I was completely soaked with not one dry piece of clothing to put on me. We spent the night huddled up too mutually heat ourselves. At the crack of dawn we were going up the slope passing Yana Cocha and Anteojos and arrived at Río Milin. The Milin had enlarged its volume in an implausible way. The water was dark, bubbling and foaming as it rapidly passed in front of us, how would we cross? We went downstream, but it was worse the river had made itself wider. We returned and looked upstream where we found a site where we could jump across.

"The porters removed our loads and piece by piece they threw them to the other side. Amador took my bundle of tied up clothes and threw them to the other side, but they rolled off the bank and into the water forever. Like an arrow my package disappeared in the turbulent water. I almost began to cry, they were the only clothes I owned! The calamity for me was not over, as upon crossing the river I fell inside. Completely wet and demoralized we arrived at Mama Rita's.

"At night I began to cough with sharp pains in the back that felt like pneumonia. But the old woman, who surely must have heard my cough, got up and put some hot dribbles on my back and covered it with a cloth. It was a smear of hot machica and the bad cough and pain was dispelled.

"We arrived at Píllaro and I had to return as quickly as possible to Quito. I had to work to buy myself new clothes and naturally for another expedition! I had seen the Lagunas de Anteojos, Yana Cocha and the remains of the Inca Trail, the passion of the Llanganatis had seized me and even today twenty-six years later will not let me loose." [Written by Brunner in 1964]

■ ■ ■

Brunner continues ... "Subsequently another expedition was mounted in 1939, under the same conditions. Ill prepared and with inappropriate equipment, the expedition did not even arrive at my final camp site of the previous year, once again defeated by the inhospitable rain and fog of the Llanganatis.

"Some expeditions I made under the same conditions as the first one. The death of José Ignacio Quinteros in the Llanganatis occurred at the same time of yet another expedition I made, in which we did not even arrive at my final camp of 1938. The causes were the same, rain, fog and inappropriate equipment. When I exited the Llanganatis this time, I was completely bankrupt.

"Afterwards I worked for a time in a plantation of orange trees and other citrus in the province of El Oro. Here I earned only two Sucres [303] daily of which one paid for the food and the other went for cigarettes to scare away the mosquitos at night. I slept in a large dog shed and a board was my bed, but in the three months that I worked there I learned a lot of Spanish. My work was the pruning of the trees. These trees were fumigated with chemical substances and when I punctured myself on one of the enormous thorns that grow on orange trees, I would quickly get an infection of yellowish-white fluid. The owner of the hacienda a Señor Rodfolfo Vincent, seeing how I suffered with my hands that were two large bags of pus, gave me two hundred Sucres so that I could return to Guayaquil.

"On the first day of September 1940 finding myself in Santa Rosa, the war exploded in Europe. In the early morning of the second I arrived in Guayaquil where I cured my hands and the 16th of the same month, I obtained administrative work in the Hotel Crespo in Guayaquil. There was news that caused me to leave this employment and directed me immediately to the Andes and the city of Ambato. The news reported more or less the return from England of Captain Eric Erskin Loch, explorer for years in the mountains of Llanganati, and that he would try climbing these mountains from the Oriental region by the Río Ila! When I arrived in Ambato Loch was already in Ila and it was impossible for me to follow him. When Loch returned, he exhibited in the Banco de Pichincha a large amount of gold that he had found in the Río Ila.

"I traveled to Quito and worked in the decoration of showcases [painting, graphics, artwork] and landing a big job at the Night Club Boris Palace. While I decorated in Boris Palace it came out in the paper the news of the

---

[303] Sucre - National currency of Ecuador from 1884 until 2000 when Ecuador converted to the US dollar.

disappearance and probable death of José Ignacio Quinteros in Llanganati. It gave me a great deal of grief, for José Ignacio was my good friend."

■ ■ ■

The story of Brunner's friend José Ignacio Quinteros, also known as "Old Q" is yet another interesting story mired in the myths and legends of the Llanganati. Old Q had by all accounts, been searching for the Valverde treasure his entire life. Countless were the expeditions Old Q made from Píllaro, where he lived. Old Q explored alone and in the company of most, if not all, the explorers' of the region during his lifetime.

Captain Loch had this to say about his contact with Old Q ... "I had always thought that the fact that the Llanganatis treasure was thrown into a lake has been given undue prominence, possibly through the romantic features attached to the story. It would appear to be of far greater importance to discover the ancient mines from which the gold had been extracted. An invaluable clew to their location would be the discovery of some ancient roadway.

"Just at this time I met Senor Quinteros, 'old Q,' as we called him, whose stories held out a hope of finding what we sought. Tall, slender, with grizzled gray beard, and forever enfolded in an ancient black swinging poncho cape, old Q might have stepped out of some old-world portrait painted in Spain's heyday. Always courteous in the extreme, he had the true grand manner.

"Scarcely had I met him and acknowledged his sweeping bow, than he rambled off on his one great dream … Valverde and the Treasure. His life was completely wrapped up in it. He knew the old Guide by heart, every version of it, and was convinced he knew where other seekers had gone wrong. Dwelling here in Píllaro, in the very shadow of those great peaks and amid mangled copies of worn old maps, penciled sketches, and diagrams he had spent his life trying to solve the Valverde riddle.

"He spent hours in my company, not by my choosing but his. Desperately anxious to join us, begging to be taken, he asked for nothing more in return than 'anything I chose' to give him should we be successful in finding the 'Lost Mines.' But I had already decided to take him—for quite a different reason. During his rambling talks of previous trips into the mountains, and he had made several, he talked constantly of a 'mountain crowned with gold' with a straight row of palm trees at its base.

"To the devil with his 'mountain of gold'! I didn't believe a word of that, but the 'straight row of palm trees'—straight—that was something. If true it meant the hand of man had been there before! The existence of palm trees on the eastern slopes of the Llanganatis was by no means beyond the realm of possibility. The more sheltered valleys on that side, on the equator as they are, drop rapidly to the low altitudes of the Oriente, and tropical foliage could be expected.

"If old Q's palm trees existed and were in a 'straight line,' it was reasonable to suppose they had been artificially planted at some time or other. This might mean an ancient roadway, and a road might lead to anything! People don't build roads for no reason. Where could one such lead to? I wondered. Old frontier posts of the Inca Empire?, Or old mines? To find such a road might lead to a discovery that would save months of indiscriminate search based on old maps, old guides, and the like. In fact, during all my explorations in the Llanganatis I was constantly on the lookout for signs of an old roadway as a first clew, far more than any 'Three Peaks,' lakes, or cascades. That there were such mines and such hoards of accumulated gold is unquestionable."

Once Loch's expedition had been in the Llanganatis a short period of time, reaching the halfway point contained within Valverde's *Derrotero*, Loch noticed a change in Old Q's temperament and behavior and would later write ... "I turned eagerly to question old Q, but to my surprise an abrupt change had come over him. He became vague in the extreme, and for a man of his natural courtesy, almost surly. He refused to sit near us, and when I asked about his 'mountain,' he answered that he didn't know, nor even the way.

"The thought of spending a night on this inhospitable knife-edge was an unpleasant one, and we were carefully feeling for a way down when the mist thinned for a few moments to show us below a long pear-shaped lake with an outline impossible to mistake … old Q's landmark, as described by him and marked on his map.

"Old Q's strange manner there on top of the pass caused me to reflect for a moment on his actions over the past few hours during our ascent to the pass. At first he had been eager to get on to his 'mountain of gold,' but of late he had hung back and had been of little use in directing our steps. Yet there was no doubt whatsoever about our being on the right line—he had described it far too often. We could get nothing out of him now, however; in fact he would hardly speak, and gave every evidence of having changed his mind, and appeared to be brooding over something.

"This became more and more apparent as we climbed down the ridge, heading for a cave under an overhanging rock. Old Q deliberately trailed behind us, making no effort to show us the way.

"By the next morning it was raining hard again, but although old Q was a little more tractable, his statements and descriptions became so confusing, involved, and contradictory that they became a menace. He had become a changed man. I tried kindness and threats. I said I would send him back if he did not help us now. Finally he gave in and, setting out, we worked our way to a chain of three lakes threaded together like huge beads upon a slender string of river.

"Before leaving that day, old Q had sworn that his 'mountain of gold' lay over this pass, at the foot of this enormous valley. This was borne out by his sketch map. But he now became hopelessly vague. 'This is the valley, Senor, this is the valley,' he mumbled; but I do not recognize the mountains, and as for my beautiful 'mountain of gold'… I do not see it.'

"By now I had lost hope of Q's line of palm trees, but the next night he came to me and told me that he was about to give me a great confidence: that he now knew where his 'mountain of gold' was. It was quite close, he said, and he earnestly wished to take us there in the morning. He was sincere and genuine in his belief, I was convinced; and, having come so far, I determined to give him one more chance on the morrow.

"Dawn came, and we awakened to see right before us, breaking through the mist, the pride and majesty of the Llanganatis, the Cerro Hermoso. This giant peak named 'Beautiful Mountain' has been vested with sacredness in the old legends. We had long since circled this peak, and were now well to the east of it; but, owing to the constant bad weather, this was the first time we had seen it.

"Everyone was soon astir, and we made an early start, old Q ahead and now apparently brisk and eager to show us his great secret. He warmed up to his subject with the old enthusiasm he had had in Píllaro. He talked quite rationally until of a sudden I saw again that strange, far-away look return to his eyes as he murmured something about the great confidence and something that had never before been seen by a white man other than himself. This was his mission, he said, and once it was accomplished he was ready for death. Such talk would have been enthralling but for that look in his eyes.

"His pace became slower and slower. He didn't seem ill, but that moroseness which I had come to recognize quickly was upon him again. He now declared he could not reach the place of the palm trees before nightfall. Then suddenly from behind me I heard a groan, and turning found he had collapsed.

"I pondered deeply on old Q and his dreams. I couldn't make him out. I am sure that he was thoroughly convinced of the truth of his statements about the palm trees and 'mountain of gold.' He believed them utterly, and it must be remembered that he had not asked me for any money at all and never did, to any extent.

"That was the end of Q as what you might call an active member of the party. When I saw him months afterwards in Píllaro he was perfectly normal. It was only when he crossed that fateful pass that he seemed to come under the influence of those terrific, awe inspiring, desolate peaks. My opinion is that years of meditating on his great dream of the treasure, mine or gold mountain, had crystallized them for him into actual fact."

Rolf Blomberg would write after the fact in *Buried Gold and Anaconas* that ... "At Píllaro Captain Loch met an old man named José Ignacio Quinteros, who had been searching for the Valverde treasure all his life and had perhaps been longer in Llanganati than D'Orsay.[304] Old Quinteros had

---

[304] D'Orsay will be discussed shortly, but at the time he may well have been the explorer with the greatest amount of experience spent exploring in the

guided the expedition with great enthusiasm to begin with, but he underwent a change, became taciturn and queer in his behavior, suddenly lost his sense of direction and one day collapsed altogether."

The story goes that once Quinteros left the Llanganatis and arrived back in Píllaro all was well again, he returned to his normal self. Neither would his calamitous defeat with Loch in the mountains, put an end to Old Q's Llanganati explorations. We know for a fact that Old Q accompanied Brunner on his first expedition in 1938, beyond that it is unclear if the two men traveled into the Llanganatis together again. What is clear is that Brunner would make forty to fifty more expeditions, while Old Q would shortly make his last.

Rolf Blomberg would erroneously write in 1955 that ... "Old Quinteros, Captain Loch's companion, was the last man who died in Llanganati.[305] He had been in the neighbourhood of the San José River with a peon who was not quite right in the head. When provisions began to run short the peon had just walked off and left Quinteros to his fate. The old man had tried to return alone, but with his strength reduced by hunger and privations he had not been able to cover the distance; he had collapsed at the foot of a tree and never got up again. It was D'Orsay, the French-American, who found the old treasure-hunter's skeleton."

Brunner told a more detailed version of Old Q's death that was related by Peter Lourie in *Sweat of the Sun, Tears of the Moon*. It appears that on one of Old Q's many expeditions into the Llanganatis he discovered a green stone, an oddity for this region. Old Q dispatched his brother to Quito with the stone to have it analyzed. His brother however, didn't make it to Quito. Instead, the brother met a jeweler in Ambato and sold him the precious stone, telling Old Q that he had lost the stone. Brunner then tells of the events that followed ... "Months later, the jeweler went to Píllaro to the store of Señor Villacresis. And, well, Old Q discovered that he had been cheated by his own brother, that the stone had not been lost, as his brother had told him.

"The jeweler said he'd come to give Old Q fifty thousand Sucres to make an expedition to get more stones like the first. But old Q went crazy. He didn't accept the money. He asked Villacresis for provisions, wheelbarrows, and food for two months. He said he wanted to dig up a landslide where he'd found the green stone. Everyone said he seemed loco. And Villacresis gave Old Q nothing.

"So the last known words of José Ignacio Quinteros were, 'Well, there is no one anymore in the world you can trust.' And he took a little raw sugar, you

---

Llanganatis. D'Orsay established a base camp and his expeditions were purported to have lasted up to eight months at a time.

[305] At least one other man that we know of died in the Llanganatis after Quinteros ... Salvador's porter in 1954. Quinteros was not the last to die in the Llanganatis as of the writing of Blomberg's manuscript, and the list of deaths within the Llanganatis would continue to grow longer.

know this panela, and some máchica, barley flour, and a few other items. And he went alone to the Llanganatis with a mute and deaf idiot Indian. One of these aberrations you find in the sierra.

"Together they went down to the valley of San José de Poaló, where Old Q slipped on a rock and broke one of his legs. This was before the road went through there. So they made a thatched roof, and put a little firewood beside him. And they put Old Q's things near him while the idiot Indian went off to Píllaro to get help.

"But instead of two and a half days, it took the idiot nine days to get out. And fifteen days to organize a search party. When he finally got into the Llanganatis again, the idiot had forgotten where he had left Old Q. They looked all over but couldn't find him."

"It appears that Brunner had learned that his friend was lost and presumably dead in the Llanganatis, through a Quito newspaper toward the end of 1940. It would not be until 1943 when yet another explorer of the Llanganatis, Richard D'Orsay, discovered the skeleton of Old Q propped up against a tree. Due to the climate of the region, the thatch roof was in complete disorder and Old Q's pants had almost rotted away, while his rain poncho and rubber hat were intact. The poor man must have suffered beyond imagination ... a slow death from exposure and starvation."

■ ■ ■

Brunner continues ... "In March of 1941 I again entered the Llanganatis. On this expedition I took a different route, through the area of Lake Auca Cocha and Pan de Azucar (Zunchu Urcu on the map of Atanasio Guzmán) up until the Soguillas. In this zone I found two pieces of the Inca Trail and a large Tola (Indian mound) in the form of a round hill. Behind the Tola on two hills there are two signs in the form of an Indian burial mound, pyramids of stone! But our supplies and food ran out so we had to return. But now I had the certainty of the truth of the *Derrotero de Valverde* because there was obvious and clear evidence that the ancient Indians traveled in these mountains, no longer were there only geographical accidents that you hear about, but the hand of man!

"During the twentieth century there were countless Englishmen and others who came to explore in these mountains. Some came simply as treasure or gold seekers, while others came as botanists, geologists, surveyors, always camouflaged in some way. Some made only one expedition others several and some even settled for decades in Ecuador, while still others traveled as a pendulum between Europe and the Republic of Ecuador in South America. Some of these explorers I knew personally, such as retired Captain Eric Erskine Loch, Scottish and tall, strong and very smart, brave and with a very commendable tenacity." [This story has been related previously and is not repeated here.]

■ ■ ■

Brunner continues ... "Also I met the French-Canadian Richard (Dick to his friends) D'Orsay.[306] We met by chance in the Cordillera de Las Torres, when I was looking for a more direct route out from there. I was descending the western slope of Rundu Uma Urcu or Sacha Llanganati with my two companions, when one of the men said ... patron, over there is smoke. I looked in the direction indicated and indeed a great banner of smoke came out of some bushes well above the gorge of San José.

"Stung by curiosity, we headed in that direction. After an hour we reached a well-built shelter and that is when I met D'Orsay. He invited us to stay for the afternoon and evening there in his camp. This night was the only time in more than forty years of exploration in the Llanganatis that I ate freshly baked bread. D'Orsay had constructed a good oven for baking bread, a sure sign that he planned to stay there for some time.

"In our conversations, I told D'Orsay that I was retiring forever from this part of the Llanganatis because I had reached the conclusions that Valverde's lake was not in this area, and that the cave of Guacharos lower down in the gorge of San José is not the socavón. D'Orsay did not respond at all, but his eyes shone through the forest of his mustache and beard. He was one of those types of men who are reserved and uncommunicative ... that hears everything and says nothing. [307] Long after this meeting I found out that Dick D'Orsay also abandoned his search in the area of Las Torres and the last year he was in Ecuador was spent exploring around the Yurac Llanganati or Cerro Hermoso.

"One afternoon we ran into each other at the Bar of the Hotel Majestic in Quito, where at that time is where you would encounter the entire world, senators, deputies, gringo tourists and gringo explorers, foreign residents, people of society, politicians and all others. The most common question in Quito at the time was who was with whom at the Majestic? Dick gave me a hug and told me that I was lucky to have found him because he was

---

306 Born about 1903, Richard F. D'Orsay was a naturalized US citizen (District Court Miami Florida 30 Apr 1929).

307 It does appear however, that D'Orsay did have a sense of humor. On 28 Jul 1946 the Sunday morning issue of the *Syracuse Herald American* carried a short article entitled *Dinosaurs in Ecuador?...* "Quito, Ecuador - Incontrovertible proof that the summers silly season has arrived was seen in 'disclosures' of the existence of live dinosaurs in the Ecuadorean jungle by Richard D'Orsay, a french explorer who has just arrived here from a trip to the interior. D'Orsay told intimates that the dinosaurs made elephants appear as pygmies in comparison, and he added that they were even larger than the prehistoric size indicated by their skeletal remains in various museums, believed to date from at least 200,000 BC. He said, straight faced, that a herd of the modern-day dinosaurs he encountered grazing in the Llanganati region set up an uproar which he compared to a prolonged clap of doom."

traveling to the United States.[308] D'Orsay explained that in the Llanganatis with each step you encounter minerals and without having any knowledge, perhaps great wealth is being passed aside.

"D'Orsay stated that he was going to the Colorado School of Mines to learn and study mineralogy and geology. At the same time he would work to raise $50,000 US dollars for further exploration of the Llanganati.[309] He promised to write and indeed I received some postcards and letters. In the last letter D'Orsay wrote that he already had $50,000 Dollars and that was soon to take his exams. But man proposes and God disposes, or perhaps it was the curse of Llanganati. While taking a class or field trip in an old

---

[308] D'Orsay departed Puna, Ecuador aboard the *Sea Nymph* on 14 Oct 1945 bound for New York, where he arrived on the first of November. D'Orsay, listed as an employee of the Rubber Development Corporation (The Rubber Development Corporation, the chief overseer of rubber acquisition, sought out other sources including establishing a rubber program that sent intrepid explorers into the Amazon.), had apparently been in Ecuador during World War II, as a field agent, surveying for possible rubber development in the country. D'Orsay's reports were classified by the US government. However, one report (circa 1944) was made available after the discovery of missionaries murdered in Ecuador during 1956. D'Orsay's report was quoted and discussed in Ed Creagh's Washington UP article *'Copter Spots 4 Bodies near Camp of Missionaries; Tribe Described.* The article was picked up and circulated throughout the US and stated in part ... "The Auca Indians, presumed slayers of five flying missionaries from the United States, are a naked, bloodthirsty Ecuadorean tribe still living in the Stone Age. This is a picture presented to a US government agency by field agents who surveyed the region for possible rubber development during World War II. Aucas use as their weapon a lance 9 to 12 feet long. One Agent, Richard F. D'Orsay, said (12 years prior) he was inclined to doubt the blood curdling stories of what they did with their lances until he saw for himself the result of an Auca hit-and-run attack: 'There were six bodies lying on the beach, two women and four children. The dead were literally poled to the ground by a 12-foot lance which was stuck in the ground like a flag.'" The complete story of the 1956 murders by the Waodani tribe is told in the docudrama *End of the Spear (2006),* still available on DVD.

[309] Research has uncovered a Winnipeg Free Press newspaper article from 26 Apr 1958 by Frank Feldman entitled *The Deadly Hoard of Inca Gold* , that confirms a portion of this statement ... "Now another seeker of fortunes [previously discussed Loch], American Richard D'Orsay, is equally sure that he will find the legendary Inca gold. D'Orsay knows the Ecuadorian Andes backwards. He has clambered in their rocky elevations for more than five years. His haul so far has however, been disappointing ... several golden nails. Yet D'Orsay is convinced that he is on the right track. When he ran out of funds he returned to the US to save up more for yet another expedition." It appears therefore, that D'Orsay was in Ecuador during WWII, left in 1945, yet according to the "Dinosaur" article was in Ecuador in 1946. In any case, during 1958 D'Orsay was still planning another expedition.

abandoned mine, a rung on an old staircase that went up a vertical pit broke, and my friend Dick fell to a depth of eighty meters, where he died." [310]

■ ■ ■

Judging from the chronological order of Brunner's story and the fact that Brunner does not mention any dates ... it is my assumption that Brunner knew D'Orsay during the 1950s. D'Orsay himself appears as one of the most elusive characters of this book. Other than D'Orsay's naturalization records, I have not been successful in uncovering any other personal documents relating to the man ... no birth, death or marriage certificates. A few newspaper articles have provided what little information is available on the man. One article in particular *Postwar Plans Of This local GI Feature Genuine Treasure Hunt,* [311] although its representation of the facts is so ludicrous as to be amusing, mentions D'Orsay and takes us back to the 17th century ... "The postwar world will mean a fortune-hunting career for Pvt. Frank M. Dampier, Jr.,[312] 1165 Hamilton Boulevard, who dreams of prospecting for a fabulous buried Inca treasure of gold and jewels in Ecuador, South America. The story is told in a special dispatch to the *Daily Mail* from the public relations officer at the Ardmore, Oklahoma, Army Air Field, where young Dampier is stationed.

"According to Dampier, his proposed expedition for a fortune estimated at 18 to 20 billion in gold and emeralds has attracted another adventure-loving local serviceman--- Henry C. Ford, of the U.S. Merchant marine, a hometown friend.

"This adventurous GI's dream of unearthing the musty wealth of the ancient Incan Empire revolves around a valuable map which a paternal ancestor, Capt. Dampier,[313] 17th century Royal Navy hydrographer turned buccaneer, looted from a Spanish church in Guayaquil, Ecuador.[314]

"The fabulous fortune which Dampier plans to seek with his own expedition after the war is known as the Valverde treasure. Valverde, a 16th century beachcomber, wedded the daughter of an Inca chief, and with the help of his wife located a buried treasure. Valverde sketched a map which is called the 'Derrotero of the Inca Treasure.' Actually, the Spanish divided the map into two parts, sending one part to the King of Spain and locking the other in the

---

[310] This portion of Brunner's story can not be independently confirmed.

[311] *Daily Mail* 24 Aug 1944

[312] Francis "Frank" Marion Dampier III [1922-1995]

[313] Genealogical research confirms Frank's paternal ancestor was William "The Buccaneer" Dampier [1652-1715]

[314] William Dampier, buccaneer, pirate, circum-navigator, captain in the navy and hydrographer, wrote four books on his voyages including *New Voyage round the world (1697)* and *Voyages & Descriptions (1699)*. The *Oxford Dictionary of National Biography* indicates that between July 1684 and August 1685, Dampier was among the pirate fleet that "scourged the coast of South America." The city of Guayaquil was ravaged in 1684.

archives of the church in Guayaquil. Unfortunately for the king, Spain was involved in a war which prevented any immediate treasure hunting.

"After Valverde's death, the church was looted by Dampier's ancestor and years later the matching half of the treasure map was found and reproduced. The King of Spain, according to legend, sent a priest to Guayaquil, but the search for the buried treasure was fruitless.

"Dampier, a Link trainer instructor of the 222nd Combat Crew Training Station (Flying Fortress), says the complete map is in his private possession. The original copy is sketched in vellum,[315] while the copy of the map purportedly held by the King and later reproduced was written in Spanish.

"About 80 years ago a retired U.S. Army colonel and his partner struck out for the treasure but after about 50 unsuccessful expeditions their bones were found by Richard D'Orsay, French naturalized American, whose writings [316] fired the interest of the Maryland soldier. Later a Captain Loch, an adventurous American Army officer, reported that he believed he had located this treasure when he uncovered pieces of gold. Loch, however, died by his own hand when he returned to Quito to form another expedition.

"Dampier has corresponded with Jack Sheppard, director of the Pan-American Society of Tropical Research, since his high school days in Haggerstown, in an effort to learn more about the needs of an expedition and the history of the treasure."

Without question many of young Dampier's second hand factual assertions (being written by a public information officer) we know to be erroneous, and do not even warrant consideration. On the other hand, Dampier's claim of a "buccaneer" ancestor has proven factual and Dampier appears to have a general knowledge of some of the "players" (Valverde, King of Spain, Brooks, D'Orsay and Loch). Considering that we know portions of the story are true and others not ... just how much credence one should give the article is uncertain.

Similar to the Bermender story, young Dampier's story raises many questions ... Is it plausible that Brooks had a partner?, ... Is it plausible that Valverde actually made his death bed *Derrotero* while in Ecuador?, ... Is it plausible that the *Derrotero* was accompanied with a map as many have assumed?, ... Is it plausible that the *Derrotero* was sent to the King and the map held in the archives of the church? ... If so, is it highly probable that the map was looted by William "The Buccaneer" Dampier?

■ ■ ■

Returning to Brunner, his story continues ... "In 1959 I was in Isabela Brooks' campsite in the valley of the same name. One day two of my

---

[315] Vellum-is mammal skin prepared for writing or printing on, common for the period.

[316] I have not been able to confirm this statement. If D'Orsay wrote any material on the Llanganati treasure I have not been able to discover it. If indeed something exists ... it would be an interesting read.

former laborers including José Lopes, that on this trip did not accompany me, unexpectedly arrived. They informed me that they formed part of an expedition of an English lady that wanted to go to the Valley of Brooks to obtain fraylejón plants.[317] This surprised me because to obtain fraylejónes or to study the environment in which this plant thrives, there was no need to suffer the ravages of a long and expensive trip into the Llanganatis, due to the fact that in the páramos of the Angel in the province of Carchi you can pick fraylejónes, almost, almost without getting out of your car! [318]

"José Lópes informed me that Mrs. N. Barclay was a botanist. Barclay's last name sounded familiar, but at that moment I did not remember why. It is worth clarifying that this lady of England never made it to the Valley of Brooks, for when she was in the swamps of Auca Cocha she was surprised by one of those storms of rain, hail, fog and hurricane force winds, that convert these sites on the Equator to something like the Siberian tundra.

"A few weeks later, once back in Quito, a friend introduced me. Where ... naturally during the five o'clock tea in the Majestic Bar. Doctor Nora Barclay was a very nice woman and I calculated her age to be from forty to forty-five years. As is logical I asked her why she had made this alleged trip into the Llanganati, mentioning that I did not believe in the story about collecting fraylejónes. She looked at me and with a very enigmatic smile on her face said ... 'Oh yes I was there because of the fraylejónes and of course for something else to!'

"Over time I finally remembered the name because it had sounded familiar. In his book *Fever, Famine and Gold* Captain Loch spoke of two cousins with the surname Barclay. One he met during the First World War while he was in a military camp in Africa. The Barclay in Africa, told Loch that he had a cousin who worked in the intelligence service at the War Office in London, where after the war Loch met him. It was there when this second Barclay introduced Loch two friends of his, Mr. William (Bill) Klamroth and Mr. Carl de Muralt. Also, these four gentlemen formed the first nucleus of the Andes and Amazon Expedition Co., of which John Barclay was a shareholder, although he was not involved in the expedition. I asked the Doctor if she was related, but the only answer I received was that enigmatic smile of hers.

■ ■ ■

---

[317] Fraylejón plant or *Espeletia picnophyla* - These plants live at high altitude in the páramo. The trunk is thick, with succulent hairy leafs disposed in a dense spiral pattern. Marcescent leaves help protect the plants from cold.

[318] Lourie in his book *Sweat of the Sun Tears of the Moon* tells this general story erroneously quoting Brunner as stating; "One guy I met once wanted to find a certain plant, no? And he hiked into the Llanganatis, five days through thunderstorms and snowstorms and hail, spending hundreds of dollars, thousands of Sucres. Why? To find a plant, he said, which he could have grabbed out of his car window on the páramo of Carchi! A kind of geranium, that was all!"

"I also met some of the young English students who were part of the 'Anglo-Ecuadorian Llanganati Expedition'[319] in 1969. This group consisted of teachers and students from several universities in England, all between twenty and forty years of age. The Ecuadorian side was represented by the Ecuadorian Institute of Natural Sciences, represented by its president, botanist and scientist Dr. Misael Acosta Solis. This club of 'scientists' worked for several months and had, that is to say their main camp was at Auca Cocha, just a day and a half from Píllaro.

"Officially their goals were notably scientific in the fields of geology, geophysics, geomorphology and botany, involving the collection of minerals, plants, flowers, rocks and water. As is logical and natural the ombudsmen and organizers of such a 'scientific' event officially informed the press, that the expedition had nothing to do with the history of the treasure of Atahualpa or the *Derrotero* of the Spanish Valverde. But ... but, I assure you that there were many buts, for example I was told by my porters who were with the 'scientists,' that the English had asked them if they knew of any virgin lakes. That is to say lakes that had not been visited by explorers or crazy adventurous treasure hunters. This is what everyone was looking for, the non scientists as well!

"Later, once they discovered one of these very rare virgin lakes, these famous scientists, especially the so-called botanists, desecrated its virgin waters with inflatable rubber boats, searching the muddy lake bottoms for decomposed vegetable matter and algae, to see if these components could be utilized for fertilizer. Really ... does all this smell of pure science? But if this is the case I ask ... is this type of exploration done from rubber boats and with metal detectors?

"For the majority of people the scientific camouflage was good, but for us crazy treasure hunters it was not. I personally am of the opinion that these 'scientists' should have applied another class of detector, that of the lie. It was published in the newspapers, the day on which man first walked the surface of the moon, that these scientists would send a message from the mountains of Llanganati. I do not know if they did or not, but in 1970 the daily newspaper of Quito *El Comercio* reported that an English magazine had published the provisional results of their investigations in the Llanganatis. I am sure they did not publish anything regarding the search for decomposed plant material with metal detectors.

■ ■ ■

"In one of my expeditions in the year 1967 I was accompanied by an Englishman, Ernest (Ernie) Trigg, and it is better that I do not remember him. This young complex man from the city of Coventry almost let me die on Cerro Hermoso when I became ill with acute pneumonia, but the gross details of this case are not relevant here. I forgive this and many other things even worse because I believe this man suffered in his subconscious a serious trauma that made him hate Germans without even realizing. He had

---

[319] Cambridge Llanganati Expedition of 1969.

lost in those terrible bombings of Coventry in World War II very close family members. Who knows?

"Two articles concerning my dilemma were published in the daily newspaper *El Comercio* of Quito.[320] At the same time it must also be made clear that this man withdrew to Quito where he gathered from several people medicine, food and money for my benefit. But this man never returned to my camp on Cerro Hermoso.

■ ■ ■

"My friend Andrés Fernandez Salvador [introduced in the previous chapter], a son of the owner of the mineral springs Güitig in Machachi, also conducted research and expeditions concerning the treasure of Atahualpa in the Llanganatis. Andrés had made some expeditions into the mountains but with Americans and with Guido Boschetti, son of Don Tulio Boschetti the leader of the Italian-Ecuadorian Llanganati Expedition of 1934. All of them are my friends, but we were never together in the Llanganatis. The son Guido I had met in 1939 when he was still a boy. Years later in 1956, both Andrés Fernandez Salvador and Guido Boschetti were associated with me when we tried to discover a Spanish galleon that sank off the coast of Ecuador.

"One fine day when I was in Guayaquil I visited my friend Andrés Fernandez Salvador. Andrés told me that he was planning an expedition to the Llanganatis using a helicopter of the Ecuadorian Air Force (FAE) and that he would call me right before he left. I told Andrés that I would like to spend a short time with my friend Father Luis López Lescurré in Manglaralto. I also mentioned that the father was one of the best clairvoyant visionaries in the world and that he possessed God's power and had also cured many, many patients. Andrés was interested in this power of the Father and he suggested we travel together on his plane to Manglaralto, to see if the father could sense something from his aerial photographs of the Llanganatis.

"Andrés and I flew there and Father Luis received us very well. He reviewed the photos that Andrés showed him and said ... 'Where you are about to look you will not find anything because what you seek is on the other side.' I was greatly surprised by Andrés reaction, instead of asking the Father in what location he should look, Andrés began to argue and stubbornly claimed that the Father was wrong. Andrés claimed that the thing he was seeking was there at the point in the photographs where he had indicated. Father Luis looked at Andrés for a long time and then laughed, telling him ... 'very well my friend, go away on your quest and you shall see that this trip will be in vain.' Andrés returned to Guayaquil and I stayed in Manglaralto. Father Luis then explained to me that my friend was tremendously mistaken and that what he wanted was exactly on the other

---

[320] Similar to Dyott's being stranded alone in the Llanganatis for many months Brunner was also stranded alone with pneumonia and without supplies.

side of the mountain, not on the east side, but on the west side. All this happened in 1963.

"Weeks passed and there was no sign of Andrés. I did not know if he really was to be found in the Llanganatis or if he recently had returned, or perhaps he was still preparing to go, I did not know. In the fifth week since Andrés departure on the plane, Father Luis called me to the sacristy and told me ... 'Eugene, you have to go immediately to the Llanganatis because Andrés is in mortal danger. Take my assistant with you and take this money.' The Father gave me five thousand Sucres and called his assistant Juan de Saraguro, indicating that he had to go with me on a long trip to the mountains, and he had given me money to buy shoes and clothes for the mountains. That very same day Juan and I were traveling in the direction of Píllaro in the province of Tungurahua.

"Once there, I was surprised by the fantastic power of perception of Father Luis. Just as we arrived, I was informed by the daughter of Luisa Moya, in whose house I had always stayed, that everyone was very distressed. It had just become known that Mr. Andrés Fernandez Salvador and companions had crashed in a helicopter and presumably everyone was dead there in the Llanganatis. I became faint and thought I was going to blackout, oh my god, Andrés and all the other deaths among the scrubby, craggy, broken grounds of the Llanganati."...the balance of Brunner's story concerning the infamous helicopter crash was related in the previous chapter.

■ ■ ■

Brunner's expeditions into the Llanganatis, as all others before him, commenced from the "town of Píllaro." Just as those before him, the landmarks and signs in the *Derrotero de Valverde* led Brunner to 'the farm of Moya,' 'Cerro Guapa,' 'Los Anteojos,' 'Yana Cocha,' the 'ravine and waterfall,' 'a deep dry ravine' and 'Margasitas' mountain. From here, as with almost all other explorers, the Valverde sign sent Brunner to the north and into the region of the "Roncadores," which Brunner explored in depth for nearly thirty years to no avail.

Once at Margasitas mountain the *Derrotero* instructs ... "which leave on thy left hand, and I warn thee that thou must go round it in this fashion." Wallace in his commentary on the *Derrotero* and hieroglyph theorizes that the "circle to be the mountain and the right-hand termination of the curve the point already reached." The question arises ... did Spruce copy the hieroglyph in the exact orientation of the *Derrotero* ... or, could the hieroglyph have been flipped ... if not by Spruce, inadvertently upon publication and republication? Below and on the left is the image of the hieroglyph as it appears in *Notes of a Botanist* ... on the right the image is flipped.

This modified hieroglyph would leave the mountain "on thy left hand" and appears just as it does on Blacke's first map ... placing the explorer on the "Way of the Inca." Perhaps it is for this intentional or unintentional difference on their map that Blacke & Chapman had no difficulty in reaching their destination. Brunner ... tracing backwards toward the north (slightly northeast) from Cerro Hermoso ... discovered that Blacke's first map accurately depicts the route of the hieroglyph which appears in the *Derrotero de Valverde*, that confounded explorers for many years, himself included. [321]

Based on the results of Brunner's discoveries after he obtained the Blacke materials from Commander Dyott, I would observe that Wallace was only partially correct [322] ... the "circle" of the hieroglyph is perhaps the mountain. However, flip the hieroglyph and commence its path on the northwest face of the mountain, leaving the mountain on your left hand. By so doing ... "the right-hand termination of the curve"...places you on a path to the southeast in order to find ... "a small plain" ... "which having crossed thou wilt come on a cañon between two hills, which is the Way of the Inca." This "Way of the Inca," incidentally turned out to be much longer than Brunner had originally imagined.

Blacke purportedly took this exact route that had been marked for him on his first map. Brooks would also decipher this same route which led him to his Valley of Brooks and Laguna de Brooks. He would later write ... "I had no trouble in finding all of the landmarks of the guide up to and beyond the 'Way of the Inca,' and I had no trouble about the correct side on which to pass the 'mountain which is all margasitas.'"

The hieroglyph of the *Derrotero,* once deciphered, had ultimately led Brunner away from the Roncadores toward Cerro Hermoso ... where he had already made numerous discoveries.

■ ■ ■

What does Spruce tell us in his translation of the *Derrotero*? ... "Look to the east"[323] from Cerro Guapa and again from Los Anteojos to "perceive the three Cerros Llanganati, in the form of a triangle, on whose declivity there

---

[321] The same principle involved completing a difficult puzzle or maze. Having started a maze from the beginning and being unable to get to the end ... you start from the other end to connect up in the middle with where you left off with the route from the beginning. In the case of the *Derrotero* the beginning is Píllaro, the middle is Margasitas Mountain and the hieroglyph, with the end being ... Cerro Hermoso.

[322] Wallace erroneously doubles the distances covered by the *Derrotero*. While it is true that the *Derrotero* mentions only four sleeping places ..."so that the whole journey occupied five days," due to the terrain and growth, the distance traveled per day was in no way equal.

[323] Regardless of ... "so that thy back be toward the town of Ambato" (old or new makes no difference), the *Derrotero* instructs to look "east" ... not ... north east in the direction of the Roncadores

is a lake" ... once again singular ... and to the east of these landmarks sits ... Cerro Hermoso. Spruce continues his translation indicating that from the "Way of the Inca"...which according to Blacke, Brooks and Brunner would face south toward the north face of Cerro Hermoso ... "thou shalt see the entrance of the socabón."[324] Spruce in completing his translation states ... "thou wilt perceive a cascade which descends from an offshoot of the Cerro Llanganati" ... and ... "to ascend the mountain" ... again singular and even without the aid of the hieroglyph, Spruce delivers the explorer to the foot of Cerro Llanganati, Gran Volcan del Topo, Yurac-Llanganati or ... Cerro Hermoso and her three peaks.

Finally, let us examine the *Derrotero* in the words of others. Spruce and all the explorers that followed him, confirm the *Derrotero's* landmarks up to Margasitas Mountain ... "all exactly where Valverde places them."

Alfred Russel Wallace stated that "...the 'Guide' is equally minute and definite in its descriptions throughout, that it agrees everywhere with Guzmán's map, and that, as it is admitted to be accurate in every detail for more than three-fourths of the whole distance, there is every probability that the last portion is equally accurate."

Luis Andrade Marin would declare that "...many have suggested that the present text of the *Derrotero* does not tally with the original, but has been altered. But to me there is nothing confusing in the *Derrotero*."

Major E. C. Brooks would be even more concise ... "Let me make this clear and emphatic that the Valverde *Derrotero* or guide is correct and that the 'three Llanganati peaks in the form of a triangle' do exist."

Blacke of course would have the last word on the matter ... his access to the *Derrotero*, Guzmán and possibly Valverde maps provided the means to write ... "It is impossible for me to describe to you the wealth that now lies in that hidden cave marked on my map, but I could not remove it alone, or with thousand's of men."

■ ■ ■

---

[324] Brunner has previously indicated that Blacke & Chapman's route took them along the Desaguadero de Yana Cocha to Parca Yacu (the junction of the rivers Desaguadero and the Rivera de Llanganati). From there they crossed the Desaguadero following it's north bank passing Margasitas mountain to a tributary called Cascadas de las Tundas on the slopes of the Roncadores ... to the "location of probably world's biggest gold mine" ... from where they could see the "Way of the Inca" from the mines to their "guayra" on Cerro Hermoso. Blacke & Chapman then returned to Parca Yacu and followed the Rivera de Llanganati until they reached Soguillas (which is a passage in which the water divides, one side flows south into the Río Topo, the other north in the Desaguadero). Brunner stated ... "Definitely Blacke & Chapman must have seen the socavón mentioned in the *Derrotero* as they walked along the Inca Trail before entering into the thick forest that is crossed by the mighty Río Topo."

Brunner would write ... "It was 1946 [325] when I met the world famous English explorer Commander George M. Dyott, far from civilization and deep in the Llanganatis. This story was related in the previous chapter [referring to his manuscript *Ecuador y sus Tesoros*] along with the history of two other English explorers of the Llanganati. Blacke & Chapman were to my knowledge, the last Englishmen who in the late nineteenth century were in the mountains of Llanganati. But now Dyott no longer kept any secrets from me and it is for this reason that I had the ability to write the complete history of these two sailors and their misadventures. I do not know what others feel when they handle and read original documents written in the years 1886-1892 but for me it sent chills down my spine. With Blacke's maps my nearly thirty years of research and exploration in the Llanganatis began to make sense. Everything became clear and the pieces of the puzzle fell neatly together.

"In 1975 I was again in the Llanganatis, but not on Cerro Hermoso, a little further north-north-west but always in the mountains surrounding Cerro Hermoso. I was in the foothills where Laguna Melliza [Twin Lake] can be found. This is the lake drawn on the second map of Barth Blacke. Also to be found in this area are all the mountains, small hills, swamps and other landmarks included in Blacke's second map. As I will explain later I had discovered these landmarks and verified Blacke's signs or clues left on his map. I was in the area trying to discover the things that Blacke had left there. But this research I could not finish but for the simple reason that the coast was not clear or rather, I was not alone on this site and that's the story I am going to recount.

■ ■ ■

"One day while returning from Ambato with provisions, when I was ascending the little road that goes to the pass of Mesa Tablón loaded like a donkey, sadly I suddenly saw a large camp in front of me. Seven huge tents and a kitchen tent with a gas stove in which a man was cutting a mountain of onions. Hello ... hola ... I yelled and the man looked in my direction, upon seeing how I was laden he came to help me. Once in the kitchen tent, rather a canvas roof that covered the kitchen, I thanked him and asked, what are the Mexicans doing up here at the dam of Pisayambo? We are not Mexican answered the man, we have come from the Military Geographical Institute and we are making plans and taking dimensions for channels and tunnels to carry water from Auca Cocha and from Cocha León to the Lake of Pisayambo dam, you are not Mr. Brunner? I stayed cool, this man knew my name, what the hell is happening here I thought. That camp over there across the valley is not yours? ... said the man again. Yes it is I said, but please explain how you know my name? Let me explain Mr. Brunner he replied, I'm Corporal Andrade and I have great pleasure to meet you. It is very simple, my Captain Ortuño told us that in Ecuador there is only a single man that comes alone into these mountains and stays sometimes three

[325] As previously stated, I believe Brunner's recollection of this date to be in error ... perhaps it was 1947.

or four months exploring and working entirely alone and unaided. This man is the Ecuadorian gringo Eugene Brunner, who is a good friend of the armed forces and the whole world in general. We chatted for a while and the Corporal gave me a cup of hot coffee, then I said good bye, gathered my things and went in the direction of my own camp.

"Around five in the afternoon two soldiers arrived at my camp and on behalf of Captain Ortuño invited me to have dinner at their camp. To make a long story short, I want to clarify that all the officers and soldiers treated me very well. Nothing I needed did I go without, they even supplied horses to me, but the tranquility of my work had vanished in the distance. Why? Of course I can explain why. Every day when I went out to explore and work, someone or some of them would always be watching me, using their telescopes or binoculars. If it appeared I was at some interesting point, perhaps an hour or hour and a half later, one or two soldiers would arrive, allegedly hunting for deer. Their hunting trips always ended in the sites that I had explored earlier!

"I had already imagined what would happen if I succeeded in my quest. If by chance I discovered the things that Barth Blacke had hidden here. I have nothing left to say but ... Blessed are the surveyors of the Military Geographic Institute (IGM). One day, over the radio the news came that the General Commander of the FAE, Brigadier General Luis Morejón Almeida crashed at the entrance to the airfield in Quito.[326] I took advantage of the funeral of this good friend, as a reason to leave that area of the Llanganatis without hurting the feelings of the friendly officers and soldiers of the IGM. I said my good byes and I was gone. Two months later I sent some Indians from San Andrés to retrieve the things from my camp, bringing them to me in Píllaro.

"In the year 1977, I was in this area for the last time. My goal was to take pictures of the signs that Barth Blacke had drawn on his second map, but the very bad weather allowed me to complete this proposition only half way."

■ ■ ■

[326] General Morejón died in a plane crash at the end of 1974 or the beginning of 1975 (Two separate articles in *HOY* indicate conflicting dates). The General was flying his military plane to Quito and on approaching the Mariscal Sucre airport, crashed 200 meters short of the south runway. The plane crashed into the house of the Viteri family, which also contained a kindergarten. Against all common sense the property also housed an enormous gas reservoir and the tragedy could have been much worse. The General died and only one member of the Viteri family suffered any type of wound other than material and economic losses.

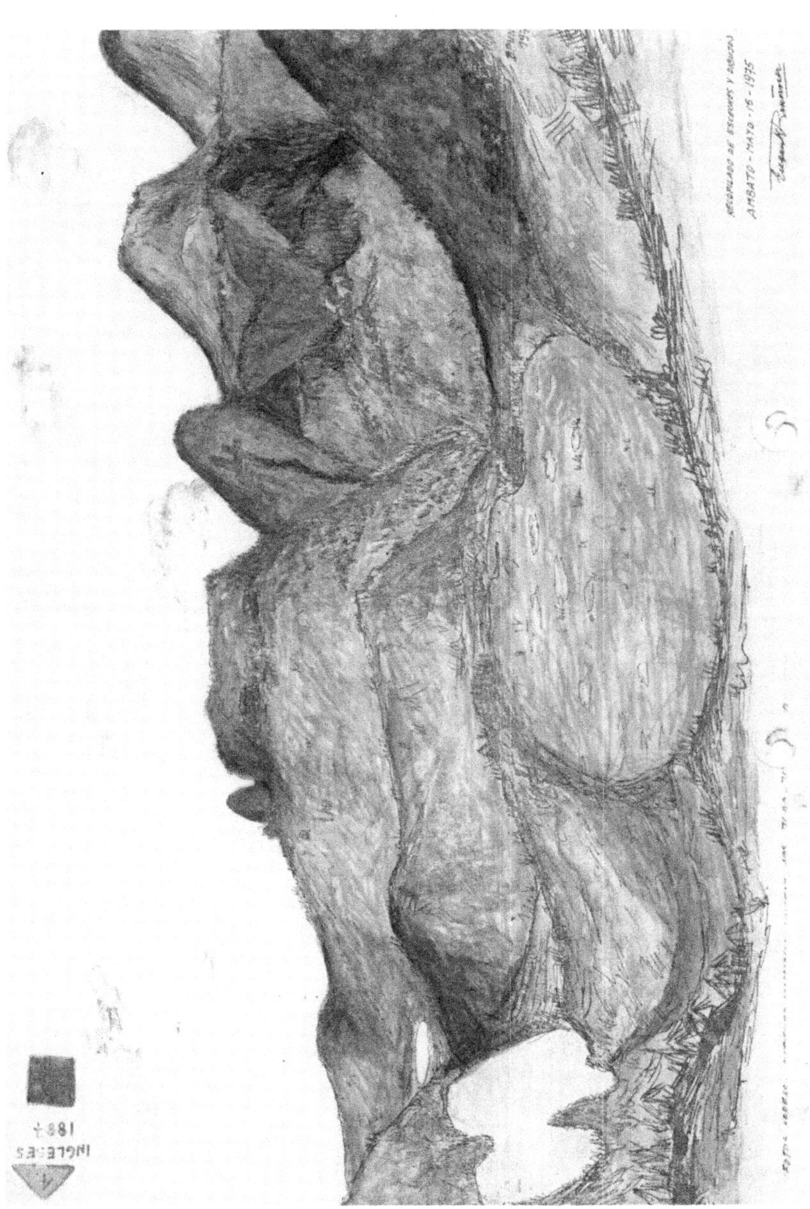

Brunner Sketch of Blacke's Landmarks

Hasta Febrero 24 encontre 4 de los seis puntos interes tn del mapa del Ingles!

1. TWin Lake
2. Extinct Lake (peligroso hay que rodear no atravezar)
3. El dibujo como pajaro (Es una Peña pelada)
4. El 4 to L. (Explicación sigue)

Brunner's Key to Sketch of Blacke's Landmarks

Eugene Brunner had ultimately taken a portion of his photographs of the Blacke signs on the second map, I know this to be true as I printed the negatives and viewed the photographs. I no longer have the photographs in my possession, but I do have Brunner's drawings and notes.[327] It is amazing how accurately Brunner's drawings and descriptions of the Blacke signs depict what I viewed in his photographs! The mound or grave of Chapman, a large mound of rocks grown over with grass and moss ... the flying bird with outstretched wings ... the small lake in the form of a painter's palate ... the marsh or extinct lake and the meaning of Blacke's notation "Look for the cross and 4 to L," all discovered and described in Brunner's own hand and verified in his photographs.

Brunner discovered that Blacke's second map depicts Blacke & Chapman's route out of the Llanganatis after the discovery of "Atahualpa's hoard" by the "merest chance" in a "hidden cave," as they were seeking a treasure not in a cave ... but in a lake. Brunner traced and verified Blacke & Chapman's route of departure after their discovery of the treasure in a cave, from a ceratin point on Cerro Hermoso.

Blacke's clue ... "Look for the cross and 4 to L" has confounded many explorers, both actual and armchair, for many years, and still does even today. Could everyone simply be over thinking the clue looking for some hidden meaning? Blacke, a mariner, had drawn the map not only for himself but as a guide for his friend, also supposedly a mariner, in case "something should happen to me." Interpretations of this clue have ranged from the simplest to the extreme with everything in between.

The simplest explanation appears to be, look for a cross, perhaps a wooden cross on Chapman's grave, then start counting the ridges to the left.[328] More complex is the theory that Blacke's being a mariner has a bearing on the clue, to a point where you look for the Southern Cross [329] and then four degrees to the left. Nevertheless, Blacke doesn't specifically indicate four degrees ... just "4 to L." Perhaps Blacke was making reference to the Crux, perhaps indicating ... look for the Crux and the four is to the left. When one considers that the *Derrotero* route comes from the northwest, it would also seem reasonable that from a certain vantage point the Crux might have appeared to be above Cerro Hermoso at various points in time. However, Blacke's second map depicts his route out of the Llanganatis and is oriented

---

[327] Brunner's drawing of the general area contained on Blacke's second map is accompanied by his explanatory notes.

[328] This explanation was attributed to Commander Dyott in *Valverde's Gold.*

[329] Southern Cross or Crux- A constellation (group of stars) that is found in the southern region of the night sky close to the constellation of Centaurus, visible all year in the southern hemisphere. The most commonly known and easily identifiable of all the southern constellations, the Crux, used by explorers and navigators to point south just as one would use the rising or setting Sun or Moon to indicate east and west.

from the southeast toward the north-northwest, which would therefore have placed the Southern Cross to his back.

Brunner's illustrations and notes clearly depict and indicate that up to this point in time in 1975, he had discovered four of the "six interesting points" on Blacke's second map. One point being the landmark of Twin Lake in the form of a painter's palate, secondly the landmark of an extinct marshy lake bed, third is the vertical surface of a cliff with its bare rock in the image of a flying bird with outstretched wings with the fourth "interesting point" to its left, a hill with the number four appearing on it.

Brunner's discoveries and observations clarified and resolved most of the clues and landmarks on Blacke's second map. "Cave here" for example, on Blacke's map has confused and diverted the attention of many explorers and viewers of Blacke's second map. Upon seeing this landmark, most have incorrectly assumed this to be Blacke's treasure cave which is shown on his first map, which it is not. Brunner's theory was that the cave marked on the map is most probably where Blacke rested after the death and burial of Chapman. Brunner's theory continues that perhaps Blacke left Chapman's knapsack with some of the treasure he could not carry in the cave, if not, it was buried with Chapman. Brunner was intent on exploring this theory but did not get the opportunity before his own death, so unfortunately this remains unclear.

One clue on Blacke's second map remains unsolved. I have never seen any mention, explanation or comment whatsoever, from Brunner or any other source, on the clue of the numbers two and five which appear to have two crossed signal flags between them. One simple explanation could have relevance to Blacke & Chapman being mariners. Brunner indicates in his manuscript that after Chapman's death, Blacke left behind a "navy telescope and broken navy compass." Perhaps Blacke also had a sextant or quintant [330] with him in the mountains. This instrument, if held horizontally, could have been used to measure the angle between two landmarks, which would then allow for the calculation of a position on a chart or map. Could this cryptic symbol actually be the intersection of two position lines that would be used to fix a position to identify the mariners' location? Or, could the two and five indicate 2/5 of a circle, 144 degrees? Unfortunately I do not comprehend the symbol's meaning and can only theorize, so this clue remains unclear.

■ ■ ■

---

[330] A sextant or quintant fulfill the same exact purpose. The name indicates that the portable instrument is furnished with a graduated arc equal to either a sixth or fifth part of a circle. A sextant is 1/6 turn or 60 degrees and a quintant is 1/5 turn or 72 degrees.

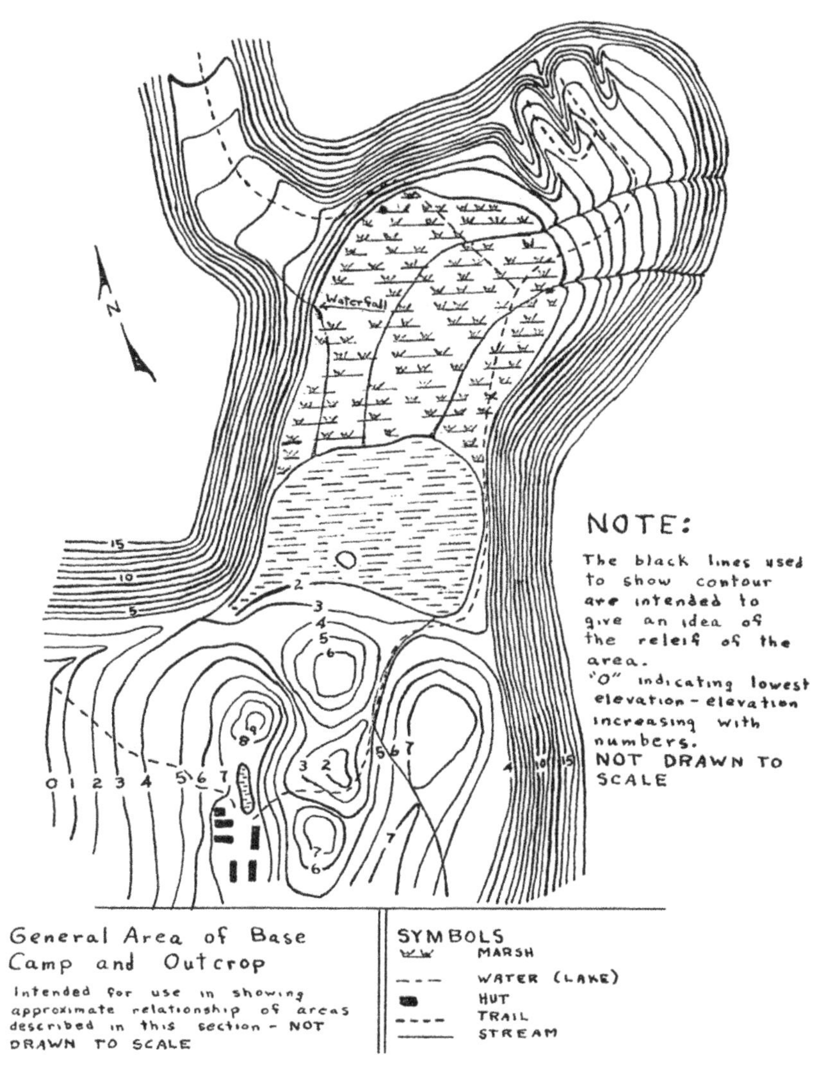
Waterfall
N
NOTE:
The black lines used to show contour are intended to give an idea of the releif of the area.
"O" indicating lowest elevation - elevation increasing with numbers.
NOT DRAWN TO SCALE
General Area of Base Camp and Outcrop
Intended for use in showing approximate relationship of areas described in this section - NOT DRAWN TO SCALE
SYMBOLS
MARSH
WATER (LAKE)
HUT
TRAIL
STREAM

Lake Brunner Relief Map

As the reader may recall from the previous chapter, another Brunner discovery during 1965 was a small lake, 320 feet wide by 500 feet long and 65 feet deep, at a high elevation of around 14,500 feet on the southwesterly flank of Cerro Hermoso, which he named "Lake Brunner." Just as Brooks before him had discovered Laguna de Brooks in the Valley of Brooks,[331] although Brooks' lake turned out to be natural, Brunner believed beyond any shadow of a doubt that he had discovered the lake "into which the ancients threw the gold" as described in the *Derrotero de Valverde.*
Some individuals have jealously indicated that Brunner was egotistical and arrogant with his choice in naming his discovery, but nothing is more illogical. Rivers, streams, lakes, mountains, hills and passes are customarily named after the discoverer. As Brunner believed the treasure was in this lake, would it have made any sense to name it Valverde Lake, Treasure Lake, Atahualpa's Ransom Lake, Rumiñahui's Gold Lake or perhaps Come Steal What I Have Discovered Lake?

Brunner had been quoted as referring to his discovery as "my treasure lake." What made Brunner so adamant that this was the "lake made by hand" mentioned in the *Derrotero de Valverde*? First and foremost must have been Brunner's knowledge from his previous explorations eliminating other regions of the Llanganatis, specifically the Roncadores region. Secondly, Brunner's exploration of the socavón, his discovery of a zig zag trail, large square hole and the Reclining Woman, all on Cerro Hermoso, limited his search to this mountain. But what made the discovery of this small lake different from every other of the hundreds if not thousands of lakes in this region one may ask ... Brunner discovered indisputable evidence that his lake was man made!

Even though the climate and topography of the Llanganatis have produced numerous similar vistas of this picture painted in the *Derrotero* ... "thou wilt perceive a cascade which descends from an offshoot of the Cerro Llanganati and runs into a quaking bog ... to ascend the mountain, leave the bog and go along to the right, and pass above the cascade, going round the offshoot of the mountain" ... Lake Brunner at first glance appears to be an exact image ... but remember, these descriptions were for the area of the socavón, not the treasure lake.

Lake Brunner appears to result from a crevice that has been dammed at one end and is fed from a large waterfall to the north that drains through a small outlet on the lakes southwest end. Brunner's illustration of the *General Area of Base Camp and Outcrop,* gives a good impression of Brunner's base camp, Lake Brunner, the bog, waterfall, pass to ascend the mountain and the steepness of the relief in the area. Brunner had determined that the narrow outlet of his lake had indeed been constructed by man and was not natural. A natural crevice and mine had been dammed at the narrow end centuries ago and the water level raised, filling with mud and silt over the passage of time.

---

[331] Located north-northeast of Cerro Hermoso.

To substantiate Brunner's findings and theories one must take into account his observations and discoveries in the general area. Brunner discovered that this area had indeed been an old mining area, whether pre-Inca or Inca I cannot say with certainty. The outcrop mentioned on the base camp illustration refers to an enormous native copper outcrop on the northeast end of Lake Brunner. Copper also resides in the sulfide deposits of malachite and azurite found in abundance throughout the mountain of Cerro Hermoso, the only non volcanic mountain in the Llanganati range.[332] At one point Brunner held a mining concession on this area and retained at least two geologists [333] who conducted surveys and wrote positive reports on the copper deposits.

Brunner obtained his most conclusive discoveries when diving[334] in his treasure lake. Brunner found evidence of mining tailings and an enormous log not indigenous to this area or altitude. Ultimately his most important discovery, a spiral staircase hand carved into the bottom of the lake through which the water drained with such a current that he could not approach very close! This discovery of water draining underground from the lake, through what is called a churry ucto,[335] combined with the previous discovery of a tunnel or socavón at a lower altitude with water running through it, one can but only recall the *Derrotero de Valverde* ... "for the water of the lake falls into it."

At one point in time, someone during one of Brunner's expeditions had attempted to use dynamite to breach the dam, which failed. Fearful of flooding out villages on the Río Verde,[336] Brunner wanted to drain his lake slowly with a pump or syphon and calculated the amount of water the lake held.

---

[332] Is it plausible that Old Q's "mountain crowned with gold" could in reality be Cerro Hermoso? Is it possible that from a certain location, the reflection of the sun off from an outcrop of native copper or other copper deposit might provide the appearance of a "mountain crowned with gold?"

[333] At least two additional geologists were hired directly by Brunner's partners or potential partners who similarly would later downplay the mineralization of Cerro Hermoso.

[334] Brunner did not dive in his lake alone he was accompanied by a Chuck Powell. A similar version of events was related to me by both Ricardo and Powell. The story goes that after diving in the lake, Brunner told Powell and his financial partner's that they dove in the wrong lake ... Ricardo added that this was due to Brunner's paranoia and for security reasons, his mistrust of Powell. Obviously Chuck and his financial partner's were furious and as Ricardo stated they "raised hell." But a point in fact ... Brunner and Powell dove in the larger lower lake ... Lake Brunner.

[335] Churry ucto - a spiral staircase carved into rock

[336] During Richard Spruce's time this river was known as Río Verde Grande, previously as Río Verde Segundo.

Lake Brunner Crevice Sketch

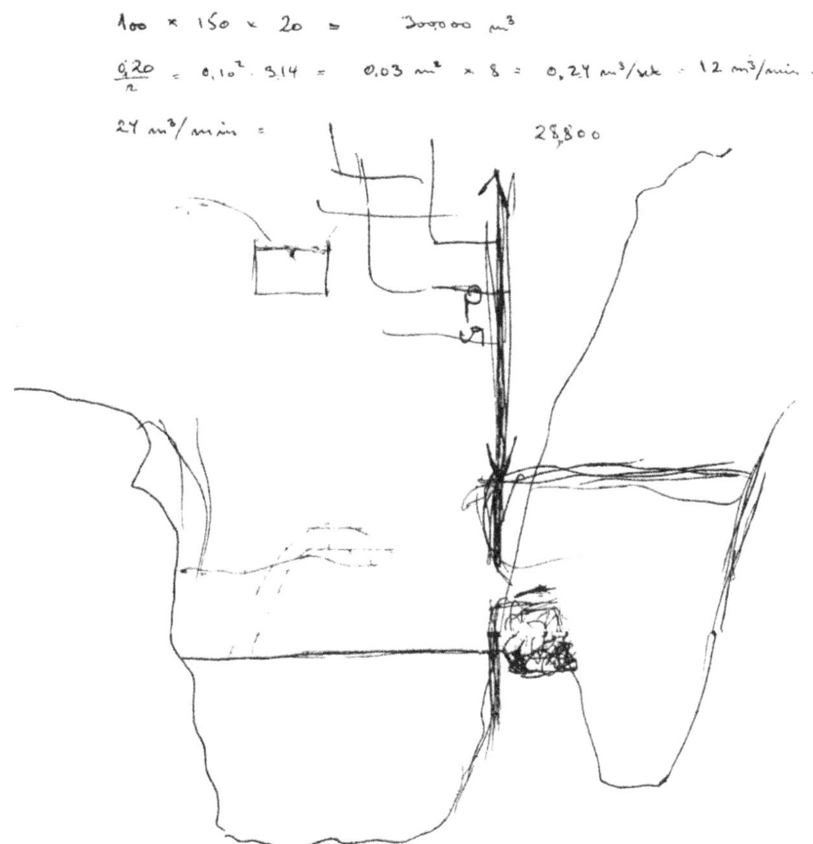

100 × 150 × 20 = 300,000 m³
0,20/2 = 0,10² · 3,14 = 0,03 m² × 8 = 0,24 m³/sek = 12 m³/min =
24 m³/min =
28,800

Lake Brunner Draining Calculations Sketch

Two of Brunner's illustrations indicate the man's rough notes, calculations and diagrams for draining his treasure lake. The first sketch clearly shows the crevice and purported treasure deposit. Brunner's second diagram raises more questions than it answers as it appears to indicate a cave on a side of the lake with the entrance blocked and perhaps underwater.

Was it possible that Rumiñahui had the most revered items of treasure, which was intended to be recovered after the conquistadores were expelled from the empire, placed in this cave, perhaps even with Atahualpa's mummy? Did Rumiñahui then have the everyday items such as tableware, gold chain, decorative wall plates and roof tiles, unworked gold from the mines and the like, thrown into the crevice ... the cave sealed ... the lake dammed ... a lake at a higher altitude then diverted and drained to fill the "lake made by hand" ... who knows? What is abundantly clear, was Brunner's ultimate interest in possibly yet another cave ... Blacke & Chapman's cave ... or are they one and the same?

■ ■ ■

Convinced that the *Derrotero* and Blacke's maps were not just completely accurate but establish that the treasure deposit was on Cerro Hermoso, and due to his advanced age and declining health, Brunner needed to find a shorter route to his "treasure lake." After countless hours pouring over newly available topographic maps [337] of Cerro Hermoso, Brunner was determined to break trail from the south to his base camp at Lake Brunner. It was 1970 when Brunner chose the small Town of El Triunfo to be his starting point. El Triunfo [338] is a small sleepy town about six to eight hours southeast of Quito at the end of a long twisting road from Patate, [339] in the province of Tungurahua.

Brunner hired forty men as porters to help cut his trail [340] the roughly twenty-five kilometers to Cerro Hermoso, up the west slope of the Llanganati cordillera. Brunner's trail leaves the town of El Triunfo and starts up a valley with a swift running river, Río Verde Chico. The steady uphill climb breaking trails along the Río Muyo, through the jungle, cloud forest and into the páramo, took Brunner and his crew fifteen days to complete. In addition to his base camp at Lake Brunner, two camps were established on the trail at roughly 10,000 feet and another at about 14,000 feet. The trail is muddy ... so muddy that at times the suction will grab a hold of your boot and not let go as you walk out of it. Due to the damp wet climate of the region the trail overgrows rapidly and in some sections it is almost vertical. However, if the trail is prepared in advance ... you are in

---

[337] Topographic maps were not available in Ecuador until 1968.

[338] El Triunfo is located on the *Sucre Topographic Map*, and is not to be mistaken with the city of the same name in Guayas province that grew with the help of the French priest in our story, Luis López Lescure.

[339] The winding route the road travels to El Triunfo can be viewed on the *Baños* and *Sucre Topographic Maps*.

[340] It would be up this trail that author Peter Lourie would later travel with Brunner's assistance.

good shape and the weather permits ... the trip can be made in one or two days.

The base camp near Lake Brunner at approximately 14,500 feet, with its thatched huts, sits in a muddy elevated area [341] on a small plateau at the south end of the lake in front of a small stagnant lake or pond. Over the years and for security reasons, many visitors to Brunner's base camp were misinformed and led to believe that Lake Brunner was this small stagnant lake! Brunner also had prepared in this location a hard surface (rocks packed firmly into the mud) for a helicopter landing pad next to this camp. Once that I know of, Brunner had a helicopter land at base camp, which proved to be an extremely difficult and dangerous maneuver due to the elevation, wind currents and weather.

■ ■ ■

Brunner continues ... "I personally followed up with the work on that terrible mountain, Cerro Hermoso. I found a very good copper mine and obtained a mining concession. Between the years of 1970-1974 I invested about 4,000,000 Sucres [roughly $200,000 US dollars] in the Llanganatis. Then during the military dictatorship, the Minister of Natural Resources, Rear Admiral Jarrin Ampudia canceled the concessions of the company 'ADA' in the Gulf of Guayaquil, and the company 'Minas y Petroleos' in the Oriente. My partners in the copper mine were equity holders in 'ADA' and 'Mining and Petroleum,' they left Ecuador and never returned. I was told on their departure that they were very sorry, but with what the government had done to them with oil, that copper mining would follow as well. I do not think I have any more to say about this, but I went into bankruptcy and stayed in the street.

"But one thing I can say is for sure ... I know now exactly where to find the lake made by hand mentioned in the *Derrotero de Valverde* that so many other people and entities have sought. We dove in this lake and know how many meters the Indians raised the water level. Atahualpa's treasure is there and I have sworn that I will continue until the end, placing it in the Central Bank for its gold to support the national currency. Or perhaps the treasure of Atahualpa, hidden by his stepbrother the glorious defender of Quito, ATI II named Rumiñahui, will finish me.

"I know the location of the lake made by the hand in the *Derrotero de Valverde* and I also know where the hidden cave [342] of Barth Blacke is. But

---

[341] Brunner was not about to make the same mistake Brooks and Loch had made being flooded out of camp.

[342] Common belief is that Blacke & Chapman discovered the treasure by chance in a "hidden cave." Clearly the pair's discovery was made by "the merest chance," as the mariners were seeking a treasure in a lake, not a cave. Therefore, if the cave had previously been sealed by an earthquake, the mariners would have had no incentive to excavate it, and there is no indication that they did. Perhaps the mouth of the cave was covered by "salvaje" just as the "socavón?" Or, could it have been that the entrance to the cave had been

on the other hand I know and I am sure that once the treasure is discovered and delivered to the vaults of the Central Bank, this will only serve to shed more blood or will serve for fighting and discord, then it is best that the treasure stays where it is now.

"The golden treasure of Atahualpa hidden in the lake made by the hand of the *Derrotero de Valverde* and hidden in the cave on Barth Blacke's first map, should serve to redeem the blood that it has already cost, to serve and assist the welfare of the people and foremost must form the basis for the integration of the Ecuadorian Indian into national life, his rightful place by heritage. Integration which must be done without removal from the agricultural sector or culture, but with dignity and guarantees. Then and only then I am ready to give my discovery to the national government and therefore to all Ecuadorians." [Written November 1979]

■ ■ ■

Perhaps due to living in Ecuador for so many years under military rule, or his interaction and involvement with the Ecuadorian military over the years, or even the loss of his mining concession, Brunner was convinced that the sole path to the recovery of the Llanganati Treasure was through the military. It was under this belief that Brunner was plotting his course. Brunner knew as do I, that regardless of whether Ecuador is ruled by a military dictatorship, military junta or a civilian government, let there be no mistake, the military controls Ecuador and civilian governments' operate at the whim and will of the military.

By the mid to late seventies Brunner was no longer searching for the Llanganati treasure, he had arrived at the final point of his quest, the recovery phase. Brunner viewed his ultimate obstacle for the recovery of this discovery as obtaining the ear and favor of military leadership ... the Generals' ... whether from the Air Force or Army, at this point in time Brunner really did not care from which branch.

In *Sweat of the Sun, Tears of the Moon*, Peter Lourie quotes Brunner as stating sometime in 1980 that "...I have worked for the military so many years in the old days. They owe me. I made rescue missions in rugged mountain passes, taking bodies from airplane wrecks so the families could have a decent burial for their sons."

Lourie continues and erroneously insinuates that Brunner was involved with the recoveries of the Quito-Cuenca air crash victims.[343] Once again quoting

---

concealed by a mound of stones loosened by time and nature to expose the mouth of a cave? Apart from the clue that the "hidden cave" is located on or near the "reclining woman," the meaning of "hidden" has never been clearly defined or its location pinpointed, beyond Brunner's statement that the cave lies "between the main peak and an adjacent stone pyramid."

[343] Two SAETA Quito-Cuenca air disasters occurred prior to Lourie's conversation with Brunner in 1980 (15 Aug 1976 and 23 Apr 1979). The crash sites however, were not discovered until 1984 and 2003. I believe Brunner was referring to military crashes and accidents.

Brunner, Lourie writes ... "To get the treasure out now, we need helicopters and men. I have a very important meeting with a friend next week, a general in the Air Force. After next week we will meet with the president himself. I think he is finally realizing the significance of finding this treasure. There's so much money involved here that they will have to revalue the Sucre to somewhere near the dollar, I think."

Brunner's meetings with the generals did not occur as he had planned. Brunner was destined to spend more years in this attempt with no success, until ...

■ ■ ■

General Map of Ecudaor

General Gribaldo Miño Tapia

General Medardo Salazar Navas

THE MILITARY & GENERALS

Without question, Eugene Brunner had a great deal of contact and interaction with all three branches of Ecuador's military throughout his many years in country. It remains unclear though, whether Brunner comprehended the dynamics of the rival factions, animosities or politics within the military during this period of time in Ecuador's history. In addition to these factors and continuos war with Peru, Ecuador's top Generals' of the period were preoccupied with a country on the brink of forming a new democracy or facing yet another coup d'etat within their ranks. Brunner may have been blinded by the proximity of the successful conclusion of his life-long quest. The Generals' at the time however, were presumably predisposed to more urgent matters of state.

■ ■ ■

Historically the Ecuadorian military establishment has alternated between direct control, as in a military dictatorship or junta, or indirect control over the elected government, by exercising an unwritten veto power over government policies that were considered to affect the military's interests. In a nutshell, the republics continued existence has always been dependent on the will of the officer corps.

Among the modern officer corps, an extreme political ideological division has existed and created factions within the military. On one hand you have the apparent left leaning pro-socialism officers and on the other hand the right leaning pro-democracy elements. This division amongst the military at times has benefitted Ecuador's struggling democracy, acting as a counterbalance [344] to the threat of a coup d'etat. Some generals even achieved such power that they left marks on their country that may never disappear.

The military in Ecuador has been more closely aligned with the business class than the landholding upper class and over time they became an institutional political force. Constitutions between 1945 and 1979 legitimized the role of the military in governmental policy making. Democracy in Ecuador has always appeared to be at the will and whim of the military, with interventions most often over issues considered basic by the military leadership. Even civilian contenders for political power would often seek the support of elements of the military to topple an administration or to forestall an electoral outcome unfavorable to them. Occasionally the military has even applied its influence to intervene indirectly to ward off political developments that it opposed.

The Ecuadorian Army is the backbone of the armed forces of the country having the larger ranks and operational competence of all the branches. Unlike the US officer ranking system that has four ranks of General, Ecuador has only three; a two star Major General,[345] a three star Lieutenant

---

[344] Counterbalancing - The division of the military into rival forces, a strategy that is common in coup-risk states.
[345] General de Brigada.

General [346] and a four star General.[347] At the head of the Ecuadorian Army is typically a four star General, the General Commander of the Army. [348]

The Armed Forces Joint Command [349] is Ecuador's highest planning, preparation and strategic body of military operations. This body advises on national defense and consists of the Chief of the Armed Forces Joint Command,[350] which is the highest position an active-duty Ecuadorian general officer can attain and is appointed by the President, and the commanders of all three branches of the Ecuadorian Armed Forces; the Army, Navy and Air Force. This body operates under the authority of the Minister of Defense [351] and the Commander in Chief of the Armed Forces [352] who, similar to the United States, is the Constitutional President of the Republic.

■ ■ ■

Ecuador has a mandatory military service law requiring nine months of service [353] for which all men eighteen to fifty-five must register and obtain a Military Identification Card, which must be shown for employment or travel outside the country. While voluntary recruitment starts at the age of seventeen, compulsory recruitment starts at eighteen with the selection process being held by lottery. As with most laws in Ecuador, loopholes for the upper middle class and elite exist. An individual can be excused from the requirements of military service under certain conditions or even pay a small fine for the privilege of non service. Thus, Ecuador's troops, except of course for the career officer corps, consisted mainly of the poor and lower classes of Ecuadorian society. [354]

Promotions within Ecuador's military are not issued on the basis of battlefield performance. The country's military is predominately a domestic force rarely seeing military action, unless of course one considers Ecuador's seemingly constant border skirmishes with Peru over the highly disputed Amazonian region, or internal coup d'etat's. Rather, a promotion is granted on the basis of seniority and participation in training courses at home and abroad, in conjunction with a soldiers record of disciplined and efficient performance in discharging his administrative responsibilities. In order to

---

[346] General de Division in the army, or General del Aire in the air force, which is the highest rank attainable in the Ecuadorian Air Force.

[347] General del Ejército.

[348] Comandante General del Ejército.

[349] El Comando Conjunto de las Fuerzas Armadas.

[350] Jefe del Comando Conjunto de las Fuerzas Armadas.

[351] Ministro de Defensa Nacional - typically a civilian, or better stated ... a retired military officer.

[352] Comandante en Jefe de las Fuerzas Armadas.

[353] In 2008 Ecuador's compulsory recruitment law changed requiring twelve months of service. The compulsory recruitment age also increased to twenty years of age.

[354] For this reason Ecuador's body of troops had an extremely high illiteracy rate.

receive their second lieutenant's commission for example, candidates must have satisfactorily completed several years of study at one of the armed forces branch military schools.[355] Advanced training therefore is a top priority, with a high percentage of Ecuador's cadets and officers getting further training through the US Army School of the Americas (SOA), [356] which is a US army training facility largely for Spanish speaking Latin American cadets and officers currently located at Fort Benning Georgia.

■ ■ ■

During World War II Ecuador was one of several South American nations to join the allies late in the war, with Ecuador joining against Germany on 2 Feb 1945. Prior to this however and without a formal written agreement, Ecuador did let the United States utilize Baltra Island in the Galapagos, to establish an American Air Force Base. The US Navy moved into the island during January 1942 and the US Army began construction in February 1942. It was May 1942 when the movement of US troops into the Galapagos Base occurred.

The US military force consisted of one heavy bombardment squadron, one reinforced infantry company, one coast artillery battery with one sea coast searchlight platoon, and an air base detachment. Crews stationed at Baltra patrolled the eastern Pacific for enemy submarines and provided protection for the Panama Canal naval base. After the war the facilities were given to the government of Ecuador and the island base continued as an official Ecuadorian military base.

World War II did have an adverse effect on the country though. In 1941 while the rest of the world was preoccupied with global war, the Peruvian army invaded again over the disputed Amazonian area. This latest war [357] devastated Ecuador's El Oro province, and the Ecuadorian forces were easily defeated. The United States and other major powers were too preoccupied with World War II to allow such a small conflict to destroy allied unity, during a peace conference at Río de Janeiro in 1942, the allies forced Ecuador to relinquish its claims too much of the Amazonian region.

The politics and government after World War II presented contradictions. On one hand, Ecuador enjoyed a long period of constitutional government and relatively free elections. From 1948-60, three presidents, beginning

---

[355] For example the Ecuadorian armies Colegio Militar Eloy Alfaro.

[356] Established during 1946 in the US controlled Panama Canal Zone, the school operated there until 21 Sep 1984 when operations were suspended in compliance with the terms of the 1977 Panama Canal Treaty. In December of 1984 the school's operations resumed at Fort Benning.

[357] As the reader may recall from previous chapters, Ecuador and Peru were also at war over the disputed Amazon region upon Richard Spruce's arrival in Ecuador. Even today this area is still in dispute with border skirmishes breaking out what appears to be every few years. This dispute has been utilized by Ecuadorian politicians and the military as a domestic rallying point of national pride.

with Galo Plaza, were freely elected and completed their terms. On the other hand, there were two long periods of pro-US military governments during 1963-1966 and again from 1972-1979.

■ ■ ■

"Two circumstances proved critical in persuading the military to overthrow President José Maria Velasco before the scheduled completion of his term in 1972. On the one hand, the state was due very shortly to begin reaping vast revenues under a 1964 petroleum concession. On the other hand, the overwhelming favorite too win the presidency in 1972 was Asaad Bucaram Elmalim.[358] Both the military and the business community regarded Bucaram as dangerous and unpredictable and unfit to be president, especially at a time when unprecedented income [359] was expected to flow into the state coffers. On 15 Feb 1972, four months before the scheduled elections, the military once again overthrew Velasco, who was sent into his final period of exile to Argentina." [360]A revolutionary and nationalist military junta led by Army General Guillermo Rodriguez Lara seized power and Lara became President (Dictator).

A bloody coup attempt during September 1975 by the Army Chief of Staff, General Raul González Alvear, occurred shortly after midnight when about one hundred-fifty soldiers and six tanks penetrated the facade, succeeded in routing the thirty-four member palace guards and captured the Presidential Palace. The revolt crumbled when troops and at least ten tanks loyal to Lara surrounded the palace. González, dressed in civilian clothes, managed to walk out of the palace unnoticed and gain asylum in the Chilean embassy. What later became known as "The Cocktail Coup" for being so poorly organized, cost seventeen lives and wounded eighty. [361]

As a result of González's failed coup attempt, others within the military and government that were believed to want a lasting military government under

---

[358] Asaad Bucaram Elmalim, born 1916, died 1981. Twice elected Mayor of Guayaquil in the 1960s. Deported to Panama in 1970 and returned in 1972. Wikipedia states ... "He is also remembered for being the first Mayor in the history of Ecuador to use a Municipal Police Force to beat up university students that protested a coup d'etat."

[359] The discovery of commercial quantities of oil in the Amazon rainforest of Ecuador in 1967, by a consortium of the foreign companies Texaco and Gulf, was heralded as the salvation of Ecuador's economy, exports began in 1972. Since this time ... "the armed forces have received 45% of the oil royalties earned by the state oil company, Petroecuador." *The New York Times* 22 Dec 2000

[360] US Library of Congress, *Country Studies, Ecuador*

[361] *The New York Times* 15 Sep 1975

avowedly rightist authoritarianism [362]were purged. Those dismissed by Lara included his Minister of Finance and Minister of Natural Resources.

Just three short months later in January of 1976, rising constitutional sentiment within the Ecuadorian armed forces resulted in yet another coup, this time bloodless, and a military junta seized power. The Supreme Council of Government, consisted of the then Commanders of the Navy; Admiral Alfredo Poveda Burbano, Army; General Guillermo Durán Arcentales and Air Force; General Luis Leoro Franco. This new military government's administration was dominated by Colonels.

The Federal Research Division of the United States Library of Congress compiles Country Studies and Profiles that present a description and analysis of the historical setting and the social, economic, political, and national security systems and institutions of countries throughout the world. Ecuador's study provides insight into the country's new military administration ... "Virtually the only item on the agenda of the new military triumvirate was to preside over a return of the government to constitutional, civilian rule. The bloody September 1975 coup attempt had revealed the depth of the breach in the institutional unity of the armed forces. Handing the government back to civilians, it was hoped, might remove the causes of divisions within the military, or at least make it easier to hide them from public view.

"The original timetable, announced in June 1976, called for a transition that was to culminate in presidential elections in February 1978. First, new government charters and electoral laws were to be drafted by appointed commissions [363]and then a public referendum would choose between two proposed constitutions. The transition was repeatedly slowed down, however, and in the end, instead of the less than two years originally scheduled, three years and eight months elapsed between the 1976 coup and the inauguration of a civilian president.

"Two reasons are commonly cited for the delay: the slowness of decision making within the Supreme Council of Government because of ongoing disagreement within the military high command and repeated maneuvering's by the military government to manipulate the electoral process, thereby controlling its outcome. Like the Rodríguez Lara government, the Council was particularly interested in ... preventing Bucaram from winning the presidency."

Commission member Oswaldo Hurtado Larrea would write in *El poder politico en el Ecuador (1977),* that while on the commission he felt pressure from the military only once, "...the purpose of which was to secure the

---

[362] The 1972 military government had expanded the economic functions of the Ecuadorian state beyond that accomplished by any previous government. The military had control over every aspect of government and society.

[363] One such commission member was Oswaldo Hurtado Larrea, who would later become Vice President and then President of Ecuador.

inclusion in the constitution and electoral law of provisions that would disqualify the presidential candidacy of CFP (Concentration of Popular Forces [364]) leader Assad Bucaram," the inclusion of which Hurtado goes on to state "he rejected." Whether Hurtado rejected its inclusion or not, in 1978 an electoral law laid down that presidential candidates must be of Ecuadorian parentage, thus excluding Bucaram, who was of Lebanese parentage but had been widely favored to win the election, thereby ending his candidacy. [365]

Bucaram's protégé, Jaime Roldós Aguilera, who was also married to Bucaram's niece, then stood in for him as presidential candidate of the CFP party. The official party slogan of the time was "Roldós in Office, Bucaram in Power." Finally after seven years of military rule and transitional delays, Ecuador and its roughly eight million people returned to democracy when Jaime Roldós Aguilera was elected as President on 16 Jul 1979 and was inaugurated on 10 Aug 1979.

Roldós openly opposed US oil companies and their involvement with Ecuadorian oil, refusing international proposals for oil exploitation. Roldós signed a humanitarian protocol between Colombia, Peru and Ecuador, which was purportedly seen by US President Ronald Reagan as a lean toward Soviet implementation. The major accomplishments of the Roldós presidency included signing presidential decrees' reducing the work week to forty hours and doubling the minimum wage to 4,000 Sucres per month, roughly $160 in 1979 US dollars.

In late January and early February of 1981, there was a military confrontation with Peru, in the Cordillera del Cóndor. Clashes occurred in the regions of Paquisha, Mayaycu, and Machinaza. Roldós chose to use diplomacy in the midst of this crisis, leaving the territorial dispute in the hands of the Organization of American States. The clash ended with a cease-fire, with three Ecuadorian outposts destroyed and the Peruvian Army in control of most of the disputed area. One can only surmise that the President's act of diplomacy may not have had the full support of his military's leadership.

■ ■ ■

Two powerful military players within the period of military government (1972 -1979) and into this new period of civilian rule, who as cadets and officers had attended the School of the Americas (SOA), were Colonel Gribaldo Miño Tapia and Colonel Reñe Vargas Pazzos. Both men rapidly furthered their careers within these governments becoming powerful Generals of the period. However, throughout their careers, these two men with apparently opposing leftist and rightist views, would become bitter rivals.

---

[364] Concentration of Popular Forces - At the time was a populist and ideologically incoherent party.
[365] The military had one other demand for elections to commence, that a senior officer must become Minister of Defense.

Gribaldo Alfonso Miño Tapia was born in El Corazón of Cotopaxi Province on 2 Aug 1929. Senior in rank to Vargas, Gribaldo Miño attended the SOA in 1950 and 1951 as a Cadet, in 1957 as a Lieutenant and again in 1966 as a Major, taking classes in Basic Weapons, Heavy Weapons, Tactics, Special Weapons & Communication, and Irregular Warfare Orientation. Miño would serve as the Commander of the First Military Zone and Gribaldo's military career advanced rapidly under the years of military rule, especially after the bloody September 1975 coup attempt, when Lara named Colonel Miño his acting Minister of Finance.[366] Two months later, Colonel Miño was assigned as Director of the Colegio Militar Eloy Alfaro [367] from November 1975 through June 1976.

It would be under the rule of the Supreme Council of Government that Gribaldo Miño's military career would rapidly advance, attaining the high Ecuadorian military ranks of General and General Commander of the Army. It would be under civilian rule that four star General Miño would attain Ecuador's highest military rank ... Chief of the Armed Forces Joint Command until 11 Jun 1984.

Under General Miño's stewardship the Ecuadorian military, through its army corps of engineers, set out on one of the most ambitious road construction projects of the country's history, building more than three hundred miles of roads within the Amazon Basin. This road construction frenzy, although appearing humanitarian, clearly had a military purpose. Not only did the project allow for migration and population of the area, it improved access and mobility for troops, heavy equipment and materials to the region [368] where Ecuador established a chain of bases in the event of further military action against her sworn enemy Peru. [369]

---

[366] As evidenced by Colonel Miño's signature on *Decreto No. 799-B*, Lara's Ley De Ejercicio Professional del Periodista of 18 Sep 1975. This Decree, under the auspices and powers of Ecuador's Ministry of Education and Culture, established and governed the life of the National Federation of Journalists of Ecuador.

[367] General Lara himself had served as Director of the Colegio Militar Eloy Alfaro from November 1969 through March 1971. General Medardo Salazar Navas, who appears later in our story, would also serve as Director of the school shortly after Colonel Miño's term, from July 1977 through August 1979. Whether mere coincidence or not, it appears that service in this post has been a stepping stone to the command of Ecuador's army.

[368] Similar in purpose to the Dwight D. Eisenhower National System of Interstate and Defense Highways created in the United States built to transport troops and missiles.

[369] A protracted border dispute continued to strain relations between Ecuador and Peru. The approximately 200,000-square kilometer area of the Amazon (the Marañón district), which Ecuador had claimed since the nineteenth century, contained the city of Iquitos on the west bank of the Amazon River and also Peru's main jungle petroleum producing region. Since 1960, when

Shortly before his retirement, pro-democracy General Miño was awarded the US Legion of Merit,[370] degree of commander, by the United States Army at the direction of President Ronald Reagan ... "for exceptionally meritorious conduct in the performance of outstanding services"[371]... during the period of 1 Feb 1982 through 15 Feb 1984, while serving as Ecuador's Chief of the Armed Forces Joint Command. [372]

■ ■ ■

Similar to Cadet Miño, Reñe Vargas also attended the School of the Americas where as a Cadet he also took classes in Basic Weapons and Heavy Weapons during 1951 and Engineering in 1952. Born in Chone of Manabi Province on 13 Apr 1932, Reñe Vargas comes from a long leftist family political history and of military tradition, his father having been an army colonel. Reñe graduated from Ecuador's military academy, Colegio Militar Eloy Alfaro, in 1953 as a second lieutenant and became an engineer in the Ecuadorian Army. As a Colonel, Vargas was assigned as general manager of CEPE,[373] and later became commander of the army's El Oro Infantry Brigade.

Even though Colonel Vargas was known to hold left-wing nationalistic, anti-capitalist and anti-oil company views, in late 1976 the military junta appointed Vargas as its Minister of Natural Resources and Energy.[374] During his short term as Minister, Colonel Vargas was involved in the forced sale of Gulf Oil Corporation's 37.5% share in Ecuador's oil consortium to the state. In the 2 Oct 1976 *New York Times* it was stated that

---

Ecuador's President Velasco declared the Río Protocol to be invalid, under which the area was recognized as Peru's, Ecuador has continued to assert its right to the disputed region and to emphasize its need for an outlet to the Atlantic via the Amazon River. In addition to minor skirmishes, at least two major wars have occurred in the Amazon, the Paquisha War of 1981 (during which General Miño served as Inspector of the Army) and the Cenepa War of 1995.

[370] The Legion of Merit - A military decoration of the United States armed forces awarded for exceptionally meritorious conduct in the performance of outstanding services and achievements. The decoration is issued both to United States military personnel and to military and political figures of foreign governments.

[371] US Army General Order 13 dated 11 May 1984

[372] The newspaper *El Universo* of 12 Jun 1984 however, states that General Miño held the post of Chief of the Armed Forces Joint Command from August 1983 through 11 Jun 1984. Ex-President Hurtado confirms in *La dictadura civil (1988)* that General Miño held the post until June of 1984.

[373] CEPE is the acronym of the Ecuadorian State Petroleum Corporation. Through CEPE the Government of Ecuador imposed itself into and participated in various petroleum related commercial ventures

[374] From *Memorandum Opinion* dated 15 Dec 1988 - US District Court for the Southern District of Florida in Norsal Oil & Mining Co. V. Texaco, and *The New York Times* 1 Jan 1977.

... "Colonel Reñe Vargas Pazzos, head of the Ecuadorean Natural Resources Ministry, said on Thursday that Gulf's deposit payment had averted cancellation of the company's contract and opened way for negotiations."

On 31 Dec 1976 the forced sale was completed and was reported in *The New York Times* of 1 Jan 1977 ... "The property of the Gulf Oil Corporation in Ecuador [it's 37.5% share] passed today to the state oil corporation, CEPE, in a forced sale caused by what the Minister of Natural Resources [Vargas] described in an interview as the 'rebellion' of Gulf against Ecuador." ... shortly thereafter in early 1977, Colonel Vargas was removed as Minister of Natural Resources and Energy.

Following in his rival's footsteps, Reñe eventually rose to the ranks of General, General Commander of the Army until 11 Jun1984 and Chief of the Armed Forces Joint Command [12 Jun 1984 - 11 Aug 1984] ... "Embassy [USA] officers in the late 1980s labeled Vargas a 'slick Schemer', highlighting his ambitious and sophisticated nature. During military dictatorships in the 1970s, he shrewdly engineered assignments to the Ecuadorian state oil corporation, also serving as Minister of Natural Resources and Minister of Energy and Mines. These assignments reputedly netted him huge illegal commissions on oil sales and contracts. He also reportedly profited from graft on purchases of Army supplies and equipment. Embassy officers at the time found that Rene had enriched himself 'on a scale unusual even in a nation where corruption is the norm.' Vargas continues to champion military participation in private businesses, from which he is presumed to have benefitted in the past." [375]

In 1994 the author Bruce W. Farcau [376] would write a clearer picture of Generals Miño and Vargas in *The Coup: Tactics in the Seizure of Power* that during 1981-1984 ... "In Ecuador, the military was divided between the faction led by Chairman of the Joint Chiefs, General Gribaldo Miño Tapia, and that led by General Reñe Vargas Pazzos, and the personal animosity between the two rival Generals Gribaldo Miño and Reñe Vargas was such that, if either seemed bent upon overthrowing the government, the other would automatically declare himself the loyal supporter of the government, regardless of the apparent reason for the planned coup, just out of spite." [377]

---

[375] *El Universo* 24 Apr 2011 - USA Quito Embassy Political Section "Secret" Cable # 95515 dated 6 Feb 2007 set to be declassified in 25 years, leaked by Wikileaks and published in the newspaper.

[376] Mr. Farcau worked at the American Embassy in Quito from 1981 to 1984 as part of the Political/Military Section at the Embassy.

[377] Through a personal communication in 2012, Mr. Farcau, in response to my questions regarding the feud between General Miño and General Vargas, clarified the matter in this manner ... " I don't believe it had to do with ideology so much, as each man headed a clique of officers within the military that competed for influence and position. There was also a personal aspect to the conflict, I believe. One concern at the time I was there was that President Hurtado was doing his best to rig the election. While I don't believe that the

General Vargas would succeed General Miño as Chief of the Armed Forces Joint Command upon his rival's voluntary early retirement on 12 Jun 1984. Vargas assumed Miño's position for a very brief period of two months, until Vargas was forced into retirement when an officer junior to him was appointed Minister of Defense and Admiral Santiago Coral Terán was appointed as incoming President Febres Cordero's Chief of the Armed Forces Joint Command on 12 Aug 1984.

■ ■ ■

In 1979 the leftist Roldós had won the election, but differences quickly developed between Bucaram and the President. Roldós distanced himself from his radical mentor by scrapping the slogan he had used during the campaign, thereby moderating his own image. Bucaram [378] had been elected President of the National Assembly of Ecuador after Roldós was sworn in, and utilized his position to obstruct Roldós in congress by forming an alliance with the Conservative party, in order to pass a series of controversial bills, many of which were then vetoed by Roldós. On 15 Apr 1980 Roldós established a committee of leaders to find a solution for the battle for power with the National Congress, presided over by his former mentor Assad Bucaram.

With the government of President Roldós besieged from broad sectors of the population, rumors of a possible military coup began to circulate. Then, on 24 May 1981, President Roldós, his Minister of Defense General Marco Subía Martinez, their wives, and all passengers and the crew were killed in an airplane crash. [379]

---

military was particularly concerned about the actual ideology of either major party, the consensus was that, if blatant rigging took place, the military would be implicated as having condoned it. Since they did not stand to gain from a Left-leaning government, they really didn't like the idea and there were constant rumors of coup plotting."

[378] I had what I would call the misfortune of meeting a sixty-three year old Assad Bucaram, during a brief encounter in his office at the National Assembly in Quito toward the end of 1979. Bucaram, apparently being a friend or acquaintance of my mother-in-law, had created a position for my wife as head of the assembly's printing office.

[379] Ecuador appears to have a very high incidence of government officials succumbing as crash victims. Just during the short period from 1975 through 1994 Ecuador lost President Roldós, two Defense Ministers', Generals' Rafael Rodriguez Palacios and Marco Subia Martinez, two Commanders of the Air Force, Generals' Luis Morejón Almeida and Augusto Flores, two Commanders of the Army, Generals' Carlomagno Andrade Paredes and Miguel Iturralde Jaramillo, a Minister of Information and Tourism along with his Sub-Secretary, and Air Force Generals' Galo Coronel and Raul Cousin. Again in 2007, within nine days of her appointment, one of the first female and civilian Minister's of Defense, Guadalupe Larriva would succumb to a helicopter crash.

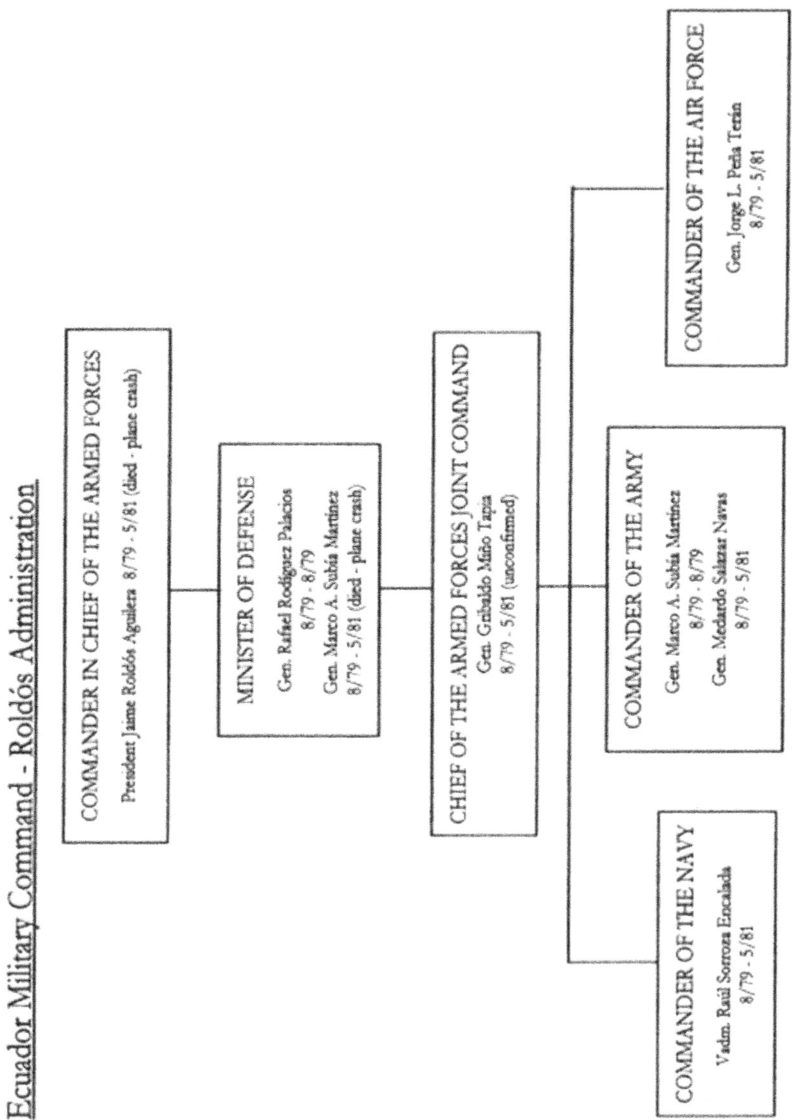

Roldós Administration Military Command

(Compiled with best available information, may be susceptible to errors.)

Questions surrounded the crash and to this day have not been convincingly explained. The Ecuadorian Air Force officially blamed the crash on the pilot, stating that the accident was a human failure. The controversy about the cause of the crash began immediately, when the Accident Investigation Committee [380] of the Ecuadorian Air Force attributed the crash to pilot error, supposedly caused by an overloading with cargo. The parliamentary commission that was formed months later, only after pressure from the families of the victims and political groups allied with the president, found contradictions and inconsistencies in the JIA report, but the commission could not reach definitive conclusions. The Zurich Police however, who had also conducted an investigation of the crash, concluded that the plane's motors were shut down when the plane crashed into the mountain. This expert opinion, which contradicted the official Air Force report, was not further investigated by the Ecuadorian government.

The cause of the accident or suspects in an assassination attempt, have never been determined. However, the plane crash led to intense popular speculation among Ecuadorians', with some attributing its cause to the Peruvian government while others blamed the United States government and the CIA.[381] There were unconfirmed reports that natives in Ecuador's amazon jungles near the crash site in Loja, confirmed they saw a fireball in the air falling down, which is how they located the "crash site." Purportedly, there is also an unconfirmed report that two key witnesses died in separate car accidents before they had an opportunity to testify.

Although the armed forces' faithfulness to democracy was severely tested during this period, in the end, constitutional legitimacy and democracy prevailed, as President Roldós was allowed to be succeeded by his Vice President Oswaldo Hurtado Larrea.

Confronted with the questionable conditions surrounding the death of Roldós, Hurtado was also faced with an ideologically split military. One faction demanding policy moves further to the left and the other further to the right. One cannot help but draw the assumption, that Ecuador's new president realized how precarious and dependent on moderation his existence truly was. Hurtado ultimately moderated the policies of his predecessor moving slightly left of center, even reversing the Roldós position on international oil exploitation.

■ ■ ■

---

[380] Junta Investigadora de Accidentes or JIA.

[381] Interestingly, what would rationally appear as the main conspiracy theory in coup prone Ecuador, a military assassination of the President, is not mentioned. Instead Ecuadorians' attributed the cause to the Peruvian government while others blamed the United States government and the CIA.

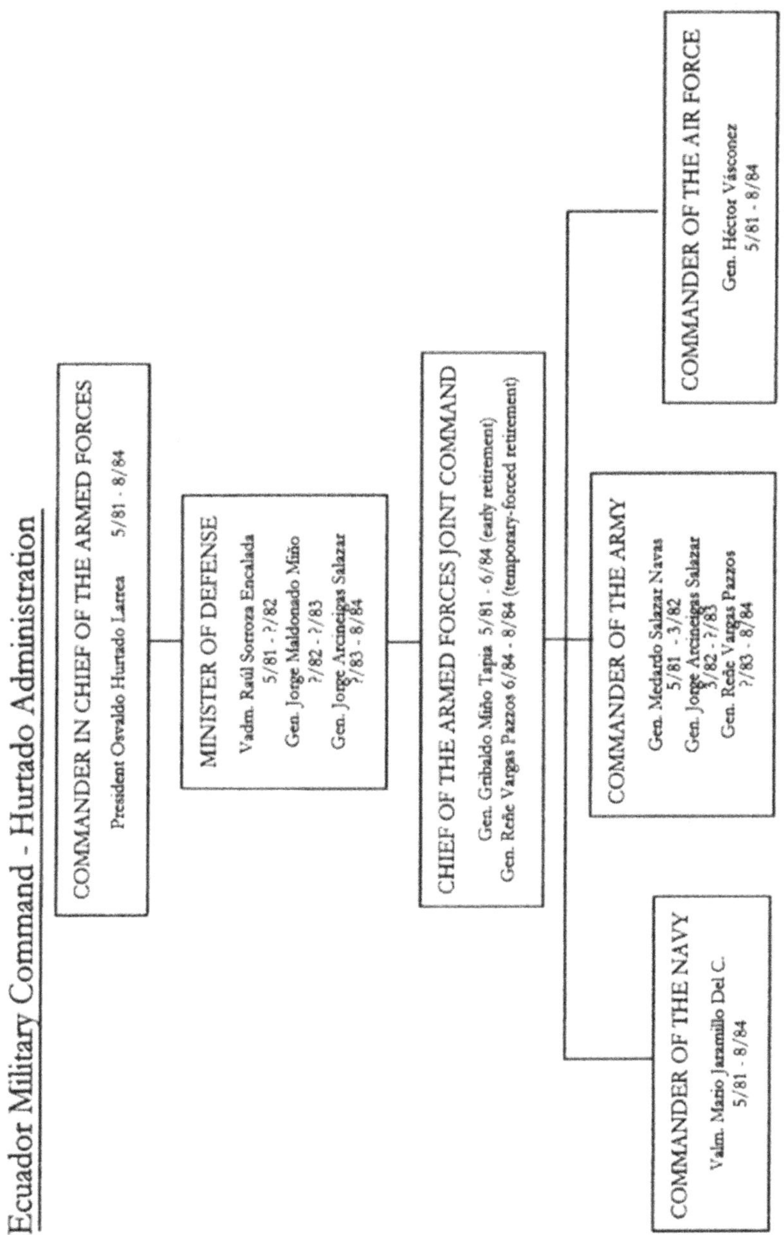

Hurtado Administration Military Command

(Compiled with best available information, may be susceptible to errors.)

Bruce W. Farcau author of *The Coup: Tactics in the Seizure of Power (1994),* establishes and clarifies in his book what was transpiring behind the scenes during Hurtado's partial term ... "The administration of Oswaldo Hurtado Larrea was extremely weak, Hurtado having succeeded to the presidency upon the death of President Jaime Roldós in a plane crash, and the rumors of coup plotting were rife. The military was divided between the factions led by Chairman of the Joint Staff, army General Gribaldo Miño Tapia, and that of army Commander Reñe Vargas Pazzos. While neither of these men had any use for the Hurtado administration, and fully agreed with the various 'institutional' military reasons being put forth for his overthrow, the animosity between Miño and Vargas was such that neither would subscribe to a coup in which the other would have the dominant role. Since power could not be shared equally between them, they both plotted continually to obtain dominant power within the military, wooing the bulk of the uncommited officer corps and conspiring with various anti-government civilian groups. However, whenever it appeared that one or the other had reached what he considered 'critical mass' for launching a coup, the other would make known within the officer corps his own commitment to the democratic process and his willingness to place his own forces on the line to oppose any coup movement by armed force. The specter of civil war was too much for most officers, and the Hurtado regime, which either wisely or inadvertently happened to keep the two factions more or less evenly balanced through the even handed policy of placement of officers of the respective alliances, sputtered along to the end of its constitutional term undisturbed by any serious military uprisings. Rumors had been flying for some time that a coup was in the works to overthrow the left - of - center civilian government of Oswaldo Hurtado Larrea, who was allegedly involved in electoral fraud to ensure the victory of another left-of-center candidate in the 1984 campaign." [382]

Another political science author, Anita Isaacs, would provide another interesting detail in her work *Military Rule and Transition in Ecuador 1972-92* ... "The prospect of a military coup ... loomed large. Opposition to the reformist policies of the Roldós and Hurtado governments led to rightist demands for military intervention ... those efforts came to nothing. According to military accounts, 'President Hurtado was forced into a corner' when a high ranking officer 'visited the North American Embassy to get a feel for how the United States would react to a coup.' Fearful lest the military intervene, Hurtado acted swiftly. The officer in question, General Luis Piñeiros, was retired from active duty."

---

[382] In 2012 a source extremely close to General Miño, whom for obvious reasons must remain anonymous, related to me that ... "The General refused to take over the government and establish a dictatorship. President Hurtado Larrea was attempting to force the General to take over in order to stop Leon Febres Cordero from obtaining the presidency."

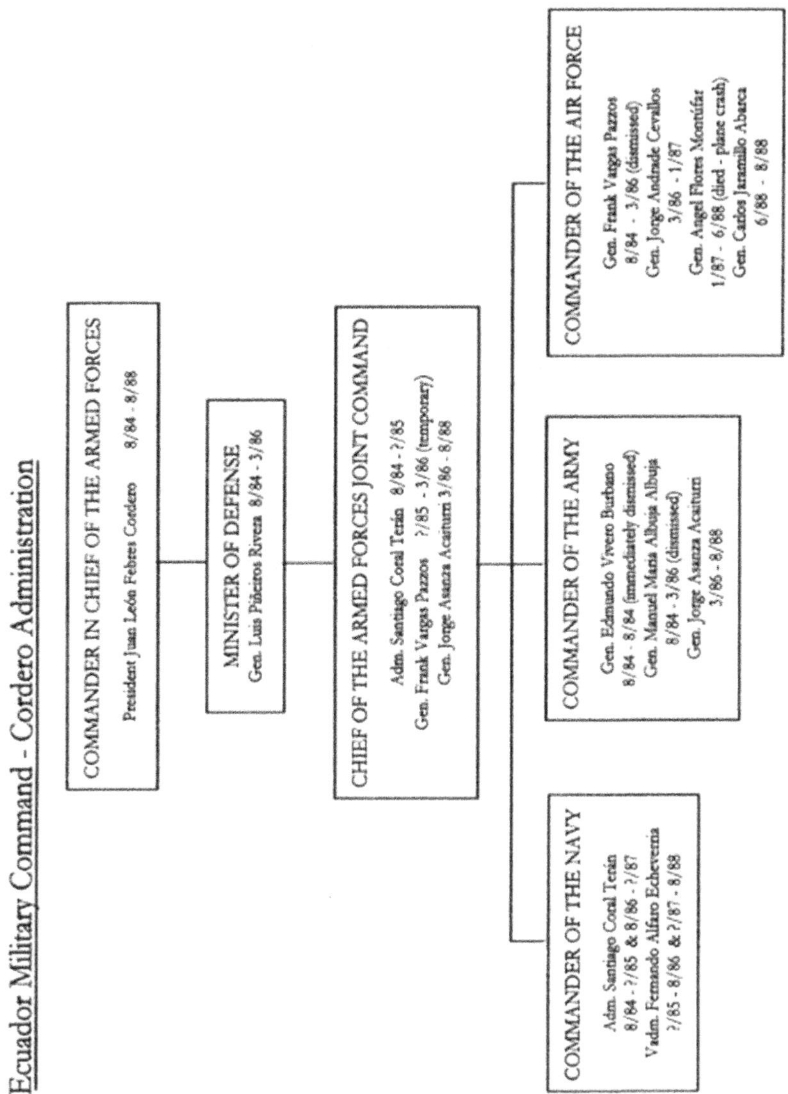

Cordero Administration Military Command

(Compiled with best available information, may be susceptible to errors.)

President Juan León Febres Cordero

■ ■ ■

The presidential elections of 1984 however, were narrowly won by Juan León Febres Cordero. A successful businessman and congressman from Guayaquil, Cordero had amassed one of the largest personal fortunes in Ecuador through his dealings in the paper, brewing, textile and energy industries. Febres Cordero was inaugurated August 10th of the same year.

Military subordination to civilian authority was not automatic in coup prone Ecuador, yet the incoming President Febres Cordero, had few qualms about employing the armed forces as an active arm of his government and freely intervened in internal military affairs when he judged it politically feasible.

Two days prior to his inauguration, Febres Cordero nominated recently retired General Gribaldo Miño Tapia as Minister of Defense [383] and the nomination was rejected by the Council of General Officers of the Armed Forces [384] on the grounds of seniority. According to the council, over which Miño's rival Vargas purportedly held influence, Miño was not the official with the most seniority or of a greater "graduacion de las Fuerzas Armadas."

---

[383] *El Universo* 9 Aug 1984

[384] Consejo de General de la Fuerza Terrestre - Ecuador's council of generals that qualifies and selects candidate's for promotion under military laws and regulations governing promotions.

Febres Cordero subsequently boldly violated military regulations by returning an officer recently retired by President Hurtado to active duty. The pro-Febres officer, Major General Luis Piñeiros Rivera, was promptly named Minister of Defense. Retired General Miño was asked to return to Panama, this time not as a student of the S.O.A., but as Ecuador's Ambassador to the recently established dictatorship of Manuel Noriega,[385] where Miño would serve until mid-1986. [386]

Military procedures and seniority were also short circuited so that the incoming President could name his own Commander of the Army, a General Manuel María Albuja. Ecuador's personnel law of the armed forces requires that the army commander is to be selected from the three most senior officers. Febres Cordero initially chose the third officer, General Edmundo Vivero Burbano, immediately dismissed him and named Albuja, who ranked sixth in succession, as Army Commander.

The temporary Chief of the Armed Forces Joint Command, General Reñe Vargas Pazzos, had assumed the position in 12 June 1984 upon the early resignation and retirement of his rival, General Miño.[387] General Vargas was forced into retirement [388] by President Febres Cordero and in August Admiral Santiago Coral Terán assumed the position as Chief of the Armed Forces Joint Command. [389]

During the first years of his conservative administration, Febres Cordero restructured the economy along free-market lines, took strong stands against drug trafficking and terrorism, and pursued close relations with the United States. His tenure though was marred by bitter wrangling with other branches of government, most specifically the leftist controlled legislature and the military.

■ ■ ■

In coup vulnerable Ecuador during the early 1980s ... "General Reñe Vargas Pazzos, then commander of the army and leader of one of two rival factions within the military, would probably not have sought out the commander of the Fighter Division located in the coastal lowlands, as the Kfir and Mirage jet fighters of the unit would be of little use in a coup. However, if Vargas was involved in coup plotting at some point, as was widely rumored, he

---

[385] Manuel Noriega was the military dictator of Panama from 15 Dec 1983 until his removal and arrest by US Forces on 20 Dec 1989.

[386] Ambassador Miño was the recipient of Panama's *Best Ambassador of the Year for 1985 in Panama* award.

[387] El Universo 12 Jun 1984

[388] *The New York Times* 19 Jan 1987 and 31 Jan 1987

[389] General Vargas was not alone in forced retirement. Dissatisfaction spread as military leadership in all three branches was restructured with many more forced retirements. One might also consider that in coup prone Ecuador, Febres Cordero faced having his army and air force under the command of brothers with well known leftist sympathies. Febres Cordero's actions, may have ensured that Ecuador continue down the path of democracy.

almost certainly would have included the air force officer in question as part of his core group, since it happened to be his brother, Frank." [390]

Lieutenant General Frank Vargas Pazzos, who had been promoted to an Air Force Brigadier General by President Roldós in 1980, was "...a figure firmly within a well-established Ecuadorian political tradition of turbulent populist leaders with an authoritarian but indeterminate ideology and a macho personal style ... Frank Vargas reached the top rank in the air force not so much because of his service record, which contains several incidents of insubordination and lack of discipline, as in spite of it." [391]

Matters reached a crisis point in Ecuador during early March 1986. Lieutenant General Frank Vargas Pazzos, then Air Force Commander and temporary Chief of the Armed Forces Joint Command, brother of Reñe, met with Minister of Defense Piñeiros on March 7. Vargas purportedly demanded the firing of General Albuja on the grounds of corruption and of mishandling funds. Specifically Vargas contended that an extra four million dollars had allegedly been overpaid [392] in the purchase of a Fokker airplane for flights of the government run airline TAME [393] to Loja. Moreover, Vargas claimed that Albuja had constructed a home using materials and manpower of the Army.

Following a stormy confrontation, some accounts indicate that shots were fired in the air, perhaps in part due to political, professional and personal jealousies of long-standing, General Vargas contended that the Minister's support of Albuja made him an accomplice in the purported corruption. Rather than Piñeiros or Albuja being dismissed, President Febres Cordero retired Vargas for insubordination, who was immediately replaced by General Jorge Andrade Cevallos as Air Force Commander and General Jorge Asanza Acaiturri became Chief of the Armed Forces Joint Command.

After he was dismissed, Vargas ordered three jets to fly over Quito in a show of support for himself. Vargas then took refuge at the Mariscal Sucre Air Base in Quito. Four hours later, Vargas flew to the Eloy Alfaro Air Base in Manta where some two hundred officers and airmen supported him, seizing the base Vargas reiterated his charges against General Albuja. The Army began to mobilize columns of mechanized infantry from Portoviejo Manta which were buzzed but not fired upon by A-37B attack aircraft based at Eloy Alfaro. After days of negotiations, it was purportedly agreed that Vargas would be judged for his actions by the Council of General Officers,

---

[390] Bruce W. Farcau in *The Coup: Tactics in the Seizure of Power (1994)*

[391] *Ecuador Fragile Democracy (1988)* by David Corkill and David Cubitt

[392] Vargas alleged that the international price for the airplane was only twelve million dollars. Therefore, Albuja had earned himself a premium of four million dollars. (Vargas himself has been reported as receiving a $250,000 USD kickback on a separate aircraft purchase, but he spent the money on the troops ... "his boys.")

[393] TAME - Acronym for the civil airline operated by the military, Transportes Aéreos Militares Ecuatorianos.

while Defense Minister Piñeiros and General Albuja would resign their positions.

On March 11, Vargas returned to Quito, surrendered and was taken prisoner, on the understanding that President Febres Cordero would dismiss both Piñeiros and Albuja. The next day, on news that Piñeiros was not going to be dismissed, Vargas determined that the President had "gone back on his word"on the purported agreement.[394] Vargas and his loyal subordinates took control of the Mariscal Sucre air base in Quito where he was under house arrest, and tried to overthrow the government, which led to armed conflict.

On March 14 about 2,000 Ecuadorian army soldiers, backed by armored personnel carriers and tanks, battled the rebels for ninety minutes and retook the base. There were four people killed and nine wounded in the fighting. Vargas was arrested at the base six hours after it was overrun. He was found in a search operation by soldiers, did not resist, and was taken to another military base. Before the end of the month, Piñeiros had been replaced as Minister of Defense by three star General Medardo R. Salazar Navas,[395] Albuja had been replaced, two senior Air Force officers loyal to Vargas had been arrested for armed subversion and Vargas himself was under house arrest at a military base awaiting trial.

The leftist anti-Cordero Legislature voted an amnesty for General Vargas in September of the same year. President Febres Cordero's administration rejected the resolution on the grounds that only the military had jurisdiction, sparking a constitutional controversy. Then, as Congress met to condemn the President, for behavior that allegedly led to his abduction, the armed forces high command issued a pronouncement aimed at limiting the debate.

The military strongly objected [396] to any form of amnesty for Vargas and the military made the point abundantly clear by publicly warning congressmen favoring impeachment against ... "using these ghastly circumstances to judge the acts of those who were offended" at the Taura Airbase "instead of those who executed the attacks." To emphasize this point, Defense Minister Medardo Salazar Navas, purportedly went to the home of Andrés Vallejo,

---

[394] *The New York Times* 14 Mar 1986

[395] In *La dictadura civil (1988)* ex-President Hurtado states ... "it was not advertised that the current Minister of Defense Medardo Salazar Navas was my Commander of the Army until March 1982, and that General Gribaldo Miño, until recently Ambassador in Panama, was also part of my administration until June of 1984."

[396] Several top commanders of the army, navy and air force were seized with the President at Taura, and Febres Cordero had been carefully courting the military since the revolt in March. Therefore, it was widely known that Western diplomats believed the ordeal had cemented the military's loyalty.

then President of Congress, and according to senior government officials, Salazar told Vallejo to "watch it." [397]

Apparently aware of the implied risk, Congress then passed a watered down non-binding resolution calling for the President's resignation, which was of course ignored by the military and the President. In the end, Congress adjourned without calling for a formal impeachment trial. "The armed forces are not about to let Congress destabilize the President, even if it is by constitutional means," said one official close to Febres Cordero. "Was it constitutional to vote an amnesty for a general who tried to overthrow the constitutional government?" [398]

Life in Ecuador during the period was best described in *The New York Times* of 22 Jan 1987 ... "In Ecuador as in many countries of Latin America, politics is a game of the elite, and whether the chief of state is a civilian or general, elected or self appointed, most people are likely to notice little change in their lives."

Another non-public version of events showing a different set of motives came out many years later in the previously cited "Secret" US Government cable ... "Reñe's brother 'crazy' Frank Vargas, with whom he has collaborated politically, was judged by Embassy officers and the Ecuadorian media to suffer from a severe personality disorder. In March 1986 Frank demanded that then-president León Febres Cordero promote him to be the first Four Star Air Force general in Ecuador's history. When LFC refused, Frank led a military uprising, which was put down, landing Frank in prison (Reñe was also temporarily held under suspicion of complicity). From prison, Frank ordered his Air Force subordinates to kidnap President Febres Cordero and hold him hostage in exchange for Frank's release, boasting he would personally behead Febres Cordero with his sword. Both men were released shortly thereafter. 'Crazy Frank' then ran three times unsuccessfully for president, with financing and other support from his brother Reñe. Reñe himself served as a member of Congress representing the Popular Democracy Party (now UDC) from 1988-92." [399]

■ ■ ■

Mariscal Sucre Air Force Base is located in the northern section of the city of Quito. This air base, scene of the bloody 1986 coup attempt, shares its runway with the adjacent civilian airport, Quito International Mariscal

---

[397] *Los Angeles Times* 31 Jan 1987: Richard Boudreaux in *Crisis Accentuated Weakness in Ecuador's Democratic System*

[398] *Los Angeles Times* 31 Jan 1987: Richard Boudreaux in *Crisis Accentuated Weakness in Ecuador's Democratic System*

[399] *El Universo* 24 Apr 2011 - USA Quito Embassy Political Section "Secret" Cable # 95515 dated 6 Feb 2007 set to be declassified in 25 years, leaked by Wikileaks and published in the newspaper. Interestingly, in 2012 it would be the Ecuadorian Embassy in London where the founder of Wikileaks Julian Assange, sought asylum.

Sucre Airport. As a tourist landing at the airport for the first time in 1978, the few military planes and helicopters on the tarmac, clearly identified with their vibrant yellow, blue and red circle insignia, framed my first impression of the country. Almost everyplace I went, the military or police were omnipresent. Traveling throughout the countryside, road blocks and checkpoints were common place, in bold contrast to the freedoms of movement that come naturally in the United States.

Naive to what I was about to encounter in this new world, I was oblivious to the dangers of political and social unrest that enveloped the country. Nevertheless, at the young age of twenty-three I arrived in the picturesque city of Quito high in the Andes, anticipating finding adventure in this dark, mysterious and unfamiliar land called Ecuador.

Even though I have always enjoyed traveling within the United States, at the young age of fifteen having spent a summer in Europe and Spain with a study group, it would never have crossed my mind to travel to South America, let alone to any country under military rule. Fate however would intervene. My best friend growing up had joined the US Peace Corps after completing college and post graduate education to become a physical therapist. "Doctor David" as he was called in Ecuador, was stationed at a small clinic in Latacunga and had invited me to visit for a few weeks of exploring.

■ ■ ■

As kids growing up in Stowe, Vermont, we spent a great deal of our summers' trout fishing, my friend had always encouraged me to more adventurous outdoor pursuits. We took a bicycle trip into Maine one summer, hiked some of the Long Trail in Vermont another and one winter snowshoed up the chin on the ridge line of Mount Mansfield, across the top of the mountain to the nose, we skied down to the regular ski trails and then on to the base of the mountain.

Mount Mansfield with its wooded slopes and rocky heights is the highest mountain in the State of Vermont. When viewed in comparison to the Andes and Llanganati mountains, it is merely a foothill. Its highest point is known as the chin and peaks at 4,395 feet above sea level. Man for centuries has delighted in the finding of his own image projected in natural features around him and Mansfield would be no exception. Similar to Brunner's discovery that Cerro Hermoso was the image of "the reclining woman," nature had left a fancied or real resemblance on the ridge line of Mount Mansfield.

When Mount Mansfield is viewed at a distance from the west [or east], one encounters the same vista seen by Commander Dyott in 1943, that of an elongated human profile, the face of a man lying on his back clearly appears. Following the ridge outline from the south, an image complete with distinct forehead, nose, upper and lower lips, chin (unlike most human faces, the chin is the highest point), and even an Adam's apple on its north end. The mountain's profile projected in natural features is completed by two caves. One cave on the nose provides the likeness of a nostril, while the second "cave of the winds," a mouth.

One peculiar fact about Mount Mansfield is quite similar to the contrast of the geologic formation of Cerro Hermoso and the surrounding Llanganati Mountains of Ecuador. Pre-Columbian rock, some 800 million years old on the geologic table, which seems to form the core of the Green Mountains of Vermont as far north as Lincoln, New Hampshire, does not appear anywhere on Mansfield.

In Vermont, similar to our story with the myths and legends of the Incas, the Abnaki Indians of the Algonquin family had a myth or legend which accounts for the mountain's formation and present day appearance. An account recorded in written form sometime in the early 1920s by Roxanna Thomas and republished by Robert L. Hagerman in *Mansfield; The Story of Vermont's Loftiest Mountain (1971)* ... "The legend begins when Mishawaka the Indian lived in the valley at Mansfield's base. The mountain was not shaped as it is today but was simply a great mound of rock without a distinguishing feature. At the very top the Indians had built an altar where they worshiped the rising sun. The trail to this was so steep and treacherous that only the strongest braves could endure the climb.

"Mishawaka was the son of the tribe's chief, a noble young brave except that he was severely crippled as a result of an accident. It was torture for him to walk even a few steps and for that reason he had never climbed the mountain to carry out the traditional worship.

"In the course of time Mishawaka's father died and custom dictated that he should become the new chief. But others of the tribe objected to having as their leader a lame weakling who had never been able to climb the mountain to worship. Word of this disaffection reached Mishawaka and he immediately resolved to correct the situation by climbing to the summit altar even if it meant dying in the effort. He left the Indian village unnoticed and for days crawled and pulled himself along despite the agonizing pain. Finally, exhausted and terribly weak, he reached the top of the mountain just as the sun was rising. Mishawaka said 'The impossible is achieved. I have reached the summit altar and I am fully repaid by the sight' and slipped to the ground dead.

"For days a terrible storm raged about the mountain and the summit was hidden by a dense band of clouds. The Indians in the village were frightened by the fury of the storm. But behold when the tempest was over and the clouds were lifted from the mountain the Indians gazed in wonder at the shape of the mountain. No longer was it simply a pile of rocks, but its outline was that of a human face ... and that face of the image of Mishawaka."

■ ■ ■

Between Mount Mansfield and Sterling Mountain to the north lies one of the most scenic deeply gorged mountain passes in New England, known as Smugglers Notch. The pass is claimed to have been formed by a mighty upheaval in prehistoric times that forced the two mountains apart, while erosion has sculpted a mighty gorge with nearly perpendicular walls of rock one thousand feet high on each side. Ice and snow through the ages has loosened and hurtled enormous rocks and boulders, weighing up to hundreds of tons each, for hundreds of feet down the cliffs, becoming randomly strewn on the bottom of the gorge.

Smugglers Notch was so named for its purported use as a route by smugglers during the War of 1812. The pass and its caves allegedly would be used to secrete themselves and their illicit goods smuggled to avoid taxation, from Canada into the United States.

Rock configurations abound throughout the gorge and pass in which the human imagination has found an image. One distinctive buttress is known as Elephants Head and appears with the top of an elephant head being the top of the cliff and the lower portion of the cliff narrows to form the trunk of the elephant. Other well known profiles and figures include the Hunter and his Dog and the Singing Bird. Unlike previously mentioned rock configurations within the notch, Smugglers Face Rock is the vertical surface of a cliff from which a rock image protrudes, forming the rough three dimensional face of a man, replete with eyes, nose and mouth. Again I find myself reminded of the similarities to the vista of Eugene Brunner's artist sketch of the "flying bird with outstretched wings" he discovered in the Llanganatis on the vertical surface of a cliff. In my imagination I can just close my eyes and see Eugene Brunner's artist hand drawing a pencil sketch to enhance the features of Smugglers Face Rock just as he did with the flying bird and reclining woman in the Llanganatis.

■ ■ ■

Travel within Ecuador with my friend was just as adventurous for me, probably due to my not speaking a word of Spanish, but also because everything we did and everyplace we traveled was a new and exciting adventure. My main impression of Ecuador that has stuck with me throughout the years, beyond the military control over every aspect of life, was the obvious poverty of the country in contrast to its extreme scenic beauty and grandeur.

"Doctor David" and I traveled by bus to Latacunga and Ambato, passing through the checkerboard countryside dotted with chozas (earthen dwellings). It was here that I experienced my first encounters with the outdoor markets and its smells, the indigenous peoples, their food, and the mandatory bargaining. When communicating with the indigenous peoples, they appeared to have a respect or general acceptance of their inbred subservient role in Ecuador's caste system. For example, I was always addressed by the respectful title of señor or patrón.

The indigenous peoples I encountered were dressed in traditional clothes, with little change from the time of Spruce and Stabler. Dependent on the region of the country (Pacific coastal plain, Andes or Oriente) that the natives inhabited, the clothing appeared to represent their lifestyle. The Indians from Otavalo, located in the northern Andes of Ecuador, well known for their skills with textiles and embroidery, wear bright colored ponchos and festive, intricately embroidered clothing. In the agricultural areas of the Andes, the clothing appeared more utilitarian. The men were typically clad in their customary cotton trousers, ponchos, wide felt hats and cloth or leather sandals. The women were seen wearing cotton skirts, with similar ponchos, hats and sandals as the men wore. It became obvious by their condition that they must have had but one change of clothes and no access to the modern amenities that we have become accustomed to.

In the countryside one would commonly see men and their donkeys burdened by their loads, especially on market day. On market days the journey would be made to a neighboring city or town in order to sell or trade their goods and produce. Heavily burdened, these men, head down and bent forward, carried loads on their backs in a basket or bundled, the weight held by a strap over their forehead. Sometimes the women carried loads in baskets on their backs as well, but typically their load consisted of a baby on their back. Public breast feeding and urination, I could not help but notice, were commonplace.

Continuing our travels, "Doctor David" and I drove to the second highest summit in the country, Cotopaxi. The world's highest continuously active volcano that reaches a height of 19,347 feet, with its almost symmetrical cone, majestically rises from a highland plain of about 12,500 feet. We climbed on its perpetual snow cap that starts at 16,400 feet, one of the few equatorial glaciers in the world, which seemed more like granular ice than the powder snow we were familiar with.

We visited the most beautiful lake I have ever seen, Quilotoa. Its eight hundred-twenty-foot deep emerald green waters, which result from dissolved minerals, fill the bottom of a two-mile wide crater in this dormant westernmost volcano of the Ecuadorian Andes. Thirty years later, I can still only describe the vista as ... not just picturesque but magnificently breathtaking!

The most memorable portion of our travels was indisputably the colorful experience of the bus rides. Once you discovered the bus stop or station you would seek a bus marked for your destination, or intermediate point, and board. Once underway you would pay the attendant, usually a young boy whose father was most probably the driver. Very inexpensive but crowded, and not always with just people, chickens and roosters or small pigs would be common place. The buses traveled on roads that wound through the constantly changing spectacular landscapes, with no traffic markings, few signs and no guardrails! Our trip took us on a bus ride from Latacunga in the Andes Mountains down into the Oriente, through Shell Mera, Puyo, Tena and Puerto Napo, to the small sleepy town of Puerto Misahaulli. Basically a town square surrounded by a few buildings, located at the end of a dirt road, at the junction of the Misahualli and Napo Rivers in the Amazon.

There we met by chance a local family that made their living by catching butterflies and selling them to universities and collectors' outside of Ecuador. I was fortunate enough to be invited into the jungle with them in search of butterflies. It was amazing the quantity of butterflies we caught, the variety of species, and their beautiful colors. My favorite as I recall, was a red, white and black butterfly about the size of a half dollar. The wings of these *Diaethria neglecta* butterflies appear to have the number 88 on them. On our jungle trek we crossed over an old rope bridge, passed an abandoned orange farm and came across a river where men in canoes were digging into the mud and dirt of the steep riverbanks. I thought perhaps mining for gem stones but was told ... "no glass."

Another day in Puerto Misahaulli, "Doctor David" and I took a canoe ride down the Napo River and hiked into the jungle for a short excursion into the rainforest in search of indigenous peoples and wildlife. I recall coming across a simple housing structure built on stilts, presumably to avoid flooding and dangerous animals, with a young girl sitting in the doorway. Although the memories of those two weeks have lasted a lifetime, I realized my friend had beer tastes, and I champagne. My very good friend enjoyed roughing it, and I enjoyed being pampered in four-star hotels. Sadly, our interests had diverged and we lost contact over the years.

■ ■ ■

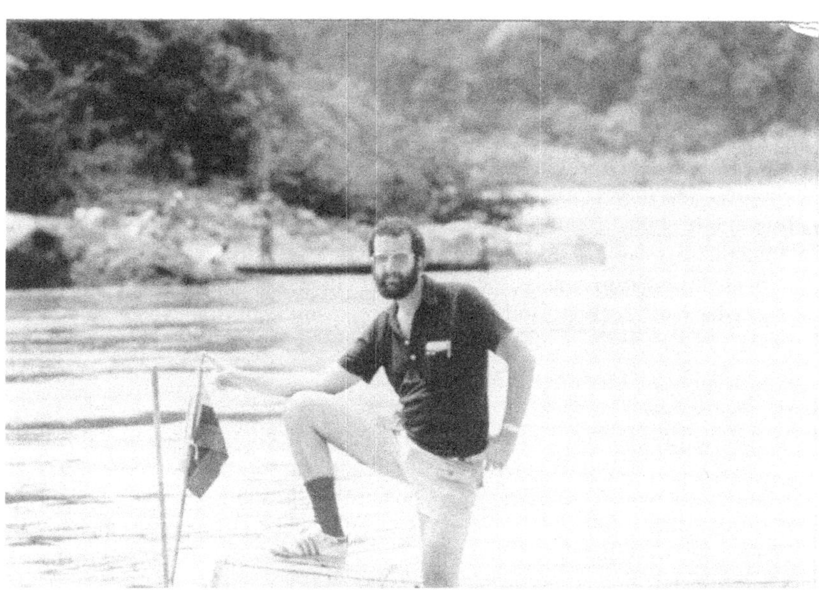

The author on the Río Napo
Puerto Misahualli, Ecuador (1978)

Arriving back in Quito for the first time on my own, I found myself in the bus station "La Terminal Terrestre de Cumandá" located south of Old Quito, the city's picturesque historical district. Protected from modernizing influences, the districts many plazas, parks, colonial buildings and flag stone paved streets are lined by white [400] two story houses with their terra cotta tiled roofs. Quito is a long city oriented north to south, located on the slope and base of the active volcano Pichincha to the west, making it almost impossible to lose your direction, so I chose not to take a taxi but to walk. My destination was a hotel in the tourist district and the best in the country, Hotel Colon [401] on Avenida Río Amazonas the city's main tourist strip.

Walking across town through its narrow streets and colonial buildings offered a close up and personal view of the city. It did not take long for me to realize this was not the best idea. Coming from the Amazon the change in altitudes from the Oriente to the Andes took its toll. I became tired, light headed and short of breath as I was entering a large cobbled square that was dominated by an enormous church. Without intent I had stumbled across Quito's oldest monumental building, the Iglesia y Convento de San Francisco with its Plaza de San Francisco in front. Groups of people were milling about in different areas of the plaza and as I was out of breath, I chose to sit, relax and take in the sights. Within minutes I perceived a weird, acrid, unfamiliar smell and instantaneously realized that some of the people milling around the plaza were indeed groups of police ... tear gas! [402]

It turned out that I had unwittingly stumbled into a common occurrence in Quito, for a long rectangular block away was the Plaza de la Independencia and the Palacio del Gobierno (Presidential Palace), where police were in the process of breaking up another student riot. I chose to leave the area immediately and was instantly stopped by a policeman. I couldn't understand what he wanted because of my lack of Spanish, so I kept saying "tourista, Hotel Colon" and he let me go on my way. I arrived safely at the hotel, rented a room in the old wing as it was cheaper, and enjoyed my first hot shower in weeks.

■ ■ ■

While waiting for the hotel's elevator, I had noticed a set of stairs to my left going down into a room that was gated, with the sign "CASINO" overhead. I thought it may have been out of business, but upon inquiry I discovered that it was only open in the evening and a jacket was required, luckily any jacket proved acceptable. That evening I went to a casino for the first time in my life, it proved to be an exciting experience.

---

[400] Old Quito's historical district zoning laws not only limit exterior remodeling, construction and signage in the district, but houses must remain painted white.

[401] Now the Hilton Colon.

[402] The film crew for *Proof of Life (1996)* would later experience a similar event in this exact same plaza during the filming of this Russell Crow movie. The film contains some excellent scenes in and around Quito, the Ecuadorian Andes and jungle.

As I walked down the stairs into the casino, the first set of tables offered the game of chance roulette. The slot machines were on the right half of the room which functioned with the national coin, a Sucre, worth four US cents at the time. On the far left side of the room was an alcove with two empty roped-off tables. At the time I assumed these tables were for highrollers or baccarat. It would be many years later that I would learn these were actually the casinos poker tables. Behind the roulette tables a little further back, was another row of tables facing out, the blackjack tables. Standing behind the players of the middle blackjack table were two attractive women, sisters I assumed. Having just come out of a relationship prior to my trip, I decided to attempt to meet one of these women. My dilemma at the time was which, the older or younger one ... I chose the younger, more attractive one.

Shortly thereafter, after roaming around the casino, I approached this blackjack table and took up a seat at third base [403] playing a few hands. The slender, long blond haired, blue eyed young woman, was now sitting at first base,[404] directly across the table. I tried to start a conversation in English but soon realized that she only spoke Spanish. Her play was terrible or just unlucky, so soon her chips were gone. I gestured and indicated to the best of my ability, having no knowledge of Spanish, for her not to leave and tossed her a few chips which were accepted and abruptly lost. As I attempted to toss a few more chips, the pit boss came over and in broken English said it would be better if we sat next to each other rather than toss chips across his table, then he added "cuidado," which I had no clue the meaning of. The young woman and I must have somehow communicated as I obtained her phone number before she left that evening.

■ ■ ■

The young woman and I began seeing each other almost daily. Even with the language barrier we seemed to connect and communicate. "Doctor David" had given me a small red pocket Spanish/English dictionary that helped us communicate one word at a time. Throughout the next few days with our broken communication and the assistance of a front desk clerk named Sebastian, who spoke English very well having studied in the United States, I learned a great deal more about this young woman.

Imagine my shock when I became aware that the older woman I had assumed to be an older sister, was actually the mother ... boy was I relieved I had picked the younger one! Was this what the casino pit boss meant by "cuidado," which I would later discover meant "be careful," or was it something else? Quito I would come to understand over time, although a large city, in some respects has a small town atmosphere, where it is quite common for someone you meet to know personally or to know about someone else that you also know. In this case I eventually discovered that

---

[403] Third base - term for the last seat on the far left side of a blackjack table, last player to act prior to the dealer.

[404] First base - term for the first seat on the right side of a blackjack table, first player to act on every hand.

the pit boss actually lived in the same neighborhood as my girlfriend and her mother.

I had also learned that this young woman was in school, her Uncle, "Tio" as she called him, got her into the military hospital [405] as a volunteer. Her father had left the family and moved to the United States when she was eight, she had a heart operation in Brazil at ten, lived with her mother, grandmother, brother, his girlfriend [406] and their two-year-old daughter. The one thing I was not able to ascertain was the young woman's age. Not knowing the legal age in Ecuador, I assumed that meeting her in a casino and the fact that she was going to school rarely, due to the amount of time we spent together, that she must be eighteen to twenty-one and in college part time, but definitely younger than me.

Days turned into weeks of walking, talking, spending time across the street from the hotel in Park El Ejido,[407] sightseeing, gambling in the casino and dining out. My hotel being located on the main tourist avenue Amazonas, offered nearby access to numerous dining experiences, especially common were the outdoor cafés where locals congregated. Typically on nights and weekends young Ecuadorians would either walk or pile into cars and cruise up and down this strip, seeking to meet up with friends or acquaintances. For many this was a customary social event and status symbol ... to be "seen" on Amazonas.

Common sights up and down Amazonas included indigenous peoples selling flowers, gum or even cigarettes by the piece. Shoeshine boys were like mice scurrying after you everywhere, persistently seeking employment. If you weren't just as persistent saying no, you'd look down and find one of the little guys had even started shining your shoes, sometimes making them appear worse than before!

---

[405] Hospital General de las Fuerzas Armadas - It was the hospital where Eugene Brunner would later die.

[406] One of my first personal encounters with the discrimination of Ecuador's caste system, was against this girl's indigenous heritage. The lack of respect, contempt, and an air of superiority on the part of the family, was quite obvious toward this young woman who in my opinion deserved better. Only due to the fact that she turned eighteen, was the couple ultimately able to get married, over the family's objections.

[407] Parque El Ejido - Large centrally located park in Quito which roughly divides the older historic portion of the city (north) from modern Quito (south). President Eloy Alfaro, upon completing his second term in 1911, moved to Europe. When Alfaro returned to Ecuador in 1912 and attempted a return to power, he was arrested on 28 Jan 1912; thrown in prison; and a group of soldiers supported by a mob, broke into the prison where Alfaro and his colleagues were detained. The mob dragged them along the cobbled streets of the city center. All were dead when the horde arrived at the city garden on the northern outskirts of town, where the mob finally burned the corpses in what later became El Ejido Public Park. Today a monument marks this site.

Of course the street beggars were just as persistent, and perhaps one and the same as the shoe shine boys. It would be common for beggars, whom appeared to be mainly young boys or crippled old men, to come up to your table at an outdoor café seeking money. Once noticed, the manager or waiter would chase them off. I recall one afternoon when my girlfriend and I were having lunch and a young street boy came up to our table stating that he was hungry and asked for money. Feeling pity, we invited the boy to sit down and gave him one of our hamburgers and fries, which he inhaled. We called over the waiter and ordered the boy another hamburger and were told that he would have to leave as they did not allow them in the restaurant. We had the boy wait on the sidewalk and when the hamburger was ready we took it out to him and gave him a few coins. As we left him on the sidewalk, he was immediately swarmed by his cohorts.

When my girlfriend and I would get together late in the day or evenings, it always seemed to be a double date with her brother and his girlfriend, where I always seemed to end up with the check. Originally I had assumed this was the difference in cultures, then at some point I discovered the truth ... this attractive young woman was seventeen and in high school, we had chaperones! At this point it was to late ... age, language, education, culture and customs weren't coming between us. I had fallen in love without truly getting to know her or her me.

Sadly, money doesn't last forever and mine was running out. My two-week vacation to visit my best friend in a strange country had run its course and lasted five weeks, and it was time to go home. But of course there was a twist to my story. I had decided to return to the States, vacate my apartment, sell my car and personal items in order that I might return to Ecuador and the girl I had fallen in love with. My departure was sad, but I knew I would return. Return I did, a short eleven days later, which seemed to have passed like an eternity.

■ ■ ■

Upon my return the taxi took me directly from the airport to Hotel Colon. After checking in I went straight to the gift shop where I purchased one dozen red roses [408] with a card on which I wrote, "Por Mi Poquito Mariposa Con Amor." Knowing that my girlfriend volunteered at the military hospital until a certain hour, I leisurely walked parallel to Park el Ejido on Avenida Patria, past Avenida 6 de Diciembre, the US Embassy and past Avenida 12 de Octubre to Calle Queseras Medio, arriving at the Hospital Militar just before the shift let out.

Quite a few people were waiting on the sidewalk next to the manned guard post that stands outside the entry gate, at the foot of the stairs leading up to

---

[408] Flowers were extremely inexpensive in Ecuador, especially when purchased from the indigenous street vendors, so these were the first of many flowers I would end up purchasing during my visits to the country.

the hospital. Hiding behind my roses as best a six-foot gringo[409] could, I spotted my girlfriend coming down the stairs talking with other young women and not paying attention. Being unaware of her surroundings, she did not see me until she was almost at the gate. I could clearly see the surprise and joy in her face, her beautiful blue eyes sparkled with happiness, at that point I knew she honestly cared for me as much as I for her. Handing her the roses, she hugged and kissed me saying ... "I thought you were not going to coming back."

One day shortly thereafter, we were sitting in Park El Ejido talking, holding hands as people in love sometimes do and enjoying ice cream from a push cart vendor, which are all common sights throughout Ecuador's parks. At some point an invitation was extended. It appears my girlfriend and her brother had convinced their mother to invite me to come stay at their "house," rather than spend such a great deal of money for a hotel. As my girlfriend and I reasoned, no hotel expense would allow me to stay longer. I believe she was afraid I would have to leave again. As we were seeing each other every day anyway, her having to travel back and forth, and the fact we were in love, made perfect sense at the time, the invitation was accepted.

The next morning I checked out of the hotel, waited for my girlfriend to arrive, then we took a cab on the same route I had walked previously with my flowers, toward la Vicentina.[410] Upon arrival at the address that was given to the taxi driver, we exited the taxi and I paid the driver. Apprehensively, I realized everything that had previously been stated to me or assumed by me, concerning my girlfriend and her family, had been predicated on outward appearances ... what people outside her family would think, and how they would be perceived. Preoccupation with outward appearances combined with the use of talented social skills in manipulative and self-centered ways, was in my opinion, the sole unflattering trait exhibited by my charming and charismatic girlfriend. I was also of the opinion that this trait had developed to a point where my girlfriend and her mother exhibited an air of superiority or entitlement. In my mind, I justified little white lies as perhaps a difference in culture, upbringing or having been placed in an environment where focused lying was necessary as a child, perhaps garnering the sympathies and support of others ... but irrespective of these traits, it was to late for me ... love concurs all!

Examining my surroundings it became painfully apparent that we were not standing in front of a "house," but some corner lots. An elevated advertising

---

409 Gringo - Term used in Ecuador for North Americans' and Europeans'. It has also been my experience that the term as used in Ecuador, shows a critical and disrespectful attitude similar to its use in Mexico. To your face you are referred to as señor, patron, jefe, amigo or hermano, while to your back you are the gringo ... or worse.

410 The same eastern section of the city I would later learn, through which Rumiñahui and the treasure purportedly departed Quito on its way toward the Llanganatis.

billboard dominated the left-hand corner of the lot, which was occupied by a metal mechanic's work area. The mechanic appeared to fabricate gates, fences, and provided the service of welding. We walked straight through the mechanics work area to a wooden fence and gate. Opening the gate, we then entered an open dirt patio area. On our left, running the entire length of the patio, was a single story building that backed up to a major street. This building had three doors, the furthest at the end of the lot was the room I would be staying in. Perhaps twelve by twelve feet my room had smooth plaster walls, a beautifully polished hardwood floor and a lightbulb hung on a wire from the ceiling for light, that operated by a toggle switch next to the double bed. Certainly nothing like any "house" that I had been accustomed to, but the room was clean, inexpensive and "home" ... which is always wherever the ones you love reside.

It would be here on the patio that I first met "Abuelita" ... grandmother ... whose dissatisfaction with my presence was immediately apparent! Clearly Abuelita had lived a long and hard life, at the time in her mid-seventies, she clearly had moral objections to the gringo staying with the family. Although I attempted to be polite and courteous, my conversations with her were one sided. My "buenas dias señora, buenas tardes señora and buenas noches señoras" were all met with silence or sputtering under her breath and the shaking of her head. If eye contact was ever made, it was a glare.

My girlfriend told me a story, which I accepted at face value. Her grandfather had been a prominent landowner holding a majority of the land in and around Quito. At some point her grandmother's distant cousin had even been President. Upon her grandfather's death, the sons and family had disposed of his assets leaving Abuelita with very little, most of which she donated to the church. The lot we were living on was the last of her grandfather's estate that Abuelita had been able to retain. The front third, occupied by the mechanic, belonged to my girlfriend's mother and the back two thirds with the building was Abuelita's. All that remained of her wealth and Hacienda was this building that had been used for storage, the "bodegas."

■ ■ ■

During the period of my stay in Ecuador, the country was experiencing the turmoil of converting from military to civilian rule. Let there be no doubt, the military still maintained firm control, but Ecuadorians experienced very little repression during this period. The political season was in full swing and students were consistently involved in political or protest demonstrations. The freedom from repression was taken full advantage of, whether over politics or tuition fees, gas prices or bus fare increases, student demonstrations were commonplace. I can recall many occasions seeing tires burning in the streets in protest.

One night I was awakened from a sound sleep by the rumbling and shaking of my room. Startled and half asleep, having never experienced an earthquake, I assumed that was what I had just encountered and returned to sleep. The next morning I asked my girlfriend's brother if he had noticed the "earthquake" last night. He responded that there was no earthquake.

When I asked him if he had felt the rumbling and the building shaking during the night, he laughed. It was explained that as a show of force, it is customary for the military to reposition tanks around the city in preparation for the next day's demonstrations. This occurs in the middle of the night and the "rumbling" I had experienced, was just tank tracks grinding along on the pavement.

■ ■ ■

Many more weeks passed of sightseeing in and around Quito and falling more in love. Finally, the reality set it. Not only was my money not going to last forever, Ecuador allowed only ninety days a year for tourist visas, even with customary extensions, at some point soon I would have to leave again. I asked my girlfriend to marry me and we would return to a better life in the United States. Enthusiastically she agreed to marry me, indicating that money meant nothing to her, she loved me so much that if we had nothing it wouldn't matter, she would live in a park with me, just to be together. The problem was not our love for each other, but it would be that at seventeen she needed her mother's permission. Reluctantly and after much persuasion from myself, her son, daughter and other relatives, permission was finally given, and even Abuelita started to warm up to the gringo.

Apparently the time had come to meet "Tio." My girlfriend and I had walked toward the tourist strip Amazonas and the street Juan León Mera, where we found Tio's house. Outside by the gate was a guard post like I had encountered at the Hospital Militar, inside was a soldier. My fiancé spoke with the guard who picked up the phone and announcing our arrival, put down the phone and let us enter. At the entrance to the house we were greeted by a slightly stocky man, perhaps in his late forties or early fifties. My fiancé hugged him and exclaimed "Tio" to which he responded, "Mi Hija" or my daughter. Finally I was introduced to "Tio" ... General Gribaldo Miño Tapia of the Ecuadorian Army. [411]

Gribaldo seemed to be a very warm, kind and generous man that in reality was not an uncle but a distant cousin. It had been the General's mother and Abuelita who were actually cousins. Gribaldo was asked to give away the bride at our wedding, which he readily accepted, responding that as a wedding present the reception would be held in his house and at his expense.

Getting married in a strange country, with a different language and customs, having no friends or family in the country, my friend "Doctor David"

---

[411] My best recollection of events when I met General Miño, is that he was introduced as Ecuador's "Commander of the Army." However, as of publication I have not been able to obtain confirmation on the issue. It is possible that I may have misunderstood and the General was introduced as a "Commander in the Army." However, it would stand to reason that for General Miño to have been the "Chief of the Armed Forces Joint Command," at some point prior to General Salazar, General Miño must have held the post of "Commander of the Army" as well.

previously having quit the Peace Corps and returned to the United States, was stressful to say the least. Not only did we get married, we were required to get married twice! In Ecuador the state doesn't recognize the authority of the church nor does the church recognize the authority of the state, you can marry in one or the other, or both. The love of my life and I legally got married in the Registrar Civil of Quito, where her mother had to sign permission, due to her being less than eighteen years of age.

Both of us being Catholic, although neither of us were practicing, my fiancé and her family wanted a church wedding. As my visa was about to expire, we did not have the opportunity to fulfill the churches pre-marriage requirement of marital classes. Through her family connections we obtained a waiver. The monsignor counseled us before giving permission, and made it clear that in our religion marriage was not to be entered into lightly. Marriage was one time and forever. It was through sickness and health, good times and bad, to love honor and obey, till death do us part and that there is no divorce in our religion. We chose life together under those conditions, out of love, forever.

Standing outside the church a few blocks away from Hotel Colon I waited what seemed to be an eternity for my bride, ultimately she pulled up in the General's car ... only an hour late! Looking at our wedding pictures, it must have appeared to have been a shotgun wedding! On my side of the isle was Sebastian, the hotel desk clerk through whom we had communicated, sitting by himself. Standing before the altar, I appear in the photos with my wife and her mother, the general and the monsignor, all of them related! It was the happiest I had ever been, the woman I loved ... had married me for the second time!

We enjoyed a one night honeymoon at Hotel Colon, where Sebastian had arranged a nice room in the new tower at the national rate. It was then that I discovered in Ecuador the hotels had a two-tier pricing system. The tourists rate and "tarifa nacional" for Ecuadorians, which at the time was less than half of what tourists pay. My then wife and I had to make the journey to Guayaquil in order to obtain her visa and file the required financial responsibility papers with the US Consulate, which for some reason, could not have been done at the Embassy in Quito. On 8 Sep 1978 we boarded a plane for our new life together in the United States of America.

■ ■ ■

Eugene Brunner spent many years in "the old days" as he called them, involved with the military. Not only had he spent more than five thousand hours diving in Ecuadorian waters, but he had helped train the navy's divers. Brunner actually had entered into a few salvage contracts with the navy in the past as well, but to the best of my knowledge they expired with no recovery. Brunner had also been involved in numerous rescue missions with the military in rugged mountain terrain, but these usually resulted in the recovery of bodies from a plane crash.

Brunner had a brown three ring binder with a military emblem on the cover, detailing his work with the military and government, over stuffed with letters of appreciation, photos and newspaper clippings. It was entirely clear that at the end of his life, with all the problems and difficulties that Brunner had endured with partners and investors, that he believed his sole course of action for the recovery of the Llanganati treasure was with the military.

Never having met Brunner in person limited my knowledge of the man or his background. But one day while living in Vermont, my wife and I received a phone call from Ecuador, it was her mother and Eugene. Of course the majority of the conversation excluded me, but from what I was able to piece together, Brunner had met my mother-in-law and perhaps had even been renting a room from her, the exact same room I had occupied in Vicentina. A relationship developed at some point and they either had already gotten married or were about to.

When the phone was handed to me to speak with Brunner, I had very little to say to a complete stranger, but indicated that we may be moving to Florida at some point as I was looking for a new direction in life. During the very few minutes we spoke, Eugene did not discuss his work or projects except to indicate that I should ... "hold on and do not move to Florida," because ... "we are all going to be rich." Brunner mentioned that in the very near future ... "the Sucre will be at par with the dollar."[412] He ended the call as it had started, telling me ... "I love you." These four statements left me feeling very uncomfortable. My original impression of Eugene Brunner was not just flaky, but a crazy old man. We never met or spoke again.

After Brunner's death, as I started to hear from my mother-in-law about his projects, I learned something very important ... Brunner at some point in time had met "Tio" just as I had, General Gribaldo Miño Tapia, then Ecuador's top General, Chief of the Armed Forces Joint Command. According to my mother-in-law, Brunner had gained the General's commitment of support for his Llanganati project. The General was going to provide the helicopters, manpower and security to remove the treasure, not to search for it. Whether by coincidence or not, Brunner was finally in contact not just with "the Generals," but with Ecuador's highest ranking active duty General. Had Brunner finally reached the goal of his nearly fifty

---

[412] It was Brunner's theory that once the Llanganati treasure was recovered, the gold and silver would be deposited in Ecuador's Central Bank and support the national currency of Ecuador (the Sucre) increasing it's value to par with the US dollar. Brunner's theory ended up being partially correct (for reasons completely unrelated to the treasure) in the year 2000 when Ecuador converted to the US dollar. The Sucre lost sixty-seven percent of its foreign exchange value during 1999, then in a one week period it nose dived seventeen percent ending at 25,000 to the dollar on 7 Jan 2000. On January 9th President Jamil Mahuad announced that the US dollar would be adopted as Ecuador's official currency. It became legal tender in Ecuador on 13 Mar 2000 and Sucre bank notes ceased being legal tender on 11 Sep 2000. Sucre notes remained exchangeable at the Banco Central until 30 Mar 2001 at the rate of 25,000 Sucres per dollar.

year search, or was this just going to be yet another story of disappointment for Eugene?

One could not help but remember Brunner's numerous disappointing attempts at gaining the ear and favor of the military for his recovery project. Brunner's last failed attempt in 1980, described previously, would have occurred during the Roldós Presidency and when Frank Vargas Pazzos was a Commander in the Air Force. [413]

The story continued ... that prior to Brunner's planned expedition with the military, presumably due to his advanced age or perhaps that he was not feeling well, Brunner wanted a complete physical and clean bill of health to proceed into the Llanganatis. For whatever reason Brunner was admitted, presumably with the General's assistance, to the Hospital Militar for tests and observation. The military hospital was a convenient choice, being just a short distance from where the Brunner's lived.

Brunner had taken some of his papers with him and was working on them at the hospital. For some unexplained reason, perhaps a premonition, Brunner started to feel uneasy, uncomfortable and apprehensive. He asked his wife to take his papers home with her that evening. When my mother-in-law returned the next morning, 3 Jun 1984, her husband of a matter of months, Eugene Konrad Brunner, was dead. Subsequently, I was told that the official cause of death on his death certificate states ... "stopped breathing!"

Years later, through phone conversations and a personal meeting with General Miño, I was able to confirm the story of the General's involvement and commitment to Brunner. However I must admit, that at the time I had no knowledge of the rivalries and events that had transpired within the military.

Researching and writing this book, I stumbled upon yet another very interesting fact, the date of the General's early retirement ... around 11 Jun 1984 [414]. . . one week after Brunner's death ... two months prior to the end of the General's term ... and of President Elect Febres Cordero's inauguration, in whose administration the General would have been Minister of Defense!

Let me be perfectly clear, in no way am I insinuating, or would I ever believe, that the General may have had any involvement in Brunner's death. That date, if known to me at the time, by sheer coincidence alone, solely would have raised yet another very important series of questions to have asked the General ...

■ ■ ■

---

[413] Whether Frank Vargas was one of the Generals that Brunner had been in contact with remains unclear.

[414] El Universo 12 Jun 1984

I, Max Cleland, Secretary of State of the State of Georgia, do hereby certify that

the photographed matter hereto attached is a true and correct copy of the Articles of Incorporation and Certificate of Incorporation for

"ECUADORAN EXPLORATIONS, INC."

a corporation created under the laws of the State of Georgia, as same appears of file and record in the Office of Secretary of State.

IN TESTIMONY WHEREOF, I have hereunto set my hand and affixed the seal of my office, at the Capitol, in the City of Atlanta, this 2nd day of September, in the year of our Lord One Thousand Nine Hundred and Eighty-Seven and of the Independence of the United States of America the Two Hundred and Twelve.

Max Cleland
SECRETARY OF STATE.

Certificate of Incorporation

THE COMPANY & PRESIDENT

Almost two years after Brunner's death, I returned to Ecuador in May of 1986 looking for a new direction in life. Despite Brunner's suggestion that I not move my family to Florida, we had moved in 1985. At the age of thirty I was considering starting a small import-export business importing Ecuadorian handicrafts for sale in the United States, exporting US-MADE clothing to Ecuador, or any other business venture I might discover. I did some traveling with my wife's brother looking into the products available from Ecuador, at the same time we examined the possibility of continuing with Brunner's projects. Although my mother-in-law preferred that we both take over Brunner's work, her son had expressed absolutely no interest in doing so, if I was interested, it would have to be done alone.

■ ■ ■

Even at this late date, all of Quito was still abuzz with the latest story in a long string of gringo expeditions into the Llanganatis in search of Rumiñahui's treasure deposit. Quito's daily newspaper *El Comercio* had published an article, if memory serves me correct sometime in early 1986, concerning a failed Llanganati expedition of an American, Bill Johnson. Wherever you went or whomever you talked with, this was the topic of conversation.

Two Americans, described as ex-military or missionary types, had come to Ecuador in search of the infamous Rumiñahui treasure deposit. Poorly equipped and outfitted, the expedition it appears was destined to fail. The pair of Americans merely hired college students as carriers or porters, who entered the inhospitable environment of the Llanganatis in light sweaters and street shoes. One member of the expedition, an American, died of exposure and the military had to go in and rescue the rest of the expedition. It is due to circumstances and events such as this, that has caused the government of Ecuador to frown upon unauthorized explorations into the Llanganatis, making it more and more difficult I would learn, for future explorers to obtain government permission. [415]

■ ■ ■

Upon initial examination the sheer magnitude of Brunner's materials astounded me. No, not just the quantity, but the quality and details of his research and documentation, changed my opinion of the man immediately, he was no longer the crazy old man. In my mind's eye it became apparent that Brunner ate, slept, and lived only for his projects, there was a method to his rituals.

---

[415] Should an intrepid soul even consider entering the Llanganatis, it is strongly advised that all government regulations and permits required (if any), to travel into the region be complied with. In addition, travel in this region is not to be taken lightly, every precaution must be taken, including but not limited to, obtaining proper equipment and supplies for the conditions, sufficient porters, a knowledgeable guide, and of course diligent security or safety precautions must be in place.

The first item that caught my attention was a large wall-size map of Ecuador. On this map were probably a hundred small colored red dots, blue triangles and yellow squares, most were numbered. Each represented either a land based treasure, sunken galleon, emerald, gold or silver mine, lost city, burial mound or other archeological site. Those with numbers had corresponding papers, folders or binders that described in detail Brunner's research, explorations and discoveries, with photos and drawings for that specific site. It became immediately apparent that this was not a hobby or pastime, but the pursuit of his life to the point of being obsessed.

Brunner's materials appeared to represent many, many years of day and night hard work. There were chapters for Brunner's unpublished book manuscript *Ecuador y sus Tesoros* that had been typed on an old manual Spanish language script typewriter. Each chapters title pages contained detailed color artwork. There was a large topographic map of Cerro Hermoso on which Brunner had marked the trail and camps of the route to his base camp on Cerro Hermoso from El Triunfo, plotted in red, similar to Wallace's version of Guzmán's map in *Notes of a Botanist*.

There was a large manila envelope from the Instituto Geográfico Militar labeled in a black marker "Por General Miño." Inside of this envelope were one large twelve-inch square [416] and twelve smaller eight-inch square satellite photographs' of Cerro Hermoso and the surrounding area. I had been told that aerial photographs in the Llanganatis are difficult to obtain as there is consistently cloud cover. But to the contrary, I held in my hands thirteen perfectly clear satellite photographs without even a hint of a cloud in sight.

Brunner also possessed a photocopy of Spruce's *Notes of a Botanist* chapter XXVIII along with Wallace's version of the *Guzmán Map*. There were also numerous dog-eared books, including Andrade's 1970 version of *Viaje a las Misteriosas Montañas de Llanganati* and *The Incas of Pedro Cieza de León*, their pages book marked with countless notations and scraps of paper.

Brunner's materials included two geological reports on Cerro Hermoso, a notepad with the story of his first trip into the Llanganatis in 1938, a large binder on other Llanganati expeditions he had assembled, yet another detailing his work with the military and government, with letters of appreciation, photographs and newspaper clippings. Among Brunner's materials were also loose notes, letters, papers, drawings, hand drawn maps, photographs, negatives, plus contracts with investors and other treasure hunters, all of this rounded out what I had to digest.

---

[416] Reproduced with the notation "Lake Brunner and arrow" as it erroneously appeared in Peter Lourie's book *Lost Treasure of the Inca (1999)*. The arrow actually indicates Brunner's base camp on Cerro Hermoso which is next to a small lake. Lake Brunner is actually the larger lake located at a lower elevation behind the arrow. Comparing the Lake Brunner diagram to the satellite photograph, one can clearly make out the summit, lake, outcrop and pass from which the waterfall flows into Lake Brunner.

Aerial Image of Cerro Hermoso

The initial problem I encountered with Brunner's materials was that absolutely everything, all of his projects, were massed together as though in the two years since Brunner's death, my mother-in-law had commingled all of his papers. Additionally, certain portions of his work, including the manuscript [417] entitled *El Tesoro en las Misteriosas Montañas de Llanganati* had reportedly been stolen. Sadly, on first examination there was not the smoking gun of the treasure's location. Perhaps this was contained within the missing manuscript, but in the papers before me, Brunner on first glance, had not pinpointed the exact location of the Llanganati treasure on one piece of paper for all to see.

Knowing that Brunner and his new wife had spent day and night working together on his paperwork and considering how detailed this work was, I questioned my mother-in-law numerous times about this lack of detail when it came to pinpointing the treasure and what he had told her. Her response was consistently adamant yet vague ... "Eugenio was digging with his hands on the last expedition to remove the treasure, not looking for it ... the treasure is behind Cerro Hermoso."

So many projects and documents, so much research, exploration and discovery, it was obvious that this project was going to be a monumental task, just to sort everything out and interpret Brunner's data! Apart from compiling and understanding Brunner's research and data, I was overwhelmed by the realization that there was much I did not know and would need to learn about map reading, Inca history, Ecuador's Patrimony Laws, contract laws, corporations, project funding, copyrights, book and movie rights, mining claims and oh yes ... about gold itself.

■ ■ ■

Immediately the paranoia of a treasure hunter began to set in. How much of Brunner's material was known by others ... how much was secret ... who were his friends ... and who were his enemies? If the story surrounding Brunner's death were true ... could I not be in danger as well? In retrospect I have asked myself on countless occasions ... if I knew then, what I know now ... would I have still pursued Brunner's project? The answer to this question has always been clear in my mind ... absolutely! I have always realized that if I turned my back on this project, the missed opportunity of what could have been ... would have haunted me the rest of my life. However, my suspicion and mistrust of others would have increased ten fold and the method's I utilized approaching and conducting this project would have been completely different ... if I knew then what I know now.

At this point in my story I must interject to remind you, that the knowledge you now possess, far exceeds that which I had at the time. Appreciate for the moment that not just previous authors, but the Llanganati explorers themselves, were not privy to as much information as you the reader now

[417] This manuscript was actually the book chapter Brunner and his new wife were recreating prior to his death. Although extremely informative containing pieces of the puzzle, there would be no smoking gun there either.

are. Without any background information or prior knowledge, I started this project with a clean slate and open mind. Some of the characters in this portion of my story have previously been introduced ... I shall relate my personal involvement with these men and others.

■ ■ ■

Commencing with a clean slate, the first step in my journey was to go through Brunner's materials sorting everything by project, compiling a list of names or cast of characters if you will. Additionally, I made notations of what I knew for a fact about each person through letters, contracts and Brunner's notes. I would then attempt to contact the individual and determine to my own satisfaction if they were friends or foes, and what they actually knew about Brunner's work.

My method to extract this knowledge would be to introduce myself through a letter or phone call [418] announcing Brunner's death, and that I was attempting to publish his manuscript *Ecuador y Sus Tesoros*. Then I would feign ignorance on the details of Brunner's work and on some occasions utilize misleading information in order to illicit a response. In this manner any information I would glean, could then be compared against the knowledge I had obtained from Brunner's materials, not solely to confirm or deny my observations, but to ascertain the parties' truthfulness, candor and motives.

My list did not include Commander George Dyott as I knew he was deceased, but it did include Michael Dyott his son.[419] Also not included were Andrés Fernandez Salvador, whose family owned Güitig, Ecuador's premiere bottled mineral water company, as I knew Brunner and he had previously been friends and partners until there was a falling out. Also absent from the list was Salvador's son-in-law Diego Arias, whom was apparent that Brunner did not like. Other names that made the list were Hermine Gruber, Chuck Powell, Robert R, Ricardo Petersmyth, Clifford Jones, Jane Dolinger, Ken Kripenne, Peter Lourie, Guillermo Barriga, Paul Chandler, and Howard Schmidt. A few other names whose letters came back from Europe stamped "No Such Addressee at This Address," are not mentioned herein.

■ ■ ■

One of the first names I was able to cross off my list was Hermine Gruber. Apparently this woman had been Brunner's secretary, whom he assumed to be the culprit that absconded with his missing manuscript chapter *El Tesoro en las Misteriosas Montañas de Llanganati y la casi Increíble Historia de los Ingleses.*

---

[418] All relevant phone calls concerning the treasure project were recorded to avoid the pitfalls of any misunderstanding, incorrect interpretation and lapses of memory, on my part or that of others.

[419] Throughout my involvement on this project, I had assumed Michael Dyott was an only child. It was not until a quarter century later researching this manuscript that I discovered Michael had a brother, then to my surprise a year later, I learned that he had yet another brother.

Within Brunner's papers was a copy of a letter sent by another member on my list to Hermine Gruber, dated 6 Dec 1982. The letter apparently indicates a partnership between the parties in this short quote ... "One thing I guess we all are hanging on the edge of our chairs about is whether we can get the support of the military with their manpower and equipment. I might be naive about the magnitude of the project ... we may be able to produce (retrieve) one or several objects without anyone else's knowledge. "

When I first contacted this person in the mid-eighties, he defensively expressed a disbelief that Gruber had taken or had Brunner's manuscript. However, in 2012 through a letter, this mans story would drastically change ... "In 1984 Gruber had your father-in-law's manuscript and when she and I came back from the Llanganatis, her apartment had been broken into and the manuscript taken. Days before "Geno" had died in the hospital."

I could find no further information or current address on Ms. Gruber, until a third member on my list, Ricardo Petersmyth, confirmed that it was Brunner's belief that she had taken his manuscript. Ricardo indicated further that he had informed Brunner, as his contact in the US State Department had informed him, Gruber was a suspected Peruvian-Soviet spy and had fled to Austria.

■ ■ ■

Ricardo Petersmyth turned out to be a great source of invaluable information and assistance in advancing my understanding of the players and the project. As it turns out Petersmyth had met Brunner only once in person during November of 1981, but Ricardo had an extensive library of tape recordings of every phone conversation with Brunner compiled over numerous years. Ricardo, drastically younger than Brunner, spoke with admiration and exuded a great feeling of respect for the man, his intelligence and accomplishments, this man he constantly referred to as ... "Gino."

I was informed by Ricardo not only of Ms. Gruber, but that indeed Brunner was passing information through him to the US State Department about Peruvian and communist cells operating in Ecuador. During one of our conversations Ricardo explained how Gino had talked about them both acquiring a book, the same book. They would then write each other letters using a common number code with each set of four numbers [420] being one word. This confirmed what I had previously gleaned from Brunner's papers, not only his paranoia, but that Brunner believed himself to be a spy for the US government, just as he had purportedly been during World War II.

At a later date I flew to a major airport on the eastern coast of the US in order to meet with Ricardo and obtain further information. At this meeting in the airport terminal, I was given information that will become relevant later in this story and was shown photographs of Ricardo with Caspar

[420] Code - First number would be the page number in a pre-chosen book, second number the paragraph, third number the line with the fourth being the word.

Wienberger,[421] Colin Powell and other US Government officials. Ricardo also stated that prior to Brunner's death he had become a minority partner sending $5000 US dollars to cover Brunner's expenses in the final expedition that was planned with the military. Again confirming what I had already been aware of through Brunner's papers. Ricardo I discovered would eventually play an indispensable role in my story.

■ ■ ■

Michael Dyott needed no introduction. I knew he was the son of Commander George Dyott. Brunner had been a partner with his father in the 1960s and through that partnership Brunner had made great discoveries utilizing Blacke & Chapman's material. I made contact with Dyott, an engineer that lived in California, and flew to Los Angeles in 1987 to meet with him. We got together over a nice lunch of Thai food in Hollywood, near the round landmark building of Capital Records. Michael seemed polite and quite reserved but open to a point. In his clearly discernable New York accent Michael informed me that similar to Brunner's papers, some of his father's journals, those covering his two expeditions into the Llanganatis, had come up missing.

Dyott further explained that his father had not given the Blacke & Chapman material to Brunner all at once. Instead, Brunner would be told to go find a certain clue or landmark in the Llanganatis and come back with the details. Brunner would make the discovery and be given another landmark to find. Michael also mentioned that he had followed his father's footsteps into the Llanganatis on at least two occasions, once in the fall and again in May, but he gave no details as to the results. Thinking out-loud I expressed ... "the treasure would have already been recovered if all the treasure hunters had worked together and shared the information from research and expeditions openly," giving Michael an opening which was not accepted, beyond general conversation on the climate in the Llanganatis.

As with all explorers the weather in the Llanganatis has been a major factor in the failure of countless expeditions and loss of life. Michael explained that very few people apart from his father and Brunner understood the conditions and realities of being in the mountains, that the weather in Píllaro and El Triunfo is opposite of that it the mountains. Michael told me ... "according to Dad, the good weather in the mountains starts at the end of September and extends until the beginning of January."

Michael continued with his own sentiment ... "It is not the weather, it's the fog that kills you. A compass is no good in the fog. You have no reference point and become disoriented. The grass grows so thick in this wet climate that it grows over streams and hangs over cliffs, you think you're stepping on solid ground and there is a void under you. You could walk right over a cliff. The problem with the growth down there, is it grows right over the cliff so you don't know that you're over the cliff until you step through the

---

[421] Caspar Wienberger - US Secretary Of Defense 1981-1987 under President Ronald Reagan.

grass and all of a sudden you find yourself falling. I almost did that three or four times."

Then Michael told me the story about one similar event on an expedition he took into the Llanganatis by himself ... Michael always went in alone [422]... "I almost fell in an underground stream once and the stream was probably flowing at what seemed like fifteen miles an hour. It surfaced as I was walking across what appeared to be a perfectly flat field which is really unusual in the Llanganatis. This stream surfaced, went about twenty-foot and went back underground, there are a lot of streams that come up and then go underground again. The grass had grown up on either side of it and crossed over, then it gets matted down just by the weight of the wet on it all the time. I heard the running water, I could hear the rush of the water but I didn't know where it was coming from. The surface of the ground looked quite even and it was in moderate fog, I just kept walking. I was just about to take a step, I would look into the distance trying to fight the fog, then I would look down where I was putting my next step and then I would look up again. I just happened to look down and I saw the white of the water through the grass and my instantaneous reaction was that I was seeing the reflection of the sky, the white of the sky. Then instantaneously I realized I couldn't be seeing the reflection of sky in the grass. I stopped and when my eyes focused I realized I was looking at white turbulent water. If I had taken that step and fallen in there, I would have gone about eight or ten-foot and then I would have gone underground like a plug. I would have become a plug in the hole where the water went underground. There is no way with the pack on my back that I ever could have fought that. I was all alone, so that there wouldn't have been anybody there to help me."

Three points about my meeting and subsequent communications with Dyott stuck in my mind. Firstly, Michael indicated that it would be "best to recover a small amount of the treasure without anyone knowing," especially the Ecuadorian government. Michael showed the same disdain and mistrust of the authorities previously credited to his father and used the same sentiment that he had written to Hermine Gruber in the letter of December 1982.

Secondly were the sentiments Michael had expressed regarding the Llanganati story and its explorers ... "Treasure stories like any other story, have a beginning, a middle and an end. Throughout any story there can be misdirection and misinformation. If a reader believes or knows a portion of the story to be true, does it not follow that the reader would then believe the entire story to be true?"

Lastly was Michael's expression of his real interest in the treasure ... a window into the past. It was Michael's belief that examination of the artifacts once recovered, could provide evidence and proof of an extra terrestrial connection with the Incas. This revelation didn't seem as off-the-

---

[422] It was not until 2012 that Michael would tell a different story about having gone into the Llanganatis with Hermine Gruber.

wall as one might think, when taken into consideration with the fact that Michael worked for Boeing and NASA as a Space Shuttle Research Specialist.

What amazed me about Michael's revelation was that Brunner had held this same theory, but it did not appear to me to be to such an extent. I informed Michael that indeed Brunner had an artifact, not made of gold but of the same material as pottery of the period, which Brunner called ... "The Astronaut." I promised to send photos and Michael sent me a copy of Loch's book *Fever, Famine, and Gold* with a note dated 4 Aug 1987 which stated ... "I'm envious that you've applied yourself and have made such headway."

■ ■ ■

Jane Dolinger [1932-1995] and Ken Krippene [ca.1899-1980] turned out to be husband and wife, travel and adventure authors that had written numerous articles and books using Brunner as a source. In the fifties and sixties Dolinger was also a successful model and pin-up girl. During 1968 Dolinger had published her book *Inca Gold find it if you can touch it if you dare*. Chapter five is entitled *Secret of the Golden Condor* and is about the Llanganati treasure. Dolinger writes ... "Today, it is generally conceded that Swiss-born Eugene Brunner, explorer and treasure-hunter, has the best chance of eventually finding the missing treasure of the Llanganatis."

Among Brunner's papers was also a copy of a letter dated 17 Sep 1968 from Dolinger to Clifford A. Jones that stated in part ... "We have known Swiss-born Eugene Brunner for over a period of fifteen years and have always relied on him for material on lost Inca treasures, Spanish treasure galleons off the coast of Ecuador, as well as other buried treasures in the vicinity. He is perhaps the only expert in this field in this entire area, and his research is thorough, painstaking, and accurate." ... giving the letter the appearance of being an introduction letter of sorts.

■ ■ ■

This brought me to the next name on my list, Clifford A. Jones Sr. [1912-2001], who not only was the recipient of the Dolinger letter, but was mentioned in Brunner's manuscript as having been involved at one time in other treasure projects. I did receive a short note from Mr. Jones in response to my letter on 22 Oct 1986 which stated in part ... "I am very sorry to hear about the death of Professor Brunner. He was indeed an outstanding man. I had the pleasure of meeting him many years ago."

Mr. Jones turned out to be a very interesting man himself, a lawyer, politician, casino owner and at one point treasure hunter. Jones had been Lieutenant Governor of Nevada from January 1947 until December 1954. At various times Mr. Jones had interests in casinos including the El Cortez, The Algiers, The Dunes, Golden Nugget, Pioneer, Thunderbird and Westerner in Las Vegas, plus international properties in France, Lebanon and Ecuador. At the time, Mr. Jones was the only Nevadan listed in the *American Edition of Who's Who*.

Mr. Jones and I never did meet in person. It seemed that every time Mr. Jones was in Ecuador, I was in the United States and vice versa. Mr. Jones and I did have numerous phone conversations concerning a matter unrelated to Brunner's materials and my project, which would in my opinion become an indicator of the difficulties one might face overcoming obstacles created by the politics and corruption that runs rampant in Ecuador.

In this nation where corruption is the norm, in my opinion non-Ecuadorians, foreigners or "gringos," all have an invisible target on their backs. An outsider succeeding in Ecuador appears to be a temporary state of events and not to be considered permanent. Once a foreign company, businessman or absentee owner succeeds, it appears that someone is always there with a hand out or worse yet, taking over (nationalizing in some manner) your investment. A good example of this would be how Ecuador's oil and gas concessions were nationalized, only after the expense of research and development had been incurred. In Ecuador, as in many developing countries, it also appeared commonplace for bribes to be demanded. Whether the person seeking a bribe was a politician, bureaucrat, government employee, judge, policeman or business partner, in made no difference, they all appear to view the process with a sense of entitlement.

Jones purportedly endured his own personal betrayal at the hands of his Ecuadorian managing partners. My memory fails me in regard to the exact details of the case and of course I had only heard one side of the story. However, to the best of my recollection Mr. Jones absentee ownership of the Ecuadorian casinos had been diminished or dissolved through Ecuador's court system. Apparently it was Mr. Jones belief that he could only receive equity and justice from an unbiased court system. Therefore, Mr. Jones initiated or was about to commence legal action in the United States, where he would have access to some of his partners financial assets and a non corrupt legal system.

Allegedly according to Mr. Jones, it had appeared that to some degree the Ecuador casinos had been losing money, or at the very least not making as much as they had been previously. Again allegedly, the theory was that his partners might have been skimming money from the casino, and transferring it to Miami, Florida, where they had investments and property. Either the partners were attempting to, or had already taken over the company as nationals, and with money comes power, so allegedly it had been an easy matter for them to utilize Ecuador's corrupt legal system. Jones was therefore seeking information on the casinos business practices for future litigation in the United States.

Once Mr. Jones had explained his situation with the casinos to me, it immediately brought to mind events that I had witnessed, which I then related. It had always seemed odd to me that whenever I played in the casino and bought in with US Dollars, the money was never "dropped"[423]

---

[423] Typically when a customer purchases gaming chips at any casino table, once the cash is exchanged for chips, the money is "dropped" through the slot

as was customary with the a buy-in of Sucres. Every time a customer would buy-in with dollars, the pit boss would be called over and the money would be exchanged at the current rate of exchange for chips valued in Sucres. The currency was taken away to the pit bosses station, recorded in a notebook and placed in a small cashbox. If you were lucky enough to have a winning session, your chips would be paid out in Sucres. However, if you asked for your dollars back you were reluctantly paid, but limited to the amount of your buy-in with Dollars, the balance was paid in Sucres.

Mr. Jones was of the opinion that this procedure created the potential for wrong doing. It must be made clear that whether any wrong doing occurred or not is uncertain, but the potential existed. Taken a step further , Mr. Jones theorized that if the money was not dropped, it was not part of the count. Any dollars that were taken in during the night might not show on the casinos books and could therefore be "skimmed." Additionally, by allegedly acquiring dollars at the casino in this manner, it would leave no paper trail, as no institutional financial transaction record would be required to obtain the foreign exchange. The US Dollars could then easily be transferred out of the country to Florida, if indeed this is what happened.

Shortly after these conversations Mr. Jones and I lost contact. Whether or not suit was filed in Florida, remains unclear. Therefore, if suit was filed, I have no knowledge as to the outcome or any settlement that may have occurred between the parties. Typically there exist two sides to every story and legal situation, I had only heard portions of one side. Whether Mr. Jones may have been a victim of private "nationalization" or of corruption, unfortunately, remains unclear.

■ ■ ■

Chuck Powell [1928-1992] was another name on the list. Chuck had been a partner of Brunner's at one point, having made three expeditions to Cerro Hermoso together in the seventies. In Brunner's papers there was an abrupt end in communication with Powell shortly after their failed expedition of November 1981. Chuck had promised Brunner money for the slow and tedious work customarily required prior to any expedition of opening the trail from El Triunfo to Cerro Hermoso and preparing base camp. The money must have arrived as Brunner had accomplished this work over a period of two months.

It appears that a group of seven investors, Ricardo among them, arrived in Quito a few days prior to this planned expedition. The plan was the investors were to stay in the hotel and await the results of Chuck and Brunner's expedition. Powell himself was to arrive the day of the expedition. Chuck however was a no show, instead at the last minute a

---

in the table that has a locked cash box below it. The box is later removed and the contents are counted and recorded in a secure environment at the end of the night.

telegram arrived canceling the expedition.[424] Brunner again was faced with the recurring nightmare that always eluded him. Brunner could never get the money together at the same time that the people were together.

Just as with Andrés Fernandez Salvador, it was clear there had been a falling out between Brunner and Powell. Brunner was worried Chuck was going into the mountains by himself. Also there was something peculiar about Powell's failure to arrive for the tediously prepared for expedition, but I could not discover what or why at the time. However, talking with Powell you would think that was not the case.

Powell talked with an apparent admiration concerning Brunner, or "Gino" as Chuck referred to him. It was as though the two men were the best of friends and still partners. Powell described their three expeditions to Cerro Hermoso in detail, what they had discovered around and diving in Lake Brunner, basically confirming what I already knew. Chuck expressed a willingness to continue Brunner's project with me but I was left with a gut feeling, just as Ricardo had warned me ... that Powell believes this to be "HIS" project and he will not be satisfied in a subordinate role.

■ ■ ■

Three of the names on the list were geologists who had completed surveys and written glowing geological reports on Cerro Hermoso for Brunner or his financial partners, one lived in Quito and I chose to contact him in person. Paul Chandler lived in Old Quito near the Plaza de la Independencia, in a dark and damp colonial building. He downplayed the mineralization of Cerro Hermoso, not knowing that I had read his report that contradicted what he was now telling me. Chandler also attempted to dissuade me from exploring Cerro Hermoso for treasure. Chandler implied that Brunner's work was invalid and that the treasure had already been discovered. He told me a story that the treasure had already been removed by a family in Peru. Paul left the room and returned shortly with a newspaper clipping from the Quito paper *ULTIMAS NOTICIAS*, dated Thursday 28 Oct 1965. Indeed, this portion of what I was being told could be true.

The second geologist, Guillermo Barriga, I discovered by chance. One day at the Insituto Ecuatoriano de Mineria[425] seeking information on filing a

---

[424] Lourie in his book *Sweat of the Sun, Tears of the Moon* refers to an expedition planned with Brunner in 1980 canceled at the last minute. Either there exists an error concerning the date on Lourie's part, or there were two failed expeditions, one in 1980 and another in 1981. Regardless, Powell had been into the Llanganatis with Brunner only on three occasions all in the 1970s, their association culminated in the failed expedition of November 1981.

[425] INEMIN -The Ecuadorian Government Institute responsible for granting mining concessions within Ecuador. At the time, INEMIN held its own mining concession in the Llanganatis which covered the northern area known as the Roncadores.

mining application for Cerro Hermoso I noticed the name Barriga, Guillermo on the building's roster. As of this writing I cannot recall what title he held, but I approached the receptionist and asked her to contact his office. I was asked if I had an appointment, when I said no, the question then became, in reference to? My response was "Cerro Hermoso. I am Eugene Brunner's son-in-law." The receptionist relayed the message and a moment later hung up the phone and stated that Barriga would be right down.

After a brief introduction the conversation shifted to Cerro Hermoso. Barriga like Chandler, made every attempt to convince me that there were no minerals of any value on Cerro Hermoso and a mining claim there would be a waste of time. Barriga explained that even if we found any commercial deposits on Cerro Hermoso, due to the mountains remoteness and geography a road to the mining claim could cost upwards of a million US dollars. Annual concession taxes Barriga continued ... just for filing a claim, would be about six thousand US dollars. All of this did not dissuade me, Barriga just as Chandler, did not seem to realize that I had read his exuberant report on Cerro Hermoso and its varied copper deposits.

Contact with the third geologist on my list, Howard Schmidt, came to fruition through Chuck and Ricardo. Powell had apparently acquired two prospective investors from the Atlanta area, an attorney and his partner, that were interested in funding Brunner's Cerro Hermoso mining concession. Schmidt had been hired by these potential investors in the early seventies to conduct a geological survey of the mountain, a report which at the time I desperately wanted to read.

Powell vainly attempted to discourage me from pursuing Schmidt or the renewal of Brunner's mining concession on Cerro Hermoso indicating that "there was nothing worth looking at." Which was in my opinion yet another apparent smoke screen. Reluctantly, Powell agreed to search through his files for Schmidt's contact information and would get in touch with him to set the groundwork for my introduction. Powell later got back to me with Schmidt's phone number and informed me that he had spoken with him and advised him that I would be in contact.

It would be a few days later that I made the call. The phone was answered ... "Schmidt and Associates." I asked for Howard Schmidt and was asked who was calling. Upon giving my name the call was transferred and Mr. Schmidt came on the line. I explained that I was Eugene Brunner's son-in-law and he acted as though he did not have a clue what I was talking about. I mentioned my call was in regards to the Cerro Hermoso concession in Ecuador, which seemed to jar his memory as Howard expressed that this had been a long, long time ago and had slipped his mind. Odd I thought, as I knew Powell had contacted him prior to giving me his number. After what appeared to be an initial charade, I got straight to the point.

Schmidt confirmed the names of the men who had hired him, also that he had been with Brunner to his camp on Cerro Hermoso and conducted a geological survey for a copper concession. Ultimately yet reluctantly,

Schmidt acknowledged that he had written a report. When asked if he still had a copy, Schmidt hesitantly replied "yes I'm sure I do somewhere." When further asked for a copy the line went dead for a moment, ultimately Schmidt responded that the report was privileged information and belonged to whomever he did the job for. I responded that I was Brunner's successor to which Schmidt replied ... "I didn't do the work for Brunner, it was done for the investors." Schmidt continued to state that if I could contact the investors and they gave permission, he would release a copy to me. However, I knew from the tone in his voice that this was a dead end.

What I was able to glean from our short conversation concerning Cerro Hermoso was very little. Schmidt kept using the adjective "miserable place" when speaking of his expedition to the mountain. Apparently Brunner and Schmidt had gone ahead with the first group as there had not been enough porters so two trips were required to get all the equipment and supplies to base camp. Schmidt indicated that ... "it had been miserable on Cerro Hermoso, wet and cold, with mud ... the miserable black mud, it was everywhere."

Discussing the substance of this conversion with Ricardo at a later date, Ricardo mentioned that he was not surprised with Schmidt's reluctance to provide a copy of his report on Cerro Hermoso's mineralization ... Brunner had told Ricardo during one of their numerous conversations that he suspected Schmidt wanted the concession for himself. This theory could just have been Brunner's rampant paranoia ... we will never know for sure ... but one thing we do know for sure ... some of Brunner's paranoia's did have a sound basis in fact and events.

■ ■ ■

Robert R and Chuck, presumably through Powell's salvage company out of Georgia, turned out to be connected, but not in a good way. All I knew about Robert was that he was an American from the western portion of the United States perhaps California, no address or phone number. When questioned, Powell implied that Robert was an investor that hadn't panned out. Rather than leave it there, I thought perhaps Ricardo could shed some light on Robert. When questioned, Ricardo stated that he absolutely did know who Robert was, left the phone for a minute to check his notes, came back and gave me a number and extension to call for the details. Ricardo did mention though that Powell had been having personal problems at the time and allegedly utilized up to $250,000 US Dollars solicited for Brunner's Llanganati projects, for personal use, money that never made it to Ecuador!

My adrenaline was racing as I dialed the number Ricardo had given me. The operator answered ... Securities and Exchange Commission[426] ... do you know your extension. I asked the operator for the investigations extension and the phone was picked up after a few rings ... "special investigations." After introductions and explaining the situation, my question to a Ms. Pat

---

[426] Securities and Exchange Commission of the Federal Government

Oliver was if the names' Robert R, Chuck Powell or his salvage company appeared within the Commissions files. I was told she would have to research her files and call me back.

Upon returning my call, Ms. Oliver stated that she could find nothing in the computer files on Robert R or the salvage company, but she did come across a Securities Violation that resulted in a *Cease and Desist Order* in 1980 against Chuck E. Powell only, not his company. She explained that the files have no specific details beyond that. Considering the State of Georgia[427] had applied for the Order, perhaps they would have more specific details on the case and she gave me the number for a Ms. Francis Pierson at the Georgia Securities and Exchange Commission.

Ms. Pierson was able to locate Chuck Powell's *Cease and Desist Order* on her computer, but she stated that it would be best to speak to the lead investigator on the case, Tom Colter, to whom I was transferred. Again after preliminary introductions, Mr. Colter explained that yes it was his case and he remembered it well. "Mr. Powell had been soliciting investments from the public, selling investments in a gold venture in Ecuador, without the benefit of being registered as required by law. There were numerous securities and exchange violations involved." When asked what the outcome of the investigation or prosecution was, the lead investigator responded "none ... other than the *Cease and Desist Order* of 3 Jan 1980."[428] Colter went on to state that ... "There were no criminal charges pressed because there were no complaining victims. There was fraud involved, but there was no complaining victim." Surprised by this response, I brought up that according to my information Robert R had invested $250,000 USD, Colter responded that ... "complainant did not live in Georgia," he was a victim in the State of his residence and was ... "advised to file criminal charges" in California.

■ ■ ■

Last but not least on my list was Peter Lourie. Mr. Lourie turned out to be an author that was writing a book based on Brunner's work and a short trek in 1982 that Lourie had made to Cerro Hermoso with Brunner's assistance, utilizing his porters and trail from El Triunfo. Lourie had answered my letter with a phone call. Looking back, it is hard to recall who was playing whom. I would ask questions to ascertain what he knew and he would do the same.

I specifically recall Lourie asking if I knew of Andrés Fernandez Salvador. Of course my response was ... "no who is he," at the same time wondering if Lourie could tell through the tone of my voice ... that I was lying! Of

---

[427] Georgia Securities and Exchange Commission

[428] It appears that at the time, Brunner was not aware of the *Cease and Desist Order* of 3 Jan 1980 against Powell or of the funds raised for his project that never made it to Ecuador. One would note that the date of the order is prior to the canceled expeditions referred to earlier in footnote nine of this chapter, so Powell was presumably still actively seeking investors.

course I knew a great deal about Brunner's old partner! If it wasn't for Andrés helicopter crash in February of 1963, Brunner would never have discovered the socavón and expanded his search to Cerro Hermoso!

In order to ascertain if Lourie was utilizing Brunner's copyrighted manuscript for his book, I asked if I could read Lourie's manuscript before publication, he quickly responded that his book wasn't finished. Lourie then stated he needed an ending for his book and questioned if he could use my involvement as an epilogue. My recollection is that I responded ... "that would be fine on the condition that I read a copy prior to publication."

Peter, unlike some of the others on my list, was hard to figure out. On one hand Lourie spoke of a great friendship and with admiration for Brunner, on the other, he spoke with nervousness and was not forthcoming to the point of being secretive with information on his book. I could not know how much of Brunner's material he was utilizing, if any, until I was able to read his manuscript.

Lourie like Chandler, asked if I knew about the family in Peru whose ancestors had removed the treasure and suggested that Brunner's search for the treasure was in vain. Again I said no, and he promised to send a copy of the newspaper clipping. What arrived appeared to be a translation of the Spanish newspaper article ...

ULTIMAS NOTICIAS Thursday 28 Oct 1965
No. 77, 167
FABULOUS TREASURE

"The Pástor family disputes a fabulous treasure which was left by a Spanish Magistrate [from Latacunga, Ecuador]. Peruvian descendants say they are nearly ready to collect the inheritance. Various Ecuadorians are shaking the dust off old papers and genealogical charts.

"The Peruvian press publishes sensational information about three families residing in Lima who are the descendants of the Puga Pástor family branch in Guayaquil. They are almost at the point of inheriting a fabulous treasure of twenty-eight thousand million sucres [about a billion dollars] which was deposited in the Royal Bank of Scotland in Edinburgh in 1803. Following the dates of ancestors, the family Puga Pástor is a direct descendant of the Magistrate Antonio Pástor y Marín de Segura, Marqués de Llosa.

"The judicial proceedings have begun before the civil judicature of Lima-The Origin: The fortune is evaluated at 460,000,000 pounds sterling and originally was sent by the ship El Pensamiento which embarked from the port of Lambayeque [429] under the command of Captains John Doigg and John Fanning. The cargo contained various crates of gold and silver bars, a great quantity of emeralds, other precious stones, gems, gold powder, gold Incan necklaces, masks, and vases. The deposit was made by Sir Francisco

[429] Lambayeque is a city in the Lambayeque region of northwestern Peru. In the 16th century, the Spanish Conquistador Francisco Pizarro traveled across this region on his way to Cajamarca.

Mollison in accordance with the authorization given him ... Don Antonio Pastor y Marín de Segura was born in Cartagena, Spain, in 1772 and his parents were Don Bartolomé Pástor y Doña Rosa Maria de Segura. His god-parents were King Charles the Third and the Queen. He came to America as Magistrate of Latacunga in 1794. Later he held other public offices in Chile and Lima ... The Magistrate died in 1804. His will requested that his great fortune be divided between his descendants in the fifth generation, several of whom reside in Ecuador and others in Peru."

Once again I was confronted with an attempt to dissuade me from pursuing Brunner's quest for the treasure! Based on an unsubstantiated newspaper claim, suggesting that the treasure had been recovered and in 1803 deposited with a Scottish bank, I was advised to abandon my project. With Brunner's indisputable evidence that the Blacke maps of 1887 were completely accurate in the back of mind, maps that indicate a vast treasure still in the Llanganatis some eighty years later, I pondered why so anxious to have me stop. The ultimate contradiction arose when Peter suggested that I shelve my work on Brunner's manuscript [430] and ... "go for the treasure!"

■ ■ ■

At this point the *Ultimas Noticias* article should be addressed briefly. Brunner paid absolutely no attention to this claim as it was not only unsubstantiated, but eighty years later Blacke & Chapman had discovered the treasure, or portions of the treasure in a cave. Therefore, even if the claim was accurate, all of the treasure could not have been removed. Even today in 2012 this claim remains not only unsubstantiated ... but perhaps even rebuked. What can be ascertained with certainty is that since the descendants of Antonio Pástor y Marín de Segura filed their initial claims in 1965, no physical evidence or record of any such deposit in the Royal Bank of Scotland or of the existence of the ship *El Pensamiento* ... has ever been found.

Nobody seems to mention if the will in question specifically indicated if the wealth of Antonio Pástor y Marín de Segura had come from a treasure deposit. The *El Comercio* article is also silent on the source of his purported wealth. Another unconfirmed article in *El Comercio,* published five months previously, adds yet another intriguing element to the story. The article recounted how an infamous pirate had plundered the mansion of the Obaya family in Lambayeque, looting among other items ... 598 bags or containers of gold and silver ... coincidently the same number of bags mentioned in the *El Pensamiento* story. Is it plausible that Antonio Pástor y Marín de Segura's wealth may have been pirates' plunder, or profits from his cinnamon business and other ventures?[431] Perhaps Marín de Segura could have even utilized his position to embezzle taxes collected for the King of

---

[430] In hindsight, my opinion is that perhaps this could have been an effort to delay publication.

[431] The Lambayeque region in Peru, similar to the region of Píllaro in Ecuador, was well known for the practice of grave robbery and looting of artifacts.

Spain as some theories suggest ... no one knows. Regardless ... no record of any shipment or deposit of any such wealth has ever been uncovered or confirmed.

Some aspects of the story however, do appear to have a basis in fact. For example ... the hostilities between Britain, France and Spain had halted the flow of treasure ships from South America to Spain. In 1802 the Treaty of Amiens created a short period of time which would have allowed the resumption of the backlogged treasure shipments.[432] The names of Captains' Doigg (or Doig) and Fanning ring true, both seafaring families having been confirmed as living in Lambayeque at the time.

■ ■ ■

Other accounts, although unconfirmed, point to Captain John Fanning of the *El Pensamiento,* as either utilizing his wealth to help finance the American Revolution or being related to the John Fanning[433] that served under John Paul Jones during the War of Independence from England. Another more intriguing account, has a portion of the missing *El Pensamiento* treasure being diverted to France by none other than Albert Gallatin, as payment for the Louisiana Purchase and funding of the Lewis and Clark Expedition. Assuming for a moment that there indeed was a ship named *El Pensamiento*, laden with treasure, regardless of the treasure's source, that disappeared at the exact time of the Louisiana Purchase, is the account plausible? If so, is it mere coincidence that more than a century later, Commander Dyott, related through marriage to Gallatin, acquired an interest in searching for the Llanganati treasure?

■ ■ ■

One can only theorize that if the will and its interpretation are accurate, and if Antonio Pástor y Marín de Segura did indeed leave a vast fortune, could he have removed a portion of the treasure from the Llanganatis, transported it from Ecuador to Peru, packed and loaded it on a ship in Peru, then shipped the treasure to Panama unloading it on Panama's Pacific shore, transporting it over the pre-canal isthmus and then loading it onto yet another ship on Panama's Atlantic shore[434] for the journey to Leith, Scotland ... without being discovered? Or, could the Antonio Pástor y Marín

---

[432] Some accounts have the ship *El Pensamiento* sailing in 1802, others indicate she sailed in 1803.

[433] Among the first commissions issued by the newly formed American Congress, 22 Dec 1775, can be found the name of Captain John Fanning.

[434] What most narrator's of this story appear to miss, is the fact that ... even if the treasure departed Peru aboard the ship *El Pensamiento,* once in Panama the treasure would have been transported across the isthmus and loaded onto yet another ship. Therefore, there would be no record of the *El Pensamiento* having ever arrived in Scotland. The only possible route for the *El Pensamiento* to take, in order to arrive in Scotland would have been around Cape Horn. Also, considering that the *El Pensamiento* carried a Spanish name ... why was it assumed that the ship, presumably a Spanish barque. . . was English?

de Segura treasure shipment have taken the risky southern route around Cape Horn? Is it plausible that such a gamble would have been taken, with such vast wealth at risk, in a location where the waters were known as a sailor's graveyard, being particularly hazardous, owing to strong winds, large waves, strong currents and icebergs? [435]

What is known as a matter of fact is that the Royal Bank of Scotland was inundated with hundreds of contacts and claims from Ecuadorians and Peruvians regarding this alleged deposit during 1965 through 1968. An extensive audit and physical examination of the banks archives and vaults in 1966 by Robert Forbes uncovered no such deposit or record thereof and even to date, no claims have ever been paid.

Theorizing that either the ship's captains, a bank employee or even the bank itself absconded with the purported fortune, although plausible, also defies common sense. Would Antonio Pástor y Marín de Segura or for that matter any individual, ship such vast wealth without accompanying it himself or sending an emissary, armed guards, or at the very least, having obtained some form of indisputable concrete evidence that he had indeed made such a shipment that had reached its destination?

Just for the sake of argument, let us consider for a moment the weight of gold and silver bullion shipped in ninety wicker baskets [436] as the story indicates. Assume a value of 460 million English Pounds on the 1803 deposit as the article suggests, and the value of gold at the time being 4.25 English Pounds [437] per troy ounce.[438] Assuming the entire deposit consisted of gold [439] ... simple math would invalidate the claim. The numbers indicate that this purported deposit would have been in excess of one hundred million troy ounces![440] Therefore, every merchant bag would have had to contain over one hundred-eighty-thousand troy ounces ... more than five tons of gold! Each and every wicker basket would have weighed more than

---

[435] The first recorded voyage through the Drake Passage was in 1616.

[436] Ninety wicker baskets purportedly contained 598 large merchant bags.

[437] Sir Isaac Newton, Master of the UK Mint, set the gold price in England at 3lb17s10d per troy ounce in 1717 where it remained the same for more or less two hundred years ... except for the periods of the Napoleonic Wars of 1797-1821 and 1800-1803 when it was 4.25 lbs per troy ounce.

[438] Troy ounce - Equivalent to 1.097 avoirdupois ounces, 31.1 grams or 480 grains.

[439] The *El Comercio* article clearly establishes that this was not the case ... "The cargo contained various crates of gold and silver bars, a great quantity of emeralds, other precious stones, gems, gold powder, gold Incan necklaces, masks, and vases."

[440] 460,000,000 English Pounds divided by 4.25 English Pounds =108,235,294.12 troy ounces. 108,235,294.12 troy ounces divided into 598 merchant bags = 180,995.48 troy ounces per bag. 180,995.48 troy ounces divided by 1.097 = 164,991.32 avoirdupois ounces, divided by 16 = 10,311.96 pounds or 5.16 short tons per bag.

thirty short tons! If the purported deposit included a great deal of silver and other materials as the newspaper article suggests, it would have required greater bulk to attain the value placed on it, weighing even more! Implausible! One would then also wonder ... is it plausible that a ship of the period transported a treasure cargo well in excess of its cargo capacity? [441]

One theory even refers to a miscalculation and misinterpretation of the will, insinuating that the deposits value was quoted in French livres.[442] With an exchange rate at the time of twenty-four livres to the pound, the deposit's value according to this theory would have been merely twenty-million English Pounds ... but still, over one hundred-thirty short tons of gold. Even if so, no record of any such deposit has ever been found. Sufficient theories abound on this purported deposit to fill a separate volume ... however, in 1887 Blacke & Chapman discovered a vast treasure in a cave ... so lust for Inca gold continued.

■ ■ ■

Upon examining Brunner's materials closer, I obtained an even better realization and respect for the man's abilities, accomplishments and the tenacity of his quests. I believe that the man lived for the pursuit of his treasures and any discovery would have been a secondary bonus. Brunner appears to have been content following Ecuador's rivers and streams, panning river beds, examining hillsides, exploring the plains, jungles and mountains, diving the ocean in search of wrecks, absorbing all that he could to educate himself and others most importantly ... documenting his discoveries ... this being the man's methodology. [443]

Any artistic work, whether that of an artist, composer, poet, novelist or the manuscript of a nonfiction writer, is an evolving process. In the case of a nonfiction work, many revisions and alterations, new facts and theories, occur over time. A manuscript is not set in stone until it is published or the author dies. Brunner's manuscript was set in stone upon his untimely death.

---

[441] Compare the purported treasure shipped on the *El Pensamiento,* to that carried aboard arguably two of the most famous treasure ships', Sir Francis Drake's prize the *Nuestra Señora de la Concepcion* carried roughly thirty tons of treasure, while Mel Fisher's *Nuestra Señora de Atocha* carried roughly forty tons of treasure. Remember as well, that Francisco Pizarro had sent his brother back to Spain "with a portion of the Royal Fifth"...obviously due to limited cargo capacity.

[442] Consider for a moment ... Is it plausible that Antonio Pástor y Marin de Segura of Peru, would have quoted the value of his wealth in his last will and testament, wealth which purportedly was on deposit in Scotland, who's monetary unit was British Pounds Sterling, in French Livres?

[443] As must be obvious by now, I have taken Brunner's method one step further by reverse engineering the story. For me this is the process of breaking the story down into individual purported factual elements and either confirming or dispelling each component of the story. Then you assimilate the facts weeding out the literary license and determine the plausibility of the entire story.

At what stage of the process Brunner's manuscript had reached upon his demise ... one may never know for sure. What is absolutely known is that Brunner's papers, most importantly his manuscripts, represented a half century of dedication, they were his life. Disturbing though, is that Brunner's papers also raised red flags and questions.

For the life of me I could not ignore some basic questions ... How can two treasure deposits be explained? ... Why after all those years of exploration and discovery had Brunner not recovered any treasure from even one of his projects? ... Why did Brunner not state in detail where the Llanganati treasure was, pinpointing its location and his plan for removal? ... If the treasure was recovered, what legal effect would the numerous old contracts Brunner entered into with partners and investors have? ... and ... What mistakes did Brunner make that I could learn from?

My first two questions, even today have no concrete answers. When my mother-in-law was asked the second question specifically, her response was that through the years Brunner had made minor discoveries of nonmetallic artifacts and obtained some raw gold prospecting that were sold to finance his expenses. Although I cannot confirm this, what I can say for a fact is, that some of Brunner's exploration projects, specifically relating to sunken treasures and lost Indian tribes in the Oriente, have subsequently been discovered and/or salvaged by others, confirming Brunner's data and research. Hopefully Brunner's Llanganati research will ultimately be proven as well ... with a recovery.

For the third question I developed an answer based on my own opinion and theory. Consider for a moment the paranoia that is inherent among treasure hunters, this alone would justify Brunner withholding certain details. The man also thought of himself as a spy or secret agent. Brunner had expressed that his life had been in danger numerous times, not just over this, but the Llanganati work as well, this too added to his paranoia. Combine these paranoias with the facts that the Llanganati chapter of his manuscript had been stolen, that Brunner had falling outs with at least two of his Llanganati treasure hunting partners and that with each prospective investor and author, data was disseminated, each time losing exclusivity to portions of his research. It is easy to understand why certain things, Brunner told no one ... but Brunner did leave clues.

■ ■ ■

One of Brunner's clues was within his manuscript *Ecuador y sus Tesoros*. Brunner's manuscript had a page, similar to a dedication page, containing a short quote. The quote was from Rudyard Kipling [1865-1936] the famous author best known for his work *The Jungle Book*. Brunner quoted Kipling's poem entitled *The Explorer*, written in 1898 ...

> "Till a voice, as bad as Conscience, rang interminable changes
> On one everlasting Whisper day and night repeated - so:
> Something hidden. Go and find it. Lost and waiting for you. Go!"

Conducting research within the library one day, I thought it would be nice if I could find Kipling's poem to verify Brunner's quote. Luckily I found a collection on Kipling's poems including *The Explorer* ...

"Till a voice, as bad as Conscience, rang interminable changes
On one everlasting Whisper day and night repeated - so:
Something hidden. Go and find it. **Go and look behind the Ranges - Something lost behind the Ranges.** Lost and waiting for you.
Go!"

I couldn't help but wonder why had Brunner misquoted Kipling and left out the sentence ... "**Go and look behind the Ranges - Something lost behind the Ranges.**" Then like a lightning bolt it struck me, what had my mother-in-law consistently and adamantly stated ... "Eugenio was digging with his hands on the last expedition to remove the treasure, not looking for it ... the treasure is behind Cerro Hermoso." Brunner was not just stating "Something hidden. Go and find it. Lost and waiting for you. Go!," Brunner was leaving a clue, "Go and look behind the Ranges - Something lost behind the Ranges!"

It immediately became clear to me that I had originally made an assumption and missed an important fact. I was starting with the knowledge that Brunner obtained over the years that proved to him and me later, that the treasure's location was on Cerro Hermoso. I knew that he had discovered Lake Brunner and why he believed that to be the treasure lake of the *Derrotero*. I knew of Brunner's shortcut trail from El Triunfo to Cerro Hermoso. I viewed Brunner's maps and data from south to north. My involvement in this project commenced from the end, not in the search but recovery, so I had missed the fact that the *Derrotero* and Brunner's explorations for the treasure, were oriented north to south. Brunner had started his quest from the beginning, but I had started mine from the end. Originally I had assumed that "behind" meant on the other side ... but Brunner's work had already placed him and me ... "behind" Cerro Hermoso!

Another clue within *Ecuador y sus Tesoros* was Brunner's story of his childhood dream. I had discovered that Brunner held the belief that dreams were glimpses into the future that represented future events or came true. I do not doubt that Brunner had a childhood dream similar to what he described, as even I can remember having childhood dreams about finding treasure as probably does every boy. However, it is my opinion and theory that Brunner included in his story of the dream, specific details on this treasure's location. Brunner's dream describes in detail a mountain, lake, pinnacle, waterfall, cave and stairs carved into solid rock, and includes the Blacke quote ... "I could not remove it alone or with thousand's of men."[444] It appears that Brunner's "dream" could not have represented any other place on earth as exactly as Cerro Hermoso and Lake Brunner. And lastly, I do not believe that Brunner's cartoon printed in the front of this book is just

[444] Brunner's quote varies from others who state ... "a thousand men."

a curious doodle. It is my opinion that this drawing was purposefully drawn, a cleverly concealed clue, indicating his helicopter pad and the treasure cave on Cerro Hermoso.

■ ■ ■

Regarding the question concerning contracts between Brunner, his partners and investors, it seemed reasonable that as no treasure had been recovered, the contracts were void or at least the statute of limitations would have expired. I made legal inquires in Ecuador and the US and confirmed that indeed this was most probably the case. In order to make absolutely positive, my mother-in-law had gone to probate court in Ecuador as Brunner's widow and received a court order on 18 Jun 1986, granting her sole ownership of all Brunner's materials, research documentation, rights and property. I personally was not aware at the time that Brunner had previously been married and had a daughter. In my opinion this seems to indicate that my mother-in-law's motives in obtaining a court order were different from mine. However, when I spoke with Michael Dyott,[445] Chuck Powell and Ricardo Petersmyth, even though none of them raised the issue, I assured them that I would consider their claims, if any.

My last question was probably the most troubling. In my opinion Brunner made two major mistakes that at the time may have made sense for the situation he was in. It is understandable that Brunner, having lived in Ecuador nearly fifty years, most recently under a military dictatorship then junta, realized you cannot do anything without military approval or involvement. In the past he had assisted or cooperated with the military on various projects and was comfortable working with them. For him the Llanganati project was no different. Brunner wanted a treasure salvage contract with the military, army or air force ... it would appear to have made no difference to Brunner which branch.

The support that Brunner required from the military included helicopters, manpower and security. Perhaps blinded by the proximity of the termination of his life long quest, Brunner seems to have ignored the fact that since the late seventies Ecuador was finally under democratic civilian rule, with the military releasing more and more of its authority over time. The laws had changed, treasure recovery and salvage rights were very limited, the Instituto Nacional de Patrimonio y Cultura now had exclusive authority over cultural heritage.

Brunner's second mistake in my view was short term funding. It seems that almost every investor or partnership was established for the next expedition of limited scope. After each expedition Brunner or his partners seemed to be broke once again, and the process of seeking new investors started all over. One or two investors with sufficient disposable income to cover the entire project, expedition after expedition, in my opinion could have resulted in

---

[445] In fact Dyott had been invited and "definitely"agreed to join any future expedition "anytime of the year."

success. The road to success in my opinion, would be to handle the materials and the resulting projects as a business, not a treasure hunt.

■ ■ ■

First order of business was to determine what projects and information was contained within Brunner's documentation. Every paper and map was assembled and sorted by subject matter. Initially, *Ecuador y sus Tesoros* the book manuscript and the Llanganati treasure projects were my main focus. All of the loose photos were gone through to sort by relevance to either project. Absolutely every negative that was found was then printed, so that no photograph of relevance would be overlooked.

After review of all the materials available to me, I chose a course of action that narrowed Brunner's work down to the three most important projects, publishing his book manuscript *Ecuador y sus Tesoros*, recovering the Llanganati treasure and reestablishing Brunner's mining concession on Cerro Hermoso that had been lost. My business plan and theory was that obtaining a mining concession would provide obvious benefits and side effects. We could be mining for copper and uncover the gold or we could be looking for the gold while people thought we were mining copper!

Ultimately I reached the conclusion that Brunner's Llanganati project had consisted of three phases ... research, exploration and recovery. My Llanganati project would need to consist of four phases ... research, permitting, exploration of specific sites, and treasure recovery. With absolutely no experience in any of these fields, I would have to learn what I could about treasure hunting, salvage contracts, funding, investors, copper mining and concessions, book publishing and Ecuador's treasure and archeological laws. Hopefully I might find some assistance in the list of Brunner contacts and his materials.

■ ■ ■

Meanwhile, my quest for knowledge and understanding continued. Having discovered so many details at the University of South Florida's Library, concerning the Incas and Richard Spruce, back to a library I went. However, on this occasion I went to the public library in Temple Terrace. I was aspiring to learn what I missed in Cub Scouts, Boy Scouts and Geography class about longitude, latitude, topographic maps, plotting points and coordinates. Hopefully this knowledge would give me a better understanding of Brunner's maps. I was reminded how my teachers always said ... "pay attention, you never know when this will come in handy!"

The most common coordinate system in use turned out to be the Geographic Coordinate System, which uses degrees of latitude and longitude to describe a location on the earth's surface. Lines of latitude run parallel to the equator and divide the earth into one hundred-eighty equal portions from north to south, or south to north. The base latitude is the equator which runs through Ecuador and each hemisphere is divided into ninety equal portions, each representing one degree of latitude and is labeled North or South. In the northern hemisphere degrees of latitude are measured from zero at the equator to ninety at the North Pole. In the southern hemisphere degrees of latitude are measured from zero at the equator to ninety degrees at the South

Pole. Wherever you are on the earth's surface, the distance between lines of latitude is the same, sixty nautical miles.

Lines of longitude labeled as West or East, in contrast do not stand up so well to the standard of uniformity. Lines of longitude run perpendicular to the equator and converge at the poles. The base line of longitude called the prime meridian runs from the north pole to the south pole through Greenwich, England. Subsequent lines of longitude are measured from zero to 180 degrees east or west of the prime meridian. At the equator and only at the equator, the distance represented by one line of longitude is equal to the distance represented by one degree of latitude. As you move toward the poles, the distance between lines of longitude becomes progressively less until, at the exact location of the pole all 360 degrees of longitude are represented by a single point. So using the geographic coordinate system, you have a grid of lines dividing the earth into squares. Therefore in Ecuador, being located on the equator, the square created between degrees is exactly sixty square miles.

To be truly useful the map grid is divided into small enough sections that they can be used to describe with an acceptable level of accuracy the location of any point on the map. To accomplish this, degrees are divided into sixty minutes, and minutes are divided into sixty seconds or 3600 seconds in a degree, represented as ' for minutes and " for seconds. So again at the equator, one second of latitude or longitude equals 101.3 feet.

■ ■ ■

All this background was a great starting point, but useless until the information could be plotted on a map pinpointing exact locations in detail. I had Brunner's topographic map from the Instituto Geográfico Militar on which he had plotted his trail that was established from El Triunfo to the backside of Cerro Hermoso and Lake Brunner.[446] But to pinpoint other sites, I would need to learn how to locate and plot these points for permit applications.

When I first looked at Brunner's topographic map, it appeared somewhat confusing and not very useful, solely because I could not read or understand it. Learning about longitude, latitude, degrees, minutes and seconds helped, but something was missing ... contours. There seem to be a few rules that topographic contours must obey and once you learn these rules the map becomes an extremely useful and easy tool to use. There seemed to be seven rules for contours to follow ... every point on a contour line represents the exact same elevation, contour lines can never cross one another, moving from one contour line to another always indicates a change in elevation, on a hill with a consistent slope there are always four intermediate contours for every index contour, the closer contour lines are to one another the steeper the slope is in the real world, a series of closed contours (the contours make

---

[446] Brunner's copy of the "Sucre" map was not available to him until at least 1968 when it was first printed. Before that, treasure hunters and explorers in Ecuador drew their own maps, many of which are printed in this book.

a circle) represents a hill, and lastly, contour lines crossing a stream valley will form a "V" shape pointing in the uphill and upstream direction.

■ ■ ■

On my return trip to Ecuador, armed with this knew knowledge and the fact that topographic maps were printed by the Instituto Geográfico Militar, which was located on the hill above the Military Hospital in Quito, I went to the Institute to obtain my own map copies. Not wanting to be seen as yet another gringo looking for treasure by the employees at the Institute, I had previously made a short list of Brunner's other project areas for future use and added the two maps I needed for the Llanganati project to the list. I entered the large multi-story lobby and upon inquiry learned that topographic map copies could be purchased upstairs. So up the long staircase I climbed.

At the top of the stairs on the wall was an enormous map of Ecuador, which went well beyond the Protocol of Río de Janeiro, containing the disputed eastern third of the country. Framed and mounted behind glass, this map was entitled ... Mapa Índice De Hojas Topográficas and was marked with the appropriate degrees of longitude and latitude. On the side margins the spaces created between lines of latitude were marked by Roman Numerals I through VIII, while on the top and bottom the spaces created between lines of longitude were labeled with the Spanish Alphabet, using letters' M through T. As I had learned at the library in Florida, these squares created between degrees near the equator were exactly sixty square miles.

By locating the square that contains Quito, I was able to discover the squares that represented my areas of interest for the Llanganati treasure project. My squares, or better stated ... the squares that correspond to the area covered by the *Derrotero de Valverde* and the *Guzmán Map* were labeled CT-ÑIII, the square where Quito is located, and directly below it CT-ÑIV, the square created between 79° West, 78° West and 1° South , 2° South ... where Brunner's areas of discovery were also located.

Within these squares on the map there were six sections labeled A through F at a scale of 1:100,000. Each of these six sections was divided into four sections and labeled from number one to four and most were titled. These sections were at a scale of 1:50,000, meaning one inch on the map equals 50,000 inches on land. In total, twenty-four individual rectangular maps commonly referred to as quadrangles or quads, were contained in the square created between degrees.

I checked my list and wrote down six map names for other projects and added the two Llanganati maps at the end. I handed the list to the clerk who upon reading the list gave me a cynical glance. Perhaps it was just my paranoia, but I could see he hadn't been fooled, his eyes said ... another foolish gringo! He left the counter and returned with seven maps, two he said were out of stock. For a second I was anxious, but to my relief the Llanganati maps were there.

Thanks to Brunner's years of research and exploration I now had at my disposal two of the relevant topographic maps printed in 1968, that corresponded to the *Derrotero de Valverde* and the *Guzmán Map*. Each rectangular map covers an area of ten miles by fifteen miles or one hundred-fifty square miles.[447] Directly below the *San José de Poaló* Map numbered CT-ÑIV-B1 (3990-IV), was the *Sucre* Map, numbered CT-ÑIV-B3 (3990-III). It is on the *Sucre* Map where Cerro Hermoso can be found, whose summit is at 1° 17' S 78° 17'W, with the small town of El Triunfo also being located here, at 1° 3' S 78° 4'W. Rather than reproduce the indispensable *Sucre* Map at a scale that cannot be read in book form, the all-important rivers of Río Verde Chico and Río Verde Grande along with the route from El Triunfo to Cerro Hermoso can more easily be viewed on the 1:250,000 scale topographic map online in The University of Texas map collection.[448]

Cerro Hermoso I would discover is the tallest Llanganati peak at 14,993 feet high and is actually a geological anomaly of the Eastern Cordillera of the Andes. It is composed of a block of Cretaceous limestone that was uplifted, faulted and thrust from the east on top of the basal metamorphic rock. Cerro Hermoso is therefore the only high peak in the main Andean chain in Ecuador that is not of volcanic origin,[449] contrary to the *Guzmán Map* description of "Hydro Volcán de Siete Bocas." This fact brings to mind Blacke's message to his friend in New England ... "treasure in dead volcano by extinct lake."[450]

---

[447] The topographic map labeled *Laguna de Anteojos* and numbered CT-ÑIII-F3, was not included on my list.

[448] One can clearly distinguish Lake Brunner and trace its outlet flowing into the Río Verde Grande., which brings to mind Stabler's statement in his paper of 1916 ... "The Río Verde is locally reputed to have its source in the lake in the Llanganati Mountains, at the bottom of which the golden vessels which formed the ransom of King Atahualpa were thrown by the Incas when news reached Quito that their ruler had been murdered."

[449] Kennerley, J.B. and Bromley, R.J. (1971). *Geology and geomorphology of the Llanganati Mountains, Ecuador*. Instituto Ecuatoriano de Ciencias Naturales, Contrib. No. 73. Quito. 16 pp.

[450] In the time of Guzmán, Spruce and Blacke & Chapman, it was falsely assumed that Cerro Hermoso was an inactive or "dead volcano." The question arises ... in this region where rain is a constant, how would a lake become extinct? Could it be the lake's source of water was diverted, or the lake drained? If so, for what purpose? Two theories come to mind ... could the lake have been drained to fill a man-made lake at a lower elevation, thereby covering the treasure deposit with water ... or, could the lake have been drained, the treasure removed, and deposited in a cave nearby?

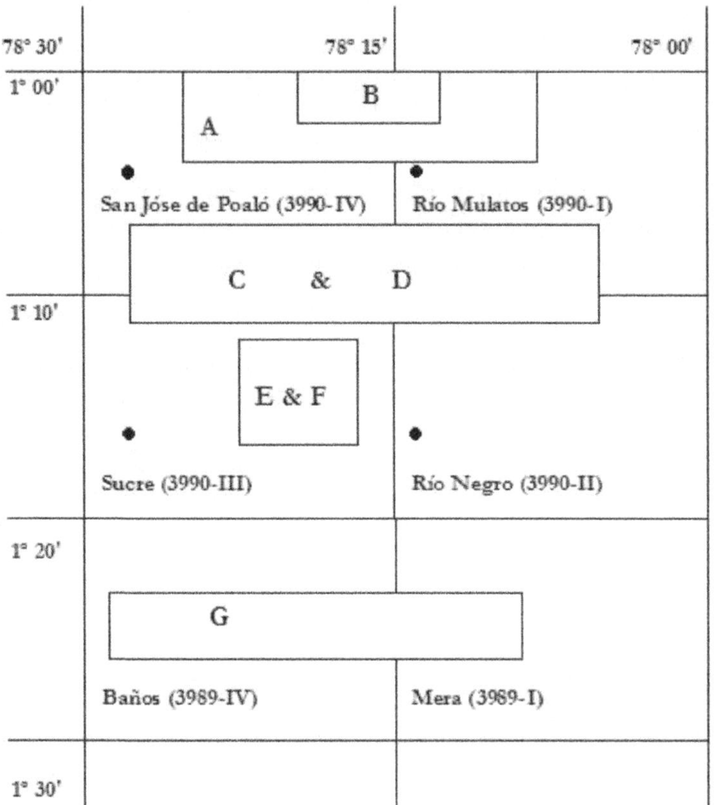

Llanganati Region Map Index Graphic

Graphic displays the rough location of all modern day maps referenced in this book. All are contained within the boundries of Guzmáns Map.

-NOT TO SCALE-

A - Brunner's map of Roncadores area – Page 240.
B - Brunner's map of Tres Cerros Llanganati – Page 241.
C - Loch's expedition sketch of the Llanganati region – Page 158.
D - Dyott's map of the area north of Cerro Hermoso – Page 191.
E - Brunner sketch of the reclining woman – Page 201.
F - Brunner map of Lake Brunner – Page 269.
G - Spruce & Stabler's route along the Río Pastaza – Page 101.
●- Corners of Ecuadorian Explorations Archaeological Project – Page 382.

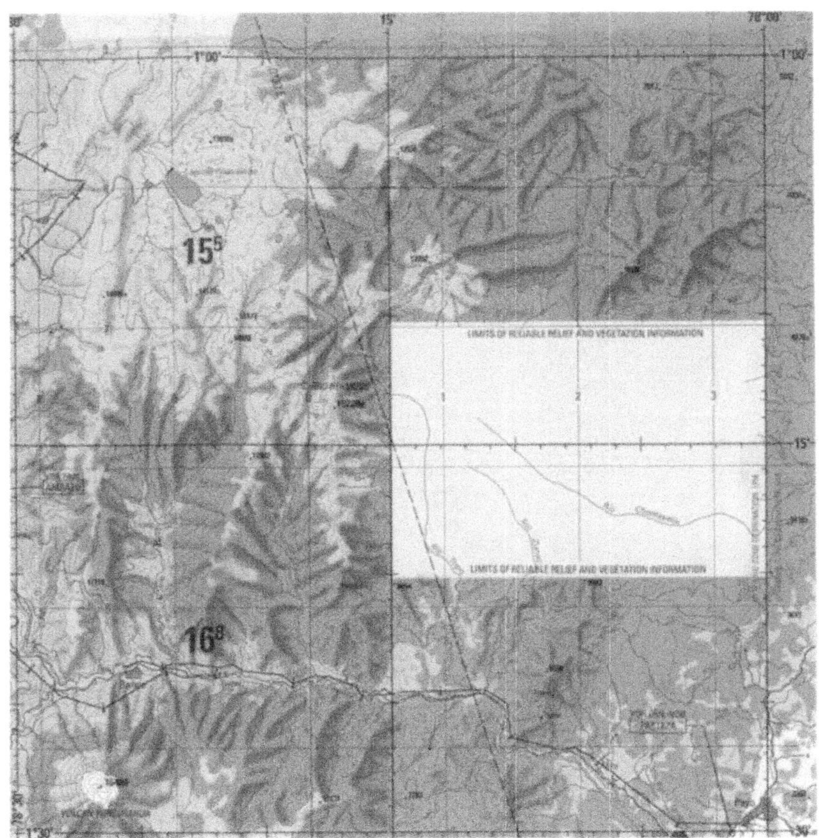

Llangantai Region Joint Operations Graphic

(Section of 1:250,000 Scale CIA Joint Operations Graphic AIR)

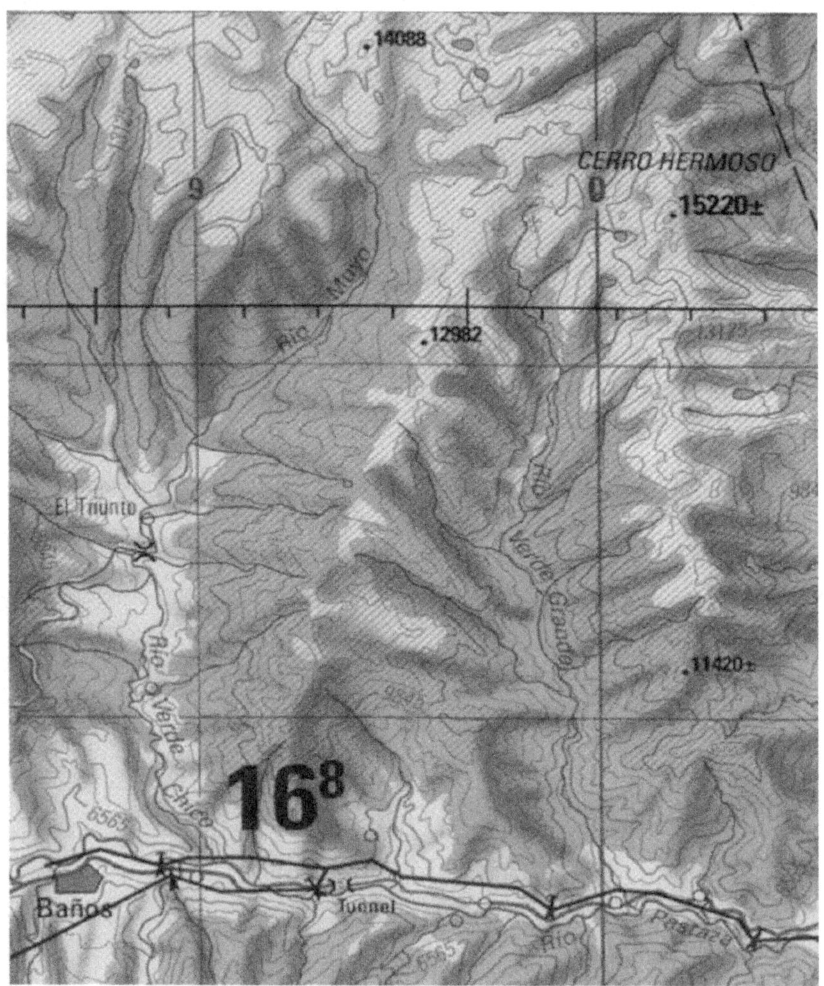

Baños & Cerro Hermoso Area Graphic

(Enlarged Section of 1:250,000 Scale CIA Joint Operations Graphic AIR)

Thanks to Brunner's years of research and exploration I now had at my disposal two of the relevant topographic maps, printed in 1968, that corresponded to the *Derrotero de Valverde* and the *Guzmán Map*. Each rectangular map covers an area of ten miles by fifteen miles or one hundred-fifty square miles.[451] Directly below the *San José de Poaló* Map numbered CT-ÑIV-B1 (3990-IV), was the *Sucre* Map, numbered CT-ÑIV-B3 (3990-III). It is on the *Sucre* Map where Cerro Hermoso can be found, whose summit is at 1° 17' S 78° 17'W, with the small town of El Triunfo also being located here, at 1° 3' S 78° 4'W. Rather than reproduce the indispensable *Sucre* Map at a scale that cannot be read in book form, the all-important rivers of Río Verde Chico and Río Verde Grande along with the route from El Triunfo to Cerro Hermoso can more easily be viewed on the 1:250,000 scale topographic map online in The University of Texas map collection.[452]

Cerro Hermoso I would discover is the tallest Llanganati peak at 14,993 feet high and is actually a geological anomaly of the Eastern Cordillera of the Andes. It is composed of a block of Cretaceous limestone that was uplifted, faulted and thrust from the east on top of the basal metamorphic rock. Cerro Hermoso is therefore the only high peak in the main Andean chain in Ecuador that is not of volcanic origin,[453] contrary to the *Guzmán Map* description of "Hydro Volcán de Siete Bocas." This fact brings to mind Blacke's message to his friend in New England ... "treasure in dead volcano by extinct lake."[454]

Apart from being the source of many articles and books on Ecuador's treasures, Brunner had himself written articles concerning the Llanganati treasure, providing sporadic sources of income. It appears that with every article or book published where Brunner was the author or source, investors would undoubtedly follow. Not only did I find clippings of newspaper

---

[451] The topographic map labeled *Laguna de Anteojos* and numbered CT-ÑIII-F3, was not included on my list.

[452] One can clearly distinguish Lake Brunner and trace its outlet flowing into the Río Verde Grande., which brings to mind Stabler's statement in his paper of 1916 ... "The Río Verde is locally reputed to have its source in the lake in the Llanganati Mountains, at the bottom of which the golden vessels which formed the ransom of King Atahualpa were thrown by the Incas when news reached Quito that their ruler had been murdered."

[453] Kennerley, J.B. and Bromley, R.J. (1971). *Geology and geomorphology of the Llanganati Mountains, Ecuador*. Instituto Ecuatoriano de Ciencias Naturales, Contrib. No. 73. Quito. 16 pp.

[454] In the time of Guzmán, Spruce and Blacke & Chapman, it was falsely assumed that Cerro Hermoso was an inactive or "dead volcano." The question arises ... in this region where rain is a constant, how would a lake become extinct? Could it be the lake's source of water was diverted, or the lake drained? If so, for what purpose? Two theories come to mind ... could the lake have been drained to fill a man-made lake at a lower elevation, thereby covering the treasure deposit with water ... or, could the lake have been drained, the treasure removed, and deposited in a cave nearby?

articles that he had written for the Quito papers, there was reference to the US magazine *Treasure*.

I contacted the publisher, a Jim Williams in 29 Palms, California, introduced myself, mentioned Brunner's death and that I was going to proceed with the Llanganati project and attempt to publish Brunner's book manuscript. Mr. Williams acknowledged that indeed they had published a two-part article either by Brunner, or with Brunner as a source and offered to send me complimentary copies. Mentioning that I had no experience in the treasure salvage field, I inquired as to where I might start looking for investors or salvage experts. I was told a good start would be to contact a man named Norman Scott who was also in Florida, Pompano Beach to be exact.

■ ■ ■

Upon contacting Mr. Scott, the man seemed extremely interested in the Llanganati project and inferred that at some point previously he had considered doing an Ecuador project with another party. Scott and his company Expeditions Unlimited Inc. had been involved in treasure search operations since 1959 with numerous successes in the sixties and seventies searching for underwater treasures. Scott was probably best known for his involvement in the thirteen-day Victoria Peak treasure expedition "Operation Goldfinder" of March 1977, on the White Sands Missile Range in New Mexico. During the period I met Mr. Scott he was involved more with his company American Cable Layers, laying underwater and underground fiber optic telephone cable.

Our first meeting was in the terminal at Miami International Airport. Norman brought me the book *Treasure of Victoria Peak* by Phil A. Koury that detailed Scott's and Expeditions Unlimited's efforts. For my part Brunner's research and discoveries on the Llanganati project were laid out in general terms. I expressed my need for an investor, salvage expert, partner or any combination thereof. Scott seemed extremely interested in the project and afterwards we continued to discuss the project on the phone and through the mail.

While reading *Treasure of Victoria Peak*, it became apparent that Scott was a man that thrived on the limelight created by being center stage, taking control of an expedition and any publicity it would generate. Similar to Powell, I feared that Scott would not be satisfied in a subordinate role. Also, tantamount to Brunner and previous explorers of the Llanganatis, Scott appeared to have had very little success with treasure recovery and appeared more interested in the thrill of the hunt, discovering the unknown and proving or disproving a theory. The most important point I would take away from my association with Norman, what set Scott apart from other Llanganati explorers, is that Norman's business model didn't require the recovery of any treasure. Scott was typically paid for his services by investors and would make his money off photo, movie, film, television or book rights.

Questions were raised regarding treasure salvage contracts in general and the legal issues that would be encountered. At some point there would need to be a contract entered into between myself and my mother-in-law. Brunner's widow had obtained a court order for sole ownership of his materials and we would need to set our agreement on paper. There could be no misunderstanding between us as to the terms of an agreement, and I wanted to be fair. Norman indicated that an up-front cash payment is not customary in the treasure business. Typically the source of information would either sell the data outright for a minimal payment or more often than not, would just receive a small percentage of recovery profits, typically around 5 percent.

Scott on the other hand was not that easy to deal with. I acquired a great deal of knowledge from Norman due to his experience, but it became obvious that he was not willing or capable of being an investor. With his experience though, he might make a capable partner, perhaps obtaining investors or at the least, working as a contractor in search and recovery efforts. Every attempt was made to come to terms and enter into a contract with Scott, rough drafts were sent back and forth and never signed. One of the sticking points seemed to have been my demand for a non-competition clause and the fact that all book, magazine, movie and television rights to the project, would belong to my company. On occasion it seemed as though he might have been stalling, seeking more specific details on Brunner's discoveries.

Our discussions and communications ranged from a partnership to actual expedition planning. Norman understandably did not want to divulge the secrets of his trade, but indicated any prospective expedition could include the use of ground penetrating radar, a magnetometer, infrared scanner, underwater remote operated vehicle, and surprisingly showed little concern over altitude acclimatization. While not only did the negotiations with Mr. Scott come to an impasse, Norman had also not been successful in obtaining possible project investors.

■ ■ ■

Upon arrival in Quito on 29 Dec 1986, my taxi whisked me directly to the new Hotel Alameda Real on Avenida Río Amazonas a few blocks north of Hotel Colon. My friend Sebastian, who had been so helpful during the courtship of my wife was now employed at the newly built Hotel Alameda. With one phone call, regardless of how busy the hotel was, even when over-booked, I was always welcomed at the national rate, upgraded to a nice mini-suite and was permitted to stay as long as I desired.

Discussing my project and plans in general terms with Sebastian one day, he informed me that indeed his father was a retired Colonel from the army and was actually employed at the Ministry of Defense. Also Sebastian's family had known Juan León Febres Cordero long before he had become President and perhaps they could assist me making contact. Weeks and months passed with Sebastian making slow headway in obtaining an audience for me with the President through his contact in the Palace, a

General Delgado.[455] I had also mounted a letter and fax campaign directly to the President seeking an audience with very limited results.

■ ■ ■

Long delays in the bureaucratic processes of Ecuador created the problem of boredom setting in, keeping oneself occupied was difficult. Traveling alone, there was very little one could do. Even when you had an appointment or desired to conduct business, Ecuador followed the Latin custom of long two hour "siesta" lunch breaks. Television at the time was limited to about three local Spanish language channels that ran Hispanic soap operas and poor slapstick comedy along with poorly translated and outdated American television series programing. As a result, I watched very little if no television while in Ecuador.

My main source of entertainment while in Ecuador became playing poker at the Hotel Colon Casino or in a private home game. I had never played poker before and the game of choice in Ecuador at the time was seven card stud, which I slowly learned at the table. At these games I met and played with basically the same people over and over again, some of us became friends, others just acquaintances.

I met my best "new" friend in Ecuador at the poker table. Walter was an American from the deep south that grew up with a father who had been a professional gambler. Walter as well, after many years of business ventures, had turned to making his living playing poker. JM was another poker player, an American who worked at Quito's US Embassy. Señor G was only one of the numerous wealthy Ecuadoran businessmen of note that frequented the poker tables. One of the younger Ecuadoran's that frequented the tables was a customs official, who at times assisted me through customs. All in all, a nice friendly group of players.

One fine evening at about midnight, after having an excellent night at the table, winning more than 100,000 Sucres, I decided it was time to cash out my winnings and make the leisurely walk back to my hotel, The Alameda. About half-way back to my hotel, a young native girl about six years old and her younger sister of about four years of age, approached me holding a bunch of flowers that they were selling by the piece. I instantly took pity on and felt empathy for these young children who were about the same age as my children, but were apparently living on the streets and being forced to work at this late hour in order for their family to survive.

Still euphoric over my winning session, I assumed that if the young girls had no more flowers to sell, they could get some sleep and/or something to eat. I asked the girls if they had more flowers and they said no, while also confirming that when these were sold they could call it a night. I asked how much for the entire bunch of flowers, two hundred Sucres was their response. Doubling their figure, I gave each child two hundred Sucres in exchange for the bunch of flowers. The girls ran over toward their mother,

---

[455] General Marcelo Delgado Alvear - At the time Jefe Militar de la Casa Presidencial.

whom I then realized had been sitting with some blankets in the vestibule of a building keeping an eye on them. As I was walking away, I became enveloped by a warm feeling of deep pleasure from my actions and I noticed that the girls were settling in for the night.

When I arrived back at the Hotel Alameda, I was greeted by the girls that staff the reception desk. I could not enumerate how often the reception staff had assisted me extending my stays and with faxes, phone calls, messages and the like. Continuing with my emotions and actions of the evening, I offered my newly acquired bunch of flowers to the staff as a gesture of my appreciation for services previously rendered. My night ended with that feeling of pride that comes from doing the right thing, of committing a magnanimous gesture that no one ever needs know occurred.

Upon the conclusion of my business on this trip, I returned to Florida, my home and my family. It was always gratifying to be welcomed home by the unconditional love of young children that were euphoric to greet their father after a prolonged absence of a week or two. However, I could sense something was amiss with my wife. She appeared not only to be reserved, but there were uncharacteristic and constant questions about my trip, what I did, whom I saw, et cetera.

Ultimately, I was confronted by the question ... "Who did you give flowers to in Ecuador?" ... I was in shock! The small town atmosphere prevalent in Quito, where everyone appears to know everyone else, produced news for the gossip mill concerning my activities in Ecuador, that had arrived in Florida before me! I reluctantly had to explain the entire story to my wife, a story that to this day is probably not totally believed. It just goes to show that ... "no good deed goes unpunished!"

It was not until the end of my travels in Ecuador that the country finally obtained satellite programing and English language programs. One morning on a day that I was leaving Ecuador, as was customary, I had the television on one of these newly acquired English channels. My mother-in-law came to my hotel to drop off some paperwork and gifts for her daughter. Even though she had been told to drop them off at the front desk, she was knocking at my door when I was getting out of the shower. Naked and running late I told her through the door to please leave the items outside the door and I would get them.

This seemingly innocent event as well, would end up causing me some friction on the home front. Once again after being away from home and family for weeks, I would arrive expecting to be welcomed by open arms ... to be greeted by hostility instead. Once again the news had reached Florida before me, that my mother-in-law had heard a woman's voice speaking English, coming from my hotel room that I would not let her into!

■ ■ ■

Irrational would be the definition of the contract talks with my mother-in-law. With solely the knowledge that the treasure could be on Cerro Hermoso and the fact that she did not have the missing book chapter, she illogically wanted $100,000 US Dollars up front for Brunner's materials.

She had even implied that the Spanish government had offered her as much. This of course I assumed to be pure fantasy, an illogical and irrational proposition. During the negotiations I almost walked away from the project. My wife at that point begged her mother to be rational and agree to terms, while at the same point begging me to accept the project.

Ultimately we came to an agreement where Brunner's widow would receive an up front fee of 100,000 Sucres or about $600 US Dollars, which at the time was roughly a years wages in Ecuador. Additionally, my mother-in-law would receive a 10 percent share of my profits. This of course was the same percentage as in Brunner's contract with Dyott, double the industry average, based on my net profit share of recovery. So there would be no misunderstanding, as I was not willing to take a chance that any possible disagreement between us in the future could destroy my family, the contract was written in English and Spanish. The wording of the contract and terms of sale ("hereby sell, assign and transfer"), what was being transferred ("including but not limited to") and its effect on the parties ("binding on all heirs and assigns"), left no room for misinterpretation.

On 7 Jan 1987 my mother-in-law and I mutually agreed to the terms and signed the contract in duplicate and payment was tendered. In exchange I received all rights, title and interest to the entirety of Brunner's materials. All of the materials were then packed in my large gray duffle bag, which must have weighed at least fifty pounds, and taken back to my hotel.

■ ■ ■

Finally after months of agonizing waiting and the uncertainty of whether I was pursuing the proper course of action, Sebastian informed me that a message had been received from General Delgado, the President would meet with me next Friday prior to leaving for Guayaquil, as it was customary for him to spend weekends at his home on the coast. This was perhaps the breakthrough I needed! What rational person could overlook the potential of what I had to offer?

On my way to Hotel Colon for dinner and perhaps some poker later, I stopped by my mother-in-law's to give her the good news. Throughout my involvement she had been against my working with the President and tonight was no exception. She had received word through an intermediary that General Frank Vargas Pazzos would urgently like to meet with me before this coming Wednesday, also that ... "he understood the value and importance of Brunner's research." Caught off-guard by this outlandish development, I told my mother-in-law I would give it some consideration and abruptly left.

Here I was, finally on the brink of dealing with the legitimate government of Ecuador for the recovery of seventy billion dollars in treasure, a move that could permanently alter the economic and political situation, not only of Ecuador, but the surrounding region, and provide our family with extreme wealth. Yet my mother-in-law was irrational enough to think that I would jeopardize this by meeting in prison, actually under house arrest on a military base, with the man responsible for a failed coup. But why was it so urgent for Vargas to meet with me prior to Wednesday? ... What could have been his motive?

While eating dinner I decided that if my friend, JM for his privacy and security, from the U.S. Embassy's Political Section[456] came to the casino to play cards that evening, I would take him aside and ask his opinion of the situation I found myself in. Nothing could jeopardize future relations with the Febres Cordero government!

I got to the Hotel Colon Casino extremely early that evening, the first poker player to arrive. Slowly players began to file in around nine o'clock, as is customary for Friday evening. I noticed a familiar lanky gringo slowly descending the stairs into the main casino, I was lucky, JM had arrived early. I got up from my chair and met JM before he could enter the poker room. Taking JM to one side, I explained the developments of the day.

Needless to say JM was extremely astonished to hear that General Vargas, could or had made contact from prison. JM's advice was just as I had predicted, to stay away from Vargas, as nothing good could become of it. JM also expressed an interest in why it was so urgent that a meeting be held by Wednesday, after all he reasoned, Vargas was in jail and had all the time in the world! Whether JM passed this information onto Washington in his official capacity or not, is unclear. What was clear to me at the time, was that in no manner, shape or form was I going to have any contact with General Vargas ... the entire situation was put behind me and forgotten.

■ ■ ■

In hindsight, the situation at the time was potentially more precarious than even I could have imagined. We now know that Ecuador's military was still split by rival factions, the nationalistic left and democratic right. According to the author Peter Lourie, in 1980 Brunner had been making contact with and seeking the support of Generals' in the Air Force and President Roldós. Was it possible that the leftist Lieutenant General Frank Vargas Pazzos, appointed a Commander in the Air Force by the leftist Roldós, was one of the Generals' whose favor Brunner had been courting? If so, that could explain the quote attributed to Vargas that ... "he understood the value and importance of Brunner's research." Is it not also plausible that Frank's brother, the nationalistic and leftist General Reñe Vargas Pazzos, then advancing within the ranks of the Ecuadorian Army, could have also become aware of Brunner's research?

Assume for a moment that my mother-in-law's theory of Brunner having been murdered while in the military hospital was accurate ... who would have had an interest in killing the man and to what end? At the time of Brunner's death Oswaldo Hurtado Larrea was President, General Gribaldo

---

[456] The Political Section (POL) is responsible for reporting to Washington on foreign policy issues and political trends in Ecuador and for representing U.S. interests in these fields. The section advises the Ambassador on political-military issues, domestic politics, labor issues, democracy and human rights, extradition, as well as indigenous movements.

Miño was his Chief of Staff, General Reñe Vargas Pazzos was Commander of the Army and his brother, General Frank Vargas Pazzos, was a Commander in the Air Force (soon to become Commander of the Air Force).[457] Even my mother-in-law must have realized, that if the military had any involvement in Brunner's death, it would have had to involve either the extreme left or right factions. Considering that the right had reached an agreement with Brunner to participate in the recovery of the Llanganati treasure, through her cousin General Miño, this fact should have removed any possible motive for the right to kill Brunner ... then who would have had a motive? I must clarify however, that even though other facts strongly suggest questionable circumstances surrounded Brunner's demise, the facts do not provide conclusive proof of any wrong doing.

Take into account the circumstantial coincidences of Brunner's premonition, the fact that Brunner sent his papers home with his wife and died that exact same evening, and Gruber's apartment had been broken into and the manuscript taken around the same period that Brunner was in the hospital. Consider the rivalry between General Miño and General Reñe Vargas and that purportedly General Miño had been experiencing difficulties with other Generals'.[458] Most importantly consider General Miño's "voluntarily"retirement within a week after Brunner had died and the General's reluctance to assist with my project until he returned from Panama. Given these factors, to this day I cannot comprehend why my mother-in-law would have considered placing me in contact with the brother of her cousin's rival ...

■ ■ ■

The weekend and beginning of the week flew past quite rapidly in relation to the normal agony of waiting for government officials and dealing with the corrupt bureaucracy. As each day passed, I fine tuned my facts and sales pitch that I would give President Febres Cordero. Considering the President spoke no English and his time would be limited, I decided to utilize Sebastian as an interpreter and my presentation needed to be accurate, specific, frank and sincere.

Thursday morning I awoke to a bright sunny day. However, something seemed amiss, and I could sense an unnatural stillness in the air. The city outside was abnormally quiet for this time of day. Absent was the hustle and bustle of the city in the morning. Car traffic was almost non-existent and foot traffic was unusually light. I quickly showered and dressed deciding to go outside and ascertain if I could discover what was going on ... a holiday or natural disaster I presumed. Only twice prior had I ever sensed such a

---

[457] It has always amazed me that in a coup prone country such as Ecuador, two brothers would have been allowed to assume command of the country's Air Force and Army during the same period of time.

[458] On one occasion prior to Brunner's death, I specifically recall my mother-in-law calling and telling my wife and I how "Gribaldo" had been having difficulties with other General's ... to a point where they had removed his private guard.

foreboding sensation. Similarly, with no prior knowledge of the events that had transpired, one occasion was as I arrived home from school on the day President Kennedy was assassinated, and the other was arriving at work in an office on September 11th.

To my astonishment I was able to piece together the fact that around 8:30 in the morning, President Cordero was kidnaped by Air Force troops loyal to General Vargas, many people had reportedly been killed. The President would be ransomed for the release and pardon of General Vargas. All that I could think of at the time was ... "Don't these idiots know that, finally after all these months, I had a meeting scheduled with the President!"

Immediately the paranoia kicked in and I started to ponder the situation and my options. My chances of meeting with President Cordero anytime in the near future were gone, perhaps if he was released I could start over later. If he was killed, where would I be left? But wait ... if Vargas is somehow involved in the kidnaping of the President, could I not be in danger as well? Would Vargas not hesitate to take my information and dispose of me as well? I called the airline and made a reservation to leave the next morning for the safety of the United States.

Once again as I was packing the paranoia kicked in. What if someone discovered what documents were in my duffel bag? I could not take the chance of checking my bags at the airport, with such important papers inside! I chose to carry the heavy duffel bag and my briefcase as carry on baggage. Eastern Airlines at the time allowed two carry-ons, but the duffel was almost three-foot long! Luckily Eastern was never very strict with their rules, especially in first class. For me, the paranoia did not dissipate until my documents were safe at home in the United States.

It was the next morning and yet the paranoia still lingered ... I drove to a gun shop and purchased a small caliber Beretta pistol easily conciliable under my suit jacket. Also, in order to provide as much protection and to inflict the utmost damage as possible with such a small caliber weapon, my purchase included a box of hollow point bullets.

■ ■ ■

On the flight back to Florida I had picked up a copy of *The New York Times* dated Friday 17 Jan 1987. Instantly I spotted an article by Joseph B. Treaster, entitled *Ecuador Troops Kidnap President And Trade Him For Jailed General*. I started reading hoping that President Cordero had not been harmed as I still considered him by far to be my best bet for a successful outcome ... "GUAYAQUIL, Ecuador, Jan.16 - A group of armed military men seized President León Febres Cordero today and released him 12 hours later in exchange for an Air Force general who had been arrested in a mutiny 10 months ago. General Frank Vargas Pazzos, the former Air Force commander and chief of Ecuador's joint military command, who had been under arrest since last march, arrived at the base here about an hour before President Cordero was freed."

To my great relief President Juan León Febres Cordero was alive and unharmed! I continued reading to discover that the President had been accompanied by the Minister of Defense Medardo Salazar Navas, the Commanders of the Navy and Air Force, his brother Nicolas, two Presidential aides, two friends and some civilians. The President and his entourage were greeted by a military band and a few moments later shots were fired by paratroopers and the Presidents bodyguards returned fire. Two of the Presidents bodyguards and two of the attackers were reportedly killed and others wounded before the President was captured.

The next day I obtained another copy of *The New York Times* in order to read an updated article about the kidnaping. The article centered around whether General Vargas played a role in capturing the President or not. The President himself stated that he did not know who was behind the incident. Members of General Vargas's family argued on his behalf "...that the general could not have directed the capture of the President because his ability to communicate from the base where he was detained was extremely limited." But I had my doubts ... just as JM from the US Embassy must have had his own.

■ ■ ■

My rapid departure from Ecuador and the long flight home gave me the opportunity to pause and reconsider my options. It would definitely take some time for circumstances to stabilize in Ecuador. I could utilize this opportunity to work on Brunner's book manuscript that I had previously spent a month laboriously typing with my hunt and peck style. I could continue seeking funding and would look into the possibilities of renewing Brunner's copper mining concession on Cerro Hermoso.

Book publishers' showed little interest in Brunner's manuscript as it was not only in Spanish but roughly written. *National Geographic Magazine* expressed an interest in a story concerning the expedition but would not fund it. I flew to California and met with Michael Dyott. While in Hollywood I met with family connections in the film industry and discussed the sale of movie rights to the treasure story and expedition.

At about this time I had also become aware that Ecuador was experiencing a modern day gold rush with mining claims and concessions being gobbled up throughout the country. I had also discovered that Cyprus Minerals Company, an American mining company, was taking part in Ecuador's modern day gold rush by actively pursuing exploration prospects in Ecuador. I made an appointment and flew to Colorado, for a meeting with the Vice President of Exploration.

With me I took a few small copper mineral samples from Cerro Hermoso that were provided Cyprus to assay, on the condition that I receive a copy of the report. Although an extremely small sample, the "VP" appeared quite interested with the results. It was explained that the company was not accustomed to seeing results with such a large showing of gold and silver byproducts, measured in parts per billion, compared to industry averages. The real monetary values of Cerro Hermoso's copper mine, if proven accurate, would come in the form of its byproducts!

Although Cerro Hermoso is extremely remote and the difficulties of building a mining road would be astronomical, Cyprus showed an interest in exploring the area. Cyprus put me in contact with the General Manager of the company's subsidiary in Ecuador, Cyprus Minera de Ecuador Corporation. Bill as he preferred to be called, offered to fund an initial expedition to the mountain, but I was not yet prepared to go into the Llanganatis. I did not want anything to interfere with obtaining a Presidential Decree. Going into the mountains without permission, was in my opinion not the correct path at the moment.

One day when visiting Bill at his office in Quito, he stated that he had something I might be interested in, as I had previously told him the Brunner story. Bill seemed reluctant, but ultimately he stated that something had come into his possession that he had given his word he would return and he could not disclose his source. Bill would share something with me, only if I gave my word that I would return it to him, which I did. Bill went into his desk pulling out a folder of papers, reaching across his desk Bill handed me a copy of the manuscript *El Tesoro en las Misteriosas Montañas de Llanganati*, Brunner's stolen book chapter that he had been recreating prior to his death!

Regardless of the number of times I questioned Bill about his source, he was true to his word and would not reveal anything. Bill told me to take the manuscript with me and read it if I wanted, but I must return it to him. It is hard to put in words the thought process I went through on this dilemma. I had in my hands a copy of something that I owned all rights to, that had been stolen ... but I had given my word to return it. I could have just kept the manuscript, but instead, kept my word. I made a copy and returned the manuscript to Bill. I retained my integrity and the possibility of a business venture with Cyprus in the future. I now had a complete copy of the missing book chapter that Brunner was redrafting upon his death, that even my mother-in-law did not have access to!

■ ■ ■

Updating Ricardo over the phone one day, I briefed him again on my need for an investor and that the situation with Norman Scott did not seem to be panning out. Ricardo replied not to worry, he had been discussing the project with a friend and his associate. Ricardo implied that these two individuals might have an interest in funding the entire project and had the wherewithal to do so. A meeting was quickly arranged so that I could describe Brunner's research and findings in detail, then make a project proposal.

Prior to the meeting I prepared a folder outlining my ownership of Brunner's materials and evidence of his discoveries with photos of Lake Brunner, the surrounding area and Chapman's grave site. As no partnership agreement had yet been entered into, Mr. Scott was invited to accompany me at his own expense, to Atlanta. Scott brought to the table his expertise, and would be a potential project contractor.

Nervous would be an under statement upon meeting my potential partners. Both men were prominent members of Atlanta society, "Partner A" was Chairman of the Board of a family owned global company and the other was Justus C. Martin Jr. [1925-1993], Chairman of the Board of The Robinson-Humphrey Company, a stock brokerage firm. My thoughts as we were escorted into Mr. Martin's conference room however were not on the project, but on the beauty and elegance of his offices. Never before or since, have I ever seen such a magnificent office, with floor to ceiling cherry wainscoting, and the wood's elegant, deep, rich, red hues.

Brunner's research and discoveries, my government contacts and efforts up to that point were laid on the table and my presentation went forward. The project would be broken into three phases ... the permit process, an exploration expedition and the recovery phase. For funding of each phase, a percentage of profits from recovery would be granted in conjunction with an option to fund the next phase. Mr. Scott then explained his background, expertise and the anticipated exploration phase. Questions were raised and answered by all parties, with the meeting ending in a commitment to fund phase one for a 10 percent interest and options on the next two phases. A contract would be drawn up and was subsequently signed on 16 Jul 2007.

Upon the conclusion of our meeting, Scott manipulated the conversation to his own interests and projects. It became apparent to me that Norman was sizing up my new financial partners as potential investors for his unrelated projects. As Norman had an earlier flight than I, we were preparing to walk out of the room when one of the partners indicated for me to stay for a moment. After Norman departed "Partner A" inquired what relationship I had with Scott. Specifically he wanted to know how much proprietary information Scott had been privy to and was he a partner, associate or contractor. My initial response was an apology for what I considered to be Scott's inappropriate sales pitch on unrelated projects. I explained that Scott had been provided a limited insight into the Brunner materials, nothing beyond what had just been disclosed in our meeting and that we had been in negotiations covering all those options, yet no agreement had been reached or signed ... "Partner A" stated ... "don't sign anything with Scott yet" indicating further that he had some experience in the past dealing with a treasure project in Egypt and that for numerous reasons other options could be available to us, even mentioning that we could get someone such as Mel Fisher [459] on our project if need be. I readily agreed that Scott would be kept at arms length as a potential contractor and that I would not disclose any further proprietary information to him.

---

[459] Later upon addressing the issue of perhaps enlisting Mel Fisher with Michael Dyott, he stated "I have heard he is a problem to work with. You need someone long on high tech and short on bossing." These are the same issues that bothered me about Scott, who appeared in my opinion to demand and thrive upon the attention and glory of being the man in charge.

ECUADORAN EXPLORATIONS, INC.

CERTIFIED RESOLUTION

I, the undersigned, Joe M. Young, Secretary of Ecuadoran Explorations, Inc., a Georgia corporation, do hereby certify that set forth below is a resolution duly adopted by the Board of Directors of said corporation by unanimous consent dated September 2, 1987, which resolution has not been amended or rescinded:

> RESOLVED, the Board of Directors of Ecuadoran Explorations, Inc. does hereby authorize and empower Steven J. Charbonneau, President of the corporation, on behalf of the corporation, to enter into negotiations with the Ecuadoran government for the purpose of securing rights for treasure exploration by this corporation, to retain Ecuadoran legal counsel to act as the legal representative of the corporation, to hire on behalf of the corporation anyone required by the Ecuadoran government to act for the corporation, and to enter into such agreements and contracts relating thereto as the President of the corporation shall deem to be in the best interests of the corporation.

IN WITNESS WHEREOF, I have set my hand and affixed the seal of the corporation this September 3, 1987.

REPUBLICA DEL ECUADOR
SERVICIO CONSULAR ECUATORIANO

JOE M. YOUNG

REPUBLICA DEL ECUADOR
CONSULADO EN MIAMI

Presentada para legalizar la firma que antecede, el suscrito Cónsul del Ecuador certifica, que es auténtica siendo la que usa el Sr. Sandra Dickerson Notario Publico en todos sus actos

Número de la Legalización 8523

13-D

$25.00

SEP 21 1987

Sandra R. Dickerson

Notary Public, Georgia, State at Large
My Commission Expires Mar. 14, 1988

Ecuadoran Explorations Inc. Certified Resolution

Never in my life had I conducted business with a man as straightforward, easy going, honest or as fair as "Partner A." After this initial meeting all my contacts were directly with "Partner A," Mr. Martin was for all intensive purposes a silent partner. When my partners made a commitment or agreement, their word was their bond. There were no attempts to change our agreement prior to signing. If I was told a check was forthcoming, it arrived as agreed. Never was there a complaint about my expenditures, which I made every effort to minimize, even to the point that my partners suggested my per diem was insufficient. To describe my association with my Atlanta partners, it could be simply stated that they were men of integrity and a pleasure to do business with.

Within days of signing our agreement, a trip to Ecuador for the first time with investor funding, was scheduled. Certified overnight delivery brought the first check from my new partners, drawn on a bank in Georgia. Upon inquiry I discovered a branch office near downtown Tampa and proceeded to the bank. Approaching the teller, I wondered if there was going to be a problem with an out-of-state check at a bank where I did not have an account. Sure enough the teller examined the check and asked if I was a customer. With no way to verify the signature and balance on an out-of-state account, she could not assist me. I asked for the manager and was directed Karen, an Operations Officer. I explained the situation and that I was leaving the next day for Ecuador, which in hindsight probably made it more difficult for her to cash the check. Due to my persistence the young woman was finally willing to make an effort and agreed to call the main office in Atlanta. As she returned to her desk, I questioned ... "any problem" ... to which she responded ... " oh no Mr. Charbonneau! ... the main office stated that this account has been with the bank 'since dirt' and they authorized me to override procedures on behalf of the account holder in order to assist you." Once again I would be bound for Ecuador, but this time with the support of a partnership and funding other than my own money.

Shortly thereafter, my company issued a Certified Resolution, authorizing and empowering me as President of Ecuadoran Explorations Inc., to ... "enter into negotiations with the Ecuadoran government for the purpose of securing rights for treasure exploration."

■ ■ ■

It was 23 Jul 1987 that I found myself again en route to Ecuador. Everything this trip would prove to be the beginning of success. Everything seemed to be coming together! So much so, that this trip lasted through August twentieth of the same year.

General Miño, whom I had been communicating with in Panama, had just returned to Ecuador. Whenever I called the General in Panama, or should I say the Ambassador, the operator always asked who was calling and within a minute or so the General would be courteous enough to accept my call. For some unknown reason though, the General always said he would not be able to help me until he returned to Ecuador. This reluctance always puzzled me, as I believed that all the General needed to do, was pick up the phone and call the President. At the time, being totally unaware of the events that led the General to his Ambassadorship in Panama, I falsely assumed that the General wanted to establish some sort of partnership first.

Once in Quito I called General Miño and was invited to visit him at home. I was warned that having just returned from Panama, everything was coming out of storage and the family was moving into a new house. Warned that it would be a chaotic mess, I was given the new address regardless. Upon my arrival, after the pleasantries and family updates, I asked Gribaldo what he knew about Brunner and the Llanganati project.

Gribaldo informed me that Brunner had convinced him of the discovery of the Llanganati treasure on Cerro Hermoso. The General acknowledged that he had agreed to provide Brunner with the support of the Ecuadorian military, its helicopters, manpower and security forces to remove the treasure, not to search for it. Brunner had entered the hospital for a checkup prior to the expedition, and died.

Gribaldo mentioned that he would be happy to assist me any way he could. Much to my surprise ... at no point did the retired General inquire what would be in it for himself.

It was then my turn to bring the General up to date on the difficulties I had been having obtaining an audience with the President and Sebastian's contacts with General Delgado. That if I could just communicate with the President I believed a contract could be entered into and my company would pay for the recovery of the treasure. A win/win situation for my company and for the government of Ecuador, as well as anyone who assisted me. Gribaldo seemed to be listening patiently until I brought up the Vargas affair and the attempted contact prior to the President's kidnaping.

Gribaldo excused himself, got up and left the room but within minutes he had returned. The General stated that he was sorry but he was going to have to cut our meeting short. He handed me a small piece of paper with a name and phone number on it which was ... General Marcelo Delgado Alvear ... Gribaldo stated ... "you have an appointment at the Presidential Palace tomorrow morning with General Delgado, tell him what you have told me and he will assist you as best he can."

■ ■ ■

Arriving at the Presidential Palace for my meeting, I passed two ceremonial guards attired in their colonial uniforms at the large entrance doors to the Palace. On the right wall as you enter the lobby, was a window with bars on it where you sign in. I announced myself and within minutes was told to enter through security. Straight ahead was a metal fence and the entrance manned by guards and a metal detector. Once through the metal detector I came upon the interior of the palace with its two sunken courtyards. In the right courtyard about twenty soldiers were exercising in formation. In the center was a grand staircase going up to the second level and the Presidential offices, where I could see two more ceremonial attired guards standing. However, I would not be going upstairs today and was directed to the first door on my right on the ground floor, wherein Brigadier General

Marcelo Delgado Alvear, Jefatura Militar de la Presidencia de la Republica [460] had his office.

After respectful personal introductions, reminding General Delgado that previously through letter, fax and my friend Sebastian I had been in contact with him, the conversation turned to how General Miño became involved. I explained the family connection with Gribaldo, Brunner and myself and told General Delgado everything I had relayed to Gribaldo including the Vargas affair. Delgado responded that ... "yes, yes, my general [referring to General Miño] contacted me and asked if I could assist you in any manner."

Similar to my conversations with General Miño, General Delgado appeared more interested in what I had to say concerning the purported Vargas contact than the treasure project. I expressed my concerns over safety issues and told the General that if he shared my concerns I would like to carry a firearm while in Ecuador. The General responded ... "that would not be a problem" ... he then asked what type of gun I had and made a phone call.

Delgado then called out for his orderly, a Sergeant, who came into the room and was told to type a note of introduction and recommendation to Lieutenant Colonel German Velasco, El Jefe de la Seccion Material de Guerra [461] at the Ministry of Defense where an appointment had been made for me the next morning. The next day I went to the Ministry, this time through the front sentry post [462] and upon receipt of the General's note, the Colonel was extremely courteous and helpful. Within minutes, in this country of more than seven million people, I was issued one of Ecuador's few gun carrying permits, number 4057 dated 2 Jul 1987.

■ ■ ■

Ultimately, I had not left my meeting with General Delgado empty handed. The General informed me that he had discussed my project with President Cordero and it had been determined that the matter should be looked into by the Ministry of Defense to determine the best course of action. A letter was typed, signed and delivered to Minister Medardo R. Salazar Navas, I was given a copy for my records and a meeting was arranged.

The letter reads as follows ... "For the disposition of the Constitutional President of the Republic, who refers for your expedient determination Mr. Steven J. Charbonneau, who declares to possess important information of an economic character, as is clear from the documents I am permitted to attach.

---

[460] Chief of the Military Household of the Presidency of the Republic - What appears on the surface to be a very powerful position, yet presumably one of the most dangerous postings in this coup prone country. Throughout modern history the palace guard has been required to fight and die defending their post, not against a foreign invader, but against their own brothers in arms!

[461] Section Chief of War Material.

[462] My first visit to the Ministry had been with General Miño in 1978. We arrived through the rear gate and in his chauffeured car with the general's flag flying, an indicator that a General was within, the snap to attention and salute of the guard seemed automatic.

"The President considers it convenient that Mr. Charbonneau shall be heard by the body that you my General deems appropriate after determining its importance and he can then be channeled through the state agencies that legally correspond to the activity of the group he represents."

■ ■ ■

El Ecuador ha sido, es y será País Amazónico

PRESIDENCIA DE LA REPUBLICA

OFICIO Nº 87-582-JCMPR-1. Quito, 28 de Julio de 1.987

Sr. General de Div.
Medardo R. Salazar Navas
MINISTRO DE DEFENSA NACIONAL
En su Despacho.

Por disposición del señor Presidente Constitucional de la República, concurrirá a su despacho el señor STEVEN J. CHARBONEAU, quien manifiesta poseer importante información de carácter económico, como se desprende de los documentos que me permito anexar.

El señor Presidente considera conveniente que el señor CHARBONEAU, - sea escuchado por el organismo que usted, mi General, estimare conveniente y que luego de determinarse su importancia, se pueda canalizar a través de los organismos del estado que legalmente corres - ponda, la actividad del grupo que representa.

DIOS, PATRIA Y LIBERTAD

Marcelo Delgado Alvear
General de Brigada
JEFE DE LA CASA MILITAR.

Letter of Introduction to the Minister of Defense

The Ministry of Defense [463] was located in the south end of the city, past the Presidential Palace and Old Quito near the Panecillo.[464] My taxi dropped me off by the security-gated driveway on the left end of the main ministry building whose facade bordered the street. Approaching the guard post I retrieved the letter of introduction that General Delgado General Delgado had supplied from my briefcase, displayed it to the sentry whom I informed of my appointment with "Señor Ministro." Another soldier was called over, who took my information and called the Ministers office, my papers were returned and I was told how to proceed to the office.

As I started to enter the grounds ... almost as an afterthought ... the realization hit me that I was an armed foreigner entering a military installation with access to the Minister of Defense. I returned to the post and advised the sentry that I was armed and took off my suit jacket and shoulder holster. As I handed over my gun for safekeeping, I advised the soldier that although the safety was on ... not only was the gun loaded ... there was also a round in the chamber.

The Minister's offices were extremely easy to locate as I learned that I had previously walked past them when obtaining my gun permit on an earlier visit. Located at the far end of the old main building facing the street I entered the Ministers enormous outer office with its high ceiling, secretary's desk and couches. In contrast to the warmth of Justus Martin's magnificent office, here I sensed a damp emptiness or coldness in my surroundings. After a short wait I was ushered by the secretary into the Minister's office which was as spacious as the outer office. Behind a desk located at the far end of the room toward the street sat a slightly stocky man dressed in a suit, whose appearance instantly reminded me of Gribaldo. The man got up and came to greet me at the front of the room ... I had just met General Medardo R. Salazar Navas, Ecuador's Minister of Defense.

The Minister, I realized, was not a man to beat around the bush. General Salazar got straight to the point, informing me that he had been contacted by the Presidential Palace and asked to determine the legal method of channeling my project through the appropriate government agencies.[465] The

---

[463] Ecuador's Ministry of Defense also houses the offices of the General Commanders of the Army, Navy and Air Force, The Armed Forces Joint Command, National Security Council, and support staff. Originally ordered to be constructed in 1908 by General Eloy Alfaro President of the Republic, for an international exhibition. The Palacio de la Exposición was inaugurated in 1909 and later utilized as the country's military school from 1912 until 1937, when it became the Ministry of Defense.

[464] El Panecillo-The famous hill and statue located in the south of Old Quito. Blomberg describes this historic landmark in *Buried Gold and Anacondas* ... "El Panecillo the height on which one of the sun temples of the Inca people is said to have stood."

[465] In hindsight, after what I have learned about the military and civilian government in Ecuador at the time, I have come to the conclusion that behind

Minister asked me to explain the basics of my proposed "activity" with the government of Ecuador and also questioned my involvement with General Miño, whom he knew well.[466]

Briefly and generally I explained to the Minister that my wife's step-father had been the leading authority on the Llanganati treasure deposit and prior to his death had discovered its location on Cerro Hermoso, that my company was willing to spend upwards of a million US dollars to recover the treasure ... at no expense to the government beyond security and helicopter transport.

As I explained my family association with General Miño to the Minister, it appeared that the air or mood of the meeting lightened. Perhaps it had been known or feared that General Miño was involved in the project as he had been previously, I do not know. Ecuadorians have proven to me over the years to be more prone to assist a countryman or foreigner with familiar ties rather than just another gringo. One thing I can say for sure, the Minister seemed genuinely willing to assist me with the advancement of my project.

It became apparent that the Minister had some advance knowledge of my project as he had already come to the conclusion, apparently prior to my arrival, that my application for a contract with the government of Ecuador for the "search and recovery of national treasures in the Llanganatis" ... as the Minister put it ... should be studied and reviewed by the ministry's legal department. I was advised that the review would occur post haste as the President was involved and awaiting the outcome.

Upon leaving the ministry after what I perhaps naively deemed to be a successful meeting, considering the project was at last advancing, I stopped by the guard post to retrieve my gun. For safeties sake in the eventuality that I needed to use my weapon, I removed the clip to verify it was still loaded, which it was. Pulling back the slide to verify that a round was still in the chamber as I had left it, I discovered that my hollow point bullet had been removed. Returning the clip and cocking a round into the chamber I had an empty feeling in the pit of my stomach and paranoia set in. What if I had just assumed my gun was as I had left it ... not verifying that it was loaded ... and for some reason I needed to fire the weapon? I would have cocked the hammer ... pulled the trigger ... and been horrified by the clicking sound of the hammer hitting an empty chamber. What if the bullet had been removed intentionally ... ? [467]

---

the scenes the President of this fledgling democracy possibly wanted to know what the military's position would be on the recovery of such vast wealth and any contract he might be inclined to enter into by Presidential Decree.

[466] I did not learn until much, much later that the Minister had actually been the Commander of the Army for a portion of the Hurtado presidency, while his superior officer, General Miño, was the Chief of Staff.

[467] I would later learn that indeed the bullet had been removed intentionally ... but not maliciously. Every single time I visited the ministry, the same event would occur, the round from the chamber would disappear. Apparently my

■ ■ ■

My journey through the "tramite" or bureaucratic process within the Ministry of Defense may have been conducted "post haste" by Ecuador's standards but not mine. I have lost track of the number of Colonels' and Generals' that I met and was passed back and forth between including the Sub-Secretary of Defense, members of the cabinet and their aides. One day when dropping off or obtaining documents from the ministry's legal advisor, I was approached by a short thin man in a suit who introduced himself, a retired Colonel that worked in the ministry, my friend Sebastian's father! The Colonel asked how everything was proceeding and reminded me that he was at my disposal if I should require any assistance.

My application, or should I say the ministry's research concerning current law, the military's' interpretation of the law and the process required to enter into a binding contract, was placed in the hands of the Asesor Jurídico del Ministerio de Defensa,[468] who at the time was Dr. Francisco Larrea Donoso. Dr. Larrea informed me that he had a strong background and experience with treasure salvage permits in the country in his previous position as the Asesor Jurídico del Comando General de Marina.[469] The navy it seems had in the past always been the source of and a party to, any and all treasure salvage contracts in Ecuadorian waters, even those entered into by Eugene Brunner. But as Dr. Larrea stated ... "the law has changed many times since then" ... he would need to do some research that should not take very long, but ultimately he believed that the legal opinion to come out of the ministry would be beneficial to my company and the project.

I cannot say if the process was proceeding normally by Ecuadorian standards or whether it was being delayed for possible personal gain ... what I can say ... is that a civilian employee of the ministry in a high position, did approach me seeking a bribe to move the process forward quickly and favorably. My response to this individual was that US Law prohibits an American company from doing so ... but I would "remember" who had helped me throughout the process once a permit was granted. I must admit that on a return visit I did give this individual a bottle of Crown Royal as a gift ... nothing more.

■ ■ ■

Considering the importance of a favorable legal opinion, it was decided by the board of directors [470] that Ecuadoran Explorations obtain a legal opinion of our own from some law firm of note in Ecuador. After doing some

---

small hollow point bullets were an oddity in Ecuador and the guards were taking one as a souvenir. This event always occurred at the ministry and never at the palace or airport.

[468] Asesor Jurídico del Ministerio de Defensa - Legal Advisor to the Ministry of Defense

[469] Asesor Jurídico del Comando General de Marina - Legal Advisor to the General Command of the Navy

[470] Board of Directors consisted of the author, "Partner A," and Justus C. Martin Jr., both in Atlanta, Georgia.

research on the matter I discovered that the law firm of Quevedo & Ponce y Carbo was well respected in the community and represented many foreign corporations in the country including Cyprus Minera de Ecuador. Interestingly, either Dr. Quevedo or Ponce not only knew the President, but at some point in time had purportedly been his personal lawyer or a part of the Febres Cordero government. This connection I had hoped, would provide me with yet another voice in the President's ear.

I made an appointment with Dr. Alejandro Ponce and once there explained my situation in detail. Dr. Ponce appeared sympathetic and understood that the company required legal research and an opinion that hopefully would substantiate and support the opinion coming out of the Ministry of Defense. Everyone involved seemed to understand the importance of the legal research and resulting opinion, as we would be setting historical precedent ... never before had Ecuador entered into a commercial treasure salvage contract.

Only one disappointing point came out of our preliminary meeting, Dr. Ponce was extremely busy and his schedule would not allow him the opportunity to personally handle our case ... which would be assigned to a junior lawyer at the firm, but Dr. Ponce indicated he would review the research and resulting opinion once drafted.

■ ■ ■

Ultimately after weeks of delays, it was now mid-August 1987, I contacted the Minister of Defense seeking to learn the status of the ministry's research. I was also hoping to move the process along at a faster rate. It appeared to me that the process had stalled. Perhaps the "tramite" was being held up by the individual hoping for personal gain. If it was being held up, I surmised that the Minister's inquiries might possibly stir up some action.

It would not be until the end of September that I obtained an official response (Oficio No.72187-MS-1) from the Minister. The letter states ...

"In response to your note of August 18 of 1987, requesting an authorization to undertake the business of searching for treasures in the area denominated Llanganatis, and the possibility of concluding a contract between the National Government and the petitioner, this body informs you that in accordance with Article 32 of the Law of Cultural Heritage, the application must be presented through the National Institute of Cultural Heritage in order to obtain the corresponding authorization."

Shortly thereafter, I obtained a copy of Dr. Larrea's lengthy favorable legal opinion on the matter which definitively provided the legal process to be followed that the Minister had advised me of. It is important to note that Dr. Larrea's opinion came to the same conclusions that the company's private lawyers had already drawn in their opinion.

EL ECUADOR HA SIDO, ES Y SERA
PAIS AMAZONICO

Oficio No. 72187 -MS-1.

MINISTERIO DE DEFENSA NACIONAL

ASUNTO: Ref. Autorizac. para explorac. y rescate tesoros.

Quito, a 29 SET. 1987 de 198

DE : MINISTRO DE DEFENSA NACIONAL

PARA : SEÑOR STEVEN CHARBONNEAU

EN : Ciudad.-

En respuesta de su nota de agosto 18 de 1987, por la que solicita una autorización para emprender en la empresa de búsqueda de tesoros en el área denominada Llanganatis, y la posibilidad de suscribir un contrato entre el Gobierno Nacional y el Peticionario, este Despacho le manifiesta a usted que de conformidad con el artículo 32 de la Ley de Patrimonio Cultural la solicitud debe presentarse al Instituto de Patrimonio Cultural a fin de obtener la autorización correspondiente.

Muy atentamente.

DIOS, PATRIA Y LIBERTAD,

MEDARDO K. SALAZAR NAVAS
GENERAL DE DIVISION
MINISTRO DE DEFENSA NACIONAL

DISTRIBUCION:
Original: Dest.
2 copias: MS-1
MRSN/FMC/YEM/1
30IX87

Letter from the Minister of Defense

Basically, the law had changed many times in the past and the changes were chronologically noted. In the past for example, Ecuador's Banco Central had purchased artifacts, but that policy had been deemed counterproductive and brought to an end. Current law provided for the finder of treasure to be entitled to 50 percent of the treasure, while the landowner was entitled to the remaining 50 percent. In our situation in the Llanganatis, the government of Ecuador was the landowner. However, all treasure recovered in Ecuador must remain in the country as it would be considered a national treasure that belongs to the state ... just the first of many contradictions in Ecuadorian law!

The National Institute of Cultural Heritage had been determined to be the sole authority over national treasures and they would be the governmental agency through whom we must proceed. However, the Institute had no authority under the law to negotiate or enter into a contract for the valuation and payment to the finder of any treasure deposit. The country's patrimony law had only envisioned the Institute's involvement to be the archeological recovery (not commercial recovery) and protection of national treasures.

Ultimately, in order that Ecuadoran Explorations receive any payment for the treasure's discovery as allowed under the law, it would be necessary to enter into a binding contract with the landowner ... the government of Ecuador. Any contract entered into would require numerous signatories including the President, Minister of Defense and Director of Patrimony ... the contract would be entered into by the National Institute of Cultural Heritage and the National Government as part of our permit process and placed into effect by Presidential Decree.

During my last contact with the Ministry of Defense I was provided a copy of Oficio No. 72197-MS-1 dated 5 Oct 1987 that was written as a letter of introduction on my behalf to the Director of the National Institute of Cultural Heritage, which states ... "Mr. Steven Charbonneau submitted an application to facilitate the development of a contract between the government of Ecuador and the company that he represents for the exclusive purpose of discovering and extracting treasures in the area denominated Llanganatis. Following the procedure indicated in the Law of Cultural Heritage the application must be directed so as to obtain the respective authorization from the technical and administrative organs of the Institute of Cultural Heritage, which is the institution according to Article 32 of the above mentioned act, that must emit pertinent legal opinion. I will be grateful if you would communicate to me the outcome or resolution that is worthy of the application formulated by the company presided by Mr. Steven Charbonneau, because this office considers it of transcendental importance to the interests of the country the results to be obtained from the company's recovery of the national treasures."

The ministry transmitted the "Oficio" to the Director of the National Institute of Cultural Heritage while an appointment was arranged on my behalf. I was also advised to get back in touch with General Delgado who would assist me in advancing through the contract and decree process with the President.

■ ■ ■

EL ECUADOR HA SIDO, ES Y SERA
PAIS AMAZONICO

Oficio No.72197-MS-1.

MINISTERIO DE DEFENSA NACIONAL

ASUNTO:

Quito, a de -5 OCT. 1987 de 198

DE : MINISTRO DE DEFENSA NACIONAL

PARA : SEÑOR DIRECTOR NACIONAL DEL INSTITUTO DE PATRIMONIO CULTURAL

EN : SU DESPACHO.-

El señor Steven Charbonneau presentó una solicitud tendiente a que se conceda facilidades para elaborar un contrato entre el Gobierno del Ecuador y la Compañía que representa con el exclusivo propósito de -- descubrir y sacar tesoros en el área denominada Llanganatis.

Siguiendo el procedimiento señalado en la Ley de Patrimonio Cultural la solicitud debe ser encaminada hasta obtener la autorización - respectiva por los órganos técnico-administrativos del Instituto de Patri mónio Cultural, Institución que según el Art. 32 de la Ley mencionada, -- debe emitir dictámen pertinente.

Agradeceré comunicarme el resultado o resolución que merezca la solicitud formulada por la Empresa presidida por el señor Steven Charbonneau, pues que este Despacho considera de importancia trascendental -- para los intereses del país los resultados que se obtengan de la Empresa de recuperación de los tesoros nacionales.

Muy atentamente.

DIOS, PATRIA Y LIBERTAD,

MEDARDO R. SALAZAR NAVAS
GENERAL DE DIVISION
MINISTRO DE DEFENSA NACIONAL

MINISTERIO DE DEFENSA NACIONAL QUITO

DISTRIBUCION:
Original: Dest.
2 copias: MS-1
MRSN/FAPC/[illegible]/1
02X87.

Letter of Introduction to Director of Patrimony & Culture

Upon my return to the Presidential Palace I entered the lobby approaching the sign-in window, announcing that I was there to see General Delgado. The soldier manning the window asked if the General was expecting me to which I responded in the negative ... I had no appointment. The soldier replied that the General was extremely busy as he left the window, but within minutes returned telling me to enter through security. As I walked through the metal detector, it went off. The soldier on duty had me open my briefcase for inspection after which I was told to proceed to the General's office. Once again as an afterthought, it occurred to me that I was an armed foreigner entering the Presidential Palace with possible access to the President, the wrong place to be discovered with a concealed weapon. I returned to the security post and advised the soldier that I was armed and placed my weapon in his care. General Delgado seemed genuinely interested in the update that I provided, although I sensed he was preoccupied or had already been briefed and was awaiting my visit.

Once again the General assisted me with a letter of introduction to the Director of the National Institute of Cultural Heritage, Oficio No. 87-743-JCMPR-1, which states ... "For the disposition of the Constitutional President of the Republic, I would appreciate it if you, Mr. Director, would arrange for the appropriate channels, to grant the facilities required by Mr. Steven Charbonneau, representative of the company Ecuadoran Explorations Inc., so they may proceed to legalize their status, for the purpose of carrying out their work of exploration in the National Territory. For the attention that you serve to dispense with this issue, in advance, Mr. Director, my cordial gratitude."

The General informed me that in order to enter contract negotiations and obtain a decree, the next step in the process would be conducted through the President's legal advisors Doctor's Paez and Castro, and Dr. Velasco the Inspector General. The General made a short call, got up from his desk and walked me upstairs to the Asesor's office which was located almost directly above his on the second level of the palace. As the General and I walked up the central staircase I noticed to my left on the opposite end of this level, two ceremonial outfitted soldiers standing at attention on either side of a doorway ... I assumed this meant the President was in his office.

The contract and decree process would proceed in the palace, with Ecuadoran Explorations providing a proposed contract and decree for legal review and study. This review would proceed concurrently with Ecuadoran Explorations permit application process at the National Institute of Cultural Heritage. I was introduced to the President's Private Secretary Simón Acosta Espinosa, and was advised that I could make further contract through him, the General had bowed out. [471]

---

[471] It would be a quarter century later when I would discover the reason behind the General's apparent preoccupation, it was on this very day, 1 Oct 1987, that General Marcelo Delgado had been appointed and assumed the position of Director Nacional de Intelligencia.

El Ecuador ha sido, es y será País Amazónico

PRESIDENCIA DE LA REPUBLICA

OFICIO Nº 87-743-JCMPR-1. Quito, 01 de Octubre de 1987

DE: JEFE DE LA CASA MILITAR DE LA PRESIDENCIA DE LA REP.

PARA: SR. DIRECTOR DE PATRIMONIO CULTURAL

EN: SU DESPACHO.

Por disposición del señor Presidente Constitucional de la República, agradeceré a usted, señor Director, se sirva disponer a quien corresponda, se concedan las facilidades que requiera el señor STVEEN CHARBONNEAU, Representante de la Cía. ECUADORAN INC. y pueda proceder a legalizar su situación, con el fin de que lleve a cabo sus labores de exploración en el Territorio Nacional.

Por la atención que se sirva dispensar a la presente, anticipo a usted, señor Director, mi cordial agradecimiento.

Atentamente,

DIOS, PATRIA Y LIBERTAD

Marcelo Delgado Alvear
General de Brigada
JEFE DE LA CASA MILITAR.

Letter of Introduction to Director of Patrimony & Culture

From the top down instead of from the bottom up, this had been my plan of action for approaching the government of Ecuador in my quest for a permit, the National Institute of Cultural Heritage would be no exception. Armed with my letters of introduction from the Minister of Defense and Presidential Palace, two legal opinions, generalized information concerning Brunner's work, and two topographic maps with the coordinates plotted for my proposed project sites, I set off for the Institute which was located to the right of the Presidential Palace in old town, on the second floor of a nondescript colonial building.

Just as in the Presidential Palace, except on a much smaller scale, the Institute had a central open air courtyard with a wide staircase in the middle leading up to the offices of the Institute. I found the Director's office at the top of the stairs in the right-hand corner of the building. Dr. José Jaramillo, a political appointee to the office, appeared to be very soft spoken, polite and courteous. My instantaneous opinion of the man coincided with his own words, that he would do whatever he could within his power to assist the advancement of my project, not for me, but to accomplish what his President had asked of him; to grant my company Ecuadoran Explorations a permit within the confines of the law.

Director Jaramillo walked me to an office on the opposite diagonal corner of the building, the Archeological Department of the Institute, a small room with a desk facing the door as you enter and two small offices to the left, where after introductions the Director left me for my first meeting. A middle-aged woman was apparently the department head and she was joined by a tall slender archeologist for our meeting.

Generalizing as much as possible, I related Brunner's background and research, my involvement and the legal processes under way at the Ministry of Defense and Presidential Palace. I presented two topographic maps ... "Sucre" and "San José de Paoló" ... with the coordinates for two concession areas plotted. The main rectangular project area clearly marked on the "Sucre" map, contained roughly fifty square miles on and around Cerro Hermoso. This project area pertained to the treasure deposit mentioned in the *Derrotero de Valverde* and on Blacke's first map. A much smaller rectangular project area, roughly a third the size of the Cerro Hermoso area, was marked for Chapman's grave and the area represented in Blacke's second map. This secondary project area straddled both maps "Sucre" and "San José de Paoló." Clearly it was put forth that my company was seeking an "excavation permit" and not a "survey permit," as Brunner had advanced our project beyond that point.

Immediately the misinformation and misdirection I would face within the department became apparent. Each comment or question that was asked of me appeared as an attempt to glean more specific information or to dissuade me from my course of action. I was informed that archeologists do not believe that the treasure exists and that there is no evidence that Quito was a large developed Inca city. Perhaps I surmised, they were merely testing my knowledge of history beyond Brunner's research or my resolve.

Roadblocks and speed bumps to a smooth permitting process were put in place instantaneously. I was informed that I must file an archeological project plan for the permitting process to begin. An archeological plan that must entail specific data on the discovery and location, historical background and research, finances and funding, personnel and curriculum vitae, method of excavation and plan of action. Additionally, that an archeological plan must be written and presented by an archeologist "certified by the department" to work in Ecuador.

As if not daunting enough, the department head then hit me with the kicker, the ultimate attempt to persuade and advise me not to continue on my course of action. You could almost feel the satisfaction in her voice when the department head stated ... "There are only a very few archeologists in the country and they are all committed on other projects for at least two years. If you choose to obtain an archeologist from outside the country, they would need to be certified by the department first, which is a very long and time-consuming process."

So there it was, I was confronted by what at the time appeared to be yet another unsurmountable hurdle. Prior to departing I had decided to approach the Director to state my gratitude and appreciation for the assistance he had provided and might be able to provide in moving the permit process along. While waiting on a bench for the Director to become available, an obscure employee of the Institute came near me and nervously said ... "Señor ... I need to talk with you but not here. I have important information for you and I will go on lunch break shortly." We agreed to meet at Kentucky Fried Chicken which was behind the Presidential Palace and across the street halfway down the block. After briefly speaking with the Director, I made my way to KFC.

For the sake of the Institute employee's privacy and safety, in our story we will be calling this person my "mole." Being the first to arrive at KFC, I sat down impatiently waiting, while speculating what "important information" the mole could have. It had been my experience in other government offices[472] for an employee, regardless of pay level or grade, to seek an audience with me hoping to obtain some form of personal gain in the advancement of my project, so this impromptu meeting didn't seem too far outside of the boundaries of ordinary in Ecuador.

The mole arrived and exhibited the same nervousness that had been displayed in the Institute. My original impression of this nervousness was guilt, conflict of conscience, or fear of being discovered. To place my mole at ease, I suggested we order and talk over lunch. As I paid for our lunches, I could sense that this had relieved some of the tension. To make the mole even more comfortable I suggested that my mole call me Steve instead of

---

[472] The only exception to this statement was the Presidential Palace. Not once did any individual, whether civilian or military, connected with the Palace make any form of request or indication that they sought personal gain for the advancement of my project.

the formal "Señor" that had been used up to that point, the mole tried but it always came out "Señor Esteve." With my mole feeling more at ease, our conversation turned toward the Institute and the point of our meeting.

The mole indicated that ... he or she ... held the personal belief shared by the majority of his or her countrymen that Rumiñahui's historical treasure deposit existed. It was also expressed how the treasure's recovery could help the country immensely. My mole continued to express a moral disagreement over how I was being treated by the archeological department of the Institute, ultimately asking if I would pay for information. My immediate response was clear ... I said "yes if the information proved important to my project."

My mole got straight to the point ... "Señor Esteve, but you have been lied to. The archeological department has no intention of granting any commercial permits. Their method of dealing with your permit application will be to stall and put roadblocks in front of you until you get disillusioned and give up. They lied that they do not believe the treasure exists. Like all Ecuadorans', they view Rumiñahui as a national hero and the treasure deposit as a national treasure. Their theory is that the treasure exists and has been hidden for hundreds of years and will remain where it is until they find it themselves or else it will remain where it is for hundreds of years more. They will ask of you more and more specific information throughout the permit process to glean as many details as they can from you, keeping the permit process in tramite."

"Señor Esteve" mole continued ... "the worst lie is that there are no archeologists in the country available for your project. The head of the department has a female friend that is an archeologist ... she is already certified in Ecuador and unemployed!" My mole then provided me with her name and contact information.

After paying for lunch I gave the mole a few hundred Sucres, all the cash that I had on me. For less than ten US Dollars I had purchased my mole lunch and given out some petty cash, I could not believe how grateful the mole appeared, almost ecstatic. It was further communicated that this information would indeed be worth more to me once it proved to be accurate, my appreciation would be expressed with more money and the possibility of a job once the permit was granted. I gave the mole my contact information and it was agreed that my mole would remain alert and vigilant for any additional relevant information.

■ ■ ■

After a few unsuccessful attempts and unanswered messages, I ultimately made contact with the archeologist who lived outside the city in a small town. Just as was the case with my wife's family, the archeologist had no phone in her house and utilized the phone of relatives next door, so it took awhile to make contact. We set up an appointment to meet at my hotel in Quito, Sebastian had always provided me with a suite containing a living room for work space and conducting private meetings at the hotel.

After initial pleasantries the archeologist told me in confidence of her reluctance to take on our project. She explained that her friend in the Institute, the department head, was surprised to hear that I had contacted her and showed an interest in discovering how I became aware that she was available and certified. I explained that I had contacts within the Institute ... vaguely insinuating that it had been the Director, to protect my real source. The archeologist continued to indicate that she had been politely warned that if she took on our project, she would not be allowed to work again on another project in Ecuador for quite some time. If the archeologist accepted our project, she would more or less become black balled in the industry as the archeologist community does not agree with the commercialization of archeological artifact recovery.

Considering this friendly advice and after much personal travail, the unemployed archeologist had relented to the idea of taking on our project as "principal investigator," which if brought to a successful conclusion would establish her position in the archeological community on a grand level. However, under the circumstances she would need to charge a great deal of money for the preliminary application paperwork, as it might be a long period before she could work again. Once and if a permit was granted, we would then need to discuss the fees for the excavation phase of the project.

Ultimately we came to an agreement on her initial fee of $1000 US Dollars solely for the permit application and project plan paperwork. Presumably from the archeologist's viewpoint and Ecuadorian standards, what amounted to a great deal of money. On the other hand, not knowing the standards of compensation prevalent in the field, I had assumed this to be a bargain. After all, the laws of supply and demand placed my company in a very weak position ... currently being the only available certified archeologist in the country ... afforded the opportunity to name her own price.

The archeologist was given a copy of Brunner's chapter *El Tesoro en las Misteriosas Montañas de Llanganati* along with an explanation in general terms on the Cerro Hermoso project area, Chapman's grave and the area represented in Blacke's second map. Also, I informed the archeologist that I had previously supplied the archeological department with two topographic maps plotting the coordinates encompassing the Cerro Hermoso and Chapman's grave project areas.

The archeologist was also supplied with my electric typewriter, although it had an English keyboard, it would ease her preparation of the project plan. It was made clear that she was not to include specific details on the sites' locations ... to be as vague as possible in her project plan ... providing the Institute with the minimum amount of data that would be required for a permit to be granted. It was further explained that once the archeological department gleaned enough information ... it was my belief that they would hold up our permit process.

One sticking point brought to light by the archeologist was that the archeological permit plan required an advance expedition to the site with an archeologist's report on the project area. I explained that since I was dealing with the government at the Presidential and Ministerial levels in an effort to obtain a Presidential Decree, an expedition into the Llanganatis prior to the signing of a decree was not appropriate. Clearly comprehending my reluctance, the archeologist interjected that with Brunner's detailed expedition notes and manuscript's ... she perhaps had sufficient information to detail the project area for the application. Considering my objection to mounting an expedition at this early stage ... the archeologist would indicate in her plan that we had made the required expedition. Ultimately, I would need to approve the plan prior to its being submitted to the Institute.

■ ■ ■

The second occasion I met with the mole was in my hotel. Once again I was contacted and informed of the urgent need to meet, that there was new and important information to relate. At this meeting I was informed that the stalling method of the department was the same method the department was utilizing on yet another permit application. To some extent the departments stalling tactics appeared to be working, as the other party's visits to the Institute were far and few between. Nevertheless, a previous and current permit application existed in "tramite" at the Institute. This second application covering the same general area of interest in the Llanganatis was from another American company, Western Explorations Incorporated and a man named William Johnson.

The department head and archeologists of the department had been stalling with this second company as well, putting up roadblocks, adding processes and requirements until Johnson stopped coming around the Institute as much, exactly the same method they were attempting with my application. Westerns survey permit application however, covered a much broader area of the Llanganatis, roughly 300 square miles, that encompassed the more specific excavation permit areas sought by Ecuadoran Explorations. This fact therefore gave the archeologists another excuse to delay the permit process. Whereas never before in Ecuador's history had a commercial permit application even been considered, the department was now confronted by the dilemma of two separate applications with overlapping coordinates.

The name William Johnson sounded familiar and sparked a memory of the newspaper article concerning the failed Llanganati expedition of Bill Johnson where one member had died. Indeed, William Johnson of Western Explorations and Bill Johnson would prove to be one and the same person.

Johnson's contact information in Rockford, Michigan, was provided by the mole in our conversation, along with two additional interesting points. Firstly, that the government through INEMIN, held a mining concession on the northern portion of Westerns survey permit area, on the Roncadores region of the Llanganatis. Secondly, Western Explorations had filed a $250,000 US Dollar letter of credit with their application.

My gratitude was again expressed and it was agreed that the mole would discreetly remain alert and vigilant at the Institute. As the mole was departing, I extended my hand to shake, folded in my palm was petty cash for me, perhaps a month's salary for my mole ... this would prove to be our last meeting. After my mole had departed, with the story of Johnson's disastrous expedition into the Llanganatis on my mind, I contemplated these new developments and the path that should be taken.

■ ■ ■

As was my habit, confronting this new situation head on would be my course of action. I was aware that the Director of the Institute had been receiving calls from the Presidential Palace and Ministry of Defense exerting pressure to move the process along, and he seemed genuinely inclined to assist in the advancement of our application. However, on the other hand the Director had to deal with the objections and resistence coming from within the Institute ... the archeological department ... he was stuck between a rock and a hard place. After much consideration I came to the conclusion that perhaps I could help the Director as much as he could help me. If I could remove the archeological department's obstacles and objections ... with pressure coming from above, the palace, the military and the director ... they would reluctantly be forced to action.

It had come to my attention through Ricardo that a large collection of Incan ceramic artifacts had been removed from Ecuador over the years and were in Georgia, an issue that definitely came under the purview and jurisdiction of the Institute. Previously Director Jaramillo had appeared quite interested in who was making expeditions into the Llanganatis without permission, another issue under the purview and jurisdiction of his Institute. If I could assist the Director with these two issues, perhaps he would be even more inclined to exert as much pressure on the archeological department as possible under the confines of the law.

My method would be to approach the Director asking for his assistance while at the same time being sympathetic to his delicate position. Furthermore, I would offer my assistance on the other two matters. I returned to the States and through my partners obtained a letter of credit similar to Westerns, showing Ecuadoran Explorations financial ability and commitment, in the amount one million US Dollars. Hopefully this would resolve another issue with the archeological department for the Director.

While in the States, inquiries were made through the US State Department's Ecuador Desk and Federal Bureau of Investigation concerning the artifacts in Georgia. Questions were raised and answered concerning US laws governing the importing, possession of and the procedures required for the return of Ecuador's artifacts. Indeed, purportedly crimes were deemed to have been committed and treaties violated. However, subject to a treaty that the United States and Ecuador were both parties to, the government of Ecuador must initiate the request for an investigation and the return of the country's patrimony.

Prior to returning to Ecuador, I acquired evidence of who had possession of the subject artifacts that were in Georgia, along with photographs of the artifacts and an audio tape recording of the individuals involved discussing how, when and where the artifacts were procured and removed from the country of Ecuador. While Brunner had been supplying the United States with information from Ecuador, I would be doing the reverse. I could not help but feel that this turn of events, ironically brought me closer to an understanding of Eugene Brunner the man.

Upon my return to Ecuador I went directly to the Institute without an appointment and announced myself to Jaramillo's secretary, she advised me that the Director was on the phone and quite busy, but to wait. Eventually the Director came out of his office, approached me and stated ... "Señor Charbonneau I am so surprised to see you, what can I do for you?" ... to which I replied ... "Señor Director, the purpose of my visit is not what you can do for me, it is what I can do for you." Watching the Director's facial expression as I spoke, I knew these words had the desired effect as I was quickly ushered into his office.

Initially I expressed to the Director my desire to help resolve one of the issues on our application for him, suggesting that Ecuadoran Explorations wanted to establish their financial ability and commitment to the government of Ecuador and our project ... while handing Jaramillo the company's certified "Irrevocable Letter of Credit." The Director politely accepted the document indicating that indeed this would resolve one of the issues the department faced on our application.

Broaching the issue of artifacts removed from Ecuador is what really appeared to have caught the Director's attention. He called on his secretary asking her to deliver Ecuadoran Explorations "Letter of Credit" to the archeological department for inclusion in our file ... and to clear his schedule as he would be tied up with Señor Charbonneau for some time. I then provided the Director with the details I had uncovered on the collection of Ecuador's artifacts in Georgia. The Director's demeanor bordered on incredulous but the evidence was overwhelming. As he viewed the photographs I played the audio tape, translating as we went along. It became apparent that this was not only mine, but it was the Director's first involvement concerning smuggled artifacts and their possible recovery.

After providing the Director an opportunity to digest the information, I asked ... "Would the Institute be interested in the return of these artifacts?" Immediately and enthusiastically he replied ... "Oh yes, yes Señor Charbonneau, what would we need to do?" I explained that I had previously made inquiries with the US government and informed the Director that for the return of the artifacts, by treaty the government of Ecuador, presumably by and through the Institute, must initiate a claim for their return. The Director appeared bewildered, indicating he did not have a clue how to proceed. Once again I was given the opportunity to display to the Director how sympathetic I was and helpful I could be ... "Señor Jaramillo" I stated ... "I have taken the liberty to discuss this matter with a friend in the US Embassy here in Quito, who is in a position and prepared to assist you with the process that will be required. His name is JM and is awaiting your call."

Trust Company Bank

Donald M. Thompson
First Vice President

September 8, 1987

To Whom It May Concern:

We hereby confirm our unconditional guaranty to issue our Irrevocable Letter of Credit in your favor, available for a sum or sums not exceeding United States Dollars One Million ($1,000,000) upon request of applicant, Ecuadoran Explorations, Inc.

This undertaking is not subject to any precondition or qualification and carries no contingent provisions.

Should you have occasion to communicate with us regarding this credit, kindly direct your communication to the attention of Donald M. Thompson making reference to this letter.

Very truly yours,

DMT(3)/ed

Notary Public, Georgia State at Large
My Commission Expires Feb. 21, 1989

REPUBLICA DEL ECUADOR
CONSULADO EN MIAMI

Presentada para legalizar la firma que antecede, el suscrito Consul del Ecuador certifica, que es auténtica siendo la
que usa el Sr. Shila Sawyer
Notario Público E de Florida
en todos sus actos
Número de la Legalización 851
Partida arancelaria 13-D
Valor Cobrado $25
Fecha SEP 21 1987

REPUBLICA DEL ECUADOR
SERVICIO CONSULAR ECUATORIANO

Walter Franco
Vice-Consul

Ecuadoran Explorations, Inc. Letter of Credit

I could sense his gratitude, almost a giddy excitement exuding from the Director, it was now time to turn the tables ... I needed some answers and assurances of my own. I explained to the Director that I had been informed about the existence of a second application, that of Western Explorations which predated our application in the Institute and the issue of conflicting, overlapping coordinates bothered me. Feeling out the Director's position on the issue I suggested, what if the companies could possibly come to an agreement altering their coordinates, would this maneuver resolve yet another issue on our application for him? Jaramillo responded ... "Yes ... yes ... if that could be arranged it would help, but I should not be to concerned with the dates of applications. Whoever completes the requirements first will be issued a permit, it will not be based on the date of application. Besides, Western's application is for a survey, while your company's is an excavation permit. Ecuadoran Explorations is much further along in the process, and also has the support of the Palace and Ministry of Defense."

In closing out our meeting, the Director himself raised the last issue by expressing his interest in who was currently making expeditions into the Llanganatis, specifically questioning if Johnson had been in since his first disastrous expedition. The Institute it appears was deeply concerned over unauthorized expeditions into the mountains in search of the country's national treasures. However, I was only able to provide the Director with outdated information on past expeditions, but informed him I would keep him abreast of any information I became privy to. As I was leaving, we were tossing around ideas on how to control access to the area, I indicated to the Director that in the United States the government controls access to public lands such as the Llanganatis, the solution in my opinion would be nothing short of declaring the Llanganatis a national park.

■ ■ ■

My next step was to contact Johnson, who would not discuss his source of information but solely to indicate "they," meaning his company Western Explorations, was in the exploration or survey stage. It appeared to me that Johnson might have had access to some of the Blacke information. When I questioned Michael Dyott about this development, Dyott stated that his mother had told him about a "missionary type" who had "visited my Dad in New York" in late 1970 or early 1971. Michael continued to state "I highly doubt that Dad would have given him the Blacke information." Dyott indicated that even though Mendell died around 1947, his grandson was still active in the search and may have been Johnson's source if indeed he had access to any of the Blacke information.

When I raised the issue with Johnson about the Dyott visit, he replied that he had never met Commander Dyott so no he was not "that" Bill Johnson. Other small talk concerned Johnson's background, he stated he had worked on ships, water salvage projects in other countries and expressed worries on the upcoming elections in Ecuador ... "two bad choices" as he put it ... and I agreed wholeheartedly.

Johnson, always speaking in plural form, stated that they ... "had given Cerro Hermoso a cursory look" ... but were not seriously interested in that specific area of the Llanganatis. To which I responded that I understood they were more interested in the northern "Roncadores" region including that on which INEMIN held a mining concession, and the Cerro Negro area. Johnson acknowledged that indeed we were "not looking in the same area." Whether misdirection, actual or feigned ignorance, Johnson replied "Cerro Negro ... do you mean Cerro Hermoso ... I've never heard of Cerro Negro." Incredibly Johnson had just expressed ignorance on the existence of one of the Llanganatis major mountain landmarks. Located to the northeast of Cerro Hermoso (Yurac-Llanganati) and across the Río Topo sits Cerro Negro (Yana-Llanganati), another mountain where some explorers have thought Rumiñahui's treasure might be located.

Having established that both parties were not interested in the same areas and mine being of such limited scope, I proposed that we adjust the coordinates of his application to exclude my companies limited areas of interest. This proposed simple maneuver would, in my opinion, remove the dilemma of overlapping coordinates faced by the Director of the Institute, a roadblock that both companies faced with our respective applications. This move would in turn provide an opportunity for the Institute to grant two separate applications instead of one only, a win/win situation all around.

Johnson gave the initial appearance of being receptive to my proposal, although he also appeared to be under the false impression that he was negotiating from a position of strength. Johnson would only go as far to state that he was ... "inclined to say that a deal can be made" ... but his company would want something in return. Always stopping short of an initial understanding or commitment, reminding me of my similar dealings with Norman Scott, Johnson stated his need to consult the company's board of directors, in other words his investors, for a ruling on the matter. In closing the conversation, Johnson stated that a member of his board would contact me with a response and final negotiations on the matter. The name of the man I was waiting to hear from was eerily ... "Gino."

A short period of time would pass, perhaps a matter of days or weeks, until I received the call from Gino. Quite similar to Johnson, it appeared that this individual as well was under the false impression that he was negotiating from a position of strength. Gino stated that his company would like to make a deal, however, they want something in return for the time and legal fees they had expended up to this point. In short, they wanted a percentage of my company or projects in return.

With the brief passage of time between phone calls, I had been given the opportunity to methodically reconsider the situation. I explained to Gino that any deal needed to be structured as a win/win situation. I was still of the opinion that my original proposal did just that, Western Explorations and Ecuadoran Explorations would each obtain a permit for their respective areas of interest, while the Institutes dilemma would be resolved for them. Furthermore, it was my opinion that if we had found ourselves in a different set of circumstances, where Western Explorations already had a permit, then indeed they would be giving up something tangible of value which would warrant a percentage of my company or projects in return. What I did not communicate to Gino were my main objections ... due to Johnson's apparent lack of knowledge and his disastrous expedition ... I would not take him or his company on as a partner in any shape or form.

Gino of course responded with reasons why he thought his company should receive compensation for any deal we might make. One such reason was that Western Explorations application had priority over ours as it had been made prior to Ecuadoran Explorations application. My response to Gino's reasoning was to loosely quote from the conversation I had with the Director of the Institute ... "A permit will be granted to whomever completes the requirements first, it is not based on the date of application, Ecuadoran Explorations is much further along." To drive my point further home, I informed Gino that even if he were correct, my application had commenced with the Presidential Palace and Ministry of Defense prior to Western's application through normal channels. We both admitted that the main problem Western Explorations faced, besides the fact that they were in the exploration phase and Ecuadoran Explorations was at the recovery phase, was that the Institute had no legal authority to negotiate or enter into a contract on percentages of recovery, a hurdle that my company was surmounting. Gino basically acknowledged at this point in our conversation that it appeared we were further along than his company, but we left the door open to future negotiations should circumstances change.

Johnson's first disastrous expedition into the northern Llanganati area I would later learn had been funded by a group of investors with rights to the results, or better stated ... profits, resulting from that one expedition only. Apparently there had been a falling out afterwards, presumably over this aspect and the utter failure of the expedition, for these investors had approached me to fund my company and/or expedition. As a partnership and the funding of Ecuadoran Explorations had previously been secured, I respectfully declined their offer.

■ ■ ■

Contacting my archeologist one day for an update on her progress, she advised me that it would be better, more cost effective and easier for her and the Institute, if we enlarged the Cerro Hermoso permit area to include the Chapman grave site. Otherwise, we would need to create two separate archeological plans, one for each project area. The pros and cons were discussed, in the end it was determined that the original coordinates for the Cerro Hermoso project area should be expanded to include Chapman's grave site. The archeologist advised me that she had already calculated the new project area to be approximately 204 square kilometers or roughly 100 square miles. With this minor change the archeological plan would be available for my review in the near future. Not long thereafter ... it would be March 1988 ... the archeologist provided me with our completed archeological plan entitled *Proyecto Llanganati,* which was then delivered to the Institute.

Having never seen an archeological plan before, the plan before me appeared to be a very professional piece of work. Over forty pages long, the document was broken into twelve sections and subsections. The sections were entitled Introduction, Project Objectives, Theoretical Framework, Background, Context of Research, Research Strategy, Recording of Material, Conservation of Materials, Storage and Packing, Project Schedule and Final Considerations. Upon perusing this document it met my expectations and was written to my satisfaction. It appeared to be as general as possible to conform with the standards required for a permit to be granted.

I will not attempt to reproduce the entire document here as more detailed information has been presented in this book than was contained in the entire archeological plan, but I will provide the reader a sampling of it's content. In general terms an archeological plan has the appearance of being nothing more than an outline of what, why, who, when, where and how you intend on conducting your project, in reality a contract between the "principal investigator" and the Institute outlining the methods and methodology to be used on the project.

The archeologist introduced our plan thus ... "A legend is above all a story told, but it is a story that has no known author or creator, only storytellers. Certainly a legend has a beginning based in reality, or has emerged from a true story, with characters and real objects, which by necessity is a first person narrative by a particular individual. But for a story to become a legend, from narration to narration the narrative is required to be precise, stripped of personal tastes, feelings or opinions which affected the first narrator's subjectivity. A legend has no other broadcaster that society itself and the listener who hears the story receives a message whose true characteristics are transformed with the passage of time." Then the archeologist continues with her narrative on the legend of the Ransom of Atahualpa and the Llanganati treasure story.

After explaining and reviewing the chronology of the legend and the *Derrotero de Valverde*, with historical references and citations from Xeres, Pedro Pizarro, Cieza, Garcilaso, Velasco, Zarate, Vargas, Sancho and Suarez, the archeologist introduces Dyott and Brunner's involvement with the legend into the plan. Thereafter in section five, the general area, climate and conditions of the Llanganatis and Cerro Hermoso are described, in conjunction with officially laying out the *Proyetco Llanganati* coordinates stating ... "The study region as a whole covers an area approximately 204 kilometers square, whose coordinates are indicated on the attached map and are as follows ...

Point A being the NW corner = 78° 21' 29" W, 1° 7' 15" S
Point B being the NE corner = 78° 15' 00" W, 1° 7' 15" S
Point C being the SW corner = 78° 21' 29" W, 1° 15' 54" S
Point D being the SE corner = 78° 15' 00" W, 1° 15' 54" S."

In this same section the archeologist describes our imaginary expedition to Cerro Hermoso from Píllaro ... "During the second fortnight of February this anthropologist carried out a survey to certain sections of the area mentioned. Without question the field research was limited in terms of personnel, time, inadequate equipment and other difficulties, therefore I could only obtain a very small sampling of this enormous region. Utilizing the basic method of prospecting data and results already delivered by other explorers and researchers [473] it was possible to obtain useful data for the termination of our research.

"Reflecting specifically on the description of the area we observed and experienced firsthand the climatic variations that during the first days were not noticed much between Píllaro and Pisayambo. Arriving at Aucacocha the temperature was already beginning to decline, although we generally encountered good weather. Near Yurac-Llanganati or Cerro Hermoso the scenery is quite impressive, though descending toward the Llanganatis one experiences the region's notorious climate changes. The intense fog appears to be a set characteristic of this sector. We could not climb Cerro Hermoso as we were not adequately equipped considering the purpose of our exploration was the evidentiary prospecting of data we already possessed. Without question we found that this region is quite rugged and full of shallow craters despite not being a mountain of volcanic origin."

I ask, how much more "general or vague" could the archeologist have been? This section of the plan bothered me for two reasons. Not only was it not true ... but I feared that anyone who had been into the "inhospitable"[474] Llanganatis, or even read any accounts of those that have, in my opinion, would instantly realize that no expedition had been conducted. However, it appeared that the archeologist's narrative satisfied the Institutes requirements, as the issue was never raised.

Quite simply, all the data contained within each section of the plan pertained to their titles. Research Strategy, Recording of Material, Conservation of Materials, Storage and Packing for example, enumerate currently accepted methods and procedures used within the archeological and scientific communities. The Project Schedule section was extremely vague and explains that ... "It is hard to predict what one is going to encounter, therefore it is difficult to indicate a term for each of the stages." Ultimately an estimate is put forth ... "Taking into account all of these considerations, should the investigation last three years we could give a tentative time for each phase ... Prospecting & Data or Document Collection six months, Excavation twenty months, and Classification of Materials ten months."

The last section of the archeological plan entitled "12 - FINAL CONSIDERATIONS," gave the archeologist the opportunity to distance herself from the politics of the project and extend an olive branch to the archeological community ... she would state ...

---

[473] The "other researchers and explorers" were Luciano Andrade Marín and Eugene K. Brunner whose writings were cited throughout the plan.

[474] Inhospitable - Common term to describe the Llanganatis, used by virtually every explorer of the region.

"In closing I wish to mention that my participation in this project is only of a technical nature, that any contractual agreement is solely between the company Ecuadoran Explorations, Inc., the National Institute of Cultural Heritage and the National Government."

■ ■ ■

With all the hurdles finally surmounted at the National Institute of Cultural Heritage, the sole remaining obstacle was the contract and decree currently under review by the President's legal advisors. By the end of March my patience and personal finances were running thin. Although company funds covered the expenses of the project and my per diem while in Ecuador, personal funds had been required to cover all costs of the project up to the point of forming a partnership and company, as well as the cost of living for my family of five. My personal financial well was running dry. I needed the contract and decree process to reach its satisfactory conclusion immediately in order to obtain personal funding and allow Ecuadoran Explorations to advance into Phase Two of the project, the exploration expedition.

In desperation I contacted the President's private secretary in hopes of moving the process forward. Señor Espinosa suggested that I proceed to the office of the Director of the Presidents Legal Advisors, at the time Dr. Manuel Castro Murillo, who he deemed would be more capable to respond to my inquiry. I could get no firm commitment from Dr. Castro beyond the fact that the proposed contract and decree were under review, which he confirmed in writing at our meeting of 30 Mar 1988. "Oficio" number 88-570-DAJ reproduced on the opposing page, is the only concrete benefit that came out of our conversation and states ... "I wish to inform you that the project of the Decree in which the National Institute of Cultural Heritage can enter into a contract with the company Ecuadoran Explorations Inc., for the search and archeological excavation of the treasure of the Llanganatis, is currently in process and being studied under the direction of the Asesoría Jurídica de la Presidencia de la República."

■ ■ ■

It would be not be until late April 1988 that a call from Ecuador came. One fine day at home in Florida, taking advantage of the beautiful weather doing yard work, my wife came outside extremely excited informing me that I had a call from Ecuador. I rushed inside contemplating who could be calling ... turning on the tape recorder that was connected to the phone ... I answered the call. The somewhat excited voice on the end of the line informed me that he was calling from the Presidential Palace of Ecuador.

Dr. Paez, Assesor Juridica de la Presidencia, indicated that he was calling to inform me that the President had given his "visto bueno" to our project. I explained that I did not understand the meaning of "visto bueno." Dr. Paez replied ... "That is to say Señor Charbonneau, you have received the President's approval for your project. I am calling to confirm when you will be available to come to Ecuador and complete the final details and sign the documents."

■ ■ ■

El Ecuador ha sido, es
y será País Amazónico

PRESIDENCIA DE LA REPUBLICA

Of. No. 88-570-DAJ

Quito, marzo 30 de 1988

Señor
Steven J. Charboneau
Ciudad.-

De mis consideraciones:

Pongo en su conocimiento que el proyecto de Decreto mediante el cual el Instituto de Patrimonio Cultural podrá celebrar un contrato con la compañía Ecuadoran Explorations Inc., para la búsqueda y excavación arqueológica del tesoro de los Llanganates, se encuentra en trámite y en estudio a cargo de la Dirección de Asesoría Jurídica de la Presidencia de la República.

Presidencia de la República - Asesoría Jurídica -

Muy atentamente,

Dr. Manuel Castro Murillo,
DIRECTOR DE ASESORIA JURIDICA, ENCARGADO

CPF/eas.

Letter from the Director of the President's Legal Advisors

Once again I would find myself climbing the central staircase of the palace, this time with the company's lawyer at my side for the meeting to negotiate the final terms and conditions of the contract to be entered into between Ecuadoran Explorations and the government of Ecuador. Once again two ceremonial attired soldiers stood guard outside the Presidents doorway. Although the President would not attend, today our meeting would be adjacent to his office, in the President's conference room. Throughout the meeting he would be routinely kept advised on our progress.

Director Jaramillo was present along with other obviously reluctant participants from the Institute, including the head of the Archeological Department. The President's legal advisors among others were present, we all settled in and took seats at the long conference table located on the left side of the room. Throughout the meeting it was constantly on my mind that the door on the right side of the room ... led into the President's office.

Most of the details for a contract having been previously presented, we still were required to go over each specific item and clause in detail. Almost every point met with objections from the Institutes Archeological Department. I must say that to his credit, the Director stepped in and made it clear that the department had been invited to the meeting to advise on technical aspects alone, the decision to enter into a contract was not within their purview, having already been decided by the President.

Ecuadoran Explorations original proposal had been developed taking into account all of the aspects required to create a win/win situation for both parties, even going above and beyond Ecuador's current law. Although Ecuador's patrimony law established a fifty-fifty split of all treasure, Ecuadoran Explorations had proposed that two classes of treasure be established. This proposal which had been mutually agreed to, established that only the first class of treasure, bulk unworked material,[475] would be divided fifty-fifty. The second category of treasure that was established included all hand crafted precious metals and stones, or artifacts. Ecuadoran Explorations would receive only 15 percent of the value of this class of treasure.

An appraisal methodology was also established to reach an acceptable valuation on these artifacts. The company and the government would each have their own appraiser determine an object's value. If the two appraisers could agree on a value, then Ecuadoran Explorations would be paid 15 percent of the artifacts appraised value. However, if the appraisers could not reach an accord, then a third independent appraiser would review the separate appraisals and determine the objects value on which the 15 percent would be calculated and paid.

---

[475] Bulk unworked material consisted of any gold, silver or precious stones that had not been crafted by man. For example ... gold and silver lumps, nuggets or powder ... non artistic wall slabs and roof or floor tiles ...uncut or crafted loose precious stones.

Of course once an evaluation of the treasure was made, the problem of payment would arise. Ecuador's patrimony law prohibited the removal of any artifacts from the country and Ecuadoran Explorations was not about to leave its assets in the country. Ecuador, being a poor developing country, simply would not have the means, sufficient foreign exchange, to meet its obligation for payment under the contract. Taking all of these factors into consideration, Ecuadoran Explorations had proposed that payment be made not only with foreign exchange, but with bulk unworked material. In this manner the country could meet its financial obligation under the contract, thereby preserving one hundred-percent of the historical artifacts' in-country, consistent with the patrimony law.

Additional points that were readily agreed to by all parties included the fact that the excavation and retrieval of artifacts would be conducted under the company's archeological permit and the purview of the National Institute of Cultural Heritage, with most importantly the company paying for the expenses of the project. The National Government would supply security for the sites and any recovered treasures through the Ministry of Defense. It was further contemplated that the military's contribution would include logistical support in the form of helicopter transport. [476]

With a few other minor details and clauses having been negotiated, our meeting came to an end. The terms and conditions of the contract between Ecuadoran Explorations and the government of Ecuador had come to its successful conclusion. All that remained was for the contract and decree to be typed and signed by the man sitting in the adjacent room ... President Juan León Febres Cordero.

■ ■ ■

Time dragged on and on. My consistent inquires whether the decree was done yet, through the President's private secretary, legal and political advisers, must have appeared to them like the question a child in a car on a road trip who constantly asks ... are we there yet ... are we there yet? Eventually I received the answer to my question, an answer which brought my inquiries and involvement in the recovery of the Llanganati treasure to an abrupt anticlimactic conclusion.

An official in the Palace, who will remain nameless, spoke with me in confidence off the record and was extremely apologetic. "Señor Charbonneau" ... he stated ... "I am sorry to inform you that on the advice of the Attorney General the President has decided not to sign your Decree. Again, I am sorry, I know we told you that the President had given his 'visto bueno' and that we had an agreement on the contract and decree, but for political reasons the President has been convinced not to sign any decree." Closing out our conversation I was informed that the Attorney General had also advised the President that we could legally continue with

---

[476] Not only logistical helicopter support of supplies, equipment and personnel, but the military would take possession of the treasure on site as it was removed and transport it back to Quito for deposit in the Banco Central.

our project under our archeological permit and Ecuador's existing law ... and the President hoped we would do so.

Overwhelmed with the shock and grief of the circumstances, I was utterly devastated. I had reached the stage where it was required that the contract and decree process reach its satisfactory conclusion in order to obtain personal funding or face financial ruin. Looking back, in some manner I could have surmounted the monetary issues, just as I had done throughout the project. But there were other issues involved in my decision making process. Not just the Vargas affair and the possibility of a coup d'etat, there had been threats on my life as well, the safety of my family must come first.

Finally, there were the legal considerations. Without a contract and decree, whether Ecuadoran Explorations would receive its 50 percent share of found treasure consistent with Ecuador's current law, would come down to a matter of trust or confidence in any future government of Ecuador ... I had absolutely none. I firmly believed that upon any recovery of treasure without a contract or decree, I would become either another gringo casualty of the Llanganatis ... or ... the treasure would be declared a national treasure that belonged solely to Ecuador. In any event, it was my opinion that the disposition of the treasure once recovered would have been mired in protracted legal battles.

After nearly two years of studying Brunner's work, doing research and becoming totally convinced that not only does the treasure still exist in the Llanganatis, but that clear and convincing evidence points to its location on Cerro Hermoso, having overcome what at times appeared to be unsurmountable hurdles, for me the game was over ... just one yard shy of a touchdown.

In my opinion the accomplishments on this roller coaster ride had been numerous. I had obtained investors, partnerships, created a corporation, established contact with the highest levels of Ecuador's government, negotiated a precedent setting commercial contract, even dealt with the corrupt bureaucratic process, but all of this was useless and meaningless without a presidential decree! Perhaps even with my successes I had been naive, lacking of experience, wisdom or judgment, out of my league, or even had become infected with a lust for Inca gold ...

■ ■ ■

THE ULTIMATE BETRAYAL: EPILOGUE

Treasure stories like any other story, have a beginning, middle and an end. Throughout any story there can be misdirection and misinformation. If a reader believes or knows a portion of the story to be true, does it not follow that the reader would then believe the entire story to be true?

These general sentiments of Michael Dyott were prevalent throughout my involvement in this project and have been a guiding light in the writing of my manuscript. Relating the entire story in detail, without deception, misdirection or the use of literary license to fictionalize my involvement as other writers have done, being my intent. In hindsight, Michael made no mention in his sentiments of the deceit and betrayal that would be a major part of any story on lust for Inca gold.

Perhaps the most perfidious act has been previous implications that the Blacke & Chapman material was merely a hoax, perpetrated by either Commander Dyott or Eugene Brunner. Hopefully the facts, evidence and discoveries related herein, have decisively and permanently laid this theory to rest. Regrettably, the Commander and Brunner never reaped the benefits of their discoveries. Quite similar to the man in whose footsteps they followed, Richard Spruce, these men passed on nearly destitute. Ironically, apart from possibly Chuck Powell, the sole individuals that have profited from the Blacke & Chapman story have been authors like Peter Lourie and Mark Honigsbaum.

Betrayals' commenced from the beginning of our story, as Atahualpa was betrayed for the power and wealth Pizarro's lust for Inca gold would provide, all sanctioned by the Crown and under the cloak of religion. Was it merely coincidence that Pizarro sent his brother Hernando, whom had developed a personal friendship with Atahualpa, who would not have permitted the travesty of a trial and execution occur, back to Spain with a portion of the Royal Fifth shortly prior to Atahualpa's trial and death? Reasonable minds can easily infer that Pizarro never had any intention of releasing Atahualpa upon the fulfillment of his infamous ransom. Plainly and simply, the Spaniards coveted Inca gold and silver but had no respect for, nor placed any value upon, indigenous life.

Throughout the conquest and even in modern day Ecuador, a caste system based on the purity of lineage thrives. Viracocha's prophecy that some foreign people from a faraway land would become the indigenous peoples' masters, not only came true, but appears to have become an accepted way of life. Ones purity of breed or Spanish blood, creates an exclusive social class in Ecuador which in general has shown little respect for the Indian race or life itself and as I have witnessed, still exists in Ecuador today. For this reason ... "the integration of the Ecuadorian Indian into national life, his rightful place by heritage," so sought after by Eugene Konrad Brunner ... has never occurred. In my opinion, upon the ultimate recovery of Inca gold hidden by Rumiñahui in the Llanganati Mountains, the indigenous peoples of Ecuador ... are sadly destined to be betrayed once again.

■ ■ ■

Did certain Incan's not betray their heritage and solemn oath's never to disclose the hiding place of Atahualpa's ransom treasure, hidden from the Spanish long ago, by revealing its location to the young Spaniard Valverde? Did Valverde, being a descendant of the Spanish conquerors responsible for unspeakable atrocities committed against the Incan peoples, meet the criteria established by legend for the disclosure of the treasures location ... merely for being in love with and marrying his native princess?

In spite of the fact that Inca legend mentions Rumiñahui's treasure location should never be disclosed, unless to someone "of good heart" or "pure of heart" ... even with the forewarning that once recovered the treasure should be utilized for the betterment of the native peoples, the treasure's location was disclosed to Valverde for his personal gain and benefit. Did this betrayal ... "invoke the curses of their forefathers upon them"[477] and cause the death of Valverde's Indian wife en route to Spain? Once in Spain (or still in Ecuador) was Valverde himself not betrayed by this new found wealth which brought him to the attention of the Crown, forcing his infamous *Derrotero* to be given?

■ ■ ■

Richard Spruce's methodical scientific research on botany was interrupted briefly, but his methodology clearly carried over to his research on the *Derrotero de Valverde* and *Guzmán Map*. Research that was not kept secret, to the contrary the majority of Spruce's findings were purportedly published in their entirety, or so we are led to believe. It was many years later, after Spruce's death, that Wallace in my view committed a betrayal of Spruce's scientific research, which was then romanticized to a point that it became a lust for Inca gold.

What form of betrayal may have occurred over Spruce's missing journals that Wallace so sought after in vain. Were the journals merely misplaced by the executor of his estate? Perhaps Spruce had given the journals' to his nephew or Stabler his friend and confidant, for safe keeping. Had Spruce's notes, journals and a purported second unpublished map, been supplied to Blacke & Chapman, making their quest for Inca gold much easier? If Spruce did possess this undisclosed second map, purportedly Valverde's companion map for his *Derrotero* ... who is to say that Spruce's translation of the *Derrotero* itself was completely accurate? If Spruce had intended on profiting from the recovery of Llanganati treasure through third parties, would he have published a clear and concise guide to its location? Or, would it have been more logical for Spruce to relate the story obscuring its location? For scientific reasons alone, would it not have made sense for Spruce, just as I have done with the indigenous guide, to also publish the *Derrotero* in its original Spanish form along with his own translation?

The hieroglyph of the *Derrotero* being the "key" for the route to the treasure, would it not have been important to verify its orientation on the original document? Could the "key" have been flipped or rotated by Spruce

[477] Quote from Captain Eric Loch in *Fever, Famine, and Gold.*

to protect his potential find? Were the document copies obtained by Spruce "pure documents" or had they fallen victim to some form of alteration over the years prior to Spruce obtaining "copies" of them? Sadly, one may never know the answer to these or many other questions ... but theories abound.

■ ■ ■

Assume for a moment that the indigenous guide to the location of Atahualpa's Treasure, introduced at the end of Chapter I and reproduced here, is a legitimate record of how to reach the treasure ... "If you yearn to achieve the wealth desired by the bearded white Spaniard, enemy of our pure race, never divulge this route I am going to provide you. Because having gone to the three Llanganatis, our hills of the Sun, and by putting your hands into the enchanted lagoon you will get gold, the desire of the bearded white men and magistrates of Tacunga and Ambato, those who our lineage have always expressed disapproval and disappointment with, uttering curses urging God Viracocha for justice, so that the gold will always remain in the possession of our land and that it will never be discovered by the bearded ones. So here I bequeath and describe the path you must follow without warning or notifying any of the whites who want to overcome our domains.

"Placed in the small town of Píllaro, soil of our great Rumiñahui, there ask for the "Moya of Rumiñahui," continue toward the cold heights until you reach our peak of "Guapa," from whose top, if the day is good, always watching in the direction where the sun rises, or to say that you will always have the town of Ambato to your backs and your eyes will always focus to the side where the sun rises, the three mountains called the Llanganatis that are in the form of a triangle, like that of the "Callo of Tacunga,"putting the mounds in a straight line toward those of "Cerro Hermoso." Follow this course downhill until you reach the green lagoon that is the same that was made by hand, ordered by Rumiñahui, who sent his brother the Chieftain of Panzaleo to throw all the gold metal desired by the ambitious white gods to free our father Atahualpa, owing to the order that the white god gave. I say continue to follow the "Cerro Guapa," always with the mountain until you arrive at the great patch of dense vegetation of large "sangurimas" that will confuse those who walk by there because they are diverted from the route by "flechas."

"I will tell you that this spot where vegetation grows thick is the guide that you will always follow on the left hand until you reach the large "juncal" in the middle of the slope, pass through it, and from the large "juncal" you will see two small lakes that we call "Los Anteojos", from having a nose in the middle, a tip of sand resembling the "Cuilcoche de Otavalos." From this site focus your eyes where the sun rises and you will see again the Llanganatis just as you saw them from the height of the great "Guapa" and I warn you do not be deceived because these lagoons you must leave always on your left and proceeding with the nose or point on your left hand you will see a large plain of straw which is the second days sleeping place. This is where you will leave the beasts and proceed on foot to reach the Black Lake called "Yanayacu," which you leave to the left, descending very carefully along the hillside, arriving at a ravine, reaching the great waterfall that is the drain or "Chorrera del Golpe," where you will pass over a bridge of three poles. And if they do not already exist, search for a site to place another bridge where you will see the hut that serves to sleep in, attached to the large stone where many routes have been drawn out.

"The next day, continue to travel by the same landslide of the mountain, reaching a very deep gorge where you put poles in order to pass with much caution, because it is very deep. This way you can always get to the pasture where the rays of heaven roar, follow the great plain; and seeing that the plain ends you come into a large canyon between the three mountains, where you come across a trail paved by the Inca and from where you will see the entrance of the "socavón" (tunnel) which is made like the outside of a Church. You will walk a good way up coming across a waterfall coming out of a son (offshoot) of the largest Cerro of Llanganati creating a soft boggy area where there is more than enough gold so that by inserting your hand you will extract grains of gold.

"But to climb the mountain leave the soft boggy area and go along to the right hand passing above the waterfall, climbing to go around the offshoot and if by chance the mouth of the offshoot is covered as it should be with "salvaje" or wild moss, remove this with your hands and encounter the entrance, from where you will see the "Guayra" (furnace) which is the oven to melt metal. If you want to return, seek the river and follow it on the right bank, taking to the beach toward the confluence, always following the canyon of the drainage of the lagoon; that you will follow on the right side until you see the nose of the "Lagunas de Anteojos" and the great "Guapa" that always resides behind the town of Ambato. Continue along to this mountain, your principal steward, then follow the cold pasture down to Píllaro."

Upon scrutinizing this document it becomes apparent that a direct route from point A to Z is not sequentially laid out. To the contrary, the guide describes what you seek …"the wealth desired by the bearded white Spaniard," the general location where it is located …"having gone to the three Llanganatis, our hills of the Sun," and once there how it can be obtained …"by putting your hands into the enchanted lagoon." The route then commences in Píllaro and travels to the top of a mountain Guapa, from where you can see your destination …"the three mountains called the Llanganatis that are in the form of a triangle." A cryptic message tells how to proceed once on the mountain, to arrive at the treasure lake …"follow this course downhill until you reach the green lagoon." The guide then returns to Guapa and describes the route to the mountain of your destination …Cerro Hermoso.

Many landmarks and names on the route that would be clearly understood by indigenous peoples follow. Once having crossed a plain and encountering a canyon the guide places the traveler on the Inca Trail, from where a socavón or tunnel can be seen on the mountain. Arriving at the mountain, the guide indicates there is also a waterfall and gold within a bog at its base. The guide instructs the follower to remove the moss from the entrance of this tunnel, without mention of entering it, and that the furnace to melt metals can be seen from the entrance. Continuing on, the guide further provides directions on how to ascend the mountain. However, the location of the treasure lake does not follow, instead the guide describes the route to return to Píllaro. Therefore, once the mountain has been ascended, you must decipher the treasure lake's location from the clues provided in the beginning of the guide ... "follow this course downhill until you reach the green lagoon."

Comparing the indigenous guide to the *Derrotero de Valverde* introduced in Chapter II and reproduced below, it also becomes apparent that they are quite similar in form and content. It can only be theorized, but Valverde may have followed this exact same indigenous guide to his treasure lake. Upon dictating the route in his infamous deathbed *Derrotero* from memory, Valverde may well have expounded on many points, utilizing landmarks and terminology that would be more understandable to a fellow Spaniard. Even so, the primary differences between these guides are quite simple ... the indigenous version makes no mention of "a mountain which is all of *margasitas* (pyrites)" or of a hieroglyph, while on the other hand, Valverde's guide provides no apparent indication on how to reach the treasure lake ... the destination of his guide!

"Placed in the town of Píllaro, ask for the farm of Moya, and sleep (the first night) a good distance above it ; and ask there for the mountain of Guapa, from whose top, if the day be fine, look to the east, so that thy back be towards the town of Ambato, and from thence thou shalt perceive the three Cerros Llanganati, in the form of a triangle, on whose declivity there is a lake, made by hand, into which the ancients threw the gold they had prepared for the ransom of the Inca when they heard of his death. From the same Cerro Guapa thou mayest see also the forest, and in it a clump of *sangurimas* standing out of the said forest, and another clump which they call *flechas* (arrows), and these clumps are the principal mark for the which thou shalt aim, leaving them a little on the left hand. Go forward from Guapa in the direction and with the signals indicated, and a good way ahead, having passed some cattle-farms, thou shalt come on a wide morass, over which thou must cross, and coming out on the other side thou shalt see on the left hand a short way off a *jucál* on a hill-side, through which thou must pass. Having got through the *jucál*, thou wilt see two small lakes called "Los Anteojos" (the spectacles), from having between them a point of land like to a nose.

"From this place thou mayest again descry the Cerros Llanganati, the same as thou sawest them from the top of Guapa, and I warn thee to leave the said lakes on the left, and that in front of the point or "nose" there is a plain, which is the sleeping-place. There thou must leave thy horses, for they can go no farther. Following now on foot in the same direction, thou shalt come on a great black lake, the which leave on thy left hand, and beyond it seek to descend along the hill-side in such a way that thou mayest reach a ravine, down which comes a waterfall: and here thou shall find a bridge of three poles, or if it do not still exist thou shalt put another in the most convenient place and pass over it. And having gone on a little way in the forest, seek out the hut which served to sleep in or the remains of it. Having passed the night there, go on thy way the following day through the forest in the same direction, till thou reach another deep dry ravine, across which thou must throw a bridge and pass over it slowly and cautiously, for the ravine is very deep ; that is, if thou succeed not in finding the pass which exists. Go forward and look for the signs of another sleeping-place, which, I assure thee, thou canst not fail to see in the fragments of pottery and other marks, because the Indians are continually passing along there. Go on thy way, and thou shalt see a mountain which is all of *margasitas* (pyrites), the which leave onthy left hand, and I warn thee that thou must go round it in this fashion:

"On this side thou wilt find a *pajonál* (pasture) in a small plain, which having crossed thou wilt come on a *cañon* between two hills, which is the Way of the Inca. From thence as thou goest along thou shalt see the entrance of the *socabón* (tunnel), which is in the form of a church porch.

"Having come through the cañon and gone a good distance beyond, thou wilt perceive a cascade which descends from an offshoot of the Cerro Llanganati and runs into a quaking-bog on the right hand; and without passing the stream in the said bog there is much gold, so that putting in thy hand what thou shalt gather at the bottom is grains of gold. To ascend the mountain, leave the bog and go along to the right, and pass above the cascade, going round the offshoot of the mountain. And if by chance the mouth of the socabón be closed with certain herbs which they call "Salvaje," remove them, and thou wilt find the entrance. And on the left-hand side of the mountain thou mayest see the 'Guayra' (for thus the ancients called the furnace where they founded metals), which is nailed with golden nails. And to reach the third mountain, if thou canst not pass in front of the socabón, it is the same thing to pass behind it, for the water of the lake falls into it.

"If thou lose thyself in the forest, seek the river, follow it on the right bank; lower down take to the beach, and thou wilt reach the canon in such sort that, although thou seek to pass it, thou wilt not find where; climb, therefore, the mountain on the right hand, and in this manner thou canst by no means miss thy way."

Throughout this manuscript, every attempt has been made to clearly transmit facts and evidence. Theories, legends and myths are just that, should be identified as such and remain so, until proven or dispelled beyond any shadow of doubt. However, indulge me for a moment and entertain one of my theories. What if, and I must reiterate ... what if ... Guzmán and Spruce's "Margasitas" mountain had no connection what-so-ever with Valverde's *Derrotero*? What if ... Valverde's mountain of pyrites and Old Q's mountain crowned with gold were one and the same ... Cerro Hermoso? What if ... Valverde's hieroglyph was not an indicator on how to arrive at the mountain as everyone has assumed for centuries? What if ... the hieroglyph was actually a key to the termination of Valverde's guide after ascending the mountain, in other words ... the route to Valverde's treasure lake? Indulge me further ... draw an imaginary circle around Lake Brunner ... from the left side of this circle mentally trace the pass located to the left of the lake, arcing around to ascend the mountain, passing through the main and secondary peaks to reach the other side of the mountain ... an image is created quite similar to Valverde's hieroglyph!

■ ■ ■

For centuries, legend, myth, an indigenous guide, the *Derrotero de Valverde* and common belief held that the gold and treasure destined for the ransom of Atahualpa was hidden in a man-made lake in the Llanganatis. Only with the advent of Blacke & Chapman's material in Ecuador was the theory of Atahualpa's gold residing in a cave in the Llanganatis broached and accepted without question or explanation. Why ... will never be known with absolute certainty ... perhaps owing to the fact that there is no verifiable explanation.

Similar to the landmarks within the indigenous guide and *Derrotero de Valverde*, the landmarks within the Blacke & Chapman material have been confirmed on location. Therefore, for the sake of argument consider for a moment the possibility ... is it plausible two treasure deposits could have occurred? There appears to be only two possibilities ... one or more of these "guides" were elaborate hoaxes ... or, all three sources are true and accurate accounts so there must have been two deposits made.

Could it have been that items required in the afterlife and religious articles, were interred with Atahualpa's mummy in his tomb ... within a cave in the Llanganatis ... while bulk and non-significant materials were ... thrown in a lake made by hand? If so, would the indigenous peoples have then left a guide to the treasure that mentioned Atahualpa's tomb, or kept that portion of the guide secret?

On the other hand, is it plausible that Valverde removed a small portion of treasure from the lake and later Don Antonio Pastor y Marín de Segura (or an undisclosed party) recovered the balance ... but how without draining the lake? Considering the time consuming and labor intensive process that would have been required for anyone to recover a treasure from the lake "that thousands of men" could not remove, is it plausible that during this lengthy process the treasure, once removed from the lake, was stored in a cave while portions were removed from the Llanganatis? Could this cave and its remnants of treasure later have been stumbled upon by Blacke & Chapman?

■ ■ ■

Could there have been some falling out between the two mariners Blacke & Chapman while in those inhospitable mountains of the Llanganatis? Had Chapman died falling into a precipice when a rope broke or had Chapman actually succumbed to a tropical disease? Chapman's death after the discovery of such wealth appears too quickly set aside in most versions of their story. A story which one must remember would have been related by the sole survivor. Paranoia and betrayal could easily have intervened in Blacke & Chapman's trek out of the mountains laden with Inca gold. Perhaps the answer lies within Chapman's grave ... "a stone mound at the foot of the snowy Atilis."

Imagine Blacke returning to England with eighteen pieces of Inca gold and precious stones during the late 1880s. This epoch found England enveloped by a long depression, high rural unemployment, emigration, internal migration to the cities, labor unrest and demonstrations. An era that included the fictional Sherlock Holmes, horse drawn carriages, gas street lamps and great poverty. What appears to have been a seemingly small amount of treasure that fit within a single backpack, even if shared with his benefactor, whether it was a nephew of Richard Spruce, Spruce's friend and confidant Stabler, or Spruce himself ... could easily have provided Blacke with a life of leisure throughout the balance of his life. Spruce however died in near poverty, so it would appear reasonable to assume that yet another betrayal may have occurred.

Had Blacke's wealth been squandered ... had Blacke retired from the Navy ... or had he been secretly acting under the authority of the Admiralty? Regardless of which version of events one subscribes to, Blacke's lust for Inca gold was renewed some years later. As Blacke was traveling back to New England and from there on to Ecuador in order to recover more treasure, whether falling overboard in a drunken stupor or tossed overboard, Blacke himself would meet the ultimate betrayal ... death.

■ ■ ■

Jordan Stabler's publication of information concerning Major Brooks expeditions into the Llanganatis could easily have been viewed as a betrayal of his confidence and of their friendship. But to the contrary, even though some of Stabler's representations were inaccurate, Brooks response was very respectful and polite in that regard.

When viewing the data that came to light from these explorers publications in the *Geographical Journal*, one would do well to remember that both of these men entered the inhospitable regions of Ecuador, a mere quarter-century after Blacke & Chapman. Stabler and Brooks did not have the benefit of modern aerial photographs, topographic maps and most probably not even access to *Notes of a Botanist* and Wallace's commentary, which had just recently been published in 1908. Brooks clearly indicated he had obtained access to Spruce's 1860 paper, and he makes no mention of Spruce's *Notes of a Botanist,* except to state in 1917 that ... "a copy is available for review in the New York Public Library."

Whether Stabler, or Brooks through his association with Stabler, had access to any other Spruce material is pure conjecture and shall remain a mystery. It seems to amaze me however, that no one has yet explored this possible connection between Jordan Stabler and Spruce's friend and confidant George Stabler. In addition, I find it odd that all writers have downplayed Brooks' expeditions in search of the treasure. It is my opinion that Brooks had been more successful in deciphering Valverde's route in two expeditions, by following not only the route of the *Derrotero* but in Blacke & Chapman's footsteps. Brooks traveled a more exact and direct route to Cerro Hermoso than others have after him in countless attempts.

■ ■ ■

What type of arrangement had Commander Dyott originally made with the Bermender family in New England ... a small percentage of treasure recovery perhaps? No one knows the answer as that issue has never been openly addressed. Had the Commander as Brunner would write, sought permission of the family to pass the information onto Brunner and Salvador? If so, what was the new arrangement between Dyott and the family, definitely a smaller share at the least. One could reasonably question ... if Dyott furnished Brunner ... "actually and permanently with all the advice and information Dyott has in relation with the so-called Atahualpa Treasure" ... for 10 percent of any recovery ... why was Brunner only permitted to copy the original documents and why would Brunner not have received them upon Dyott's death? These of course being the same documents and expedition journals that the Commander would deposit at the British Embassy for his son Michael, which would turn up missing after Dyott's death and bring to light yet other possible betrayals.

With the passage of time a clearer overall picture develops. Through the writings of authors Lourie and Honigsbaum, covering a span of more than twenty years, it appears Dyott's missing journals ended up in the hands of Andrés Fernandez Salvador ... who by contract would have had only a shared interest in with Brunner. From the outset Salvador denied having Dyott's journals, indicating that he was referring to his handwritten notes of conversations with Dyott over the years. With the passage of time the story evolves to Salvador making the claim that after Dyott's death, the journals were sent to him anonymously.[478] A claim that in my opinion just doesn't make sense, and brings to mind the possibility that yet another betrayal may have occurred.

---

[478] I contacted Michael Dyott mentioning ... "Regarding who has your dad's journals, all indicators point to Andrés Fernadez Salvador" and asked if Mike had ever discussed this with Andrés. Michael's response was ... "I have not asked Andy about my dad's journals but when I was at his place, he got dangerously drunk, admitted (bragged about) several things but never insinuated that he had my dad's expedition journals. By that I mean that he never implied that he had any special information or even said that he intended to go back into the Llanganatis ... but he eventually did at seventy-two ..."

■ ■ ■

What manner of betrayal had occurred between these two friends Andrés Fernandez Salvador and Eugene Konrad Brunner, during their partnership and mutual friendship of admiration and respect? Was it just a coincidence that at this same point in time, Andrés and his new son-in-law Diego Arias had visited Commander Dyott at Hacienda Delta prior to his departure for New York, purportedly obtaining more details of Dyott's Blacke information? Could Salvador have been Andrade's "secret source" for the Dyott, Blacke & Chapman story, a story which Brunner considered intellectual property? Or was it merely that Andrés lost interest or confidence in Brunner no longer funding his expeditions, choosing instead to fund his son-in-law Diego's Llanganati expeditions?

Over the years Brunner does not appear to have betrayed his friendship with Andrés. I have not discovered any negative comments in Brunner's writings about his old friend and partner except to state that he had been disappointed by Ecuador's elite many times. Even in the stories told by others ... friendship, admiration, respect, even regret appears to have played on Brunner's mind as he spoke of Andrés. Salvador's thoughts and commentary concerning Brunner on the other hand, as presented by authors' Lourie and Honigsbaum, shows an inkling of the same deep friendship, admiration, respect and regret which appears to have been altered with the passage of time.

Lourie's conversations with Salvador concerning Brunner took place while Brunner was still alive, in the early 1980s. They were then published in *Sweat of the Sun, Tears of the Moon* in 1991. At this point in time Andrés was still referring to his old friend and partner as ... "the true expert on these mountains." Salvador's admiration and respect for Brunner and his work on Cerro Hermoso continued beyond this comment with statements of ... "The importance of Brunner's work ... "; "Brunner made the connection; Brunner's done valuable work up there ... "; "He's the greatest aficionado of the Llanganatis."; and "The old German has gone more times to the Llanganatis than any man alive." Salvador had even made statements confirming the validity of some of Brunner's theories. But even still, you could notice at that time a certain air of envy, jealousy or rivalry in Salvador's changing attitudes, also referring to Brunner as ... "odd, even crazy."

Honigsbaum's conversations with Salvador would take place some twenty years later. According to Honigsbaum's account in *Valverde's Gold*, absent from these conversations was any mention of Brunner. When ultimately questioned about Brunner, gone were Andrés sentiments of admiration and respect for the man ... "Eugenio was a dreamer, that is all. Dyott and I sponsored him-until we got bored" ... and ... "I was the one who sent him to Cerro Hermoso, but Eugenio became fixated on the mountain. He wouldn't consider any other possibility. Dyott thought he was a fool."

Even if Commander Dyott had thought Brunner a fool, at least at one point in time Dyott had a very different opinion of Brunner, as Dyott entrusted

Brunner with the Blacke material to continue a search which he himself had abandoned. A search that even Dyott, with all his experience and expertise, had unwittingly been brought to the point of ... "staring up at the ramparts of Cerro Hermoso."

Andrés Fernandez Salvador was not included on my list of contacts as I knew Brunner and Andrés had previously been friends and partners until there was a falling out. Also absent from this list was Salvador's son-in-law Diego Arias, whom was apparent that Brunner did not like. At the time I could see no benefit to any contact or relationship with either party. Having the benefit of hindsight after reading Lourie and Honigsbaum's accounts of their alcohol induced interviews with Salvador and Arias, my intuition appears confirmed. In my opinion Andrés admiration and respect for Brunner and his work, apparently had been supplanted over time by envy, jealousy, rivalry and ego. With the passage of time Salvador had evolved into the central character while Brunner had become trivial, almost nonexistent.

Salvador's apparent pride of heritage coupled with bravado, machismo and alcohol in my opinion, is the epitome of Ecuador's elite. It has been my experience in Ecuador to witness these distant descendants of the conquistadores, "the elite," displaying in their actions and way of life an utter disdain for the country's natives. Pizarro and the conquistadores placed no value on Indian life or culture, except as a source of cheap goods and labor. Nearly five hundred years since, "the integration of the Ecuadorian Indian into national life, his rightful place by heritage" has not occurred, the status quo remains intact. Consistent with Inca myth and legend, perhaps this inherent flaw apparently found within Salvador and Arias, the lack "of good heart" or being "pure of heart" toward the natives, may have attributed to their failures as they lusted for Inca gold.

■ ■ ■

What of the geologists' that were hired over the years to examine Brunner's Cerro Hermoso concession? Whether betrayals were committed or not remains unclear. What is clear is that the geologists' written reports conflict with their later verbal accounts. Is it plausible that some of these individuals wanted the mining concessions for themselves? Perhaps lust for Inca gold had expanded to other minerals ... from Inca gold to silver and copper ... all to be found in abundance on Cerro Hermoso.

■ ■ ■

Robert R definitely felt the sting of betrayal as his investment disappeared. Whether Brunner knew about Robert at the time, or of the magnitude of funds Powell was purportedly raising in the name of Brunner's project, pennies of which were ultimately reaching Ecuador and Brunner, remains unclear. However, considering the time-line of events, it appears obvious that this possible betrayal could have been the reason for Brunner's falling out with Powell. Just imagine for a moment, Brunner's possible feelings of shock, anger and betrayal upon discovering that sufficient funds might have been available to successfully complete his life-long project ... yet were possibly diverted for personal uses.

■ ■ ■

To this day unanswered questions abound concerning General Gribaldo Miño. It was not until I commenced my research for this manuscript, that I came to the realization that I had known Gribaldo the man. I had no inkling who Gribaldo the General was, or the power he wielded in this small country. Whether the General had been betrayed, or had himself been part of some betrayal, will presumably never be ascertained with complete certainty.

As has been reported, events must have transpired that caused the General to resign his post only months prior to the end of his term. I know for a fact that the General was having difficulties with another General, presumably Reñe Vargas. At one point Miño had even complained about his house guard having been removed, but the extent of the personal animosity between the two rival Generals Miño and Reñe Vargas Pazzos, I was never aware of.

Speaking of the possibilities of a coup in Ecuador during the end of the Hurtado administration, Bruce Farcau provides an insight within his book *The Coup: Tactics in the Seizure of Power*, into the extent that personal animosities within the officer corps could have on such an event. Mr. Farcau made every effort to remain discreet, without naming names, for the story he relates is an unconfirmed third hand account of events. It must also be kept in mind that Ecuador's officer corps has dozens, if not a hundred or more, active duty and retired Generals at any given point in time. Therefore, it is not my intent reproducing Mr. Farcau's story here, to attribute the events to any specific character within this book. [479]

"One of the most prominent candidates to lead the coup we shall delicately identify as General 'A', who enjoyed considerable prestige for his professional competence and strong ties to the commanders of a number of strategically located military units.

When I asked a military contact if General 'A' were likely to launch a coup, this officer merely chuckled and said that he didn't think so. When I elaborated on why General 'A' should be a logical choice to take such an action, adding that he was rumored to have a personal feud going with President Hurtado, the officer agreed with me on every point ... The officer explained to me that it was simply because everybody knew that General 'B' had been having an affair with General 'As' wife and that, while the army might easily enough be led into a coup, it would not follow a cuckold into one. Whether the story was apochryphal or not, I cannot say, but it is a fact that General 'A' never did launch his coup."

---

[479] In May of 2012 Mr. Farcau would elaborate in an email ... "I don't believe it had to do with ideology so much as each man headed a clique of officers within the military that competed for influence and position. There was also a personal aspect to the conflict, I believe, although I do not believe that either one (Miño or Vargas) was either General A or General B."

It would stand to reason that any rivalry between these Generals' could have stemmed from opposing political ideologies or personal animosities, even possibly being connected to a long-standing feud between General Reñe Vargas and President Febres Cordero. One would do well to remember that Cordero's nomination of recently retired General Miño as Minister of Defense was rejected by the Council of General Officers of the Armed Forces, over which then Chief of Staff and Commander of the Army General Reñe Vargas, may well have wielded his influence.

Events that have been related herein later were to transpire, after General Reñe Vargas had been sacked by Febres Cordero, involving Reñe's brother Lt. General Frank Vargas Pazzos. Had these events been an attempted coup d'etat, a continuation of the family feud, the well-intentioned righteous complaint of a patriot, a combination of all or just the personal ambitions or one man?

Whether General Miño's resignation occurring so near Brunner's sudden demise in the military hospital was mere coincidence and the reasons behind the General's reluctance to become involved in assisting the advancement of my project while still in Panama, will never be known.[480] I missed my opportunity to ask these questions and others of the General and his family remains silent on the matter. It has always bewildered me why the General insisted that he must physically be in Ecuador prior to any assistance being provided ... my General obviously knew something that I did not!

■ ■ ■

Conducting research for this manuscript in April of 2010, I discovered the online source of an Ecuadorian historian and biographer from Guayaquil, Rodolfo Pérez Pimentel, entitled *Diccionario Biográfico Ecuador*. This source includes sixteen hundred short biographies on important people in Ecuador's history. As there was no entry for Gribaldo Miño Tapia an email was sent to Mr. Pérez requesting any information that he might have on the General. The following brief response was received ... "Dear Steven: As you must be an American, you ignore that there are usually one hundred generals in active service, distributed between the three branches of the armed forces and the police in Ecuador. Many Generals' swords are virgin, because they have never smelled gunpowder or attended any fighting, this causes their names to pass unnoticed. You imagine the importance which they will have. They are promoted from time to time, only for taking approved courses and to warm positions.

---

[480] In 2012 a source extremely close to General Miño, whom for obvious reasons must remain anonymous, related to me that ... "Yes, indeed General Miño was the upcoming Minister of Defense under Cordero, the best way to keep the General safe was to send him away and keep him out of Ecuador, Febres Cordero sent him away to Panama as Ambassador. The death of General Miño within two years of his return from Panama, was under very, very suspicious circumstances!"

"Of course there is no shortage of decorations and when they move into passive service, their names are forgotten and they fall into absolute anonymity. Perhaps in Quito not so much because they have clubs bringing them together, but in Guayaquil and the rest of the country, what remains of them and their memory is nothing but silence. It is a pity that it is this way, but blame the system, since an army of no more than five to ten thousand members, should only have - at best - three to five Generals. In my dictionary, what could be said of many, many generals, that they were born, married and died, their medals, their studies and courses abroad, their jobs within the armed forces, in other words, their curriculum and nothing more. That's why I do not include them, it would be a waste of time. Very cordially, Rodolfo Pérez Pimentel"

On the surface I found Mr. Pérez's reply quite reasonable. With thousands of generals in Ecuador's past and present, I must agree that to compile a biography on each General would be meaningless and time consuming. But what of the Generals' that played an important role in Ecuador's history and our story? Surely I thought, there must be some mention of these men and others in our story, especially due to the importance of this period of transition from military to civilian rule within Ecuador. I set out to examine the *Diccionario Biográfico Ecuador* to discover which biographies pertained to characters from our story.

Obviously I assumed that the country's rulers, both military and civilian, must have been listed in such a work. Much to my surprise only two biographies of characters from our story were included ... President Oswaldo Hurtado Larrea and General Frank Vargas Pazzos ... but the central characters who shaped Ecuador's history from military dictatorship to democracy were not. Biographies from the past however were prevalent and included those of Atahualpa, Rumiñahui, Francisco Pizarro, Cieza de León, Oveido, Padre Valverde, José Valverde (*Derrotero de Valverde*), Guzmán, Marin de Segura, Spruce, Hassaurek, Thur de Koos, Luciano Andrade Marin and Andrés Fernandez Salvador. Commander Dyott and other characters from our story did not have individual biographies, but were mentioned within the biographies of others.

A biographical narrative is required to be precise, stripped of personal tastes, feelings, opinions, biases or political affiliation which effect the narrator's subjectivity. In my opinion, the reader of certain biographies relevant to our story, does not receive an accurate and unbiased message. Sadly, it became obvious that Mr. Pérez had utilized Luciano Andrade Marin's writings as a source for much of the information in his biographies regarding people connected to the Llanganati treasure story. Therefore, any false assumptions, misinformation or misdirection within Andrade's works, have once again been presented as factual material.

Mr. Pérez's biographies on Andrés Fernandez Salvador and Frank Vargas Pazzos appear in my opinion to be biased, presenting these men as those who could be admired for their courage or outstanding achievements. Perhaps I myself am guilty of presenting biased views as well. For on the other hand, reviewing the available facts, it has been my opinion that these men were more villainous than heroic. It has been my intent throughout this narrative to provide biographical data on the characters of our story, in order that the reader may comprehend the true character of the individual. Data has been provided on characters who are interesting men in their own rights, including Edwards Brooks, Eric Loch, George Dyott, Eugene Brunner and Gribaldo Miño, so that their names and accomplishments are not forgotten before ... "they fall into absolute anonymity."

■ ■ ■

Las Vegas, Nevada, is where my family found ourselves living years after my involvement in the Llanganati project. It would be during 1993 when the work of compiling memories, details and facts on the project for a possible manuscript commenced. Once again, just as the project had begun for me, I found myself within a public library. I was at the main Clark County Library examining micro films of old *New York Times* articles on the military in Ecuador when feelings of betrayal confronted me.

Searching the library's card catalog I discovered that Peter Lourie had ultimately completed and published his manuscript under the title *Sweat of the Sun, Tears of the Moon.* Reason prevailed as I determined that perhaps my feelings of betrayal were premature, I was willing to withhold judgment until I had read Lourie's book. Again giving Peter the benefit of the doubt, perhaps he had attempted to make contact and provide a copy of the manuscript prior to publication as had been discussed. It was beyond Lourie's control that my family and I for security reasons had disappeared at the end of the project and left no trail for mail to be forwarded or traced.

Upon obtaining a copy of the book *Sweat of the Sun, Tears of the Moon,* I jumped directly to Lourie's epilogue. Sure enough, Peter had partially been true to his word and utilized my involvement with Brunner as an ending for his manuscript. Even today I can remember as I read further, the feeling of betrayal that returned and rapidly developed into anger.

Had my method of extracting information during the project by feigning ignorance on the details of Brunner's work and discoveries, on some occasions utilizing misinformation to elicit a response, not solely to confirm or deny my observations, but to ascertain Lourie's truthfulness, candor and motives, been so successful that I had appeared to be unknowledgeable, eccentric and even foolish? The further I read the more apparent it appeared to me that Peter's liberal use of literary license had the effect of making every other character in his book appear in this same manner, thereby placing himself as the central dominating character. As I had my method, this most obviously in my opinion was Lourie's method.

I must admit that Lourie's writing style did make for easy reading, almost like reading a novel. But Michael Dyott's sentiment ... "If a reader believes or knows a portion of the story to be true, does it not follow that the reader would then believe the entire story to be true?," conversely stuck in my mind as I read Lourie's epilogue. Knowing portions of Peter's epilogue to be false, even taking into account any misdirection or misinformation on my part, cast a shadow over his story in its entirety.

Throughout *Sweat of the Sun, Tears of the Moon* it became obvious in my opinion, that Lourie did not have a copy of Brunner's missing manuscript, or if he did, he was consistently making erroneous conclusions and representations. Nevertheless, certain portions of Lourie's book did appear in my opinion to result in copyright infringement on Brunner's writings, unless of course there exists some form of release, written permission, agreement or contract between the two. One thing I knew for certain, both as a private individual and the legal copyright holder of Brunner's materials, I had signed no such release.

Threats of prosecution or litigation being my only recourse, I contacted Lourie's publisher on 11 Nov 1993. More than two months later having received no response, I again contacted the publisher on 25 Jan 1994 stating in part ... "Researching historical records for my manuscript, I discovered *Sweat of the Sun, Tears of the Moon* by Peter Lourie, published by Atheneum in 1991. On November 11, 1993 Atheneum was advised by U.S. Mail that a large amount of *Sweat of the Sun, Tears of the Moon* [may have] resulted from copyright infringement on United States copyrights TXu 270-451 and TXu 298-422. Once again, to avoid future litigation, I request copies of all written permission, agreements, contracts, and/or tape recordings by and between Mr. Lourie and Mr. Brunner be provided if they exist. If it is found that Eugene Brunner did give Peter Lourie a release, the matter may be dropped."

Shortly thereafter I received a response from Macmillan's legal department. Basically the publishing company washed their hands of the issue, taking the position that the matter was between myself and Lourie. Any claim of possible copyright infringement, according to Macmillan's legal department, was therefore to be directed to Mr. Lourie, whose contact information was provided.

Macmillan had called my semi-bluff and the time had come for me to re-analyze my position and options. Two factors needed to be considered. Mainly, whether or not any copyright infringement had occurred, and if so, could it be proven in a court of law? Some soul searching would also be in order ... were my emotions and feelings of betrayal clouding my judgement? More importantly, if infringement occurred and could be proven, was my family which had recently grown to seven, in the financial position to commence a protracted legal action in Federal Court? This question at least had an immediate answer ... no, we were not.

Whether emotions were clouding my judgement or not was unclear. However, I could not dispute the fact that I had been upset over my character's portrayal in Lourie's epilogue. Beyond that point it must be admitted that I was also unhappy with what I considered to be insinuation's in Lourie's book concerning other characters that in my opinion did not conform with acceptable standards of propriety or taste. The inference for example that Dyott had settled in Ecuador, as far away from New York as he could ... "because it was the farthest he could get from his wife" ... whether true or not, was in my mind clearly inappropriate.

Brunner as well faced what I deemed as inappropriate insinuations within *Sweat of the Sun, Tears of the Moon*. For Lourie to have professed such an admiration of Brunner, purportedly having been privy to Brunner's extensive body of work, one would think that even though Lourie would dismiss the claims of Brunner being a fraud, charlatan, thief or imposter, that an effort would have been made to avoid such a topic. Lourie's conjecture that a child in El Triunfo could have possibly been Brunner's, in my opinion was also beyond acceptable standards of propriety or taste. What actually bothered me the most, was that Lourie had made no contact with Brunner's widow, or at the least, provided the family with a copy of the manuscript (or book) as agreed.

Personal feelings aside, the facts and evidence had to be examined before any decision on litigation could be reached. Although Brunner's manuscript disappeared roughly at the time Lourie had departed Ecuador, and Lourie himself wrote in *Sweat of the Sun, Tears of the Moon* ... "Part of me, I admit, wanted to grab those maps and run ... ," Brunner's manuscript would later surface in Ecuador. I concluded therefore that Lourie had not absconded with Brunner's manuscript. [481]

The question was then raised if Lourie had somehow obtained a copy that was being used as a source of material for his book. Certain of Brunner's stories, such as his childhood treasure dream, were presented by Lourie almost verbatim, while other stories contained erroneous inconsistencies. Closely examining *Sweat of the Sun, Tears of the Moon*, I came to the conclusion that, in general, Lourie must have been writing from notes taken or recorded during conversations with Brunner. I also took into consideration that names, titles, slogans, short phrases, ideas and facts cannot be protected by copyright. It was my opinion that if Lourie had possessed a copy of Brunner's manuscript, Lourie would have probably spelled Blake as Blacke and other erroneous inconsistencies would have been avoided. For all these reasons and more, the matter was dropped.

One of Lourie's quotes from Brunner within *Sweat of the Sun, Tears of the Moon* brings to mind yet another possible betrayal. Speaking about his life's work Brunner states ... "All this will go to someone when I die, so my work will not be lost. I will carry on, even when I am dead." In the back of my mind has always been the question ... Did my failure to bring the Llanganati project to a successful conclusion betray Brunner's legacy ... and does this book help establish his legacy?

■ ■ ■

Norman Scott's curriculum vitae, as presented to Ecuador's National Institute of Cultural Heritage in the eighties, listed Norman's involvement on international projects conducted through his company Expeditions

---

[481] Of course my conclusion was later confirmed when Michael Dyott admitted that Gruber had Brunner's manuscript at the time.

Unlimited. While conducting research for this manuscript during 2010, I discovered Scott's current curriculum vitae online, which also included projects made through his company Global Explorations. A mere four years after our association, I discovered that Scott or his team had made an expedition to Cerro Hermoso and Brunner's base camp in 1992! Instantaneously I experienced feelings of betrayal, but was not surprised with this new revelation in the least. In reality, this information only confirmed my suspicions on why Scott had been reluctant to sign a non-competition clause.

During our negotiations Scott had insinuated that other proposed projects in Ecuador were under review with third parties and he would not limit his options, which was understandable, but in my opinion to proceed with the same project, was not. In my opinion, it now appears that my original gut feeling and possibly that of "Partner A," correctly assumed that Scott was seeking information and intended on proceeding with the project, with or without me.

Two Ecuadorian projects appear on Scott's current curriculum vitae, which indicates that in 1992 Scott ... "Conducted full geophysical survey for Discovery II at 13,000 feet in the Llanganati Mountains of Ecuador in search of the treasure of Atahualpa, the last Inca King, using ground penetrating radar, magnetometer, infrared scanner, remote operated vehicle, and global positioning system." Another entry for 1995 indicates Scott's company conducted a ... "Magnetometer survey for Maritime Explorations in Ecuador trying to locate the *Capitana* off Chanduy Reef. Have located an ancient vessel."

Norman Scott, always the self indulging publicist, wisely makes his money from investors or print, television and movie rights not treasure recovery, conducted an interview with Barbara Stewart, a reporter for the Orlando Sentinel. The interview and article appeared in the 9 Aug 1992 edition and the relevant portion is reproduced here ... "'We started out as treasure hunters,' he says the 'we' being either royal or a reference to whoever was around at the time. 'But the word is taboo to us now.' These days, Scott has awarded himself a loftier, if wordier, title: 'Cultural asset recoverer.' Global Explorations Inc. in Gainesville, which he heads, and which is supported by a few investors, is a 'geophysical company ... for scientific expeditions.' 'We market history for profit,' Scott says. He doesn't hunt treasure to keep, like Mel Fisher. He used to, but he didn't find much. Now he hunts treasure with a past, treasure steeped in history hunts that won't make him billions but do make great party stories. Such as a hunt going on right now for gold in Ecuador, hidden by Incas some 500 years ago from marauding Spanish explorers some 750 tons of it, more than all the gold in Fort Knox, gold that, if found, the Ecuadorian government will claim. This afternoon, he is summoned to talk to his hired mountaineers, calling in on a radio 14,700 feet up in the Andes Mountains ..." [482]

---

[482] Used with permission of the *Orlando Sentinel* ©1992

Scott's other Ecuadorian project coincidentally shared a common interest with Brunner's endless research on shipwrecked treasure. Having spent thousands of hours diving in Ecuadorian waters, Brunner recorded his exploits and discoveries during the fifties and sixties in his manuscript *Ecuador y Sus Tesoros.* Brunner's manuscript contains stories similar in content to Brunner's Llanganati adventures, including Mar Bravo, the Isla de Plata and Chanduy Reef treasures.

It would be in 1996 that a Robert McClung, former Director of Field Operations for Maritime Explorations, discovered the shipwreck of the famous Treasure Galleon of 1654, *Jesus Maria La Limpia de Concepcion* (*The Capitana*), in the waters off Chanduy, Ecuador. Under contract with a private group of Ecuadorian investors an estimated $25 million US Dollars worth of treasure and artifacts were recovered under McClung's expedition leadership. *The New York Times* published an article written by Dana Jean Schemo entitled "Search for a Galleon off Ecuador Yields a Shipwreck and a Dispute" in its 14 Apr 97 edition, a portion of which is reproduced here ... "After scouring historical records and following a trail of broken pottery scattered on the ocean floor, an American diver appears to have found the largest Spanish galleon built in the New World, which sank off the coast of Ecuador nearly 350 years ago. The diver, Robert McClung ... traced the legendary ship to an almost irritatingly logical place: under 30 feet of water a mile offshore from El Real, the coastal village founded by the wreck's survivors. Treasure seekers believe that the ship, the Capitana, carried silver coins and gold worth millions of dollars.'When I actually recovered the first coins, there was no doubt in my mind that I had the Capitana,'said Mr. McClung, now the lead diver on a major undersea expedition being carried out under the watch of two Ecuadorean warships here. 'I said, This is it.'"

Though the discovery of the *Capitana* would have seemed to reward years of labor, McClung's elation was short lived. For as I had predicted a decade earlier, the discovery of any lost treasure would attract intrigue, confusion, and conflicting claims of ownership that exhibited a sense of entitlement on the part of others. As it became known that Mr. McClung had discovered the wreck, a second group of treasure hunters disputed McClung's find. This group was led by an Ecuadorean history buff named Rony Almeida and a Don Johnson, who was under investigation in Florida on suspicion of cheating investors. In 1993 the Securities and Exchange Commission had also issued a *Cease and Desist Order*, just as they had against Chuck Powell in Georgia, banning Mr. Johnson's investment activities in Connecticut. The group had argued that the *Capitana* was really some five miles away, where they had a permit to search.

As Dana Jean Schemo continued to relate in her *New York Times* article ... "The atmosphere of uncertainty has prompted the director of Ecuador's Institute of Cultural Patrimony to withhold judgment until further testing of the relics. But archeologists from the institute and from the Ecuadorean merchant marine said in interviews on board the recovery ship that they believed that the trove of undersea coins, silver bars and cannon balls proved that the wreck was the Capitana." [483]

As with any treasure story many different versions of events abound. Apparently, Sub-America Corporation, owned by Argentine Herman Moro and financed by Dave Horner, first obtained a lease on the site in 1996 and discovered the wreck site with a magnetometer. However, about the same time of the magnetometer discovery and before Sub-America's divers could verify the site, diver Rob McClung who was working for another company which held the adjacent lease, also stumbled upon it and filed a discovery claim before Sub-America could verify its own discovery. Confusion and legal threats followed. However, after some initial acrimony, the two groups agreed to work together to conduct the salvage. The subsequent work was conducted legally and in cooperation with the Ecuadorian Navy and members of the National Institute of Cultural Patrimony, with both organizations having many representatives present during the recovery work. A conservation lab was established at the Salinas Naval Base and all of the artifacts were processed at that location before being transferred to the Central Bank to await division. The division was held about a year later and the Americans were allowed to take their share out of Ecuador for sale in the United States.

Later, another group out of Florida again involving Rob McClung, obtained a sub-contract from Sub-America in 2002 and returned with an even larger ship to re-excavate the site. It was alleged that McClung had fabricated a story and convinced new investors that the work had been terminated early due to interference from the Ecuadorian Navy and a dispute with the government over the ownership and division of treasure. Implicitly the viewer was left with the assumption that the work had not been completed and much treasure was left behind. [484]However the story continues, nothing

---

[483] "At the invitation of the Institute of Cultural Patrimony of Ecuador and of Sub-America Discoveries, Inc. Company, I have inspected an assemblage of cultural material excavated from a 17th-century shipwreck located 1 nautical mile offshore from the town of El Real, Ecuador, in 10 meters of water. From Saturday, March 29th through April 3rd, 1997, I was aboard the R/V Explorer, and inspected a wide variety of cultural materials being excavated from the wreck site. Over two thousand silver coins and one gold coin were brought up during that particular period, along with a large silver bar, pottery shards, encrusted objects, some tentatively identified as iron (fe) fasteners, and copper-based (Cu) cannon balls. Based on all the cultural material and organic remains (woods) that I have examined I can safely state that the ship being presently excavated is the Jesús María de la Limpia Concepción, also known as la Capitana. There is not one single element that could suggest another identity or dating for this particular shipwreck." *Archeological report of John de Bry aboard the R/V Explorer, off El Real, Ecuador 2 Apr 97.*

[484] In the summer of 1997 researchers located in the Jesuit archives in France, extensive new information that the Spanish had employed their own recovery operations on the *Capitana* for ten years between 1654 and 1663, having left

of the kind had ever transpired. The account of Rob McClung, which even appeared on television at one point, allegedly had no basis in reality although sufficient persons bought into it and financed another expedition to the site.

After the large salvage expeditions of 1997 and 2002, it was no longer economically feasible to continue further salvage operations and the site was abandoned after 2003. Sub-America did not bother to renew their lease, and no one else applied for the concession, because the wreck was widely believed to have been worked out. Only recently was a new lease on the site obtained by a new Ecuadorian company.

To this day I recall inadvertently discovering the Ecuadorian treasure salvage program about McClung on educational television. Regrettably, at the time I was flipping channels and only caught a few minutes of the program, so at the time I did not realize that the shipwreck being discussed was the *Capitana*, for if I had, I would have taken a closer look at Brunner's documentation on the site. From what little I saw of the program, I was under the impression that a Spanish shipwreck near the Gulf of Guayaquil was being salvaged. It appeared that there was a dispute over the ownership and division of artifacts, which were whisked away by the military and deposited in the Central Bank. The program left me with the visual image of an omnipresent soldier (or a sailor) in the background and his automatic weapon.

McClung's story had hit very close to home. I had always been of the opinion that upon the recovery of any treasure, while operating under an archaeological permit without the benefit of a companion contract and presidential decree, a dispute with the government just as McClung had described, would occur. After viewing the program I felt vindicated, but now that appears not to be the case, as there ultimately was a division of treasure that was allowed to be removed from Ecuador.

On the other hand, it was also obvious to me that it should be taken into consideration that the Llanganati treasure consisted of handcrafted Inca artifacts and bulk materials, while the *Capitana's* treasure consisted mainly of coinage, thus two separate and distinct categories of "cultural heritage" existed. Furthermore, Ecuador (and the international community for that matter) had a great deal of prior experience and precedent to follow when dealing with shipwreck salvage rights, but never before had a commercial land-based salvage operation such as ours, ever been considered in Ecuador.

Throughout my involvement with the Llanganati project, consternation over the unknown, what would transpire upon the recovery of such a massive treasure, was omnipresent. I feared the obvious, that the world's lust for

---

little unrecovered treasure behind. The Spanish documents found in the Jesuit archive categorically state that they quit recovery operations on the wreck in 1663 after reporting to creditors in France that the wreck had nothing further to yield and that they had already recovered over five times what had been officially manifested.

Inca gold would not end with any recovery ... the lust for Inca gold would only be fueled.

How many years of legal battles would lay ahead dispensing with the claims of governments, companies or individuals, all seeking a share of Inca gold discovered through the labors of Eugene Brunner? The list of possibilities of course appeared endless ... the governments of Ecuador, Peru, Spain and England, Brunner's heirs, associates, sub-contractors, investors, partners and all their heirs. Beyond that, would the rightful heirs, the descendants of the Inca Atahualpa, consider the treasure as their inheritance and demand its return? And most important, what position would the indigenous peoples themselves take on such a massive recovery of cultural heritage?

One only needs to review the events that transpired over the *Capitana* recovery and the mere mention of a possible distribution of the purported *El Pensamiento* treasure, to realize that the discoverer of the Llanganati treasure will be inundated with claims, some perhaps valid, some definitely not. Brunner would write in 1979 ... "I am sure that once the treasure is discovered and delivered to the vaults of the Central Bank, this will only serve to shed more blood, or will serve for fighting and discord, then it is best that the treasure stay where it is now."

■ ■ ■

Many years would pass and events would transpire on continents far removed from Ecuador, which would appear to vindicate my fears, as lust for Inca gold would once again rear its ugly head. One can help but be struck by the hypocrisy of the situation and that of the central entity to the story I am about to relate. This entity was indisputably responsible for the greatest mass destructions of cultural heritage in history. Aztec, Mayan and Incan precious metal artifacts were not admired for artistic beauty or preserved for posterity, they were destroyed and melted into bars, ingots or coinage. Indigenous peoples and their realms were conquered, looted, pillaged, raped, murdered and exploited, all in the name of the church and the Kingdom of Spain.

It would be 2007 when once again an American company based out of Florida, Odyssey Marine Exploration, Inc., would find itself center stage in an international case of treasure recovery. At stake in the matter was ownership of a recovered sunken treasure consisting of an estimated 500,000 gold and silver coins, with a purported value of $504 million US Dollars. The treasure's recovery in international waters and subsequent transfer to Florida, peaked the interest and legal challenges of many, including the government's of Spain and Peru.

Odyssey took the position that the treasure was discovered in international waters. Therefore, the company acted legally and appropriately in the recovery of the artifacts. Odyssey indicated further that it did not know with certainty what ship the treasure came from, as there was absolutely no provenance of any vessel or human remains located at the recovery site and the treasure was discovered directly on the sea floor. Despite that, several countries expressed interest in the matter, most notably Spain and Peru.

Irrespective of the lack of provenance required by the archeological community to substantiate a find, both countries shared the belief that the treasure was from the shipwreck of the *Nuestra Señora de las Mercedes*, which was sunk by British warships in 1804. [485]

The Kingdom of Spain claimed "sovereign immunity" and argued that Spain had ... "not abandoned its ownership and other rights in cargo or other property of the Kingdom of Spain on or in its sunken vessels." Peru entered the mix filing a claim contending that the treasure coins were minted in Lima and made with Peruvian silver and gold belonging to the Inca's. Many of the descendants of passengers on the *Nuestra Señora de las Mercedes* joined the suit as well, claiming that 75 percent of the cargo aboard was commercial and did not belong to Spain but to their relatives, a fact that was never disputed.

The evidence, including accounts from Spain's "experts" and her own contemporaneous diplomatic communications, proves that the *Mercedes* was on a commercial mission on her final voyage, a fact that would legally void Spain's claim of immunity under settled international law and conventions, as a distinction between cargo and vessel is allowed and even required by settled admiralty law. According to the manifest of the *Mercedes*, the vast majority of cargo on board did not even belong to Spain, even Spain conceded the cargo was "articles of Spanish citizens." Even if the treasure was from the *Mercedes*, Odyssey held the unequivocal belief that the ship was on a commercial voyage, rendering its contents open to salvage law. Had it been on an official mission for the government, like a warship, only then could the matter have been interpreted otherwise. A United States Federal Judge ruled there was enough evidence to confirm the recovery site was that of the *Mercedes* and that the vessel and its cargo were subject to sovereign immunity.

Regardless of the facts, evidence and legal precedent, some say with US State Department interference on Spain's behalf and an alleged behind the

---

[485] The *Nuestra Señora de las Mercedes* was a Spanish frigate which was sunk by the British off the south coast of Portugal on 5 Oct 1804. While traveling in a small fleet returning to Spain from South America in 1804, the *Nuestra Señora de las Mercedes*, carrying enormous quantities of gold, silver and jewels, was blown up by the British off Cape Santa Maria, Portugal. Spain was at the time a neutral country, but was showing signs of declaring war in alliance with Napoleonic France. Acting on Admiralty orders Vice-Admiral Sir Graham Moore required the Spaniards to change their course and sail for England. The senior Spanish officer refused and opened fire on the British, leading to a short battle during which the *Mercedes* blew up. The English Prize Office removed 4,773,153 gold and silver pesos from the three captured ships, 1,307,634 of which belonged to the King of Spain. Another estimated $1,000,000 in gold and silver, including a solders' fund of 143,070 pesos, was estimated to have gone down with the *Mercedes*. After the incident Spain declared war on England.

scenes political deal, the case was decided in favor of Spain. The case was then immediately appealed to the United States Court of Appeals for the Eleventh Circuit who confirmed the lower courts ruling. The United States Supreme Court rejected Odyssey's appeal and the $504 million US Dollars worth of treasure was ordered to be returned to Spain. Two Spanish Hercules transport planes were then dispatched to collect Spain's "national treasure."

Throughout Odyssey's protracted five year legal battle, the company, correctly in my opinion, held the position that the trial's outcome would have a significant impact on shipwreck recoveries and claims ...

"From an archaeological and historical standpoint, shipwrecks will no longer be properly documented, recovered and conserved. Potential owners will neither receive notice nor an opportunity to have their claims adjudicated, and there will be no forum in which merits rulings on the status and disposition of property lost at sea can be obtained. At stake in this appeal is nothing less than preserving the integrity of a forum for resolution of shipwreck disputes; otherwise, this historic resource may be forever lost." [486]

Regrettably, it is my opinion that the archeological community themselves, those that ascribe to the wait and see philosophy, the methodology of allowing others to spend massive amounts of time, money and manpower discovering a countries lost "cultural heritage," then confiscating the fruit of their labors, are committing a betrayal against what they are intent on preserving ... a country's cultural heritage. Without considering the consequences of their actions, an atmosphere has been created and perpetuated over many decades, where the discoverer of any lost treasure will be inclined not to report or preserve any great find for posterity. We can only hope that the desecration of Incan cultural heritage by the Spanish in the sixteenth century, does not become the norm during the twenty-first century.

Understandably, Ministries or Institutes of Culture and Patrimony do not have the financial resources or manpower to search out lost cultural heritage. Therefore, the groundwork for commercial assistance on such projects should be laid out on terms favorable to all parties in advance, just as my company attempted in Ecuador. Otherwise, a country's lost treasures are destined to be discovered and removed from the country piece-meal, just as occurred with Valverde and Blacke. Who knows how many countless others may have already quenched their lust for Inca gold with a knapsack of treasure that once removed provided sufficient wealth to live comfortably for the rest of their lives?

■ ■ ■

---

[486] From Odyssey Marine Exploration, Inc. VS. The Kingdom of Spain in United States Court of Appeals for the Eleventh Circuit, *Appellant's Opening Brief* dated May, 2010.

For me personally, the most devastating and ultimate betrayal throughout centuries of lust for Inca gold, came many years after Eugene Brunner's demise and developed through what I considered a most unlikely source. A source so close to my heart, that betrayal on such a scale and magnitude was hard to contemplate and even harder to endure. This betrayal would occur during 2006 and culminated in December of the same year, breaking my heart.

It would be 10 Jan 2006 that the call arrived announcing "Abuelita" had died of respiratory arrest and pneumonia at 101 years of age ... just two months shy of one hundred and two. Considering her advanced age, one could say it would have been reasonable and normal to expect such a call. It appeared to me however, that my spouse was devastated beyond normal grief, almost to the point of being hysterical, as though a much younger person had met a sudden and unexpected end. Based on current and past behavior, and the fact that it requires two people to fall in love in order to get married, but only one to fall out of love to get divorced, I predicted that my nearly thirty year relationship would be over within a year, or at the least, my spouse would be living in another state with her ... "real family."

In my opinion, it appears more common than not, that the number one pitfall in any relationship is that the main issue a couple argues about would be extended family ... or nothing at all! Complaints being perceived as an attack also escalate any conflict, often resulting in a defensiveness and a failure to take responsibility for ones actions, stonewalling or silent treatment. Rather than accept responsibility or apologize, either hoping to avoid the issue or perhaps trying to calm down and not make it worse, a spouse stonewalls. The result of doing so, is of course the exact opposite, as when one is faced with somebody who is silent like that, the argument escalates.

I believe this pitfall occurred in my relationship as well, which in my opinion was destined to fail. For in my opinion not only was there a lack of respect in the relationship, but there was contempt, the best predictor of divorce, and an air of entitlement similar to what I had previously encountered. Everything always appeared to be about outward appearances, what people outside the family would think or how events would be perceived.

What transpired for our family over the following year was the most turbulent year of my marriage.[487] My love, contentment, or just a desire to

---

[487] It is not my intent to imply that I was a perfect husband and my wife was the devil reincarnate. The woman had and has many kind and enduring traits that not only caused me to fall in love, but to have five children and remain in a troubled relationship for nearly thirty years. There is always two sides to every story and like everyone, I have made mistakes and done things that one might not be proud of. Regardless, my priority in life has always been my wife and children. I personally would rate our overall relationship as ... worst than some ... better than most!

maintain the family unit, enabled me to justify normally unacceptable behavior. I consistently opined that perhaps it was my fault, or blamed the irrational behavior on the differences of customs, culture, education, language, age, upbringing or peer pressure. However, in my mind nothing could ever justify that a husband and children were secondary to a grandmother, mother or brother, who were referred to as "my real family." Upon "Abuelita's" death, everything became more and more about my spouse's ... "real family."

■ ■ ■

In order to relate the events that were about to transpire, I must re-establish that my research and draft for this book commenced in the early nineties. Over the ensuing years our family moved numerous times between California, Nevada and Vermont. During a portion of this period of time, Brunner's materials and my personal papers were boxed and in a storage unit in Nevada. It would be in late 2002 when our family returned to Nevada, removing our personal property and the Ecuador papers from storage we discovered that some electronics (such as my computer scanner) had been ruined by the heat.

Nearly a year later, in late 2003, with the purchase of a new flatbed scanner, work on my manuscript resumed in earnest. Brunner's illustrations, maps, short stories, contracts, correspondence and notes, along with the documentation from my involvement with the project, were all scanned into digital files and stored on the computers hard drive. Digital working copies of Brunner's illustrations were also made and I spent many hours cleaning up the scans. One thing led to another and the project was once again moved to the back burner of my mind ... until mid-2006.

Still to this day I can remember the sense of anger and hostility that permeated the air, on every occasion that my wife witnessed me working with the project papers. Of course being clueless, I had incorrectly assumed that my spouse was upset over something I had done, did not do, or might have done. Normally, as was her habit, my wife would avoid raising an issue that was bothering her, but I could clearly sense an unexplained anger and hostility. Finally one day, my wife apparently could not hold it in any longer, exploding in a rage she stated ... "those are not your papers, they are my mother's!"

Certainly my wife did not desire to hear the rational conversation that followed. Over a twenty year period, there was only so much that could be said or repeated on the matter, the facts would always remain the same. For some reason my wife could not, or would not, understand that when we purchased Brunner's materials from her mother some twenty years past, a binding contract had been entered into and money changed hands. We clearly had not entered into any form of partnership with her mother, so if money was made, her mother would have stood to share in the profits according to the contract, yet if a loss occurred just as it had, her mother would not share in that loss or the expenses of the project.

Additionally, some of the Brunner materials were obtained from other sources as explained herein and I personally had devoted two years to the project, with our family losing a great deal of money on the venture. So as could be expected, I explained once again that it had always been my intent to recoup some of our loses with the publication of one or more books on the subject. The only response I would ever receive was always that I had "stolen" the papers from her mother by only paying a small fee and a percentage of profits.

Rather than deal with the hostility over the issue any further, I chose to continue working on the illustrations and writing sections of my manuscript only when my wife was out of the house, thereby avoiding any more hostility or confrontation. After a short while, either paranoia or one of those gut feelings of impending disaster came over me. For the time being at least, I chose to pack the majority of the project materials, which had previously been scattered in almost every room of the house, into one large plastic storage container. To further avoid any confrontation with my spouse, the container was then placed in our master bedroom walk-in-closet, along with nine other such containers that were filled with children's old toys and personal memorabilia that had already been stored there. Out of sight ... out of mind, the issue was forgotten ... at least by me.

At some point in time the hard drive on my computer crashed. As I only had made working backup copies of Brunner's illustrations and a small portion of the documentation, the computer was entrusted to a technician with the instruction to recover all of the files from the "Book folder" before reformatting the drive. Upon the return of the repaired computer, I was horrified to realize that the files backed up by the technician were not consistent with my request! Although I still possessed all of the hard copies, a great deal of time and labor was lost. At that moment I felt fortunate to still possess my working copies of the important illustrations for the Ecuador project. In short, every illustration reproduced within Chapters V and VI, along with Brunner's copy of the *Guzmán Map*, had been preserved for posterity and everything else could be re-scanned.

Around Thanksgiving our eldest child had for the first time expressed an interest in viewing the Ecuador project documentation, but due to my procrastination, the process of assembling and providing her with the relevant materials slipped my mind. Sometime in the beginning of December, one night while I was trying to go to sleep, my spouse was cleaning the master bedroom closet, a process that lasted into the wee hours of the morning. In itself, not something out of the ordinary, as when my wife was mad with me or trying to avoid me, she would clean late into the early morning hours. An event that had previously grown to the point of becoming a family joke ... that if I wanted the house cleaned, I just needed to annoy my spouse! But once again, paranoia or that gut feeling of impending disaster came over me ... something was amiss.

The next day, after my spouse had left the house, my curiosity got the best of me. Examining the closet, everything appeared to be organized and in order. The plastic storage containers were all there and neatly stacked, but upon closer examination I discovered that every container was now filled with just toys and personal memorabilia! The Ecuador papers, all of Brunner's and my work was nowhere to be found! I expanded my search to every other closet and container within the house and garage ... except for the original Ecuadoran Explorations and Ecuadorian government documents within a file folder and my digital copies ... everything was gone! Outraged, I also began to wonder if the crash of my hard drive had been random after all, but I gave my wife the benefit of doubt, as I did not believe she was capable of such an act. Needless to say, December turned out to be one of the worst months of our relationship.

It would be early Sunday morning, 6 Jan 2007, just a few days shy of the anniversary of "Abuelita's" demise, that my wife of nearly thirty years left a note on the refrigerator that stated ... "I'm going to see my brother out for breakfast. Be back by?" The day passed agonizingly and just as I had predicted nearly a year prior, my wife had left the State. Within the month and without further discussion, I was served divorce papers. [488]

■ ■ ■

Three months' after my wife left, we actually got back together for about a week, which was in my opinion, one of the best periods of our entire relationship. During our time together my wife admitted that she had removed the Ecuador papers a little at a time so that I would not notice. Whether this statement was the truth or not I'll never know with certainty,[489] for sadly there had always been difficulties with the truth, a flaw that would work to my benefit throughout the court proceedings.

As has been previously stated, everything for my wife and her "real family" was always about outward appearances. Sometimes this would be taken to the point of making up stories and at the same time believing them to be true,[490] at least in public. It was my opinion that lying was almost a normal and reflexive way of responding to questions, bending the truth about everything, large and small. When caught in a lie, she would become hostile or try to disregard the fact she lied, often playing it off as a joke or misunderstanding.

What my wife did not understand or refused to understand, was that not only had a portion of the Brunner materials been electronically scanned into my computer, but the mere taking and holding of these materials would not

---

[488] All references and quotes concerning the parties relationship and dispute over the "Brunner, Ecuador or personal papers" come from public records. All reference to events and personal information, although a matter of public record , that are not relevant to the "Brunner, Ecuador or personal papers," have been omitted to protect the parties personal privacy.

[489] In an attempt to obtain confirmation of this allegation, the question was put forth as a *Request for Admission,* and "denied."

[490] This reminds me of the quote attributed to Lenin ... "A lie told often enough becomes truth."

convey ownership or title, specifically to items such as registered copyrights. Ironically at this point in time, just the mere act of telling the truth, would have confirmed my wife's community property interest in the Brunner materials and copyrights.

Any divorce is basically an accounting process where the assets [community property] and liabilities of the marriage are equally divided. Therefore, similar to property issues in a bankruptcy, once court papers are filed, everything comes under the jurisdiction of the court. Any community property removed or transferred from the jurisdiction of the court by either party prior to divorce, of course, becomes subject to closer scrutiny. Unwittingly, my wife had set the stage in motion for an uninterested third party, a judge, to determine the disposition of the Brunner materials and my personal papers.

Considering that for twenty years my spouse had never exhibited any personal interest in the Brunner materials or my personal papers, and through legal filings in the beginning of the divorce claiming no community property interest in the materials, it was obvious by her actions and words that she wanted them only for her mother. How far she would go to keep the Brunner materials became evident when it was asserted in her initial court filing, after moving out-of-state and residing with her mother ... "That there is no community property or community debts of the parties to be adjudicated in this action."... the first of many contradictory and conflicting positions taken under oath.

After the initial shock of being served with divorce papers, I researched the law and prepared my *Answer and Counterclaim for Divorce,* in which all community property and debts were listed as required. At the time, trying to be as reasonable and fair as possible, this court filing proposed that my wife be awarded ... "Physical possession of all 'Brunner' papers" and I would obtain ... "Physical possession of all other project papers." Through her attorney an *Answer to Defendant's Counterclaim* was filed under oath indicating that "...the 'Brunner' papers do not belong to either party but are the property of Plaintiff's mother; also the 'project papers' named herein do not belong to either party but are the property of Plaintiff's mother."

After numerous failed attempts to resolve the issues within our divorce, I filed a Motion with the Court in May of 2007 seeking in part, the return of personal property (Copyright Certificates, Brunner & personal papers) thoroughly detailed in Exhibit 23. The lengthy Motion stated in part ... "Defendant contends that plaintiff did willfully remove personal property of Defendant, that is an issue of this action, from the jurisdiction of this Court. That Plaintiff should be ordered to return said property to the Courts jurisdiction, and held by her attorney of record, until said issue is adjudicated."

Clearly hoping to delay the issue, an *Opposition* was filed stating in part ... "The Defendant asks for the return of personal property but lists no personal property that he believes should be returned to him. It would be impossible to comply with his requests without knowing what he thinks is his personal property. Clearly property issues are matters for trial, but if Plaintiff knew what personal property the Defendant was referring to, perhaps its return could be negotiated."

Upon learning that my soon to be ex-mother-in-law was planning a trip to Ecuador in the near future, another *Motion for the Return of Personal Property,* placed all parties on notice that the "Ecuador papers" were under the court's jurisdiction and that there would be consequences to any transfer or removal. In order to resolve the issue once and for all, a *Motion* was also made to join my mother-in-law in the lawsuit, these were filed at the beginning of July and stated in part ... "It came to the attention of the Defense that subject property has been removed from the jurisdiction of this Court and taken to ... , where the Plaintiff and her mother reside. It has also become known to Defendant, that Plaintiff's mother is leaving for Ecuador in July and that said property, whose subject matter covers lost and unrecovered treasure in Ecuador, may be removed from the country at said time."

It would not be until the end of July after much legal negotiation, process and posturing that the matter would finally be argued in front of the Judge. After explaining to the Judge what the personal property in question consisted of, in response to a question from the Judge, I explained that the most important document required for trial was the contract of sale for the Brunner materials which would provide indisputable proof of ownership. In a contradictory statement my wife's attorney argued that … "These are not documents relating to the community. They are things of personal interest to him that there is a question as to whether they are community or separate. They have nothing to do ... I believe it is a trial issue. They have nothing to do with bills, community interest, debts, that sort of thing."

The Judge's response to the lawyers argument ... "Well then, he can have them back then" ... apparently caught the attorney off-guard, as his immediate response was ... "Huh!"...the judge repeated ... "He can have the documents back then can he not? Or no?" The lawyer replied ... "Well she thinks they are hers ... they are papers from a relative [my wife spoke up and said "My Mom"] ... that they both believe are their personal property." The Judge then decided that copies be made for me, the lawyer interjected that it should be at my expense due to the multitude of materials, I acknowledged that it indeed was a large plastic tub full of papers, but that I only required a copy of the contract to prove ownership. The Judge stated ... "Yeah, well give him that document at the very least," to which the attorney responded ... "I will give him a copy of everything."

In hindsight I must admit that I was a little surprised with the lawyer's contradictory claim that the documents were not community property and my wife claimed they were her personal property.[491] Based on my experience and past history dealing with stories, I had expected to be

---

[491] This claim also contradicted the initial sworn statement that they "do not belong to either party but are the property of Plaintiff's mother."

confronted with a complete denial that the papers ever existed, were in my possession and removed, that my wife had them or any knowledge of where they were. Understandably, I was ecstatic with the fact that we would just be dealing with the legal issue of ownership at trial, which I knew could be established beyond question. As for the Judge's final decision on the issue, I could not have hoped for anything more ... "Just give him [me] everything and he can make copies of what he wants. But make sure they are inventoried before they go over. Sir, you inventory them immediately upon receipt. Copy what you want and send it back. Have copies made and I'll decide at trial [ownership]."

My ecstacy would not last long. It is my assumption that due to the attorney's agreement to produce the materials and with no objection from my wife, who had been an active participant in the argument, the Judge, apparently assuming the transfer would occur forthwith, failed to establish a time limit for the transfer to occur. On three separate occasions I asked my wife for a date that she would produce the materials as the Judge had Ordered. The responses were not what I had hoped for ... "we'll see what I have to do or not," ... "you need to drop the paper's issue, I want my mom to be happy"...and ... "I don't care what the Judge said." Frustrated, I emailed her attorney, who clearly must have understood that compliance with the Judge's Order was mandatory, and requested a date for production. To my astonishment a reply came that stated in part ... "I have spoken with my client and she informs me that she does not have the 'Ecuador papers' and therefore she cannot comply with the Court Order to produce them to you because she doesn't have them. If you disagree with this, we will take it up at the time of trial."

Deferring the issue until trial had always been this attorney's position and the letter seemed to dictate a take it or leave it attitude. It also appeared that the stalling tactic had allowed the documents to be removed from the country and taken to Ecuador.[492] Ultimately this lawyer and his firm were in for a rude awakening.

Reviewing my position, I realized that I still possessed digital copies and originals of the most important materials, those concerning the Llanganati treasure. Shrewdly, Brunner's manuscripts had been copyrighted and deposited in the Library of Congress just for this eventuality. Meaning of course that they could easily be replaced if lost or stolen. Brunner's other project documentation was not of any immediate interest as well, so I realized that I only needed a copy of the contract of sale, the ultimate proof of ownership.

Knowing that twenty-five years prior, copies of this contract had been supplied to my partners, the Government of Ecuador, and submitted with my copyright application, obtaining a copy would be difficult but not impossible. Later, hoping that my financial partners had retained a file on

[492] It is my opinion that although a portion of the documents may have been taken to Ecuador, I do not believe that they were removed in their entirety.

our project, an email was sent stating ... "A voice from the past seeking your assistance. As you may remember, after two years of negotiations for our company, obtaining the final approval for a Presidential Decree, I went to Ecuador to sign the decree as negotiated and the deal fell through. At that point I could no longer continue with the project. Absent that decree [in my opinion], the government would have robbed us of any recovery. In addition, there were threats on my life and we personally went broke on the failure of this project. We lost our entire life savings, house, and went into debt over this project and moved to California. I could not continue and would not ask you to invest any more.

"I do not regret the decision to have attempted this project. I enjoyed the learning experience, especially meeting people and dealing with yourself and Justus. I had considered at the time to let things die down and perhaps continue the project at a later date. (I did see that Norman Scott at some point, has made an expedition to Cerro Hermoso as well.) I have always considered writing a book about the treasure, Brunner's involvement and mine. However, twenty years have passed. The documents to base my story upon, all the Brunner materials and my correspondence with you detailing events of the negotiations have all been removed from my possession and transferred to a third party.

"Currently I am involved in a court case ..., seeking the return of my papers. In court documents, I have stated that a portion was transferred to Ecuadoran Explorations, Inc., I have not named you or Justus to protect your privacy. I know you are a very busy man and perhaps you no longer have the file or do not desire to help. However, if you still have the file, I would greatly appreciate a copy of the contract entered into between me and (my mother-in-law) where I purchase the Brunner documents and the letter where I transfer ownership of the Llanganati papers to our company. Otherwise, if the file was destroyed over this great period of time, would it be possible to obtain a notarized statement indicating the existence of said documents and your recollection thereof, if not, I totally understand."

A short, clear and concise email response came shortly thereafter indicating ... "This will respond to your email. We do not have any of the documentation you are requesting and I would not be comfortable providing a notarized statement because I cannot remember all the documents we had."

The thought had occurred to me that just in case I could not obtain a copy of the contract, it might be possible to get my wife to inadvertently acknowledge the truth, that we had purchased the Brunner materials from her mother. To this end I utilized and submitted a legal *Request For Admissions*, obtaining an affirmative response (admission) under oath to this specific question ... "Admit that Plaintiff has asserted to Defendant numerous times that her mother had been offered $100,000 for the 'Ecuador Papers' and that Defendant had 'stolen' them from her mother by paying only $600 and 10 percent of recovery in the contractual agreement of twenty years past."

In conjunction with this effort, a *Motion for Order to Show Cause* was filed with the Court seeking that my wife and her attorney ... "be ordered to appear before this Court to show cause, if any they have, why they should not be found in contempt for willfully disobeying the judgement of the Court ... ," the Judge agreed and signed an *Order to Show Cause* directing both the lawyer and my wife to appear before him on a contempt charge.

Opposing the Judge's Order the attorney indicated that "...the manuscript and the property interest therein were trial issues ... while it is true that the Court ordered ... the subject copies of the 'papers' to be turned over to him ... she doesn't have the 'papers' to turn over, that they are with a third party over whom she has no control."

In an apparent effort to distance themselves from any contempt it was also stated ... "If (our client) is lying to her counsel or misrepresenting facts to her counsel and she does in fact have these 'papers' in her possession or in her control and did not produce them ... but, absent some proof of that fact there is no way that she can produce what is not in her possession or control."

On the day of the hearing, my wife and her attorney were no shows. Appearing on their behalf was another partner of the law firm.[493] Although the Judge readily accepted the provided excuse for the lawyer's failure to appear, my wife and the partner that did appear, were not so lucky. The Judge quickly dispensed with the attorneys arguments that my motion was frivolous and their claim for $1500 USD in sanctions, stating in effect that ... to Mr. Charbonneau's credit I remember Ordering that the documents be produced and I want her here to explain where they are! The attorney did some verbal backpedaling and informed the Judge that if the papers had been transferred or removed to Ecuador, they would do everything in their power to have them returned to the Court's jurisdiction. The Court then Ordered that my wife also file financial documents and the contract between the parties for the "Ecuador papers," that I had originally requested. The matter was continued and it was Ordered that my wife "MUST BE PRESENT at the return date."

At that instant it did not look good for my wife. Taking the property in question out-of-state and transferring it to her mother would have been bad enough, but once ordered to produce the property, not doing so and stalling until it could be removed from the country, or lying that it had been, would be worse if that is what happened. It seemed to me that the only way out of the situation she had created for herself, would be to lie once again. Therefore, realizing that my wife would possibly do or say anything to keep

---

[493] Whether true or not, I had been informed by a friend that was also a well-known family court lawyer of many years, that it would not be uncommon for a lawyer to not appear and send another attorney in their place. Assuming the attorney or client in question was found in contempt and not there, a fine could be imposed of $500 USD, if on the other hand a person was present, they could be incarcerated.

the "Ecuador papers" for her mother, it was my opinion that I needed to prepare all my evidence prior to the next hearing.

The evidence supporting my claims was overwhelming, including such items as legal title to the Brunner manuscripts (copyright certificates), confirmation of the contract of purchase, physical evidence and affidavits' confirming that the "Ecuador papers" had been in my exclusive possession for more than twenty years, and last but not least, witness testimony to the fact that the property was in my possession and removed without my permission, and contrary to a previous denial of an admission under oath, that taking the property and transferring it had been admitted to third parties.

Moments prior to our case being called for hearing, possibly owing to being confronted with overwhelming incontrovertible evidence and a possible contempt ruling, my wife's attorney frantically struggled to reach a settlement in the divorce. Basically we came to an agreement where my wife would forfeit any and all legal interest in the "Ecuador papers," it was acknowledged that a contract existed between my mother-in-law and me, and that I could then sue my mother-in-law for the return of the property. We came to an agreement and with obvious relief the Judge accepted it and ordered ... "IT IS FURTHER ORDERED, ADJUDICATED, AND DECREED that there are papers that are at the heart of this matter and the Plaintiff has no personal or community property interest therein. The papers issue, referenced throughout this action as the "Ecuador, Brunner and/or personal papers," more specifically described in detail in Defendant's Exhibit 23 on file herein, shall be between Plaintiff's mother and Defendant, which is a contract." [494]

Ironically, the mere act of telling the truth and accepting the terms of divorce that I had proposed a year previously, would have resulted in a completely opposite outcome for my wife and in turn her mother. Ultimately and at another hearing, irrespective of my objection (none being voiced by his client) my wife's lawyer withdrew (quit) informing the Court ... "The Plaintiff and I have reached a point which we can no longer work together effectively."

After the Judge's approval and withdrawal of my wife's attorney, the Judge read and approved the terms and format of our *Decree of Divorce*. The Court then asked my wife to read and affirm the terms and conditions of the decree. After a period of time my wife acknowledged acceptance of all the terms and conditions contained therein. As the Judge was preparing to sign the decree, my soon to be ex-wife asked to read a paper that her brother had just handed her which stated in part that "...the books that he (me of course) stole from my mom, we have discovered through this court that he has registered without my moms permission and it does not belong to him, but if he is planning not to return anything to my mom, I should be entitled to 50 percent of ownership of the books. In reference to my attorney ... he has

---

[494] *Court Order* Entered 19 Feb 2008.

misrepresented me from day one, and I think he should not be able to simply abandon me in this case for his multiple mistakes made throughout this court."

Glancing at the Judge, his demeanor appeared to indicate to me that through these contradictory statements, inconsistent with what had just occurred, been agreed to and affirmed ... the man might have finally realized what her attorneys and I had been experiencing! The Judge signed the *Decree of Divorce* and the matter was closed.

Irrespective of horrendous stories and allegations that were made against me, as I had predicted the evidence and truth had prevailed. Sadly, just as with most divorce cases, it was a devastating process to all involved, an experience not recommended or to be wished upon my worst enemy.

Without the custody, unconditional love, respect, emotional and financial support of all five of my children, before, during and after the divorce, life would have had little meaning. Although it may appear on the surface that my main concern at the time was the "Ecuador papers," I must clearly and emphatically once again state that ... "the world's greatest treasure was already in my possession, my children."

■ ■ ■

Of course the effect of our divorce settlement meant that my mother-in-law had not been joined in the action. Although I held legal title to the "Ecuador papers" through contract, US Copyright Registration and District Court Order, if I wanted the hard copies returned, I would need to file suit against my now ex-mother-in-law. As expected, through procrastination or the reluctance of facing yet another confrontation, I chose to let the matter rest, as long as no commercial use of the materials was made.

It became apparent working on this manuscript, that in order to be as accurate as possible relating events, it would be best to confirm my memory of events with my personal documentation. To that end, I drafted what I considered a fair and equitable offer for my ex-mother-in-law, a portion of which follows ... "It has taken a quarter of a century, but I have finally completed the rough draft of my first book; *Lust for Inca Gold: The Llanganati Treasure Story & Maps*, based on the writings of Eugene Konrad Brunner concerning solely the Llanganatis. My intent is to publish the complete factual story, which has been expanded and includes information that even Brunner did not possess at the time. Due to the ... [loss] of my personal papers, I have been required to write the chapter concerning my involvement in the project from memory. I would like to make one final settlement offer to you, in order that I may verify the accuracy of the data to be published within my book ... I hereby make the following compromise offers:

"1) I would like you to return my personal papers or copies so that I can confirm my factual representations and memory of events. The following are the items requested; ...[what follows is a list of all non-Brunner documentation from Exhibit 23] ... I would also appreciate a photograph of Eugene in the Llanganatis for inclusion in my book.

"In exchange I would grant you all legal rights and title to some of the Brunner materials you now have in your possession. Specifically, I would transfer the ownership of the manuscript and copyright for *Ecuador y Sus Tesoros* and *Mar Bravo*, unconditionally to you. To be clear so there is no misunderstanding ... not included in this offer are the chapters *Llanganati* [covered by copyright TXu-270-451] and *El Tesoro en las Misteriosas Montañas de Llanganati* [covered separately by copyright TXu-298-422]. These chapters, along with other writings of Brunner concerning the Llanganatis, have been translated into English and edited for inclusion in my book. After the publication of my book, I would consider, dependent of course on the rights acquired by my publisher, to allow the one-time inclusion of these chapters within your possible publication of *Ecuador y Sus Tesoros.*

"2) If you choose not to accept the above offer, alternatively, I shall provide you with yet another option; Rather than an exchange as above, I would be willing to transfer the ownership of the manuscript and copyright's to you as specifically mentioned above, for the sum of $5000 US Dollars.

"Regardless of your decision, my book *Lust for Inca Gold: The Llanganati Treasure Story & Maps* ... will be published as is, or hopefully with the benefit of verified facts concerning my involvement. Many books have been written concerning the Llanganati story, however, with the passage of time the theories have become fact, events have been misrepresented and misinterpreted, and Eugene's involvement has been minimized and trivialized, my book tells the complete story and will revive Brunner's memory."

Having patiently awaited any form of response for three months, it became apparent that Chapter VIII of this book must be published without the benefit of confirmation, so my offer was withdrawn. Obviously with documents in hand more specific's on the negotiations and agreements could have been related, but rest assured that every effort has been made to relate a complete and accurate account of all events. It has never ceased to amaze me that people so concerned with outward appearances, always seem to prefer to ignore situations rather than seek an equitable resolution. But, be that as it may, it appears that my next book project will be *Ecuador y Sus Tesoros*.

■ ■ ■

A full, complete and honest analysis cannot occur without looking deep within. Searching my conscience I must ask myself ... who may I have betrayed in this story? Did I betray Brunner's expectations that ... "All this will go to someone when I die. So my work will not be lost. I will carry on, even when I'm dead." Did I betray my partners or mother-in-law by walking away from the project, or had I given it my best effort? Had I unintentionally betrayed my "mole" at the Institute or my archeologist, by leaving them exposed to the consequences of any assistance which they provided? Had I betrayed Scott by picking his brain without compensation, or was that just the consequence of his inaction?

■ ■ ■

Reading Honigsbaum's *Valverde's Gold* some twenty years after my involvement on this project I found myself again reminded of Michael Dyott's words ... "If a reader believes or knows a portion of the story to be true, does it not follow that the reader would then believe the entire story to be true?" Would it not also stand to reason that the converse of Dyott's sentiment is also relevant? If a reader believes or knows a portion of the story to be false, does it not follow that the reader would then believe other portions of the story to be suspect. Taken a step further as Judge Judy [495]so adeptly states ... "If it doesn't make sense, it is not true, it's a lie."

Honigsbaum himself quotes Dyott's similar sentiments as well " ... a story has a beginning, a middle, and an end, and all through those pieces there can be misinformation. If the listener knows, or believes, any of the pieces, it gives credence to the others and the misinformation gets passed on as a 'fact.'" Reading *Valverde's Gold* I have consistently encountered misinformation being presented as fact, on numerous occasions my story brings some of them to light.

Mark Honigsbaum from England, billed as "a journalist and historian" on the back cover of *Valverde's Gold*, which is set forth as a serious historical work, appears in my opinion to have made numerous historical and factual errors. A historian from England purported to have spent countless hours researching in the archives of England and Spain failed to correct the implication in his story that Spruce's "grandson" could have been Dyott's source of the Blacke material. Simple research on Honigsbaum's part into Spruce's heredity would have dispelled this misinformation in a matter of minutes. In my opinion further investigation could have shown whether any of Spruce's nephews had been studying to become an officer during the time period and if they had, another route to investigate would have been whether Blacke & Chapman were teachers, or on staff at the academy.

The apparent misspelling of Blacke, of which Honigsbaum must have been aware through Brunner's manuscript,[496] could perhaps have produced different results in his search. According to Brunner, Dyott was able to confirm that Blacke & Chapman had indeed been in the service. Could Dyott have had access to military service or Royal Geographic Society archives that the public did not? In modern times sensitive military service

---

495 Judge Judith Sheindlin - Presiding judge of America's most watched courtroom series in history.

496 Even though unpublished and protected by copyright, Honigsbaum listed Brunner's *El Tesoro de Atahualpa en las Montañas de Llanganati y la casi increíble historia de los ingleses desde 1857 hasta hoy* as "Further Reading." (Honigsbaum has privately admitted to having had a copy of Brunner's manuscript.) Incidentally, simple online research of Brunner's name or mine (which was published in *Sweat of the Sun, Tears of the Moon*), would have also provided both Lourie and Honigsbaum with the knowledge that Brunner's materials were protected by US Copyright.

records, such as Dyott's, remain classified. How did the Admiralty deal with sensitive matters in the late 1800s?

Honigsbaum's book mimics Lourie's both in content and its characters, with a similar story line placing the author as the central character, ending in their own expeditions into the Llanganatis in search of Valverde's gold. In my opinion the only gold these men have discovered, is that generated by the sale of their respective literary works, which are based on the extensive labors of the Llanganati explorers, just as mine is.

Speaking of Diego Arias, Andrés Fernandez Salvador's son-in-law, Honigsbaum relates that ... "In 1990 he set up a foundation dedicated to the preservation of the Llanganatis unique flora and fauna and began lobbying the Ecuadorian government to declare the Llanganatis a national park - a goal that was finally achieved, four years later, in 1994."

From all that has been written of the man, this exhibits a major contradiction of character, in short ... "it doesn't make sense." Although Arias may have done just that, one must consider that such a magnanimous gesture brings to light possible ulterior motives, including the exclusion of other treasure seekers from the Llanganatis, just as I had opined to the Director of the National Institute of Cultural Heritage some two years' prior. The lust for Inca gold, once again in my opinion, continued under the auspices of science and botany.

■ ■ ■

My purpose and intent throughout this book in pointing out erroneous statements of other authors, including Brunner, is not to malign their work or impute their character, it is solely a method to clarify and correct misinformation and misdirection. Ecuadoran Explorations archeologist would write in the company's archeological plan "...from narration to narration the narrative is required to be precise, stripped of personal tastes, feelings or opinions which affected the first narrator's subjectivity ... the listener who hears the story receives a message whose true characteristics are transformed with the passage of time."

Michael Dyott's sentiment that ... "misinformation then gets passed on as a fact," has been evident throughout the Llanganati treasure story. Wallace's somewhat erroneous critique of Spruce's work resulted in some misinformation and misdirection over the years. Stabler's article contained misinformation that was corrected by Brooks. The author's Andrade, Blomberg, Dolinger, Brunner and yes perhaps even myself, have all fallen victim to misinformation being passed on as fact in their own narratives. Therefore, the reader should not be surprised to discover that Lourie and Honigsbaum fell victim to misinformation as well.

Just as I have critiqued and corrected misinformation and misdirection on the part of others, I would expect that at some future point in time others shall critique this work. Perhaps I myself have unwittingly misinterpreted data and drawn erroneous conclusions or theories in this narrative, but for me it is clear and has always been clear ... that lust for Inca gold will reach its successful conclusion only when the narrative is stripped of all misinformation and misdirection ... and the cards everyone is holding ... are laid face up on the table for all to see.

■ ■ ■

Eugene Brunner always exhibited his interest in the well being of the indigenous peoples and strived to achieve his goal of their integration into national life. Some people in Ecuador's cultural elite actually believe that integration has finally occurred or at the very least is occurring. Oswaldo Hurtado Larrea for example, would write in *Portrait of a Nation: Culture and Progress in Ecuador* (2010) concerning the great progress the country had made in this regard during the 1990s stating "...perhaps the most important transformation for the indigenous peoples was the recovery of the cultural values of their race and a sense of personal dignity."

On the surface this appears to be a major accomplishment for the country to be proud of. However the reality of the situation, in my opinion, shows this to be merely a grandiose statement. Ecuador is still a country where a third of the population, especially the indigenous peoples, exist below the poverty line.[497] As Hurtado continues writing on the subject, one catches a glimpse of the cultural elites skewed definition of transformation and integration ... "Currently, not only do many Indians drive vehicles, but they also own them. The donkeys that used to be part of the rural landscapes in backward countries have disappeared in Ecuador's countryside, and horses, bicycles, motorcycles, and in some cases pickup trucks have taken their place. It is a shame to have to admit it, but only fairly recently - for the first time in hundreds of years - Indians can wear shoes (instead of their traditional cloth sandals) and have more than one change of clothes."

With all due respect ... transforming the indigenous people of Ecuador into consumers and debtors does not meet my definition of inter-mixing these highly segregated peoples into society while retaining their cultural values.

■ ■ ■

So here we have the complete story of the Llanganati Treasure, whose details have been mutilated by time and evolved over the centuries, revealed through more than forty years of the sweat and toils of a man of "good heart" ... Eugene Konrad Brunner. A man who departed this world without reaping the benefits of his labors and discoveries. But I am positive that the events and history in Ecuador since Brunner's death have just confirmed his belief that the treasure is better off where it is now, until a point in time when it can "serve to redeem the blood that it has already cost, to serve and assist the welfare of the people and foremost must form the basis for the integration of the Ecuadorian Indian into national life, his rightful place by heritage. Integration which must be done without removal from the agricultural sector or culture, but with dignity and guarantees." [498]

Brunner's ultimate explanation of the location of his beloved treasure trove and for his fixation on this "beautiful mountain" Cerro Hermoso, shall live

---

[497] *CIA World Hand*book June 2010

[498] Quote from Eugene Konrad Brunner, written November 1979.

forever here in print, without deception, misdirection or the use of literary license. Not all questions surrounding this story have been answered and many more have been raised, but of one thing I am certain ... the treasures hidden within the Llanganati Mountains of Ecuador await an intrepid sole within a certain cave on Cerro Hermoso. One day an intrepid sole will climb this mountain on its east side, reaching the summit and the passage that exist between the main peak and secondary peaks, by which he can descend to the west side of the mountain. It is at this site near Lake Brunner, between the main peak and an adjacent stone pyramid, in a "hidden cave" that has been sealed by earthquakes [499] common in the region ... where lust for Inca gold must end for some ... but for that intrepid sole ... it shall be just the beginning!

###

[499] Brunner specifically cites Ecuador's major earthquake of 1949 which destroyed Píllaro and transformed the Llanganatis.

WORKS OF STEVEN J CHARBONNEAU

Lust for Inca Gold: The Llanganati Treasure Story & Maps

ISBN: 978-1478146063 REPLACED BY A SECOND EDITION

Lust for Inca Gold provides a fascinating insight into the insatiable pursuit of Atahualpa's ransom treasure, untold quantities of Inca gold spirited into the mysterious Llanganati Mountains of Ecuador. This intriguing and mesmerizing story is related utilizing vivid firsthand accounts of Francisco Pizarro's conquistadores, botanist Richard Spruce, Colonel E. C. Brooks, Captain E. E. Loch, Commander G. M. Dyott and Eugen K. Brunner. Adventurers, explorers and armchair travellers alike will relive history on this adventurous journey in search of Valverde's gold, gaining knowledge of discoveries within a region where few have gone before. The narrative paints a visual image of the conditions, hardships, deprivations, successes and failures endured on expeditions into the Llanganati Mountains. Numerous original maps and illustrations also provide a means to trace expedition routes into this unknown territory. Going well beyond what has previously been written, this book relates portions of the story that have never been told, while clarifying what has been. Behold the explorers' quest for knowledge concerning the solution to the riddle of Inca gold hidden deep in the Llanganati Mountains, the thrill of discovery which drove their personal quests, or in some cases ... a ***Lust for Inca Gold***. This book is the author's initial work, written using pseudonyms for certain characters, to protect both the innocent and guilty.

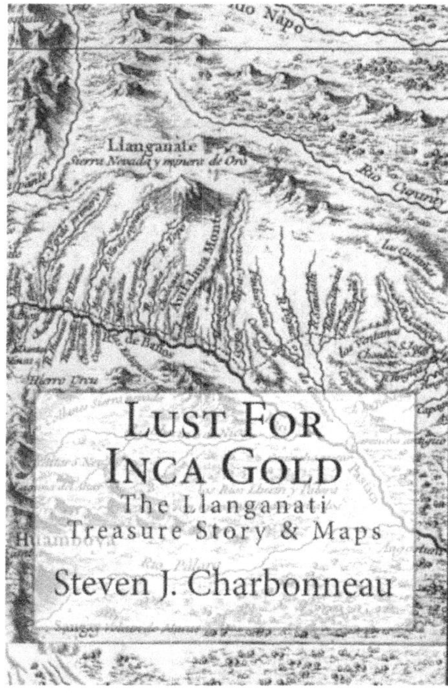

Lust for Inca Gold: an intriguing true story of Exploration, Discovery, Murder, Espionage & Treasure

ISBN: 978-1480049253 **EXPANDED SECOND EDITION**

Lust for Inca Gold is a masterful blend of history, biography, legend and storytelling, providing a definitive account of the centuries-old quest for Inca gold from Atahualpa's ransom secreted in the mysterious Llanganati Mountains of Ecuador. This fascinating you-are-there narrative also exposes political conditions and events in Ecuador during the country's transition from military to civilian rule, including the government's role in attempted recoveries of the Llanganati treasure. An expanded second edition, this book unmasks pseudonyms retaining all initially published information, revealing much more. New evidence is disclosed and misinformation, misdirection, myths, and theories are corrected or dispelled. Numerous sources with personal connections to the story help fill in gaps and expose intriguing twists, providing exciting new material. New events and characters are introduced concerning the central character Eugen Brunner, providing a unique insight into events, the man and his paranoia. This genre busting literary adventure has something for everyone; folklore, history, botany, biography, autobiography, memoirs, politics, military, murder, mystery, espionage, adventure, exploration, discovery, travel, romance and treasure lore. Live the odyssey and join in a quest for Valverde's gold secreted in a certain "lake made by hand" and "hidden cave" within the Llanganati Mountains.

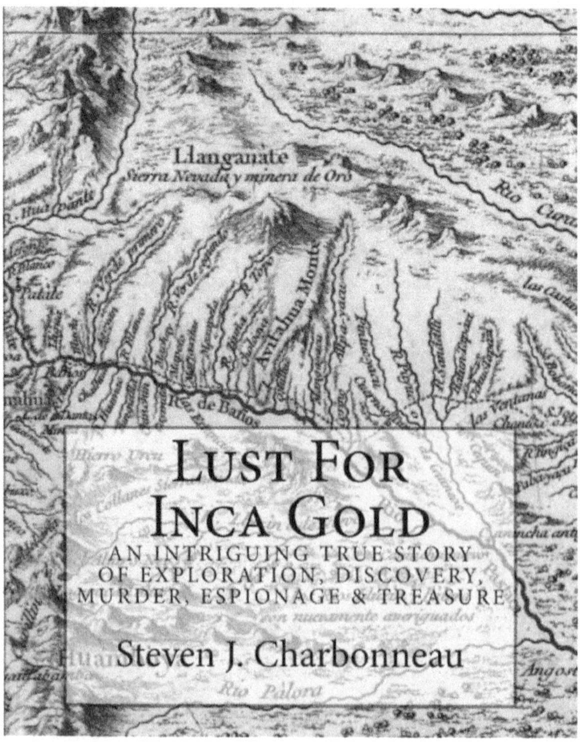

The Inca's Ransom
ISBN: 979-8593196071

Prepare to embark on a journey back in time into the realm of the unknown with the conquistadores and Francisco Pizarro as ***The Inca's Ransom*** relates a fascinating and engrossing story of an indigenous people, their social structure, culture, religion, military, administration, myths, legends and conquest. With the aid of historical resources gain knowledge of unfathomable and unparalleled events that transpired during this epoch of pillaging, looting, kidnapping, torture, murder, rape, and destruction of cultural heritage, fueled by the Kingdom of Spain's insatiable lust for Inca gold. The beginning of this three part compilation relates tales of Atahualpa's ransom and murder, the Inca conquest and much more. Not merely a story about the conquest of a civilization, but also of the legends that subjugation inspired, including the legend of Valverde's Gold spirited into the Llanganati Mountains of Ecuador. A snapshot in time, the second portion of this compilation provides a clear understanding of the harsh conditions travelers and treasure seekers of the period experienced on their journey in Ecuador during the late-1880s. An intriguing tale of fiction completes this compilation and was chosen for inclusion due to bearing uncanny similarities to future events and discoveries concerning the legendary Llanganati treasure deposit, leaving one speculating where the author's relation of fact ends and fiction begins!

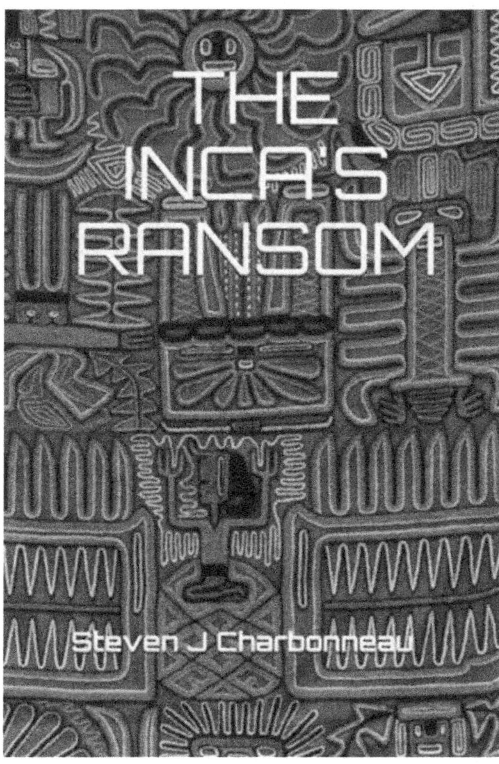

Valverde's Gold: The Royal Geographical Society Llanganati Papers
ISBN: 978-1479274956

Three captivating and obscure historical papers, sources of fascination for over a century, published as a compilation. Originally presented to the Royal Geographical Society, these papers provide a foundation for the quest of Inca treasure in the Llanganati Mountains of Ecuador. Portions have been utilized by adventurers, explorers and treasure seekers for decades, with many lacking a complete knowledge of the papers contents. Botanist Richard Spruce's paper *On the Mountains of Llanganati* contains Spruce's translation of the *Derrotero of Valverde*, a guide to an Inca treasure deposit, and hand-copied *Guzmán Map* of the region, Holy Grails for those in quest of Valverde's gold. Jordan Stabler, previously the Secretary of the American Legation at Quito, presented a paper and map of the route followed on his travels entitled "Travels in Ecuador." Merely an interesting period travel guide until Stabler divulges previously unknown information concerning his friend Major E. C. Brooks having made two expeditions into the Llanganatis in search of Valverde's gold. "Taken by surprise" with this breech of confidence, in correspondence to the Society published as "The Inca Treasure of Llanganati," Major E. C. Brooks indicates Stabler "forced my hand" and sets the record straight disclosing many interesting facts. All three works can now be read together and in their entirety, relating an intriguing and timeless tale.

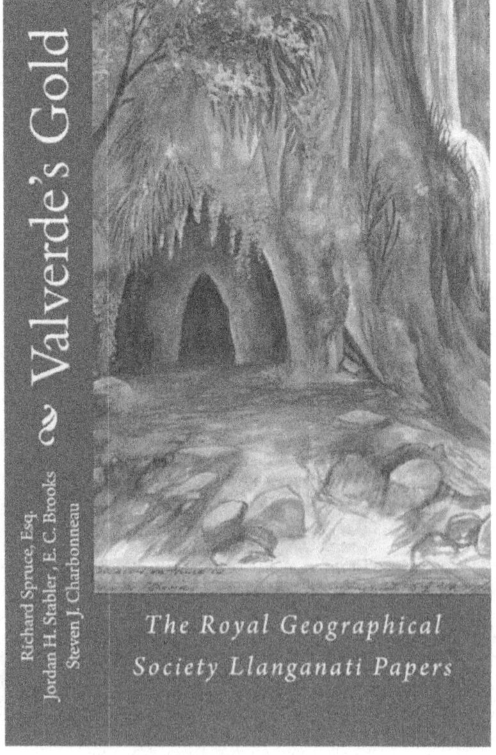

The Treasure in the Mysterious Mountains of Llanganati
and the incredible story of the English
ISBN: 978-1480049277
SPANISH LANGUAGE EDITION ISBN: 978-1479308484

Eugen Brunner fled Nazi Germany for Ecuador and devoted the majority of his life researching the country's history and exploring its jungles, rivers, mountains and ocean. He was a man of many tales, yet withheld many more secrets. A renowned explorer of the mysterious Llanganati Mountains, Brunner's trials, tribulations and discoveries on a fifty-year quest for Inca treasure, portions of Atahualpa's ransom known as Valverde's gold, are related in his own words. Brunner seemed to possess an uncanny ability of knowing at what point in his stories to leave out details and information, protecting secrets, loved ones and himself. Very little leaked out about Brunner's family, European past, involvement with the Nazis, CIA, or Llanganati discoveries, until now ... a quarter of a century after his death. This story discloses Brunner's personal secrets and evidence supporting his conclusion that the cache of Inca gold he sought was hidden on Cerro Hermoso in the Llanganati Mountains. This is the publication of one of Brunner's manuscripts and three of his maps, preceded by the tale of their theft and recovery. An insight into Brunner's true nature and character is also presented through an intriguing short biography. One of the last true explorers of the Llanganati, a picture is painted of an adventurer and historian, not a stereotypical treasure hunter. Even so, Brunner's paranoia appears more than justified!

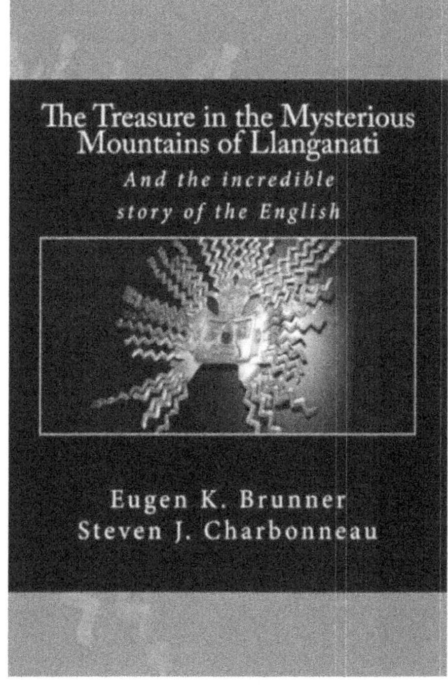

Beyond West Point: A Tale of Character, War & Nation Building

ISBN: 978-1500240646

SAME CONTENT DIFFERENT TITLE & COVER:

Quest for Inca Gold: Colonel E. C. Brooks' 1910 Llanganati Expeditions

ISBN: 978-1984133322

Intriguing yet sometimes embarrassing, this multi-biography provides an insight into the life and times of Colonel E. C. Brooks, his family, friends, associates and comrades-in-arms. Similar to many West Point graduates Brooks rose from obscurity to witness history in the making and became an active participant in the shaping of the world at the turn of the century, an odyssey that commences with deep family roots in the history of Oregon and Washington Territories. Brook's journey through life is documented from birth to West Point and carries on through careers as a cavalry officer, college instructor, Auditor of Cuba, railroad engineer, treasure hunter, entrepreneur, commission agent and traveling representative. Brooks' role in the Indian Wars, death of Sitting Bull, Spanish American War, Philippine Insurrection and construction of Ecuador's Railroad in the Sky are exposed, as is a connection with the Great Chicago Fire and Crosby Mansion "Tawasentha." Although Brooks mounted two expeditions in search of a fabled Incan treasure, Valverde's Gold, these adventures were but minor acts in the life of E. C. Brooks. His is not merely a tale about a treasure, but of a man who spent a few months in search of Inca gold. An accurate and complete story of one of the most interesting, elusive and obscure explorers of the Llanganati Mountains of Ecuador that begged to be told, this is Brooks' story ... ***Beyond West Point***.

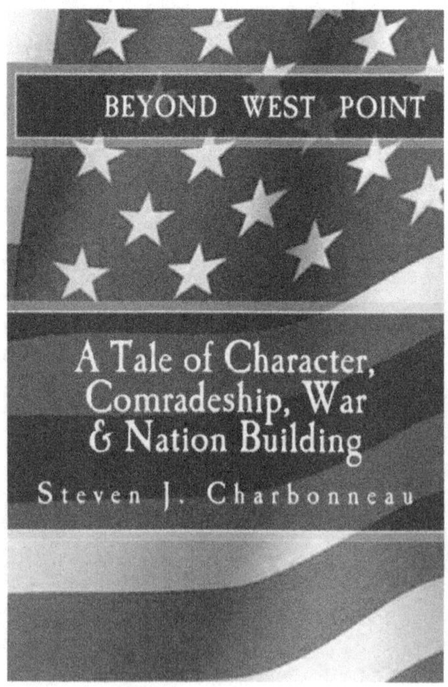

Quest for Inca Gold:
Commander G.M.Dyott's 1947 Llanganati Expedition
ISBN: 978-198413397

This book relates a story of treasure lore founded in real events and fact, a quest for Valverde's gold, portions of the Inca Atahualpa's ransom spirited into the Llanganati Mountains of Ecuador. In treasure lore the closer one comes to a first person narrative, the nearer one is to the truth. Previously, Commander Dyott's involvement within the Llanganati treasure story relied on intermediate sources that blurred the lines between fact and fiction. ***Quest for Inca Gold*** bestows clarity related through never before published firsthand accounts in the form of extensive personal correspondence between Commander Dyott and the mysterious "family in New England." These accounts are not paraphrased, but reinforced with background information and clarification in order that the circumstances that form the setting for events, statements and ideas can be fully understood and assessed. Once and for all the fog of misinformation, misdirection and literary license which has obscured the truth for decades is lifted. With the characters unveiling the story in their own words as it developed, the reader is provided an experience like none other. This intriguing story provides sufficient background information and new evidence that exposes a different version of events. Regardless if you are an active explorer, treasure hunter, historian or armchair adventurer, the true story of Commander Dyott's journey into the unknown awaits within.

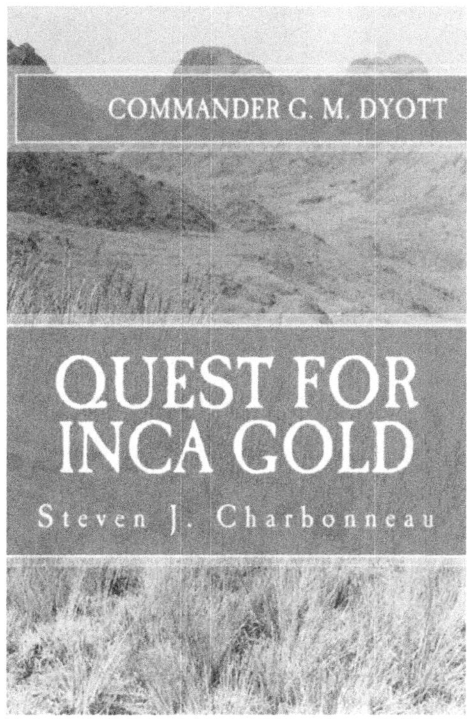

Made in United States
North Haven, CT
02 April 2022